THE GLORY OF
GOD'S GRACE

FAITH AND REASON
Studies in Catholic Theology and Philosophy

The series aims at publishing scholarly studies that serve the project of "faith seeking understanding." We hope to assist in making available in English valuable work being done by theologians and philosophers abroad; in this regard we recognize a special place for the ongoing renaissance in French-language Thomistic theology and philosophy. In addition to translations, we intend to publish collections of essays and monographs from a range of perspectives, united by their common commitment to the ecclesial and sapiential work of "faith seeking understanding" so as to build up the Church and proclaim the Gospel afresh.

PUBLISHED VOLUMES

    Serge-Thomas Bonino, OP, ed., *Surnaturel: Reflections on Nature and Grace*
    Gilles Emery, OP, *Trinity, Church, and the Human Person: Thomistic Essays*
    Lawrence Feingold, *The Natural Desire to See God*
    Matthew L. Lamb, *Eternity, Time, and the Life of Wisdom*
    Guy Mansini, OSB, *The Word Has Dwelt among Us*
    Thomas G. Weinandy, OFM, Cap., *Jesus: Essays in Christology*
    Thomas Joseph White, OP, *Wisdom in the Face of Modernity*

THE GLORY OF GOD'S GRACE

DEIFICATION ACCORDING TO ST. THOMAS AQUINAS

Daria Spezzano

SAPIENTIA PRESS
OF AVE MARIA UNIVERSITY

Sapientia Press
of Ave Maria University
5050 Ave Maria Blvd.
Ave Maria, FL 34142
800-537-5487

Distributed by:
The Catholic University of America Press
c/o HFS
P.O. Box 50370
Baltimore, MD 21211
800-537-5487

Cover Image: *Annunciation* by Fra Angelico, Museo Nacional del Prado, Madrid

Printed in the United States of America.

Library of Congress Control Number: 2014952266

ISBN: 978-1-932589-72-6

In laudem gloriae gratiae suae,
in qua gratificavit nos in dilecto Filio suo
—Ephesians 1:6

Contents

Acknowledgments   viii

Introduction   1

1. The Divine Source and End of the *Imago Dei*   17

2. The Image of God and Its Perfection   72

3. The Grace of the Holy Spirit   105

4. The Incarnation and Participation in the Divine Nature   152

5. Charity in the *Summa theologiae*   211

6. Wisdom, Charity, and Christ   265

7. Deification in the *Summa theologiae*   328

APPENDIX A. A Brief Survey of Deification in the Christian Tradition before Aquinas   347

APPENDIX B. The Disputed Question of "Created Grace" in the *Summa theologiae*   359

Bibliography   367

Index   383

Acknowledgments

This work could not have been completed without the guidance and friendship of many. I am deeply indebted to all who have offered advice and encouragement throughout the development of this project. Among these I remember with gratitude my professors at Notre Dame and the Liturgical Institute, especially John Cavadini, Larry Cunningham, David Fagerberg, Thomas Prügl, and Joseph Wawrykow. I will always be grateful as well to the Sisters of Our Lady of Grace Dominican Monastery, especially Sr. Mary Ann, OP, and Sr. Maria of the Angels, OP, who, along with the Dominican friars, first shared with me their knowledge and love of St. Thomas. Special thanks goes to those who have offered encouragement, helpful suggestions, and constructive criticism on the manuscript, including Fr. Bernard Blankenhorn, OP, Daniel Keating, Matthew Levering, Fr. Thomas Joseph White, OP, and my colleague at Providence College, Ian Levy. Any errors are of course my own. Finally, my love and gratitude go to my husband, Frank Spezzano, for his unfailing support, prayer, and encouragement throughout the years it took for this project to come to fruition.

THE GLORY OF GOD'S GRACE

Introduction

See what love the Father has bestowed on us, that we may be called the children of God.

—1 John 3:1

Christianity makes the radical claim that God creates human beings with the possibility of sharing, as God's adopted children, in the divine life—indeed, that all creation exists for the fulfillment of this purpose and awaits it "with eager longing."[1] Those predestined in Christ, and signed with the Holy Spirit, are called by God's will to live forever "for the praise of his glory."[2] And yet human beings are incapable of attaining this goal by their own powers and, because of sin, are completely unfit to live in God's company.[3] They must be transformed by grace, reconciled to God, and even—in the mystery of divine generosity—made "partakers in the divine nature,"[4] becoming "like God" in order to "see him as he is" in eternal life.[5] The Christian tradition, drawing from Scripture, teaches that salvation must also in some sense be deification, or the "attainment of godlikeness and union with God."[6] This rather startling doctrine, which demands theological nuance to safeguard it from unorthodox expression, has informed Christian

---

1. Rom 8:19.   2. Eph 1:12–13.

3. Gen 3:8–24; Rom 5:6–11.

4. 2 Pet 1:4: "May grace and peace be yours in abundance through knowledge of God and of Jesus our Lord. His divine power has bestowed on us everything that makes for life and devotion, through the knowledge of him who called us by his own glory and power. Through these, he has bestowed on us the precious and very great promises, so that through them you may become partakers in the divine nature, after escaping from the corruption that is in the world because of evil desire."

5. 1 Jn 3:2.

6. Dionysius, *Ecclesiastical Hierarchy* (*EH*) 1.3 PG (3.376A).

understandings of sanctification since the earliest centuries of the Church. While deification (sometimes called divinization) is frequently associated only with Eastern Christianity, in which it has traditionally been a central doctrine, some recent publications have emphasized its presence and ongoing relevance in the theological tradition of the West.[7] These publications are witness to a current upsurge of interest in the question of deification; it might be said that this ancient doctrine is currently a hot topic. St. Thomas Aquinas in particular has received attention as a Western theologian who employs the concept of deification in his theology of human sanctification.[8]

A study of deification in Aquinas might proceed with either of two major intentions. One could approach the subject from a primarily comparative or external viewpoint, seeking to examine the correspondence—or disjunction—of his thought with other theologians or schools in the Christian tradition. Most treatments of Thomas's theology of deification thus far have taken this external approach, providing a fruitful, though at times controverted, perspective on his place within the larger tradition. But no major study has examined Thomas's theology of deification on its own merits, nor attempted to fully delineate his understanding of sanctification as deification within the overall context of his vision of the human journey by

---

7. E.g., A. N. Williams, *The Ground of Union: Deification in Aquinas and Palamas* (New York: Oxford University Press, 1999); Robert Puchniak, "Augustine's Conception of Deification, Revisited," and Myk Habets, "Reforming Theōsis," in *Theōsis: Deification in Christian Theology*, ed. Stephen Finlan and Vladimir Kharlamov (Eugene, OR: Pickwick, 2006), 122–33, 146–67; Nancy J. Hudson, *Becoming God: The Doctrine of Theosis in Nicholas of Cusa* (Washington, DC: Catholic University of America Press, 2007); Veli-Matti Kärkkäinen, *One with God: Salvation as Deification and Justification* (Collegeville: Liturgical Press, 2004). Michael J. Christensen and Jeffrey A. Wittung, eds., *Partakers of the Divine Nature: The History and Development of Deification in the Christian Tradition* (Madison, NJ: Fairleigh Dickinson University Press, 2007), includes essays on deification in Anselm, Luther, Calvin, and Wesley, among others. Daniel Keating also notes a current resurgence of interest in the topic of deification and provides references for modern Eastern and Western treatments of the subject, as well as numerous passing references to deification in the Western tradition throughout his book, in particular in the theology of Augustine and Aquinas. *Deification and Grace* (Naples, FL: Sapientia Press, 2007), 2–5. See also the sections on Leo the Great and Augustine in his *The Appropriation of Divine Life in Cyril of Alexandria* (Oxford: Oxford University Press, 2004).

8. E.g., Williams, *Ground of Union*; Daniel Keating, "Justification, Sanctification and Divinization in Thomas Aquinas," in *Aquinas on Doctrine: A Critical Introduction*, ed. Thomas G. Weinandy, Daniel A. Keating, and J. P. Yocum (New York: T&T Clark, 2004), 139–58. See discussion later in this chapter.

grace to beatitude.[9] The intention of this book is to offer such an in-depth examination of the nature of Thomas's mature teaching on deification in the *Summa theologiae*, the reasons for its development, and its highly significant—though sometimes hidden—role internal to his entire theological project.

In the *Summa theologiae* Thomas Aquinas treats the "advance of the rational creature towards God"—God who is the creature's beginning and end, in whose image it was made, by whom and in whom it is perfected through the grace of the Holy Spirit flowing from Christ and his sacraments, for a share in God's own eternal life.[10] The *Summa* represents Thomas's most mature thought on human sanctification; in it he presents a fully developed account of the graced movement of the elect toward God. Thomas's primary definition of grace in the *Summa*—as a created *habitus* that is a "participation in the divine nature" (cf. 2 Pet 1:4)—is one indication that he thinks of this process as deification. In this journey of transformation, the human creature is both conformed to and moved by the Trinitarian divine exemplar, the source of both its creation in a rational nature, and its re-creation by grace through the divine missions. The Holy Spirit, who "proceeds temporally for the creature's sanctification,"[11] is dynamically involved at every point of the human being's journey to the deiformity of beatitude through grace, the theological virtues, and the gifts of the Spirit. The Spirit's role in deification, though not always explicit, can be traced

---

9. I am grateful to Joseph Wawrykow for underlining the importance for Aquinas of this metaphor of human sanctification as a graced journey to beatitude, which is foundational to my project.

10. *Summa theologiae* Ia q2, prol.; cf. I-IIae q1, prol. Translations from the Latin are mine, although the English translation of the *Summa* by the Fathers of the English Dominican Province (New York: Benzinger Brothers, 1948; reprint, Christian Classics, 1981) provided assistance at many points. Because of the necessity of brevity, the Latin text has been included only where it might be needed for clarification of particular points. Latin editions of Thomas's works are readily available. For translations of the *Summa*, I consulted the Leonine edition (in *Opera Omnia iussu impensaque Leonis XIII P. M. edita*, vols. 4–12 [Ex Typographia Polyglotta S. C. de Propaganda Fide, Romae, 1888–1906]) as well as the Ottowa edition (Instituti Studiorum Medievalium Ottaviensis, 5 vols. [Ottawa: Commissio Piana, 1953]). The online Corpus Thomisticum website gave invaluable assistance for this project (incorporating the Index Thomisticus of Roberto Busa, SJ), edited by Enrique Alarcón, SJ, for the Fundación Tomás de Aquino, at www.corpusthomisticum.org.

11. *ST* Ia q43 a3.

wherever grace and its effects are at work. The Spirit's role correlates with that of the Son, who is the principle and model of the perfection of God's children by grace. This scheme has its foundation in the Ia *pars*—in Thomas's treatment of the Trinity, the missions, and the human person made to the Trinitarian image—and unfolds through his treatment of grace, virtues, and gifts in the IIa *pars*, and their transmission and perfection in the Christology and sacramentology of the IIIa *pars*.

In the *Summa*'s moving picture of graced human persons toward beatitude, the virtue of charity and the gift of wisdom play a primary role among all the virtues and gifts, involving both divine and human action in the attainment of "conformation to the image of the Son" through the "Spirit of adoption" (Rom 8:14–15, 29). Deification by grace constitutes the elect as God's adopted children, called to share in the fellowship of beatitude. Charity and wisdom, flowing from grace, transform the powers of adopted children so as to enable them to attain that goal. As participations in the likeness of the Spirit and Son, charity and wisdom make the perfection of the *imago Dei* a true conformation to the Trinitarian Persons: charity is a created participation of the Holy Spirit,[12] and by wisdom—especially the Spirit's gift of wisdom—the soul is assimilated to the Son, the "Word breathing forth love."[13] Charity and wisdom thus can be said to deify the will and intellect of adopted children, ordering them through their own graced activity to eternal fellowship with God as participants in the Son's own relationship to the Father.

Because the gifts of grace, charity, and wisdom are created *habitus* in the human person, which are yet participations in the uncreated divine life and activity of the Trinitarian Persons, they lie at the dynamic interface where the divine elevates human nature and activity. Therefore one important factor in Thomas's account of deification is his understanding of the relationship between divine and human causality. Within the last several decades of Thomist scholarship, a renewed recognition has emerged of the dynamic character of Thomas's mature conception of the process of human sanctification. Thomas comes in his later works to stress both the absolute causal primacy of God—operatively and cooperatively working through the grace

12. *ST* IIa-IIae q23 a2.
13. *ST* Ia q43 a5 ad2; IIa-IIae q45 a6.

of the Holy Spirit—and the proper instrumental causality of the graced human subject, whose intellect and will informed by the theological virtues and gifts are actively engaged in full freedom in their movement toward the end of beatitude. The divine delicacy in bringing about this interplay of freedoms—expressed beautifully by Thomas's Dominican brother Fra Angelico in the courtesy of the archangel Gabriel to Mary at the Annunciation[14]—requires, to be understood, a robust philosophical and theological construct. One must account for God's simultaneous transcendence and immanence to the created order, and so for the possibility of true freedom under grace, and, on the part of the creature, it must be explained how attaining a share in the divine nature and activity is possible (and even fitting) without pantheism or monism. Thomas provides such a construct in his mature teaching as he builds a comprehensive picture of God's manifold causality as end, mover, and exemplar in the plan of divine providence to bring rational creatures to communion with himself.

My goal in this study is to elucidate Thomas's mature account in the *Summa* of Christianity's "precious and very great promise"—God's deification of the human person—within the overall context of his vision of the human journey by grace to beatitude. In doing so, I demonstrate the important, though not always obvious, way in which his understanding of deification shapes his larger theological project. To this end I explore what Thomas actually means by deification, and how it operates within the larger body of his teaching, by undertaking a close reading of texts relevant to Thomas's teaching on deification throughout the *Summa*—with attention to their organization, use of Scripture, and other authorities from the tradition—and to possible developments in his mature teaching by select comparisons with his other writings. I draw especially on links to Thomas's scriptural commentaries on biblical texts central to his notion of deification to investigate the influence that the writing of such commentaries may have had upon his mature formulations. I argue that Thomas's theology of deification in the *Summa theologiae* clearly demonstrates his mature commitment to a vision of God's loving and sapiential ordering of predestined human beings to communion with himself, by a progressive participation

14. Museo Nacional del Prado, Madrid. The *Annunciation* appears on an altarpiece originally painted by Fra Angelico for the monastery of San Domenico in Fiesole, Italy.

in the divine likeness and activity, which accounts for both the absolute primacy of divine causality in all of its modes and the fullness of graced human freedom.

The Vocabulary of Deification

By the time Thomas began to think about deification in the thirteenth century, there was already a rich heritage of Christian teaching associated with this doctrine, rooted in Scripture and developed in the theological traditions of both East and West.[15] Thomas was heir to many of the most important sources from both traditions; by the time he wrote the *Summa theologiae*, a number of works by the Greek Fathers had become available to the Latin West in translation, from which he drew freely in his terminology. The notion of deification, its biblical roots shaped by the language of Hellenism, was first understood and articulated by the early Church in the language of metaphor—employing themes such as assimilation, participatory union, the attainment of incorruptibility, divine adoption, and imitation—to talk about the soul's ascent to God.[16] By the sixth century, this metaphorical understanding came to be expressed in a more conceptual and dogmatic manner; deification became a technical term for Christian theology, receiving from Dionysius a formal definition: "Deification (*theosis*) is the attaining of likeness to God and union with him so far as is possible."[17]

Dionysius and Augustine were the most important patristic authors in the communication of a doctrine of deification to the Latin West and were both significant sources among the many that shaped Thomas's own teaching.[18] The Dionysian writings furnish a rich store of concepts that Thomas

15. See Appendix A for a summary introduction to this complex history, with attention to sources that are relevant to Aquinas's thought. Besides the references listed there, the reader is referred to such recent historical overviews as Paul Collins, *Partaking in Divine Nature: Deification and Communion* (New York: T&T Clark, 2010), and Christensen and Wittung, *Partakers of the Divine Nature*, which is especially recommended for the quality of its essays and extensive bibliography by Jeffery Wittung, of sources on deification throughout the Christian tradition: "Resources on *Theosis* with Select Primary Sources in Translation," 294–310.

16. Norman Russell, *The Doctrine of Deification in the Greek Patristic Tradition* (Oxford: Oxford University Press, 2004), 8–15.

17. Ibid., 1. See Dionysius, *EH* 1.3 PG (3.376A).

18. M.-D. Chenu remarks that Dionysius is Thomas's second-most frequently quoted authority (1,702 times) after Augustine. *Toward Understanding Saint Thomas: Translated with*

and other scholastics associate with deification: procession and return, likeness and union with God, participation in the divine attributes, illumination of the intellect, mediation of the divine gifts through a universal hierarchy by means of the symbols of the earthly liturgy. From Augustine, Thomas derived key elements of his doctrine on the Trinity, the perfection of the human person to the image of God, and especially the graced journey to beatitude.[19]

Thomas's direct use in the *Summa* of the terminology of deification developed in the Latin West (*deificatio, deificare, deiformitas*) is somewhat sparse, as other scholars have noted.[20] Yet, though such direct references are limited in the *Summa* to a few specific contexts, they are significant ones. They occur in two forms. Thomas speaks of "deiformity" in the *Summa* in relation to the life of *comprehensores*: in his treatment of the beatific vision (belonging to believers in heaven and to Christ *in via*) and the habitual perfection of the angelic intellect.[21] "Deification" refers to the life of *viatores*: the deification of believers on the journey, divinely caused by grace,[22] through the charity that is an effect of the Eucharist,[23] and the deification of Christ's humanity by its union with the Word.[24] In his early *Scriptum on the Sentences*, by contrast, besides frequent Dionysian references to the deiform intellect of the angels, Thomas also attributes deiformity to those in this life who possess grace and charity or who have received baptism.[25] In his later

---

Authorized Corrections and Bibliographical Additions, Library of Living Catholic Thought, trans. A. M. Landry and D. Hughes (Chicago: H. Regnery Press, 1964), 127.

19. See Appendix A for more on the teaching of Dionysius and Augustine on deification and their influence on the Latin Middle Ages.

20. Williams, *Ground of Union*, 34; Bruce Marshall, "*Ex occidente lux*? Aquinas and Eastern Orthodox Theology," *Modern Theology* 20, no. 1 (2004): 26. Williams considers "direct references to deification" to include any reference to participation in the divine nature (although not listing them all). By "direct reference" I mean the use of the actual terminology of deification/deiformity, although Thomas thinks that participation in the divine nature by grace *is* deification.

21. *ST* Ia q12 a5, a6; Ia-IIae q50 a6. In the course of discussing the perfection of the contemplative life of the religious, Thomas also quotes from Dionysius, *EH* VI (Dionysius makes an analogy between angels and ecclesiastics), which states that by contemplation of invisible things monks enter into "a deiform unity and perfection beloved of God" (*ST* IIa-IIae q184 a5; cf. q188 a2 ob1, ad1.

22. *ST* Ia-IIae q112 a1.   23. *ST* IIIa q79 a8.

24. *ST* IIIa q2 a1 ad3, q16 a3.

25. *Scriptum* bk2 d26 q1 a4 ad3; bk3 d14 q1 a3 qc3 ad2, d27 q2 a1 ad9; bk4 d3 q1 a3 qc1 ad2.

work, Thomas seems to be more careful to say that deification begins in this life, but deiformity is attained only in the next. In other words, his mature teaching presents deification in a more dynamic manner, as a *process* that is completed only in glory.

Like the authorities from whom he drew, Thomas is profoundly shaped by his meditation on Scripture as he develops his vocabulary of deification. He employs a wide range of the scripturally based terms associated with the concept of deification in the Christian tradition: participation in the divine nature, assimilation, communication of divine goodness, perfection of the divine image, adoption by grace (through Christ and the Holy Spirit, by means of the sacraments), and unifying conformity of the soul to God by knowledge and love in the beatific vision. Thomas integrates all of these concepts into his understanding of the journey to beatitude as deification yet goes far beyond the use of what was by his time a fairly common and traditional lexicon, describing the very structure of the sanctification of the human person—through grace, the theological virtues, and the gifts of the Holy Spirit—in terms of an increasing participation, already begun from creation, in God's own Trinitarian nature and activity.

Literature on Deification in the Writings of Thomas Aquinas

To date, only one extensive treatment of Thomas's theology of deification has been published—*The Ground of Union: Deification in Aquinas and Palamas*, by Anna Williams[26]—a work that, as is evident from the title, has specific concerns rather different from the present volume. Williams undertakes a comparative study of deification in Thomas's *Summa theologiae* and Gregory Palamas's *Triads in Defense of the Holy Hesychasts* and *Capita Physica*, with an avowed ecumenical intent. Noting the prevalent perception of a fundamental opposition between Palamite and Thomistic theology, as representative of East and West—and the issue of deification in particular as a theological locus that has been claimed to divide them[27]—Williams seeks by an analysis of the mature writings of these authors to evaluate the extent to which, in their respective teachings on deification, they in fact share common ground.[28]

---

26. Williams, *Ground of Union*.   27. Ibid., 6.
28. Ibid., 7. Williams points out that the doctrine of deification is particularly significant

Williams locates fundamental criteria in the patristic tradition to identify the core elements of a doctrine of deification. She identifies the "two poles of deification" as the "simultaneous emphasis on the unbreachable divide between creature and Creator and on the creature's likening to the Utterly Other," noting that "what is most characteristic of a doctrine of deification is the delicate balancing and negotiation of these two themes."[29] Around these two poles cluster several concepts that Williams considers specifically to be markers of a doctrine of deification as opposed to some other model of human sanctification: reference to human participation in divine life, union of God and humanity (though not, in her view, in association with the idea of divine indwelling), adoption (in her view a weaker marker than the others), and some way of articulating divine transcendence. With reference to the presence of these themes, Williams analyzes the texts of Aquinas and Palamas in order to evaluate the basic consonance of their teaching and thus the implications for dialogue.[30]

Williams's analysis of, and comparison with, Palamas need not concern us here, but her evaluation of Thomas's doctrine of deification in the *Summa* is relevant. Beginning with the loci where Thomas makes direct reference to "deification, deiformity and participation in divine nature," she traces connections to related texts to build a network of theological loci in the *Summa* associated with the notion.[31] She focuses on an important subset of the texts related to deification.[32] From these direct references, Williams moves

---

as a point of comparison because it is linked to a number of other fundamental doctrines—entailing discussion "not only of sanctification and theological anthropology generally, but also the doctrines of God and the Trinity, religious knowledge and theological method." Major issues that divide East and West—and Aquinas and Palamas in particular—revolve around these doctrines; for instance, the Western doctrine of divine simplicity versus the Eastern distinction between the divine essence and energies, the question of the direct vision of God, and the "apparently intractable" question of created grace (14–15). What is most basically at stake is the question of the relationship between God and humanity, a relationship that any doctrine of deification seeks to describe.

29. Ibid., 28.

30. Ibid., 32–33.

31. If Williams counts reference to 2 Pet 1:4's "sharing in the divine nature" as direct reference to deification, she underestimates Thomas's use of it in the *Summa*; it is also significant that he uses it much more often in this and other later works than in his earlier writings.

32. Williams identifies questions on the theological virtues (Ia-IIae q62) and the *visio Dei* (Ia q12) as the primary loci of reference to deification. In his treatment of the theological virtues, Thomas brings forward important points relevant to his teaching on deification: that hu-

to an analysis of the *Summa*'s treatments of the doctrine of God, theological anthropology, and participation and union of the image with God from nature to grace and glory, especially through charity, as relevant places to look for Thomas's doctrine of deification. Williams points out that, with his claim that a human subject can participate in the divine nature, Thomas "lays the foundation for the bridge that is any doctrine of divinization, a qualified spanning of the chasm between Uncreated and created."[33] This allies with her identification of the "two poles of deification," the "simultaneous emphasis on the unbreachable divide between creature and Creator and on the creature's likening to the Utterly Other." Throughout her treatment of texts in the *Summa*, Williams seeks and finds the presence of these two poles and their associated themes.[34] Williams observes in her analyses of questions on God as One and as Trinity, and on creation and grace, that Thomas negotiates the two poles as he describes how the transcendent God draws creatures into a share in the divine life through a participation that begins with existence. She notes, as I do, that the likening of the image to God is progressive, from nature to grace and glory, and ultimately Trinitarian in pattern, through the activity of the intellect and will shaped by the virtues. Williams thus highlights the theological virtues, especially charity, that assimilate and unite the creature to God, again emphasizing Thomas's concern to hold the two poles of deification together "in creative tension."[35]

In Williams's analysis of Thomas's treatment of grace she finds confirmation of the two-pole scheme discovered elsewhere. Williams does not advert to many other elements of Thomas's teaching on grace.[36] As I argue, however,

---

man beings participate the divine nature belonging to God essentially, and that by doing so they receive new principles of supernatural activity proportionate to this share in a higher nature, which has a supernatural end (Ia-IIae q62). Williams also notes that charity emerges as important in Thomas's account of deiformity, determining the level of the intellect's participation in the light of glory (Ia, q12). *Ground of Union*, 35–39.

33. Ibid., 36.

34. Ibid., 41. In accord with the intent of her study, Williams is also concerned with addressing related issues that seem to divide East and West, such as Thomas's foundational emphasis on God's simplicity, which, she argues, secures God's uniqueness and therefore transcendence. The question then becomes, she observes accurately, how humanity can be related to the "Utterly Other."

35. Ibid., 81. This approach shapes her analyses of charity and grace as created, another question disputed between East and West (for a response, see Appendix B).

36. Ibid., 82.

insight into Thomas's larger view of the functioning of grace in the sanctification of the image is needed to understand how the creature is progressively likened to God.[37] Her treatment of glory begins with a look at texts on the Incarnation, as bringing about "human sanctification-unto-glory" both by the renovation of human nature itself through the hypostatic union and its effects in individual human subjects.[38] This study also asserts that Thomas's teaching on the Incarnation is a key element in his understanding of sanctification as deification; but it will go into considerably more depth than Williams's brief treatment, especially on the grace of Christ and the teaching on divine adoption, which is central for Thomas in explaining the effects of Christ's grace in deification. Williams ends by discussing beatitude, in which the image knows and loves God by a participation in God's own self-knowledge and love. The gist of Williams's conclusion on Thomas's doctrine of deification is that it "emphasizes resoundingly the two themes characteristic of any classic exposition of theosis."[39] In her final comparative analysis of Thomas and Palamas, she finds this to be a basis of common ground between the two theologians in their doctrines of deification, although she concludes that each leans more to one pole or the other with respect to various elements of their teaching.[40]

Partly in response to Williams's monograph, the question of deification in Thomas Aquinas has become a contested issue. While a number of responses by Orthodox writers have naturally focused on her presentation of Palamas, some have also challenged the idea that Thomas has a true doctrine of deification. Gösta Hallonsten[41] and Paul Gavrilyuk[42] caution against a too-facile conflation of what Hallonsten calls the "real *doctrine of theosis*," which is "found only in the East,"[43] with the presence of some of the themes

---

37. E.g., Thomas's teaching on predestination, and the nature and role of habitual and auxiliary grace in shaping the image's activities on the journey to beatitude, provides the context for the connection between grace and glory, which Williams views as missing from the treatment of grace until the final question on merit (ibid., 86).

38. Ibid., 90.   39. Ibid., 159–60.

40. Ibid., 173–74.

41. Gösta Hallonsten, "*Theosis* in Recent Research: A Renewal of Interest and a Need for Clarity," in *Partakers of the Divine Nature: The History and Development of Deification in the Christian Tradition*," ed. Michael J. Christensen and Jeffrey A. Wittung (Madison, NJ: Fairleigh Dickinson University Press, 2007), 281–93.

42. Paul Gavrilyuk, "The Retrieval of Deification: How a Once-Despised Archaism Became an Ecumenical Desideratum," *Modern Theology* 25, no. 4: 647–59.

43. Hallonsten, "*Theosis* in Recent Research," 292n43. Italics in original.

of deification theology in Western authors. Hallonsten defines the doctrine of deification as a "comprehensive doctrine encompassing the whole economy of salvation," which comprises

a certain view of creation, especially of human beings; a soteriology, including the meaning of the Incarnation; a view of Christian life as sanctification connected to Church and sacraments; and the final goal of union with God. The whole structure of this comprehensive doctrine is determined by a teleology that implies that creation and human beings from the very beginning are endowed with an affinity and likeness that potentially draws them to God.[44]

According to Hallonsten, the doctrine of deification, properly so called, is characterized by a "dynamic anthropology" of image and likeness, in which "the fact of being created in the image of God is linked dynamically to the goal" (participation in divine life and union with God); "the meaning of Christian life is to assimilate to God, to grow according to the prototype."[45] The Incarnation is the central point of the economy of salvation, for "this prototype, the real Image of God, is Christ."[46]

In Hallonsten's view, there must be a fundamental difference between Eastern and Western doctrines of participation of human beings in divine life, because the East, drawing from the Platonic concept of participation, sees creation as a participation from God in "its very beginning ... grace cannot be separated from creation but inheres in it and potentially leads it to union with God." Hallonsten argues that in the Eastern view God causes creation "in the sense of formal causality, whereas in the Western view efficient causality takes its place: God and the world are distinct beings, even if the world participates in Being in an analogical sense." Williams's analysis ultimately falters, Hallonsten believes, because she does not adequately make this distinction and thus equates "having a doctrine of deification" with "having a doctrine of participation of whatever kind, together with the use of words like deification, partaking of the divine nature, adoption and filiation."[47] Gavrilyuk likewise comments that "Williams deploys

---

44. Ibid., 284–85.   45. Ibid., 285.
46. Ibid., 287.
47. Ibid., 286. In chapter 1, I argue that Thomas's notion of participation integrates both Neoplatonic and Aristotelian elements, supporting a view of God's causality as all-encompassing (final, efficient, and exemplar) and underpinning a conception of human beings as created from

the broadest definition of deification possible—participation in God—and then finds various instances of this idea in Thomas's theology," agreeing that there is a need for greater precision in using the terminology of participation, and that a definition of deification must include certain assumptions about Christology, anthropology, and sacraments as well as reference to a host of notions associated with every aspect of the spiritual life.[48]

Daniel Keating, in response to Hallonsten, defends the presence of a true doctrine of deification in Thomas Aquinas (and key Western fathers), which, though "its potential is not as fully explored and exploited as it is in the East," nevertheless shares the same patristic roots and "gives important shape to Christian theology."[49] Keating, in a brief though substantial essay titled "Justification, Sanctification and Divinization in Thomas Aquinas," examines a number of aspects of Thomas's teaching on how "the human race receives divine life and is transformed through grace into the image of Christ."[50] Keating begins his analysis not with the *Summa*, but with Thomas's biblical commentaries, a method that demonstrates effectively the truth in his contention that these commentaries provided a scriptural foundation for Thomas's mature thought in the *Summa*, a place where he worked out in depth the scriptural insights to which he refers more tersely in his later systematic work and that contribute to the "profound biblical basis" of the *Summa*'s systematic presentation of doctrine. This book, although it centers on analysis of texts from the *Summa*, draws upon Thomas's commentaries on scriptural loci relevant to his doctrine of deification in order to shed light on the biblical perspective of the *Summa*'s teaching.

Keating examines texts in Thomas's commentaries on John and the Pauline letters, showing the presence in Thomas's account of salvation of several interrelated themes that echo the patristic tradition. First is the centrality of

the outset with a likeness to God that dynamically orients them to the possibility of union with God in beatitude.

48. Gavrilyuk, "Retrieval of Deification," 651–52: "The list of such notions includes filial adoption, deliverance, spiritual battle, liberation from the power of the demonic, purification, forgiveness, justification, reconciliation, illumination, perfection, healing, sanctification, transfiguration, glorification, regeneration, imitation of Christ, incorporation into Christ, communion, second creation, election, eschatological consummation, recapitulation, deiformity, appropriation, sophianization, mystical union, and so on."

49. Keating, *Deification and Grace*, 6n8.

50. Keating, "Justification, Sanctification and Divinization in Thomas Aquinas," 139.

the Incarnation, the purpose of which is "the graced transformation, even the divinization, of the human race."[51] Related is the important role of the Holy Spirit, for "our participation in Christ's own transformed life comes about through participation in the Holy Spirit." Thomas's teaching on the Holy Spirit's role in sanctification is closely linked to that on grace and justification, for the indwelling Spirit with his gifts is the source of all grace.[52] This study's analysis of the *Summa* confirms many of Keating's conclusions drawn from the biblical commentaries. Keating considers how the relationship between grace and human freedom fundamentally shapes Thomas's views of justification, sanctification, and divinization,[53] and how Thomas draws from deep patristic roots in his use of 2 Peter 1:4 and the notion of participation in the divine nature to describe union with God through Christ.[54] Keating concludes that "Thomas not infrequently uses 2 Pet 1:4 as the biblical medium … for his doctrine of grace" and points out that Thomas's characterization of human transformation by grace as a participation in the divine nature refutes the notion that Thomas presents "a doctrine of grace that is cut off from its source in God."[55] On the basis of his analysis, which shows Thomas's emphasis on both the priority of grace and the free cooperation of transformed human nature in salvation, Keating concludes with the suggestion that Thomas's treatment of the virtues in the *Summa*'s IIa *pars* may be seen as "perhaps the most developed account in the Christian tradition of the possibilities for the divinization of human nature in the present age."[56]

Keating's study, though not claiming to be exhaustive or systematic, touches on a number of the central components of Thomas's theology of deification to be discussed in greater depth in this book; Williams also brings forward important aspects of Thomas's teaching, for instance, in her identification of the "two poles of deification." As these authors assert, there is warrant to think that Thomas does have a developed doctrine of deification, perhaps even one that accords with the comprehensive requirements

51. Ibid., 140.   52. Ibid., 150–51.
53. Ibid., 143.   54. Ibid., 153–54.
55. Ibid., 154. See also Marcel Sánchez Sorondo's study of Thomas's use of 2 Pet 1:4: *La gracia como participación de la naturaleza divina según Santo Tomás de Aquino*, intr., Cornelius Fabro, Bibliotheca Salmanticensis 28 (Salamanca: Universidad Pontificia de Salamanca, 1979).
56. Keating, "Justification, Sanctification and Divinization in Thomas Aquinas," 155.

of Hallonsten and Gavrilyuk. As noted above, however, it is not my intent to support a claim that Thomas's teaching on deification is (or is not) the same as the Eastern doctrine.[57] Rather, I seek, like Keating in his essay, to understand how the teaching on deification functions internally to Thomas's theology. I also accept, with Keating and Williams, that Thomas's repeated identification in the *Summa* of grace as a "participation in the divine nature" bestowed by God, who "alone can deify" (cf. Ia-IIae q112 a1 and 2 Pet 1:4), is a primary referent for his understanding of the notion of deification, as it was for so many of the Church Fathers.[58] The limited literature review of Thomas and deification above serves to raise the point that a fuller and more systematic understanding of what Thomas means by deification is clearly desirable.

The Larger Context of Deification in the *Summa*

The topic of deification falls at the intersection of many areas of Thomas's thought. Studies of Thomas's theology of the Trinity, image, beatific vision, missions, grace, virtues and gifts (especially charity and wisdom), Christ, Holy Spirit, adopted sonship, and sacraments are all relevant to this project. Of particular importance will be a number of these that have brought to the fore the significant evolution of Thomas's thought, from his early *Scriptum on the Sentences* to the *Summa theologiae* and other works of his later years, toward an increasingly dynamic understanding of the integrated roles of divine and human action in the movement of graced human beings to beatitude.[59] As many of these studies show, Thomas stresses in his mature

---

57. I would argue, however, that a fuller understanding of Thomas's own teaching is needed before making accurate comparisons, and so perhaps this study may prove useful in furthering that wider discussion.

58. E.g., Cyril of Alexandria; see Russell, *Doctrine of Deification*, 12, 200–202.

59. E.g., Joseph Wawrykow, *God's Grace and Human Action: "Merit" in the Theology of Thomas Aquinas* (Notre Dame, IN: University of Notre Dame Press, 1995); Bernard Lonergan, *Grace and Freedom: Operative Grace in the Thought of St. Thomas Aquinas*, ed. Frederick E. Crowe and Robert Doran (Toronto: University of Toronto Press, 2000, reprint, 2005); Henri Bouillard, *Conversion et grâce chez S. Thomas d'Aquin* (Paris: Aubier, 1944); see also, in relation to the divine missions, Gilles Emery, "Trinity and Creation," in *The Theology of Thomas Aquinas*, ed. Rik van Nieuwenhove and Joseph Wawrykow (Notre Dame, IN: University of Notre Dame Press, 2005), 58–76, and in relation to the perfection of the Trinitarian image, D. Juvenal Merriell, *To the Image of the Trinity* (Toronto: Pontifical Institute of Medieval Studies, 1990). Some have emphasized

teaching God's manifold causality as end, mover, and exemplar in the plan of divine providence to bring rational creatures to communion with himself.

It is within the context of this larger picture that I begin to locate Thomas's theology of deification. Before he presents his treatments of grace and the theological virtues and gifts in the *Summa*, he establishes a comprehensive framework within which the interplay of divine and human causality operates in the journey to beatitude. A sketch of this framework in chapter 1 provides the necessary background for understanding God's inner operation in the intellect and will of the human person brought to beatitude. There are two essential convictions at the heart of this causal picture: first, that God is the primary cause of created causality in every respect and, second, that God works with creatures according to the nature bestowed on them by creation or grace. As I describe in later chapters, because human beings are made to the image of God insofar as they are created with intellect and will, they are, like God, the principle of their own activity, "having free will and control of their actions,"[60] whether for their natural or supernatural end. So God, as the source of their free activity, works through their very freedom to bring them to the end ordained for them in divine providence. We must begin, though, by considering why Thomas thinks that to reach the supernatural end of beatitude the human person must be deified in the first place.

---

the integral, though at times hidden, place of the Holy Spirit working through grace and the infused virtues and gifts, which is an important element in Thomas's theology of deification: Servais Pinckaers, *The Sources of Christian Ethics*, trans. Sr. Thomas Mary Noble (Washington, DC: Catholic University of America Press, 1995), esp. chap. 7, and *The Pinckaers Reader: Renewing Thomistic Moral Theology*, ed. John Berkman and Craig Steven Titus, trans. Sr. Mary Thomas Noble et al. (Washington, DC: Catholic University of America Press, 2005); Ulrich Horst, *Die Gaben des Heiligen Geistes nach Thomas von Aquin* (Berlin: Akademie Verlag, 2001); Eugene Rogers, "The Eclipse of the Spirit in Thomas Aquinas," in *Grammar and Grace: Reformulations of Aquinas and Wittgenstein*, ed. Jeffrey Stout and Robert MacSwain (London: SCM Press, 2004), 136–53; Joseph Wawrykow, "Christ and the Gifts of the Holy Spirit According to Thomas Aquinas," in *Kirchenbild und Spiritualität: Dominikanische Beiträge zur Ekklesiologie und zum kirchlichen Leben im Mittelalter. Festschrift für Ulrich Horst zum 75. Geburtstag*, ed. T. Prügl and M. Schlosser (Paderborn: Schöning, 2007), 43–62. It has become evident that Thomas's progressive mastery of traditional sources, owing to both the new availability of translations in his lifetime and his more profound assimilation of the teaching of certain patristic theologians—Augustine in particular—had much to do with developments in his thought (see, e.g., Merriell, *To the Image of the Trinity*, 210ff; Wawrykow, *God's Grace and Human Action*, 269–76).

60. *ST* I-IIae prol.

CHAPTER 1

The Divine Source and End of the *Imago Dei*

We shall be like him, for we shall see him as he is.

—1 John 3:2

Thomas Aquinas's theology of deification describes God's gracious resolution of a providential paradox: the creation of human beings with the capacity to receive an end beyond their grasp, with the unfulfilled potential for an elevation so great that its realization is the highest manifestation of the divine goodness in God's wise plan of providence. Thomas inscribes the pattern of this resolution into the very structure of the *Summa theologiae*. He maps out his plan for the *Summa* in the prologue to Ia q2:

Because the principal aim of *sacra doctrina* is to hand on the knowledge of God—not only as he is in himself, but also as he is the source of things and their end, and especially of rational creatures, as is clear from what has already been said—we intend to set forth this doctrine by treating first, of God; second, of the advance of rational creatures towards God; third, of Christ, who as man is the way directing us to God.[1]

In referring to "what has already been said" about God as source and end, Thomas makes an allusion to q1, where in the first article of the *Sum-*

---

1. For the sake of consistency and accuracy, I have generally chosen to translate the term *homo* and its derivatives in Thomas's text using "man" or "mankind" in the traditional gender-inclusive manner, to indicate the state of belonging to the human race. Use of the term "human" in translation reflects a form of the actual underlying term *humanus*.

ma he begins by talking about the end.[2] God is the end of human beings, he says in q1 a1, and this poses something of a paradox, for human beings as rational creatures are "directed to God, as to an end that surpasses the grasp of reason." *Sacra doctrina*, divinely inspired knowledge revealed by God through Scripture, is therefore necessary for salvation because "the whole of human salvation, which is in God, depends on knowledge of this truth." That the last end of rational creatures exceeds their own grasp emphasizes their absolute dependence on God to attain the goal toward which he orders them; that the goal is God himself requires human beings to possess knowledge of God, so that, Thomas says, they may "direct their thoughts and actions to the end."

While human thought and action must be engaged and directed to God, they are insufficient for this task on their own. The question on *sacra doctrina* anticipates the theological anthropology of the *Summa*, a teaching on human beings made to the image of God and transformed by grace to share the divine life. Regarding the attainment of the end, Thomas in Ia q1 a1 quotes Isaiah 64:4: "Eye has not seen, O God, without you, what you have prepared for those who love you." Not surprisingly, this text and its New Testament partner, 1 Corinthians 2:9, appear elsewhere in the *Summa* where Thomas refers to the beatific vision and the impossibility of its attainment through human thought and action alone.[3] At least three of these references occur in contexts especially relevant for Thomas's theology of deification. In the beginning of the IIa *pars*, where Thomas presents beatitude as the goal of human life, he asks whether we can reach this happiness by our natural powers and answers in the negative:

2. Cf. also Ia q1 a7.

3. 1 Cor 2:9: "Eye has not seen, nor ear heard, neither has it entered into the heart of man, what things God has prepared for those who love him." Note that Thomas's text for the Isaiah passage (here and elsewhere in the *Summa*) is "Oculus non Deus absque te quae preparasti *diligentibus* te," which differs from the Vulgate's *expectantibus te* but brings the text into harmony with 1 Cor 2:9: "quod oculus non vidit nec auris audivit nec in cor hominis ascendit quae praeparavit Deus his qui diligunt illum." On the other hand, when Thomas quotes the latter passage, he frequently (and always in the *Summa*) grammatically conflates it, by the use of the dative, with that of the Isaiah passage (i.e., *quae praeparavit Deus diligentibus se*). This may serve at least as an indication of their immediate relationship in his mind, and the interpretation he places on both seems to connect the beatific vision as the last end of rational creatures with the love that leads those creatures there. For the Isaiah text, see also *ST* IIa-IIae q175 a3; IIIa q55 a1.

Man is naturally the principle of his own action, by his intellect and will. But the final happiness prepared for the saints exceeds the human intellect and will; for the Apostle says (1 Cor 2:9): "Eye has not seen, nor ear heard, neither has it entered into the human heart, what God has prepared for those who love him." Therefore man cannot attain happiness by his natural powers.[4]

At the outset of his treatment of the moral life, Thomas signals that something must be added to human beings called to beatitude to enable them to successfully "direct their thoughts and actions to the end."

Thomas describes these added powers later in the IIa *pars* when he discusses the theological virtues in Ia-IIae q62. Remarking again that the human intellect and will "fall short of the order of supernatural beatitude according to 1 Cor 2:9: 'Eye has not seen,' etc.," he argues that human beings must "receive certain supernatural principles"—faith, hope, and charity—added to intellect and will in order to attain the happiness described by Paul.[5] But at the origin of these new principles is the transformation of grace, for not only are the natural powers of intellect and will incapable of attaining supernatural beatitude on their own, but also human nature, as their source, is itself radically insufficient, ontologically underproportioned for eternal life and so incapable of producing the acts necessary to get there. In q114 on merit, at the end of the Ia-IIae *pars*, Thomas again refers to Paul's text, writing:

Now eternal life is a good exceeding the proportion of created nature; since it also exceeds its knowledge and desire, according to 1 Cor. 2[:9]: "Eye has not seen, nor ear heard, neither has it entered into the human heart." And thence it is that no created nature is a sufficient principle of an act meritorious of eternal life, unless there be added some supernatural gift, which is called grace.[6]

Not only the natural powers, then, but also created human nature itself as the principle of these powers and their acts must be changed by grace, making it proportionate to eternal life, so that human knowledge and love can be raised to the happiness of the saints.

What exactly does it mean for human nature to be proportioned to eternal life? The primary scriptural authority for Thomas on the possibility of the beatific vision is 1 John 3:2: "We shall be like him, for we shall see him as he is." So the transformation that takes place in the "advance of rational

4. *ST* I-IIae q5 a5 s.c.   5. *ST* I-IIae q62 a3.
6. *ST* Ia-IIae q114 a2.

ὅμοιοι αὐτῷ ἐσόμεθα, ὅτι ὀψόμεθα αὐτὸν καθὼς ἐστιν

creatures" to the vision of God must consist in becoming more like God. Before we can understand exactly how Thomas thinks of this transforming journey as deification, however, we must consider what he has to say in the beginning of the *Summa*'s treatment of the divine nature, about the relationship between God and creation, which grounds the movement of all creatures, according to their natures, toward their Creator.

The Divine Source and End of Creatures

Most scholars agree that the organizational principle of *exitus* and *reditus*, derived from Neoplatonism, which holds that everything returns to its originating source, influences the *Summa*'s structure to some degree. Marie-Dominique Chenu, who proposed that the *exitus-reditus* scheme mapped in a straightforward way onto the Ia and IIa *pars*, first offered this insight in 1939.[7] As others pointed out, however, this seemed to relegate the IIIa *pars*, which treats Christ and his sacraments, to the role of an appendage. Albert Patfoort notes that Thomas already makes reference to the notion of the *reditus* of creation in the Ia *pars*, and the IIIa *pars* treats the *reditus* as well, for the return of human persons to God takes place precisely through Christ.[8] Marie-Vincent LeRoy proposes that the *exitus-reditus* scheme applies only to Thomas's treatment of the divine economy, beginning with Ia q44, on creation, and continuing through the IIIa *pars*, that is, after the "theology" or treatment of God *in se*.[9]

As Jean-Pierre Torrell points out, Thomas's use of the Neoplatonic construction of procession and return is not an attempt to impose a philosophical schema upon Christian doctrine; it is governed by faith and the Creed. The Incarnation is far from a disruption to the scheme in his thought; rather, it is precisely through the Incarnation that the movement of *exitus* and *reditus* achieves its fruition.[10] Most fundamentally, Thomas grounds his use

7. Marie-Dominique Chenu, "Le plan de la Somme théologique de saint Thomas," *Revue thomiste* 47 (1939): 93–107.

8. Albert Patfoort, "L'unité de la *Ia Pars* et la mouvement interne de la Somme théologique de S. Thomas d'Aquin," *Revue des sciences philosophiques et théologiques* 47 (1963): 513–44. Reprinted in Patfoort, *Thomas d'Aquin: Les clefs d'une théologie* (Paris: FAC Éditions, 1983), 49–70.

9. Marie-Vincent Leroy, Review of *Thomas d'Aquin: Les clefs d'une théologie*, by Albert Patfoort, *Revue thomiste* (1984): 298–303.

10. Jean Pierre Torrell, *Saint Thomas Aquinas*, vol. 1, *The Person and His Work*, trans. Robert

of the *exitus-reditus* principle in the Christian doctrine of creation; everything comes forth from and returns to God, as caused by divine knowledge, freely willed by divine love, and ordered to its end by divine wisdom. So the *Summa* is properly theological or theocentric as a whole. Thomas's theology of deification is perhaps the clearest example of the fulfillment of the *exitus* and *reditus* of rational creatures through God's creating and redeeming Word.

The first thing to be studied, as the "source of things and their end," is God in himself. But even in the first questions (Ia qq2–11), which purport to be about the divine nature itself—that is, whether God exists, and if so, how—there is an economic element, as these questions contain foundational claims about created beings and their relationship to the divine nature, upon which Thomas builds in later, more properly economic, sections. This is perforce the case because of Thomas's theological method in these questions, which is to work from the known to the unknown, from effects to causes, so that from God's effects (i.e., all of creation) something about God can be known (Rom 1:19–20).[11]

God's existence can itself be demonstrated, Thomas argues, by the ne-

---

Royal (Washington, DC: Catholic University of America Press, 2003), 153–55. Cf. Torrell, "Imiter Dieu comme des enfants bien-aimés," in *Novitas et Veritas Vitae: Aux Sources du Renouveau de la Morale Chrétienne*, ed. Carlos-Josaphat Pinto de Oliveira (Fribourg: Éditions Universitaires, 1991), 53–65.

11. *ST* Ia q2 a2 s.c. Indeed, Ia q12, on "how God is known by us" (or "how God exists in our cognition," q12 prol.), and Ia q13, on the names of God (i.e., on how God can be spoken about by us), might seem somewhat out of place in the midst of a treatment of God's substance and operations (qq2–26) unless one recognizes that for Thomas, because God is both the object of knowledge under consideration and the source of the power of knowing, questions about the latter, as effect, are integrally related to those about the former, as cause. Cf. *ST* Ia q12 a2. Thomas will explore in q13 the limitations of human language about God, who is *in se* beyond human comprehension and linguistic categories. Yet, he says, we can speak about God by analogy with created things, for God is related to them as the cause of creaturely perfections, and in God those perfections first exist preeminently. We can speak truly, though imperfectly, about God, by using words derived from the experience of the partial perfection of creatures because the full reality signified by the words exists first in God (a6). Before Thomas can present this teaching on theological analogy to describe God by way of words first used for God's effects, though, he must demonstrate that there is a basis for the use of analogy by establishing that there is the kind of ontological relationship between God and creation that this analogy presupposes. He does this from the beginning of the questions on the divine nature. On Thomas's doctrine of theological analogy, see Gregory Rocca, *Speaking the Incomprehensible God* (Washington, DC: Catholic University of America Press, 2004).

cessity of a primary cause of change, of causality itself, and of contingency, perfection, and the goal-directedness of all things to an end (q2 a3). These are claims about the universal cause, "which we call God," but also about the way in which things in the world are causally dependent upon and governed by God. In q3 a4 the most fundamental reason for this dependence becomes clear. In discussing God's simplicity, or lack of composition, Thomas argues that God's essence and existence are one, and in so doing sets out the principle that governs his understanding of the metaphysical relationship between God and the created order: God's essence is to exist, whereas everything else exists by participation in God's existence, "just as that which has fire, but is not itself fire, is on fire by participation."[12] To have an essence apart from existence implies potentiality and composition because existence is to essence as actuality to potentiality. But because God is the first existent, there can be no potentiality in him. God is "Pure Act," preceding and causing the existence of everything else, which is potential relative to God.[13] The relationship of the participated existence of creatures to God's essential existence is that of potency to act.

In q4 a1 ad3 Thomas argues that existence itself (*ipsum esse*) is the greatest perfection, for it actuates everything: "Nothing has actuality except insofar as it exists, hence *ipsum esse* is the actuality of all things and even of their forms."[14] The notion that God, as *ipsum esse*, actualizes all things as the participated source of existence and perfection is fundamental to Thomas's conception of God as both transcendent to and actively immanent within the created order—and especially to his teaching on deification. As Thomas begins the properly economic section of the *Summa* with his discussion of creation in Ia q44 a1, he refers to this notion to argue that everything that exists must be created by God, who is *ipsum esse per se subsistens* and so is the source of all participated being, "as iron is ignited by fire."[15] Thomas con-

---

12. *ST* Ia q3 a4.

13. *ST* Ia q3 a1, a2: "Deus est purus actus, non habens aliquid de potentialitate."

14. *ST* Ia q4 a1 ad3.

15. *ST* Ia q44 a1: "It must be said that everything that in any way exists, does so from God. For whatever is found in anything by participation, necessarily is caused in it by that to which it belongs essentially, just as iron is made fiery by fire. Now it has been shown above (q3, a4) in treating of the divine simplicity that God is his own existence subsisting through himself (*ipsum esse per se subsistens*) ... Therefore it remains that all things apart from God are not their own existence, but participate existence."

sistently uses the traditional metaphor of an object heated by fire to illustrate the idea of participation by creatures, through the gifts of creation and grace, in what belongs to God essentially.[16]

Participation and Perfection

On a philosophical level, Thomas's understanding of the fundamental relationship between God and creatures is that of participated cause to participating effect. God, as *ipsum esse subsistens*, participates to every creature existence and perfection; each is thus related to and dependent upon him as effect to cause, and as potency to act.[17] Thomas applies the notion of participation in varying ways throughout the *Summa*, in contexts having to do with the relation of creatures, and especially rational creatures, to their divine source and end. Most often, especially in the Ia *pars*, he speaks in terms of participation in the divine goodness or likeness, whether simply by existing, or by living, or also by knowing and understanding, as in the case of the image.[18] References to participation in the divine goodness later in

16. E.g., *ST* Ia q3 a4, q4 a2, q6 a3, q8, a1, q44 a1, q45 aa6–7; Ia-IIae q62 a1 ad1, q112 a1; IIIa q62 a1.

17. For helpful recent overviews of the twentieth-century recovery by Thomist metaphysicians of the notion of participation as central to Thomas's thought, which provide summaries of significant features of Thomas's doctrine, see John Rziha, *Perfecting Human Actions: St. Thomas Aquinas on Human Participation in Eternal Law* (Washington, DC: Catholic University of America Press, 2009), chap. 1; and Gregory T. Doolan, *Aquinas on the Divine Ideas as Exemplar Causes* (Washington, DC: Catholic University of America Press, 2008). The writings of Cornelio Fabro provided major early contributions to this recovery—largely summarized in "The Intensive Hermeneutics of Thomistic Philosophy: The Notion of Participation," *Review of Metaphysics* 27, no. 3 (1974): 449–91—and Louis-Bertrand Geiger, *La participation dans la philosophie de S. Thomas d'Aquin* (Paris: J. Vrin, 1952). Significant recent contributions include John Wippel's "Thomas Aquinas and Participation," in *Studies in Medieval Philosophy*, vol. 17, ed. John Wippel (Washington, DC: Catholic University of America Press, 1987), 117–58, in which he also discusses the work of Fabro and Geiger. Wippel likewise devotes a chapter to Thomas's doctrine of participation in *The Metaphysical Thought of Thomas Aquinas: From Finite Being to Uncreated Being* (Washington, DC: Catholic University of America Press, 2000), 94–131; see also his article on "Metaphysics," in *The Cambridge Companion to Aquinas*, ed. Norman Kretzmann and Eleanor Stump, 93–95 (Cambridge: Cambridge University Press, 1993). William Norris Clarke provides a number of helpful essays on the topic of participation in *Explorations in Metaphysics* (Notre Dame, IN: University of Notre Dame Press, 1994). A recent major treatment is Rudi te Velde's *Participation and Substantiality in Thomas Aquinas* (Leiden: E. J. Brill, 1995).

18. E.g., *ST* Ia q4 aa2–3, q6 a4, q14 a6, q44 aa3–4 ad3, q47 a1, q57 a1, q93 a2, q106 a4; Ia-IIae q1 a8; IIae-IIae q2 a3.

the *Summa* tend to refer more specifically to the fuller participation in this goodness, which belongs to grace and glory in both angels and humans.[19] Thomas defines grace in the *Summa* as a "participation in the divine nature"; he describes wisdom and charity too as participations in the likeness of the Son and Holy Spirit—a combination of formulations that, used systematically, appears only in his mature work.

The notion of participation thus provides a metaphysical hermeneutic for his teaching on both creation and grace in the *Summa*. Its significance becomes evident when Thomas's unique understanding of participation itself is considered, with its implications for the relationship between God and the created order.[20] Participation, as Thomas defines it most basically in his commentary on Boethius's *De hebdomadibus*, means that something receives in particular fashion what belongs to another in universal or total fashion.[21] While he distinguishes various types of participation in this commentary, he refers most often in his later works, especially in relation to creation, to the ontological participation of an effect in its cause.[22] He

19. E.g., *ST* Ia-IIae q110 a2; IIae-IIae q172 a2; IIIa q1 a2, q20 a1 ad3, q27 a5, q56 a2 ad1, q57 a4. As discussed in this chapter, Thomas also talks about nature, grace, and glory in specific relation to the knowledge of God as increasing participations in the light of the divine intellect. E.g., *ST* Ia q12 a2, a5, a11 ad3; q79 a4; Ia-IIae q91 a2 (cf. a3 ad1, where Thomas also describes human reason as a participation of divine wisdom).

20. Te Velde suggests that the frequency of Thomas's use of the notion of participation as a way of conceiving of creation increased from his earlier to later works, acquiring maturity and precision as he moved toward his own original view of the concept. As te Velde points out, this was likely associated with his closer reading in his later career of Dionysius's *De divinis nominibus* and Proclus (in the newly translated *Elementatio theologica* as well as the eponymous *Liber de causis* drawn from it). *Participation and Substantiality in Thomas Aquinas*, 3–4.

21. Thomas Aquinas, *Exp. Lib. Heb.* lect2 no24.

22. Ibid. Aquinas's classification in *De Hebdominabus* 2.23–24 is discussed in Wippel, "Thomas Aquinas and Participation," 119ff, and "Metaphysics," 93–95. Thomas distinguishes between three types of participation: it may be purely logical, as when an individual participates in a species; this is a case of participation in a universal concept. Participation may also be ontological or real in one of two ways. First is in the case of a given subject and a received perfection, resulting, e.g., in the real composition of a substance and its accidents. The second type of ontological participation is that of an effect in its cause, especially when it is not equal to the power of its cause. As te Velde has shown, Thomas adjusts the notion of participation that he received from Boethius, who had problematized the concept by opposing participation and substantiality—Boethius asked whether things are good by participation or by their substance and thus associated participation only with accidentality. *Participation and Substantiality*, 15ff. Te Velde also notes that in his later works Thomas shifts the primary focus from participation in goodness to participation in being (44ff).

holds that such participation can be on the level of substance; a created substance itself participates in being (and thus in all other perfections), on a level higher than that of essence, its existence and essence created *ex nihilo* in unity as co-principles of its actual existence.[23]

Thomas was original in integrating the Aristotelian structure of act and potency into the Neoplatonic system of participation, which he derived from sources such as Dionysius's *On the Divine Names* and *Celestial Hierarchy* as well as the *Liber de causis*.[24] The concept of participation underlies Dionysius's scheme of procession and return (*exitus-reditus*), presented in the context of relating the created world to its supereminent divine Cause. The universe is seen in terms of a Neoplatonic participation structure in which all things come forth from the transcendent Good, which "contains everything beforehand within itself,"[25] and return to it through desire, rational beings becoming deified by the illumination of their intellects, each after their own fashion.[26] Everything exists in an ordered hierarchy by participation in this providential Cause of the universe, "[who] in the beautiful, good superabundance of his benign yearning for all is also carried outside of himself in the loving care he has for everything."[27] The first gift of the transcendent Goodness, which preexists all things and in which everything participates, is the gift of existence, and all other perfections are rooted in participation in Being.[28] The deifying return of intellectual beings to the Good takes place as the Good "draws sacred minds upward to its permitted contemplation, to participation and to the state of becoming like it."[29]

Thomas retains the Dionysian sense of God's transcendence and universal causality, securing what Robert Sokolowski has called "the Christian distinction" between God and the world,[30] a distinction essential to Thom-

---

23. See te Velde, *Participation and Substantiality*, 158–59.

24. Thomas frequently refers to Dionysian sources in Ia qq2–13 and was writing his commentary *De divinis nominibus* either concurrently with the Ia *pars* or shortly beforehand. On Thomas's originality in this regard, see Clarke, *Explorations in Metaphysics*, 79–82.

25. Dionysius, *Divine Names* 1.7. Translated by Colm Luibheid as *Pseudo-Dionysius: The Complete Works* (New York: Paulist Press, 1987), 56.

26. Ibid., 1.5–6. Luibheid, *Pseudo-Dionysius*, 54.

27. Ibid., 2.5, 4.4, 4.13. Luibheid, *Pseudo-Dionysius*, 82.

28. Ibid., 5.5–6.

29. Ibid. Luibheid, *Pseudo-Dionysius*, 50.

30. Robert Sokolowski's comparison of pagan and (Judeo-) Christian notions of divinity shows that for pagans the divine is always part of the world, albeit the noblest part. Even when

as's doctrine of deification. For Thomas, though, God is transcendent to the whole created order not because he is above being but because in his own nature he has the subsistent, unlimited fullness of being (and of all perfections), in which all creatures participate.[31] The very existence of creatures is a share in the subsistent existence of God, who is their primary cause. Furthermore, because God, as *ipsum esse*, is the absolutely transcendent source of all things, he is also completely immanent. Concerning God's presence in created things, Thomas explains:

Now since God is existence itself through his own essence, created existence must be his proper effect, just as to ignite is the proper effect of fire. Now God causes this effect in things not only when they first begin to exist, but as long as they are preserved in being ... being is innermost (*magis intimum*) in each thing and most deeply within all things (*profundius omnibus inest*), since it is formal with respect to everything which is in a thing ... Hence it must be that God is in all things, and innermostly (*intime*).[32]

God is therefore in all things continually "as an agent is present to that upon which it works."[33]

---

the divine is source of all that exists, as for Plato, the divine and the world are still part of one eternal structure of necessity, one order of things. Thus, when the divine enters the world in human form (as in the pagan myths), it must displace or limit the human element. The gods are in competition with human beings and are subject to the same external laws of fate. With its doctrine of creation, Christianity makes a radical departure: God is recognized as totally other than the world, complete and perfect; the existence of creation is gratuitous. Thus, for Christianity, the entrance of the divine into the world as both God and man in the Incarnation may be understood as a "coherent mystery." Because God is radically transcendent to the world, he is not defined in contrast to other beings in the world. The divine nature can even be united to a human nature without displacing or truncating it. Sokolowski calls this shift in cosmology based on revelation "the Christian distinction." *The God of Faith and Reason: Foundations of Christian Theology* (Notre Dame, IN: University of Notre Dame, 1982), 23.

31. While Dionysius refers to God as "being itself," in order to say that God is the cause of being insofar as he is above all being (*Divine Names* 11.6), for Aquinas, as discussed above, the term *ipsum esse* applies to God not only causally—in that God is the cause of all beings— but also substantially. See te Velde, *Participation and Substantiality*, 265. As te Velde notes, this means that for Thomas there is a positive identity in God of Being itself and other divine perfections such as Life itself and Understanding itself, and God can truly (though defectively) be named as such, while for Dionysius God *in se* remains ineffably above the divine perfections, which are variously manifested (and thus named) by their participations in creatures. For Thomas, the perfection of being in God includes every other perfection; see Ia q4 a2.

32. *ST* Ia q8 a1.

33. Ibid.

The Christian distinction implies that God is present and active within the created order in a noncompetitive manner. God does not displace or replace anything in the creature, as if he were another substance in the created order that would compete with it for metaphysical space, nor does God enter into composition with creatures as a form (which would result in pantheism).[34] Rather, because God as *ipsum esse* is totally other than the world, he can be, and must be, causally present as the ontological precondition for the creature's existence and activity in the first place. This insight is fundamental to Thomas's understanding of the working of created causality in God's providential plan to bring creatures to the perfection he ordains for them, and so it grounds his doctrine of deification.

Thomas's unique integration of the Aristotelian notion of act and potency into this Neoplatonic participation structure frames his understanding that all created things are related to God through a hierarchy of perfection, in which each creature, while causally dependent on God (who is their source, exemplar, and end), nevertheless has its own proper metaphysical reality and causality.[35] In Ia q4 a1 Thomas establishes that because God is the first principle, and so most "in act," he is most perfect, having the perfection of existence that "actuates all things, even their forms" (ad3). On the basis of the participation relationship between God and creatures, Thomas argues that every created perfection flows fundamentally from partici-

34. Responding in *ST* Ia q3 a8 ad1 to the objection (drawn from Dionysius, *CH* 4) that God must enter into composition with other things because "the being of all things is that which is above being—the Godhead," Thomas replies that "the Godhead is called the being of all things as their efficient and exemplar cause, but not as being their essence."

35. As early as the *De ente et essentia* (*Opera Omnia*, vol. 43; Rome: Editori di San Tommaso, 1976), 315–81, Thomas had argued for a composition in creatures of form and existence, taking Aristotle's hylomorphism to a new level: something actualizes form itself. *Esse*, subsistent in God, who is pure actuality, becomes the ground of actuality and thus perfection in creatures. Thomas is able to place the whole hierarchy of created composite beings into a causal picture in which God is Pure Act and therefore the giver of existence/perfection to each existent creature, in which existence is received and therefore "limited and restricted to the capacity of the recipient nature" (5.4; 4.8–10, 5.1–4). Whether spiritual or corporeal, creatures are differentiated by their degree of perfection, which depends on "their distance from potentiality and their closeness to pure act" (5.8). In the *De ente* Thomas does not yet systematically employ the language of participation to describe how this hierarchical causal picture works. But the essence/existence distinction is a necessary foundation for understanding how God shares his existence and thus his perfections in varying degrees with creatures: how the many can participate in the act of existence of the One, and in the divine perfections, without being God.

pation in God's subsistent existence: "all perfections pertain to the perfection of existing, for things are perfect insofar as they have being in a certain way" (q4 a2). Thus Thomas says in q4 a3 that creatures can truly be said to resemble God, "although by analogy only, as God is a being by essence, and other things [are beings] by participation" (ad3). This predication by analogy is based on an ontological participation relationship in reality. In creating, God causes creatures to share to varying degrees in the perfect act of divine being. A creature's degree of perfection is thus constituted by its degree of participation in being—that is, by its degree of actuality—insofar as it participates to the extent proper to its nature in God's own perfect act of being.[36]

Thomas refers to the way that human creatures participate in the divine perfections early in these questions on the divine nature. In q3 a1, on whether God is a body, Thomas answers an objection that humans, according to Genesis 1:26, are "made to the image" but are corporeal: "It is according to his intelligence and reason, which are incorporeal, that man is said to be according to the image of God" (ad2). In the *sed contra* of q4 a3, on whether any creature can be like God, Thomas refers again to Genesis 1:26, and to another Scripture text that will be central in his discussions of the divine image in human persons, their deification, and their perfection in glory: "When he appears we shall be like him" (1 Jn 3:2). Although Thomas does not specifically discuss these Scripture verses in his reply to q4 a3, he seems to be indicating, by bringing them forward as his authorities in the *sed contra*, that he is preparing the ground for his treatments of the progressive perfection of the resemblance of human beings to God (and therefore their increasing actualization or participation in being), by creation in the divine image, and deification by grace and glory.

Thomas's integration of an Aristotelian act-potency structure into the Neoplatonic scheme of participation has been said to "represent a peculiarly original stroke of genius" because it allows for the proper metaphysical unity of creatures. If a metaphysical entity has its own unity, it is capable of its own proper actuality or reality and is the principle of its own activity.[37] Thomas follows Aristotle (rather than Plato) in his acknowledgment

---

36. *ST* Ia q44 a1.

37. Clarke, *Explorations in Metaphysics*, 80–81, 95. Thomas adopts the basic Neoplatonic structure of an unlimited perfect source (the supreme perfection of *esse*), limited by reception

that every creature has full reality in itself, even though, because it exists and acts by participation, it is totally dependent on the Creator.[38] Creatures have their own proper act of being (according to their nature); therefore they also have their own proper share in the perfections that flow from being, and first of all in goodness:

> From the First who is being and good, through his own essence, everything can be called good and a being, inasmuch as it participates in it by way of a certain assimilation, although remotely and deficiently … Everything therefore is called good from the divine goodness, as from the first exemplary, effective and final principle of all goodness. Nevertheless, everything is called good on account of the similitude of the divine goodness inhering in it, which is formally its own goodness, denominating it as good.[39]

Such an understanding gives full weight to the goodness of created things in themselves, as well as to the causal primacy of the divine goodness in which they participate. God is the "first exemplary, effective and final principle" of creatures who originate from God not only as from an efficient cause but also by sharing in God's own existence and perfection as exemplar cause; so their *reditus* to God as final cause takes place precisely through their own perfection in God's likeness according to their nature. In desiring their own perfection, creatures desire God, the source of their perfection,[40] and the perfection proper to rational creatures in desiring God is to know God *secundum seipsum*.[41]

By the time Thomas gets to Ia q12, where his main subject is the knowl-

---

in the created essences of participating subjects (75–79). At the same time, he identifies *esse* as an actualizing principle relative to the potency of created essence. This synthesis (from the *Summa contra Gentiles* onward), Clarke argues, safeguards the metaphysical unity of creatures as ontological and operating subjects in their own right, a unity threatened in the traditional Neoplatonic participation scheme, which "habitually left vague, unexplained, and dangerously ambiguous the unity of the composite resulting from the superposition of participated on participant" (79). In a unified composite subject, one of its components must function as act and the other as potency, for two entities in act cannot be completely united: "In every composite there must be act and potency. For many cannot become simply one unless there is something which is act and something else which is potency." (Cf. Aquinas, *SCG* I.18; *De spir. creat.* 3. See Clarke, *Explorations in Metaphysics*, 96.) A composite being cannot have intrinsic unity unless it is unified by a single higher act (Clarke, *Explorations in Metaphysics*, 18–19).

38. Fabro, "Intensive Hermeneutics of Thomistic Philosophy," 449.

39. *ST* Ia q6 a4.   40. *ST* Ia q6 a1, a2.

41. *ST* Ia q6 a1 ad2.

edge of God in the beatific vision as the goal of all human knowing and desiring, he has already established a great deal about the parameters of the
transformation necessary for humans to attain this final perfection. We already know at this point that while all creatures share God's goodness, and
in a sense become more like God as they move toward the fullest share in
divine perfection possible to them, human perfection is a true deification
because it consists in an increasing share in existence as a specific resemblance of God, in the divine image and likeness. Human beings are made in
God's image "according to intellect and reason,"[42] and to know God is the
highest fulfillment of the human intellect. Thus, in the full participation of
humans in the divine perfection, there is a level of union and intentionality
lacking in the perfection of nonrational creatures. And, as is evident from
the very first questions of the *Summa*, this "advance of the rational creature
towards God," which consists of "seeing him as he is," can only take place if
human nature and its proper activities are elevated by grace to this supernatural end, for it is "an end that surpasses the grasp of reason."[43]

The Vision of God in Glory: Goal of the Journey

In Ia q12 Thomas examines the possibility and means of humans attaining
to this knowledge of God. As in q1, Thomas begins his treatment by directing our attention first to the ultimate end of human knowledge of God; the
first ten articles of q12 ask not how we can know God in this life, but how
the blessed will know him in the next. The beatific vision is presented as the
goal and perfection of all human knowing and loving, which must involve a
greater participation in the likeness of God. And so, as q12 unfolds, Thomas
introduces the language of "deiformity" for the first time.

First, however, Thomas must address the objection that it seems impossible for a created intellect to see God at all. In the background to q12 is a
controverted history of debate over the possibility and mode of the *visio
Dei*, which in 1241 had been resolved, juridically at least, by the formal declaration of Bishop William of Auvergne and the Masters of Paris that "we
firmly believe and assert that God will be seen in his essence or substance by
the saints, by angels, and by glorified souls."[44] Two central issues emerged

---

42. *ST* Ia q3 a1 ad2.   43. *ST* Ia q1 a1.

44. Bishop William and the Masters condemned those who taught the opinion that the

in the history of this discussion—first, the problem of the lack of proportionality between the human mind and God, emphasized in the writings of Greek Fathers such as Dionysius and John Chrysostom and newly discovered by the West, and, second, the need—according to Aristotle—for a medium or similitude in all knowledge, which the notion of an immediate vision of the divine essence, taught by Augustine, seems to contradict.[45] After 1241, theologians had to explain how a finite created intellect can be proportionate to the vision of the uncreated essence of God, and how God can be seen in the beatific vision without any intervening extrinsic medium.

By the time of the *Summa*, Thomas offers an answer to these questions more radical than many of his contemporaries, and more nuanced in at least one significant way than an earlier treatment in the *De veritate* (hereafter *DV*). Whereas some theologians in the Fransciscan tradition (e.g., Bonaventure in the *Itinerarium*) essentially bypassed the problem of intellectual proportionality by proposing a supraintellectual affective union in the vision,[46] Thomas (following Albert the Great) posits that the intellect

---

vision of God in heaven must be indirect at best. Their declaration was something of a triumph for Augustinianism in the Latin tradition, which, with its confidence of the immediacy of the beatific vision as promised in Scripture (1 Jn 3:2), had been predominant in early scholasticism. Henri Dondaine, "L'objet et le 'medium' de la vision béatifique chez les théologiens du XIIIe siècle," *Recherches de théologie ancienne et médiévale* 19 (1952): 60–130.

45. Opposition to the notion of the direct vision of God arose in the twelfth and thirteenth centuries with the introduction to the West of the Greek Fathers as well as Aristotle, which raised both metaphysical and epistemological challenges to this "Christian hope." Translations of Dionysius, John Damascene, and John Chrysostom seemed to undermine the possibility of the full vision of God, with their teaching on God's absolute incomprehensibility to the human mind; it seemed he could only be known in "brilliant darkness" by means of theophanies (as taught by Eriugena), reflections of his essence in the creatures he illuminates. The challenge is one of proportionality; the objection is that the finite human mind is unable to encompass the infinite uncreated reality of God. Aristotelian epistemology, too, challenged the possibility of the immediate vision of God with its demand for a medium or similitude in all knowledge (Dondaine, "L'objet et le 'medium'"). The problem of the need for a medium drove discussion, and some attempted to reconcile Augustine and Aristotle by employing the solution of "avicennizing augustinianism," in which God, in the role of the agent intellect, impresses a form like a mirror by interior illumination on the passive possible intellect. See Christian Trottmann, *La vision béatifique: Des disputes scolastiques à sa définition par Benoît XII* (Rome: École Française de Rome, 1995), 150ff. This impressed form in which God is seen, however, is still a medium extrinsic to the intellect, and such solutions were rejected by the condemnation, which demanded an immediate vision of the essence itself.

46. Trottmann, *La vision béatifique*, 197ff, 343–44.

itself is reproportioned by the gift of a supernatural intrinsic disposition in the soul, by which God can be seen immediately: the light of glory. Thomas, however, goes beyond Albert's contention that the knowledge of God in the beatific vision is nonquidditative.[47] Whereas in this life we can know only *that* God is, Thomas says in the *De veritate* that in the beatific vision we will see God *quid est*: not only that he is, but *what* he is.[48] Only in this way can the beatitude of intellectual substances be complete.[49]

Thomas works out his solution to the problem of the medium in the vision of God *quid est* within the terms of Aristotelian epistemology while moving beyond this framework to make a radical claim that the divine essence is both the object and the medium of the vision.[50] The Aristotelian noetic holds that in all knowledge there is a species abstracted by the agent intellect from the intelligible object, which informs the possible intellect so that it united with the object. The species itself is not the object of knowledge but the medium by which the object is seen. In *De veritate* q8 a1, therefore, Thomas states as his premise that all vision requires a medium "by which the one who sees beholds what is seen." How, then, can the vision of God be immediate? His answer is that the essence of God itself becomes for the intellect the medium of the beatific vision (playing the role of species by informing the intellect). This cannot be by means of any likeness or similitude; the divine essence directly relates to the intellect "after the manner of a form" so that the intellect is able to share in God's own comprehension of himself (and therefore his beatitude), albeit not fully as God comprehends himself.[51] To see *per essentiam*, Thomas argues (against Albert's position in the *De resurrectione*), means precisely to see the *quid est*.[52]

The reproportioning of the created intellect by the light of glory disposes it for union with the divine essence, making it perfectible by the divine essence as form by giving it a higher potency suitable for such a higher ac-

47. Albertus Magnus, "*De resurrectione*, 9.1; *De divinibus nominibus* 1.21–27, 13.27," in *Opera Omnia*, ed. A. Borgnet (Paris, 1890–99).

48. *DV* q8 a1. See Henri Dondaine, "Cognoscere de Deo 'quid est,'" *Recherches de théologie ancienne et médiévale* 22 (1955): 72–78.

49. Thomas thus clearly distinguishes between the knowledge of God possible *in via* and *in patria*.

50. See Dondaine, "Cognoscere de Deo 'quid est.'"

51. *DV* q8 a2 ad5.

52. *DV* q8 a1 ad8.

tualization.[53] In the *De veritate* Thomas argues for the necessity of this re-proportioning but does not specify what kind of new disposition the light of glory bestows. In q12 a1 and a2 of the *Summa* Thomas's position evolves further. He again addresses the two issues at stake in the claim that a created mind can see the essence of God: that of proportionality and the need for a medium or similitude. His arguments, though quite similar to those in the *De veritate*, are nevertheless different in their emphasis: in the *Summa* he gives more attention to the participation relationship between the Creator and rational creatures, who are already, by virtue of their share in existence and intelligence, proportioned in a preliminary though insufficient way to the vision of God.

In both the *De veritate* and *ST* Ia q12 a1 Dionysius and Chrysostom appear in the objections, which all center around the incommensurability of created and uncreated. In Dionysian terms, God is above all created intellect because he is above all being and therefore all intelligibility. *DV* q8 a1 ob6 presents this difficulty in an Aristotelian mode:

The intellect must be proportionate to the intelligible since the intelligible is the perfection of the one who understands. But there can be no proportion between the divine essence and an angelic intellect, for they are separated by an infinite distance, and there is no proportion between such widely separated things. Consequently, an angel cannot see God through his essence.

Thomas answers that because "proportion" can refer not only to commensurability but also to relation,

a created intellect is proportionate to the sight of the divine essence inasmuch as, in some way, it is related to the latter as to an intelligible form, even though the perfections of the two are incommensurable because an infinite distance lies between them.[54]

His solution in this text is simply to say that, because "act and potency always belong to one genus," the light of glory gives the created intellect a (unspecified) higher disposition, putting it in the supernatural order so it can be perfected by the divine essence.[55]

ST Ia q12 a1 ob4 is almost identical to *DV* q8 a1 ob6:

53. *DV* q8 a3.
54. *DV* q8 a1 ad6.
55. *DV* q8 a3. In *DV* q15 a1 ad8 Thomas remarks that understanding of spiritual substances

There must be some proportion between the knower and the known, since the known is the perfection of the knower. But no proportion exists between the created intellect and God, for there is an infinite distance between them. Therefore the created intellect cannot see the essence of God.

But while Thomas will still maintain (in a2) that the created intellect requires a higher disposition by the light of glory, giving it potential for a higher actualization, his answer to the objection in the *Summa* acknowledges some fundamental proportion of rational creatures to God by virtue of the participation relationship brought about by creation, even prior to that effected by union to the divine essence in the beatific vision:

> We can speak of a proportion between the creature and God inasmuch as it is related to him as effect to cause, and as potency to act: and according to this the created intellect can be proportioned to knowing God.[56]

In contrast to the *De veritate*, Thomas places his reply in the context of the potential bestowed by creation itself for the rational creature to attain a greater proportion to God, who is the perfecting object of its knowledge. In answer to the problem of proportionality, we see in the *Summa* a more comprehensive notion of the perfection of the rational creature, which views the light of glory as the radical culmination of a participation in the divine perfections rooted in existence itself.

Underlying the objections about God's intelligibility to creatures is a recognition of the absolute metaphysical distinction between the two, which seems to rule out the possibility of any real human relation to God. Thomas has already demonstrated in *ST* Ia qq2–11 that he takes this difficulty seriously; in asking about what God is in himself, he acknowledged, we can only proceed by way of negation. And yet he has been at pains to establish that God is nevertheless the participated cause of creatures, and

---

belongs to the next life, when (like the angels) our intellect will be deiform. But this deiformity does not seem to be in itself the necessary disposition given by the light of glory for the vision, as in the *Summa*. In *DV* q8 a3 ad16 Thomas states that the deiformity of the angelic intellect consists in their greater natural conformity to God than human beings, because their cognition does not take place through sensibles, and he distinguishes this "natural" deiformity from the supernatural disposition bestowed upon angels by the light of glory for the beatific vision. In *DV* q15 he says that the glorified human intellect will be deiform because it will be able, like the angels and God, to understand without sensibles.

56. *ST* Ia q12 a1 ad4.

so there is at least between God and creatures a relationship of cause and effect, potency and act. Thomas's answer to q12 a1 ob4 and much of his discussion in q12 a1 and a2 are based on this relationship of dependence: the rational creature has a proportion to God because God is the source of its existence (a1) and so of its power of sight, which is itself a sort of similitude of God, as a participation in the light of the divine intelligence (a2).

In the *corpus* of q12 a1 Thomas asserts that both faith and reason demand that the blessed see the essence of God, placing in the *sed contra* at the head of his reply a partial quote of 1 John 3:2: "We shall see him as he is." He begins by acknowledging that God is not fully intelligible by the human intellect, and yet, precisely because God is Pure Act, he is in himself supremely knowable. Thomas's premise is the Aristotelian principle that the ultimate beatitude of rational beings is the highest operation of their intellect. Thus those who held that the created intellect could never see the essence of God deny to it the promise of beatitude, which is opposed to faith. Thomas then introduces a Neoplatonic principle that places the entire discussion in the context of the movement of the rational creature to God by the actualization of its capacities: "The ultimate perfection of the rational creature lies in that which is the source of its being; for each thing is perfected only insofar as it attains to its source." The *reditus* of intellectual creatures must take place through knowledge of their source, and perfect knowledge of their source must be knowledge of its essence.[57] Thomas thus argues that it is against reason to claim that the blessed do not see the essence of God; he makes an argument from the natural desire of rational creatures to know the causes of things, which would remain unfulfilled apart from the vision of God, who is first cause. This argument, though historically controversial, is nevertheless closely related to the two principles already proposed in the *corpus* and raises the same paradox that Thomas first indicated in q1 a1: the last end of human beings is beyond their grasp, and so something must be added to human nature to attain it. The picture that Thomas sketches in q12 a1 of that attainment is as yet incomplete, and the questions that he raises about how human nature is elevated to the vision of God will only be fully answered when he has presented his teaching on grace, charity, and the gifts.

---

57. See Brian Shanley, *The Treatise on the Divine Nature, Summa Theologiae I 1–13* (Indianapolis: Hackett, 2006), 303.

In a2 Thomas addresses the second challenge to the doctrine of the *visio Dei*, that of the need for a medium or similitude in all vision. Thomas's teaching on the *lumen gloriae*, in comparison to the *De veritate*, adds a new level to the notion of the similitude involved in the beatific vision—the soul itself becomes a kind of intrinsic disposing medium for the vision by virtue of its likeness to God (and it is this which proportions it for the vision). In the *De veritate* Thomas was simply concerned with establishing that the vision must take place *per essentiam* and not *per similitudinem*; and so, in answer to the objection that "all knowledge takes place through assimilation," he replies that assimilation between knower and known (as ordinarily takes place through the medium of an intelligible species) is only needed for union, but in the vision the divine essence gives a direct union with itself more perfect than if it had taken place through a likeness, so no assimilation is necessary.[58] In *ST* Ia q12 a2, however, the burden of Thomas's reply is precisely to establish that "to see the essence of God, there is required some similitude in the visual faculty, namely, the light of glory strengthening the intellect to see God," even though "the essence of God cannot be seen by any created similitude representing the divine essence itself as it really is."

In the *corpus* of a2 Thomas stresses that the potential for this participated similitude is founded in the natural likeness of the intellect to God in the first place. God can raise rational creatures, to whom he has given the natural gift of the intellectual power, to the source and highest object of that power—the divine essence itself. The intellect is already a participated similitude of the essence of God, who is the First Intelligence. So the natural light of the intellect—and any further perfections of it by grace and glory—are all to varying degrees participations of the light of the divine intellect:

The power of understanding in the creature (since it is not itself the essence of God), must be a participated likeness of the one who is the first intellect. So in a certain manner the intellectual power of the creature is called an intelligible light, derived from the first light, whether this is understood of the natural power or of any perfection of it, superadded by grace or glory.

---

58. *DV* q8 a1 ad7: "Ad septimum dicendum, quod ad cognitionem non requiritur assimilatio nisi propter hoc ut cognoscens aliquo modo cognito uniatur. Perfectior autem est unio qua unitur ipsa res per essentiam suam intellectui, quam si uniretur per similitudinem suam. Et ideo, quia essentia divina unitur intellectui Angeli ut forma, non requiritur quod ad eam cognoscendam aliqua eius similitudine informetur, qua mediante cognoscat."

Thomas anticipates his teaching on the perfection of the image by grace and glory. In q12 a2 ob1 the full quote of 1 John 3:2 appears: "We shall be like him, for we shall see him as he is." The objector argues that this must mean that the created intellect will see God "through some likeness"; Thomas replies by saying that this authority refers to "the likeness which is by participation in the light of glory," that is, in the intellect itself.[59]

As in the *De veritate*, Thomas argues that the intellect perfected by the light of glory itself becomes a medium by which (not in which) God is seen.[60] And in both works the divine essence itself becomes the form of the intellect in the beatific vision, bringing it from the new higher potency given by the light of glory to act.[61] The *Summa* makes clear, however, that the new potency or disposition given to the intellect must specifically be a greater share in the divine likeness itself; this transformation makes it proportionate, and an intrinsic medium for the vision.[62] Thomas's larger vision in the *Summa* of God as "the source of things and their end, and especially of rational creatures,"[63] made in the divine image is in evidence here. It is precisely by a process of increasing similitude to God that the intellect is disposed to receive the vision. Thomas draws a larger picture of continuity between the vision proper to nature, grace, and glory as increasingly perfect participations of the creature in the light of the divine intellect, resulting in a more and more perfect likeness to God.[64]

59. *ST* Ia q12 a2 ad1.

60. Here Thomas cites Dionysius, and is in agreement with the Eastern tradition, in saying that there can be no created medium in which God is seen, no similitude that can represent the divine likeness. Cf. *ST* Ia q12 a5 ad2.

61. *ST* Ia q12 a2 ad3.

62. "To see God there is required some similitude to God on the part of the visual power, by which the intellect may be efficacious for seeing God." Cf. *SCG* III.51–63, on the vision of God through the divine essence. *SCG* III.53.2 clearly argues that in the vision of God's substance "the divine essence cannot become the form of a created intellect unless the created intellect participates in some way in the divine likeness."

63. *ST* Ia q2, prol.

64. The likeness of the light of glory does not subsume the creature's individual being in some monistic manner, but rather perfects it. As Thomas Gilby puts it, "The union is immediate, the vision direct, its objective content the uncreated being of God. Yet since by knowing the knower becomes the known without ceasing to be itself, this epistemological union with God blots nothing out. He is not the exclusive One, but the simple cause of the Many, not a devouring flame, but the Father of lights; his zeal, says Dionysius, does not consume, but cherishes. All is God, as known and loved, yet the psychological identity of the creature is not

Against the background of this continuity Thomas marks in q12 a4 the radical difference between the vision possible to the creature by nature and by grace.[65] Something is actually known when the "known is in the knower," but the way the known can be in the knower depends upon the knower's mode of knowing, which is proper to its nature. But God's way of existing exceeds human powers of knowing. God cannot be present in the human knower by the operation of his own natural powers, to which it is connatural only to know corporeal things, for the human soul is embodied. But the human mind, because it already possesses by nature an intellectual element above the material, "can be elevated above its nature by grace to something higher."[66] The creature's participation by nature in the divine intellect makes it capable of this elevation. In the *De veritate* Thomas adverts to the properly gratuitous or superadded character of grace and glory as supernatural forms—that is, their discontinuity with nature—but by the time of the *Summa*, he seems to work out more clearly the way in which the rational nature is in fact the ground of grace. He clarifies how there is both continuity and discontinuity between nature and grace, both characterizing them more clearly in terms of a progressively greater participation in the divine perfections and explaining how grace elevates the rational creature to a completely new state of existence and activity.

In the *corpus* of a5 Thomas immediately continues this train of thought by looking more closely at what sort of likeness to God is bestowed by the light of grace and glory. The light of glory that elevates the created intellect to the "sublimity" of receiving the divine essence itself illuminates the mind, increasing the power of the understanding. Thomas places in the *sed contra* Psalms 35:10, "In your light we see light"; he referred to this verse in a2 also,

---

absorbed or destroyed; substance and accidents remain, in a heightened likeness to God, the *lumen gloriae*, which strengthens the creature to see and delight in his presence." "Introduction," in *St Thomas Aquinas: Summa Theologiae*, vol. 3, *Knowing and Naming God (Ia 12–13)*, ed. Herbert McCabe (Manchester: Blackfriars, 1964), xxvii.

65. By the word "grace" in this article, Thomas actually primarily refers to glory, the fulfillment of grace. The scriptural texts he uses in the *sed contra* are Rom 6:23, "The grace of God is eternal life," and Jn 17:3, "This is eternal life, to know you, the only true God." And yet, as discussed below, even in this life, for those who possess the grace proper to wayfarers, God is present to the mind in a special way beyond that possible to nature, "as the object known is in the knower and the beloved is in the lover" (*ST* Ia q43 a3).

66. *ST* Ia q12 q4 ad3.

where he argued that the light of glory is a likeness of the "first light" of the divine intelligence. This verse for Thomas expresses the participation relationship of greatest similitude between the divine and the created intellect in the state of glory. In the beatific vision, this greatest similitude is realized; by the light of glory, the society of the blessed are made "deiform—that is, like to God, according to 1 John, 'When he appears, we shall be like him, for we shall see him as he is.'" The blessed, made as like God as possible, are disposed to receive a share in God's own vision of himself and his effects through the divine essence. Their intellects are brought to a higher potency, which is actualized by the divine essence as intelligible form.

Although this intelligible form is the same for all, Thomas argues in a6 that all do not see the essence of God equally in eternal life. He examines the question of the creature's possible predisposition *in via* for receiving the light of glory to a greater or lesser extent. A difference in capacity for the vision can only be due to one having a greater participation in the light of glory than another (and therefore being more deiform). This cannot depend on any difference in the natural intellectual faculty (which is insufficient for the vision). But one quality on the part of the creature can predispose it to receive this greater share. The light of glory is participated more fully by the one who possesses more charity:

because where there is greater charity, there is greater desire; and desire in a certain manner makes the desirer apt and prepared to receive what is desired. Hence the one who has the more charity, will see God more perfectly, and be more beatified.[67]

With this first mention of charity in the *Summa* Thomas begins to flesh out the trajectory by which the human creature is elevated above its nature by grace so as to be more like God, that is, so as to be brought to deiformity.

The beatific vision is the fulfillment of faith, hope, and charity because the blessed see God, possess him as eternally present, and enjoy him as the ultimate fulfillment of desire.[68] Only later in the *Summa* will Thomas fully explain how charity, as a deification of the will, directs all of human life to perfect union with God in heaven. It also becomes more clear why the vision—although its substance, as vision, consists in the activity of the glorified intellect—has both intellectual and affective dimensions; it is, like its

67. *ST* Ia q12 a6 c.
68. *ST* Ia q12 a7. Cf. Ia-IIae q3 a8, q4 a3.

earthly foreshadowing in contemplation, a "love-knowledge,"[69] an experience of fully savored communion in which charity reaches perfection. Even though the deiformity given by the light of glory belongs only to the next life, it is nevertheless the perfection of powers already belonging to the creature *in via*, and the degree of deiformity possible in glory depends on the disposition of those powers by the fullness in this life of charity (itself, however, bestowed by and likening the creature to God).

The last articles in q12 move from a consideration of the beatific vision as the final goal of human knowing to examine the knowledge of God possible prior to its attainment by natural reason and grace. Except by a miracle, God's essence cannot be seen by a human being still living in the flesh because the embodied soul, dependent on knowledge received through the senses, cannot perceive a purely intelligible object.[70] By natural reason, God's existence and some truths about God can be known through God's effects (q12 a12).[71] But by grace a more perfect knowledge of God can be had; the light of grace elevates the natural light of reason to know God's effects more fully, and revelation informs the mind with divine truths beyond the reach of natural reason (q12 a13).[72] In the *sed contra* of a13 Thomas places this "revelation of grace" in a sapiential context and distinguishes it from the natural knowledge of God available to the philosophers, by quoting Paul, preaching to the Corinthians about the divine wisdom, which "God has revealed to us through his Spirit."[73] By the end of q12 Thomas has sketched out the advance of rational creatures toward God through an increasingly greater participation in the light of the divine intellect, in nature, grace, and glory, a movement of knowledge and love, leading to final deiformity and union.[74]

---

69. See Thomas Gilby, "Appendix 10: The Dialectic of Love in the *Summa*," in *St Thomas Aquinas: Summa Theologiae*, vol. 1, *Christian Theology, Ia, 1* (Cambridge: Blackfriars, 1964), 126.

70. *ST* Ia q12 a11.   71. *ST* Ia q12 a12.

72. *ST* Ia q12 a13 c., ad1.

73. 1 Cor 2:8; *ST* Ia q12 a13 s.c. Cf. *ST* Ia q1 a2, a3, and a6; see chapter 6.

74. Article 13, with its reference to the graced knowledge of revelation as wisdom given to us through the Spirit, also makes a clear connection to Ia q1 a6 on *sacra doctrina*. In the latter, Thomas argues that *sacra doctrina* is "wisdom above all human wisdom" because it is the consideration of God as the highest cause—not only as the philosophers knew him through creatures but "also so far as he is known to himself alone and revealed to others." The principles of *sacra doctrina* come from God's own knowledge (*scientia*), "through which, as through the highest wisdom, all our knowledge is set in order" (q1 a6 ad1). Thomas has argued in q1 a2 that

Source of the Image: God's Word and Love in Creation and Providence

The picture that Thomas has drawn so far of the movement of human beings toward God is founded in the special kind of participation relationship they have with God from creation: as Thomas explains more fully in his treatment of the *imago Dei* in Ia q93, rational creatures are made "to the image of God" specifically by reason of their intellectual nature (i.e., they possess intellect and will),[75] and so the perfection of that image consists in reaching a likeness to God "chiefly in this, that God understands and loves himself."[76] This kind of likeness to God sets rational creatures above everything else in creation. It is truly deification, for God's self-understanding and loving are God's primary activities, identical with the divine essence and existence: God, in his one essence, is his own act of self-understanding and loving.[77]

God's self-understanding and loving in the unity of the divine essence, as immanent processions, constitute the Trinitarian relations that are the divine Persons and at the same time, through the Word and Love, are the ground of God's extra-Trinitarian activities in creation and providence.

---

sacra doctrina is a science because it proceeds from established principles, known not by the light of the natural intellect but by the light of a higher science—that of God and the blessed. Thus *sacra doctrina* is "a certain impression of the divine science" in the human intellect (Ia q1 a3 ad2). The completion of this teaching in Thomas's treatment of the Spirit's gift of wisdom, and especially its Christological dimensions in relation to the teaching on the Son/Word in the Ia *pars* (and the Word Incarnate in the IIIa *pars*), must wait until a later chapter. But q12 a13 adds to Thomas's consideration of *sacra doctrina* as wisdom in q1 a clearer delineation of how grace elevates the natural light of the intellect, disposing it to be informed with the divine truths that impart a share in God's own knowledge of himself, though not as full as what the blessed have in heaven. If the intellects of the blessed are disposed by the light of glory to receive the divine essence itself as actualizing form, and so share in the most perfect way possible in God's own knowledge of himself and his effects in the beatific vision, the intellects of those in this life elevated by the light of grace are disposed to receive the wisdom of *sacra doctrina*, which is likewise a certain participation in God's knowledge of himself and his effects as revealed through Scripture—though not, as in the beatific vision, a knowledge of God *quid est*, which belongs only to deiformity.

75. *ST* Ia q93 aa1–2.

76. *ST* Ia q93 a4.

77. On God's self-understanding, see *ST* Ia q14 aa1–4; on God's self-loving, Thomas says that the divine will is God's own existence essentially (Ia q19 a2 ad1), and that by the act of his will—i.e., his love—he wills for himself his own perfect goodness (Ia q20 a1 ad3).

Thomas has described in q12 the deformity that is required for the blessed to enjoy the vision of God, but as yet has said nothing specific about how God brings individuals there nor of what enables the rational creature to make this journey to perfect participation in the divine likeness. The doctrine of the divine ideas—through which God, in knowing and loving himself, also knows and loves all creatures—provides the foundation of Thomas's thought on two important constituents of his teaching on the journey of the image to beatitude in the *Summa*: the divine *ordinatio* of providence by which God manifests his goodness, particularly as he predestines and brings the elect to eternal life, and the Trinitarian basis of the divine exemplarity that is especially imaged in the rational creature, both in its creation by nature and its re-creation by grace.

The Divine Ideas and God's Causal Knowledge and Will of What Is Not God

God, by one perfect cognition, knows himself and all things in himself. In God, who is absolutely simple, the divine intellect, its object, species, and act of understanding are all identical with the divine essence. God is his own subsistent act of understanding, by which he understands himself through his own essence. In doing so, God also knows things other than himself, because God knows in himself all the effects that preexist in him as cause.[78] Furthermore, knowing himself perfectly as their cause, God has a perfect knowledge of each of his effects. God not only knows all things in general, but also knows each created form in its own proper individuality, as a certain way in which his perfection can be participated.[79] God's knowledge of things other than himself is not only speculative (as a builder knows speculatively how a house is made) but also practical—it is the cause of things that he wills to make, as a builder's practical knowledge is the cause of things to be built.[80] What is more, God, in knowing the divine essence, knows as its effect the whole order of the universe, which is the highest good existing in things; just as a builder must conceive of the whole

78. *ST* Ia q14 aa4–5.
79. *ST* Ia q14 a6. And so, in a certain sense, the divine essence, as the transcendent source of all created forms, "can be taken as the proper *ratio* of each thing according to the diverse ways in which it can be participated or imitated by diverse creatures" (ad3).
80. *ST* Ia q14 a8, a16.

as well as of each part of a house to be built, in the divine mind exists the idea of the order itself of the universe as well as the proper ideas of each of its parts.[81]

This is the basis of Thomas's teaching on the divine ideas in Ia q15, both as they are the source, in God's creative intellect, of every creature, and as creatures are ordered one to another in all their variety in the divine wisdom.[82] God knows his essence "as it can be participated in by creatures according to some degree of likeness," and the proper species of each creature is constituted precisely by the limited degree to which it participates in the likeness of the divine essence (i.e., God knows his essence to be imitable to that degree as the particular idea of that creature).[83] Insofar as that idea is the principle of something that God actually makes by his causative knowledge, it can be called an exemplar.[84] Thomas's doctrine of the divine ideas shapes his teaching on deification in two ways: it grounds his understanding both of the divine exemplarity of the *imago Dei* and of the ordered plan of providence, within which the image journeys to beatitude. We consider first Thomas's teaching about the divine *ordinatio*, which governs the advance of the rational creature to God.

The Divine *Ordinatio*

The term *ordinatio* in the *Summa* has a variety of meanings, centering on the fundamental concept of God's wise ordering of the universe toward the end for which he wills it. This end, as Thomas repeatedly states, is to communicate and thus manifest the divine goodness.[85] On this deepest level the

81. *ST* Ia q15 a2.

82. Cf. *ST* Ia q44 a3. For a useful discussion of the notion of the divine exemplarity (which is at the heart of the concept of the divine ideas) in the *Scriptum* (I d36 q2 aa1–3), *DV* (q3 aa1–8), *SCG* (I.51–54), and *ST* (Ia q15 aa1–3, q44 a3), which takes into consideration Thomas's use of classical and patristic sources, see J. L. Farthing, "The Problem of Divine Exemplarity in St. Thomas," *Thomist* 49 (1985): 183–222.

83. *ST* Ia q15 a2. Rudi te Velde points out that for this reason the essence of each creature is at once a self-distinction by God from God and (for the same reason) a relation to God: "The distinct essence is part of the divine likeness in each creature, as God intends its effect to be different from himself. The otherness of creation is therefore not a self-alienation on the part of God. Even in the otherness of created being God relates to himself, as his likeness in creatures entails a determinate negation with respect to how God is in himself." *Participation and Substantiality*, 159.

84. *ST* Ia q15 a3.

85. E.g., Ia q19 a2; Ia q44 a4.

term signifies Thomas's "sapiential" understanding of God's entire plan of creation and redemption.[86] Thomas presents divine providence in the *Summa* (Ia q22) as the type that exists in the divine mind of the order of things in the universe toward the end of divine goodness; the notion of providence as Wisdom governs his discussion, as evidenced by his references in q22 and elsewhere to the scriptural figure of Wisdom, who "reaches from end to end mightily and orders all things sweetly" (Wis 8:1). It belongs to the wise person to order, and to God above all, as the wise architect of creation, to order the whole of the universe as well as each of its parts. The knowledge and will of God, by which God "loves all things that exist" (Wis 11:25) is the cause of things and of their ordering to the end through the divine ideas.

God's causative knowledge of things, by which they participate in his existence and perfection, is thus an order of wisdom and love, not a kind of necessary Plotinian emanation. Because there is intellect in God, there is will, and as the divine intellect is identical with the divine essence, so is the divine will, says Thomas in Ia q19.[87] As God knows creatures in himself, so God, in his love, wills them to share in his own perfect goodness, the proper object of his will. Because it is the perfection of the will to communicate to others the good it possesses, it belongs especially to the divine will to communicate its goodness to others by bestowing on them a likeness to itself. And because all things are good by participation in the divine goodness, they are ultimately inclined toward the divine goodness:

He wills both himself, and other things, to be. But himself as end, and other things as ordered to that end (*ad finem*), inasmuch as it befits the divine goodness that other things should also participate it.[88]

While Thomas often makes reference, as he does here, to the Dionysian maxim that the good is diffusive of itself (*bonum est diffusivum sui*), he makes from his earliest works the Aristotelian clarification that goodness is self-diffusive in that it moves as a final cause.[89] God's goodness is not self-

86. See Joseph P. Wawrykow, *God's Grace and Human Action: "Merit" in the Theology of Thomas Aquinas.* (Notre Dame, IN: University of Notre Dame Press, 1995), 149–64.

87. *ST* Ia q19 a1.

88. *ST* Ia q19 a2.

89. See *ST* Ia q5 a4 ob2, ad2: "Ad secundum dicendum quod bonum dicitur diffusivum sui esse, eo modo quo finis dicitur movere." Cf. *Scriptum* bk1 d34 q2 a1 ad 4: "Ad quartum dicendum,

diffusive in the sense that he cannot help pouring out the divine goodness to others, as would be the case in a Neoplatonic model of necessary emanation of the Good. God's perfect goodness draws things to himself as end; his goodness is the primary object of his own will, and "in willing an end we do not necessarily will things that conduce to it, unless they are such that the end cannot be attained without them."[90]

Therefore God need not have willed anything other than his own goodness. Rather, God acts in perfect freedom by virtue of the activity of the divine intellect and will, which together are the cause of things and their goodness. Within God's one free act of understanding everything through his essence and willing all things in his goodness, he graciously wills the order of things in the universe, conceived by the divine ideas, as means toward the end of his goodness.[91] When Thomas asks in q19 a2 whether God wills things apart from himself, and answers that it is most fitting to the divine goodness that it should give others a participated share in itself, he chooses as his authority in the *sed contra* a quote from 1 Thessalonians 4:3: "This is the will of God, your sanctification." The sanctification of human beings is the clearest manifestation of God's will to communicate his goodness to others.

Created Causality and Predestination

The notion of the divine *ordinatio* shapes Thomas's understanding in the *Summa* of how God brings the elect to beatitude. In the divine plan of wisdom, by which God communicates his goodness, he ordains that creatures should be involved as secondary causes in bringing about the effects that he wills to fulfill that plan by acting according to their natures. "God wills effects to proceed from definite causes, for the preservation of order in the universe,"[92] even in the contingent causality of free rational creatures. In the divine foreknowledge, God knows and so brings about even contingent things infallibly; they are future contingent events from the perspective of their own causes, but to God they are eternally present. In the case of the

---

quod bonum dicitur diffusivum per modum finis, secundum quod dicitur quod finis movet efficientem." Cf. Aristotle, *Physics* II.3.

90. *ST* Ia q19 a3.   91. *ST* Ia q19 aa3–5.

92. *ST* Ia q19 a5 ad2.

free choices of rational creatures, he knows them from eternity—that is, God knows and therefore causes what will have actually taken place, however contingently this state of affairs comes about.[93]

Thomas places his teaching on the predestination and salvation of individuals within the sapiential context of God's entire plan of creation and redemption. As God orders every action to its appropriate effects, so he ordains elected human beings to eternal life with himself, and also brings them to that end by means of their graced activities. In Thomas's mature thought, this ordination thus includes both the plan of God's predestination of elected individuals and God's actual ordering of their good works by grace to the appropriate reward of eternal life.[94] The entire graced journey of the human person to beatitude is properly understood as a particular manifestation of God's goodness, willed in the plan of divine wisdom for that individual. Thomas places it within the larger context of the communication of divine goodness, which is the *ratio* of creation and the effect of divine love, for "the love of God infuses and creates goodness."[95]

A primary locus for reflection on these questions early in the *Summa* is in Ia qq19–23, on God's causative will and love, providence, and predestination. These discussions provide the foundation for later treatments of the movement of rational creatures toward God in the questions on grace, virtues, and gifts in the IIa *pars*, and the role of Christ as the author of grace and

93. See *ST* Ia q14 a13 s.c., c.

94. See *ST* Ia q22–23. Joseph Wawrykow, in his study of merit in the thought of Thomas Aquinas, highlights the important role of the divine *ordinatio* in Thomas's mature understanding of the way in which God brings the elect to the supernatural end of glory. In their "journey to beatitude," the elect—both by the meritorious involvement that derives from the activity of their own graced free will and by the unmerited gifts of conversion and perseverance—are moved by the prevenient grace of God. Wawrykow shows that Thomas came to his mature teaching in the *Summa* by drawing on the mature teachings of Augustine on grace in the *De dono perseverantiae* and *De praedestinatione sanctorum*. *God's Grace and Human Action*, 266–76. Wawrykow builds on the work of Bouillard (*Conversion et grâce*), who noted the importance of these writings of Augustine in shaping Thomas's mature theology of grace, though Bouillard did not address the question of merit. As Wawrykow points out, when Thomas cites the divine ordination to establish the possibility of merit in the *Summa*, he places merit in a sapiential context, showing that it is designed to manifest God's goodness in a special way (33, 267). Cf. *ST* Ia-IIae q114 a1; Ia q23 a5.

95. *ST* Ia q20 a2; cf. q19 a2: "[God] wills both himself, and other things, to be. But himself as end, and other things as ordered to that end (*ad finem*), inasmuch as it befits the divine goodness that other things should also participate it."

exemplar of the predestined in the IIIa *pars*. The election of some people to eternal life is the communication of a particular good—eternal salvation—that is brought about because of God's love for those people.[96] God's love for a creature is his causal will for its goodness; God in his wisdom wills for some a better good (i.e., loves them more) and thus elects them for eternal life.[97] To those whom God elects, he communicates grace and glory, by which they are so transformed as actually to reach the end of beatitude.[98] As I outline in subsequent chapters, Thomas thinks that God especially communicates and manifests the divine goodness in those whom he wills to transform and bring to fellowship with himself through grace, charity, and wisdom. God infuses into them these created gifts, working in them to transform them, elevating their own nature and activities of will and intellect to a higher end, and so involving their own free action in reaching that end.

Thomas's mature understanding of providence and predestination thus includes the notion that God works through human persons as secondary causes, involving human activity under grace to infallibly accomplish the divine purpose, without compromising human freedom or genuine causal involvement.[99] "The abundance of God's goodness" is especially shown in that "the dignity of causality is imparted even to creatures."[100] God is the cause of all created causes, not only by creating causal agents but also by ordering their activity to their ends and applying every agent to its activity. Rather than competing with creatures causally, God makes it possible for them to be causes at all by participating in his causality. In fact, in the plan of creation, it might be said, God puts into place an ordered pattern of causality that he infallibly accomplishes through the secondary agency of acting creatures.[101]

---

96. *ST* Ia q23 a4 c., ad1.   97. *ST* Ia q20 a4.

98. *ST* Ia q23 a4.   99. *ST* Ia q23 a6.

100. *ST* Ia q22 a3. Thomas lays the groundwork for this possibility at the outset of the *Summa* with his explanation of the participation relationship between God and God's creatures. God, as the universal first cause of existence as well as source and end of creation, is absolutely transcendent to the created order. So God is also absolutely immanent, "intimately" or innermostly present in all things, as the ground of their existence and activity: "Esse autem est illud quod est magis intimum cuilibet, et quod profundius omnibus inest, cum sit formale respectu omnium quae in re sunt, ut ex supra dictis patet. Unde oportet quod Deus sit in omnibus rebus, et intime" (*ST* Ia q8 a1).

101. The type of all causes and their effects exists in the divine mind, "the type of the order of things foreordained towards an end, and the execution of this order" (*ST* Ia q22 a3). The

God's goodness is both the efficient and final cause of predestination generally speaking; however, in the working-out of the actual journey of the
predestined, he "wills one thing on account of another," preordaining that
the meritorious works of the free will flowing from grace will play a role by
moving the person along the path to attain glory. The journey thus involves
both the primary causality of the divine goodness and the secondary, subordinated causality of the graced free will.[102] Thomas's awareness of the seeming difficulty this raises with respect to the freedom of rational creatures,
especially in light of sin, is evident in his finding it necessary to repeatedly
address potential objections. In *ST* Ia q19, on the will of God, Thomas asserts that the indefectible will of God is the universal cause of things, so it
is impossible that it should not produce its effect. Yet, as he has established
in discussing God's foreknowledge of contingents, while God's will is infallibly accomplished, it does not impose necessity on all things. Not only is
everything that God wills done, but also it is done in the way God wills it;
God wills some things to be done necessarily and some contingently, "so
that there be order in things, for the completion of the universe."[103] God
prepares contingent causes for the effects that he wills to happen contingently, and should it be otherwise, "there would perish free will and counsel, and all other such things."[104] The human free will is a secondary contingent cause within the overall plan of God's causative knowledge and will.

In q22 a2, on whether everything is subject to God's providence, Thomas responds that all things are subject "not only in general, but even in their
own individual selves" because the universal causality of God, as the source
of being, extends to all being, even the individualizing principles of things.
He answers the objection that because God "left man in the hand of his own
counsel" (Sir 15:14) it seems that human beings are exempt from providence

---

"execution of this order," by which God leads created things to their ends, thus giving them
perfection, belongs to providence but is more specifically called the divine government (*ST* Ia
q103 a1).

102. *ST* Ia q23 a5.

103. *ST* Ia q19 a8: "Cum igitur voluntas divina sit efficacissima, non solum sequitur quod fiant ea quae Deus vult fieri; sed quod eo modo fiant, quo Deus ea fieri vult. Vult autem quaedam
fieri Deus necessario, et quaedam contingenter, ut sit ordo in rebus, ad complementum universi."

104. Ibid., *sed contra*: "Omnia bona quae fiunt, Deus vult fieri. Si igitur eius voluntas im-
ponat rebus volitis necessitatem, sequitur quod omnia bona ex necessitate eveniunt. Et sic perit
liberum arbitrium et consilium, et omnia huiusmodi."

by explaining that God causes the very act of free will, by which they act of themselves in taking counsel and making a choice. Unlike irrational creatures, humans are not predetermined, as causes, to one fixed effect; they can choose to direct themselves to alternative ends. But that they can do this is itself part of divine providence: God's providence includes human providence "as a particular under a universal cause" God does, however, "have providence in a certain more excellent way for just people than for the impious; inasmuch as he does not permit anything to happen to them which would finally impede their salvation." Thomas quotes Romans 8:28: "To them that love God, all things work together for the good."[105] Because of their free will, human beings are subject to praise or blame for their actions and so can merit reward or punishment.[106] Thomas goes on to say, in discussing the role of merit in the journey to beatitude in q23 a5, that what flows from the meritorious graced free will, as a secondary cause, is also part of predestination, which is the first cause of the movement of the elect to salvation.

God orders the effects of each acting individual toward its end and has immediate providence over each, causing the divine ordination to be worked out through each individual's activity.[107] In fact, as Lonergan points out, Thomas's understanding of predestination develops from the *Scriptum* to the *Summa* precisely with respect to his later affirmation that God's providence is certain in particular cases because he is the universal cause, applying every agent to its act.[108] Each predestined individual is the object of God's special election and

---

105. *ST* Ia q22 a2 ad4: "Sed quia ipse actus liberi arbitrii reducitur in Deum sicut in causam, necesse est ut ea quae ex libero arbitrio fiunt, divinae providentiae subdantur, providentia enim hominis continetur sub providentia Dei, sicut causa particularis sub causa universali. Hominum autem iustorum quodam excellentiori modo Deus habet providentiam quam impiorum, inquantum non permittit contra eos evenire aliquid, quod finaliter impediat salutem eorum, nam 'diligentibus Deum omnia cooperantur in bonum,' ut dicitur Rom. VIII."

106. *ST* Ia q22 a2 ad5. God allows some people to fall away from the end of eternal life through the sinful actions deriving from their own free will, on account of which they can merit or be at fault; Ia q23 a5 ad3. Thomas points out that God cannot be said to be unjust on this account, but rather that the gratuity of predestination must be preserved. Reprobation does not cause sin but simply leaves the human free will on its own (*ST* Ia q23 a3 ad2; in saying this, Thomas avoids a doctrine of "double predestination"). Eternal life exceeds what is due to anyone, and reprobation is the just punishment for sin. Yet God's justice always presupposes God's mercy, and the latter exceeds the former (*ST* Ia q21 a4).

107. *ST* Ia q22 a3 c., ad2.

108. Bernard Lonergan, *Grace and Freedom: Operative Grace in the Thought of St. Thomas*

love, and the gifts of grace and glory work to bring each one on their journey of deification to the end of personal union with God; so God communicates and manifests his goodness in a special way in each individual.[109]

Divine Exemplarity through the Word and Love

Before Thomas gets to his *ex professo* treatment of the created image and its re-creation by grace in Ia q93, he completes the necessary context for understanding the notion of "image" by his teaching on the Trinitarian structure of the divine exemplarity. We know from the questions on the one divine nature at the beginning of the *Summa* that creation is the common work of the entire Trinity; God causally knows and loves in himself the idea of every creature as a particular way in which the divine essence can be participated. But by the time Thomas gets to the questions on creation, after his treatment of the Trinity, he is much more specific about the role of each divine Person in creation: "God the Father made the creature through his Word, which is his Son; and through his Love, which is the Holy Spirit."[110] Thomas can say so much more at this point about the specifically Trinitarian form of the divine exemplarity in creation because in his treatment of the Trinity

---

Aquinas. *Collected Works of Bernard Lonergan*, vol. 1, ed. Frederick E. Crowe and Robert Doran. (Toronto: University of Toronto Press, 2000), 76–80.

109. *ST* Ia q23 a4 c., ad1. God's goodness is especially manifest in Christ, the Blessed Virgin, and the created beatitude of the saints; these all have "a certain infinite dignity from the infinite good, which is God. And on this account, there cannot be anything better than these, just as there cannot be anything better than God" (Ia q25 a6 ad4). Wawrykow, who discusses the characterization of Thomas's teaching on merit as "personalist," argues that while the term is not inappropriate because people do enter into personal communion with God by their merits, the personal realization of human beings is secondary, as regards Thomas's teaching on the purpose of merit, to the achievement of God's will within God's plan of divine wisdom to manifest the divine goodness. Thus Wawrykow prefers to designate Thomas's teaching on merit as "sapiential." *God's Grace and Human Action*, 30–32, 32n73.

110. *ST* Ia q45 a6. In q44 a3 Thomas introduces his treatment of creation by recapitulating first his teaching on creation by the one God through the divine ideas: "It is manifest that things made naturally receive determinate forms. This determination of forms must be reduced to the divine wisdom as to the first principle, which thought out (*excogitavit*) the order of the universe, which consists in the distinction of things. So it must be said that in the divine wisdom are the types (*rationes*) of all things, which we called above ideas, i.e., exemplary forms existing in the divine mind (Ia q15 a1). These can be multiplied with respect to things, but are not really other than the divine essence, as its likeness can be participated in diverse ways by different things. Thus therefore God himself is the first exemplar of all things."

he has identified the immanent processions of God's knowing and loving—the divine intellect and will—with the generation of the Word, or Son, and the procession of Love, or the Holy Spirit.

Trinitarian Foundations of Creative Causality

The Word proceeds as the intellectual concept that God has of himself—an exact likeness of his source and sharing in the one divine nature—because in God the act of understanding and existence are the same.[111] The procession of Love in God follows on that of the Word because "nothing can be loved by the will unless it is conceived by the intellect," even though in God the intellect and will are the same, and identical with the divine substance. These processions are immanent, or terminate within God as an intellectual agent. By analogy with the human intellect, the loved object is in the lover by the procession of love, as by the conception of the word the known object is in the knower.[112] There is a difference, however, between the processions of word and love; in the procession of the intellect a likeness of the object conceived actualizes the intellect, whereas the will is actualized "by way of impulse and movement towards an object." So love proceeds in God, Thomas says, not as generated or begotten like the Son, but "as Spirit, which name expresses a certain vital movement and impulse, as anyone is described as moved or impelled by love to perform an action."[113] The proper name of the Holy Spirit, then, is Love, as Word is the proper name of the Son,[114] and the Holy Spirit is the subsistent relation of love between the Father and Son.[115]

Even in the heart of this discussion of the Trinitarian Persons and their immanent relations Thomas has in mind its implications for his teaching on the nonimmanent activities of God, those that have an exterior effect in creation. In Ia q32 Thomas locates the very purpose of a teaching on the Trinity itself, the reason for the necessity (on our part) of a revelation of God as

---

111. *ST* Ia q27 a2.

112. *ST* Ia q27 a3 c., ad3. Cf. q27 a5.

113. *ST* Ia q27 a4. While the name "Word" can properly apply to the Son, who proceeds by way of an emanation of the divine intellect (Ia q34 a2), the name "Holy Spirit" is fitting for the Person proceeding by way of love, for "spirit" signifies impulse and motion, and "it is a property of love to move and impel the will of the lover towards the object loved" (Ia q36 a1).

114. *ST* Ia q37 a1.

115. *ST* Ia q37 a1 ad2–3.

Trinity—a mystery inaccessible to reason alone—in the salvific knowledge it imparts about God's activity in creation and redemption:

> Knowledge of the divine Persons was necessary for us in two ways. In one way, in order to think rightly about creation. For in saying that God made all things by his Word, the error of those who propose that God produced things by a necessity of nature is excluded. By saying that in him there is a procession of love, it is shown that God produced creatures not out of need, nor because of any other extrinsic reason, but because of the love of his own goodness ... In another way, and principally, that we may think rightly about the salvation of the human race, which is brought about by the Incarnate Son, and by the gift of the Holy Spirit.[116]

Faith in the revelation of God as Trinity safeguards the truth that God's activity *ad extra* in creation and redemption is a freely willed plan of wisdom to communicate the divine goodness through the divine intellect (Word) and love (Holy Spirit). Most importantly, the teaching on the Trinity leads us to a right understanding of the salvation received through the Incarnation and gift of the Spirit. As Gilles Emery points out, Thomas places the soteriological dimension of Trinitarian doctrine to the fore. Trinitarian theology is the study of the triune God in whom, as their end, human beings find salvation and beatitude: "For this reason, the reading of Thomas's Trinitarian theology leads to the Trinitarian dimension of creation and, above all, the salvific dimensions of the revelation of the mystery of the Trinity (divine missions)."[117] God acts through his Word and Love, both in creation and in the re-creation of the image through grace.

Thomas adverts to these activities of the Trinitarian Persons *ad extra* even in the midst of his discussion of their proper names, where he remarks that "the proper name of any person signifies that whereby the person is distinguished from all other persons."[118] In Ia q34, on "Word" as the name of the Person of the Son, Thomas says that because God knows every creature by knowing himself, God's "only Word is expressive not only of the Father but of all creatures."[119] Similarly, in Ia q37, on "Love" as the name of the

---

116. *ST* Ia q32 a1 ad3.

117. Gilles Emery, "The Treatise on the Trinity in the *Summa theologiae*," in *Trinity in Aquinas*, trans. Teresa Bede and Matthew Levering (Ypsilanti: Sapientia Press, 2003), 123.

118. *ST* Ia q33 a2.

119. *ST* Ia q34 a3. With regard to creatures, the Word is not only cognitive but also operative. Thomas refers here to his teaching on God's causal knowledge of things other than himself.

Holy Spirit, Thomas extends his teaching on the Holy Spirit as the love between Father and Son to include the dynamic role of the Holy Spirit in the love of God for creatures:

As therefore it is said that a tree flowers by its flowers, so the Father is said to be speaking, by the Word or the Son, both himself, and his creatures; and the Father and the Son are said to love both each other and us, by the Holy Spirit, or by Love proceeding.[120]

As it is through the Word that the knowledge of God is causal with respect to creatures (by giving them a share in the divine likeness), so it is by the Holy Spirit that the love of God is causal (by making everything share and be ordered toward the divine goodness):

So it is clear that relation to the creature is conveyed both in the Word and in the Love proceeding, as if secondarily, inasmuch as the divine truth and goodness are the principle of understanding and loving all creatures.[121]

At the heart of his treatment of the Trinity, Thomas establishes that the spring of creation flows from the dynamic and free activity of the very knowledge and love that constitute the personal relations of God's triune nature.

Having already drawn this causal connection in the questions on the Trinity between the processions of the Persons and creation, it is not surprising that in Ia q45 a6, on creation itself, Thomas argues that within one divine action the divine Persons each have a certain causality with respect to the creation of things:

For as was shown above [cf. q14 a8; q19 a4] when treating of the knowledge and will of God, that God is the cause of things by his intellect and will, as the craftsman is of the things made. Now the craftsman works through the word conceived in his intellect, and through the love of his will, for what he renders. Hence also God the Father worked the creature through his Word, which is his Son; and through his Love, who is the Holy Spirit. And thus these processions of the Persons are the type of the productions of creatures (*rationes productiones creaturarum*), inasmuch as they include the essential attributes, which are knowledge and will.

---

120. *ST* Ia q37 a2.
121. *ST* Ia q37 a2 ad3.

Emery has shown that Thomas, from his earliest works, thought of this divine causality in Trinitarian terms (both with regard to the *exitus* of creatures in creation and their *reditus* by grace) while maintaining the unity of operation of the divine Persons in the works of God *ad extra*.[122] "The eternal processions of the Persons are the cause and reason (*ratio*) of the production of creatures," Thomas says in the *Scriptum*, in terms similar to those in q45 a6 above.[123] The Trinitarian processions have an efficient, final, and especially exemplar causality with respect to the participated communication of being and perfection to creatures by God, which is analogous to the full communication of being and perfection between the divine Persons within the Trinity. The immanent activities of God are the basis of God's transitive activities and their *ratio*.

But it is not until Thomas's later works, because of the development of his understanding of the Trinitarian processions themselves, that he specifies the mode of causality of the Persons in terms of the processions of knowledge and will, as in the quote from *ST* q45 a6 above.[124] Beginning with the *Summa contra gentiles*, Thomas characterizes the procession of the Word as a procession by mode of intellect, and that of the Spirit in more dynamic terms, as a procession by mode of will with the note of an "affection toward" (*affici ad aliquid*), or impulse toward the object of love, rather than as a static informing of the will by the good as in the *Scriptum*.[125] So the Son and Spirit share in the united efficacy of God's works *ad extra* according to their personal properties as Word and Love—that is, according to the processions of intellect and will—that provide the reason of that efficacy, and this is why, as Emery points out, the proper names of Word and Love can include a relation to creatures.[126]

---

122. Gilles Emery, "Trinity and Creation," in *The Theology of Thomas Aquinas*, ed. Rik van Nieuwenhove and Joseph Wawrykow (Notre Dame, IN: University of Notre Dame Press, 2005), 58–76; "Trinitarian Action," in *Trinity, Church and the Human Person: Thomistic Essays* (Naples, FL: Sapientia Press, 2007), 115–53.

123. *Scriptum* bk1 d14 q1 a1.

124. In the *Scriptum* Thomas teaches that the Son proceeds by mode of nature (not intellect) and conceives of the Spirit's procession by mode of will in more static terms than in later works. Emery, "Trinity and Creation," 62, 66. See *Scriptum* bk1 d10 a1.

125. Emery, "Trinity and Creation," 66. Cf. *SCG* IV.19.

126. Emery, "Trinity and Creation," 69.

Causal Roles of the Divine Persons

God acts efficaciously through the Word and Love, then, in every work of creation and grace, insofar as the divine knowledge and will are the principle of causatively understanding and loving all creatures. For this reason, Thomas indicates in q45 a6 ad2 that there is an ordering of the modes of action of the Persons in creation, which reflects the intra-Trinitarian ordering of the Persons themselves, based on their personal properties.[127] As the Son receives the divine nature from the unbegotten Father and the Holy Spirit receives it from both, so the power of creation belongs to the Son "through whom all things were made" (Jn 1:3), as to a principle that comes from a principle. It belongs to the Holy Spirit to "govern and quicken" what is created by the Father through the Son. Thomas associates these modes of acting in creation with the appropriations to each Person of the essential divine attributes of power, wisdom, and goodness on the basis of their personal properties. *Power*, which chiefly appears in creation, is appropriated to the Father as principle; *wisdom*, "through which the intellectual agent acts," is appropriated to the Son; and *goodness* is appropriated to the Holy Spirit, for to goodness belongs, "both government, which brings things to their proper end, and the giving of life—for life consists in a certain interior movement; and the first mover is the end, and goodness."[128]

127. Emery comments that "this teaching reveals a profound personalism" in Thomas's account of Trinitarian action in creation and redemption (ibid., 71).

128. *ST* Ia q45 a6 ad2. This discussion is based on a similar earlier treatment in the questions on the Trinity of the appropriations of power, wisdom, and goodness (*ST* Ia q39 a7; cf. q32 a1). Our knowledge of each divine attribute is analogous, drawn from creatures, in which it exists in a limited way; these similitudes of the essential attributes give us some knowledge of the divine Persons, even though the Trinity itself cannot be proved by demonstration. The appropriation to the Father, Son, and Holy Spirit of power, wisdom, and goodness (among other triads of attributes) is traditional (cf. Augustine, *DT* 6.1–7, 7.4–5, 15.29; Bonaventure, *Breviloquium* 6). Thomas reflects on the appropriation of wisdom to the Son in the context of 1 Cor 1:24 ("Christ the power of God and the wisdom of God"), as does Augustine, to whom he refers (*DT* 6.2) for the teaching that an appropriation of essential attributes to the Persons does not mean that the attributes belong exclusively to any one (q39 a7 ad2). Earlier in the Middle Ages, Peter Abelard had attempted to identify the attributes of power, wisdom, and goodness as unique personal properties of Father, Son, and Spirit, such that a consideration of these attributes could lead to a purely philosophical knowledge of God as Trinity; like his contemporaries, Thomas holds that the Trinity cannot be known by natural reason (Emery, *Trinity in Aquinas*, 4–9, 124). Cf. Peter Abelard, "Book I, ch. II, ch. V" and "Book II, ch. IV, no. 103," in *Theologia summa boni*, ed. Constant J. Mews (Turnhout: Brepols, 1987), 86–88, 92–99, 150–51.

Given this discussion, it might seem that Thomas would go on to say simply that God's efficient causality should be appropriated to the Father, exemplar causality to the Son, and final causality to the Holy Spirit, but he does not.[129] Rather, Thomas indicates that particular created effects can be appropriated primarily to particular persons as exemplar cause based on the divine attributes of power, wisdom, and goodness appropriated to them; that is, creation to the Father, order to the Son, and mercy and justification (i.e., the work of grace) to the Holy Spirit.[130] The implication is that the divine Persons in some sense have appropriated exemplary roles with regard to certain effects, within the one divine action of creation and redemption.

In the *Summa contra gentiles* Thomas states this explicitly. There he indicates that we can speak of both Spirit and Son in terms of divine exemplarity, while all three Persons are identically the efficient cause of every effect. Every effect of God in us is related to God both as to an efficient and as to an exemplar cause, because divine power effects something in us that is accomplished by means of an imitation of God in some respect. Nevertheless, an effect in us may properly be "representative" of a particular person with whom that attribute is associated ("the love by which we love God" with the Holy Spirit and "the word of wisdom by which we know God" with the Son) and thus can be said to be in us especially through them (i.e., as exemplar).[131] Thomas builds on this notion in the *Summa theologiae*, in his theology of the image and its perfection.

---

129. Bonaventure does, however: *Breviloquium* 6.1,4.

130. Thomas apparently concedes the objection that "any determinate mode of causation ought not to be attributed to one Person more than to another," because every essential attribute causes every divine effect in creatures. Thomas's reply to that objection is framed simply in terms of the effect, which "can be reduced to that attribute with which it is naturally connected," so that the order of things can be reduced to wisdom, justification and mercy can be reduced to goodness, and creation itself to power (*ST* Ia q45 a6 ob3, ad3).

131. *SCG* IV.21.2: "Sciendum tamen est quod ea quae a Deo in nobis sunt, reducuntur in Deum sicut in causam efficientem et exemplarem. In causam quidem efficientem, inquantum virtute operativa divina aliquid in nobis efficitur. In causam quidem exemplarem, secundum quod id quod in nobis a Deo est, aliquo modo Deum imitatur. Cum ergo eadem virtus sit patris et filii et spiritus sancti, sicut et eadem essentia; oportet quod omne id quod Deus in nobis efficit, sit, sicut a causa efficiente, simul a patre et filio et spiritu sancto. Verbum tamen sapientiae, quo Deum cognoscimus, nobis a Deo immissum, est proprie repraesentativum filii. Et similiter amor quo Deum diligimus, est proprium repraesentativum spiritus sancti."

Trace and Image: Degrees of Likeness

Thomas draws on the idea that created effects can be representative of particular divine Persons as exemplar in Ia q45 a7, where, following Augustine, he distinguishes between the representation of "image" and the "trace" of the Trinity that is found in every creature.[132] Not all creatures participate in the divine likeness to an equal degree. Different kinds of effects represent their cause in different ways—some represent only the causality of the cause but not its form, and this is the representation of a trace; some represent the form by a likeness to it, and this is the representation of an image. In all creatures there is a trace of the Trinity because everything subsists in its own existence (representing the Father by showing that it has a principle), with its own form and species (thus representing the Word, "as the form of the thing made by art is from the conception of the craftsman"), and has relation to something else (so representing the Holy Spirit, "inasmuch as he is love," because the order of an effect to something else is from the will of the Creator). In a sense, every creature manifests the Trinitarian nature of the Creator in some way by pointing to the essential attributes of power, wisdom, and goodness appropriated to the divine Persons, "from whom, and through whom, and in whom, are all things" in their ordered causal roles in creation.[133]

In the rational creature, however, there is a representation of the divine Persons not only as cause but also by a likeness of form, a likeness to the personal modes of the Trinitarian processions that act as exemplars:

The Son proceeds as the word of the intellect, and the Holy Spirit proceeds as love of the will. Therefore in rational creatures, in whom is intellect and will, there is found the representation of the Trinity by way of image, inasmuch as there is found in them the word conceived, and love proceeding.[134]

Thomas's mature view, that the procession of the Word is by mode of intellect, and the Holy Spirit's by mode of will, is evident. The rational creature is constituted as rational specifically by a likeness to the Word and Love—in intellect and will, respectively. Not only does God effect the work of creation in the image through the Word and Love (insofar as the divine intellect and will carry out all his works), but also God bestows in it a likeness to the per-

---

132. *DT* 7.10.   133. *ST* Ia q45 a7 ad1.
134. *ST* Ia q45 a7 c.

sonal properties of Word and Love, so that the divine Persons have a unique kind of appropriated exemplary causality for the rational creature. In the image there is a specific representation of the Trinitarian processions, which now have an exemplary role both because the creature reflects the Trinity as cause and because of a specific likeness in form to the mode of procession that personally distinguishes each Person within the Trinity. The rational creature, in its nature an intelligent principle like the Father, is like the Word insofar as it has a form and species and also because in its intellect it represents the Word. And it is like the Spirit in having relation to another and also because its will represents Love proceeding. Thomas anticipates in the beginning of his treatment of creation his full examination in later questions of the Trinitarian image and its perfection.

Even earlier in the *Summa*, in each of his treatments of the divine Persons themselves, there is a question that sheds light on their exemplarity both in the creation of the image and in its deification by grace. In Ia q33 a3, in the course of a discussion of the name "Father" as principle in the Trinity, Thomas discusses paternity and filiation in God, and of God with respect to creatures. The Son has an exemplar role in the different degrees of "filiation" of creatures to God, according to their likeness to the Son. The "perfect *ratio*" of paternity and filiation are found in Father and Son, who share one nature and glory,

But in the creature, filiation is found with respect to God, not in a perfect *ratio*, since there is not one nature of Creator and creature, but according to some likeness, which is more perfect the nearer we draw to the true idea (*ratio*) of filiation.

Likeness of the creature to the Creator relates specifically to the degree to which this likeness approaches the perfect idea of filiation found in the Son. God is called Father of irrational creatures "only by the similitude of a trace," but of rational creatures "by reason of the similitude of his image." Thomas locates their imagehood in their representation of the Son as son, as generated by the Father. His focus is on participation in the Son's relation to the Father rather than in the Word's mode of procession. It might be said that the former is a consequence of the latter.

In fact, Thomas foreshadows the substance of the theology of deification as divine adoption, which he develops in later parts of the *Summa*. He goes on to say that God is called Father of those who (in a greater degree of likeness to the Son) have "the similitude of grace," on account of which "they are also called adoptive sons, as ordained to the heritage of eternal glory by the gift of grace which they have received, according to Rm. 8:16,17: 'The Spirit Himself gives testimony to our spirit that we are the sons of God; and if sons, heirs also,'" and of others "by similitude of glory, inasmuch as they have obtained possession of the heritage of glory according to Rm. 5:2: 'We glory in the hope of the glory of the sons of God.'" The relation of filiation to God applies to creatures in the measure to which they are like the Son, in the increasing degrees of likeness of nature, grace, and glory. Common terms that signify relations of creatures to God

come after proper terms which signify personal relations; because the Person pro-ceeding in the divinity proceeds as the principle of the production of creatures ... The Son proceeds from the Father before the creature, to which the name of filia-tion is applied as it participates in some likeness of the Son, as is clear from what is said in Rm. 8:29: "Whom he foreknew and predestined to be conformed to the image of his Son."[135]

In this question early in the *Summa* Thomas establishes an important foundation for his theology of deification: the Son is exemplar not only of the coming forth of the variety of creatures in the *exitus* of creation, but also of the diverse and progressive likening of predestined human creatures to God by participation in his sonship, in the *reditus* of grace.

In his treatment of the Person of the Son, Thomas includes a question on the name of the Son as Image (Ia q35). With the same references to Augustine and Hilary of Poitiers that he will make in q93 on the *imago Dei*, he defines the idea of image as requiring both likeness and origin.[136] Clarifying why the Holy Spirit is not also called Image (because it is spirated, not begotten), he argues that the name of Image is properly applied to the Son; as Scripture says, he is "the image of the invisible God."[137] Thomas distinguishes between the imagehood belonging to the Son and that belonging to the human being who is "the image and glory of God" (1 Cor 11:7). He differentiates an image

135. *ST* Ia q33 a3 ad1.

136. *ST* Ia q35 a1. This distinction drawn from Augustine will also be repeated in q93; follow-ing Augustine, too, Thomas will build upon the notion of humans made to the image in his dy-namic account of the movement of the soul toward God through the activity of intellect and will.

137. *ST* Ia q35 a2; cf. Col 15, Heb 1:3.

sharing a specific nature ("as the image of the king is found in his son") from one that is of a different nature from its exemplar ("as the king's image on the coin"). In the second way, humans are called the image of God, but the divine image is imperfect in them, and so they are called not "the image" simply, as the Son, but "to the image" (*ad imaginem*; Gen 1:26).[138] Thomas interprets this distinction in terms of the potential for a dynamic image perfection, remarking that by the phrase "to the image' … is expressed a certain movement of tendency to perfection."[139]

In q38 Thomas associates this dynamism with the exemplar and efficient causality of the Holy Spirit. As Love proceeding, the Holy Spirit has a relation to creatures because the divine goodness is the principle of God's love for creatures, ordering them to the end of God's goodness. The Holy Spirit is so called because "spirit" signifies impulse and motion, and "it is proper to love to move and impel the will of the lover towards the beloved."[140] The rational creature's special share in the divine goodness that God's causal love bestows in the Holy Spirit places in them a likeness in form to Love proceeding (i.e., the created will), which orients them toward that divine goodness.[141] It is by a further divine gift, Thomas says in q38 a1—that of the Holy Spirit itself—that the rational creature alone can be moved to know and love God. It is only the rational creature, created with intellect and will, who can be "made partaker (*particeps*) of the divine Word and of Love proceeding, so as freely to know God truly and to love God rightly." Participating in the divine Persons in this way, the creature can be said to possess and enjoy the divine Persons because the object of love is the possession and enjoyment of the beloved. The power to do so, however, cannot come from the creature but must be given from above. So a divine Person can be given and can be a gift.[142] Gift in fact can be said to be a personal name of the Holy Spirit, because while the Father gives both the Son and the Spirit, the reason for the Father's gift is love, his well-wishing toward those who receive it: "love has

---

138. Cf. *ST* Ia q93 a1 ad2.

139. *ST* Ia q35 a2 ad3; cf. *DT* 7.12.

140. *ST* Ia q36 a1.

141. Thomas discusses the natural inclination of the will toward the good, or the last end of happiness, in Ia q82 aa1–2, on the will; in Ia q105 a4, on the divine government, he discusses God's movement of the created will by giving it its interior inclination toward the good. I say more of this below.

142. *ST* Ia q38 a1.

the nature of a first gift, through which all free gifts are given. So since the Holy Spirit proceeds as love ... he proceeds as the first gift."[143]

In each of these three questions on Father, Son, and Holy Spirit, in the heart of his treatment of the Trinity in itself, Thomas reminds us of the primary *ratio* of Trinitarian theology; that is, to teach us to think rightly about God's extra-Trinitarian works in both creation and redemption. Taken together, these questions reinforce the importance for Thomas of thinking about God's causality *ad extra* in Trinitarian terms. Each provides some insight not only about what he will have to say about the creation of the image and its deification, but also about how this deification brings about a new relationship between creature and Creator. In each question Thomas refers to the special likeness, albeit imperfect, that rational creatures have to the Trinitarian Persons, and to the potentiality that is thus bestowed on them by creation for a further participation in their exemplar. Rational creatures image God by sharing in the relationship of the Son to the Father in their generation, and as they grow in likeness to the Son, this relationship of filiation is perfected. While the image of God in human beings is imperfect—they are not the Image, *simpliciter*, as is the Son—they are made "to the image" in an inherently dynamic orientation toward such perfection by likeness with their source. Finally, the rational creature already created with this orientation toward its Trinitarian exemplar by its possession of intellect and will may (by the "first gift" of God's love, which is the Holy Spirit) be brought toward this perfection by participating in the Word and Love "so as to freely to know God truly and to love God rightly," and so be united to God in full possession and enjoyment of the divine Persons.

The Missions of Word and Love in the Graced Intellect and Will

In the final question of his treatment of the Trinity—Ia q43 on the divine missions, which "include the eternal procession, with an added temporal

143. *ST* Ia q38 a2 c., ad1. Thomas draws in q38 from the traditional appropriation of the name Gift to the Holy Spirit found in numerous places in Augustine's *De trinitate* and quoted by Lombard in *Sent.* I d18. In particular, Thomas refers to *DT* 4.20—"As 'to be born' is, for the Son, to be from the Father, so, for the Holy Spirit, 'to be the Gift of God' is to proceed from Father and Son"—and *DT* 15:34. By the gift, which is the Holy Spirit, many particular gifts are portioned out to the members of Christ." Both are found in Lombard, *Sent.* I d18 ch1–2.

effect"[144]—Thomas examines more closely the Trinitarian exemplarity at work in this perfection of the graced rational creature, in which God comes to be present within it "as the object known is in the knower, and the beloved in the lover."[145] We know by q43 that the Trinitarian processions are causal exemplars in creation; in the missions they have an even greater exemplar role. Thomas's placement of the question on the missions in the culminating final position of his treatment of the Trinity—where it also functions as a kind of entrée to his treatment of God's extra-Trinitarian works which is the subject of the rest of the *Summa*—emphasizes again that the chief purpose of a teaching on the Trinity is to "think rightly about the salvation of the human race, which is brought about by the Incarnate Son, and by the gift of the Holy Spirit."[146] We are alerted by the organization of the questions on the Trinity itself that God's work in creation will culminate in the gift of grace, given through the Incarnation for the sanctification of human beings.[147]

The missions of the Son and Spirit are extensions of their eternal intra-Trinitarian processions, with an added external temporal effect, by which they begin to exist in a new way in creatures. The notion of mission includes a double relation of the one sent: a relation both to their origin or sender and to their term, the end to which they are sent. The mission of a divine Person thus includes both the notions of their procession of origin from the

144. *ST* Ia q43 a2 ad3.   145. *ST* Ia q43 a3.
146. *ST* Ia q32 a1 ad3.

147. I.e., the structure of the treatment of the Trinity, as exemplar in its examination of the eternal processions and then the temporal missions, is reflected in the structure of the rest of the *Summa*, which treats first creation then grace. In his prologue to the questions on creation in Ia q44 a1 Thomas draws a parallel between the teaching on the eternal processions and the production of creatures: "After treating of the processions of the divine Persons, we must consider the procession of creatures from God." The teaching on the divine missions finds its parallel in the treatment of the Trinitarian image re-created by grace and its activities led by the Holy Spirit; it is completed by the treatment in the IIIa *pars* of the visible mission of Christ in the Incarnation, and his sacraments, the source and means of grace. In the questions on the Trinity, Thomas thus lays the foundations for his teaching on both creation and grace by placing them at the outset in the perspective of their source in the causal exemplarity of the divine Persons. Herwi Rikhof makes a similar point that Ia q43 is "not only the culmination of the preceding *quaestiones* but also the bridge to what follows: first, the subsequent *quaestiones* that deal with the *processio* of the creatures from God (qq.44ff.), and second, the other parts of the *Summa*." "Trinity," in *The Theology of Thomas Aquinas*, ed. Rik van Nieuwenhove and Joseph Wawrykow (Notre Dame, IN: University of Notre Dame Press, 2005), 43.

Father, which is eternal, and of a new way of existing in their created term, which is a temporal effect.[148] The Son and Spirit each have both visible and invisible missions for the creature's sanctification. The Son, who proceeds eternally as God the Word, is sent temporally by becoming human in his visible mission, and by dwelling in the human being by grace in his invisible mission. Likewise, the Holy Spirit, proceeding eternally as Love, is sent visibly by means of signs such as the figure of a dove descending upon Christ at his baptism, and invisibly in the divine indwelling by grace.

In the gift of grace, by which "the soul is conformed to God" by being assimilated to the divine Persons, the rational creature is perfected so as to possess and enjoy them.[149] God is then present to the creature in a special mode belonging only to the rational nature; God not only exists there as he does in all things—by his essence, power, and presence—but also actually dwells within it "as in his own temple." God is said to be present in the rational creature, who attains to God by its graced operations of knowledge and love, "as the object known is in the knower, and the beloved in the lover."[150] Both Son and Spirit are sent in the gift of grace and, dwelling in the soul along with the Father, are possessed and enjoyed by the creature.[151] Thomas places "the gift of grace which makes one pleasing" to God in the foreground of q43[152] as the "root" of the divine missions, specifically devo-

---

148. *ST* Ia q43 a1, a2 ad3. The new existence of a divine Person in someone involves a change, not in the divine Person but in the creature (Ia q43 a2 ad2).

149. *ST* Ia q43 a5 ad2, a3 ad1.

150. *ST* Ia q43 a3: "Super istum modum autem communem, est unus specialis, qui convenit creaturae rationali, in qua Deus dicitur esse sicut cognitum in cognoscente et amatum in amante. Et quia, cognoscendo et amando, creatura rationalis sua operatione attingit ad ipsum Deum, secundum istum specialem modum Deus non solum dicitur esse in creatura rationali, sed etiam habitare in ea sicut in templo suo."

151. The Father gives himself also in the gift of grace with the Son and Spirit, from whom he cannot be separated, though he cannot be sent, and therefore has no mission (q43 a4).

152. This phrase is often translated as "sanctifying grace." However, while Thomas does refer to *gratia sanctificationis* later in the *ST* (e.g., IIIa q34 a1), he does not do so here, although he indicates that this grace sanctifies (cf. q43 a3, *sed contra*). Jeremy Wilkins notes insightfully that Thomas's use of this term as his "typical expression for the effect of the Spirit's mission ... is another index of the priority of the interpersonal situation created by divine favor, because it emphasizes how grace constitutes a created person in a new relationship to God, rather than how grace is immanently perfective of the creature." "Trinitarian Missions and the Order of Grace According to Thomas Aquinas," in *Philosophy and Theology in the Long Middle Ages: Essays in Honor of Professor Stephen Brown*, ed. K. Emery, R. Friedman, and A. Speer (Leiden: E. J. Brill,

ting two articles to the relationship of the divine missions to grace (a3, on the missions in the gift of grace, and a6, on the missions in the various stages of grace's transmission and increase).[153] That the missions take place by grace is also the central consideration in arguing for the fittingness of the Son's invisible mission (a5). This gives an explicit focus to the importance of the notion that the missions take place according to the gift of grace. And, as Herwi Rikhof points out, because most attention is given in q43 to the invisible rather than visible missions, Thomas especially emphasizes the role of the Spirit.[154]

In a3, which asks "whether the invisible mission of the divine Person is only according to the gift of grace which makes one pleasing," it is almost exclusively the invisible mission of the Holy Spirit that is highlighted. Thomas places in the *sed contra* a quote from Augustine to support his argument that the divine missions, being for the sanctification of rational creatures, take place through the gift of grace. As Thomas quotes this text from the *De trinitate*, Augustine writes that "the Holy Spirit proceeds temporally for the creature's sanctification."[155] The emphasis seems to be on the Holy Spirit's role in sanctification in the invisible mission in particular. Actually, Thomas takes Augustine somewhat out of context and changes his words in

---

2011), 689–708, esp. 696. In the questions on grace, too, Thomas refers to *gratia gratum faciens*. Cornelius Ernst points out that this term includes not only the form of habitual grace but also the divine *auxilium*. "1a2ae 106–114," in *St. Thomas Aquinas: Summa Theologiae*, vol. 30, *The Gospel of Grace 1a2ae 106–114*, ed. Cornelius Ernst (New York: McGraw-Hill, 1964), 125nb. Thomas's various use of this terminology remains a subject for further study.

153. There is something of a difference here from Thomas's earliest treatment in the *Scriptum*, where, though he certainly talks about grace in the questions dealing with the divine missions, parallel loci to a3 and a6 in the *Summa* are subordinated to treatments of other matters ("whether the temporal procession of the Holy Spirit takes place according to all of his gifts"; "to whom the missions of the Son and Spirit are sent": *Scriptum* bk1 d14 q2 a2, d15 q5 a1).

154. Rikhof, "Trinity," 44–45. Just as Thomas says that in creation there is an ordering of the roles of the Persons, which reflects the intra-Trinitarian ordering of the processions of the Persons themselves, the missions of the Son and Spirit in the gift of grace are ordered in a certain manner not only by their origin (as the Son's generation is distinguished from the Spirit's procession) but also by the respective priority given to their visible and invisible missions, their differing temporal effects in the invisible mission, and the differing roles that their visible missions have in the economy of salvation. The Trinity acts as one in the works of creation and grace; yet, within this one action, each divine Person acts "according to the mode of his relative personal property." Emery, "Trinitarian Action," 115–53, esp. 133.

155. "*Sed contra* est quod Augustinus dicit, XV *de Trin.*, quod spiritus sanctus procedit temporaliter ad sanctificandam creaturam."

a way that underlines, more than Augustine does, this activity of the Holy Spirit and indicates the emphasis Thomas wishes to place on the role of the Holy Spirit's invisible mission.[156]

At the end of the *corpus* of q43 a3, Thomas again focuses primarily on the Holy Spirit when concluding his argument that the invisible missions take place in the gift of grace:

We are said to possess only what we can freely use or enjoy. To have the power of enjoying the divine Person is only according to the grace that makes one pleasing. And yet in the gift itself of the grace that makes one pleasing the Holy Spirit is possessed, and indwells man. Hence the Holy Spirit himself is given and sent.

Thomas clarifies in his answer to the first two objections that, contrary to "the error of those who say that the Holy Spirit is not given, but that his gifts are given,"[157] the gift of grace perfects the rational creature so that it

156. In the *De trinitate* text from which Thomas appears to be working (there is no exact parallel), Augustine quotes from his Tractate 99.9 on John to make the somewhat different point that "the Holy Spirit does not proceed from the Father in the Son, and then from the Son to sanctify the creature; rather, [the Holy Spirit] proceeds from both at once." *DT* 15.27.48: "Spiritus autem sanctus non de patre procedit in filium, et de filio procedit ad sanctificandam creaturam; sed simul de utroque procedit" (PL 42.1095). Thomas's addition of *temporaliter* may be drawn from Peter Lombard, *Sent.* I d14 ch. 1, in which, while referring to the same quote from Augustine, Lombard specifies the Spirit's procession *ad sanctificandam creaturam* as *temporalis*: "Praeterea diligenter ad notandum est, quod gemina est processio Spiritus sancti, aeterna videlicet, quae ineffabilis est, qua a Patre et Filio aeternaliter et sin tempore processit, et temporalis, qua a Patre et Filio ad sanctificandam creaturam procedit. Et sicut ab aeterno communiter ac simul procedit a Patre et Filio, ita et in tempore communiter et simul ab utroque procedit ad creaturam. Unde Augustinus in decimo quinto libro de Trinitate ait: 'Spiritus sanctus non de Patre procedit in Filium et de Filio procedit ad sanctificandam creaturam, sed simul de utroque procedit; quamvis hoc Filio Pater dederit, ut sicut de se, ita etiam de illo procedat.'"

157. *ST* Ia q43 a3 ob1. It is unclear who "those" are, who err in this way, but Thomas follows Peter Lombard, who names Bede as their authority and Augustine as the counterauthority. Lombard, *Sent.* I d14 ch2: "There are some who say that the Holy Spirit, God himself, is not given, but his gifts, which are not the Spirit himself. And as they say, the Holy Spirit is said to be given, when his grace, which, however, is not himself, is given to man. And this they say Bede meant in the words above, in which he says that the Holy Spirit proceeds, when his grace is given to man, although not as if he himself were given, but his grace. But that the Holy Spirit himself, who is God and the third Person in the Trinity, is given, Augustine openly shows in *De trinitate,* Bk. 15, saying, 'We should not doubt that the same Holy Spirit is given, when Jesus breathed [on the disciples], about which he then said: "Go, baptize all the nations in the name of the Father and of the Son and of the Holy Spirit." He himself is, therefore, also the one who was given from Heaven on the day of Pentecost. How, therefore, is God not the one who gives the Holy Spirit? Even more, how much is God the one who gives God?'"

may not only "freely use" the created gift of grace but also "enjoy the divine Person himself." With reference to the maxim at the end of the *corpus* that "we are said to possess only what we can freely use or enjoy," both the created gift of grace and the divine Person himself are given to and truly possessed by the creature.[158] Again with reference to the Holy Spirit, Thomas explains in ad2 that the Holy Spirit is not only the cause of the gift of grace but also that, by means of this grace, the soul is disposed to possess the divine Person, and "this is signified when it is said that the Holy Spirit is given according to the gift of grace that makes one pleasing." Some new disposition or *habitus* is placed in the soul, allowing it to possess and enjoy the gift of the divine Persons. Furthermore, gratuitous graces such as the gift of prophecy manifest the presence of this grace, and thus of the Spirit; "Hence gratuitous grace is called the 'manifestation of the Spirit'" (1 Cor 12:7).

The focus in this article is primarily on the Holy Spirit as both Gift and Giver of grace, and so the invisible mission of the Spirit has a certain priority in sanctifying the creature. The Holy Spirit, to whom, as Love proceeding in the divine will, the divine goodness is appropriated, is the divine Person in whose mission the gift of sanctification, by which God especially shares his goodness, is primarily bestowed.[159] Furthermore, Thomas says in ad1, the perfection of the rational creature that disposes it to possess and enjoy the divine Persons as gift comes about through the created gift of grace, especially associated with the invisible mission of the Holy Spirit. In ad2 Thomas refers to Romans 5:5 as authority for the teaching that the gift of grace is from the Holy Spirit: "the charity of God is poured forth in our hearts by the Holy Spirit."[160] We can expect that in the perfection of the rational creature through the gift of grace, the Holy Spirit and charity will have some close connection to the participated likeness of the divine goodness that sanctification bestows.

Thomas's special association of the gifts of grace with the Holy Spirit

---

158. *ST* Ia q43 a3 ad1.

159. Recall that in q19 a2, which asked whether God wills to share the goodness of existence with things apart from himself, Thomas framed his response by placing 1 Thess 4:3 ("This is the will of God, your sanctification") in the *sed contra*, so offering the example of God's will for human sanctification as a primary instance of the divine will to communicate the divine goodness to creatures by bestowing on them a participated likeness to that goodness.

160. *ST* Ia q43 a3 ad1–2. In chapter 5, I explore the importance of Rom 5:5 in guiding Thomas's mature thought on the Holy Spirit, grace, and charity.

is unsurprising, given the traditional scriptural warrant. When he turns to the invisible mission of the Son in a5, he must answer the objection that it seems unfitting in addition to the Spirit's invisible mission precisely because "all gifts of grace belong to the Holy Spirit, according to 1 Cor 12:11: 'One and the same Spirit works all things.'"[161] Thomas explains in the *corpus* that the invisible mission of the Son is fitting for the same reason as is the Holy Spirit's. The whole Trinity dwells in the soul by grace, and because the Son, like the Spirit, has his origin from another, he is also sent in the gift of grace. Thomas's reply to the objection tells us more about the distinctive role of the Son's invisible mission in relation to creatures and to the invisible mission of the Spirit. Thomas agrees that all the gifts are attributed to the Holy Spirit, as the first gift, "since he is Love;" nevertheless, those gifts that belong to the intellect are appropriated "in a certain way" to the Son, and it is in this respect that we speak of the invisible mission of the Son.

The invisible mission of the Son, from the perspective of the way in which its temporal effects are bestowed in creatures, seems in a certain sense to take place through the invisible mission of the Spirit, the divine Gift of love "through which all free gifts are given."[162] But in terms of the nature of the effects themselves, the invisible missions of Son and Spirit are manifested in distinct ways in the creature: the invisible mission of the Spirit has its effect in the creature's will, consisting in the "enkindling of the affection," and that of the Son in "the illumination of the intellect which breaks forth into the affection of love." The result of the missions is a likening of the will to the Spirit, who is Love by the gift of charity, and of the intellect to the Son, who is "the Word breathing forth Love" by wisdom.[163] In this way "the

---

161. *ST* Ia q43 a5 ob1.

162. *ST* Ia q43 a5 ad1.

163. *ST* Ia q43 a5 ad2: "By grace the soul is conformed to God. So when a divine Person is sent to someone by grace, an assimilation must come about to the divine Person who is sent by some gift of grace. And because the Holy Spirit is love, the soul is assimilated to the Holy Spirit through the gift of charity; whence, the mission of the Holy Spirit is applied through charity. The Son, however, is the Word, not any kind of word, but the Word breathing forth Love, as Augustine says in Bk. 9, *De Trinitate*: 'the word which we mean, is knowledge with love.' The Son is not sent, therefore, in accord with just any perfection of the intellect, but according to the instruction of the intellect which bursts forth in the affection of love, as it says in John 6 (45): 'Everyone who has heard from the Father, and has learned, comes to me'; and in the Psalm (38:4), 'in my meditation a fire shall flame forth.' And thus Augustine clearly says (*De Trin.*, 4.20) that the Son is sent, when he is known and perceived by anyone, for perception

soul is conformed to God by grace," the "root" of the missions,[164] and is able to possess and enjoy the divine Persons dwelling in the soul by grace in an objective union.[165] A full discussion of the relation of the invisible missions to charity and wisdom must wait until a later chapter; but recall that Thomas (in q38 a2) has already said that the way in which the rational creature comes to "know God truly and to love God rightly," so as to possess and enjoy the divine Persons, is by becoming "a partaker in the divine Word and Love proceeding."

The missions take place in everyone who has the gift of grace, by which "the soul is conformed to God."[166] When Thomas treats grace itself—the "root" of the missions—he will define it in terms of this deifying likeness to God. In the answer to an objection in q43 a6 Thomas anticipates another element of his treatment of grace, its progressive increase in those being sanctified. He already alluded to this in q12 in terms of a progressive intellectual perfection from nature to grace to glory, and in the questions on providence and predestination (qq22–23), when he introduced the notion of the journey to beatitude of the elect, whose own graced works play a causal role in the meriting of further grace and of glory. The missions are to "all who participate grace," and the invisible mission is sent not only when

---

signifies a certain experiential knowledge. And this is properly called wisdom (*sapientia*), a kind of savored knowledge (*sapida scientia*), according to Ecclesiasticus 6:23: 'The wisdom of doctrine is according to her name.'"

164. *ST* Ia q43 a5 ad2–3.

165. A comparison of the teaching on the missions in the *Scriptum* and *Summa* is beyond the scope of this work, but Gilles Emery offers a thorough examination of the development of Thomas's Trinitarian theology in several studies. He argues that, with regard to the way in which the Trinitarian indwelling takes place, Thomas moves from a more static "ontological" model in the *Scriptum*, where the missions imprint on the soul a likeness of the personal properties of Son and Spirit, in the gifts of charity and wisdom, to a more "objective" model in the *Summa*, which completes the first and lays the emphasis on how the missions unite the person to God in knowledge and love, as the "known in the knower and the beloved in the lover." Thomas's thought develops toward the idea of a dynamic objective union as the characteristic of the Trinitarian indwelling because of his mature understanding of the processions of the Word and Love. Emery, *Trinity in Aquinas*, 161–63. In this regard, a text from the *Scriptum* (bk1 d15 q4 a1) is worth noting. Thomas, while saying that the missions of Spirit and Son cause in the soul "received likenesses" of the proper relations of the Persons to the Father in the gifts of charity and wisdom, nevertheless presents these assimilations in a static way as impressed forms, by which the Persons are in the soul as a reality is in its likeness, and as the power of an impressing agent is in an impressed form.

166. *ST* Ia q43 a6; cf. q43 a5 ad2.

grace is first given (as it was even to the patriarchs) but also throughout the journey to beatitude.[167] Progress in virtue or increase of grace signals an increasingly intensified new way of existence of the Persons in the creature, according to the creature's growing capacity to perceive and be united to them. In the blessed experiencing the beatific vision, to whom the divine presence cannot be intensified because their intellect is united directly to the divine essence, the invisible mission takes place not by an increasing intensity of grace but by its extension in the ongoing revelation of mysteries.[168] Having outlined the activity of the missions in the "advance of the rational creature to God" on which he will focus in the IIa *pars*, Thomas also adverts in a6 to the missions to Christ in his humanity, and Christ's sacraments, the means of grace, treated in the IIIa *pars*.[169]

Thomas's treatment of the fittingness of the Spirit's visible mission in q43 a7 not only sheds light on the purpose of the visible missions in general, but also further specifies the relationship between the missions of the divine Persons and thus their activity in sanctification. Thomas remarks at the beginning of the *corpus* that, because "God provides for all things according to their nature," the invisible missions of the divine Persons had to be made manifest by visible creatures, because human beings must be led by visible things to the invisible things of God. He offers the same kind of reasoning in the IIIa *pars*, in the first article of his treatment of the Son's visible mission, the Incarnation, which asks whether it was fitting for God to become incarnate.[170] He makes a similar argument again in IIIa q60 a4 regarding the necessity of sensible things for the sacraments, remarking there

---

167. *ST* Ia q43 a6 ad2.

168. *ST* Ia q43 a6 ad3.

169. Christ, in his human nature, received the invisible mission from the moment of his conception, when "he was filled with all wisdom and grace" (Ia q43 a6 ad3). Possessing the fullness of grace, Christ as the Head of his Body is the source of grace for his members, who participate in his grace by means of his sacraments (cf. IIIa *pars* qq7–8). The sacraments cause grace instrumentally insofar as they share in the sanctifying causality of the Word working through Christ's humanity, and specifically through the power of his Passion from which the sacraments are derived (cf. IIIa q62 a5); the invisible mission is sent to those who receive grace through the sacraments (ad4).

170. *ST* IIIa q1 a1 s.c.: "On the contrary, it would seem most fitting that by visible things the invisible things of God should be made known; for to this end was the whole world made, as is clear from the word of the Apostle (Rom 1:20): 'For the invisible things of God … are clearly seen, being understood by the things that are made.'"

as he does in Ia q43 a7, on the visible mission of the Spirit, that God (or divine Wisdom) provides for each thing according to its nature, leading humans from the sensible (or visible) to the intelligible (or invisible).[171] In the visible mission the Spirit's gift of sanctification is given through the Son (who sends the Spirit) by means of his sanctified humanity, and is manifested by visible signs for "the confirmation and propagation of the faith."[172] There is thus, it might be said, a sacramental aspect to the visible missions of both Son and Spirit. Conversely, in the economy of grace, caused by the sacraments as instruments of Christ's humanity, there is also a revelation of the divine missions at work in an ongoing way through Christ's Body, the Church.

In the invisible missions, rational creatures receive all of the gifts of grace through the dynamism of God's love in the Holy Spirit to order them to the end of his goodness, the highest manifestation of which is God's will for their sanctification. The effects of this divine benevolence are twofold: the rational creature, already created as Trinitarian image by the similitude in its intellect and will of the Word and Love (cf. q45 a7), is assimilated even more closely to the Word and Love, whose invisible missions add to their eternal processions (the exemplars of the creation of the image) a further temporal effect of a greater likeness to themselves. And so the Persons begin to exist in a new way in creatures and can be possessed and enjoyed by them as the object of their knowledge and love.[173]

Summary and Conclusion

From the outset of the *Summa* Thomas lays the philosophical and theological groundwork for his treatment of the advance to glory of those rational creatures who are predestined by God to reach eternal life, manifesting in the highest way God's goodness in the divine *ordinatio*. Participating in

---

171. In I-IIa q101 a2, on the ceremonial precepts of the Old Law, Thomas relates the need for sensible signs and external actions in worship to the twofold nature of the human being, composed of body and soul. Outward worship is ordained to the interior worship by which the soul "is united to God by the intellect and affections." Through external worship—which consists in the outward use of the sacraments in this life and the eternal praise of God, seen by the blessed in the next—the effects of the invisible missions are accomplished in human souls.

172. *ST* Ia q43 a7 ad6.

173. *ST* Ia q43 aa2–3.

God's existence and likeness in creation, the elect are further transformed by the gift of grace to share by participation in God's own inner life of knowledge and love through assimilation to the divine Persons. In this way, their intellects and wills are transformed so as to move them, with God's help, along the path to glory, where they can possess and enjoy God in fullness, attaining their perfection as they become "like God" by "knowing him as he is." By the time he wrote the *Summa*, Thomas understood this journey as a progressive participation in the divine perfections that proportions the creature to the vision of the divine essence, as its soul becomes an intrinsic disposing medium for the vision by the light of glory.

In God's wise plan of creation and grace, God is the universal cause, knowing and loving every creature as a certain participation of himself. God's creative and sanctifying causality has a Trinitarian form, the production of creatures flowing from the eternal processions of the Persons as reason and cause. In Thomas's later work he comes to understand the processions of the Word and Love as taking place in the modes of intellect and will, and so prepares the way for his mature thought on the exemplar causality of the Trinitarian Persons in both the creation of the image and its re-creation by grace. Through the missions of the Son and Holy Spirit, flowing from the gift of grace, participation in the Word and Love transforms the creature's intellect and will so that it may begin to possess and enjoy the indwelling divine Persons. The question on the divine missions is the Trinitarian foundation of Thomas's treatments of the perfection of the image, grace, charity, and wisdom, and so we must return to it in later chapters. Thomas has already established in Ia q12 that the goal and substance of the rational creature's perfection are the perfect knowledge and love of God. But the teaching on the Trinity allows us to begin to understand more clearly how this perfection comes about, by the conformation of the image to its Trinitarian exemplar, through the "efficient, exemplar and final" causality of God in the divine Persons.[174]

---

174. Cf. *ST* Ia q44 a4 ad4.

2

The Image of God and
Its Perfection

The light of thy countenance, O Lord, is signed upon us.

—Psalms 4:7

From his treatment of the divine knowledge and will as the cause of the existence and order of all things to his identification of the eternal processions of the intellect and will with the Trinitarian Persons of the Word and Love—as exemplars in creation and grace—Thomas develops a Trinitarian hermeneutic for understanding the creation and perfection of creatures by participation in their divine exemplar. The image, bearing a formal and not only a causal likeness of its Trinitarian source, reflects its exemplar specifically in its nature and activities as an effect manifesting its cause. Such a creature manifests God's goodness in a special way, sharing in the likeness of God's own immanent processions of intellect and will, and so representing "by way of image" the divine Persons of Word and Love.[1] The deiform perfection of the rational creature is the knowledge and love (and so the possession and enjoyment) of God as object. This is a level of participation in the divine goodness that begins with, but goes far beyond, the participation in being and divine perfection possible to those creatures that bear only a trace of the Trinitarian likeness; it is the intentional participation of a personal being in the life of the Persons of the Trinity.

1. Cf. *ST* Ia q45 a7.

The loci examined in the Ia *pars* so far have allowed us to view the creation and perfection of the human being from the perspective of its Trinitarian cause and end—God, the divine operator of creation and grace. This chapter examines Thomas's presentation of the complementary doctrine in his treatment of the creation of humans at the end of the Ia *pars*, considering the effect: the product of this operation, the image itself. Subsequent chapters in turn examine the movement of the image toward God as a principle of its own natural and supernatural activities, a caused cause both operating and operated upon, participating in the outworking of God's plan of wisdom in the divine *ordinatio*. The framework that Thomas builds for understanding the participation of rational creatures in the divine causality according to their nature and proper activities provides the immediate context for his teaching on deification—the higher participation possible to that nature elevated by grace, and the interplay of divine and human action that brings it to a new and higher end through the theological virtues and gifts.

Image of Creation: The Rational Nature

In *ST* Ia q93 Thomas examines the human person as the *imago Dei*. The overall structure of q93 witnesses the relationship of exemplarity that Thomas has prepared us to expect in considering the image as an effect of its divine cause. The question consists of nine articles: the first three treat the rational creature as the image insofar as it is a likeness of the one divine nature, the fourth treats the progressive perfection of the image by an increasing likeness to God in the immanent activities of the essence, the next three treat the image of God according to the Trinity of Persons, and a final article considers the distinction between image and likeness. The development of the question thus more or less follows the structure of the development of Thomas's entire treatment of God, in which he examines first the unity of the divine essence and then the Trinity of Persons. Pointing this out, D. Juvenal Merriell notes that the structure of q93 also reflects developments in Thomas's treatments of the image from the time of his *Scriptum super Sententiis*; aa1–3 and a9 are parallel to the four articles on the image in the *Scriptum* II d16, while aa5–8, on the image according to the Trinity, find parallels in Thomas's later treatments of the image in *De veritate*, albeit with significant developments characteristic of his most mature thought.[2] Merriell makes the case that Thomas's treatment of the image of the Trinity in aa5–8 reveals a shift in his mature thought toward a more dynamic account of the activity of the Trinitarian image as a representation of its divine exemplar (see below). He attributes this shift to Thomas's rereading and appropriation of Augustine's most developed account of the image of the Trinity based on the processions of word and love in the *De trinitate*, noting the "saturation" of quotes from the latter work in aa5–8.[3]

Articles 1, 2, and 3 of q93 examine the likeness to God found in humans, irrational creatures, and angels, respectively, and argue that only rational beings, properly speaking, are made to God's image; that is, they possess by nature the "image of creation" insofar as they share a likeness to God's intellectual nature, and so rational beings come nearer to God than any other kind of creature, as Augustine says.[4] As Augustine also says, however, an image does not necessarily imply equality.[5] Perfect likeness belongs only to identity of nature; only the Son is the perfect image of God, but humans are said

2. D. Juvenal Merriell, *To the Image of the Trinity* (Toronto: Pontifical Institute of Medieval Studies, 1990), 170–71, 190–91.

3. Ibid., 191, 191–93, 208–10, 240–43. In support of Merriell's argument, Thomas's use of Augustine in the earlier articles on the image of unity in q93 also seems to show an awareness of heterogeneity in Augustine's own thought on the Trinity. In each of the first three articles of q93, where Thomas establishes that rational creatures are made to the image of the divine essence according to their intellectual natures, he makes reference to Augustine's treatments of the image of God in intellectual creatures in *83 div. quaest.* q51, q74 and *De Genesi ad litteram.* As J. Sullivan notes, in these works, written before the *Confessions*, Augustine tends to focus on the image viewed from the aspect of its relation to the unity of the divine nature, although he attributes proper roles to the divine Persons in the human being's creation and re-creation to the divine image, and in relation to the triple causal role of the Persons in creation he sees the traces of the Trinity in every creature. Beginning with the *Confessions*, however, and most fully in the *De trinitate*, Augustine develops his teaching on the "psychological trinity," or the specifically Trinitarian aspect of the image in the human mind, which allows it to be used as an analogy for the relations within the Trinity itself. J. E Sullivan, *The Image of God: The Doctrine of St. Augustine and Its Influence* (Dubuque, IA: Priory Press, 1963), 38–39, 70n1. Thomas of course would not have been able to historically order Augustine's works, yet he effectively follows the development of Augustine's thought in q93, considering the image with respect to the unity of the divine nature (and referring to Augustine's earlier works) in the first articles, and then moving in aa5–8 to a treatment of the image according to the Trinity (for "one follows from the other") with frequent reference to the *De trinitate*, first of all to justify this double treatment of the image (cf. q93 a5 ad4; Augustine, *DT* 12.6, 7)

4. *ST* Ia q93 a2, a3 ad2. Thomas refers to Augustine, *83 div. quaest.* q51.

5. *ST* Ia q93 a1; Augustine, *83 div. quaest.* q74.

to be both "image" because of their likeness to God and made "*to* the image" because they are imperfect likenesses of the exemplar.[6] Thomas has already referred to this distinction of Augustine in q34, on the Son as Image, where he observed that the phrase "to the image" expresses "a certain movement of tendency to perfection."[7] He makes a similar comment in a1: "The preposition *to* signifies a certain approach, as of something at a distance."[8] There is at once separation and an inherent dynamism toward union. The dual likeness and unlikeness of humans to God in the image of creation is a function of the specific extent to which they all participate by nature in the perfection of God: enough, as intellectual creatures, to be called "made to God's image," but less than the angels, who, because of their more perfect intellectual nature, are more like God.

Thus these first three articles of q93 place human beings in the ordered hierarchy of the universe, a hierarchy of perfection structured by each creature's specific degree of participation in God's existence and likeness.[9] The dynamism of the image is inherent in this hierarchy; Thomas, like Augustine, employs a Neoplatonic view of the universe in which creatures come forth from and return to their principle; a dynamic tendency of the image to return to its exemplar is proper to the Augustinian notion of image from which Thomas draws.[10] The image moves toward its perfection as all creatures desire their own perfection, "which is the likeness of the divine perfection and goodness."[11] So humans show forth the divine goodness in their proper way in the divine *ordinatio*, and in desiring and reaching their own perfection move toward their divine source and end.

To have a human nature is to participate in being and thus in the likeness of the divine perfection in a particular manner. Although God is the exemplar cause of all things, which all therefore have some likeness to God, rational beings have a likeness in species or kind, and so alone are properly said to be made to God's image.[12] Although there can be no real common species between God and human beings because God is *sui generis*, this can be called a specific likeness and unity with God "according to a certain anal-

---

6. *ST* Ia q93 a1 ad2.   7. Cf. Augustine, *DT* 7.12.
8. *ST* Ia q93 a1.

9. As Thomas states in *De ente* 5.8, the position of each creature in the hierarchy places them at a certain "distance from potentiality and closeness to pure act."

10. Sullivan, *Image of God*, 17.   11. *ST* Ia q44 a4.
12. *ST* Ia q93 a2.

ogy or proportion."[13] In a2 Thomas explains, with reference to a passage from Augustine's *83 div. quaest.* q51, that the intellectual creature is the image of God because it not only exists, and lives, but also understands; so it has a likeness in nature not only to God as the First Being, and as the First Life, but also as the Supreme Wisdom.[14] God causes an analogical likeness to himself in the image by granting to it a participation in his own highest perfection, an intellectual nature.

Perfection of the Image

The dynamic hierarchy of perfection traced in aa1–3 is the foundation for Thomas's subsequent examination of the perfection of the image by grace and glory. The movement toward perfection in any creature is a process of actualization in which God causatively knows and wills that his own essence be increasingly imitated, and the creature becomes more fully "itself" the nearer it approaches to the likeness of its divine source. In the case of the image there is a yet higher level of dynamism toward God; the divine operations of knowing and loving in which the rational creature participates are intentional in nature and have God as their highest object. The progressive perfection of the image of God—that is, its deification—will thus involve an increasing likeness to God precisely by means of the intellectual activities that unite the image to God as object.

Article 4 considers the three progressively perfect levels of the image of God possible to human nature within the universal hierarchy of perfection.[15] Thomas says that the human being, made to the image by having an intellectual nature, is most perfectly like God when it best imitates God in his intellectual nature. And the intellectual nature imitates God best when it does so by having God himself as the object of knowledge and love. A progressive likening to God "most of all in this—that God understands and loves himself" constitutes the perfection of the image;

Hence the image of God can be considered in man in three ways. First, inasmuch as man has a natural aptitude for understanding and loving God; and this aptitude

---

13. *ST* Ia q93 a1 ad3.
14. *ST* Ia q93 a2 c., ad4.
15. As noted by Merriell, *To the Image of the Trinity,* 171–72.

consists in the nature of the mind itself, which is common to all mankind. Secondly, inasmuch as man actually or habitually knows and loves God, even though imperfectly; and this is the image through the conformity of grace. Thirdly, inasmuch as man knows and loves God perfectly in act; and this is the image according to the likeness of glory. Whence on the words, "the light of thy countenance, O Lord, is signed upon us" (Ps 4:7), the gloss distinguishes a three-fold image, namely, of creation, and of re-creation, and of likeness. The first is found in all mankind, the second only in the just, the third only in the blessed.[16]

The image's three stages of nature, grace, and glory (or creation, re-creation, and likeness) represent increasingly perfect participations of the divine likeness, in which the image is united in a progressively closer fashion to God. In this progression there is both a continuity—because the natural substrate that constitutes the likeness (capacity for the intellectual operations of knowledge and love) remains the same—and a radical discontinuity—because in the more perfect image of grace and glory, the object of these operations is actually and not only potentially God. There is a movement, as the image becomes more God-like, from aptitude or potentiality for the knowledge and love of God, to the actual and perfect activity. Or, to look at it another way, God actualizes the creature's potential by causing it to participate more fully in God's own divine life of knowledge and love.

When Thomas describes the threefold perfection of the image in terms of a progression from nature to grace to glory, he is doing so within an established context. As described in chapter 1, Thomas has already prepared the reader to understand the significance of this progressive movement of perfection in his treatments of the beatific vision, Trinity, and divine missions. The perfection of the image takes place in the context of the journey to beatitude of the elect by a movement toward deiformity. And this transformation comes about through the bestowal of new dispositions, which allow them to share in God's knowledge and love of himself, likening them to the divine Persons of Word and Love by wisdom and charity and so bringing them into a new relationship of sonship with their divine exemplar.

In q93 a4 Thomas's business is to describe this journey from the point of view of the ontological progression of perfection in the image itself (i.e., from the perspective of the effect produced rather than of the divine cause).

16. *ST* Ia q93 a4 c.

The image of likeness found only in the blessed (a *deiformitas* more perfect than the *conformitas* of grace) is the terminus of this journey insofar as an ontological state of human nature is concerned. As Merriell notes, Thomas introduces Ia q93, on the image, by saying in this question's prologue, "We now treat of the end or term of the production of man (*de fine sive termine productionis hominis*), inasmuch as he is said to be made 'to the image and likeness of God.'" Merriell makes the argument that in q93 "Thomas locates the ground of the image of God in man in the formal cause of man, his soul," realizing in the *Summa* that "the formal cause of man, his rational soul, can also be viewed as the final cause of his production."[17] In other words, the end of the production of the human being, with which q93 is concerned, is the form that constitutes the rational creature, a communicated likeness of God.

Merriell contends, however, that Thomas intends to treat in q93 only the bestowal of the form of the rational nature (the human soul) in creation, and not its perfection. As he puts it, "Creation ends at form; growth and perfection come after."[18] Considering the image as the *finis productionis hominis*, Merriell distinguishes between the *finis operis* (end of the work) of the creation of human beings, which is the production of the image itself, and the *finis operantis* (end of the worker), which is God's purpose to communicate the divine goodness to creatures, both in creation and perfection.[19] While the *finis operis* of creation is the form of the creature (in the case of the human being, the rational soul), the *finis operantis* extends to include the perfection God intends for the creature. In creatures with a rational nature, this perfection comes about as the creature strives by its own operations, with God as its final cause, "to realize its likeness to God as fully as possible." Merriell thinks that the consideration of this perfection belongs to the treatment of the creature's operations, not of its nature, "which is the *finis operis* of the first stage of assimilation to God, which takes place

17. Merriell, *To the Image of the Trinity*, 181.

18. Ibid., 166, cf. 180. Merriell contrasts his position with that of L.-B. Geiger, who interprets the prologue of q93 "in terms of the ultimate end of man." Cf. Louis-Bertrand Geiger, "L'homme, image de Dieu: A propos de *Summa Theologiae*, I, 93, 4," *Rivista di Filosofia Neo-scolastica* 66 (1974): 511–32.

19. For the distinction between the *finis operis* and *finis operantis* upon which Merriell draws, see IIa-IIae q141 a6 ad1.

in the act of creation."[20] Merriell thus argues that the *finis productionis* in the prologue of q93, and the purpose of q93 itself, should be understood only in terms of an investigation of the production of "the form of man as the terminus of God's communication of His likeness in the act of creation," and not with reference to the ultimate human end of beatitude.[21] He proposes that Thomas's treatment of the perfection of the image (through its activities), which is included in the ultimate *finis operantis* of the Creator, is reserved to the IIa *pars*.[22]

Merriell's conclusion is based on the premise that in q93 Thomas is thinking of only one kind of *form* as bestowed on the creature—the rational nature—while the creature's perfection comes about through its *operations* in grace and glory.[23] Merriell points out rightly that for Thomas the "nature" of a thing signifies its formal principle, and it is the principle of its activities. In the human being the soul is the formal principle, which is the principle of its operations.[24] Thomas introduces the IIa *pars* with a quote from Damascene signifying that he will now turn to a consideration of the image of God "insofar as the image implies 'an intelligent being endowed with free-will and self-movement'"; that is, insofar as the image is, like God, "the principle of his own actions."[25] These actions would include those moving the image toward its ultimate end of beatitude. Merriell argues that, by contrast, q93 is concerned with the principle itself, as the rational nature that is the terminus of the act of creation. In Merriell's interpretation of a4 he emphasizes that, in Thomas's description of the degrees of perfection in the image, at each stage the human intellectual nature "does the imitating according to which man is made to the image of God." In grace and glory, "the acts of knowing and loving God take man beyond the moment of his creation and lead him towards his ultimate end," but Thomas "only mentions the state of beatitude here in terms of the perfection that it gives to the image of God rooted in man's nature."[26]

While Merriell is undoubtedly correct in his assertion that the *finis productionis* to which Thomas refers in the prologue to q93 is the form of the

20. Merriell, *To the Image of the Trinity*, 164. See also Ia q44 a4.

21. Merriell, *To the Image of the Trinity*, 169.

22. Ibid., 169–70.   23. Cf. ibid., 164.

24. Ibid., 189.   25. *ST* Ia-IIae, prol.

26. Merriell, *To the Image of the Trinity*, 189–90.

human being rather than the end of beatitude itself, it seems nevertheless that the production of "the form of man as the terminus of God's communication of his likeness" not only includes the bestowal of the form of the rational nature but also extends to the bestowal of the new forms or perfecting dispositions (i.e., *habitus*) of grace and glory, by which God communicates to the image a new participation in the divine likeness that it did not possess before, making it a new *kind* of human creature, not only a human creature with new activities—in fact, it is only because it becomes a new kind of creature that it is capable of new activities. It seems clear from the loci examined earlier in the *Summa* that Thomas is thinking in terms of such a transformation by the gift of new formal dispositions (and not only the addition of new operations) as the creature progresses from nature to grace to glory. In other words, although q93 falls within his treatment of creation, Thomas (in a4) arguably maps out for us the ontological form of the image as the *finis sive terminus productionis hominis*, not only in the state of created nature but also after God has elevated the image to having a new nature with a new end and therefore to being the end (*finis*) of a new work (*operis*) of God. In q93 Thomas treats the image as an ontological state of human nature, in all of its stages on the journey to beatitude, though he will examine how it actually gets there as the re-created principle of its own graced activities later, in the IIa *pars*.[27]

In q93 a4, then, Thomas presents us with the formal transformation of the image as God's *finis operis* at every stage of the journey, and this is consistent with his general treatment of the rational creature in the *Summa* from the perspective of its movement toward glory by means of a progressively increasing participation in the divine likeness. As noted in the analysis of q12 aa1–2 above, Thomas's treatment in the *Summa* of the *lumen gloriae* shows some development by contrast to its parallel in the *De veritate*.[28] In the *Summa* he founds his explanation upon an understanding of the created intellect itself as already participating in the likeness of the divine intellect, a participation increasingly perfected by grace and glory. Again, Thom-

---

27. As Merriell insightfully remarks with respect to those activities, "the *finis operantis* of the Creator includes the *finis operantis* of the creature, for the creature cooperates with the Creator by striving towards the end to which He has ordained it, the perfection of its nature" (ibid., 164). See Ia q44 a4.

28. *ST* Ia q12 aa1–2; *DV* q8 a1 ad6.

as sees both continuity and discontinuity in this movement of the creature toward God, but he consistently thinks overall from the perspective of the entire journey. A comparison of Thomas's references to the degrees of the image in the *Summa*, *De veritate*, and *Scriptum* reveals what is apparently a related difference between later and earlier treatments.

In q93 a4 Thomas ties his threefold classification of the image of creation (nature), re-creation (grace), and likeness (glory) to the Gloss on Psalms 4:7 ("the light of thy countenance, O Lord, is signed upon us"), which has as one of the glosses on this verse, "Imago creationis, ratio; recreationis, gratia; similitudinis, tota Trinitas."[29] Merriell notes that, in the *Summa*, Thomas "gets the Gloss' order of the triple image right, in contrast to his odd interpretation at the end of book 1, distinction 3 of the *Scriptum*."[30] In the *Scriptum* Thomas changes the order of the gloss, assigning its final Trinitarian "similitude" of the image to the intellectual nature given in creation, and not referring to glory at all in connection with the threefold image.[31] In the *De veritate* Thomas also quotes the gloss on Psalms 4:7 in connection with the image; he does not refer to an "image of likeness," though,[32] and notably absent, as

---

29. *Glossa ordinaria* (PL 113:849d): "'Signatum est super nos lumen,' etc. (AUG.) Hoc lumen est totum, et verum hominis bonum, quo signatur, ut denarius imagine regis. *Lumen.* (AUG.) Lumen, id est, luminosus vultus, et illuminans nos, imago qua cognosceris. (CASS.) Vel: Crux nobis impressa est, in signum regis nostri, quae est lumen vultus: quia in talibus radiat Deus. Imago creationis, ratio; recreationis, gratia; similitudinis, tota Trinitas."

30. Merriell, *To the Image of the Trinity*, 184. In the *Summa*, reference to the Trinitarian Persons is removed to later articles, where Thomas treats the image of the Trinity (188, 190ff).

31. The issue in this text of the *Scriptum* is whether sin destroys or only deforms the image of God in the human person. Thomas is arguing for the permanence of the image founded in the rational nature. He distinguishes between the image of creation, "which is reason, insofar as it approaches the imitation of the divine intellectuality"; the image of likeness, "which consists in the distinction of the powers representing the Trinity of Persons"; and the image of re-creation, "which consists in graced habits (*habitibus gratuitis*), and imitates God in act." The difference between the first two and the latter is that the image of re-creation is lost by sin (*Scriptum* bk1 d3 q5 a1 expos.).

32. Thomas refers directly to the gloss on Ps 4:7 that assigns degrees to the image twice in the *De veritate*, although there, oddly, the gloss is interpreted as calling the image two-, not threefold. In both cases the gloss appears in an objection. In *DV* q27 a6 obs, on whether grace is in the essence of the soul, the objector says, "The image of recreation corresponds to the image of creation, which two-fold image is distinguished in the Gloss on Ps 4:7, 'the light of thy countenance, O Lord, is signed upon us.' But the image of creation is applied with respect to the powers, namely, memory, intellect and will, which are the three faculties of the soul, as the Master says in *I Sent.* d3. Therefore grace is taken with respect to the powers of the soul." In his answer

from the *Scriptum*, is any mention of glory in relation to the image, possibly because at that time he did not think of the light of glory within a continuum of progressive participation in the divine likeness from nature to grace and glory.[33] In the *Summa*, his reference of the Gloss's *similitudinis, tota Trinitas* to the "likeness of glory" returns the gloss to its right order and confirms his teaching on the deiformity of the souls of the blessed as the perfection of the soul's participation in the divine likeness, through the knowledge and love of God. In *ST* Ia q93 a4, then, Thomas presents his most complete picture of the progression of the image to perfection, from the perspective of the transformations of its ontological state by increasing participation in the divine likeness, as God bestows new forms or dispositions, which allow it to be the principle of the new and higher activities of knowing and loving him.

By nature, the image shares in the capacities for intellection and will, God's own primary immanent activities. Thomas further specifies in a4 that humans possess, because of these powers, a "natural aptitude for understanding and loving God," that is, as object. Without grace and glory the image does not attain to the maximal imitation of God, by which it actually or habitually knows and loves God as God does himself, yet by its very nature the rational creature has this potential. Merriell points out that, in specifying God as the potential object of the natural image's intellectual activities, Thomas differs from his description of the natural image in the *De potentia*, where he draws an analogy between God's self-reflexive activities and the activities of the image in knowing and loving itself.[34] Thomas has

---

(ad5) Thomas appears to accept the twofold distinction but clarifies that the image of creation "consists both in the essence and the powers, as the unity of the divine essence is represented by the essence of the soul, and the distinction of the Persons by the distinction of the powers. Likewise, the image of re-creation consists in grace and the virtues." Where in the *Scriptum* he had separated the representation of the divine intellectuality and of the Trinity in the image, calling the former the "image of creation" and the latter the "image of likeness," he combines the two into the one image of creation, and the image of likeness drops out of the picture. In the *De veritate* too there is a correspondence between the essence of the created soul and the unity of the divine essence in the image of creation, rather than of the created reason and the divine intellect, as in the *Scriptum*. So the analogy can be made with the image of re-creation, in which grace is referred to the essence of the soul, and virtues to the powers (also see *DV* q29 a1 ob12).

33. As Merriell points out, however, in *DV* q10 a3, Thomas does analyze the image of the Trinity in terms of imperfect and perfect levels of imitation, an insight that carries over in a general sense to the progression of levels of perfection of the image in the *Summa*. *To the Image of the Trinity*, 185, 187, 190.

34. Ibid., 187–88. Cf. *De pot.* q9 a9, resp.

alluded earlier in the *Summa* to a corollary teaching on the natural image as *capax Dei*, where he argued that there is a certain natural knowledge and love of God belonging to all rational creatures, in that God is the universal good on whom every natural good depends; in effect, God is known and loved as the source of all that is known and loved.[35] The natural inclination of the intellect and will toward truth and goodness is the ground of possibility for the progressive elevation of the intellect and will, in the image re-created by grace and made God-like by glory, to God himself, the source of truth and goodness, as object.

Image of the Trinity

In aa5–8 Thomas considers the image and its perfection insofar as it is the image of the Trinity, specifically representing the divine Persons in its operations. In a5 he establishes that in humans there exists the image of God, both with regard to the unity of the divine nature and to the Trinity of Persons. In aa6–7 he considers how the image exists as Trinitarian (in the mind, and especially in the acts of the soul). In a8 he examines the Trinitarian image and its intellectual activities in the different degrees of perfection, which, as he described in a4, depend upon the extent to which God is the actual object of those activities. In a9 he addresses the traditional question of whether there is a distinction between image and likeness.

Thomas bases his argument for the Trinitarian image of God in a5 on the exemplar relationship between God and human beings, drawing from what he has already established about God as both unity and Trinity. Because the distinction of the divine Persons by relations of origin is suitable to (*convenit*) the divine nature, "to be to the image of God by imitation of the divine nature does not exclude being to the image by representation of the three Persons, but rather one follows from the other." Because God is three Persons in one nature, the image of God is in human beings "both as regards the divine nature and the Trinity of Persons."[36] The reader of the *Summa* already

---

35. *ST* Ia q60 a5 ad4, q12 a12. Thomas refers to these texts in q93 a8 ad3, where he argues that although the meritorious knowledge and love of God can be in us only by grace, there is a certain natural knowledge and love of God by means of which the image of the Trinity exists in all humans. Cf. Ia q82 a2; Ia-IIae q109 a3 ad1.

36. *ST* Ia q93 a5, c.

familiar with Thomas's earlier presentation of God's knowledge and love of himself as the processions of Word and Love, and the special exemplarity of the Word and Love for the image in both creation and grace, will easily follow the progression of Thomas's discussion of the image in terms of its progressive imitation of its divine exemplar by knowledge and love of God in a4, to its imitation of God by the representation of the divine Persons in a5, to (in the subsequent articles) the way in which, created as a rational being and perfected by grace, it imitates God by representing the Word and Love in its processions of intellect and will, less or more perfectly depending upon its object.

In aa6–8, where Augustine's *De trinitate* as authority comes to the fore, Thomas undertakes the heart of his discussion of the Trinitarian image. This work of Augustine, of course, has already informed his treatment of the Trinitarian exemplar earlier in the Ia *pars*. As both Emery and Merriell have shown, Thomas came, in his mature understanding of the Trinity, to characterize the mode of the processions of Word and Spirit in terms of the dynamic processions of intellect and will as one of the results of his fuller appropriation of Augustine's own mature teaching in the *De trinitate*.[37] Merriell argues too that Thomas makes substantive shifts in his treatment of the image from the *De veritate* to the *Summa theologiae*, as a result of his rereading and deeper grasp of Augustine's text, especially emphasizing the processions of word and love owing to a new recognition of the significance of Augustine's final formulation in *DT* 15. In particular, Merriell points out that in the *Summa* Thomas makes extensive use of quotes from *DT* 14–15 to argue that the image of the Trinity exists dynamically in the word and love proceeding in act.[38]

In a6, which asks "whether the image of God is in human beings only according to the mind," Thomas returns to the distinction that he has already made in q45 a7, on creation, between the trace of the Trinity as cause represented in all creatures and the representation of the Trinity "by way

37. See, e.g., the ubiquitous references to the *De trinitate* in Thomas's treatment of the Son as Word proceeding by mode of intellect, and Spirit as Love proceeding by mode of will (*ST* Ia q34, q37) among other questions on the divine Persons. See Gilles Emery, "Trinity and Creation," in *The Theology of Thomas Aquinas*, ed. Rik van Nieuwenhove and Joseph Wawrykow (Notre Dame, IN: University of Notre Dame Press, 2005), 64–66; Merriell, *To the Image of the Trinity*, 148–50, 154, 208.

38. Cf. Merriell, *To the Image of the Trinity*, 212–16.

of image," found in rational creatures whose intellect and will bear a for-mal likeness to the Word and Love proceeding. The articles are similar in their explanation of the general difference between image and trace.[39] But the *sed contra* of a6 links two Pauline texts to argue that because "the renew-al that consists in putting on the new man" both belongs to the mind (Eph 4:23–24) and is ascribed to the image who "is renewed in the knowledge of God" (Col 3:10), "therefore to be to the image of God pertains only to the mind."[40] Thomas goes beyond simply specifying the intellectuality of the image to argue that it belongs to the mind because it is the mind that is capable of being renewed, evidently by the re-creation of grace, in light of a4.[41] In the responses of aa6–8 Thomas examines exactly how the image represents the likeness of God both as unity and Trinity, specifically in the mind. He founds his argument on the repeated premise that "a certain rep-resentation of the species belongs to the nature of an image."[42]

To understand exactly how the image represents God as Trinity, we must examine what Thomas means by "representation of the species." Ear-lier in q93 Thomas refers twice to a text from Hilary to say that "the nature

39. On this subject Thomas clearly has in mind *DT* 6.10.2, which he had placed in the *sed contra* of q45 a7, although he does not refer to it here, as he is now interested in locating the im-age in a more refined way within the human mind alone, not in the rational nature in general. Cf. Augustine, *DT* 6.10.12: "The trace of the Trinity appears in creatures."

40. *ST* Ia q93 a6, s.c. It is perhaps worth noting that Thomas inserts "of God" into his quota-tion of Colossians—"putting on the new man, who is renewed in knowledge *of God*"—in keep-ing with his understanding in the *Summa* of the image's intellectual activities, referring to God as object, potentially by nature, and actually so when the image is perfected by grace and glory.

41. In his *Commentary on Colossians*—Col 3:10: "induentes novum hominem, qui reno-vatur in agnitionem Dei, secundum imaginem eius qui creavit eum" (you have put on the new man, which is being renewed in knowledge [of God], to the image of its Creator)—Thomas at-tributes the renewal of the mind in the "new man," which is the renewal of the image, to grace (*nova creatura est gratia innovans*), and, more precisely, to the faith that comes from grace's healing of the mind subjected to sin, and leads the interior man from ignorance of God to knowledge of God. "Interior homo vetus per ignorantiam Dei, renovatur per fidem et agnitio-nem Dei … Sed ubi est haec renovatio? Ibi, scilicet ubi est imago Dei, quae non est in potentiis sensitivae partis, sed in mente. Unde dicit secundum imaginem, id est, ipsa Dei imago, quae est in nobis renovata, et hoc secundum imaginem eius, scilicet Dei, qui creavit eum." In Ia q43 a6, on the divine missions, Thomas says that in the creature receiving the missions two things take place: the indwelling of grace and "a certain renewal by grace (*innovationem quandam per gra-tiam*)." His use of the latter phrase is something of a textual link between the questions on the divine missions and the image.

42. *ST* Ia q93 a7.

of an image requires likeness in species."[43] This text also appears in an objection arguing that human beings cannot be the image because they have no common species with God: "Hilary says (*De Synodis*) that 'an image is of the same species as that which it images'; and again he says that 'an image is the undivided and united likeness of one thing co-equating to another.'"[44] But Thomas will not argue, as the objector supposes, that humans can actually share the same species with God, for God transcends every genus and species.[45] Rather, he clarifies that only of the perfect image (i.e., the Word) can it properly be said that "one thing equates to another" with respect to God, and thus perfectly shares the same species, but, he says, humans can share the oneness that belongs to the notion of species with God—that is, have unity or agreement (*convenientia*) with God—"according to a certain analogy or proportion."[46]

The few other instances in the *Summa* and elsewhere when Thomas speaks of the *convenientia creaturae ad Deum* clarify his use of the term; he places *convenientia* in the context of discussing the participation of creatures (and specifically of the image) in God, which creates between them a relationship of proportion. The *convenientia* of creatures to God arises by virtue of their existence as participated likenesses of God.[47] In Ia q13, on analogy, Thomas describes God as a kind of universal analogical agent, producing his own likeness in all creatures so that names apply to them according to their relationship of proportion to God.[48] What does it mean, then,

---

43. *ST* Ia q93 a2. This refines his definition of "image" somewhat from that of q45 a7, where he said that an image represents its cause "by the likeness of its form."

44. *ST* Ia q93 a1 ob3.

45. In the questions on the divine nature, he has already said that in the relationship of agent to effect by which God communicates form to creatures, no likeness of creatures to God can be affirmed on account of a communication of genus or species common to God and creatures, but only "according to analogy, for the reason that God is a being by his essence, and other things by participation" (*ST* Ia q4 a3 c., ad3).

46. *ST* Ia q93 a1 ad3: "Ad tertium dicendum quod, cum unum sit ens indivisum, eo modo dicitur species indifferens, quo una. Unum autem dicitur aliquid non solum numero aut specie aut genere, sed etiam secundum analogiam vel proportionem quandam, et sic est unitas vel convenientia creaturae ad Deum. Quod autem dicit rei ad rem coaequandam, pertinet ad rationem perfectae imaginis."

47. Cf. *Scriptum* bk2 d16 q1 a1 ad 3–4; *DV* q2 a11 c. Cf. *ST* III q3 a8, on the *convenientia* of the Word to all creatures and especially to humans as exemplar, as the Word of Wisdom through which God creates and perfects humanity. It is through the Word that there is a *convenientia* between creatures and God.

48. *ST* Ia q13 a5.

when Thomas says that in the case of rational creatures there is a special representation or likeness of *species*, a special proportioning? In Ia q12 Thomas also uses the language of analogy or proportion to refer to the participated likeness of the rational creature in the divine intellect by its nature, a participation that is raised by the gifts of grace and glory to a higher level, giving it a new potency so that it "can be proportioned to knowing God," and even to seeing God as he is through the divine essence as actualizing form. The proportioning of humans to God has to do with their participation in the divine intellect, and thus their capacity to know God.

Given this proportion already existing between the human intellect and God, what Thomas says about the divine intellect in Ia q14 sheds light on what a "specific" likeness to that intellect involves. In fact, the articles of q93 on the image of the Trinity echo to some extent q14, on God's own knowledge, by describing the image of God as "representing the species" in its intellectual nature (a6), its act (a7), and its object and intelligible species (a8).[49] In q14 Thomas devotes several articles to the consideration of the divine intellect, its act, intelligible species, and object. In the human act of cognition the intelligible species of the object informs the intellect, which is in potentiality to its object. Because God is pure act without potentiality, the divine intellect, its object, and its intelligible species are all the same, identical with the divine essence: "the intelligible species itself is the divine intellect itself, and thus God understands himself through himself."[50] The immanent act of understanding in God, by which he understands (and so loves) himself through himself as his own intelligible species, is also identical with the divine essence.[51]

From this act of divine cognition flow the species of all creatures and, in a special way, of rational creatures. In Thomas's discussion of the divine knowledge and divine ideas in Ia qq14–15, he establishes that God's causal knowledge of everything in the universe in relation to himself is the source of the universe's ordered hierarchy; in terms drawn from q13 it could be said

49. Cf. *ST* Ia q14 a1, a2, a4.

50. *ST* Ia q14 a2: "Cum igitur Deus nihil potentialitatis habeat, sed sit actus purus, oportet quod in eo intellectus et intellectum sint idem omnibus modis, ita scilicet, ut neque careat specie intelligibili, sicut intellectus noster cum intelligit in potentia; neque species intelligibilis sit aliud a substantia intellectus divini, sicut accidit in intellectu nostro, cum est actu intelligens; sed ipsa species intelligibilis est ipse intellectus divinus. Et sic seipsum per seipsum intelligit."

51. *ST* Ia q14 a4.

that the universe represents him analogically "as many things are proportioned to one."[52] The *convenientia* of creatures to God is fundamentally the *convenientia* that obtains in any act of cognition between a similitude—here, the creature—and that of which it is a similitude—God himself.[53] God, in perfectly knowing his own essence, knows also every way in which creatures can participate in it, and his knowledge joined to his will is the cause of things. God's knowledge of his own essence as participable in a certain way, "according to some degree of likeness," constitutes the proper species of each creature.[54]

If *rational* creatures participate in the divine essence "according to the representation of the species," it means that God causally knows them as being capable of some degree of participation in his own self-knowledge and love—in the activities of the divine intellect and will that have God as their object and the divine essence itself as intelligible species. These conditions are most perfectly fulfilled, as established in Ia q12, in the beatific vision, with God as the object of the creature's knowledge and love, the divine essence as intelligible form directly united to the created intellect, and that intellect disposed by a higher participation in the divine intellect.[55] The more the rational creature is likened to God by participating in the divine intellect—and in the divine intellect's own act, object, and intelligible species—the more it fulfills the potential of its nature; the perfection of the "representation of the species" is participated deiformity. So the image's representation of the species of God proportions it to God for the knowledge and love of God. Furthermore, because Thomas identifies God's act of self-understanding with the procession of the Word, and God's act of self-loving with the procession of Love, the creature's participated representation of the species will involve a representation of the divine Persons. God knows rational creatures as creatures that represent the way God knows and so loves himself—through the processions of the Word and Love, or Son and Holy Spirit.

---

52. Cf. *ST* Ia q14 a6 ad3: "Ad tertium dicendum quod idem non potest accipi ut ratio diversorum per modum adaequationis. Sed divina essentia est aliquid excedens omnes creaturas. Unde potest accipi ut propria ratio uniuscuiusque, secundum quod diversimode est participabilis vel imitabilis a diversis creaturis."

53. Cf. *DV* q8 a1.   54. *ST* Ia q14 a8, q15 a2.

55. *ST* Ia q12 a2 ad3.

In a6 Thomas examines the intellectual nature of the image of the Trinity. He begins by saying that, as to the likeness of the divine nature, rational creatures "seem, in a certain manner, to attain to the representation of species, inasmuch as they imitate God, not only in that he exists and lives, but also in that he understands (*intelligit*), as was said above (a2)." That is, the image of God is found in the mind. Similarly, with respect to the Trinity of Persons,

as the uncreated Trinity is distinguished according to the procession of the Word from the Speaker, and of Love from both of these … so it can be said that in rational creatures, in which are found a procession of the word in the intellect, and a procession of love in the will, there is an image of the uncreated Trinity, by a certain representation of the species.

Just as in the uncreated Trinity there is "the procession of the Word from the Speaker, and of Love from both of these," so the image imitates God's Trinitarian intellectual nature in that there exists in it "the principle of the word, and the word and love."[56]

This formulation comes into play as Thomas discusses the acts of the soul in a7, arguing that the image of the Trinity exists in the soul, where the soul approaches the nearest to the representation of the species of the divine Persons; that is, not just in its habits and powers but also in its actual ordered activity:

In our soul word "cannot exist without actual thought," as Augustine says (*DT* 15.7). And therefore, first and principally, the image of the Trinity is found in the

---

56. *ST* Ia q93 a6. It might seem that there is little difference from what Thomas said in q45 a7, where he also refers to his earlier treatment of the Trinitarian processions of Word and Love in q27 a3 to locate the way in which the rational creature images the processions of the Persons in its intellect and will. Here, however, he includes the notion of the ordering of the Trinitarian processions with respect to their principle (discussed first in q27 a3 ad3 and foundational for his subsequent treatment of the Trinitarian relations and Persons) as an aspect of the species that the image represents. Question 93 a6 adverts more explicitly than q45 a7 to all three divine Persons as the image's exemplar—"the principle of the word, and the word and love"—and draws attention somewhat more to an ordered activity within the image as it represents the species of the Persons. In aa7–8 Thomas will continue to advert to the exemplary distinction of the divine Persons in their ordered activity, in a way that follows most closely the texts of Augustine to which he refers. Cf. *ST* Ia q45 a7: "Now the processions of the divine Persons are referred to the acts of intellect and will, as was said above (q27). For the Son proceeds as the word of the intellect; and the Holy Spirit proceeds as love of the will. Therefore in rational creatures, possessing intellect and will, there is found the representation of the Trinity by way of image, inasmuch as there is found in them the word conceived, and the love proceeding."

mind according to act; that is, as from the knowledge which we have, by thinking we form an interior word, and from this we break forth into love.

Because the Trinity itself is inherently dynamic, the soul represents it most nearly in its own dynamic state, although the image exists virtually in the principles of its acts, the habits, and powers. As Merriell has shown, it is especially in these articles that Thomas evinces a mature reconsideration of the *De trinitate*, reading Augustine more accurately, particularly with respect to his emphasis on the processions of word and love in book 15.[57]

Merriell also notes a development in Thomas's understanding of the mind's acts as imaging the Trinity. In the *Summa* Thomas presents the image of the Trinity as found not in the mind's memory, thinking, and willing, as he did in the *De veritate*, but according to its acts. In the *Summa* the terms that proceed in the acts—the inner word and love—best represent the second and third divine Persons, not the acts of thinking and willing themselves.[58] This was clear too in q45 a7, where Thomas says that the representation of the Trinity is found in rational creatures "by way of image, inasmuch as there is found in them the word conceived, and the love proceeding." Although Merriell does not pursue this point, it is significant in relation to Thomas's consideration of the object of the image's activities in a8, as well as in his conception of the roles of charity and wisdom in the perfection of the image.[59]

If aa6–7 provide a Trinitarian explication of the basic definition of the image in a4, as a perfectible principle with the capacity for the potential or actual knowledge and love of God, a8 completes this unpacking by consid-

---

57. Merriell, *To the Image of the Trinity*, 208, 213.

58. But Thomas comes to the same conclusion in the *De veritate* and in *ST* q93 a7 based on *DT* 14, that the image of the Trinity is principally to be found in the mind with respect to its acts, and secondarily to its habits and powers. Merriell, *To the Image of the Trinity*, 213.

59. It also demonstrates further Thomas's accurate reading of Augustine's *DT* 15, where Augustine says that it is in the production of the prelinguistic *verbum cordis*, "begotten of the knowledge abiding in the consciousness" of the human as rational being, that "the likeness of the made image approaches as far as it can to the likeness of the born image, in which God the Son is declared to be substantially like the Father in all respects." Likewise, after discussing the Holy Spirit as Love in the Trinity, Augustine goes on to say that in the image human love "proceeding from knowledge and joining memory and understanding together … has in this image some likeness, though a vastly unequal one, to the Holy Spirit" (*DT* 15.20, 43). Cf. *ST* Ia q34 a1, where Thomas quotes *DT* 15.10 in reference to the *verbum cordis* as "the likeness of that Word of whom it is said: 'In the beginning was the Word.'"

ering the image of the Trinity with respect to the degrees of perfection by
which it is likened to God as its object. The rational creature images God
precisely in having God himself as the potential or actual object of its intellectual activity, just as God is the object of his own knowledge and love. In
the perfection of the image, the human person knows and loves God perfectly and so shares in the likeness of glory (a4). By a8 Thomas has established that the word and love produced by the active processions of knowledge and love in the image represent the species of the Persons of Word
and Love in the Trinity, for the divine Persons are "distinguished from each
other according to the procession of the Word from the Speaker, and the
procession of Love from both."[60] Thomas now adds that "the Word of God
is born of God according to his knowledge of himself; and Love proceeds
from God according as he loves himself." If the word and love produced in
the image are to adequately represent God's Word and Love, they must have
the same object as God's knowledge and love:

It is clear that diversity of objects diversifies the species of word and love, for in the
human heart the word conceived from a stone and from a horse are not alike in
species, nor is the species of love alike. Hence the divine image in man is found according to the word conceived from the knowledge of God, and to the love derived
as a result.[61]

Some intelligible species is required in all human knowledge, which the
intellect abstracts from the object, as a result of which it conceives an inner
word.[62] The species of the divine Persons are best represented in the human
mind (and so it most perfectly images God) insofar as the word and love
produced in the mind are alike in species to the Word and Love proceeding in God's mind, and species is determined by the object of cognition. A
likeness in object results in a likeness in intelligible species, completing the
parallel of the image's knowledge with God's own (Ia q14).

In a8 Thomas is interested both in God as the object of the image's
knowledge and love and in the intelligible species involved, by which an inner word and resulting love are produced. When the human mind has God
as object, it abstracts an intelligible species of this object and produces an
inner word and love that "represent the species" of the Word and Love—

---

60. *ST* Ia q93 a8.   61. Ibid.
62. Cf. *ST* Ia q85 a2 ad3.

so the mind itself, in which the intelligible species resides, is the medium for movement toward God by knowledge and love. This is why Thomas establishes at the outset of a8 (with the mature Augustine) that the image of God belongs permanently to human nature, though it may be obscured or defaced by sin.[63] As in a4, the image may have God as its object potentially, habitually, or actually (imperfectly or fully), depending upon its degree of perfection. The image by nature always has God as its potential object: "the image of God is found in the soul in that it is led to God, or is formed to be led to God."[64] Again Thomas shows his insight into Augustine as he emphasizes the principle of referral of created things toward God that permeates Augustine's thought and ultimately structures the De trinitate;[65] the image is, of its nature, a medium of referral for the human being to "be led to God."

This notion of the image as a medium is integral to Thomas's understanding of the way in which the image is assimilated to God as it turns toward God. He goes on to say,

The mind may be led to something in two ways, in one way, directly and immediately, in another way, indirectly and mediately; as when anyone, seeing a person in a mirror, is said to be led towards that person. And so Augustine says (De Trin. 14.8), that the mind remembers itself, understands itself, and loves itself, [and] if we perceive this, we perceive a trinity, not, indeed, God, but even so, the image of God. But this is so, not because the mind is led towards itself absolutely, but rather that thereby it can ultimately be led to God.[66]

63. Cf. DT 14.6–11, the context of the passages Thomas quotes here.

64. "Et sic imago Dei attenditur in anima secundum quod fertur, vel nata est ferri in Deum." Thomas clarifies in ad3, however, that while there is a certain kind of natural knowledge and love of God as cause, by virtue of the possession of reason, the image without grace may be clouded in those without reason, or obscured and disfigured by sin; he refers here also to DT 14.6.

65. In the De trinitate Augustine presents a spiritual pedagogy on the reformation of the divine image "to train the reader in the things that are made, in order to know him who made them," for, "to the memory, sight, and love of this supreme trinity, in order to recollect it, see it, and enjoy it, all of human life should be referred" (15.1, 39). Cf. Augustine's discussion of things to be used (uti) and things to be enjoyed (frui), according to the principle of the ordering of loves toward the enjoyment of the Blessed Trinity (De doctrina christiana 1). Cf. John Cavadini's discussion of Augustine's teaching in the De trinitate on the role of faith in Christ in directing the human mind to the knowledge and love of the Trinity, a teaching that Thomas seems to have absorbed. "The Structure and Intention of Augustine's De trinitate," Augustinian Studies 23 (1992): 103–23.

66. ST Ia q93 a8.

The authority to which Thomas refers is a passage from the same text of Augustine that he places in the *sed contra*:[67]

Augustine says (*De Trin.* 14.12): "The image of God is not in the mind because it remembers itself, and loves and understands itself; but because it can also remember, understand, and love God by whom it was made."[68]

Thomas's contrast of the "direct and immediate" or "indirect and mediated" knowledge of God as object ties his reply to his discussion of the beatific vision in Ia q12. Only in the beatific vision is God known "directly and immediately" (i.e., without any extrinsic created medium); there the divine essence directly united to the created intellect plays the role of the intelligible species, the medium required in all vision, for there can be no adequate created similitude of God in which (*in quo*) God is seen *quid est*. And yet even in the vision the light of glory must transform the created intellect to become a kind of intrinsic medium by which (*sub quo*) God is seen, without taking away the immediacy of the vision.[69]

In this life, no extrinsically unmediated knowledge of God is possible. The intellect that participates in the light of grace is still raised above its nature and strengthened (by the theological virtues and gifts that flow from grace) for a higher knowledge and love of God than is possible by natural reason, and so, like the light of glory, grace functions as an intrinsic disposing medium (or as a *medium sub quo*), giving a higher capacity. God can be known in this life even by grace, however, not directly but only through his effects, both in the graced soul and by means of those things known by revelation.[70] When God is the object of human knowledge prior to the beatific vision, the intelligible species drawn from his effects must mediate this knowledge, and the more those effects participate in the divine likeness, the more closely will their intelligible species, and the inner word and love produced, resemble the divine source of those effects.

When Thomas talks in a8 about the mind being led to God "indirectly and mediately; as when anyone, seeing a person in a mirror, may be said

---

67. Merriell notes that Thomas had not used it in the *De veritate*. *To the Image of the Trinity*, 217.

68. In *DT* 14.15 Augustine characterizes the image's remembrance, knowledge, and love of God as participations in God's eternal light of wisdom.

69. *ST* Ia q12 a5 c., ad2.

70. *ST* Ia q12 a12.

to be led towards that person," he clearly means—as does Augustine in *DT* 14–15[71]—that the mirror is the mind itself, which, reflecting upon itself as God's effect and similitude (though an imperfect one), is led to "remember, understand and love God by whom it was made." As Thomas defends the permanence of the image in the rational soul, which can make use of its reason to understand God, he places his answer into the context of a quote from *DT* 14.6, which as Thomas explains it describes the degrees of perfection of the image, from being almost nonexistent in those without the use of reason to being "'clear and beautiful,' as in the just."[72] The more God-like

---

71. Cf. *DT* 14.8, 14.23–24; 15.14ff., esp. 15.14–16, 15.21–26, 15.40–44.

72. *ST* Ia q93 a8 ad3. "Ad tertium dicendum quod meritoria Dei cognitio et dilectio non est nisi per gratiam. Est tamen aliqua Dei cognitio et dilectio naturalis, ut supra habitum est. Et hoc etiam ipsum naturale est, quod mens ad intelligendum Deum ratione uti potest, secundum quod imaginem Dei semper diximus permanere in mente, sive haec imago Dei ita sit obsoleta, quasi obumbrata, ut pene nulla sit, ut in his qui non habent usum rationis; sive sit obscura atque deformis, ut in peccatoribus; sive sit clara et pulchra, ut in iustis, sicut Augustinus dicit, XIV de Trin." In this text Thomas refers to his earlier teaching on the possibility of "some natural knowledge and love of God." Merriell argues that "the image of the Trinity can exist at the active level even in the state of nature. Nevertheless, it would seem that grace is usually required to conform and assimilate the mind to God so that the mind can participate in the divine processions of the Word and Love." By "active level" Merriell apparently means that the mind is conformed and assimilated to God in a way that "usually" requires grace; i.e., he believes that Thomas allows for some possibility of a natural knowledge of God in which God is present and possessed as the mind's object as he is in grace and glory, though "in fact, [one] often fails to know God when he is not aided by grace." "Trinitarian Anthropology," in *The Theology of Thomas Aquinas*, ed. Rik Van Nieuwenhove and Joseph Wawrykow (Notre Dame, IN: University of Notre Dame Press, 2005), 134–35; cf. *To the Image of the Trinity*, 224. But Thomas's earlier references to the natural knowledge and love of God in the *Summa* make it clear that he thinks of these as possible only in terms of God as the cause of creatures and universal good, because God is known naturally only through creatures (cf. Ia q1 a2, q12 a12, q56 a3, q60 a5, q88 a3). For God to be the object of the rational creature's operation of knowledge and love, "as the known is in the knower and the beloved in the lover," to which it is therefore united and likened, is possible only by grace (q43 a3). Later, in the questions on grace, Thomas devotes an article (Ia-IIae q109 a3) to showing that fallen humans cannot naturally, without the help of grace, love God above all things. In the course of this article he argues that even in the state of "perfect nature" (i.e., before the Fall), human beings would love God naturally—as do *all* creatures, even irrational and inanimate ones, "according to the manner of love proper to each creature"—under the aspect of their end, as God is the universal good to which their own good is referred. In the answer to ob1 he distinguishes between the love of charity, which loves God as the object of beatitude, and natural love, which loves God "inasmuch as he is the beginning and end of natural good." Only the theological virtues infused by grace can direct the intellect and will toward God as object, and not only as the "beginning and end of nature" (Ia-IIae q60 a1 ad3).

the image becomes, the more it can function as a clear mirror in which God can be perceived through his likeness, producing a more perfect word and love, until he is seen no longer in a mirror but face to face.[73] The "word conceived from the knowledge of God, and the love derived therefrom"—to which, Thomas says, "we refer the divine image in man"—are the word and love deriving from the image's actual knowledge of God as its proper object, its source, exemplar, and end. As the image's knowledge of its relation to God is perfected, the word and love produced increasingly assimilate the image to God by an active representation of the species of the divine Persons of Word and Love.

Image and Likeness

In the final article (a9) of q93, Thomas considers whether Genesis 1:26 teaches that there is a distinction between "image" and "likeness." At first reading, this article may seem somewhat perfunctory, simply addressing a traditional question. Yet on closer examination his treatment shows evidence of his mature reflection on the progressive perfection of the image, specifically in terms of its activity. Thomas is aware of different views in the tradition and must explain some difficulties arising from the treatment of this question in Lombard's *Sentences*. He brings forward as authorities both Augustine's *83 diversibus quaestionibus* q51 and John Damascene's *De fide orthodoxa*, neither

---

73. In a question on the soul's knowledge of immaterial substances (Ia q88 a3 ad3), Thomas answers the objection that God must be the first object of human knowledge because "what is first known in the image is the exemplar to which it is made; but in our mind is the image of God, as Augustine says, *De Trin.*, Bk. 12 4.7." Ceding the premises, he replies that if there existed a perfect image of God in our souls (as in the Son) we *would* know God at once. In Ia q94, on Adam's intellect in the state of innocence, Thomas says that Adam's knowledge of God was more perfect than ours because he was more able, without the distraction of sensible things, to contemplate God in his "intelligible effects" (a1); following Dionysius, he describes the soul's movement toward knowledge of the angels and God as taking place first through knowledge of the intelligible things within itself; that is, its own intellect (a2), in which God can be seen as in a mirror (a1 c., ad3). The angels are more perfectly to the image of God than humans, but as creatures, they can still by nature only know God through the mirror of the divine image. In q56 a3, on angelic knowledge, he says that because "the angelic nature is itself a kind of mirror representing the divine image," the angels' knowledge of God by their own natural principles "approaches the specular kind" of knowledge, much as "we, too, are said to see God in a mirror." In glory, however, even temporal things are known "in God"; that is, through the divine essence. *ST* Ia q93 a8 ad4; cf. *ST* Ia q12 aa9–10.

of which appeared in his treatment of the same question in the *Scriptum*.[74] From the *De fide* he draws a text that will have some significance in his presentation in the beginning of the IIa *pars*, of the image as the principle of its own activities.[75] Thomas allows that there may be two senses of the term "likeness," thus enabling it to be distinguished from "image" either as a preamble to the image—in the general sense in which likeness to God is found in all things and so is more universal—or as subsequent to it, in the sense that likeness signifies "the expression and perfection of the image." It is with reference to this latter sense that Thomas quotes Damascene, who says "that the image implies an 'intelligent being, endowed with free-will and self-movement, whereas likeness implies a likeness of virtue [or power; *similitudinem virtutis*], insofar as this is possible in man' (*De fide orth.* 2.12)."[76]

Thomas takes advantage of Damascene's use of the phrase *similitudinem virtutis* to answer a difficulty arising from a text in Lombard's *Sentences*: "the image consists in the knowledge of truth, and the likeness in love of virtue." As obj4 points out, the first belongs to the intellect and the second to the will, both of which are part of the image. But in the *corpus*, commenting on Damascene's text, Thomas points out that if there is a "likeness in virtue" there must also be a love of virtue; by implication, the latter, like the former, is associated with the likeness, which is the "expression and perfection of the image." The likeness must not only belong to the will as part of the image but also be the perfection of it. In his answer to the objection, Thomas distinguishes between the love of knowledge that is natural to the image and the love of virtue that belongs to likeness, as virtue itself belongs

---

74. *Scriptum* bk2 d16 q1 a4.

75. Michael Dauphinais also notes Thomas's use of the quote from John Damascene in these two places, and makes the argument that Thomas draws in an integrated way from both Augustine and Damascene in his teaching on the image to present a teaching in which the image, dynamically oriented to the knowledge and love of God, is perfected in the likeness of God by the love of virtue—i.e., by a participation in God under the influence of the Holy Spirit, so that "anthropology spills over into morality." "Loving the Lord Your God: The *imago Dei* in Saint Thomas Aquinas," *Thomist* 63, no. 2 (1999): 241–67, esp. 266–67. This project confirms Dauphinais's brief though insightful analysis.

76. *ST* Ia q93 a9. Thomas was also familiar, from his *Catena on John*, with a text from Hilary's *De synodis* on the Trinitarian Persons, which states that "likeness in power follows upon likeness in nature" (*Cat. in Ioh.* ch5 lect6); this applies by analogy to the image, upon which a higher participation in the divine nature is bestowed by grace, and thus a higher participation in the divine activities.

to likeness. While Thomas teaches that some virtues naturally exist in the soul, "at least, in their seeds" (ad3), and thus that there can be said to be a natural likeness to God in the soul, he is clearly speaking in the *corpus* and ad4 of the likeness that signifies perfection—the "likeness of virtue"—that belongs to the higher levels of the image in grace and glory.

This attention to the notion of perfection in distinguishing likeness from image is completely absent from Thomas's treatment of the same subject in the *Scriptum*, where he gives quite a different interpretation of the text from the *Sentences*.[77] There he states that likeness can only be distinguished from image by way of defect. Only "image" perfectly conveys the specific notion of the intellectual nature. Likeness can, as in the *Summa*, be prior to image in the sense that it signifies what is common to the genus containing the species (e.g., that which follows from having an essence; an example would be unity), but it does not signify what follows from having a rational essence (such as incorruptibility). Or likeness may defect from image in things subsequent to the possession of an intellectual nature—either the order of natural power to natural power or the order of power to habit. In the former case, because the will and its act follow that of the intellect, Thomas says, quoting Lombard's text, "'the image pertains to the knowledge of truth,' which first shows forth the intellectual nature; but, 'the likeness to love of virtue.'"[78] Nowhere in his *Scriptum* analysis of this question does he imply that the likeness may be the "expression and perfection of the image." Recall that in the *Scriptum* he had associated the Gloss's "image of likeness" not with grace or glory but with the Trinitarian image of creation. In the *Summa*, with the help of a new text from John Damascene, Thomas expands his definition of the likeness to include the notion of perfection of the image; he arguably highlights this interpretation of Genesis 1:26 by placing it at the conclusion of the *corpus* of q93 a9 and so at the end of his entire discussion of the *imago Dei*.

77. Although Merriell notes that Thomas's use of the term *similitudo* in the *Summa* to refer to the perfection of the image differs from his treatment in the *Scriptum*, he contends that *ST* Ia q93 a9 "departs little from the comparable article of the *Scriptum*, although it shows a superior organization and clarity." *To the Image of the Trinity*, 183. In fact, Thomas's treatment in the *Summa* has quite a different orientation than that in the *Scriptum*, being organized to a significant extent around that notion of perfection.

78. *Scriptum* bk2 d16 q1 a4, c.

The Image and the Divine Missions

Thomas's teaching in q43 that in the divine missions the intellect and will receive God as their indwelling object, and so are likened to the Word and Love, would seem to have obvious connections to his teaching in q93 about the representation of the species of Word and Love in the perfection of the image. Merriell points out, however, that Thomas "does not mention the image in his treatment of the indwelling, and vice-versa," and so—while acknowledging a "similarity" and a "close relation" between Thomas's teaching on the missions in Ia q43 and that on the image in q93, which he attributes primarily to the use of Augustine's psychological analogy of the Trinity from the *De trinitate* in both questions—he argues that Thomas actually fails to explicitly indicate any connection between the two doctrines in the *Summa*.[79] Torrell too considers the connection between the two loci to be "allusive," although "the teaching about the indwelling of the Trinity is the crowning achievement of the teaching about the image of God," and so it is appropriate for Thomas's commentators to develop what he did not.[80]

If an explicit connection between the two loci depends upon Thomas's use of the same terms, the point must be ceded. But early in the *Summa* Thomas identified the image with the rational creature, the term used in q43. In the three questions on the divine Persons examined earlier, Thomas has already said that humans, as rational creatures, possess "the likeness of image" by nature (q33 a3), are made "to the image" (q35 a2 ad3), and have the capacity to become "partakers of the divine Word and Love proceeding, so as freely to know God truly and love God rightly" (q38 a1). In the very beginning of his treatment of God, too, Thomas established that "it is according to intelligence and reason" that human beings are said to be "to the image of

---

79. Merriell, "Trinitarian Anthropology," 142n67, 135–38; cf. *To the Image of the Trinity*, 230–34, 242, where Merriell attributes this to Thomas's focus on the image of creation in q93: "The image is based on the intellectual nature's capacity for knowing and loving God. Although this capacity is fulfilled by the acts of a man's life and perfected by the vision and love of God that the saints enjoy in heaven, Thomas insists that the image rests on this capacity and so is rooted in man's nature from the moment of his creation. For this reason, he never makes any explicit connection between the indwelling of the Trinity and the image of the Trinity, although in the *Summa* we are almost justified in assuming such a connection because there is such a close resemblance in the analysis of both the image and the indwelling."

80. Jean-Pierre Torrell, *Saint Thomas Aquinas*, vol. 2, *Spiritual Master*, trans. Robert Royal (Washington, DC: Catholic University of America Press, 2003), 92.

God" (q3 a1 ad2). Outside of q93, in fact, Thomas usually refers to the human being in the *Summa* generically as "the rational creature" rather than as "the image" or "to the image," but he establishes early on that the terms are equivalent. It is not remarkable that in q43 he would use the former term because he had not yet treated the image *ex professo*, and yet he might expect his readers to make the connection between the two questions.[81]

As argued above, the structure of Thomas's treatment of the Trinity as exemplar, in its examination of the eternal processions and then the temporal missions, is reflected in the structure of the rest of the *Summa*, which first treats creation then grace. Question 43, on the missions, is the Trinitarian foundation of Thomas's treatment of the sanctification of the rational creature by the grace of the Holy Spirit given through the Son in his visible mission. In q43 this sanctification is treated from the perspective of its divine cause; later in the *Summa* Thomas examines the sanctification of the rational creature from the perspective of the effect in the creature, both in terms of the ontological states produced in the perfection of the created image (treated in q93) and the transformation of the creature's nature and activities that brings it to the end of beatitude, treated in later questions on grace, the virtues, and gifts in the IIa *pars*.

The connection between q43 and q93, then, can be viewed as the connection between treatments of cause and effect, which can be seen with respect to the two central and related aspects of the creature's sanctification by grace: the objective presence of God in the soul and the resulting assimilation of the creature to God. Recall in q43 a3 that Thomas says there is a special mode of God's existence in the rational nature "in which God is said to be present as the object known is in the knower, and the beloved in the lover" because

the rational creature, in knowing and loving, attains by its operation to God himself, according to this special mode God is said not only to exist in the rational creature but also to dwell in it as in his own temple.

81. Also, in Ia q43 a primary reference for Thomas is Augustine's own treatment of the missions in *De trinitate*; Thomas repeatedly quotes 4.20.28. In that section of the *De trinitate* Augustine himself speaks of the "rational creature" rather than the image. In the beginning of book 4, too, Augustine says that the purpose of the Word's mission was to bring about our enlightenment, which "is to participate in the Word, that is, in that 'life which is the light of men,'" so "he applied to us the similarity of his humanity to take away the dissimilarity of our iniquity, and becoming partaker of our mortality he made us partakers of his divinity" (4.4).

It seems clear enough that Thomas is presenting substantially the same teaching as in q93 a8, on God as the object of the image's knowledge and love, but from the perspective of the cause rather than the effect. The use of the phrase "sicut cognitum in cognoscente et amatum in amante" in q43 is itself something of an indirect reference to the notion of the rational creature's representation of the divine species, which Thomas discusses in q93, because he has earlier in the *Summa* consistently used these or similar words to describe God's knowledge and love of himself as object, from which proceed the Persons of Word and Love.[82]

A text early in the *Summa* may be helpful in connecting Thomas's use of such words describing God's presence to the graced rational creature in q43 to what he has to say about the graced image of re-creation in q93 a4. In q8 a3, on God's presence in creation, Thomas first mentions the special way in which God is said to be present in rational creatures "as the object known and loved (*sicut obiectum cognitum et amatum*)":[83]

God is said to be in a thing in two ways; in one way, in the mode of a causal agent; and thus he is in all things created by him. In another way, as the object of operation is in the operator; which is proper to the operations of the soul, according to which the thing known is in the knower, and the thing desired in the one desiring (*secundum quod cognitum est in cognoscente, et desideratum in desiderante*). In this second way God is especially in the rational creature who knows and loves him actually or habitually. And because the rational creature has this through grace, as will be shown later, God is said to be in the saints in this way through grace.[84]

Thomas's comment that God is especially in the rational creature that "knows and loves him actually or habitually" seems to be a clear reference to what he will say later in q93 a4, where he describes the image of re-creation, which "consists in the conformity of grace" as the image that is in the human being "inasmuch as he actually or habitually knows and loves God, though imperfectly." Thomas uses the phrase "actually or habitually" with reference to the knowledge and love of God only in these two places

82. See, e.g., Ia q27 a3, q37 a1.
83. *ST* Ia q8 a3 ad4.
84. *ST* Ia q8 a3. In his reply to obj4 Thomas stresses that grace alone "renders God present in anything as the object known and loved; therefore only grace constitutes a special mode of God's existence in things"; God is never present as object actually or habitually to the rational nature without grace (i.e., to the image of creation).

in the *Summa*. The text from q8 a3 above seems to proleptically link God's objective mode of presence in the graced person "sicut cognitum in cognoscente et amatum in amante" (discussed in q43) with the resulting ontological state of the graced person who has God as the actual or habitual object of knowledge and love (in q93).

The way in which the two questions describe the creature's assimilation to the divine cause can likewise be analyzed in terms of cause and effect. Merriell notes as one point of textual similarity between q43 and q93 Thomas's use of the unusual phrase "to burst forth in love" *prorumpere in amorem* in both places to describe the dynamic activity of the procession of love. In q93 a7 Thomas uses it where he says that the image of the Trinity is principally represented in the mind through its acts, inasmuch as "from the knowledge which we have, by thinking we form an interior word, and from this we break forth into love."[85] In q43 it describes the causal exemplarity of the Son, "the Word breathing forth Love," to whom the soul is assimilated by wisdom:

The Son is sent not in accordance with any and every kind of intellectual perfection, but according to a certain instruction of the intellect, by which it bursts forth into the affection of love (*prorumpat in affectum amoris*), as is said in John 6: "Everyone who listened to my Father and learned from him, comes to me."[86]

The "bursting forth into love" of the intellect instructed by the Word of the Father is presented in q43 as a likening to that Word, who breathes forth the Love of the Holy Spirit. When Thomas talks in q43 of the missions as effecting the assimilation of the soul to the Word and Love, by the "illumination of the intellect and kindling of the affections," he seems to be presenting the same teaching as in q93, on the likening of the intellect and will to the divine Persons by the representation of the species of Word and Love, in response to the objective presence of God, but again, in q43, from the viewpoint of the divine cause.

Recall that in his discussion of the divine missions Thomas emphasized that the invisible missions take place "according to the grace that makes one

---

85. *ST* Ia q93 a7, s.c.: "Et ideo primo et principaliter attenditur imago Trinitatis in mente secundum actus, prout scilicet ex notitia quam habemus, cogitando interius verbum formamus, et ex hoc in amorem prorumpimus."

86. *ST* Ia q43 a5 ad2.

pleasing" and are to "all who participate grace."[87] Question 43's primary focus is on the way in which, from the perspective of the divine cause, the Persons are sent, but Thomas has already established that there are two aspects of this sending to be considered. The divine Persons are given—as the soul's object possessed by knowledge and love—according to the gift of grace, but this can only be so because the created gift of grace itself is given, which "disposes the soul to possess the divine Person."[88] The perfection of the rational creature takes place through this gift of grace, by which "the soul is conformed to God,"[89] and because of this assimilation the invisible mission is to all in whom there is "the indwelling of grace, and a certain renewal by grace."[90] To the eternal processions of the Persons is added a temporal effect in the invisible mission, by which the divine Persons dwell in the creature. But that the divine Persons exist newly in someone, and are possessed by them temporally, can only come from a change not in the divine Persons but in the creature; the gift of grace that transforms the creature is the temporal effect of the mission, "the reason why the divine Person is in the rational creature in a new mode."[91]

There are thus two aspects to the gift of grace, which Thomas considers in q43 from the perspective of cause, and in q93 from that of effect. There is both an ontological change on the part of the creature (its assimilation to the divine Persons) and a resulting new intentionality with respect to God's objective presence "as the known is in the knower and the beloved in the lover." Thomas highlights this intentional aspect of the gift of grace in his discussion of the missions in the *Summa*[92] and also emphasizes this dynamic activity in his treatment of the perfection of the image. Question 43 treats the way in which the missions, from the point of view of the causal

---

87. *ST* Ia q43 a3, a6.

88. *ST* Ia q43 a3 ad1: "By the gift of grace (*donum gratiae gratum facientis*) the rational creature is perfected so that it is able not only to freely use the created gift itself, but also to enjoy the divine Person himself. And so the invisible mission is made according to the gift of grace, and yet the divine Person himself is given."

89. *ST* Ia q43 a5 ad2.   90. *ST* Ia q43 a6.

91. *ST* Ia q43 aa2–3.

92. *ST* Ia q43 a3, a5 ad2–3. Gilles Emery discusses Thomas's two approaches to explaining God's presence in the just (ontological, and operative or intentional), both of which are found in the *Summa*; the *Scriptum* focuses primarily on the notion of ontological presence by means of assimilation. *The Trinitarian Theology of St. Thomas Aquinas*, trans. Francesca Aran Murphy (New York: Oxford University Press, 2007), 373, 378–79.

exemplar, extend and perfect God's work of creation by increasing the divine likeness in rational creatures by grace so as to permit God's Trinitarian indwelling. The perfection of the image by the re-creation of grace and glory discussed in q93 (which involves both an ontological assimilation to the divine Persons and a new intentionality toward God as object) is the *finis productionis hominis*, the end product of God's gracious work.

Summary and Conclusion

In the Ia *pars* of the *Summa* Thomas has consistently stressed the notion of progression in the perfection of the divine image, one that culminates in deiformity. The rational creature predestined for eternal life is on a journey of transformation toward the beatific vision, which takes place by increasing participation in the divine likeness, beginning from its creation with a nature that shares in the light of the divine intellect. The participation in the divine likeness that belongs to grace and glory involves an assimilation such that the image shares not only in God's intellectual nature but also in its proper object, act, and—in glory—even its intelligible species, the divine essence itself. Each stage of this journey involves the bestowal of a new and higher perfection, the communication of a greater share in the divine goodness to the rational soul, disposing it by virtue of new capacities to be a more perfect intrinsic medium for the knowledge and love of God.

These effects in the creature flow, on God's side, from the divine plan to manifest God's goodness, brought about through God's causal knowledge and will, by which God participates to his creatures, in varying degrees, a share in the divine perfections. God knows and wills for rational creatures a share in his Trinitarian existence of knowledge and love. The rational creature represents its divine cause by imaging the processions of the Son and Holy Spirit; in the acts of its intellect and will one can see, as in the Trinity, the "principle of the word, and the word and love."[93] The graced rational creature is brought by a further gift to an even greater share in the divine likeness, "when it is made partaker of the divine Word and of Love proceeding, so as freely to know God truly and to love God rightly," and so even to possess the divine Persons.[94]

The image's ontological transformation, by which it represents more

93. *ST* Ia q45 a7, q93 a6.   94. *ST* Ia q38 a1.

perfectly the species of Word and Love in its intellect and will, involves concomitantly a new intentionality toward God as the actual or habitual object of its knowledge and love, for the species of knowledge is determined by its object.[95] This intentionality is dynamic. While the image of the Trinity exists secondarily in the habits and powers of the soul, it is found chiefly in its acts, producing a word and love that most nearly represent the active processions of Word and Love in the Trinity.[96] This dynamism on the part of the image finds its source in the dynamism of the divine Persons toward the image, in creation and especially in the missions, which temporally extend the processions in the gift of grace. This dynamic giving is especially associated with the love of God in the Holy Spirit, who is "the gift itself of sanctification" while the Son is its author.[97]

The dynamic advance of the rational creature toward God, which Thomas says he will treat in the second part of the *Summa*, has thus already received considerable attention in the first. Thomas has laid the foundation for examining the actual process of the rational creature's transformation by treating its efficient, final, and exemplar cause—God—and also the effect produced; that is, the image itself, in its different stages of perfection, likened to God by participation in his own activities of knowledge and love. Thomas has established too that, although creatures are completely dependent on God for their actualization and perfection, their existence in their own nature, as well as the activities flowing from that nature, are nevertheless truly their own. By participation in God's goodness and causal activity, the creature's goodness and causality will be proper to itself. The image, like its divine exemplar, is the principle of its own activities, according to its nature as an intelligent, free, and self-moving being. Chapter 3 examines how the gift of a new participation in the divine nature by grace transforms the image to become the principle of new and higher activities that bring it toward the perfection of glory, a process in which both divine and human action play a part. The following chapters show more clearly just how, through the divinely bestowed *habitus* of charity and the gift of wisdom shaping human action, the image is raised to an active likeness of the divine Persons of Word and Love, and, so deified, comes to share as God's adopted son or daughter in the Trinitarian life of beatitude and communion.

95. *ST* Ia q93 a8.　　　　　　　　96. *ST* Ia q93 a7.
97. *ST* Ia q38 a1, q43 a3, a7.

CHAPTER 3

The Grace of the Holy Spirit

For those who are led by the Spirit of God are children of God.

—Romans 8:14

Thomas opens his treatment of the rational creature's advance toward God through the moral life in the IIa *pars* of the *Summa* by anchoring it in the context he has already established for the image and its perfection in the divine likeness. Having examined the perfection of the image from the perspective of its Trinitarian cause, and the ontological shape of its progress from nature to grace and glory as it is increasingly likened to its exemplar, he is ready to treat this progress from the point of view of the creature's own activity as cause in the journey to beatitude:

Since, as Damascene states [*De Fide Ortho.* 2.12], man is said to be made to God's image, in so far as the image implies "an intelligent being possessing free-will and power through itself," now that we have treated of the exemplar, i.e., God, and of those things which came forth from the power of God in accordance with his will, it remains for us to treat of his image, i.e., man, inasmuch as he too is the principle of his own actions, as having free-will and power over his actions.[1]

The rational creature's share in God's likeness gives it a participation in God's intellectual activities and thus in God's power as a free intelligent cause. As in Thomas's treatment of the image, this participation is perfected by the gifts of the new dispositions or forms of grace and glory, assimilating

1. *ST* Ia-IIae q1, prol.

the creature's knowing and loving to God's own; with reference to the same text of John Damascene, Thomas argued that the resulting "likeness in virtue" is the "expression and perfection of the image."[2] This chapter examines why and how Thomas thinks that the deifying perfection of grace makes the image the free principle of its own supernatural activities leading to beatitude.

Form is the principle of activity. Creaturely activity, while causal in its own right, is also caused, because the creature itself is caused and receives its form from another. As Thomas will later say in his *Commentary on the Book of Causes*, "whatever participates a property belonging to something is likened to it not only in form but also in action."[3] This is the foundation of the secondary causality of the created order. Because God causes all created forms by participation in his own perfections, all created action is at bottom secondary and instrumental. And because the first cause is the source of the substance and activity of the second cause, it is really more the cause of effects produced by the created second cause than the second cause itself.[4] And yet, though participated from another, the creature's form and activity are properly its own, even (and especially, it might be said) the free activity of rational creatures. When the new creation of grace transforms the rational creature's nature, giving it a new and higher share in the divine nature, its new nature becomes the principle of new activities capable of bringing it to a higher end, to the full participation in God's knowledge and love, which is the perfection of the image in the blessed. In the IIa *pars* Thomas will examine the natural and supernatural principles given to the rational creature, and the divinely caused free activity flowing from them that moves the elect along the way to beatitude.

---

2. *ST* Ia q93 a9.

3. *Super de causis* l.23: "Quod autem ... participat proprietatem alicuius rei, assimilatur ei non solum in forma sed etiam in actione." Cf. *SCG* III.69 no. 14: "Si [Deus] igitur communicavit aliis similitudinem suam quantum ad esse, inquantum res in esse produxit, consequens est quod communicaverit eis similitudinem suam quantum ad agere, ut etiam res creatae habeant proprias actiones."

4. *Super de causis* l.1. For a discussion of Thomas's doctrine of causality in relation to his *Commentary on the Book of Causes*, see Michael Dodds, "The Doctrine of Causality in Aquinas and *The Book of Causes*: One Key to Understanding the Nature of Divine Action," in *Aquinas' Sources: The Notre Dame Symposium, Proceedings from the Summer Thomistic Institute 2000*, ed. Timothy Smith (South Bend, IN: St. Augustine's Press, 2008); and Brian Shanley, "Divine Causation and Human Freedom in Aquinas," *American Catholic Philosophical Quarterly*, 72 (1998): 99–122.

Human Activity in the Divine Government

Thomas introduces the subject of the causal involvement of free human activity in the plan of divine providence early in the *Summa* (see chap. 1). In the Ia *pars* he begins to address the apparent problems raised, arguing that the divine causation of human causality, which includes ordering the activity of human agents to their ends, does not compromise but rather guarantees their freedom. In predestining some to beatitude, God "wills one thing on account of another," preordaining that by the gift of grace the meritorious good works of the elect will bring them to the end of glory.[5] The human free will (*liberum arbitrium*) *must* be free in order to merit, but "human providence is contained under divine providence as a particular under a universal cause."[6] Thomas thinks that this plan of the divine *ordinatio* in which "the dignity of causality is imparted even to creatures" manifests the "abundance of God's goodness."[7] Discussions of the human free will and its involvement in the divine government later in the Ia *pars* provide some necessary further background for our consideration of the graced involvement of human activity in the journey to beatitude.

Just before his treatment of the divine image, Thomas examines the intellect and will that distinguish humans from irrational creatures. The first article in Ia q82, on the will, takes up the issue of the will's freedom. Thomas distinguishes different meanings of necessity with respect to willing. The natural movement of the will, as an appetitive power, is an inclination toward something. Any opposition to this inclination does violence to the will, imposing a necessity of coercion, which is repugnant to it. There is, however, a kind of natural necessity belonging to the will in that it naturally desires happiness and so by its own inclination must tend toward it. Such an inclination is by definition voluntary. Furthermore, the choice of those means, necessitated by the end desired by the will, is also voluntary; if one wills to cross the sea, one must also wish for a ship. Thomas holds that the will necessarily (and voluntarily) desires the ultimate good, which can be found in God alone; in effect, we have no choice about desiring this end, given full knowledge of it; rather, the capacity of human choice has to do with the means to the end.[8] Before the certitude of the beatific vision, how-

---

5. *ST* Ia q23 a5.
7. *ST* Ia q22 a3.
6. *ST* Ia q22 a2 ad4.
8. *ST* Ia q82 a1 ad3.

ever, the will may adhere to many lesser goods (i.e., lesser ends) that do not necessarily lead to ultimate happiness, because the necessary connection between those things that lead to God and the ultimate end is not seen, and other things promising a lesser happiness are chosen instead.[9]

The power of the will, informed by reason, to make a choice of the means to happiness in any given situation, is the free will (*liberum arbitrium*). In Ia q83 a1, on free will, Thomas places a quote from Sirach—"God made man from the beginning, and left him in the hand of his own counsel"—first explained in Ia q22 a2 in response to an objection against the subjection of human beings to divine providence. Now this text functions as an authority in the *sed contra*: humans must have free will, as rational creatures, and if they did not, external instruction, punishment, and reward would be useless. Humans can choose opposite courses in contingent matters using the judgment of reason. Again, because it is also known from revelation that God directs the minds and hearts of human beings,[10] Thomas must explain to his objectors that the free will, though the cause of its own movement, is nevertheless not its own first cause; God is the very cause of voluntary action, moving voluntary causes to act freely, because "he operates in each thing according to its nature."[11]

The free will itself is by definition undetermined, a power indifferent to good or evil choice. But free will, as Thomas understands it, proceeds from the activity of the intellect and will, which are naturally inclined toward truth and goodness, and so the end of happiness, for the sake of which the free will chooses the means of attainment.[12] The perfection of freedom is to choose the means in conformity with the highest end. Sin's effect is to limit freedom by turning the intellect and will away from that end to lesser ones. Free will thus requires God's help to choose those things that lead to true happiness, a help given it by grace, which restores to it not natural liberty or freedom from coercion (which was not lost by sin) but "freedom from fault and unhappiness,"[13]

---

9. *ST* Ia q82 a2.   10. Prv 21:1; Rom 9:16; Phil 2:13.

11. *ST* Ia q82 a1 ad3.   12. *ST* Ia q83 a4; Ia-IIae q13 a3.

13. *ST* Ia q83 a2 s.c., c., ad3. On Thomas's conception of human freedom as "freedom for excellence," see Servais Pinckaers, *The Sources of Christian Ethics*, trans. Sr. Thomas Mary Noble (Washington, DC: Catholic University of America Press, 1995), esp. 354–99. See also the close parallels to Thomas's teaching here in *De malo* q6, written around the same time as Thomas began the Ia-IIae.

the freedom enjoyed by Adam before sin in the first graced state of righteousness.[14]

Thomas places the activity of the human free will into the scheme of the divine ordination again in Ia qq103–5, on the divine government, where he focuses on the idea of God bringing creatures to their perfection according to the natures he has willed for them. God's government is the actual carrying-out of the divine ordination willed in the design of providence, by which God in his goodness leads all things to the perfection of their end.[15] Question 103 a5 is a parallel article to Ia q22 a2, which asked whether everything is subject to God's providence (and especially human free will); here it is asked whether all things are subject to the divine government. Again, Thomas answers that because God is the cause of the being of things, both universally and in particular, he is also the cause of bringing each of them to their perfection.

Thomas stresses throughout q103 that the end of the divine government is the divine goodness; God in bringing things to perfection especially shows his goodness by governing even the very least creature, according to the nature with which he has endowed it. The divine goodness is even more manifest in that God causes some things to govern others, causing goodness in them.[16] As secondary causes, humans first of all have the capacity to govern themselves. In a5 ad3 Thomas explains that the divine intellect and will must nevertheless govern and perfect the rational creature's intellect and will; God works in rational creatures interiorly and gives them exterior help such as commandments, rewards, and punishments to induce them toward the good.[17]

In q105 a3 and a4 (on change in creatures) Thomas has sufficiently prepared the ground to address directly the question of whether God immediately moves the created intellect and will, following up in a5 with a discussion of the causal scheme required for God to operate in things that are themselves operators. God as first cause of being and intelligibility both

---

14. Cf. *ST* Ia q95.   15. *ST* Ia q103 a1.

16. *ST* Ia q103 a6; cf. q22 a3.

17. *ST* Ia q103 a5 ad2. Thomas seems to anticipate his division of the texts on law and grace, in which God is described as the extrinsic principle of human acts moving to good, both by the instruction of the precepts of the Law, and the interior assistance of the New Law of grace; see Ia-IIae q90, prol.; q109, prol.

gives the power of understanding (natural or supernatural) to the intellect and impresses on it the intelligible species of things by which it understands. The intellect is a secondary cause, with respect to God, of its own intellectual operation (a3). Similarly, the will is moved by God, who both gives it the power of willing and is the only fully sufficient object, as the universal good, of the will's potentiality. In giving the power of willing, God inclines the created will interiorly toward the universal good (a4). In each of his answers to the objections in a4 Thomas addresses the seeming difficulty that God's inclination of the will raises with respect to its freedom, in a way that should by now not surprise the reader. God does not force the will by giving it a natural inclination by which it moves voluntarily.[18] But Thomas specifically adds an emphasis on the interiority of this inclination, which makes it voluntary, although it derives from God as an exterior cause:

To be moved voluntarily is to be moved from oneself, that is, by an intrinsic principle, yet this intrinsic principle can be from another extrinsic principle; and thus to be moved from oneself is not repugnant to being moved by another.[19]

Because the will moves itself, although it is moved to do so by another, it is responsible for its actions and subject to praise or blame.

In q105 a5 Thomas looks more closely at the way in which God "works in every worker," alluding again to God's sapiential ordering of the universe: created things would be purposeless (*inane*) if they lacked the operation proper to them, so "God works in things in such a manner that they have their proper operation." God, as the universal good and first cause of existence in particular natures and of the activity proper to those natures, works in all things "intimately." God is the end of every action, he gives creatures form, preserves them in existence, and "applies them to act."[20]

Human Action, Freedom, and the End of Beatitude

This understanding of the instrumental role of the image's free activity in the plan of divine providence is in place when Thomas says in the prologue

18. *ST* Ia q105 a4 ad1

19. *ST* Ia q105 a4 ad2; i.e., in terms of the objection, for God to move the will and for the will to be voluntarily moved from within are not impossibly contradictory.

20. Cf. *De pot.* q3 a7.

to the IIa *pars* that he intends to treat "man, inasmuch as he too is the principle of his own actions, as having free-will and power over his actions." The
first questions of the IIa *pars* return us to the last end of human life, which
"is stated to be happiness (*beatitudo*),"[21] now looking closely at the end-
orientedness of all human action, especially in relation to the highest end attainable, the "final and perfect happiness" of the beatific vision.[22] Question
1 a1 establishes the foundation of human action, *qua* human, in the fact that
humans are masters of their actions through reason and will, from which
the free will proceeds. Properly human actions, proceeding from a deliber-
ate will, are directed toward "the end and the good," which is the object of
the will. All humans desire the last end of complete happiness, which fulfills
their own perfection, though not all recognize the end that will completely satisfy their desire—to know and love God, who is the universal good.[23]
The journey to beatitude has as its goal the vision, comprehension (in the
sense of possession), and enjoyment of the divine essence itself, in which "final and perfect" human happiness consists, and which is not possible in this
life, as Thomas showed in Ia q12.[24] By the possession of intellect and will,
humans are created with the potential capacity for this goal, though they
are unable to attain it on their own because the vision of God infinitely surpasses the nature of every creature.[25]

By comparison with Ia q12, Thomas considers the last end in these questions with respect not to the knowledge of the vision that belongs to the intellect, but to the resulting beatitude belonging to the will's attainment of the
highest good. The focus is on human action now, and the part that it plays
in this attainment. Only God can bring humans to the happiness of the last
end; yet "in the order of divine wisdom" he wills that humans be involved
in obtaining beatitude "by many movements of works which are called merits," so that they may achieve the rectitude of will (or right-ordering of will to
the last end) that is necessary for them to receive it.[26] Thomas is more specific than before about how God exercises the divine causality to carry out this
plan of wisdom in the economy of salvation. Just as God created the first creatures perfectly disposed to propagate their nature to their progeny, so through

---

21. *ST* Ia-IIae q1 a1, prol.
23. *ST* Ia-IIae q1 a7, q2 a8; cf. q5 a8.
25. *ST* Ia-IIae q5 a1, a6.

22. *ST* Ia-IIae q3 a8.
24. *ST* Ia-IIae q3 a8, q4 a3, q5 a3.
26. *ST* Ia-IIae q5 a7.

Christ, who from conception shared in beatitude, is beatitude bestowed on the children of God.[27] Grace, given in baptism, is the principle of this human movement that tends toward beatitude.[28] In the divine *ordinatio*, God brings human persons, baptized in Christ as God's children, to beatitude by their own graced movement.

If grace is the principle of the human acts that lead to beatitude, Thomas must show that it gives rise to the freedom essential to the definition of fully human action. In the background is his general consideration of human acts. Thomas begins in Ia-IIae q6 with the criterion of voluntariness and subsequently returns repeatedly and with increased precision to the notion of an intrinsic principle, which he has already flagged as the chief mark of voluntary action. To be perfectly moved by an intrinsic principle is to be moved by an interior inclination on account of one's own knowledge of the end, something possible only to intelligent beings. Humans especially know the ends for which they act, and move themselves to action, and so human action especially is voluntary. But Thomas immediately returns to repeat what he has already said in Ia q105 on the divine movement of the will: it is not contrary to voluntariness that an intrinsic principle be moved by an extrinsic one; God moves the will itself from without as the first mover, but the movements of the will come from within the human person as a moved mover.[29]

Again, in Ia-IIae qq9–10, Thomas returns to the movement of the will by God as an extrinsic principle moving an intrinsic one. In each question Thomas works from the general consideration of what things move the will (q9), or how (q10), to a final article on God's movement of the will from within. In q9 a6 Thomas brings into play the whole causal picture, grounded in creation, that he has already constructed: the reason why it is only by God that the will can be moved from outside, and yet still act in a voluntary way, is because God is the Creator, who, in bestowing the form of the rational soul, is the cause of the will and its natural movements. God is the cause of the will's movement both because it is a power caused by God (God is the

27. *ST* Ia-IIae q5 a7 c., ad2: "Beatitude was to be bestowed on others through Christ, who is God and man, *who*, according to Heb 2:10, 'had brought many children into glory.'" Thomas teaches in the IIIa *pars* that this grace flows from Christ as Head to his members (*ST* III q8).

28. *ST* Ia-IIae q5 a7 ad2–3.

29. *ST* Ia-IIae q6 a1 c., ad1, ad3; cf. q9 a4.

exemplar cause of its form and powers) and also because God is the universal good, toward which the will is inclined (God is its final cause).

God not only gives the will its power and object but also moves it efficiently to "the exercise of its act" (q9 a4). A text from Aristotle's *Eudemian Ethics*, which Thomas seems to have discovered in the form of the *Liber de bona fortuna* during the time of writing the *Summa contra Gentiles*, is significant in the discussions of God's movement of the will in his later works. This text argues that there must be an external first mover of the will from potency to act in order to avoid an infinite regress:

> We must of necessity suppose that the will advances to its first movement in virtue of the instigation of some exterior mover, as Aristotle concludes in a chapter of the *Eudemian Ethics* (7.14).[30]

Thomas understood this initiating movement of the will by God as a special instance of the principle that God is responsible not only for creation and conservation in being but also for the application of each creature to its proper act.[31]

---

30. *ST* Ia-IIae q9 a4. Cf. *SCG* III.89; *De malo* 6; *Quod. 1* a7; *Super II Cor.* ch3 lect1. On Thomas's discovery and use of this text, see Henri Bouillard, *Conversion et grâce chez S. Thomas d'Aquin* (Paris: Aubier, 1944), 123–34; Bernard Lonergan, *Grace and Freedom: Operative Grace in the Thought of St. Thomas Aquinas*, ed. Frederick E. Crowe and Robert Doran (Toronto: University of Toronto Press, 2000, reprint, 2005), 99ff; Alister McGrath, "The Influence of Aristotelian Physics upon St. Thomas Aquinas' Discussion of the 'Processus Iustificationis,'" *Recherches de théologie ancienne et médiévale* 51 (1984): 223–29; Cornelio Fabro, "Le *Liber de bona fortuna* de *L'Ethique à Eudème* d'Aristote et la dialectique de la Providence divine chez saint Thomas," *Revue Thomiste* 88 (1988): 556–72. Thomas's engagement with the writings of the Arabian philosophers and his rejection of both Ash'arite occasionalism and Averroist determinism influenced his account in later works of God as the transcendent cause of causes, even contingent ones; on Thomas's solution of this Arabian "causal dilemma" with his mature doctrine of divine providence, see Majid Fakhry, *Islamic Occasionalism and Its Critique by Averroës and Aquinas* (London: George Allen & Unwin, 1958); *SCG* III.69, 97.

31. Cf. *ST* Ia q105 a4. The question of determinism inevitably arises, and Thomas clearly rejects it. In q10 a4, on whether God moves the will of necessity (*ex necessitate*), Thomas again places the quote from Sirach on human free will in the *sed contra* and reiterates the principle that divine providence works in everything according to its nature: "[Providence] moves all things in accordance with their conditions; so that from necessary causes through the divine motion, effects follow of necessity; but from contingent causes, effects follow contingently. Since, therefore, the will is an active principle, not determinate to one thing, but having an indifferent relation to many things, God so moves it, that he does not determine it of necessity to one thing, but its movement remains contingent and not necessary, except in those things

On the part of the creature, the movement of the will as an intrinsic principle is shaped by its own dispositions. As stated above, the powers of the human soul are in themselves undetermined, able to operate in diverse ways, and therefore can act either well or badly in bringing the subject to its proper end. Therefore the powers must be disposed to their natural operations by means of *habitus*.[32] *Habitus* are settled dispositions, principles of human action that are intrinsic and therefore result in free activity. Thomas draws from the *Metaphysics* for his initial definition of *habitus* as "a disposition whereby that which is disposed is disposed well or ill, either in regard to itself or in regard to another."[33] Thomas understands Aristotle to mean "in regard to its nature, or in regard to its end," so that *habitus* implies a disposition in relation to a thing's nature, and consequently to its operation (and the end of its operation), which is the end of its nature.[34]

Good *habitus* are perfections chiefly found in the operations of the soul, where they are necessary so that the powers of the soul—which are in a state of potentiality, indifferent to evil or good—may be determined toward the good.[35] *Habitus* allow the good to be performed virtuously—joyfully, promptly, and easily. The necessity of *habitus* thus derives from a state of potentiality with respect to that toward which the creature is disposed.[36] Human virtues are good *habitus*, shaping the powers of the soul that flow from the image as principle of free activity, for good operation and the production of good works, inclining the powers toward a good end.[37] The good *habitus* of the natural virtues develop from the exercise of good acts, through which the subject comes to participate more perfectly in the form of the *habitus*.[38]

---

to which it is moved naturally." Having established in earlier parts of the *Summa* that by virtue of God's transcendence to the created order God is also the immanent cause of causes, Thomas can expect the reader to understand that God causes the will, as a free cause, to act freely by reducing it from potency to act (cf. q9 a4).

32. *ST* Ia-IIae q49 a4 ad1.

33. *ST* Ia-IIae q49 a1. Cf. Aristotle, *Metaphysics* 5.20.

34. *ST* Ia-IIae q49 a2.

35. *ST* Ia-IIae q49 a4 s.c., ad3; q50 a2.

36. And so God has no *habitus*; *ST* Ia-IIae q49 a4. The angels, because they are in potentiality to God and can attain God through their intellect and will only by participating the divine wisdom and goodness, require the deiform *habitus* that Dionysius attributes to them (*ST* Ia-IIae q50 a6); cf. Dionysius, *CH* 7. It is still necessary, however, for God to reduce the higher potentiality bestowed by the *habitus* to act.

37. *ST* Ia-IIae q55 a3.

38. *ST* Ia-IIae q51 a2, q52 a2, q55 a3.

The "New Creation" of Grace and Human Freedom

There are at least two things that Thomas stresses as he defends the freedom of the will moved by God in the natural order: first, that God as extrinsic principle can move the will of the created rational being as intrinsic principle to act in a voluntary manner because God himself is the exemplary cause of the creature's form and powers and, second, that God's efficient movement of the will to its act does not curtail but permits its own proper free activity. When Thomas examines grace as a "new creation," giving rise to free activity that leads to the higher end of beatitude, he must likewise establish two things. First, just as God extrinsically moves the intrinsic natural principle of the will, shaped by its own *habitus*, in its free action toward natural goods, so God moves the will through grace as an extrinsic principle moving an intrinsic one toward supernatural good. Grace must operate as an intrinsic formal principle—which is some more perfect participation of the divine exemplar than that of nature—in the will, to give rise to voluntary action. Second, he must explain how God moves the will freely by grace to "the exercise of its act" in the journey to beatitude.

Thomas will do both in his treatment of grace, where he argues that God does not "provide less for those he loves, that they may acquire supernatural good, than for creatures, whom he loves that they may acquire natural good."[39] God provides for those whom he wills to move toward the supernatural good in two ways: (1) by giving them a new form and powers (in the gift of habitual grace—a new intrinsic principle or *habitus*—which reorients the human person toward the good on the level of their being, strengthening their will to act toward the supernatural good end), and (2) by actually moving them by a divine help (*auxilium*, or auxiliary grace) to freely will and act so as to attain the end.[40] That the graced will acts freely is essential, so that its good works may be meritorious, although the value of the merit ultimately derives from the work of the Holy Spirit within.[41] In the gifts of habitual and auxiliary grace, God both gives the creature a new inclination and sets that inclination into motion.

39. *ST* Ia-IIae q110 a2.
41. *ST* Ia-IIae q114 a3.

40. *ST* Ia-IIae q109 a1, q110 a2, q111 a2.

Grace and the New Law

As he prepares for his primary treatment of grace at the end of the Ia-IIae, Thomas seems to highlight the notion of habitual grace first, in his three questions on the New Law, which is "chiefly the grace itself of the Holy Spirit, which is given to those who believe in Christ."[42] Questions 106–8 on the New Law form the end of the treatment of law, which comprises a unit with the treatment of grace; in both law and grace, God is the extrinsic principle moving humans to good acts, for he "both instructs us by means of his law, and assists us by his grace."[43] Like all law, grace—as the New Law—governs human reason to act toward the good end, which is happiness.[44] All law ultimately derives from the eternal law, which is "the very idea of the government of things in God the ruler of the universe," that is, divine providence.[45] Thomas emphasizes the idea of the divine *ordinatio* as he explains that all plans of government in secondary movers (insofar as they participate in right reason) are ordained to fulfilling the plan of divine wisdom of the "chief governor," God.[46] The natural law regulating the human reason is itself a participation of the eternal law, by which the rational creature "participates in a share of providence, by being provident both for itself and for others."[47]

Thomas indicates that this teaching is grounded in the doctrine of the image that he laid out earlier in the Ia *pars*; it is so because the light of natural reason "is nothing else than an imprint on us of the divine light."[48] Referring to Psalms 4:7—"The light of thy countenance, O Lord, is signed upon us"—Thomas notes that the psalmist responds to one who asks what the works of justice are. So, he says, by the light of natural reason, as a participation of the divine light, we discern good from evil. If the eternal law is the idea of the way that God governs the world through divine providence, the natural law is the way that God governs rational creatures, by leading them to govern themselves through their own participation in the eternal reason. In his late commentary on Psalm 4, Thomas gives a similar interpretation of this verse and adds that, over and above the light of natural reason that is

---

42. *ST* Ia-IIae q106 a1.

43. *ST* Ia-IIae q90, prol.

44. *ST* Ia-IIae q90 aa1–2.

45. *ST* Ia-IIae q91 a1.

46. *ST* Ia-IIae q93 a3; cf. a1.

47. *ST* Ia-IIae q91 a2.

48. Ibid.

"signed upon us" as the likeness of the light of divine truth, we are further signed with the sign of the Spirit.[49] The Gloss on Psalms 4:7 was Thomas's primary authority in Ia q93 a4 for the threefold image of nature, grace, and glory.

Thomas thinks that grace is, as the New Law, a rule and measure governing human acts toward the highest happiness of eternal beatitude. It is the way that God governs the graced image through a special participation in his providence, which causes it to be self-governing on its journey toward the highest end. This rule, which is revealed in a law written down in human words, as was the Old Law, is first of all written on the heart.[50] It is precisely as an interior law that Thomas understands the grace of the Holy Spirit to be an infused *habitus*, which governs the creature from within as a principle in its movement toward beatitude. In the context of the *Summa* the teaching on grace as an internal law or *habitus* grounds its place in the divine *ordinatio* for the free activity of the elect moving toward their supernatural end. This can be seen in Thomas's primary identification of the New Law of grace as the "law of perfect liberty" (Jas 1:25). Grace makes one act freely because it "inclines one in the mode of a nature [i.e., as a second nature];" it does so because "the grace of the Holy Spirit is like an interior *habitus* infused in us, inclining us to work rightly, [which] makes us do freely those things fitting to grace and avoid what is repugnant to it."[51] The New Law is the law of love; the interior inclination it bestows is the work of charity inwardly shaping the will. In this it differs from the Old Law because grace confers "the Holy Spirit, by whom 'charity ... is poured forth in our hearts' (Rom 5:5)."[52]

The questions on the New Law form one of the three "zones of pneumatological concentration" in the *Summa* noted by Patfoort, the other two being the questions on the gifts, beatitudes, and fruits of the Spirit, and of course the treatment of grace.[53] Thomas repeatedly emphasizes the role of the Holy Spirit in q106 on "the New Law in itself," with reference in three

49. And so, he says, "we should daily make the sign of the Cross, which sign was impressed on us in baptism. Songs 8: 'Place me as a sign upon your heart.'" *Super psalmos* 4.5.

50. *ST* Ia-IIae q106 a2.   51. *ST* Ia-IIae q108 a1 ad2.

52. *ST* Ia-IIae q107 a1 ad2.

53. Albert Patfoort, "Morale et pneumatologie: Une observation de la IaIIae," in *Thomas d'Aquin: Les clefs d'une théologie* (Paris: FAC Editions, 1983), 71–102; esp. 85–88.

out of its four articles to Romans 8:2: "the law of the spirit of life in Christ Jesus has set me free from the law of sin and death." This text, and Augustine's commentary on Paul in *De spiritu et littera*, informs much of Thomas's thought in this question. In a1, after quoting Romans 8:2 with Romans 3:27, on the "law of faith," he links two texts from Augustine, in which Augustine speaks of the "law of faith inscribed on the hearts of the faithful" (*De spir. et litt.* 24) and of the "divine laws written by God himself on our hearts," which are "the very presence of his Holy Spirit" (*De spir. et litt.* 21). Here he adverts to the gift both of the Spirit and of a created effect received in the gift of grace. In Thomas's own commentary on Romans 8:2, he also gives two ways of thinking about the "law of the spirit": it may be "the law which is the Spirit," for "the Holy Spirit dwelling in the mind not only teaches what is to be done by instructing the intellect but also inclines the affections to act aright." In another way, he says, the law of the spirit "can be the proper effect of the Holy Spirit, namely faith working through love." And so "this law of the spirit is the New Law, which is the Holy Spirit himself, or something which the Holy Spirit produces in our hearts."[54] In other words, in thinking of the role of the Holy Spirit in the New Law of grace, Thomas has in mind both the motivating presence of the Spirit itself and the created effect it produces in us.

The liberty of the New Law depends, insofar as a formal cause is concerned, on grace being an intrinsic *habitus*, but the true freedom to which this new inner disposition tends is the freedom of the Spirit;[55] this liberty derives from the presence and activity of the Holy Spirit, leading believers by the gift of grace to greater perfection by the operation of the theological virtues flowing from grace—faith working through love. Grace as a *habitus* disposes the image in such a way that it is adapted for movement by the Holy Spirit, a helping motion that Thomas later identifies as auxiliary grace. Thomas alludes to this divine motion in q108 a1 after he describes grace as an "interior *habitus*," when he says that the New Law can be called the law

---

54. *Sup. Rom.* ch8, lect1.

55. See Thomas's commentary on 2 Cor 3:17: "Where the Spirit of the Lord is, there is freedom": "This is by the Holy Spirit, who perfects the mind interiorly by a good *habitus,* so that one avoids [evil] out of love, as if commanded by divine law; and thus he is called free, not as though he is not subject to divine law, but because out of a good *habitus* he is inclined to do what the divine law ordains." *Sup. II Cor., reportatio* ch3 lect3.

of liberty inasmuch as we "comply freely" with its precepts "through the interior promptings of grace" (*ex interiori instinctu gratiae*).[56]

As Torrell has pointed out, Thomas "almost constantly" speaks of grace as "the grace of the Holy Spirit,"[57] whose *instinctus* moves the creature interiorly toward God.[58] In the Ia *pars* Thomas especially associates the movement of rational creatures toward God with the *instinctus* of the Holy Spirit, as Love proceeding. Its personal names—Spirit, Love, and Gift—signify the impulse of motion, the movement of will of a lover toward the object, and the "first gift" of the Father's love "through which all free gifts are given." Thomas especially emphasizes the role of the Holy Spirit in discussing the invisible missions, in which both the Spirit and the gift of habitual grace—a temporal created effect or disposition—are bestowed on the creature.[59] In q93, on the image, Thomas indicates that this habitual gift does not exhaust the "gifts of grace." The creature images the Word and Love more perfectly in actually, and not only habitually, having God as the object of its knowledge and love. It is chiefly in the acts of the soul that the Trinitarian image is to be found—potentially in the *habitus* of grace but most completely in the movement of the newly disposed soul to its act. Thomas clarifies in the questions on grace that the initiation of all such movement toward God—even that which precedes the gift of habitual grace—although operated by the one Trinity, is appropriated to the Holy Spirit working in the divine *auxilium*. The freedom that comes from the New Law, "which is the Holy Spirit," thus depends on both habitual and auxiliary grace.[60]

---

56. *ST* Ia-IIae q108 a1 ad2: "Sic igitur lex nova dicitur lex libertatis dupliciter. Uno modo, quia non arctat nos ad facienda vel vitanda aliqua, nisi quae de se sunt vel necessaria vel repugnantia saluti, quae cadunt sub praecepto vel prohibitione legis. Secundo, quia huiusmodi etiam praecepta vel prohibitiones facit nos libere implere, inquantum ex interiori instinctu gratiae ea implemus. Et propter haec duo lex nova dicitur lex perfectae libertatis, Iac. I."

57. Jean-Pierre Torrell, *Saint Thomas Aquinas*, vol. 2, *Spiritual Master*, trans. Robert Royal (Washington, DC: Catholic University of America Press, 2003), 177.

58. Ibid., 206ff.

59. *ST* Ia q43 a3 c., ad2.

60. The role of Christ—as the author rather than the gift itself of the New Law of grace—is a rich subject to which Thomas also gives considerable attention in the questions on the New Law; cf. chapter 4, on the Incarnate Word as the principle of grace for others. As Thomas prepares for his treatment of grace, he keeps in view the provident plan of salvation in the New Law, carried out through the invisible and visible missions of the divine Persons.

Grace and Human Action on the Journey to Beatitude

Thomas opens his treatment of grace—through which God, as "the exterior principle of human acts," helps us to do right[61]—with a consideration in q109 of the necessity of grace, both habitual and auxiliary, for the natural and supernatural operation of the image's distinctive faculties, the intellect and will. As Joseph Wawrykow has noted, Thomas employs the model of life as a journey to beatitude in the questions on grace.[62] Keeping in mind Thomas's association of grace with the Holy Spirit, the Spirit's continual involvement in this journey is clear. In q109 this model helps to structure the overall organization—especially in the final six articles, which consider the role of grace in carrying out the journey to God—from the initial possibility of meriting the end to the preparation of the will for grace, conversion, the ongoing avoidance of sin, and final perseverance. The first four articles examine the capacity of the intellect and will—by which we move toward God as end—to know the truth and do the good, both natural and supernatural, without grace.

Thomas thinks that the human intellect and will are capable of the knowledge of natural truths, and the doing of some natural good, without the supernatural help of grace. Yet he is quick to establish in a1 that all movements of creatures, even on the natural level, require God's help, first in bestowing the form that is the principle of the movement, and then by moving it to its act. God is both the First Mover and the one who bestows all formal perfections, and as such is always at work in the thinking and willing of rational creatures; all of this follows from what has already been established in earlier parts of the *Summa*. It soon becomes evident in q109 a2, however, that Thomas takes seriously the damage done by sin even to our natural capacities, and especially the will. In the state of corrupt nature after the Fall, humans cannot even reach their natural good ends perfectly. They must be helped by grace both to fulfill all that is possible to their own natural powers and to will and act for supernatural good; so grace is both healing (*sanans*) and elevating (*elevans*).

The elevation of the soul to a new supernatural end involves both the infusion of a new form and the movement to actualization of the new po-

---

61. *ST* Ia-IIae q109, prol.

62. Joseph Wawrykow, "Grace," in *The Westminster Handbook to Thomas Aquinas* (Louisville, KY: Westminster John Knox Press, 2005), 63–68.

tency this form bestows. The free will is truly free, as Thomas explained in his earlier treatment of human nature, when it can choose the good unhindered by the effects of sin.[63] In q109 a2 ad1 Thomas refers again to Aristotle's text from the *Eudemian Ethics* to argue that the human free will, especially when weakened by sin, needs God to move it even to the good that pertains to its nature.[64] Likewise, in addition to the "gratuitous strength superadded to natural strength" required for the doing of supernatural good, the divine *auxilium* is also needed so that the creature may be moved to do that good. Auxiliary grace is a special example of God's free movement of the will to the exercise of its act. To those reasoning creatures whom God wills to reach the end of beatitude he gives, in spite of the damage originally done to the intellect and will by sin, the natural inclination to freely choose the particular goods that will bring them to their supernatural end (i.e., he bestows on them a new *habitus*), and he causes them to actually choose those goods freely (with the help of auxiliary grace).[65]

This picture of the manifold workings of grace that Thomas presents in the *Summa* emphasizes the primacy of divine action in turning the predestined human person from sin and moving them to God. As several scholars have pointed out, however, Thomas developed this depth of understanding only over time. These authors see a shift toward an increasing dynamism and involvement of grace in free human activity from the *Scriptum* to the *Summa theologiae*, in which Thomas moves from an exclusive focus on habitual grace as a form in the soul to a model in which the emphasis is instead on God's prevenience as mover of the free will by auxiliary grace. A brief examination of this development will help to indicate the significance and implications of Thomas's treatment in the *Summa*.

Henri Bouillard examines the development of Thomas's views on the respective roles of human preparation and divine action in the reception of sanctifying grace and justification.[66] In the *Scriptum* grace is understood only

---

63. *ST* Ia q83 a2.

64. A reference to this text also appears in *ST* Ia-IIae q68 a1, on the gifts of the Holy Spirit, to support Thomas's point that there is a twofold principle of movement in the human person, "one within him, viz. the reason; the other extrinsic to him, viz. God."

65. This seems to avoid the charge of determinism in that God still does not determine the will "of necessity to one thing, but its movement remains contingent and not necessary, except in those things to which it is moved naturally." *ST* Ia-IIae q10 a4.

66. Bouillard, *Conversion et grâce*.

as a habitual form, in a model based on the composition of matter and form. In this early model Thomas held a view of justification that he later abandoned—that human acts can remotely prepare and dispose the person for the reception of grace. Here grace acts as a perfecting formal cause upon the "prepared matter" of the human action. In a sense, grace "remains exterior to conversion itself," a conversion that really begins through the material causality of human acts.[67] This view expressed the common twelfth-century scholastic opinion that "to those who do what is in them God will not deny the grace."[68] But Bouillard observes that at some time before Thomas wrote the *Summa contra Gentiles*, he "discovered" the Pelagian error, which later came to be called semi-Pelagianism, and realized that he must take steps to avoid it.[69] Thomas became aware of this error and recognized its similarity to his early position, Bouillard believes, through his reading of Augustine's later works, *De praedestinatione sanctorum* and *De dono perseverantiae*.[70] In the *Summa contra Gentiles*, Thomas argues against this kind of "Pelagianism," emphasizing that matter cannot move itself to its own perfection but must be moved by something else. The soul cannot prepare itself for grace except by God causing it to do so.[71] It is only from the time of the *Summa contra Gentiles*, as Bouillard points out, that Thomas employs the principle from the *Eudemian Ethics*, that there must be a superior first mover of the will from potency to act, to avoid an infinite regress. Thomas begins to argue at this time that God must provide an immediate and interior movement of the will to its acts in conversion.[72] In the *Summa theologiae* Thomas continues to emphasize a dynamic view of grace as God's prevenient action in us.[73] Bouillard thus sees a shift from the *Scriptum* to the *Summa* in three ways: (1) Thomas highlights the divine initiative and necessity of divine help in hu-

---

67. Ibid., 86.

68. "Facienti quod in se est, Deus non deneget gratiam." I.e., God has infallibly promised to grant grace to those who take the first step by doing the best they can. On the history of this phrase, see Wawrykow, *Westminster Handbook to Thomas Aquinas*, 54–56.

69. Semi-Pelagianism holds that the beginning of faith can be made by human effort, without the help of grace, while God's increase and preservation of that faith complete the work of salvation; grace is still required for salvation, but we can take the first steps.

70. Bouillard, *Conversion et grâce*, 113–14.

71. *SCG* III.149; see III.147, 152.

72. Ibid., 123ff.

73. Thomas underlines this prevenience by teaching that the gift of grace is an effect of God's eternal plan of predestination, not the result of human acts; ibid., 137–40.

man preparation for grace, (2) he comes to think that this help must be an interior and immediate divine movement of the will, and (3) he subordinates the notion of grace as a static form or *habitus* to the idea of divine action.[74]

Bernard Lonergan demonstrates that over time Thomas developed an understanding of the necessity of the actual grace of divine *auxilium* with both operating and cooperating dimensions.[75] Like Bouillard, Lonergan shows that in the *Scriptum* Thomas thinks of grace only as habitual, while in the *Summa* Thomas has a clearer grasp of the necessity of the divine pre-motion in every movement of the will, and so develops the notion of actual auxiliary grace in addition to habitual grace. Furthermore, Thomas's understanding of the operative and cooperative aspects of both habitual and auxiliary grace has been clarified. By the time of the *Summa theologiae*, Thomas teaches that, because of the necessity for the divine initiative, the divine *auxilium* is always required, both before (operatively) and after (cooperatively) the will itself begins to act (see the discussion of q111 a2 below for more on operative and cooperative grace). Operative auxiliary grace, by which the will is moved simply, is always necessary in willing good ends, especially in the case of conversion.[76]

Joseph Wawrykow takes up the work of these authors in his study of the development of Thomas's teaching on grace and merit.[77] Wawrykow demonstrates Thomas's increasing understanding of the primacy of divine action in salvation, in the context of his teaching on the predestination of the elect in the divine *ordinatio*. In the *Summa*—as a result, in part, of his reading of Augustine's *De praedestinatione sanctorum* and *De dono perseverentiae*—Thomas firmly places the notion of merit in the framework of grace's movement of the predestined to beatitude.[78] Thomas recognizes the necessity of auxiliary grace

---

74. Ibid., 91. Thomas nevertheless always retains the notion of grace as a *habitus*, on the principle that an intrinsic *habitus* is necessary for meritorious acts (159–60). In Bouillard's view, God's initial movement of the will to cooperation is instantaneous with this infusion of habitual grace, as a specific case of God's general concursus, rather than a special supernatural actual grace (196), although several authors have criticized this last point, among them Bernard Lonergan and Joseph Wawrykow; cf. Joseph Wawrykow, *God's Grace and Human Action: "Merit" in the Theology of Thomas Aquinas* (Notre Dame, IN: University of Notre Dame Press, 1995), 40–41.

75. Lonergan, *Grace and Freedom*.

76. Ibid., 432–34.

77. Wawrykow provides a thorough analytical summary of Bouillard and Lonergan's work. *God's Grace and Human Action*, 34–55.

78. Ibid., 266–73.

in addition to habitual grace, especially in the context of the temptation to sin; only with God's help can "the human person in fact do the good. Thus, in the *Summa*, *auxilium* refers not only to God causing human action but indeed to God causing *correct* human action."[79] Cooperative *auxilium*, because it involves the action of the free will, allows for human merit. The gift of final perseverance, however, like the gift of conversion, is an example of operating auxiliary grace, which is thus excluded from merit; so Thomas underlines his teaching that the journey of salvation from beginning to end is entirely the gift of God.[80]

The mature picture that Thomas presents in the *Summa* includes both the gift of habitual grace, which is "the principle of meritorious works" (as a disposition of the free will), and the action of auxiliary grace, which actually moves and assists the will to do those works; in this picture he strongly underscores the primacy of divine action without excluding the role of human cooperation. In q109 aa5–10 Thomas sketches the way in which this twofold gift of God's grace causes the recipient to progress on the journey to beatitude. Habitual grace, though it may be increased, need be given only once, unless it is lost and restored, because it is an enduring form in the soul, giving it a new potential for new and higher activities and making it pleasing to God. But auxiliary grace is needed at every step of the journey, as the first efficient cause of every movement taken toward the end. One cannot merit everlasting life without grace (a5). Even before habitual grace is bestowed, the will must be prepared for its reception by the divine *auxilium* moving the soul inwardly toward the good (a6). Only God, the First Mover, can turn the free will to himself as a special end so that it can receive the light of grace and rise from sin (a7). Likewise, God's continual help is necessary to uphold the soul in good, especially because of the damage done by original sin to the carnal appetite, which is not healed by grace but continually drags the restored reason downward (a8, a9). Finally, the divine *auxilium* is necessary for one to persevere in the good to the end of life against the attacks of the passions (a10).

79. Ibid., 172. Italics in original.

80. Ibid., 228. Thomas emphasizes in the *Summa* the "sapiential dimensions of merit," showing how God's will to allow the predestined to merit on the way to beatitude is part of the divine plan of wisdom. Such a picture of merit in the divine *ordinatio* manifests the divine goodness (ix, 149–64, 180ff). See also *ST* Ia-IIae q109 a9, q114 a9.

Thomas is at pains to establish throughout the *Summa* that God's transcendent causality does not compete with the proper operation of created causes on the natural level. Likewise, on the supernatural level, God's bestowal of a new habitual form and movement of the will to its act does not interfere with human freedom but causes it, allowing the free will to become a subordinate cause of its own movement toward God. In q110 a2 Thomas looks more closely at what it means that grace is an infused *habitus* or quality of the soul, but he also makes an important point about the way in which habitual and auxiliary grace work together to move the creature through its own movements to the supernatural end in the wise plan of providence. He begins by reminding the reader that God's gracious will helps the human soul both by moving it to its acts (i.e., by the divine *auxilium*) and by the infusion of a habitual gift. As in q109, he frames these effects of grace in those chosen to reach supernatural good as a fitting provision, *a fortiori*, of the love of God, who provides even for his natural creatures all that they need to acquire natural good:

Now he so provides for natural creatures, that not only does he move them to their natural acts, but he bestows upon them certain forms and powers, which are the principles of acts, in order that they may of themselves be inclined to these movements, and thus the movements by which they are moved by God become connatural and easy to creatures, according to Wisdom 8:1: "she ... orders all things sweetly." Much more therefore does he infuse into those whom he moves towards the acquisition of eternal supernatural good, certain forms or supernatural qualities, whereby they may be moved by him sweetly and promptly to acquire eternal good; and thus the gift of grace is a certain quality.

God's loving wisdom provides both habitual and auxiliary grace, so that "the movements by which they are moved by God" may become as natural and easy as those of nature. God gives grace, as an infused *habitus* so that he may sweetly (i.e., in accord with the *ordinatio* of divine Wisdom) and promptly move the creature to beatitude. The essential function of habitual grace is thus to dispose the creature to be moved toward God by the divine *auxilium*.

Thomas's mature understanding of God's transcendent "omnicausality" in the divine *ordinatio* is clear. God is the "first exemplary, efficient and final principle" of all things in creation. In the new creation of grace, God is exemplar, acting through the formal cause of habitual grace to bestow a new kind of nature with the potential for higher operations, which God, as efficient cause, also brings into act by divine *auxilium*. God moves the rational creature toward union with himself in beatitude as its final end by giving it an increasing participation in the divine likeness, specifically in the exemplary likeness of the divine Persons. Thomas's identification of habitual grace in the *Summa* as a "participation in the divine nature," discussed below, helps us to understand this causal picture as deification, giving a new depth of meaning to grace's formal function and efficient activity.

Thomas examines more closely in q111 a2 the relationship of divine and human causality in the graced journey to beatitude as he presents his mature understanding of the distinction between operating and cooperating grace. He begins once again by recalling that God works two ways in the gift of grace: in the divine *auxilium* and by means of a habitual gift. In each of these ways he identifies two effects of God's action in the soul, one in which God alone is at work (operating grace), and one in which both God and the soul are at work (cooperating grace). This follows logically from Thomas's teaching so far, that God is at once the First Cause of movement and of form, and also the transcendent source of the rational creature's own free movement and causality. In the case of operating auxiliary grace, the mind is moved by God but does not itself move; the operation is attributed to God alone. When the mind is moved by God and also moves itself (still by reason of God's moving it), then grace is said to be cooperating, with the operation attributed to both God and the soul. Operating and cooperating grace are not different instances of the divine *auxilium*, but two effects of the same grace of God, who both initiates and works with creaturely operation.

Bernard Lonergan has shown clearly not only that a doctrine of operating auxiliary grace appears for the first time in the *Summa theologiae* but also that at this time Thomas redefines operating and cooperating grace, distinguishing them with reference to the act of will.[81] In q111 a2 Thomas relates these two effects of grace to the act of the will, which is double in

---

81. Lonergan, *Grace and Freedom,* 132, 140–42, 407. Lonergan shows that in the *Scriptum* Thomas thinks of grace only as habitual, both operative and cooperative (God operatively infuses the new form of grace and then cooperatively helps the person to the external acts flowing from this form). By the time of the *Summa,* Thomas not only develops the notion of actual auxiliary grace in addition to habitual grace, but also clarifies his understanding of operative and cooperative grace, both in the case of habitual grace and in auxiliary grace. For an extended discussion, see 390–438.

the sense that it has both "interior" and "exterior" aspects. What Thomas means by these terms is not immediately clear from the *corpus* of the article. He says that operating grace is at work in the interior act of the will, "and especially when the will, which hitherto willed evil, begins to will good"; under operating auxiliary grace, especially in the case of conversion, the will is passively moved by God. Cooperating auxiliary grace is at work in the exterior act of the will, an act that the will itself, moved by God, commands.

The reply to obj3 clarifies the meaning of the interior and exterior act. The objector argues that no grace should be called cooperating because co-operation seems to belong only to a secondary agent, while God is always the principal agent in our willing. This objection would actually oppose the activity of God and the free will, excluding God from continued causal involvement in operation. Thomas explains that God is involved both in orienting the will toward the good end and in helping the will to move toward that end:

One thing is said to co-operate with another not only as a secondary agent to a principal agent, but [also] as something helping to a presupposed end. Now man, through operating grace, is helped by God that he might will the good. And so, the end being already presupposed, grace subsequently co-operates with us.

From this text it seems that the interior act of the will is the willing of the end, and in this the will is simply moved by God to will the good by operating grace (and especially in the case of conversion; as Thomas said in q109 a6 ad1, "free-will can only be turned to God when God turns it"). The exterior act of the will is its movement to attain the good end, in which the free will is active while God's cooperating grace moves it in an instrumental way. Lonergan's careful study of this question concludes that the exterior act includes the act of the free will commanding the execution of bodily acts as well as the execution itself.[82] As Lonergan also points out, Thomas's

82. Ibid., 140. Wawrykow points out a difficulty in squaring Thomas's division of human action into two parts with his analysis earlier in Ia-IIae qq8–17 of the human act, which breaks it down into three: the conceiving and willing of the end, the deliberation about and choice of means, and the execution of the act. The question is significant in relation to merit: the choice of means must be the effect of cooperating grace in order to fall under merit. Wawrykow thinks it most likely that it does, as it is the act of the free will that Thomas considers distinctive of human action. Thus Wawrykow's analysis supports Lonergan's conclusion. *God's Grace and Human Action*, 174–75.

teaching in q111 a2 implies that operating auxiliary grace is at work not only in special cases such as conversion but also in every good act that moves the creature toward its supernatural end, causing it to will the good end while cooperating grace acts with the will, causing it to move toward the end.[83]

In q111 a2 Thomas argues that habitual grace also has both operating and cooperating effects. He associates the double effect with the metaphysics of form, which also might be said to have an interior and an exterior dimension. That is, every form has, first, being and then operation (which flows from its way of being). In other words, form is the principle of activity. The operating effect of habitual grace is that it "heals and justifies the soul or makes it pleasing to God." In this way the soul is passively transformed by God, and given a new and better kind of existence. Habitual grace is cooperating "inasmuch as it is the principle of meritorious works, which proceed from the free will." While auxiliary grace has to do with God's efficient movement of the principle of the soul into action and may work, in the case of operating *auxilium*, even before the bestowal of the new form, habitual grace is what reshapes the soul itself as the principle of new supernatural activities, thus making it capable of being moved by cooperating *auxilium* toward the end.

Does Thomas's undoubted emphasis on the primacy of divine action in the *Summa's* theology of grace relative to his earlier works, evidenced by his increased attention to the role of the divine *auxilium*, indicate the "declining importance of habitual grace" or its move to the background in his view of the workings of grace, as some have proposed?[84] I argue that it does not, that Thomas came to a deeper appreciation of both the nature of habitual grace and its role in the divine *ordinatio* in coordination with auxiliary grace. By the very nature of the perfection in existence that it bestows on the soul as principle, and the transformation of the soul's powers through the theological virtues and gifts that flow from it, habitual grace disposes the creature to be moved and led by the Holy Spirit's grace in the divine *auxilium*, participating by its own activity in the unfolding of the plan of predestination ordained for it by the divine wisdom. Thomas's mature view of habitual grace, in its operating and cooperating effects, expresses his most

83. Lonergan, *Grace and Freedom*, 126.
84. Ibid., 44; cf. Wawrykow, *God's Grace and Human Action*, 52–53.

fully developed understanding of the primacy of divine causality in general, and exemplar causality in particular, and works together with his particular emphasis on the primacy of divine efficient causality (through auxiliary grace) in the dynamic journey of the predestined to beatitude.

The Graced Image: Partaker of the Divine Nature and Principle of Supernatural Activities

What kind of new existence, bestowed by operating habitual grace, can proportion the human soul to beatitude? What kind of form could be the principle of new activities that can reach that end, especially shaping the creature to "be moved by God sweetly and promptly to acquire eternal good" by the *auxilium* of the Holy Spirit?[85] In Ia-IIae q50 (on *habitus* in general) Thomas remarks that in the essence of the soul no *habitus* is to be found "if we speak of human nature" because the soul is the actualizing form of the body (i.e., not in potency toward it) and needs no disposition with respect to the latter; however,

if we speak of a higher nature, of which man can become a partaker, according to 2 Peter 1:4, "that we may become partakers of the divine nature," nothing prevents some habit, namely grace, from being in the soul in respect of its essence, as we shall state later on.[86]

Thomas only hints at what he will say "later on" in Ia-IIae q110 of grace as an essential intrinsic *habitus* that is at the same time a participation in the divine nature—a kind of participation in the divine likeness exceeding that belonging to any creature by nature. According to Thomas's developed definition of *habitus* as "a disposition in relation to a thing's nature, and to its operation or end, by reason of which disposition a thing is well or ill-disposed thereto,"[87] we can infer that grace as a *habitus* is a perfection disposing the soul in relation to its share in a higher nature, and to its operation toward a higher end, to which it is in potency.

The "participation in the divine nature" that constitutes the infused *habitus* of grace is the "principle and root" of the theological virtues and gifts that direct the rational creature to God, that is, of its operation toward a

---

85. *ST* Ia-IIae q110 a2.
87. *ST* Ia-IIae q49 a4.

86. *ST* Ia-IIae q50 a2.

higher end.[88] Habitual grace, like every form, bestows a new being and so constitutes the soul as a principle of new activity. Thomas argues in Ia-IIae q51 a4 with reference to the infused virtues (shaping the intellect and will) that God infuses some *habitus* into the human person in order to dispose them to an end exceeding the proportion of human nature, that is, beatitude. Grace is the principle of the theological virtues, as nature is the principle of activity. Just as the *habitus* of the natural virtues shape the activities of the human intellect and will, which flow from the rational nature as principle of free natural activity, so the infused *habitus* of the theological virtues and the gifts, shaping the intellect and will, flow from the new *habitus* of grace as the principle of free supernatural activity. The image that has received the disposition of grace thus can truly be called the "image of re-creation," sharing in a new and higher nature, which gives it the capacity for new and higher activities.[89]

To understand the full meaning of Thomas's identification of grace as a participation in the divine nature in the *Summa*, it is necessary to bring together elements of his thought—on the divine missions, the image, grace, virtues and gifts, predestination and sonship, and the Incarnation—and to make connections between them that, though implicit, he does not explain definitively in one place. This picture will not be complete without examining his treatment of the theological virtue of charity and the gift of wisdom in later chapters. To begin, we must examine Thomas's use in the *Summa* of this definition of grace to see why it is an important element in his mature understanding of habitual grace as the intrinsic principle of supernatural activities, which disposes the creature to be moved by the divine *auxilium*.

Use of *Participatio Divinae Naturae:* Development and Sources

Thomas predominantly refers to grace as a sharing or participation in the divine nature only in his later works, and systematically only in the *Summa theologiae*. His scriptural authority throughout is 2 Peter 1:4: "Through [Christ] he has given us the precious and very great promises, that we may become sharers in the divine nature (*consortes divinae naturae*)." In contrast to multiple references to 2 Peter 1:4 in the *Summa*, he refers to this scriptural text only once in the *Scriptum*, once in the *De veritate*, and once in the

88. *ST* Ia-IIae q110 a3, q62 a1.
89. Cf. *ST* Ia q93 a4 and chapter 1.

Summa contra Gentiles.[90] The contexts of Thomas's earliest references to 2 Peter 1:4 are interesting, though, as they touch on different elements that appear in frequent conjunction in his treatment in the *Summa*.

In the *Scriptum* bk2 d23 q1 a1 Thomas denies that a creature can by its own nature be made incapable of sin (this would be contrary to freedom of will) but says that the creature may be confirmed in good by the gift of grace, "by which we are made sons of God, and in a certain manner sharers of the divine nature (*divinae naturae consortes*)." In *DV* q27 a6 Thomas refers to the notion in the context of discussing whether grace is in the essence of the soul. He distinguishes between grace and virtues, rejecting the opinion that they are essentially the same; the virtues perfect the powers for operation, while grace perfects the soul itself, "insofar as it gives it a certain spiritual existence, and makes it by a kind of assimilation a sharer of the

90. Marcelo Sánchez Sorondo notes the paucity of references in earlier works, though he misses the reference in the *Scriptum*, placing Thomas's first reference to 2 Pet 1:4 in the *De veritate* text. As Sorondo points out, in the *Scriptum*, while Thomas does employ the notion of participation in relation to grace, he most often refers to grace as a participation in the divine life or being. *La gracia como participación de la naturaleza divina según Santo Tomás de Aquino*, intr., Cornelius Fabro, Bibliotheca Salmanticensis 28 (Salamanca: Universidad Pontificia de Salamanca, 1979), 118–21. In the *Scriptum*, where Thomas frequently refers to the notion of the participation of creatures in the divine goodness in general (e.g., *Scriptum* bk1 d8 q3 a1 ad1; d14 q2 a2; bk2 d1 q2 a3; d32 q2 a2 ad4; bk4 d50, q2 a4 qc. 3), he sometimes also applies it more specifically to grace, charity, or glory, as a special instance of participation in goodness, as he does in the *Summa* (e.g., *Scriptum* bk1, d14 q2 a2; d17 q2 a2 s.c. 2; bk3 d19 q1 a5 qc1.) Charity is described as requiring the "participation in the divine life," which is given through grace (*Scriptum* bk3 d27 q2 a4 qc4: "cum caritas sit amicitia quaedam, quae requirit convictum inter amatos, non potest esse carita, nisi sit participatio divinae vitae, quae est per gratiam, ideo caritas sine gratia esse non potest"; cf. ad3; d28 q1 a3 c., ad1). Thomas refers to "participation in divinity" only in its fullness, however, in connection with "the Church triumphant" or the reward of beatitude (*Scriptum* bk4 d13 q2 a3; d49 q5 a1; cf. bk4 d15 q4 a5 qc2 s.c. 2). Employing a Dionysian phrase, he refers to the angels' "participation in divine things" according to their degree of distinction in the possession of grace. Thomas also speaks of grace (and charity) as bringing about deiformity in this life: "Grace confers on the soul perfection in a certain divine being, and not only with respect to operations but also such that those having grace are constituted as deiform in a certain manner, on account of which, as sons, they are called free for God." (*Scriptum* bk2 d26 q1 a4 ad3: "Gratia confert animae perfectionem in quodam divino esse, et non solum respectu operis, secundum quod quodammodo gratiam habentes deiformes constituuntur, propter quod, sicut filii, Deo grati dicuntur." Cf. bk3 d27 q2 a1 ad9: "Ad nonum dicendum, quod inquantum homines per caritatem deiformes efficiuntur, sic sunt supra homines, et eorum conversatio in caelis est; et sic cum Deo et Angelis ejus conveniunt, inquantum ad similia se extendunt, secundum quod dominus docet: estote perfecti, sicut et pater vester perfectus est.")

divine nature (*consortem divinae naturae*), as 2 Pet 1:4 says." In *SCG* IV 4.3 Thomas is dealing with a Christological question. He rejects the "Photinian" opinion that Christ was "like other men, a son of God by the spirit of adoption, begotten of God by grace, and by a kind of likeness to God, called 'God' in scripture not by nature but by a kind of sharing in the divine nature (*consortium divinae naturae*) as is said of the saints in 2 Pet 1:4." In these scattered loci Thomas briefly refers to the idea of grace as a sharing in the divine nature to make points about freedom of the will under grace, the relationship between grace and the virtues, and the adopted sonship of the saints in contrast to Christ's natural sonship.

These references anticipate the close linkage between these ideas in the *Summa*, where 2 Peter 1:4 and the idea of participation in the divine nature appear in association with a constellation of Pauline texts referring to the notion of predestination and adopted sonship (which, it becomes clear in the IIIa *pars*, is a participation in the sonship of Christ). Thomas's understanding of the "freedom of the children of God" led by the grace of the Holy Spirit on their journey to beatitude also has much to do with the identification of grace as an essential *habitus* that is the root and principle of the theological virtues.

In these earlier texts, however, Thomas does not ever identify the *consortium* of 2 Peter 1:4 with the notion of participation (*participatio*) as he does, though not always consistently, in the *Summa theologiae* and some other works from the period just after the *Summa contra Gentiles*. In his *Catena aurea* and scriptural commentaries on John and Paul, which derive from Thomas's teaching after 1264–65 (i.e., around the time he finished the *Summa contra Gentiles* and began the *Summa theologiae*),[91] he not only refers to 2 Peter 1:4 and *consortium* in the divine nature with greater relative frequency than in earlier works, but he also begins to associate it with the notion of *participatio*.[92]

The first place in Thomas's works where the scriptural text is rendered as *participatio divinae naturae* seems to be in the *Catena on Luke*, in two sepa-

---

91. Torrell, *Saint Thomas Aquinas*, vol. 1, *The Person and His Work*, trans. Robert Royal (Washington, DC: Catholic University of America Press, 2003), 332–33, 340.

92. Thomas refers to the notion of participation in the divine nature in several writings roughly contemporary with the writing of the *Summa*, primarily scriptural works (*Cat. in Lucam* ch4 lect1, ch7 lect28; *Sup. Ioh.* ch15 lect2; *Sup. Eph.* ch3 lect5; *Sup. Tit.* ch3 lect1; *Sup. Heb.* ch8 lect2), but also in the *De anima* (a7 ad9) and *Comp. theol.* (2.4).

rate quotes attributed to Cyril of Alexandria. This raises the intriguing possibility that Thomas was influenced in his interpretation by that great Eastern theologian of deification, in whose teaching on human sanctification, 2 Peter 1:4, and the doctrine of participation in the divine nature play such a central role.[93] Some texts of Cyril quoted by Thomas allude to a connection between participation in the divine nature and the sonship given by "participation in the Holy Spirit," for instance, in the *Catena on Luke* 4:1:

Cyril. God said in the past: My spirit will not remain in those men who are of the flesh; but when we have been enriched by regeneration through water and the spirit, we are made partakers of the divine nature through participation in the Holy Spirit (*divinae naturae participes per spiritus sancti participationem*). The First-Born among many brethren was the first who received the Spirit, and he is also giver of the Spirit, that the grace of the Holy Spirit might also come to us.

Thomas comes to identify "participation in the Holy Spirit" as the virtue of charity, with its associated gift of wisdom in the sons of God, flowing from the grace of the Holy Spirit.[94]

It is perhaps impossible to be absolutely certain of the source from which Thomas drew these texts from Cyril, but he had available to him a *catena* on Luke by Nicetas of Heraclea.[95] This is a most likely source for the *expositiones doctorum graecorum*, of which Thomas says in his introduction to the first volume (on Mark) of the *Catena aurea* that he commissioned a translation into Latin.[96] The Latin translation of this text may have thus played a role in identifying the Vulgate's *consortium* for 2 Peter 1:4 with the *participatio* found in Cyril's text in association with this verse;[97] at least one

93. Russell, *The Doctrine of Deification in the Greek Patristic Tradition* (Oxford: Oxford University Press, 2004), 191ff; 200–202; Daniel A. Keating, *The Appropriation of Divine Life in Cyril of Alexandria* (Oxford: Oxford University Press, 2004), 144–90.

94. *Cat. in Lucam* ch4 lect1. Also, see *Cat. in Lucam* ch7 lect4: "Cyril. Mystically, when he shows the prerogative of John among those born of women, he opposes to him something greater; namely he who through the Holy Spirit was born the Son of God: for the gift of the kingdom is the Spirit of God. So although in works and holiness we may be less than those who followed the mystery of the law, whom John signifies, yet through Christ we attain greater things, being made partakers in the divine nature (*participes facti sumus divinae naturae*)."

95. Torrell, *Saint Thomas Aquinas*, vol. 1, 137n71.

96. See J. Sickenburger's discussion of this conclusion based on the manuscript tradition in *Die Lukaskatene des Niketas von Herakleia*, Texte und Untersuchungen zur Geschichte der altchristlichen Literatur 22/4 (Leipzig: Akademie Verlag, 1902), 65–66.

97. This association was made in the Alexandrian tradition as far back as Origen, who was

precedent existed in the West for such a shift, in the Gloss on 2 Peter 1:4, with which Thomas seems to have been familiar.[98]

"Participation in the Divine Nature" in the *Summa*

Thomas's references to grace as a participation in the divine nature in the *Summa* are distributed throughout the work, and most often associated directly or indirectly with the text of 2 Peter 1:4. Sometimes 2 Peter 1:4's *consortium* alone is used, although often with textual links that indicate it is equivalent to *participatio*. On occasion, the *Summa* also refers to grace as participation in divinity, or as giving a share in the divine *esse*.[99] These latter ways of speaking about grace can also be found in his earlier works. As noted above, however, explicit references to the idea of grace as participation in

---

the first to integrate the philosophical notion of participation in a structured way into Christian thought. He also taught that, through participation in the Spirit and in the Son of God, human beings become sons of God by participation (as opposed to Christ who is Son of God by nature); see Russell, *Doctrine of Deification*, 147–54, esp. 152 (where he mentions Origen, *Sel. in Psalm*. 135, PG 12.1656A).

98. *Glossa ordinaria 1603 version, folio 679*: "Bede. a. c. *Nobis promis. de.* Vel ideo nobis, qui natura sumus Iudaei, qui magisterio ipsius corporaliter usi sumus omnia sacramenta reservavit, et ideo maxima et pretiosa spiritussancti promissa donavit, ut per hoc etiam vos qui ex Gentibus estis, qui carnaliter Christum non vidistis, divinae suae naturae donaret esse participes." "To us, who by nature are Jews, who enjoyed his teaching in the body, he revealed all of his sacraments [or: mysteries, *sacramenta*], and so gave us the greatest and most precious promises of his Holy Spirit, that through these he might grant that you also who are Gentiles, who have not seen Christ in the flesh, should be partakers (*participes*) in the divine nature." The gloss is apparently derived from Bede, though the text has been somewhat modified from the original. Bede, *In epistulas septem catholicas*, Corpus christianorum series latina 121 (Turnhout: Brepols, 1983): "Ideo, inquit, dominus nobis qui natura Iudaei, qui sub lege sumus nati, qui magisterio ipsius etiam corporaliter imbuti, omnia diuinae uirtutis suae secreta reserauit, ideo nobis suis uidelicet discipulis maxima et pretiosa spiritus sui sancti promissa donauit ut per haec etiam uos qui ex gentibus estis, qui eum corporaliter uidere nequiuistis, diuinae suae naturae donaret esse participes, nobis scilicet uos quae ab ipso audiuimus docentibus, uos per eius mysteria consecrantibus." Note the glossator's interpretation of the original *secreta* as *sacramenta*. Bede makes the jump from *consortes* to *participes*, as does Thomas in so many places where he uses 2 Pet 1:4 in his later works, while for Thomas this transposition carried with it a new depth of meaning, as this project attempts to show. The connection with the *sacramenta* (understood as sacraments) as the means by which Christ bestows "the promises of his Holy Spirit" through which we receive a participation in the divine nature is also of course in accord with Thomas's teaching.

99. E.g., *ST* IIIa q2 a10 ad1: "Gratia quae est accidens, est quaedam similitudo divinitatis participata in homine." *ST* IIIa q62 a2: "Gratia, secundum se considerata, perfecit essentiam animae, inquantum participat quandam similitudinem divini esse."

the divine nature are limited almost exclusively to later works, including the *Summa*, where this formula emerges as Thomas's primary definition.

The context for this formula is Thomas's unique metaphysics of participation. By grace, a new participation in the divine life is given that radically increases the share in the divine goodness already belonging to the creature by nature. The new disposition of grace is a new potency in the creature and so must be created—but at the same time it is truly a likeness of the divine exemplar so great that it is nothing less than deification.[100] Thomas thus continues to maintain both discontinuity and continuity between created participation in the divine perfections from nature to grace. Grace as a new creation—participation in the divine *nature*—is in continuity with the participation in the divine goodness belonging to all creation, and yet the *habitus* of grace is a kind of participation in the divine likeness that radically exceeds every natural kind. Exactly what significance does this formulation have for Thomas, how is it different from other kinds of participation in the *Summa*, and how does it relate to his discussions of the perfection of the image? To answer these questions, it is useful to consider the contexts in which he has chosen to use this definition in his text.

Participation in the Divine Nature Makes the Image a Principle of Supernatural Activity   Reference to the participation of creatures in the divine nature first appears in an objection in Ia q13 a9, on whether the name of God is communicable. The first objector argues that it is because "the name *God* signifies the divine nature, which is communicable to others, according to 2 Pet 1:4 ... 'we may be made sharers (*consortes*) of the divine nature.'" In the reply, Thomas explains that because the divine nature cannot be multiplied, the name of God is incommunicable in reality; but "this name *God* is communicable, not in its full signification, but in some part of it by way of similitude; so that those are called gods who share in divinity by likeness, according to the text, 'I have said, you are gods' (Ps 81:6)."[101] Thomas

---

100. *ST* Ia-IIae, q112 a1; see below.

101. Thomas elsewhere interprets this psalm verse, which reads in full "I have said, you are gods, and sons of the most high," to refer to divine adoption by grace (e.g., *Super psalmos* 49.1). Furthermore, because of its quotation by Jesus in Jn 10:36 ("Is it not written in your law, 'I said, You are gods'? If it calls them gods to whom the word of God came"), it is also particularly associated with the notion of participating in the wisdom or divinity of Christ the Word by sharing in the words of revelation brought by Christ (e.g., *Sup. Ioh.* 10.6).

follows up in his reply to obj1 by using the language of participation in the divine nature evoked by 2 Peter 1:4, answering "the divine nature is only communicable according to the participation of a similitude (*secundum similitudinis participationem*)." In the context of q13, which deals with the use of analogy in naming God as the source of participated creaturely perfections, this comment might seem unremarkable. But it is worth noting because this is Thomas's first identification in the *Summa* of the *consortium* in the divine nature of 2 Peter 1:4 with the idea of *participatio* in the divine nature, with all of its metaphysical implications.

In q13 Thomas also gives a hint as to the uniqueness and significance of this kind of participation. He differentiates in q13 a9 (ad3) between the name *God* (communicable only by likeness) and names such as *good* and *wise*, derived from the perfections proceeding from God to creatures, which signify the divine perfections and not the nature, and are thus communicable "in truth." While creatures possess their own proper goodness (which is nevertheless also a participation by likeness of the divine goodness), their "godness" on the level of nature is never properly their own nature but always only god-likeness in nature—they do not actually become God. Thomas also specifies that the name God is "given to God from his own proper operation, which we experience continually, to signify the divine nature." He refers to the preceding article, q13 a8, where he notes that the name God particularly signifies God's continual operation of universal providence over all things. One might infer that participation in a similitude of the divine nature has something to do with a participation in God's own operation of exercising providence through the divine government.

This inference seems warranted by many of the principal references to grace as a participation in the divine nature that follow in the IIa and IIIa *pars* of the *Summa*. These occur within the context of Thomas's teaching on grace as the principle of new activities on the journey of the rational creature to beatitude—that is, in its participation as secondary cause in working out God's providential plan of predestination for its own salvation. The activity of the image as free principle of its own actions is the overarching subject of the IIa *pars*. The first reference in the IIa *pars* to 2 Peter 1:4 has already been noted—it takes place in Thomas's general discussion of *habitus* in Ia-IIae q50, where he mentions the possibility that grace, as an intrinsic *habitus*, can be in the essence of the soul, disposing it well in relation to a "share in the divine nature," for its own operation toward the end of that nature (i.e., beatitude).[102] We can infer that the soul's share in the divine nature by habitual grace, having to do with an elevation in essence, relates to habitual grace's operating effect, while its cooperating effect relates to the inclination it gives the soul to higher activities.

In I-II q62 a1 Thomas delineates further the relationship between the soul's share in a higher nature and its operations toward the higher end of beatitude, for which it is disposed by the *habitus* of grace; the theological virtues that flow from grace as their source govern these operations of the intellect and will. Thomas explains that just as natural virtues are necessary for humans to be perfected in actions that lead to natural happiness, so supernatural virtues are necessary to reach supernatural beatitude. Natural happiness is proportionate to human nature as principle of actions, but the latter

is a happiness surpassing human nature, to which man can come only by divine power, by a kind of participation (*participatio*) of divinity, about which it is written (2 Pet 1:4) that by Christ we are made "sharers (*consortes*) of the divine nature." And because this kind of happiness exceeds the proportion of human nature, the natural principles of man, from which he proceeds to act well according to his proportion, do not suffice to direct him to the happiness of which we speak. Hence it is necessary for some divine principles to be superadded to man, by which he may be ordered to supernatural happiness, just as by his natural principles he is ordered to his connatural end, not however without divine assistance. Such kind of principles are called theological virtues: first, because they have God as object, inasmuch as through them we are rightly ordered to God; secondly, because they are infused in us by God alone; thirdly, because these kind of virtues are made known to us only by divine revelation, in Sacred Scripture.[103]

The soul, made godlike by the gift of grace, receives the capacities in its intellect and will, which enable it to participate as secondary cause in God's own operation of bringing it to beatitude, ordered to God by means of an increasing share in God's own knowledge and love of himself as object.

This teaching on the theological virtues continues to fill out Thomas's earlier teaching on the beatific vision, the divine missions, and the image on the journey to beatitude. We now know that it is by means of the *habitus* of the theological virtues (and their associated gifts) that the intellect and will

102. *ST* Ia-IIae q50 a2, q49 a4.
103. *ST* Ia-IIae q62 a1.

are actively conformed to the Word and Love, proportioned to God, so that God himself becomes the object of the rational creature's knowledge and love. The theological virtues are genuinely principles belonging to the person, although of divine origin, and this is only possible by participation, as Thomas clarifies in his answer to the first objection in q62 a1. The objector argues that "what is divine is above human nature. Therefore the theological virtues are not human virtues." Thomas answers:

A certain nature may be ascribed to a certain thing in two ways. In one way, essentially: and in this way the theological virtues exceed human nature. In another way, participatively, as burning wood participates the nature of fire: and thus, in a certain manner, man becomes a partaker of the divine nature (*particeps divinae naturae*), as said above. And so these virtues are fitting to man according to the participated nature.[104]

The theological virtues are proportionate to the human person who participates in the divine nature by grace because they proportion that person for the supernatural happiness that has become their new end. They belong to the person's new participated nature, and so to the person, just as the reason and will that they shape belong to the created nature. "The reason and will, according to their nature, are not sufficiently directed to God insofar as he is the object of supernatural happiness."[105] The theological virtues are the principles in the intellect and will that "rightly order us to God" through our own graced activity on the journey to beatitude, while the gifts of the Spirit, as Thomas goes on to say in q68, perfect the operation of the theological virtues by disposing the reason to be easily moved on this journey by the prompting of the Holy Spirit.[106]

Grace as a Created *Habitus* That Is a Participation in the Divine Nature
Thomas's central treatment of grace as a participation of the divine nature is found in Ia-IIae q110, on "the grace of God as regards its essence." He sets the stage in a1 and a2 by speaking of it as a participation of the divine goodness and by defining it as a created quality, thus placing it in the context of all creation as the highest manifestation of the ways in which God shares the divine goodness with his creatures. In q110 a1 Thomas begins by identi-

---

104. *ST* Ia-IIae q62 a1 ad1.   105. *ST* Ia-IIae q62 a1 ad2.
106. *ST* Ia-IIae q68 a1.

fying grace as an effect of God's "special love" for the creature, which gives it a "participation of the divine good." The question in a1 is "whether grace places anything in the soul," and his answer negotiates the relationship between eternal uncreated grace or favor on God's part—the divine love—and the gift of grace that is bestowed as an effect of God's causal love, whereby some good is given to the creature and belongs to it by participation. In establishing that grace can be said to be "something" in the soul—a good that is a created effect of God's love—Thomas distinguishes in q110 a1 between the natural good of existence that God's love causes in all creatures and the higher good bestowed by the special love that God has for those he wills to bring to himself as end:

It is clear that every love of God is followed by some good in the creature caused at some time, but not co-eternal with the eternal love. And according to the difference of this kind of good, the love of God to the creature is considered differently. One is common, whereby he loves "all things that are" (Wis 11:25), according to which he bestows natural being on created things. But the other is a special love, according to which he draws the rational creature above the condition of its nature to a participation of the divine good. And according to this love he is said to love anyone simply, because it is according to this love that God simply wishes the eternal good, which is himself, for the creature. So therefore when one is said to have the grace of God, there is signified something in them coming forth from God.[107]

Every creature participates by likeness in the divine goodness (by its participation in being), and so all things are drawn toward God in some way as their final cause. The graced creature, however, is drawn—by means of "something in them coming forth from God"—to a participation in the eternal good, which is God himself.

Thomas has already placed predestination as a higher gift in the context of God's plan of wisdom to manifest his goodness in the divine *ordinatio*. To the elect, God communicates by his causal love the particular good of eternal salvation. Thomas connects back to this teaching from Ia q23 a4 as he goes on to say,

Sometimes the grace of God is said to be God's eternal love itself, according to which it is also called the grace of predestination, inasmuch as God gratuitously,

---

107. *ST* Ia-IIae q110 a1.

and not from merits, predestines or elects some; for it is written (Eph 1:5): "He predestined us to the adoption of children ... for the praise of the glory of his grace."[108]

In q110 a1 the "participation of the divine good," which is grace, is this particular good of predestination to sonship, which leads to eternal salvation (bringing the creature to the eternal good of God as end in the divine *ordinatio*); here we learn too that this participation is attained, more specifically, as God "draws the rational creature above its nature." In other words, predestination to sonship involves not only a new juridical status as son, which results in a new inheritance, but also a change in nature that actually makes one into a new kind of creature capable of a filial relationship with God.[109] From the Ia *pars*, we know that this change involves a conformation to the Word and Love that brings about the perfection of the divine image. In the context of q109, too, we can understand that Thomas is teaching that the purpose of this elevation in nature is to transform the creature for the journey to beatitude, in which God will continually actualize in the creature the new higher potency bestowed by the *habitus* of grace as a special participation in the divine goodness, with the help of auxiliary grace. And, in doing so, God will especially manifest the divine goodness.

In q110 a2 Thomas asks "whether grace is a quality of the soul," examining grace as a *habitus* per se. Thomas writes that it is by infusing the habitual gift of grace, as an intrinsic quality of the soul, that God disposes it to be moved by auxiliary grace toward the supernatural good. Just as God gives natural forms and powers so that creatures are naturally inclined to "the movements whereby they are moved by God," *a fortiori* God also gives supernatural qualities to those whom God wills to bring to the supernatural good, "whereby they may be moved by God sweetly and promptly to acquire eternal good." Thomas's analogy with the natural forms and powers that God provides as the principles of natural acts in creation makes it clear that God provides the *habitus* of grace as the intrinsic principle of acts leading toward beatitude.

108. Ibid.

109. Luc-Thomas Somme notes that from the *Scriptum* to the *Summa theologiae* a shift in emphasis is noticeable in Thomas's treatment of the celestial heritage belonging to our divine filiation. The movement is toward a notion that is less juridical and more linked to grace and merit, one that is defined by the idea of adopted sonship as a participated similitude by grace of Christ's divine filiation by nature. *Fils adoptifs de Dieu par Jésus Christ: La filiation divine par adoption dans la théologie de saint Thomas d'Aquin* (Paris: J. Vrin, 1997), 88.

In the reply to a2 obj3 Thomas clarifies that grace must be an accidental quality of the soul because "what is substantially in God, becomes accidental in the soul participating the divine goodness"; grace is above human nature and so cannot be a substantial form of the soul. An accident has being with reference to its subject, and so grace is

said to be created, in that men are created according to it; that is, they are constituted in new being, from nothing; that is, not from merits, according to Eph 2 (10): "Created in Christ Jesus in good works."[110]

Because grace is above the creature's nature, it must be an accidental form; yet it becomes an intrinsic principle elevating that nature, giving its subject new being. *Qua* accident, this participation in the divine nature that is a new created disposition in the creature has existence in this creature only insofar as this creature exists. *Qua* intrinsic principle, this new created disposition transforms the creature to be the proper principle of its own supernatural activities.[111]

In Ia-IIae q110 a3, as in Ia-IIae q62, Thomas explicitly identifies grace as a participation in the divine nature, and again does so in the context of the relationship between grace and the theological virtues. Disagreeing with Peter Lombard, who held grace and virtues to be essentially identical (*Sent.* II d27), Thomas distinguishes between them on the basis of a text from Aristotle's *Physics*: "virtue is a disposition of what is perfect—and I call perfect what is disposed according to its nature":[112]

Now from this it is clear that the virtue of a thing has reference to some pre-existing nature, from the fact that everything is disposed with reference to what is congruous to its nature. But it is manifest that the virtues acquired by human acts of which we spoke above are dispositions, whereby man is fittingly disposed with reference to the nature by which he is man; whereas infused virtues dispose man in a higher way and towards a higher end, and so also they must be ordered to some higher nature. That is, ordered to the participated divine nature (*naturam divinam participatam*), according to 2 Pet 1: "He has given us the great and most precious promises; that by these you may be made sharers of the divine nature." And according to the reception of this nature, we are said to be born again as sons of God.[113]

---

110. *ST* Ia-IIae q110 a2 ad3.
111. See Appendix B, on the question of Thomas's adherence to a doctrine of created grace.
112. *Physics* VII.17.   113. *ST* Ia-IIae q110 a3 c.

Once again Thomas employs his definition of grace as a participation in the divine nature with reference to the theme of nature as the principle of activity, and graced nature as the principle of activity on the journey to the higher end of beatitude. Grace is "a certain disposition which is presupposed to the infused virtues as their principle and root";[114] the light of grace "which is a participation of the divine nature (*participatio divinae naturae*) is something besides the infused virtues which are derived from and are ordained to this light."[115]

Participation in the Divine Nature Regenerates the Children of God for Beatitude   In the above passage from q110 a3 Thomas links the definition of grace as a participation in the divine nature, and as the principle of new activities on the journey, to the "rebirth" of divine adoption.[116] He reiterates this connection with a quote from Ephesians 5:8—"For you were once darkness but now you are light in the Lord; walk then as children of the light"—as he describes the infused virtues as those that belong to the "children of light" and "enable one to walk as befits the light of grace." Question 110 a4 takes up this theme again as Thomas completes his consideration of the question first raised in I-II q50: "whether grace is in the essence of the soul as in a subject or in one of the powers?" The *sed contra* of q110 a4 introduces the connection to sonship, which is central to the article's argument:

By grace we are born again sons of God. But generation terminates at the essence prior to the powers. Therefore grace is in the soul's essence prior to being in the powers.

Grace involves a new "generation," which takes place on the level of the nature of the soul, changing its subject essentially and thus giving rise to new powers that engage in new activities:

Grace, as it is prior to virtue, has a subject prior to the powers of the soul, so that it is in the essence of the soul. For as man in his intellective powers participates in the divine knowledge through the virtue of faith, and in his power of will participates in the divine love through the virtue of charity, so also in the nature of the soul does he participate in the divine nature (*participat naturam divinam*), after the manner of a certain likeness, through a certain regeneration or re-creation.[117]

---

114. *ST* Ia-IIae q110 a3 ad3.
115. Ibid.
116. Cf. Jn 1:12–13; Rom 8; Gal 4:5–7; Eph 1:5.
117. *ST* Ia-IIae q110 a4 c.

The adopted children of God are those in whom grace, by a participation in the divine nature that changes them on an essential level, is the principle and root of the theological virtues that "flow into the powers of the soul from grace," moving them to act. And so grace is to the will "as the mover to the moved."[118] Thomas seems to mean that, as he indicated in q110 a2, habitual cooperating grace disposes the soul to be moved to beatitude by the divine *auxilium*. This takes place more specifically through actualization of the new powers flowing from grace, the theological virtues in intellect and will. For this reason, Thomas says, "grace is the principle of meritorious works through the medium of the virtues, just as the essence of the soul is the principle of vital works through the medium of the powers."[119] By the elevated activity of their free will flowing from their new participation in the divine nature, the children of God can merit so as to move along the path to beatitude that God has predestined for them in the divine *ordinatio*.

The children of God are no longer slaves but free, heirs of the promise (cf. Gal 3:29–4:7). In a passage from his *Commentary on Galatians* where he focuses on the Holy Spirit's role in this journey, Thomas provides a powerful organic metaphor for the way in which the new generation of grace leads God's adopted children to beatitude. It is worth briefly considering this metaphor in connection with the idea of transformation by participation in the divine nature. He is commenting on Galatians 4:6: "Because you are sons, God has sent the Spirit of his Son into your hearts, crying, '*Abba*, Father.'" He first points out that the conversion of the Gentiles is especially attributed to the Holy Spirit, through whom "we are united to Christ and by that fact adopted as the sons of God." He goes on to say:

He says "into your hearts" because there is a two-fold generation: one is carnal and comes about through fleshly seed sent to the place of generation. This seed, small as it is, contains in its power the whole. The other is spiritual, which comes about by spiritual seed transmitted to the place of spiritual generation, i.e., the human mind or heart, because we are born sons of God through a renewal of the mind. Furthermore, the spiritual seed is the grace of the Holy Spirit: "Whoever is born of God does not sin: because the generation of God preserves him," etc. (1 Jn ult.). And this seed contains in its power the whole perfection of beatitude. Hence it is called the pledge and earnest of beatitude (Eph 1:14).[120]

---

118. *ST* Ia-IIae q110 a4 ad1.   119. *ST* Ia-IIae q110 a4 ad2.

120. *Sup. Gal.* ch4 lect3. In his commentary on Eph 1:14 quoted here, Thomas discusses the

The grace of the Holy Spirit is a spiritual seed generating children of God from within; like the carnal seed, which, though small, contains the potential of the mustard seed to generate a fully developed new natural life, the seed of the Holy Spirit's grace bestows the potential within the person for the fullness of a new order of existence and operation leading to eternal life.

This idea of the grace of the Holy Spirit as a spiritual seed "containing in its power the whole perfection of beatitude" captures well the dynamism of Thomas's mature understanding of grace's place in the divine *ordinatio*, as well as the way in which it transforms the person from within. The image (with its reference to 1 Jn 3) does not appear, as far as I can tell, before two mentions in Thomas's commentaries on the Pauline epistles, and then somewhat rarely.[121] It does appear in a few places in the *Summa*, first in *ST* Ia q62 a3, where Thomas argues that the angels were created in grace.[122] In Ia q62 a3 Thomas writes,

For we see that all things which, in the process of time, being created by the work of divine providence, were produced by the operation of God, were created in the first fashioning of things according to seedlike forms (*seminales rationes*), as Augustine says (*Gen. ad lit.*), such as trees, animals, and the rest. Now it is evident that grace (*gratia gratum faciens*) bears the same relation to beatitude as the seedlike form in nature does to the natural effect; hence (1 John 3:9) grace is called the "seed" of God.[123]

---

way in which the Holy Spirit is sign, promise, and pledge of our inheritance, specifying the role of charity, as a participation in the divine love, in bringing the children of God to their promised inheritance.

121. Thomas also briefly mentions this idea in his *Commentary on Romans*, where he considers "how those who are led by the Spirit of God *are sons of God*. This is clarified by a likeness to natural children, who are produced by the natural seed coming from the father. But the spiritual seed proceeding from the Father is the Holy Spirit. Therefore, through this seed some are born as sons of God: 'No one born of God commits sin, because the seed of God abides in him' (1 Jn 3:9)" (*Sup. Rom.* ch 8 lect 3). In the *Scriptum* Thomas speaks of the word of God as a spiritual seed producing "wreaths and fruits" of joy in those who labor in the conversion to spiritual things (bk4 d49 q5 a2 qc1).

122. Thomas may have been inspired to develop this metaphor by Augustine's doctrine of the *seminales rationes* in the Divine Wisdom's unfolding plan of providence, presented in *Super Genesim ad Litteram*. The passage to which Thomas refers is in bk8.3 of Augustine's text, but other passages explain the doctrine at greater length, such as 5.4 and 6.11.

123. *ST* Ia q62 a3 c.

Thomas argues that the seed of grace was planted in the angels from the beginning, as the "principle of right operation," the end of which is glory.[124] He refers in the above quote to his constant scriptural referent for the doctrine, 1 John 3:9: "Whoever is born of God, commits no sin, for his seed abides in him." It is perhaps no coincidence that a more famous passage in 1 John 3, about the glorious destiny of the children of God to be fully assimilated to the divine likeness, was Thomas's primary scriptural referent in his treatment of the *visio Dei* in Ia q12, that is, "We shall be like him for we shall see him as he is." The seed of grace is planted, in God's providence, in those whose operations will bring them to "the perfection of beatitude." Like the *seminales rationes* in the order of creation, grace bestows a new potential that flowers in time into the fullness of life in the supernatural order.

It makes sense that Thomas refers to this notion also in his treatment in Ia q70 a1 of the fruits of the Holy Spirit named in Galatians 5:22–23. The fruits are the "virtuous deeds in which one delights," produced in us by the Holy Spirit,[125] and so Thomas calls them "our works, insofar as they are produced by the Holy Spirit working in us."[126] Although Thomas does not mention grace per se in the following passage, it is clear that he is speaking of its work in those who are "born of God":

If then human operation proceeds from man in virtue of his reason, it is said to be the fruit of his reason: but if it proceeds from him in respect of a higher power, which is the power of the Holy Spirit, then human operation is said to be the fruit of the Holy Spirit, as of a divine seed, for it is written (1 Jn 3:9): "Whoever is born of God, commits no sin, for his seed abides in him."[127]

Once again we see the close connection between the ideas of interior transformation by grace, divine adoption, and the activity of the Holy Spirit in leading the children of God through their own graced activity to beatitude. When Thomas says in q110 a4 that a new participation in the divine nature regenerates the sons of God in the essence of their soul, he seems to have in mind something like his teaching on Galatians 4:6—"God has sent the Spirit of his Son into your hearts, crying, '*Abba*, Father'"—and the idea of grace as a spiritual seed, containing the whole perfection of beatitude.

---

124. *ST* Ia q62 a3 ad3.   125. *ST* Ia-IIae q70 a2.
126. *ST* Ia-IIae q70 a1.   127. Ibid.

In q112 a1 Thomas identifies the essential change that takes place in the children of God as deification, an effect that only God can cause,

since it is nothing short of a participation of the divine nature, which exceeds every other nature. For it is as necessary that God alone should deify, communicating a share in the divine nature by some participated similitude, as it is impossible that anything but fire alone could ignite.[128]

Thomas adds in this article a sacramental and ecclesial dimension, again emphasizing the role of the Holy Spirit. In the economy of salvation, God instrumentally bestows the deifying gift of grace by means of Christ's humanity and the sacraments derived from it,

and principally by the power of the Holy Spirit working in the sacraments, according to Jn 3:5: "Unless one be born again of water and the Holy Spirit he cannot enter into the kingdom of God."[129]

This mention of the work of the divine Persons in the rebirth of the sons of God through the grace of the sacraments, which, as Thomas explains in the IIIa *pars*, "derive their saving power from the divinity of Christ through his humanity,"[130] is also a reminder of the source of this deification in the divine missions. When Thomas discusses Christ's humanity as the source of grace and his sacraments as its instruments in the economy of salvation, he will return to the idea of grace as a participation in the divine nature. It is specifically by being joined to Christ through the grace of the Holy Spirit that God's adopted children are deified.

Question 114 a3, the next place in the questions on grace where Thomas adverts to the idea of grace as a participation in the divine nature, nicely continues the trajectory of thought outlined above, as he considers in what way the adopted children of God, moved by the Holy Spirit, can merit eternal life. In q114 a2 Thomas established that grace, bestowed by God's preordination to eternal life, is necessary for them to do so, first because their natural

---

128. "Respondeo dicendum quod nulla res agere potest ultra suam speciem, quia semper oportet quod causa potior sit effectu. Donum autem gratiae excedit omnem facultatem naturae creatae, cum nihil aliud sit quam quaedam participatio divinae naturae, quae excedit omnem aliam naturam. Et ideo impossibile est quod aliqua creatura gratiam causet. Sic enim necesse est quod solus Deus deificet, communicando consortium divinae naturae per quandam similitudinis participationem, sicut impossibile est quod aliquid igniat nisi solus ignis."

129. *ST* Ia-IIae q112 a1 ad2.

130. *ST* IIIa q62 a5.

principles are insufficient to attain the end on their own, and second because of the impediment of sin. Article 3 asks whether one who has the grace of the Holy Spirit can merit eternal life condignly (i.e., in such a way that the merit is equal to the reward). Thomas distinguishes between two causes for the meritoriousness of human works: the divine action of the Holy Spirit, by which we merit condignly, and the action of the free will, by which the works have congruous merit or merit on account of an equality of proportion, a reward being given by God to the one who makes good use of his own powers. The condign merit proceeding from the activity of the Holy Spirit in us can truly be attributed to our works done under grace, because those works spring from grace working intrinsically to move the free will; and yet the value of the merit derives from the power of the Holy Spirit,

moving us to eternal life according to Jn 4:14: "It shall become in him a fount of water springing up to eternal life." And the worth of the work depends on the dignity of grace, by which man, made a sharer of the divine nature (*consors factus divinae naturae*), is adopted as a son of God, to whom the inheritance is due by right of adoption, according to Romans 8:17: "If sons, then heirs also."[131]

The Holy Spirit does not just move the children of God but moves them freely from within; the dignity of grace belongs to them because by it they share in the divine nature.

Thomas's reference to Romans 8:17 in the passage above underlines the notion of the end of beatitude that is the reward of this Spirit-led, yet free, activity of the children of God. It is no surprise that in his *Commentary on Romans* this theme is the subject of his treatment of Romans 8:14–17, where he outlines Paul's argument in these verses: the sons of God obtain the inheritance of glory, and those who are ruled by the Holy Spirit are the sons of God. Therefore all who are ruled by the Holy Spirit obtain the inheritance of glory. With regard to being "led by the Holy Spirit" (Rom 8:14), Thomas says that in addition to being instructed by the Holy Spirit, those who are led are actually moved by a higher instinct. So the spiritual person "is inclined to do something not as though by a movement of his own will

131. Interestingly, Thomas here uses 2 Pet 1:4's language of *consortium* rather than *participatio* to refer to the idea of grace as a participation in the divine nature, possibly simply as a way of introducing his authority (which he does not quote explicitly for a change). Nevertheless, at this point in the *Summa*, preceding questions establish the connection between the two terms, and the reader can be expected to supply it.

chiefly, but by the prompting of the Holy Spirit." Yet this movement of the will under the Spirit's prompting does not diminish the person's freedom: "This does not mean that spiritual men do not act through will and of free choice in them, as it says in Phil 2:13, 'God is at work in you both to will and to work.'" As already noted, Thomas frequently returns in his later works to the idea of the *instinctus* of the Holy Spirit, especially in his original treatment of the gifts of the Spirit.[132] In the *Summa* Thomas joins to this later emphasis on the primacy of God's action in the Holy Spirit, the formal definition and systematic use of the idea of grace as a participation in the divine nature. The sons of God in the *Summa*, then, are those whom, by a participation in the divine nature that is the grace of the Holy Spirit, the Spirit leads to the end of beatitude.

Yet it would seem that no work done in this life, even under grace, can be equal to the reward of everlasting life (q114 a3 ob3). Thomas answers again with his organic metaphor reminding the reader of the dynamism of grace in those who share in the divine nature (and thus possess the divine indwelling):

> The grace of the Holy Spirit, which we have at present, although unequal to glory in act, is nevertheless equal to it virtually as the seed of a tree, in which the whole tree is virtually. And similarly by grace the Holy Spirit, who is the sufficient cause of everlasting life, dwells in man; whence he is said to be the pledge of our inheritance (2 Cor 1:22).[133]

Grace is virtually equal to glory, as leading to and resulting in it, so the works of the elect done under grace receive value—retroactively as it were—because they are the first sprouting of the supernatural life that will flourish fully only in heaven. The presence of the Holy Spirit guarantees this growth as pledge; a pledge, it seems, in the sense both of the promise of continuing causal activity moving the person to everlasting life, and of a foretaste in the divine indwelling (through the divine missions) of what is to be possessed and enjoyed fully by knowledge and love in that life of heaven. Thomas goes on to argue in q114 a4 that graced human acts merit eternal life chiefly through the theological virtue of charity, both because it is by this virtue that one eternally enjoys the divine good that is the end of God's ordination

---

132. Torrell, *Saint Thomas Aquinas*, vol. 2, 206ff.

133. *ST* IIa-IIae q114 a3 ad3.

to beatitude, and because it is charity that gives the greatest voluntariness to acts of the free will.

In the references to grace as a participation in the divine nature in the *Summa* discussed so far, it seems that Thomas particularly adverts to this idea when he wants to consider how the grace of the Holy Spirit is a new principle of the predestined rational creature's free (and so meritorious) activities—as the reborn son of God—on the journey to beatitude, and the root of the theological virtues (and their associated gifts) that are the medium of these activities. Thomas's next reference, in IIa-IIae q19 a7 on the gift of fear—that is, filial fear, which is born of charity and is the beginning of wisdom—provides some confirmation of this idea. Thomas asks "whether fear is the beginning of wisdom," and in his reply he begins by defining wisdom as "the knowledge of divine things," with reference to q45 on wisdom. Yet, he says, wisdom "as considered by us" is different from philosophical wisdom:

For, seeing that our life is ordered to the enjoyment of God [lit., divine enjoyment], and is directed according to a certain participation of the divine nature (*participationem divinae naturae*), which is by grace, wisdom according to us is not only considered as being cognizant of God, as it is by the philosophers, but also as it is directive of human life, which is not only directed according to human reasons but also according to divine reasons, as is clear from Augustine, *De trinitate*, Bk. 12.[134]

He goes on to argue that for this reason faith can be said to be the beginning of wisdom, as supplying the articles of faith, the first principles of wisdom.[135] But filial fear is the beginning of wisdom in that it is its first ef-

---

134. It seems from his explanation that Thomas does not quite represent Augustine's thought. In *DT* bk12–14 Augustine distinguishes between knowledge (of temporal things, leading to action in this life) and wisdom (contemplation of eternal things), not exactly between human versus divine reasons that direct human life. Augustine's temporal things include the salvific truths about the Incarnation, through which God has revealed his love for fallen humanity. By faith in these one moves from knowledge to wisdom and is able to rise to the contemplation of the Trinity through knowledge of the self as created to the divine image.

135. In a question on the act of faith, Thomas argues that "the perfection of the rational nature consists not only in what belongs to it by nature but also in that which it acquires through a supernatural participation of the divine goodness" in the vision of God. Faith is thus necessary to arrive at the creature's perfection, the beatific vision, because the human mode of learning is to proceed little by little, and to do this the learner must believe God, who teaches him (IIa-IIae q2 a3). Believing God is thus the first step on the path of wisdom.

fect: to begin to regulate one's life by wisdom, one must first fear God and submit oneself to God, "for the result will be that in all things [one] will be ruled by God." In the second article of this question, Thomas beautifully compares filial fear to the "chaste fear" that belongs to a wife with respect to her husband. Both, he says, are based on the bond of affection:

Hence filial fear and chaste fear pertain to the same thing, because by the love of charity God becomes our Father, according to Rom 8:15: "You have received the spirit of adoption of sons, by which we cry out, *Abba!* Father"; and by this same charity he is also called our spouse, according to 2 Cor 11:2: "I have espoused you to one husband, that I may present you as a chaste virgin to Christ."[136]

The filial fear that is a gift of the Holy Spirit causes the adopted child of God to revere God out of love, so as to fear offending and being separated from him. Filial fear is thus the first in the ascending order of the gifts of the Holy Spirit, which make the graced person amenable to the Spirit's prompting and all the more so as he loves God more.[137] The adopted children of God receive this gift of filial fear from the Holy Spirit to dispose them to live by the wisdom that belongs to the life of grace. At the root of the direction of their lives according to divine reasons (*rationes divinas*) is their participation of the divine nature, which directs the lives of those ordered to the enjoyment of God in beatitude.

Summary and Conclusion

In this chapter, we have examined Thomas's thought on the way in which the image, as principle of its own activities, is deified by grace to become the free principle of new activities on the journey to beatitude. Thomas uses his mature definition of grace as a participation in the divine nature in the Ia and IIa *pars* of the *Summa* in association with the idea of the divine *ordinatio*, of God's wise plan to manifest and share his goodness with the rational creatures he has chosen for eternal life, by raising them to a new level of being and thus to a participation in the unfolding of his plan of salvation for them. The infused *habitus* of grace perfects the conformation of rational creatures to God begun in creation—as a participation in the divine nature,

---

136. *ST* IIa-IIae q19 a2 ad3.
137. And so filial fear increases with charity; *ST* IIa-IIae q19 a9, a10.

grace deifies the re-created image so as to make it capable of the supernatural intellectual activities of knowing and loving God that bring it to beatitude through the medium of the infused virtues and gifts. In this way, grace as a participation in the divine nature gives the predestined creature the new being and the capacities that fit it for the journey to supernatural happiness in the freedom of an adopted son.

If we read what Thomas has to say about grace as a participation in the divine nature and principle of the infused virtues and gifts, in light of his teaching on the perfection of the image by the divine missions, we can see a clear, though implicit, link between the two. Humans are created to the image of the one and the triune God. Grace bestows on the image a more perfect participated likeness to the divine nature not only in its one essence as principle of government (cf. Ia q13 a9) but also in the Trinitarian aspect of the divine nature as principle and exemplar of the supernatural activity of intellect and will, by perfection of the image's assimilation to the divine Persons. Habitual grace enables the image to share as the principle of God-like activities in the divine government, like the one divine essence, and conforms the intellect and will to the Trinitarian Persons of Word and Love in the divine missions through the medium of the infused virtues and gifts. It is thus by conformation to the Word and Love that the image is disposed for the action of the divine *auxilium*, which moves it to be likened to the divine Persons in act, causing it to actually possess and enjoy God, imperfectly by grace and perfectly in glory. Thus participation in the divine nature orders the adopted children of God toward beatitude by making them like the one and triune God in their nature and activities, disposing them to be led by the Holy Spirit to move freely to that new end in filial obedience. In later chapters, we will see that Thomas fills out this picture with his teaching on charity and wisdom, the infused virtue and gift flowing from grace that especially conform the intellect and will to the Word and Love. First, though, we must complete our examination of Thomas's teaching on grace as a participation in the divine nature by considering his teaching in the IIIa *pars* on how and why this participation is bestowed through Christ, and why, therefore, it is also a participation in the sonship of the Word, who is one in nature and love with the Father.

CHAPTER 4

The Incarnation and Participation in the Divine Nature

Those he foreknew he also predestined to be conformed to the image of his Son.

—Romans 8:29

The bulk of references in the *Summa* to grace as a participation in the divine nature occur in the IIa *pars* and are associated with the subject named in its prologue—the human being as principle of his actions, both natural and supernatural. Thomas places this teaching in the context of a rich complex of associated ideas and scriptural texts that center on predestination to adopted sonship and the primacy of the Holy Spirit's activity in "leading the sons of God" in freedom to their inheritance through the divine *auxilium*. Before examining, in chapters 5 and 6, Thomas's further teaching in the IIa *pars* about how charity and wisdom, flowing from the gift of grace, specifically shape the will and intellect of adopted sons for beatitude, I continue my examination of his teaching on grace as a participation in the divine nature by considering what he has to say about the grace of Christ—for it is in Christ that we can see the highest expression and overflowing cause of human grace, charity, and wisdom. Christ's own eternal sonship is the exemplar of adopted sonship, and his participation in the divine nature by grace, the principle and model of ours. The example of Christ instructs us about what it means to be God's adopted children.

Thomas links the Incarnation and the gift of participation in the divine nature in a number of his later works. I begin by looking at several places in his Scripture commentaries, written just before or at the same time as the *Summa*, where he reflects on Christ as the one through whom this gift is given. References to 2 Peter 1:4 are relatively abundant compared to his earlier works, where, as noted in chapter 3, he mentions the verse in only a few instances. It seems that, consistent with his more frequent use of it in the *Summa* in connection with the idea of grace as a participation in the divine nature, 2 Peter 1:4 gained in importance for him in his later thought in general. A brief survey of representative passages serves to establish a consistent connection in his teaching in the commentaries between the Incarnation and participation in the divine nature, and its association with the themes of grace and adopted sonship. The IIIa *pars* echoes many of his scriptural insights; here, as Thomas said at the outset of the *Summa*, he treats "of Christ, who as man, is our way to God."[1] We can expect that references in the III *pars* to grace as a participation in the divine nature will be found in the context of thinking about how the image's graced journey, as adopted son, takes place through the "way" of Christ the Son and his sacraments, and of how the "Savior of all" bestows his benefits on the human race.[2]

The Incarnation and 2 Peter 1:4

The text of 2 Peter 1:4 provides the most obvious source for the connection Thomas makes between the Incarnation and the benefits of participation in the divine nature:

May grace and peace be yours in abundance through knowledge of God and of Jesus our Lord. His divine power has bestowed on us everything that makes for life and devotion, through the knowledge of him who called us by his own glory and power. Through him [or, by which: *per quem*], he has bestowed on us the precious and very great promises, so that through these you may come to share in the divine nature, after escaping from the corruption that is in the world because of evil desire.

Unfortunately, Thomas wrote no commentary on the Petrine letters. But he consistently interprets this text to mean that a share in the divine nature, which follows the escape from sin, is given to us through the "pre-

---

1. *ST* Ia q2, prol.
2. *ST* IIIa q1, prol.

cious and very great promises" (containing "everything that makes for life and devotion") bestowed through "Jesus our Lord." That we should share in the divine nature is thus the end result of the promises given specifically through the Incarnation for those who know Christ. Every time Thomas uses this verse in his scriptural commentaries, without exception, he does so with reference to Christ or some teaching about the Incarnation—that is, it is specifically "through Christ" that the promises are bestowed.[3]

What are the benefits or great promises leading to a share in the divine nature to which Christ gives us access? Thomas refers to this first half of verse 4 at least nine times in his scriptural commentaries.[4] In these places, there is some indication of what he thinks those promises are. For instance, in his *Commentary on 1 Corinthians*, he writes that because grace is the first "salvific good" given to us by God, and peace the last (in beatitude), "in these all others are included." These gifts come "from God the Father,"

and, he [Paul] adds, "from the Lord Jesus Christ," through whom, as it says in 2 Peter 1, "God gave to us the greatest and most precious promises." Jn 1:17: "Grace and truth came through Jesus Christ."[5]

The text's reference to "from God our Father" can be understood as meaning "the whole Trinity, by which we were created and adopted as sons," whereas when "the Lord Jesus Christ" is added, it refers to his other (hu-

---

3. The text could be interpreted otherwise, as the referents for the nominatives and for *per quem* are not clear. *Per quem* (or possibly *per quae*, as abbreviated in medieval manuscripts) might refer to "knowledge," "glory and power," "everything that was bestowed," or "him" in the preceding phrase, and so does not necessarily refer directly to Christ or God. An interlinear gloss in the *Glossa ordinaria* explains that it may mean either "per quem Christum vel per quae dona" (a preceding gloss names "everything that was bestowed" as the *dona*). In spite of this ambiguity, however, it seems that Thomas did generally interpret these words as referring to Christ or the Incarnation wherever he employed this part of the text.

4. But never before; as with the rest of the verse, 2 Pet 1:4a seems to have become more important in his later works.

5. Thomas also juxtaposes Jn 1:17 and 2 Pet 1:4 in his *Commentary on Ephesians*, in the midst of a discussion of the "mystery of Christ ... that the Gentiles should be fellow heirs and of the same body, and co-partners of his promise in Christ Jesus, by the gospel" (Eph 3:4, 3:6). Through faith, he says, the Gentiles receive the inheritance, are joined to the body, and are admitted to a participation in the promised grace. "The Gentiles have acquired all this, not through Moses, but 'in Christ.' Jn 1:17: 'For the Law was given through Moses, grace and truth came through Jesus Christ.' 2 Pet 1:4: 'Through whom he gave us the greatest and most precious promises.'" (*Sup. Eph.* ch3 lect1).

man) nature. Thomas goes on to explain that Paul is silent about the Holy Spirit either because he is "the bond of Father and Son, and understood by both, or because he is the gift of both, understood by the gifts, of which he says 'grace and peace,' which are given through the Holy Spirit."[6] The promises, then, are the gifts given from the Trinity, through Christ, by the Holy Spirit, that lead us to salvation—grace, truth, and the peace of beatitude. Through these gifts we become sharers in the divine nature.[7]

Elsewhere Thomas refers more directly to glory as the great and precious thing bestowed through Christ, for instance, in his *Commentary on Philippians*, where he discusses Philippians 4:19: "My God will fully supply whatever you need, in accord with his glorious riches in Christ Jesus." God, Thomas says, will do this

truly in glory, namely his glory, because there all desire will be completely fulfilled. Ps 17:15: "I will be satisfied when your glory appears." Ps 103:5: "He fulfills your desire with good things." And this is "in Christ," that is, through Christ. 2 Pet 1:4: "Through whom he gave us the greatest and most precious things."[8]

Glory is identified as one of the great promises of 2 Peter 1:4 also in a brief passage in the *De anima*: "Grace, glory, and charity" are the "perfections of grace [that] befit the soul and the angel by a participation in the

---

6. *Sup. 1 Cor.* ch1 lect1. There is a hint that Thomas's reading of the *Glossa ordinaria* on 2 Pet 1:4 may have shaped his interpretations. In his *Commentary on 1 Corinthians* Thomas is discussing the end of the letter's salutation: "Grace to you and peace from God our Father and the Lord Jesus Christ." An interlinear gloss on 2 Pet 1:4's "that by these [i.e., promises] you may be made sharers," etc., reads: "'*Grace to you and peace*,' that by these." That is, the Gloss on 2 Pet 1:4 refers to 1 Cor to explain that we receive a share in the divine nature by the promises of grace and peace. Thomas makes this same link between the texts in his 1 Cor commentary. Although the *Glossa ordinaria* was fairly standardized by the thirteenth century, it had not yet reached its most stable form. Research remains to be done that would definitively show which manuscripts of the glossed Bible were available to Thomas when he was writing his scriptural commentaries and the *Summa theologiae*. As Mark Jordan has noted, however, the 1480 edition printed by Adolf Rusch in Strasbourg "does reflect the text and arrangement of some twelfth-century copies of the *Glossa*," although Thomas does not always read the Strasbourg version. See the reprinted facsimile by Karl T. Froehlich, Margaret T. Gibson, eds., *Biblia latina cum glossa ordinaria* (Turnhout: Brepols, 1992); Mark Jordan, *Rewritten Theology: Aquinas after His Readers* (Oxford: Blackwell, 2006), 21n8.

7. For other places not discussed here where Thomas refers to Christ as the source of the precious and great promises of 2 Pet 1:4, see *Sup. Eph.* ch4 lect3; *Sup. 2 Thes.* ch1 lect1; *Sup. 2 Tim* ch1 lect1; *Sup. Heb.* ch1 lect4, ch13 lect3.

8. *Sup. Phil.* ch4 lect2.

divine nature." Here too Thomas directly equates 2 Peter's *consortium* with *participatio*.[9]

God bestows all of his gifts of grace through the visible and invisible divine missions of Son and Spirit. In his *Commentary on Hebrews*, in a discussion of the gratitude that is due for the "great benefits" of the Incarnation, Thomas identifies those benefits as stemming from God's first gift to us of

> the greatest and most precious thing he had, namely, his only-begotten Son. 2 Pet 1:4: "By whom he has given us the greatest and most precious promises." He also gave us the Holy Spirit. Joel 2:28: "I will pour out my spirit upon all flesh." Rom 5:5: "The charity of God is poured out in our hearts by the Holy Spirit who is given to us."[10]

The missions of the Son and Holy Spirit—and, through the Holy Spirit, the gift of charity—are God's first and most precious gifts, through which the benefits of the Savior of all are bestowed on the human race.

The connection for Thomas between the Incarnation and the gift of a share in the divine nature is also clear in places in his scriptural commentaries where he refers to the *consortium divinae naturae* of the second half of 2 Peter 1:4. Three examples will suffice.[11] In his *Commentary on Ephesians* Thomas discusses the way in which God "is able to accomplish far more than all we ask or imagine, by the power at work within us" (Eph 3:20). He says that the profusion of the divine power in us

> becomes apparent once we consider what he has wrought in us. For the human mind and will could never imagine, understand or ask that God should become man, and man become God and a sharer in the divine nature, which nonetheless he has worked in us according to his power, and this in the Incarnation of his Son. 2 Pet. 1:4: "that through this (*per hoc*) you may be made sharers in the divine nature."[12]

---

9. The *Q. d. de anima* was written around the time of the Ia *pars*. Here he is responding to an objection concerning the specific difference between angels and human souls. The objector argues that "the angel and the soul are perfected by the same perfections, namely, grace, glory, and charity. Therefore they are specifically the same." Thomas answers: "The perfections of grace befit the soul and the angel by a participation in the divine nature. So it says in 2 Pet 1: 'Through him, he has bestowed on us the precious and very great promises, so that through these you may come to share in the divine nature,' etc. Therefore it cannot be concluded that the angel and the soul are specifically the same because they have these perfections in common" (*Q. d. de anima* a7 ad9).

10. *Sup. Heb.* ch10 lect3.

11. See also *Sup. Heb., rep. vulgata*, ch8 lect2.

12. *Sup. Eph.* ch3 lect5.

The marvelous exchange brought about by the Incarnation is the prime example of God's power at work in a way that exceeds human understanding. Yet, as Thomas explains in a beautiful passage preceding this one, it is given to the saints by faith and charity to "comprehend," to the degree possible to human nature, "the breadth and length and height and depth" of God's power, eternity, nature, and wisdom, "and to know the charity of Christ which surpasses all knowledge" (Eph 3:18–19). For "to know Christ's love is to know all the mysteries of Christ's Incarnation and our redemption [that] have poured out from the immense charity of God."[13]

God's love in Christ as the cause of our participation in the divine nature is also the subject of a passage in Thomas's *Commentary on John*, where he treats the text "As the Father has loved me, so I have loved you." Christ did not love his disciples exactly as the Father loved him, but rather by a certain likeness of that love. With respect to the Son's divine nature, the Father loved him by communicating to him his own nature; with respect to his human nature he loves him so that he is at once God and man. But the Son did not love his disciples so as to make them gods by nature, nor to unite them to God so as to form one person with God:

But he did love them up to a similar point; he loved them to the extent that they would be gods by participation in grace (*dii per participationem gratiae*). Ps 82:6: "I say you are gods." 2 Pet 1:4: "through whom he has granted us precious and very great promises, that through this we may be made sharers of the divine nature." And he loved them to the extent that they would be united to God in affection. 1 Cor 6:17: "He who is united to the Lord becomes one spirit with him." Rom 8:29: "For those whom he foreknew he also predestined to be conformed to the image of his Son."

Thomas's teaching that the Son loved his disciples with a likeness of the Father's love for him cannot but make the reader think of the Holy Spirit and its role in bestowing a participation in the divine nature by grace. Although Thomas does not pursue the point here, his references to 1 Corinthians 6:17 and Romans 8:29 are significant; they point to particular effects of participation in the divine nature that result in union with God through the Incarnation. The text of 1 Corinthians 6:17 is key for Thomas where he talks about the way in which charity brings about union by conformity

13. Ibid.

with God,[14] and also in discussions about the connaturality with God bestowed by the gift of wisdom, rooted in charity.[15] Romans 8:29 refers to the predestined who are to be conformed not only to the divine image but also specifically to the image of the Son as adopted children. Thomas also associates this idea of participated sonship especially with the gift of wisdom.

In his *Commentary on Titus* Thomas identifies the regeneration given in baptism by the Holy Spirit, which makes sons of God, as a participation in the divine nature given through Christ. Thomas refers to 2 Peter 1:4 in connection with the saving "bath of rebirth and renewal by the Holy Spirit, whom [God] richly poured out on us through Jesus Christ our savior, so that we might be justified by his grace and become heirs in hope of eternal life" (Tit 3:5–7), saying the effects of the bath are

"regeneration and renewal." By which it is to be understood that man lacked two things in the fallen state, which he obtained through Christ, namely participation in the divine nature (*participatione divinae naturae*) and the putting off of the old state … The first of the effects we obtain through Christ, namely through participation (*participatione*) in the divine nature. 2 Pet 1:4: "that through this we may be made sharers (*consortes*) of the divine nature." But a new nature is not acquired except by generation. Yet this nature is given such that ours also remains, and so it is superadded. For thus participation is generated in the Son of God [or, into a son of God], by which man is not destroyed. Jn 3:7: "You must be born again." And this is called generation. Ja 1:18: "He willingly gave birth to us by the word of his truth." Through Christ man also puts off the oldness of sin, renewed in the integrity of his nature, and this is called renewal. Eph 4:23: "Be renewed in the spirit of your minds."[16]

The "regeneration and renewal" of the sacrament correspond to the elevating and healing effects of grace, respectively, discussed by Thomas in *ST* Ia-IIae q109 a2. The participation in the divine nature, which brings about regeneration without destroying human nature, is the elevation of grace, here described as bestowed through Christ. As noted by the bracketed words, this text is one of those outside the *Summa* where Thomas clearly equates the *consortium* of 2 Peter 1:4 with the idea of participation. Thomas

14. E.g., *Scriptum* lib3 d27 q1 a1 c.; *SCG* lib4 cap34 n2.; *ST* IIae-IIae q27 a4; *De virtutibus* q2 a1 ad3; *Comp. theol.* lib1 cap214 c.

15. E.g., *Scriptum* lib3 d34 q1 a2 c.; lib3 d35 q2 a1 qc3 c.; *ST* IIae-IIae q45 a2 c.

16. *Sup. Tit.* ch3 lect1.

goes on (with reference to Gal 4:6 and Rom 8:15) to identify the Trinitarian cause of these effects of baptism as the Holy Spirit, given through Jesus Christ in the sacraments by the Father for the regeneration of the sons of God, who cry out "*Abba*, Father."

This partial survey of the places where Thomas refers to 2 Peter 1:4 in his scriptural commentaries shows that, in every case, he does so in connection with Christ, through whom, and because of whose Incarnation, the Holy Spirit can bestow on human beings the gift of a share in the divine nature. Thomas follows the context of his scriptural text whether he is focusing on the "share in the divine nature" and sonship given through the Incarnation, or on the "precious and very great promises," or the gifts through which Christ brings this about—grace, truth, and finally the peace and glory of beatitude. Given this constant association, it might seem surprising that in the Ia and IIa *pars* of the *Summa theologiae*, much of which was written after or at least concurrently with the scriptural commentaries, Thomas directly refers only once to Christ where he uses 2 Peter 1:4 (in q62 a1 on the theological virtues). The idea that those who receive a participation in the divine nature through grace become the adopted sons of God was certainly present, as seen in chapter 3, but the focus was on the role of the Holy Spirit in leading the sons of God to their supernatural end.

This finding makes pedagogical sense in light of the *Summa*'s unfolding structure, however. Where Thomas deals with the graced image in the Ia *pars* (the subject of which is "God" in himself), he is concerned with the image's relationship of similitude to God: to the divine nature in its activity of government, to the divine essence in the beatific vision, to the Son by filiation to the Father, to the Word and Love in the divine indwelling. In the IIa *pars* (the subject of which is "the rational creature's advance towards God") Thomas's business is to focus on the activity of grace in the image itself, as a new principle of higher activities for the predestined leading to beatitude. In the IIIa *pars*, however (which treats "Christ, who as man is our way to God"), Thomas takes up and more fully examines the way in which Christ, the Incarnate Word, bestows a participation in the divine nature by grace specifically as participated sonship.

The Grace of Christ and Participation in the Divine Nature

Thomas alludes to 2 Peter 1:4 or the notion of grace as a participation in the divine nature through Christ in each of the first three questions of the IIIa *pars*, as well as in questions on the grace of Christ, his priesthood, and his sacraments. The idea of grace as a participation in the divine nature has both Christological and soteriological significance. It plays an important role in explaining why Christ's habitual grace is also his grace of headship, and so is the principle of grace for his members as well as making him their perfect moral exemplar. Participation in the divine nature is linked to adopted sonship because, through Christ, it bestows a participation in Christ's own relationship with the Father. And it is in this context that charity and wisdom emerge as the virtue and gift most characteristic of adopted sons.

The opening article of the questions on the Incarnation sets the framework in which Thomas will present these teachings. IIIa q1 asks "whether it was fitting that God should become incarnate." Thomas argues that it was manifestly fitting because God's very nature is goodness, and it befits the essence of the highest goodness to communicate itself to others; this is brought about in the highest manner by God's joining created nature to himself in the Incarnation. As he did in his considerations of God's willing in creation, and of the essence of grace, Thomas places his entire discussion of the Incarnation in the context of God's plan of divine goodness for his creatures.[17]

Against this background, he goes on in a2 to argue for the necessity of the Incarnation to restore the human race—a necessity not absolute because God in his omnipotence could have restored humanity in some other way, but necessary in the sense that by it the end was attained "better and more fittingly." Thomas gives ten reasons why the Incarnation was such a fitting way for God to save humanity, grouped into two categories: in the first, reasons for our furtherance in good; in the second, reasons for our withdrawal from evil. Thomas anticipates what he will say later in the IIIa *pars* about Christ as the source of grace, as these two categories correspond to the two primary reasons for the necessity of grace for fallen human beings described in Ia-IIae

17. Cf. the discussion in chapter 1 of Ia q19 a2, on the fittingness of God's willing other things than himself on account of the divine goodness, where Thomas's authority in the *sed contra* is 1 Thess 4:3: "This is the will of God, your sanctification"; and Ia-IIae q110 a1 on grace as a participation in divine goodness, discussed above.

q109 a2, where he said that God's help is necessary to enable humans to wish and do supernatural good (i.e., to elevate nature) even in the state of integrity; in the fallen condition, grace is needed to heal corrupt nature even to do natural good. Grace acting on corrupt nature thus has two roles: to heal and to elevate nature. In IIIa q1 a2 Thomas considers the latter first.

The Incarnation was so fitting for our furtherance in good for five reasons. The first four of these reasons have to do with the Incarnation's pedagogical role in revealing and teaching humanity about God's goodness. Drawing on a rich assortment of quotes from Augustine, Thomas says that the Incarnation makes our faith more certain, strengthens our hope, and kindles our love by revealing to us the depth of God's love; it teaches us how to act well by giving us an example to follow. Finally, it is fitting with regard to

the full participation of divinity, which is mankind's true beatitude and the end of human life. And this is bestowed on us through Christ's humanity, as Augustine said in a sermon on the Nativity of the Lord, "God became man that man might become God."[18]

This fifth reason is of a different kind. With this mention of the marvelous exchange, Thomas points to the way in which the Incarnation not only reveals the highest end of human life but also brings us there, elevating us to the full participation of divinity in beatitude. This gift "is bestowed on us through Christ's humanity"—the Incarnation has some causal role (not yet fully specified) in our deification.

Thomas goes on to present the five reasons why the Incarnation was also "useful for our withdrawal from evil." Again, the first four reasons have to do with the pedagogy of the Incarnation, and the fifth with Christ's causal role; he freed us from sin by making satisfaction for us.[19] By the Incarna-

---

18. *ST* IIIa q1 a2. Augustine's influence on Thomas's thought in this article can hardly be overstated, as he is the authority for every one of the ten reasons Thomas gives; Pope Leo adds his weight to two of them. The reference seems to be to Augustine's *Sermon 292.3*. Thomas refers to this text of Augustine on the marvelous exchange only twice, here and in the prologue to the *Catena on Matthew*, in spite of his understanding of sanctification as deification. Interestingly, a similar formula was the object of Christological dispute about the deification of Christ's humanity, dealt with by Thomas in IIIa q16 a7; Thomas may be conscious of the potential dangers of the claim that "man is made God" if wrongly interpreted with regard to Christ in a Nestorian manner.

19. Cf. IIIa q40 a1 ad3, on Christ's manner of life as a preacher, where Thomas places the traditional axiom "Christ's every action is our instruction." The axiom can be found in other

tion we are taught not to honor the devil, to recognize our dignity and so withdraw from sin, and to shun presumption by the realization that we are saved without merit; furthermore, the humility of the Incarnation convinces us to overcome our pride. Thomas includes an explicit reference to 2 Peter 1:4 in a homily by Pope Leo in support of the second pedagogical reason. His first authority is Augustine, who in the *De vera religione* underlines the dignity of human nature in the scheme of creation, to which the Incarnation gives testimony: "God has proved to us how high a place human nature holds amongst creatures, inasmuch as he appeared to mankind as a true man." He then quotes Pope Leo, who exhorts those who have received a new nature by the grace of baptism: "Recognize, O Christian, your dignity; and being made a sharer of the divine nature (*divinae consors naturae*), do not return by a degenerate conversion, to your old worthlessness."[20] In addition to causing our deification, the Incarnation also teaches us how great a dignity this gift confers on us, for God has already placed humans above other creatures by taking on human nature, and in Christian baptism, further elevates that nature to share in his own.[21]

---

places in Thomas's works as well, including the *Scriptum* (e.g., lib 4 d15 q4 a2 qc2 s.c.2). Richard Schenk traces the source of the saying, also found in the work of other scholastic authors, to Cassiodorus; the *Glossa ordinaria* and the *Glossa* of Peter Lombard refined the axiom into its standard formulation. "*Omnis Christi actio nostra est instructio*: The Deeds and Sayings of Jesus as Revelation in the View of Thomas Aquinas," in *La doctrine de la révélation divine de saint Thomas d'Aquin*, Studi Tomistici 37, ed. L. J. Elders (Vatican City: Libreria Editrice Vaticana, 1990), 104–31. Joseph Wawrykow points out that this saying "nicely conveys Aquinas' conviction about the importance of Christ as moral exemplar," and so is well placed in *ST* IIIa q27–59, in which Aquinas, in a move that departs from many other scholastics of his time, deals extensively with the mysteries of Christ's life. Furthermore, Aquinas's use of the saying relates well to the "close link that Aquinas draws between creating and saving" in the action of the incarnate Word. "Omnis Christi actio est nostra instructio," in *The Westminster Handbook to Thomas Aquinas* (Louisville, KY: Westminster John Knox Press, 2005), 99–100.

20. This reference to 2 Pet 1:4 in Pope Leo's *Sermon 21.3* on the Nativity is one of the few instances of the use of this text by a patristic author in the West. In fact, 2 Pet 1:4 was used more often in the East as a key text for the doctrine of deification, primarily in the later Alexandrian tradition, and especially by Cyril of Alexandria. Daniel A. Keating, *Deification and Grace* (Naples, FL: Sapientia Press, 2007), 36.

21. In his commentary on the Apostles' Creed, which has been dated to 1273 (and therefore to the same period as the IIIa *pars*, near the end of Thomas's life), Thomas makes a similar comment as in q1 a2, about how reflection on the Incarnation should lead us to consider the dignity of our nature, and quotes from the whole text of 2 Pet 1:4: "[Human nature] was a nature so ennobled and exalted by being conjoined to God, because it was accepted for partnership (*con-*

Three points are worth noting with respect to the Incarnation and grace as a participation in the divine nature. First, the Incarnation has a dual role in deification (the final term of the salvation brought by Christ and bestowed through his grace): Christ in his humanity is both cause and pedagogical model of participation in the divine nature by grace.[22] Thomas will consider this dual role when he examines the fullness of grace belonging to Christ in his human nature, which is also the source of grace for his members. Second, in the conjunction of the two texts by Augustine and Pope Leo above is a linkage that Thomas often makes between human nature's progressive share in the divine likeness from creation to the recreation of grace; yet in the IIIa *pars* he will develop further his reflections on the special role of the incarnate Word in these related moments of God's unfolding plan of providence for his creatures.[23] Finally, in his all-encompassing role as cause of our salvation, Thomas indicates, Christ (as the cause of grace) both heals by satisfying and elevates by deifying; the Incarnation is the fitting means by which God brings fallen creatures on the entire journey from sin to beatitude.

Before leaving q1, a word must be said about the last two articles (a5, a6), in which Thomas considers the fittingness of the Incarnation's timing in salvation history. In these articles he develops a teaching on the Incarnation as the principle of perfection for human nature. This is a foundation

---

sortium) with a divine Person … and so one dignified by this exaltation ought to disdain making himself and his nature vile through sin. Thus blessed Peter says 'through whom he has given us good things, that you may be sharers in the divine nature, fleeing,' etc." (*Coll. Credo in Deum* 5; my translation). Latin text provided by Nicholas Ayo, *The Sermon-Conferences of St. Thomas Aquinas on the Apostle's Creed* (Notre Dame, IN: University of Notre Dame Press, 1988), 62. On the dating, see 2–3.

22. For Thomas, the incarnate Word plays a central role in salvation in both his visible and invisible mission—i.e., both as visible exemplar and as source of ontological change. There is an interesting parallel to Cyril of Alexandria's teaching on deification. See Daniel A. Keating, *The Appropriation of Divine Life in Cyril of Alexandria* (Oxford: Oxford University Press, 2004), and Norman Russell's discussion in *The Doctrine of Deification in the Greek Patristic Tradition* (Oxford: Oxford University Press, 2004), 191–204, esp. 197–200.

23. Joseph Wawrykow has pointed out that Thomas does so in particular in q3 a8, on the fittingness of the Son as the divine Person who assumed human nature. I say more of this in discussing conformation to the Word by the gift of wisdom. "Wisdom in the Christology of Thomas Aquinas," in *Christ among the Medieval Dominicans: Representations of Christ in the Texts and Images of the Order of Preachers*, ed. Kent Emery Jr. and Joseph Wawrykow (Notre Dame, IN: University of Notre Dame Press, 1998), 182ff.

for Thomas's later argument that Christ is the author of grace as the possessor of the divine nature, who gives a share in that nature to others through
his own participation of it as human. It was most fitting for the Incarnation
to take place when it did, Thomas says, rather than at the beginning of the
human race (a5) or at the end of the world (a6). In a5 he again underlines
the role of the incarnate Word (as the source of grace) both in healing and
elevating the human race. As "medicine is given only to the sick," so the divine physician who "decreed everything by his wisdom" did not give the
remedy of the Incarnation until after humanity had fallen ill on account of
sin. Quoting the Gloss, Thomas adds that in the divine wisdom the Incarnation did not take place until humans had been humbled by the knowledge of their own incapacity, "so that having recognized their infirmity they
might cry out for a physician, and beseech the aid of grace." Also, the timing of the Incarnation took place according to "the order of furtherance in
good, whereby we proceed from imperfection to perfection"; the authority
here is 1 Corinthians 15:46–47, on Adam as the earthly, and Christ as the
heavenly, man.

In Thomas's scriptural commentary on this passage he distinguishes between Adam and Christ as two "principles of the human race: one of natural life, namely Adam, the other of the life of grace, namely Christ." He
argues that the Holy Spirit made Christ perfect in his humanity, so that
he became "both living and life-giving," and the principle of perfection for
others.[24] When Thomas says in a5 that the timing of the Incarnation was
fitting "on account of the order" of our furtherance in good, using the text

---

24. Thomas explains in *Sup. I Cor., reportatio vulgata,* ch15 lect7 that to have a living soul
(or "animality") is derived by all people from the first principle; to be spiritual derives from
the second. Commenting on Paul's teaching that the first Adam became a living soul, the last
Adam a life-giving spirit—"factus est primus homo Adam in animam viventem, novissimus
Adam in spiritum vivificantem"—Thomas explains that as Adam attained the perfection of his
being through the soul, so Christ attained it, insofar as he was human, through the Holy Spirit.
Christ became both living *and* life giving and so had the power of giving life to others. Christ
is called the heavenly man because in him the divine nature, from heaven, was united to the
human nature. As the second man was heavenly, "that is, spiritual and immortal, so we will all
be spiritual and immortal." He goes on to say that there are two ways in which we can be conformed to the heavenly man, "namely, in the life of grace and of glory, and one is the way to the
other; because without the life of grace, one cannot arrive at the life of glory." We must move
from the "likeness of Adam" (i.e., the "earthly image") to the "heavenly image" by putting on
the "'new man,' namely, Christ (cf. Col 3:9)."

from 1 Corinthians 15:46–47 as his authority, he seems to be implying that it was necessary for human nature to proceed from its state of imperfection in Adam to its perfection in Christ, in that Christ is both himself perfectly spiritual and the principle of spiritual perfection for others.[25]

Thomas goes on in q1 a6 to argue that it was fitting for the Incarnation not to have been put off until the end of the world. He continues his consideration of the ultimate perfection of human nature in Christ, brought about by union with the divine nature, and its role as cause of perfection for others:

In the Incarnation human nature is led to its highest perfection, and so it was not suitable that the Incarnation should take place at the beginning of the human race. But the incarnate Word is the efficient cause of the perfection of human [nature], according to Jn 1:16: "Of his fullness we have all received"; and so the Incarnation ought not to have been put off till the end of the world.[26]

Because Christ is both divine and human, he is at once the prior cause and the ultimate instance of human perfection. Thomas also seems to anticipate a distinction he will clarify in his discussion of the grace of Christ, between the grace of union, by which human nature in Christ is raised to its highest possible dignity, and Christ's fullness of habitual grace, by which he not only possesses grace to the most perfect degree but is also the author of grace for others. And so, although, as an objector argues, "the highest perfection of human nature is in the union with the Word" (and might have been put off to the end of the world as the summit of perfection), "the work of the Incarnation is to be viewed not merely as the terminus of a move from imperfection to perfection, but also as a principle of perfection to human nature."[27]

---

25. Thomas uses the same text as authority in the *sed contra* of an earlier parallel question on the New Law of grace, in which he argues that it should not have been given before the coming of Christ (Ia-IIae q106 a3). When he asks whether the New Law ought to involve external works, Thomas also grounds his affirmative answer in the teaching on the Incarnation: because the Word was made flesh, it is fitting that we receive grace through sensible objects, and that we perform external works moved by inward grace, for we "become receivers of this grace through God's Son made man, whose humanity grace filled first, and thence flowed forth to us" (Ia-IIae q108 a1). Thomas anticipates his full teaching on the incarnate Word as the principle of grace for others, on account of his own fullness of grace, which is shared through the sacramental economy.

26. *ST* IIIa q1 a6 c.

27. *ST* IIIa q1 a6 ob2 ad2.

In q2 a10 Thomas begins to make this distinction between the grace of union and habitual grace in Christ, and it starts to become evident that the crux of this distinction depends upon his definition of grace as a participation in the divine nature. In this article he is focusing only on the grace of union, to begin to clear away some possible confusions about Christ's grace deriving from erroneous Christologies. The article asks "whether the union of the Incarnation took place by grace." If grace for human beings called to beatitude is a participation in the divine nature, what can the "grace" of union mean for Christ, who, as the Person of the Word, already possesses the divine nature? The union of the Incarnation took place by grace—that is, by God's gratuitous willing and unmerited gift—but not by any *habitus* of grace.[28] This means it took place substantially, not as an accident. The habitual grace that is an accident in the souls of the saints

is a certain likeness of the divinity participated in man. But by the Incarnation human nature is not said to have participated some likeness of the divine nature, but is said to be conjoined to the divine nature itself in the Person of the Son. Now the thing itself is greater than its participated likeness.[29]

In IIIa q2 a6 Thomas spent some time distinguishing the orthodox position on the hypostatic union—two natures in one hypostasis—from contemporary opinions presented by Lombard, which Thomas identified as forms of Nestorianism: the *homo assumptus* and *habitus* theories. The first maintained two hypostases in Christ, while the second maintained an accidental union. The *habitus* theory held that the soul and body of Christ were united to the Word only accidentally; as Thomas points out, this is no different from Nestorius's claim that the Word is united to the man Christ "by indwelling, as in his temple."[30] From such a union it would follow that the Person of the Word is distinct from the man in whom the Word dwells. This latter theory may be what Thomas is rejecting in q2 a10, as this kind of indwelling is the union with God that belongs to the saints, by the accident of habitual grace.

28. Thomas differentiates between two ways in which God lifts up human nature to himself: "in one way, by operation, as the saints know and love God; in another way, by personal being, and this way is singular to Christ, in whom human nature is assumed so as to belong to the Person of the Son of God." For an operation to be perfected, as in the first case, its power requires a *habitus*; but for a nature to exist in its own suppositum, no *habitus* is required.

29. *ST* IIIa q2 a10 ad1.

30. *ST* IIIa q2 a6 c.

Thomas's explanation in a10 not only underlines the unity of Christ's personal being as the supposit for both of his natures but also distinguishes between the divinity belonging to Christ, because of this unity of his being, and the deification belonging to the saints, who are divine by participation. The difference is between "the thing itself" and its "participated likeness," between what is substantial and what is accidental by participation—for, as Thomas says in places in the *Summa* where he adverts to God's sharing of perfections (including grace) with his creatures, "what is substantially in God becomes accidental in the soul participating the divine goodness."[31] While precluding some Christological confusion, which is Thomas's main concern here, his response also makes the distinction between what belongs to the one Christ by nature because of the grace of union and what belongs to the saints by participation because of habitual grace, which runs through and underlies following explanations of Christ as the causal source of participated grace to others.

Thomas takes up the grace of union and habitual grace in Christ again in q6 a6, an article that at first seems more or less to repeat the topic of q2 a10; q6 a6 asks "whether the human nature was assumed through the medium of grace." Thomas's concern, however, is quite different, and prepares for his treatment of Christ's habitual grace in q7.[32] He indicates that, on account of the unity of natures in Christ, Christ's habitual grace is unique, flowing as it does from the grace of union. While the grace of the saints acts as a medium between them and God, raising them up by its higher nature,[33] Christ's habitual grace is not a medium for the assumption of his human nature to the Word, because it is

31. *ST* Ia-IIae q110 a2 ad2; cf. Ia q6 a3.

32. Thomas summarily reminds the reader of his answer to q2 a10 in the *sed contra*: "Grace is an accident in the soul, as was shown above. Now the union of the Word with human nature took place in the subsistence, and not accidentally, as was shown above. Therefore the human nature was not assumed by means of grace," i.e., by means of an accidental habit. He then moves on to the substance of this article.

33. In the background of the question is the notion, established in q6 a1, that lower things are directed to God through higher things, which act as a medium in a hierarchy of causality. To say that something is the medium for the assumption of the human nature to God is to say that it has a higher dignity than that nature. Thomas first establishes in a6 that the grace of union cannot be a medium for the assumption of Christ's human nature to the Word, because it is itself the term of the assumption, as "the personal being that is given freely from above to the human nature in the Person of the Word."

an effect following the union, according to John 1:14: "We saw his glory, as of the Only-begotten of the Father, full of grace and truth"; by which we are given to understand that this man is the Only-begotten of the Father, through the union [and so] he is full of grace and truth.

Christ's habitual grace does not mediate between his human nature and the Word but flows from the union itself. So, even though Christ's habitual grace is a participation in the divine nature, like that of the saints (as Thomas will teach in a7), it is not, as it is for them, something coming down upon a preexisting nature; from the moment of the union, Christ has the fullness of grace and truth. This is a Christological teaching about the unity of natures in Christ that also prepares the way for Thomas's proper discussion of the grace of Christ in his human nature in q7, alerting the reader that Christ's habitual grace is both like and unlike that of his members.

In q7 a1 Thomas gives three reasons why we must suppose habitual grace in Christ's human nature. The first has to do with the union, the second with the operation of his human nature, and the third with his role as principle of perfection for others. To each reason that Thomas gives corresponds the reply to an objection, which clarifies the reason further. First, because Christ's soul was united to the Word, it was "most fitting" that it should receive the influx of divine grace, for "the nearer any recipient is to an inflowing cause, the more it participates its influence. Now the influx of grace is from God, according to that psalm: 'The Lord will give grace and glory.'"[34] The principle that "the nearer any recipient is to an inflowing cause, the more it participates its influence"[35] can be found elsewhere in Thomas's works; it is a principle of participation metaphysics, which is expressed most clearly in the same terms as the *Summa*, in his commentary on the *Liber de causis* and also in other earlier works in slightly different language.[36] Here Thomas applies it to grace as a participation in the divine nature. In the answer to the first objection, which quotes 2 Peter 1:4 to argue that

34. *ST* IIIa q7 a1. The reference is to Ps 84:12.
35. "Quanto enim aliquod receptivum propinquius est causae influenti, tanto magis participat de influentia ipsius."
36. *Sup. de causis* 24: "Si enim diversitas receptionis influxus causae primae provenit in rebus secundum diversam virtutem recipientium, cum illa quae sunt propinquiora causae primae sint maioris virtutis, sequitur quod perfectius recipiant causam primam et eius influxum." Cf. *SCG* III.64.8: "Quanto aliquid propinquius est causae, tanto plus participat de effectu ipsius."

"Christ is not God by participation, but in truth," Thomas points to the hypostatic union as the very reason that Christ should have habitual grace:

> Because with the unity of person there remains distinction of natures, as was made clear above, the soul of Christ is not divine through its own essence. So it is fitting that it be made divine through participation, which is according to grace.

Thomas applies the distinction between what is divine "by nature" and "by participation" to Christ's soul, rather than to his person, to show that while in his person he has the divine nature, in his human nature he participates in it like other humans, by grace. The definition of grace as a participation in the divine nature serves well to anchor his Christological point.

Thomas's second reason that Christ should have habitual grace has to do with the elevation, by grace, of the operations of Christ's intellect and will—that is, it focuses on the virtues and gifts flowing from his human participation of the divine nature, which direct his soul to beatitude (in Christ's case, from the moment of conception). Thomas will treat these in subsequent articles of q7. He argues that Christ must have habitual grace because of the dignity of his soul, "whose operations were to attain so closely to God by knowledge and love, to which it is necessary for human nature to be raised by grace." The accompanying second objection is made on the basis of a mistaken understanding of Christ's operation, which again fails to advert to the distinction of natures: because Christ is the natural Son of God, he already receives the inheritance of eternal life, and as Word already does all things well, so it seems he has no need of grace. Thomas answers, though, that the human soul of Christ is itself not capable of God's uncreated act of knowledge and love, so it needs grace to attain to God by a created act of fruition. Further, Christ's human operation, which was distinct from his divine operation, made it "necessary for him to have habitual grace, whereby this operation might be perfect in him." The virtues and gifts flowing from his graced soul as principle perfected his soul's powers, to be led by the Holy Spirit in their operation to a preeminent degree.[37]

The third reason is on account of Christ's role as the principle of perfection for the human race: as human, he is the mediator between God and human beings; "hence it was fitting that he should have grace also overflow-

---

37. *ST* IIIa q7 a5. See below.

ing to others, according to Jn 1 (:16): 'From his fullness we have all received, grace for grace.'" The third objection is based on a mistaken understanding of the maxim taken from John Damascene that "Christ's humanity is the instrument of his divinity."[38] The objector thinks that no *habitus* is needed in such an instrument. But, Thomas answers, Christ's humanity was not an inanimate instrument but rather "an instrument animated by a rational soul, which is so acted upon as to act. And so, as fitting to such action, it was necessary that he have habitual grace." This language about the rational soul being acted upon so as to act is familiar to us from Thomas's discussions of God's movement of the free will by the divine *auxilium* to both its natural and graced operation. As in us, the *habitus* of grace in Christ both perfects and increases the freedom of his will and consequent action, but unlike in us, it makes of his humanity a causal instrument in giving grace to others.

These three reasons why Christ should have habitual grace—on account of the union, for the perfection of his operation, and because he is a principle for the perfection of others—are reflected in q7 aa9–10, where Thomas discusses Christ's fullness of grace, and in q8, where he treats Christ's grace as head of the Church. In each of these places, John 1:14 has a prominent place: "We saw his glory, the glory as of the only-begotten of the Father, full of grace and truth." This verse appeared in q6 a6, when Thomas argued that Christ's habitual grace was an effect of the union, and John 1:16 ("of his fullness we have all received") did, too, in q7 a1, in association with the notion of Christ's grace as principle of perfection. Earlier in the *Summa*, in the questions on the New Law of grace "given to those who believe in Christ,"[39] Thomas writes:

Now mankind became receivers of this grace through the Son of God made man, whose humanity grace filled first, and from there flowed on to us. Hence it is written (Jn 1:14): "The Word was made flesh," and afterwards: "full of grace and truth"; and further on: "Of his fullness we all have received, and grace for grace." Hence it is added that "grace and truth came by Jesus Christ."[40]

Thomas's thought on the grace of Christ, and the way in which it becomes the source of grace for us, might be seen as an extended meditation on John 1:14–17.

---

38. *De fide orthodoxa* 3.15.
40. *ST* Ia-IIae q108 a1.

39. *ST* Ia-IIae q106 a1.

In q7 a9, John 1:14 appears in the *sed contra*. In the *corpus* of a9 Thomas goes on to argue for three ways in which Christ has the fullness of grace. The first two have to do with fullness in the sense of intensity or quantity, and the last with fullness regarding power in the operations and effects of grace. Christ has grace in the most perfect way possible and in the highest degree, first, because of the union: Christ's soul is so near to the cause of grace, and the nearer a recipient is to the cause, the greater influx it receives (an echo of the participation principle given in a1). Second, in that as the effect of this intensity, Christ's soul is the principle of perfection: the soul of Christ received such grace that grace is poured out from it upon others. Because of this intensity of grace, Christ also has fullness of grace in that, as a "universal principle in the genus of those who have grace," his grace extends itself to all of the operations and effects of grace—"which are the virtues and gifts, and other things of this kind." Because Christ is uniquely "full of grace and truth," his fullness of grace extends itself not only to the perfection of his own operation but also to that of others through the virtues and gifts that flow from the grace he bestows.

Christ's habitual grace, though like ours a participation in the divine nature, is not exactly like our own, either in origin or effect. As an instrument, Christ's human nature has its own proper form and operation,[41] and his human nature alone, uniquely perfected by grace, is able to operate causally in carrying out the activity that belongs to God as the principal agent of salvation, in the one Person of the Word. Because of Christ's fullness of grace, by which his humanity participates most perfectly in the divine nature by virtue of its nearness to the source in the union, he is able to be the true mediator between God and humankind, at once the causal principle and highest example of human perfection by grace. As Thomas has already indicated from the outset of his discussion of the Incarnation, Christ is both the exemplar cause and pedagogical model of human holiness. The differences between Christ's habitual grace and ours are what make it possible for his humanity, elevated by that grace, to be the singular subordinated causal principle of participating grace to others as well as the perfect moral exemplar.[42]

---

41. *ST* IIIa q19 a1.

42. Jean Pierre Torrell discusses this distinction in "Le Christ dans la 'spiritualité' de saint Thomas," in *Christ among the Medieval Dominicans: Representations of Christ in the Texts and*

Christ as Perfect Moral Exemplar

To examine Christ's moral exemplarity, a comparison with Adam is instructive. For Christ truly to be our moral exemplar, he must set an example that we can follow. That is, in his moral life as human, he must have been subject, as we are, to the conditions of temptation and suffering, with the same need for God's assistance to reach the end. And as the perfect moral exemplar, he must have done this in a way that demonstrates the greatest potential of the human condition elevated by grace. Scripture teaches that Christ, though tested in every way, did not sin.[43] In fact, Christ was sinless from the moment of conception.[44] Yet his lack of sin does not remove him from the human condition, because Adam too was created without sin. Both had the gift of sanctifying habitual grace from the beginning, and both needed the help of auxiliary grace. Yet because Christ had the fullness of grace flowing from the union (and thus the greatest possible participation in the divine nature), he could, as the second Adam, perfectly respond to the divine *auxilium* and attain the end for which humanity was created, on behalf of all.

In Ia q95 a1 Thomas teaches that Adam received grace at the time of his creation. This was a disputed opinion, but Thomas argues that it must be so, because if Adam's original righteousness were natural, it would have remained after sin.[45] Grace was not natural to Adam, though he received it from the beginning as a gift infused into his preexisting nature, to which his free will would have consented from the first moment of his existence.[46] In this question in the Ia *pars*, Thomas has not yet laid out his explanation of the different kinds of grace required on the journey to beatitude, but he is evidently talking about habitual grace. And it follows that some auxiliary grace would have been required to move Adam's preexisting free will to his initial consent, reducing his potency to act and resulting in good moral action. Thomas explains more fully in his treatment of grace that it is above natural human powers to wish and do supernatural good even in the state of

---

Images of the Order of Preachers, ed. Kent Emery Jr. and Joseph Wawrykow (Notre Dame, IN: University of Notre Dame Press, 1998), 197–219.

43. Heb 4:15.   44. *ST* IIIa q34 a1.

45. *ST* Ia q95 a1.

46. *ST* Ia q95 a1 ad5: "As the motion of the will is not continuous there is nothing against the first man having consented to grace even in the first moment of existence."

integrity (i.e., that of Adam). God must still move the free will unweakened by sin to its act in accomplishing the good natural to it, and even more so in the case of supernatural good.[47] Because Adam was sinless, an initial operating *auxilium* would not have involved conversion of the will from sin, as it does for all humans born with original sin, but it would have moved his will to a higher end than that of nature. In the state of innocence, grace was in a sense more copious in Adam than in us, because it met with no obstacle that hindered its effect.[48] But because Adam had not yet reached the perfection of beatitude, his grace, like ours, was still the grace given to a wayfarer to bring him into future union with God. As such, it gave rise to the virtues of faith and hope proper to those who have not yet reached the goal of their journey.[49]

Adam was given grace to bring him into union with God but was still in potentiality to that union. In Christ, however, habitual grace follows upon the initial union of his human nature to God as its consequence. It does not bring him from a preexisting state of being nongraced (which is true for Adam, at least conceptually, because grace was added to Adam's nature, which already had its own independent and proper act of existing). Rather, Christ is already the Word in his personal act of existence; when his human nature began to exist as the Word, it began to exist as already perfectly holy, already in possession of a full participation of the divine nature by habitual grace.[50] Habitual grace did not dispose Christ for the union, to which he was never in potentiality, but was a stable disposition following the perfection he had already obtained, just as heat, "which was a disposition to the form of fire, is an effect flowing from the form of an already existing fire."[51]

In Christ the "fire" of the union with the divine nature already exists and radiates the "heat" of a participation in the divine nature by grace into his human soul by virtue of his very existence. So, in a certain manner, habitual grace in Christ can be called a natural property, according to Augustine in the *Enchiridion*.[52] Yet this should not be misunderstood. It is still a gift to his human nature, which has its own distinct operation and which,

---

47. *ST* Ia-IIae q109 aa2–4, a6.   48. *ST* Ia q95 a4.

49. *ST* Ia q95 a3.

50. *ST* IIIa q34 a1; cf. IIIa q17 a2, on the unity of Christ's personal being, which follows from the hypostatic union.

51. *ST* IIIa q7 a13 ad2.   52. Ibid. Cf. *Enchiridion* 15.

without grace, would not be able to attain to God by knowledge and love, as Thomas said in a1. Thomas explains that Augustine means that the grace of Christ is natural by a likeness to natural properties, as existing from the very beginning of his soul's creation.[53] While this was true for Adam as well, according to what Thomas said in the Ia *pars*, it would seem that because the grace of Christ is an effect of the union, it is also natural to him in the sense that it cannot be lost (as it was for Adam).

If Christ's habitual grace is a consequence of the union, did he still need auxiliary grace, which even in the case of sinless Adam was necessary to move the free will to consent to the gift of habitual grace? Thomas does not raise this question, or directly mention auxiliary grace in Christ by name, although he holds that Christ had a free will sanctified by grace from the moment of his conception, by which he was from that time able to merit by moving his free will toward God.[54] Having previously explained the multifaceted working of grace, is Thomas assuming the reader will take the working of auxiliary grace in Christ as given? The objection might be raised that, because Christ was already in union with God from the first moment of his existence at conception, and already a *comprehensor*,[55] he had already in a sense completed by virtue of his personal existence the journey to beatitude, which in us requires auxiliary grace to move us gradually toward the goal. If this were the case, the role of the Holy Spirit, closely associated with the action of auxiliary grace in moving the will and so "leading the sons of God," would seem to be rather diminished with respect to the movement of Christ's human nature.

But there are hints that Thomas did take it as given that Christ, in his human nature, not only received the gift of habitual grace but was also moved by the divine *auxilium*. And what Thomas has to say about Christ, as the highest exemplar, allows us to see with greater clarity the full extent of the Holy Spirit's activity in all those who follow Christ on the way to beatitude. In Ia-IIae q114 a6, on merit, Thomas says that Christ, as head of the Church and author of salvation, can merit condignly for others as well as for himself because his soul "is moved by God through grace not only to reach the glory of life everlasting but also to lead others to it." Thom-

---

53. *ST* IIIa q34 a3 ad2.   54. Ibid..
55. *ST* IIIa q34 a4.

as has already established in q114 a3 that the condign merit of meritorious works "proceeds from the grace of the Holy Spirit moving us to everlasting life." As Wawrykow points out, although Thomas does not use the language about different kinds of grace that he established in earlier questions, it seems clear that Thomas is referring at this point in a3 to the grace of *auxilium*.[56] Thomas also seems to refer merit to habitual grace in a3, when he attributes the worth of the work to "the dignity of grace, whereby man, being made partaker of the divine nature, is adopted as a son of God, to whom the inheritance is due by right of adoption." The condignity of merit for humans other than Christ depends upon the presence and causal activity of the Holy Spirit in both the habitual grace that makes them God-like and adopted sons of God and the *auxilium* that moves them to the acts befitting their state.[57] When Thomas says that grace moves Christ to merit condignly for himself and others, we can assume he means that the Holy Spirit's grace gives the greatest possible worth to the meritorious works Christ carried out by his free will because he, who is the natural Son of God, participates most fully in the divine nature in his humanity and so must be of all humans most disposed to be moved by *auxilium* to his act. God's movement of Christ's soul by grace to merit for himself and others is ultimately founded in the divine *ordinatio*, in which Christ, ordained to be the savior of all, is given grace in such a high degree that it is sufficient for the salvation of all, as principle and highest exemplar. He illustrates in the highest manner the dignity and perfection of all whom God causes to merit by grace.[58]

Thomas's discussion of Christ's habitual grace and possession of the virtues and gifts in IIIa q7 seems to confirm the idea that Christ provides the highest example of the way in which habitual grace disposes the soul to be

---

56. Wawrykow, *God's Grace and Human Action: "Merit" in the Theology of Thomas Aquinas* (Notre Dame, IN: University of Notre Dame Press, 1995), 194–95n100.

57. Cf. also *ST* Ia-IIae q114 a3 ad3, where Thomas says that the Holy Spirit, whose grace is the seed of glory, dwells in the human being (i.e., in habitual grace) as the sufficient cause of everlasting life.

58. See Wawrykow's discussion in *God's Grace and Human Action*, 233–47, esp. 238ff. As Wawrykow also points out, Thomas does not think that Christ merited for himself the increase of habitual grace and the beatific vision as do we, because he was already a *comprehensor* from the moment of his conception (see *ST* IIIa q34 a4). Christ merited the secondary features associated with the beatific vision, which by dispensation he did not possess in the world, such as the glorification of the body (see IIIa q49 a6 ad3).

moved by the *auxilium* of the Holy Spirit. In the *sed contra* of q7 a1 he places a quote from Isaiah 11—"The Spirit of the Lord shall rest upon him"—
and so frames this reply and the whole of q7 in the context of the activity
of the Holy Spirit—"which, indeed," he remarks, "is said to be in man by
habitual grace"—in bestowing the gifts of grace. Wawrykow observes that
in q7 Thomas takes "the grace of Christ as an individual man" to cover not
only habitual grace but also Christ's possession of the virtues, gifts, and gratuitous graces, all of which flow from habitual grace and thus from the presence and activity of the Holy Spirit.[59] Isaiah 11:2–3 also figured prominently
earlier in the *Summa*, where Thomas treated the gifts of the Holy Spirit (as
will be discussed in more depth in chapter 5), anchoring his explanation of
the gifts as "in-spiration," by which the Holy Spirit moves the graced person
to "follow well the promptings of God."[60] The gifts are "perfections of the
soul's powers, inasmuch as these have a natural aptitude to be moved by the
Holy Spirit."[61] They dispose the person, whose reason is informed by the
theological virtues, to be led by the Holy Spirit in their perfect operation
toward the supernatural end. In q7 a5 Thomas argues that Christ, giver of
the Holy Spirit in his divine nature, possessed the gifts in his human nature
"to a pre-eminent degree."[62]

   Of all the gifts of the Spirit belonging to Christ, Thomas singles out in
q7 a6 the gift of fear for special examination. He does so, it seems, precisely
to underline Christ's docility in his human nature to the promptings of the
Holy Spirit. Christ did have the gift of fear, as is clear from its description
among the gifts attributed to him in Isaiah 11:3, which Thomas places in
the *sed contra*.[63] Yet fear is especially associated earlier in the *Summa* with
the virtue of hope, which, as the first objector argues, Thomas has denied
to Christ as *comprehensor*. Because Christ on earth already experienced the
beatific vision, according to Thomas, he had neither faith nor hope, virtues
attendant upon the imperfection of the knowledge and possession of God

---

59. Joseph Wawrykow, "Christ and the Gifts of the Holy Spirit According to Thomas
Aquinas," in *Kirchenbild und Spiritualität: Dominikanische Beiträge zur Ekklesiologie und zum
kirchlichen Leben im Mittelalter. Festschrift für Ulrich Horst zum 75. Geburtstag*, ed. T. Prügl
and M. Schlosser (Paderborn: Schöning, 2007), 58–59. The virtues and gifts in Christ are discussed more fully in chapter 5 in relation to charity and wisdom.

60. *ST* Ia-IIae q68 aa1–2.   61. *ST* IIIa q7 a5.
62. Ibid.
63. "He shall be filled with the spirit of the fear of the Lord" (Isa 11:3).

experienced by those who are only wayfarers in the present life.[64] As Waw-rykow points out, however, it is the virtue of charity that primarily radicates the gifts of the Spirit, so the absence of fear and hope in Christ does not affect the gifts.[65] In Thomas's earlier discussion of the gifts in general, he says that "whoever has charity has all the gifts of the Holy Spirit, none of which one can possess without charity." This is so, Thomas says, because the Holy Spirit dwells in us by charity.[66] Christ, who was filled with the grace of the Holy Spirit, possessed the virtue of charity superabundantly. Furthermore, it should not surprise us that Christ, although a *comprehensor*, possessed the gifts that make the soul docile to the Spirit's promptings in the divine *auxilium*—even though he had in a manner of speaking already attained the end of his journey to beatitude—because the gifts, along with charity, remain in heaven.[67] There, their operation is most perfect because "the movement of the Holy Spirit will be especially realized in heaven, when God will be 'all in all,' and man entirely subject to him."[68] That is, it is especially in beatitude that the soul is fully subject to the Spirit's *auxilium*.

With regard to this complete subjection to God in heaven, the gift of fear is especially significant—the filial fear that causes the child of God to revere God out of love, and so to obey him. The more one loves God, the more one fears to be separated from him, so one's degree of filial fear is in proportion to one's charity, and to the wisdom that prompts those who participate in the divine nature to order their life to the enjoyment of God.[69] It is clear that when Thomas talks about Christ's gift of fear he is referring to this filial fear,

on account of which the soul of Christ was moved towards God by an affection of reverence (*affectu reverentiae*), led by the Holy Spirit. Hence it is said (Heb 5:7) that in all things "he was heard because of his reverence." For Christ, as man, had this affection of reverence towards God more fully and beyond all others. And so Scripture attributes to him the fullness of the fear of the Lord.[70]

Christ's enjoyment of the beatific vision as *comprehensor* is the very reason he had the gift of filial fear in such fullness. His human will, perfect-

---

64. *ST* IIIa q7 aa3–4.
65. Wawrykow, "Christ and the Gifts of the Holy Spirit," 61.
66. *ST* Ia-IIae q68 a5.
67. *ST* Ia-IIae q67 a6, q68 a6.
68. *ST* Ia-IIae q68 a6.
69. See *ST* IIa-IIae q19 a7.
70. *ST* IIIa q7 a6.

ly ordered by love for God and rendered docile by the gifts of the Spirit, of which filial fear is the first, was continually led by the Holy Spirit's *auxilium* toward the enjoyment of and complete subjection to God, already possessed in the vision.

Christ was thus perfectly obedient in his human nature to the movement of the Holy Spirit; that is, to God. This was manifest in his life in the subjection of his human nature to the Father, to whom he became "obedient unto death" (Philippians 2:8).[71] In a sense it could be said that his perfect obedience flowed as a consequence from the hypostatic union; his human operation is fully subjected to his divine operation because his humanity is the conjoined instrument of his divinity.[72] Christ's human will, like ours, was free, and perfected like ours in its operation by grace, virtues, and gifts.[73] His humanity is made a perfect instrument by its perfect participation in the divine nature by grace and the perfect conformation of his intellect and will to the Word and Love through the infused virtues and gifts. Christ is thus the perfect model for us of docility to the Spirit's movement in the journey toward the union with God that is the terminus of our own participation in the divine nature. Christ teaches us what it means to participate as an instrumental cause in God's plan of salvation, perfected so as to be moved sweetly and promptly by God toward the end. Christ's habitual grace, as a participation in the divine nature like ours (though more perfectly so) disposes Christ's soul to be perfectly moved by the Spirit's *auxilium*, and thus grounds Christ's moral exemplarity, which is manifested in all the ways in which "Christ's every action is our instruction" that Thomas will treat in subsequent parts of the IIIa *pars*.[74]

71. Cf. IIIa q7 a3 ad2, q20 a1, on Christ's subjection to the Father.

72. See *ST* IIIa q2 a6 ad4, where Thomas points out that to say, as Damascene does, that Christ's humanity is an instrument "in the union of the hypostasis" (i.e., a conjoined instrument) is not the same as the Nestorian position that the humanity was *only* an instrument (i.e., a separated instrument) of the Godhead; cf. q62 a5, where Thomas distinguishes Christ's humanity as conjoined instrument of the bestowal of grace, and the sacraments as separated instruments deriving from his humanity.

73. *ST* IIIa q18 a1, a4, a6; cf. q19 a1: and so Christ could merit by his obedience (a3).

74. See *ST* III q40 a1 ad3. For a thorough discussion of Thomas's uses of this traditional axiom in its historical context, see Schenk, "*Omnis Christi actio nostra*," 111: Thomas cites this traditional axiom at least seventeen times in his works throughout his career.

Christ's Grace as Principle of Participated Perfection

The singular causal role of Christ's grace as the principle of perfection for others seems to be related, like his moral exemplarity, to the perfect participation in the divine nature of his humanity as the instrument of his divinity. Although Christ's fullness of grace makes him our imitable moral exemplar, it is also unique as the principle of perfection for others, exceeding the greatest possible participation of grace by the saints, because of his role in the economy of salvation. Although anyone can be said to be full of grace in the sense that they possess it fully "to the extent assigned by God" (e.g., the Blessed Virgin), only in Christ is the absolute limit of grace attained "inasmuch as grace is possessed in its highest possible excellence and in its greatest possible extension to all its effects," and so the fullness of grace is proper to Christ alone.[75]

In q7 a9, as mentioned above, in the course of arguing for Christ's fullness of grace, Thomas says that Christ has grace in its highest possible degree because his soul is so near to the cause of grace, and "the nearer a recipient is to the inflowing cause, the more it receives." Thomas follows this mention of the participation principle he introduced in q7 a1 by adding that Christ's soul received so much grace,

that in a manner it is poured out from it upon others. And so it was fitting that he should have the greatest grace, as fire which is the cause of heat in all hot things, is the hottest one.

Thomas uses participation language to express the way in which Christ's habitual grace, itself a participation in the divine nature to the highest degree, is therefore able to be a principle of participation to others. The intensity of habitual grace in Christ is compared to a fire, which as the hottest thing is also the cause of heat to others. Thomas uses this same metaphor consistently in places in the *Summa* (and elsewhere) where he talks about the way in which what is essential in God is participated to creatures in creation and grace: in the participation and upholding of existence itself,[76] of

75. *ST* IIIa q7 a10.

76. *ST* Ia q3 a4, q8 a1, q44 a1. Cf. *SCG* II.155, III.66.7; *Sup. Ioh.* pr1 (also 1.5, 5.5, 10.6). This fire metaphor in connection with participation in general can be found even in Thomas's early work, the *De ente et essentia*, where he refers it to Aristotle's *Metaphysics*, though Aristotle him-

perfections,[77] of goodness,[78] and in three separate places of the participation in the divine nature given by grace.[79] With reference to the causation of accidental forms in things by substances that possess the greatest intensity of a quality, it can apply to participation within the created order (where the quality in the cause is maximally present but univocal in nature with that in the accident), and also to participation of creatures in the divine perfections (which subsist in God essentially but not in creatures), as Thomas uses it most often in the *Summa*.[80]

The role of Christ's human nature per se as principle in participating grace to others must be of the former kind. Grace belongs to his human nature maximally but not essentially; it is still, like ours, only a participation in the divine nature, although it is subordinated to his divine activity in an instrumental way. As head of the Church, he gives grace authoritatively as God but instrumentally as human.[81] Christ's humanity is the instrument of his divinity not only with respect to his own moral perfection (thus making him the model for others) but also, on account of his own fullness of grace, with respect to the communication of grace to others, as the author

---

self does not use participation language in connection with it. *De ente et essentia* 6.3: "Quod dicitur maxime et verissime in quolibet genere, est causa eorum quae sunt post in illo genere, sicut ignis qui est in fine caliditatis est causa caloris in rebus calidis, ut in II metaphysicae dicitur, ideo substantia quae est primum in genere entis, verissime et maxime essentiam habens, oportet quod sit causa accidentium, quae secundario et quasi secundum quid rationem entis participant." Cf. Aristotle, *Metaphysics* II 1 993b24. David L. Whidden recently published an interesting study of Aquinas's use of the metaphor of light in which he similarly notes the role of participation metaphysics, especially in relation to participation in the illumination received through Christ in creation and grace. *Christ the Light: The Theology of Light and Illumination in Thomas Aquinas* (Minneapolis: Fortress Press, 2014).

77. *ST* Ia q4 a2.

78. *ST* Ia q6 a3. Cf. *SCG* I.40.3.

79. *ST* Ia-IIae q62 a1 ad1, q112 a1; IIIa q62 a1. In his *Commentary on Colossians*, in a discussion of the way in which the angels are named from their participation of divine properties, Thomas remarks that "in Sacred Scripture, what is divine is signified by fire: 'The Lord your God is a devouring fire' (Dt 4:24). And so the highest order of angels is called the seraphim, as though on fire with God and having a divine property" (*Sup. Col.* ch1 lect4).

80. As discussed below, Thomas places a text from John Damascene containing this metaphor as his authority in the *sed contra* of an article on the Eucharist to argue that the fire of our charity is hindered by venial sins. Damascene compares the Eucharist to the burning coal taken from the altar and placed on the lips of the prophet Isaiah: "by participation of the divine fire we are enkindled and deified." *ST* IIIa q79 a8.

81. *ST* IIIa q8 a1 ad1.

of salvation. We have seen that with respect to his own perfection his perfect participation in the divine nature by his habitual grace makes him perfectly obedient to the divine *auxilium*. How exactly does the instrumentality of Christ's human nature in communicating grace to others as head relate to its perfect participation in the divine nature by habitual grace? How does this definition of grace as a *participatio divinae naturae* in the *Summa* shape Thomas's understanding of how Christ's humanity communicates grace as the instrument of his divinity?

Thomas's understanding of instrumental causality in general, and of the instrumental role of Christ's humanity in particular, seems to have evolved over the course of his career.[82] In the *Summa* he presents a fully developed picture of the way in which secondary created causes participate in and are noncompetitively subordinated to the action of the primary divine cause. J. R. Geiselmann observes that in the *Scriptum*, discussing Christ's grace of headship, Thomas speaks of Christ's humanity as fulfilling only a preparatory or dispositive role in the bestowal of grace, one that makes it possible to be graced but does not accomplish this work itself.[83] In the *Scriptum* Thomas says that grace flows from God through the "disposing medium" of Christ as

82. On this, see Theophil Tschipke, *L'humanité du Christ comme instrument de salut de la divinité*, Studia Friburgensia: Neue Folge 94, intr. B. D. de La Soujeole, trans. P. Secretan (Fribourg: Academic Press, 2003). Tschipke's study accords well with the findings of this project. He shows that Thomas's understanding of the instrumentality of Christ's humanity develops between the *Scriptum* and the *Summa theologiae*, under the influence of his exposure to the later Greek Fathers, and is first fully articulated in its mature form in the *Summa contra Gentiles*. Thomas's early conception "excludes a true efficacious communication of grace by Christ's humanity," assigning to it only a prevenient role and reserving true efficacy to the divinity alone (117). Later, because of his deepening understanding of the concept of "instrument" in general, Thomas moves to the idea that Christ's humanity participates instrumentally in the works of the divinity with one efficacy (125, 131ff). In *SCG* IV.41 Thomas first describes Christ's humanity as the proper and conjoined instrument of his divinity by consequence of the hypostatic union; this notion completes his understanding of the participated divine efficacy of Christ's human action (124–25, 138) and leads to the development of his thought on the communication of the work of salvation through Christ's sacraments as separated instruments (cf. 140, 163ff). For an excellent study of the development of Thomas's understanding of the instrumental efficient causality of Christ's human will in the work of salvation, see Corey Barnes, *Christ's Two Wills in Scholastic Thought: The Christology of Aquinas and Its Historical Contexts* (Toronto: Pontifical Institute of Mediaeval Studies, 2012).

83. "Eine die Begnadung ermöglichende, nicht aber bewirkende." J. R. Geiselmann, "Christus und die Kirche nach Thomas von Aquin," *Theologische Quartalschrift* 107 (1926): 198–222, esp. 217.

human, "for he disposes the whole human race for the reception of grace"—
as the object of our justifying faith; by removing the obstacles to grace in
satisfying for sin and meriting and interceding for us; and, by virtue of the
union, making human nature more acceptable to God.[84] At the very end of
the *De veritate*, Geiselmann shows, Thomas moves to a truly instrumental
role for Christ's humanity in causing grace.[85] A parallel overall development
in Thomas's understanding of the proper subordinated instrumentality of
secondary created causes may be observed in Thomas's understanding of sacramental causality [86] and, it might be argued, in his view of grace and merit in the predestined, discussed above. In all of these cases there is a general
shift toward the idea that created causality, while proper to the creature in
itself, is also fully subordinated to the divine causality of its source.

One reason seems to be the increasingly central place that Thomas gives
to the idea of participation in his metaphysics, and thus in the philosophical underpinnings of his theology. Te Velde shows that, by the time of the
later *De potentia* at least, Thomas has developed the concept of instrumental causality "further along Neoplatonic lines" to explain how God is immanent as an active cause in the activity of nature itself. In *De pot.* q3 a7 Thomas argues that "an instrument is in a certain sense the cause of the effect of
the principal cause, not through its own form or power, but inasmuch as it
participates through its movement something of the power of the principal

---

84. *Scriptum* bk3 d13 q2 a1: "Deus immediate format mentem nostram quantum ad ipsam
perfectionem gratiae; et tamen potest ibi cadere medium disponens; et sic gratia fluit a Deo
mediante homine Christo: ipse enim disposuit totum humanum genus ad susceptionem gratiae; et hoc tripliciter. Uno modo secundum operationem nostram in ipsum: quia secundum
quod credimus ipsum Deum et hominem, justificamur; Rom. 3, 25: 'quem posuit Deus propi-
tiatorem per fidem in sanguine ipsius.' Alio modo per operationem ipsius in nos, inquantum
scilicet obstaculum removet, pro peccatis totius humani generis satisfaciendo; et etiam inquantum nobis suis operibus gratiam et gloriam meruit; et inquantum pro nobis interpellat apud
Deum. Tertio modo ex ipsa ejus affinitate ad nos; quia ex hoc ipso quod humanam naturam
assumpsit, humana natura est magis Deo accepta."

85. J. R. Geiselmann, "Christus und die Kirche nach Thomas von Aquin," *Theologische
Quartalschrift* 108 (1927): 233–55, esp. 240. See, e.g., *DV* q29 a3 ad5.

86. H. F. Dondaine has noted a strengthening of Thomas's notion of instrumental causality
in the sacraments from the *Scriptum* to the *Summa* (which he attributes to a shift from Avicennian to Averroist Aristotelianism), such that the sacraments move from a purely dispositive role
to operation as true efficient causes subordinated to the divine causality. "A propos d'Avicenne et
de S. Thomas: De la causalité dispositive a la causalité instrumentale," *Revue thomiste* 51 (1951):
441–53.

cause." That is, as te Velde explains, the instrument produces an effect that it could not produce by itself because it participates in the primary cause, whose power is immanent in it.[87]

Something of this understanding of instrumental causality with respect to Christ's own grace already seems to be at work in the *DV* q29 a5, where Thomas considers whether Christ, as head, requires habitual grace:

As Damascene says, the humanity of Christ in some sense "was the instrument of the divinity"; and thus his actions could be salvific. Inasmuch as it was specially the instrument of the divinity, then, it had to have a certain special connection with the divinity. The nearer anything is to God's goodness, the more fully it participates in that goodness, as Dionysius makes clear (*Cel. Hier.* 12). So the humanity of Christ also, because it was connected with the divinity more closely than others and in a more special way, participated in a more excellent way in the divine goodness through the gift of grace. From this it was suitable that it should not only have grace but also that through it grace should be poured out to others, as the most shining bodies transmit the light of the sun to others. And because in some sense Christ inflows (*influit*) the effects of grace to all rational creatures, this is why he is in some sense the principle of all grace in his humanity, just as God is the source of all being. So that, as all the perfection of being is united in God, in Christ the fullness of all grace and virtue is found, through which he is not only able for the work of grace himself but can bring others to grace as well. For this reason he has the headship.

Although Thomas has not yet arrived at his mature understanding of grace as a participation in the divine nature, the participation principle applied in the *Summa* (which he here identifies as deriving from Dionysius) is already at work.[88] Because Christ's humanity is so close to the divine source of grace, it participates in the divine goodness through the gift of grace in the highest way, and so is an instrument able to communicate it to others.

---

87. Rudi A. te Velde, *Participation and Substantiality in Thomas Aquinas* (Leiden: E. J. Brill, 1995), 165–66.

88. Geiselmann also notices that the "inner reason" for the place of Christ's humanity as true instrument of the Godhead in giving grace is given in this article as the Neoplatonic doctrine according to which "a partaker *per eminentia* becomes capable as well of giving a share to others." "Christus und die Kirche" (1927), 248. Tschipke observes that the Neoplatonic doctrine of the diffusion of light in this article is not sufficiently explanatory and is completed in later works by the Aristotelian principle that "everything acts in the measure in which it is in act" (cf. below, on *ST* IIIa q8). *L'humanité du Christ*, 124.

The instrumentality of Christ's humanity in bestowing grace to others depends specially upon its participation in the divine source. To put it in a way that is more obvious in the *Summa*, Christ's habitual grace, because it flows from the grace of union by a perfect participation, is also the grace of headship.

By way of contrast, it is interesting to briefly examine Thomas's early thought on the relationship between these three kinds of grace in Christ in the *Scriptum*, where, as noted above, Geiselmann has shown that Thomas sees the role of Christ's humanity as dispositive rather than fully instrumental in bestowing grace on others as head. If Christ's humanity only makes the bestowal of grace possible as a disposing cause, rather than actually bestowing it instrumentally, then it is not involved, even in a subordinated manner, in one and the same causal activity as the principal agent. This would lead one to expect that in the *Scriptum* Thomas does not yet understand the relationship between Christ's grace of union, his habitual grace, and his grace of headship in terms of the participation principle outlined above—that Christ is the principle of grace for others as head because of his own perfect human participation of the divine goodness in his habitual grace flowing from the union.

In the *Scriptum* bk3 d13 Thomas examines the grace of Christ. In contrast to his order of proceeding in the *Summa*—where he treats the grace of union first and much earlier (in IIIa q2 aa10–12) than Christ's habitual and capital grace (in qq7–8)—he does not consider the grace of union in the *Scriptum* until the third and last question of d13, beginning instead with a question on the grace of Christ as an individual man—that is, his habitual grace (parallel to *ST* IIIa q7)—followed by a question on Christ's grace of headship (parallel to *ST* IIIa q8). This alone should tell us that he does not yet view Christ's habitual grace and grace of headship as ineluctably flowing from the grace of union. In d13 q1 a1 Thomas argues that Christ, as an individual man, must have a created form of grace in his soul (i.e., a *habitus*), which fulfills the two roles of grace: the perfection of his spiritual being (which in him was "most perfect") and the perfection of his human operation. The principal concerns here are to emphasize the perfection of Christ's humanity and its distinction from his divine nature. Thomas does not yet understand habitual grace as a participation in the divine nature. The main point is that because Christ truly has a human nature and operation, a *ha-*

bitus is required for their perfection. This teaching does not disappear from Thomas's later treatment, but in the parallel article in the *Summa*, IIIa q7 a1, Thomas grounds his argument for habitual grace in Christ not simply in the requirements of his distinct human nature within the union but in the dynamic effect of this union: because Christ's soul is so close to the divine nature, it fittingly received the greatest influx of grace for the elevation of its own operations, and so this grace could overflow to others (i.e., the participation principle). In the *Summa*, this dynamic frames Thomas's reference to and clarification of Damascene's teaching, which appears in both the *Scriptum* and the *Summa*, that Christ's humanity is a rational instrument of the Godhead, which acts as well as being acted upon and thus requires a *habitus*.[89]

When Thomas turns to Christ's fullness of grace in d13 q1 a2 qc1, one difference with the parallel article in *ST* IIIa q7 a9 immediately appears. In contrast to his treatment in the *Summa*, where Christ's fullness of grace refers only to his habitual grace, in the *Scriptum* Thomas treats Christ's grace of union, habitual grace, and grace of headship as different aspects of his fullness of grace, organizing them all into a threefold scheme of Aristotelian causes.[90] The fullness of Christ's grace of union is to be understood according to the *ratio* of final causality. That is, because the end of grace is to unite us to God, and Christ's humanity was personally united to God, "his grace most fully followed his end."[91] He has fullness of the grace of headship according to the *ratio* of efficient causality because "he has grace through which he is perfected in himself, and also from him it overflows to others." Additionally, Christ has the fullness of individual (i.e., habitual) grace "according to the *ratio* of formal causality," for, in a manner exceeding that of

---

89. There is a slight but possibly significant difference between the *Scriptum* and *Summa* in the way that Thomas expresses this characteristic of the rational (or animate) instrument. In the *Scriptum* (bk3 d13 q1 a1 ad4) he says the soul of Christ is *instrumentum animatum*, which *et agit et agitur* (both acts and is acted upon). In the *Summa* (IIIa q7 a1 ad3) he describes Christ's humanity as "*instrumentum animatum anima rationali, quod ita agit quod etiam agitur*" (is so acted upon as also to act). The participation of the causal activity of Christ's humanity in that of his divinity seems clearer in the *Summa*.

90. There may be some link to Albert the Great's treatment of the *triplex* grace of Christ in his *Sentences* commentary, although in terms of causality he focuses only on the efficient causality of Christ's grace of headship. Albertus Magnus, "*Commentarii in III Sententiarum* bk3 d13 a3," in *Opera Omnia*, ed. A. Borgnet (Paris: Vivès, 1890–99).

91. "*Gratia ipsius plenissime consecuta est finem suum.*"

all the saints, Christ's grace perfected him in every virtue and use of virtue, gave to him all of the gratuitous graces, and made him completely sinless.

Thomas would later abandon the slightly awkward attempt to fit the traditional three graces of Christ under the simple rubric of three Aristotelian causes as a way of framing the relationship between them. He comes to attribute Christ's fullness of grace to his habitual grace in particular, flowing from the union and overflowing in his grace of headship, apparently for scriptural reasons that are most explicit in his treatment in the *Compendium theologiae*, written later in his career, but are also in evidence in the *Summa*. That is, according to John 1:14–16, "the very fact that the Word was made flesh entailed the consequence that he was full of grace and truth," and "since the man Christ possessed supreme fullness of grace ... grace overflowed from him to others." Thomas observes in the *Compendium*:

The Evangelist presents these three kinds of grace in due order. Regarding the grace of union he says, "The Word was made flesh." Regarding Christ's individual grace he says: "We saw him, as it were the only-begotten of the Father, full of grace and truth." Regarding the grace of headship he adds, "And of his fullness we have all received."[92]

Here, as in the *Summa*, Christ's habitual grace is a kind of central causal link between his grace of union and his grace of headship, and it is a point about the causal chain relating the three graces, eventuating in the bestowal of grace on others, that Thomas wishes to make, rather than a simple systematization according to different causal categories.

In the context of the *Scriptum*'s treatment of the grace of union, Thomas considers the ordering of the three graces in a quaestiuncula that roughly corresponds to *ST* III q7 a13. *Scriptum* bk3 d13 q3 a2 qc3 asks "whether Christ's personal grace precedes the grace of union." Thomas's answer once again is a straightforward systematization of the three graces, which "can be attributed to Christ under diverse considerations." Christ can be considered in himself or in comparison to others. If Christ is considered in himself as God, the grace of union is attributed to him—if, as human, his individual grace is attributed to him. Considered in comparison to others, he has the grace of headship. Because someone is considered in himself first, the grace of headship must follow the other two graces. The grace of union is prior to

---

92. *Comp. theol.* 1.214. Cf. *ST* Ia-IIae q108 a1; IIIa q1 a6; q6 a6; q7 a1, a7, a9, a10, a12; q8 a1, a5.

his personal grace in the order of nature and understanding, although not of time, because every grace and human perfection belongs to Christ, on account of God's union with humanity in his Person.

A comparison with Thomas's treatment in the *Summa* shows once again a quite different focus in the latter. *ST* IIIa q7 a13 asks "whether the habitual grace of Christ followed after the union." Thomas has already established, with reference to John 1:14, that Christ's habitual grace is an effect following the union "because this man (as a result of the union) is the only-begotten of the Father, he is full of grace and truth."[93] He says in q7 a13 that "the grace of union precedes the habitual grace of Christ, not in order of time, but in nature and understanding." This basic answer to the question is the same as in the *Scriptum*. The reasons Thomas gives are quite different, however, and draw on teaching he has established elsewhere in the *Summa* to reveal a deeper reflection on grace itself.

His first reason is grounded in the order of the divine missions: the Son is principle of the union in his mission, the Holy Spirit principle of habitual grace when he is sent to dwell in the mind by charity. The mission of the Son is prior in nature to that of the Holy Spirit because "the Holy Spirit proceeds from the Son, and love from wisdom." So the union is prior to habitual grace by nature. Second, grace is caused by the presence of the Godhead in us, "as light in air by the presence of the sun," and God is present in Christ by the union, so habitual grace follows this union "as light follows the sun." Third, grace is ordained to action, which presupposes the operating hypostasis; the hypostasis in Christ's human nature did not exist before the union, so the union precedes habitual grace in thought. We know from earlier articles that the nearness of Christ's soul to the presence of the Godhead because of the union (to which the second reason refers) causes in him the fullness of habitual grace from the beginning of his existence, so, as Thomas puts it in the reply to an objection, habitual grace in Christ is not something disposing for the union, but rather a perfection following the union as heat "is an effect flowing from the form of already existing fire."[94]

Unlike in the *Scriptum*, here the fullness of grace in Christ consists in the perfection of his habitual grace alone; the fullness of his habitual grace is not just one aspect of Christ's fullness of grace, "according to the *ratio* of

93. *ST* IIIa q6 a6.
94. *ST* IIIa q7 a13 ad2.

formal causality," but is the entire effect of the causal influx of the conjoined divine nature upon his human nature, the perfect participation of the latter in the former, which makes of it in turn an instrumental principle of participation to others as head, according to the participation principle established earlier. This makes clearer the identity between Christ's habitual grace and grace of headship, which cannot be fully explained in the *Scriptum*. Christ's fullness of habitual grace refers only to his possession in himself of the greatest formal perfection of grace, while the fullness of his grace of headship is what signifies the efficient causality of his grace in that, perfect in him, it overflows to others—only in the sense, however, that his graced humanity disposes them for the reception of grace from God themselves. The two graces are compared to each other as to a relation either to himself or to others. While their identity is implied, as two aspects of the one grace of Christ, the true reason for their identity has not been worked through as in Thomas's later work, where he has clarified his thought on the nature of habitual grace itself. In the *Scriptum*, where Christ's humanity, though formally perfected in itself by grace is not yet understood to be the instrumental cause of bestowing that *same* grace on others, the grace of headship cannot be seen as the extension to others of God working through the fullness of Christ's own habitual grace in his humanity in a single causal action. In the *Summa* Christ's own participation in the divine nature by his habitual grace flowing from the union, by virtue of thus being a principle of participation to others, makes his habitual grace instrumentally the grace of headship.

So Thomas argues in III q8 a5 that Christ's fullness of habitual grace flowing from the union is the reason his habitual grace and grace of headship are the same:

It is written, "Of his fullness we have all received" (Jn 1:16). He is our head, in that we receive from him. Therefore, he is our head, inasmuch as he has the fullness of grace. Now he had the fullness of grace, inasmuch as personal grace was perfectly in him, as was said above. Therefore according to his personal grace he is our head. And so his capital grace and personal grace are not distinct.[95]

To the extent to which we are able to receive it, we receive from Christ what he has himself in fullness.[96] On account of his fullness of personal

---

95. *ST* IIIa q8 a5, *sed contra*.
96. In the *Scriptum*, as Geiselmann points out, in speaking of Christ as minister of the

grace, flowing from the union, Christ can be the principle of grace to others. Thomas explains this in the terms he has used before when he established the participation principle in earlier articles, stressing the identity of Christ's grace and that given to others. He employs the language of potency and act used throughout the *Summa* in connection with participation:[97]

Everything acts insofar as it is a being in act. It is necessary that it be the same act by which something is in act and acts, and so it is the same heat by which a fire is hot, and by which it heats. But not every act by which something is in act suffices to make it the principle of acting on others, for "the agent is nobler than the patient" as Augustine says (*Super Gen. ad Litt.*, 12.16) and the Philosopher, in *De Anima* (3.19), that which acts on others must have a certain eminence of act. But it was said above that grace was received by the soul of Christ in its maximum eminence; and so from the eminence of grace which he received, it belongs to him that that grace (*illa gratia*) is derived to others, which pertains to the *ratio* of a head. And so the personal grace by which the soul of Christ is justified, is the same in essence as his grace as head of the Church justifying others, although they differ according to *ratio*.

Christ himself is eminently in act in his humanity by his personal participation in grace. His grace could not increase because he already participates as a subject as fully as possible in the form of grace, because "air cannot increase in heat when it has reached the utmost limit of heat which can exist in it" and also because that form itself reaches its utmost perfection in him: "e.g., if we say that there cannot be a more perfect grade of heat than that which fire attains."[98] And so, his humanity, conjoined to the Word whose personal *esse* is Pure Act, is able to work as the perfect instrument of the Word in actualizing others by bestowing on them the new being of grace.

Like the blessed, Christ has already attained the highest possible level of actuality possible to him by grace, in his case because he "was a true and

---

Holy Spirit in his humanity, Thomas explains Jn 1:16 by saying that "there is some likeness in what is handed over, but it is not properly a handing over": there is a likeness because one and the same uncreated Spirit descends undivided from head to body; there is an unlikeness, however, because "that same gift, by which the Holy Spirit dwells in us ... is not handed over from subject to subject." In the *Scriptum* it is God alone who gives grace, while Christ as minister in his humanity bestows the Holy Spirit, who is its source. *Scriptum* bk3 d13 q2 a1 ad1, ad2. See Geiselmann, "Christus und die Kirche" (1926), 214–15.

97. As Geiselmann puts it, in the *Summa theologiae* Thomas completes the Neoplatonic principle in an Aristotelian sense. "Christus und die Kirche" (1927), 248.

98. *ST* IIIa q7 a12.

full comprehensor from the first instant of his conception."[99] But unlike the blessed and the angels, Christ in his humanity is the cause of bringing others to beatitude, by virtue of the preeminence of his own knowledge of God in the vision. Christ had to have this preeminence in order to bring humans, who are in potentiality to the knowledge of the blessed, to their end, for, Thomas repeats again in IIIa q9 a2, "what is in potentiality is reduced to act by what is in act; for that whereby things are heated must itself be hot." Christ is indeed the head of all human beings, who even outside of the visible Church are in potentiality to union with him.[100] Christ is thus the "author of salvation" and the "first universal principle in the genus of those who have grace" because he participates most fully by his habitual grace in what he participates to others—a share in the divine nature itself, by which the image is ultimately perfected in its essence and activities for the "light participated from the divine nature" that is beatitude.[101]

Christ's Sacraments and Participation in the Divine Nature

The questions on Christ's priesthood and his sacraments are the last places in the *Summa* where Thomas uses his definition of grace as a participation in the divine nature, which perfects the essence of the soul, flows into its powers through the virtues and gifts, and provides "a certain divine assistance" in attaining the end of each sacrament in the Christian life.[102] The "participated likeness of the divine nature" that is grace extends from God as principal cause through the conjoined instrumental cause of Christ's humanity to his sacraments as separated instrumental causes of grace.[103] The sacraments, then, are instrumental causes of deification.

Christ, as priest and victim on the Cross, is mediator between God and the human race, bestowing the Incarnation's divine gifts of reconciliation and a share in the divine nature.[104] And the sacraments as his instruments "derive their power especially from the Passion of Christ, the power of which is in a manner united to us in receiving the sacraments."[105] More will be said of all this in chapter 6, after examining Thomas's treatments of

---

99. *ST* IIIa q8 a5.
100. *ST* IIIa q8 a2.
101. *ST* IIIa q9 a2 ad1; cf. Ia q12.
102. *ST* IIIa q62 aa1–2.
103. *ST* IIIa q62 a1, a5.
104. *ST* IIIa q22.
105. *ST* IIIa q62 a5.

charity and wisdom, for it is especially through charity and wisdom that we are conformed through the sacraments to Christ in the priestly sacrifice of his Passion. But here we can consider how grace itself, as a participation in the divine nature, is the root of this deifying conformation. When Thomas discusses the Passion of Christ, he says that Christ merited salvation by his Passion "not only for himself, but likewise for all his members" specifically because "grace was bestowed on Christ, not only as an individual, but inasmuch as he is head of the Church, so that it might overflow into his members."[106] The sacraments derive their power, then, from the fullness of Christ's grace in its effects. As head, Christ could atone for our sins, offer satisfaction for us, redeem us from guilt, and reconcile us to God by his sacrifice, and so it is as head that he is our priest.[107] His Passion "accomplishes human salvation efficiently" because "all Christ's actions and sufferings [in his humanity] operate instrumentally by the power of his divinity, for human salvation."[108] This is the power at work in us in the sacraments, which give us a participation in the divine nature that is, in a sense, derived from Christ's own. Christ's graced human nature is thus a kind of primary mediating principle of participation in the divine nature, as a conjoined instrument in a pattern of mediation of grace that extends through the sacraments, as separated instruments of his humanity.

Christ's humanity, as God's chosen instrument for the sanctification of others,[109] was itself perfected in its proper activity by the fullness of grace, so that as Mediator his grace might overflow onto others.[110] By Christ's Passion, because of his own fullness of grace and headship, we share in his grace and so participate in the divine nature. In his participation of the divine nature in his graced humanity, he is our model, and the principle of our perfection, as exemplar cause. Through our participation, we become in some sense what he is, and we do what he does. So his resurrection too is the cause of ours—the efficient cause of the resurrection of the wicked and just alike, but for the just alone who will rise with him in glory, the exem-

---

106. *ST* IIIa q48 a1.   107. *ST* IIIa q48; q22 a1 ad3; cf. q49.
108. *ST* IIIa q48 a6.

109. For a good discussion of the instrumental causality of Christ's humanity in Thomas's works, cf. Paul Crowley, "*Instrumentum divinitatis* in Thomas Aquinas: Recovering the Divinity of Christ," *Theological Studies* 52 (1991): 451–75, esp. 473.

110. *ST* IIIa, q7 a1 c., ad3; cf. aa9–10.

plar cause as well, for they have been "conformed to his sonship, according to Rom 8:29."[111] As discussed in chapter 6, it is especially through the Eucharist—memorial of Christ's Passion, bond of communion, and pledge of future glory—that we are brought by charity and wisdom into the fellowship of the Son, and so to a participation in his sonship that will be made perfect in heaven.

Participation in the Divine Nature as Participation in Christ's Sonship

We begin to arrive at the full meaning of Christ's gift to us of a participation in the divine nature by grace. Earlier I noted that in places in the IIa *pars* where Thomas referred to this notion he often did so in the context of passages from the Pauline letters that illustrated his teaching on the journey to beatitude of the predestined, led by the Holy Spirit, as adopted sons. Made like the one and triune God by grace, the children of God become, by virtue of their conformation to the Word and Love, the principle of new supernatural activities, prompted by the Holy Spirit and responding in filial obedience. Participation in the divine nature by grace is, in effect, adopted sonship. It is not surprising, then, that Thomas thinks that when Christ gives us a share in the divine nature, which belongs to him in his Person, and is instrumentally participated to us through his humanity, he is giving us nothing other than a participation in his own sonship.

Among the reasons Thomas gives that it is fitting for Christ to be called head of the Church in III q8 a1, his first one equates Christ's bestowal of grace with the conformation to his sonship described in Romans 8. Like a human head, Christ is principle of his body because

on account of his nearness to God his grace is the highest and first, though not in time, since all have received grace on account of his grace, according to Romans 8:29:

---

111. *ST* IIIa q56 a1 ad3. Torrell remarks that the mysteries of Christ's life "bring about an assimilation to Jesus ... and, through him, to God himself. Or more exactly: God the Father, by acting in us through the grace which he bestows on us through the mediation of Christ, conforms us to the image of his first-born Son. Our grace is a grace of adopted sons, but also of suffering, of death, of resurrection and of ascension through him, with him and in him. We are here at the heart of ontological exemplarism and of the mystery of Christ-conforming grace." "Le Christ dans la 'spiritualité,'" 207 (my translation).

"For those whom he foreknew, he also predestined to be conformed to the image of his Son; that he might be the first-born of many brethren."

Christ's fullness of grace and his power of bestowing it on others, according to John 1:14–16— the other reasons for Christ's headship—thus receive new significance as the fullness of Christ's sonship and his power as head to participate a share in it to others. In Thomas's reflection on John 1:14 in his *Commentary on John*, he says of Christ as the "only-begotten of the Father, full of grace and truth":

If we consider the Son, insofar as sonship is conferred on others through a likeness to him, then there are many sons of God through participation. And because they are called sons of God by a likeness to him, he is called the first-born of all: "Those whom he foreknew, he also predestined to be conformed to the image of his Son; that he might be the first-born of many brethren" (Rom 8:29). So, Christ is called the only begotten of God by nature; but he is called the first-born insofar as from his natural sonship, by means of a certain likeness and participation, a sonship is granted to many.[112]

On account of Christ's fullness of grace in his humanity, the elect are given grace to participate in the natural sonship of the one who is the only begotten of God. This share in Christ's sonship is not only a share in his "legal" status as son and heir to the kingdom, but also a true participation in the divine nature in the manner of a *son*, through a specific conformation to the divine Persons by charity and wisdom, as discussed in chapter 6.

The idea that adopted sonship is a participation in Christ's natural sonship, or in the likeness of the Son, appears several times in the *Summa* as an established formula,[113] almost always in connection with Romans 8:29: "Those whom he foreknew, he also predestined to be conformed to the image of his Son." Thomas, with reference to this scriptural text and others, thought of the gift of grace as "the grace of adoption" bestowing an adopted sonship analogous to Christ's natural sonship from the time of the *Scriptum*.[114] But it is not until the time of his Scripture commentaries—as it was

---

112. *Sup. Ioh.* ch1 lect8.

113. *ST* Ia q33 a3 ad1, q41 a3; IIae-IIae q45 a6; IIIa q3 a5 ad2, q3 a8, q23 a4, q24 a3, q45 a4 ad1.

114. E.g., *Scriptum* bk3 d4 q1 a2 qc2 ad2: "Ad secundum dicendum, quod Christus dicitur primogenitus in multis fratribus secundum humanam naturam, non quasi univoce filius cum aliis, sed per analogiam: quia ipse est filius naturalis propter unionem in persona, alii

for the idea of grace as a participation in the divine nature—that he describes adopted sonship as a participation in the natural sonship of Christ. In fact, one of the first places this formulation appears is near the beginning of the *Commentary on Romans*, in connection with a discussion of Christ's predestination and ours:

> Now it is obvious that anything which exists of itself is the measure and rule of things which exist in virtue of something else and through participation. Hence, the predestination of Christ, who was predestined to be the Son of God by nature, is the measure and rule of our life and therefore of our predestination, because we are predestined to adoptive sonship, which is a participation and image of natural sonship: "Those whom he foreknew, he also predestined to be conformed to the image of his Son" (Rom 8:29).[115]

Thomas goes on to say in this passage that the goal of predestination is thus "to be the son of God in power." This is the outcome of the participation in the divine nature by grace given to the predestined, which brings the children of God, through their own activities led by the Holy Spirit, to their inheritance.

God predestined those who participate in the divine nature by grace to be "conformed to the image of his Son." In what does this conformation consist, and how do the children of God thus attain their eternal inheritance? Luc-Thomas Somme, in his study of the theme of adopted sonship in Thomas's works, notes that while divine adoption is consistently related to predestination by Thomas from the *Scriptum* to the *Summa*, and to the notion of a right to inheritance promised by the scriptural texts (e.g., Rom 8:17: "If sons, then heirs"), Thomas's later work presents a less juridical perspective of this right. That is, in the *Summa* Thomas instead emphasizes that the right to inheritance is linked to grace and merit; "its foundation is to be found in the essence of grace as a participation in the divine nature and the seed of glory, and in the Trinitarian indwelling." Through the

---

autem filii adoptivi per assimilationem ad Deum quae est per gratiam; sicut etiam dicitur primogenitus creaturae inquantum, secundum Basilium, accipere commune habet cum creatura. Unde non oportet quod ad eumdem patrem omnino referantur." See the extensive references in Luc-Thomas Somme, *Fils adoptifs de Dieu par Jésus Christ: La filiation divine par adoption dans la théologie de saint Thomas d'Aquin* (Paris: J. Vrin, 1997).

115. *Sup. Rom.* ch1 lect3. Cf. *Sup. Rom.* ch8 lect3; *Sup. Eph.* ch1 lect2; *Sup. Heb.* ch1 lect3, ch2 lect3; *Sup. Ioh.* ch1 lect8, lect11.

participation in the divine nature bestowed by grace, the Holy Spirit makes us truly merit the inheritance of sons.[116] In comparison to Thomas's earlier work, "the juridical perspective of the 'right to the inheritance' gives way to that of the 'capacity to receive it'; this acquisition is referred to the link uniting grace to glory, merit to eternal life."[117] Somme's observations accord well with the development in Thomas's mature thought discussed in chapter 3, of the definition of grace as a participation in the divine nature, and the association of this definition with the notion of the transformation and meritorious free movement of the sons of God toward beatitude.

Somme's study confirms that, in the *Summa*, Thomas shifts to and develops the notion of divine sonship by adoption as a participated likeness of divine sonship by nature. As generation defines filiation, this participation brings about a spiritual regeneration analogous to the generation of the Son.[118] Christ, as the natural Son of God, cannot be adopted, though he possesses the fullness of habitual grace that he bestows on others to make them adopted sons; as discussed earlier in this chapter, this is because Christ's habitual grace is an effect of the union and makes of him the model and principle of perfection for others.[119] Somme observes that Thomas is consistently concerned in his discussion of divine adoption about making a Christological point, that is, underlining the distinction between Christ's natural sonship as the Word and our participated sonship by grace, eliminating the possibility of adoptionism with regard to the Son and elevating our gaze to the exemplar.[120] Thomas expresses the simultaneous distinction and causal exemplarity of Christ's natural sonship to ours in a juxtaposition of scriptural terms that signify this "Christological equilibrium": Christ is both *Unigenitus* (Jn 1:14) and *Primogenitus* (Rom 8:29).[121] Somme notes that in the *Summa* Thomas also develops his attribution of our divine adoption to the Holy Spirit—through grace, charity, and the gifts of the Spirit, particularly wisdom. The latter especially assimilates us to the Son, who is uncreated Wisdom.[122] To this last point, Somme relates the perfection of the image by assimilation to the divine intellect, which reaches its culmination in the beatific vision, commenting that

---

116. Somme, *Fils adoptifs*, 59. See Ia-IIae q114 a3.
117. Somme, *Fils adoptifs*, 88.
118. Ibid., 90, 347ff.
119. *ST* IIIa q23 a4, c., ad2.
120. Somme, *Fils adoptifs*, 90.
121. Ibid., 159, 383.
122. Ibid., 64–71, 89.

divine sonship and the knowledge of God are proportional: the heavenly inheritance of the sons of God is none other than the vision of the divine essence. Divine sonship by adoption involves many states of conformity to the Son of God by nature: that of baptismal grace, and that of glory.[123]

Somme's findings—especially regarding the important role in the *Summa* of the Spirit's grace, charity, and wisdom in bestowing a participation in the sonship of Christ—are valuable and suggestive for this study, although his focus is not deification as such.

A closer look at the way in which Thomas presents adopted sonship and its goal, as the *Summa* unfolds, reveals relatively greater emphasis in later sections on the transformation of the adopted son by grace, charity, and wisdom, reflecting the increasingly nuanced picture Thomas builds of the journey of the graced image to beatitude. The roles of charity and wisdom emerge as central in conforming the image, as adopted son, to its Trinitarian exemplar, and thus as primary in deification by grace. To see this progression in the *Summa*, it is instructive to return to its first reference to the idea of divine adoption in Ia q33 a3, and to compare it with two later loci, IIIa q3 a8 and q23.

In Ia q33 Thomas is discussing the Person of the Father and his paternity. As noted in chapter 1, Thomas distinguishes different degrees of filiation in creatures with respect to God the Father, according to a likeness "which is more perfect the nearer it approaches the true *ratio* of filiation" found in God the Son. God is Father of some by the likeness of grace,

and these are also called adoptive sons, as ordained to the heritage of eternal glory by the gift of grace which they have received, according to Rom 8:16–17: "The Spirit himself gives testimony to our spirit that we are the sons of God; and if sons, heirs also." Of others [God is Father] by likeness of glory, as they have already obtained possession of the heritage of glory, according to Rom 5:2: "We glory in the hope of the glory of the sons of God."[124]

The "name of filiation is applied" to the creature, Thomas further explains, "as it participates the likeness of the Son, as is clear from the words of Rom. 8:29: 'Those whom he foreknew, he also predestined to be conformed to the image of his Son.'"[125]

---

123. Ibid., 330–31; cf. 326–28.   124. *ST* Ia q33 a3, c.
125. *ST* Ia q33 a3 ad1.

In this passage the degree of the creature's filiation corresponds with the degree of its likeness to the Son, a connection, Somme points out, not yet developed in Thomas's discussion of adoption in the *Scriptum*, where he distinguishes three kinds of filiation—by nature (i.e., that of the Son), by creation, and by adoption.[126] Yet in *ST* Ia q33 a3 the gift of grace, to which is attributed the creature's adoptive sonship, is simply described as having the function of ordaining the creature to the inheritance of glory, which the adopted son who has the likeness of glory has already received. There is no reference as yet to the means by which grace accomplishes the conformation of the creature to the Son. In terms of its "juridical perspective," this text differs little from passages in the *Scriptum* that accord the same role to grace without explaining how its effect comes about in the adopted son.[127]

In the III *pars* of the *Summa*, where Thomas has already treated from multiple perspectives the perfection of the image by grace in its journey to beatitude, much more is said about just how adopted sonship conforms one to the Son. Thomas makes reference to adopted sonship in q3 a8, early in the questions on the Incarnation. In this article, in the section where Thomas is considering the mode of union on the part of the Person of the Word, he addresses the question of why it was most fitting that the Son, rather than another divine Person, should assume human nature. As in Ia q33 a3, he sketches a progression of likeness by participation in the Son but now considered as the Father's Word. He gives three reasons; first, it was most fitting that the Person of the Son should become incarnate, as the Father's Word is the exemplar cause in which rational beings especially participate, both in creation and in grace:

The Person of the Son, who is the Word of God, has, in one way, a common agreement [or proportion—*convenientia*] with all creatures, because the word of the craftsman, i.e. his concept, is the exemplar likeness of the things he makes by his

---

126. Somme, *Fils adoptifs*, 71–74. Cf. *Scriptum* bk3 d10 q2 a2 qc 1.

127. E.g., *Scriptum* bk3 d10 q2 a1 qc1 c. "Respondeo dicendum, ad primam quaestionem, quod adoptatio transfertur ad divina ex similitudine humanorum. Homo enim dicitur aliquem in filium adoptare, secundum quod ex gratia dat jus percipiendae hereditatis suae, cui per naturam non competit. Hereditas autem hominis dicitur illa qua homo dives est; id autem quo Deus dives est, est perfruitio sui ipsius, quia ex hoc beatus est, et ita haec est hereditas ejus; unde inquantum hominibus, qui ex naturalibus ad illam fruitionem pervenire non possunt, dat gratiam per quam homo illam beatitudinem meretur, ut sic ei competat jus in hereditate illa, secundum hoc dicitur aliquem in filium adoptare."

handiwork. Hence the Word of God, who is his eternal concept, is the exemplar likeness of all creatures. And thus as through the participation of this likeness, creatures are established in their proper species, though movably, so through the union of the Word with a creature, not participatively but personally, it was fitting that the creature should be restored in order to its eternal and immoveable perfection; for the craftsman by the conceived form of his art, by which he creates his handiwork, restores it, if it collapses. In another way, [the Word] has a particular agreement with human nature, since the Word is a concept of the eternal Wisdom, from whom all the wisdom of mankind is derived. And hence man is perfected in wisdom, which is his proper perfection, as he is rational, when he participates the Word of God, as the disciple is instructed by receiving the word of his master. Hence it is said (Sirach 1:5): "The Word of God on high is the fountain of wisdom." And so for the consummate perfection of mankind it was fitting that the Word of God himself should be personally united to human nature.

Thomas draws on a "Wisdom Christology," which, arguably, is present from the very outset of the *Summa*.[128] The Word, to whom wisdom is appropriated in all of the Trinity's works of creation and grace,[129] is especially the exemplar for the perfection of the human person by wisdom, which is a participation of the Word of God. Although Thomas is not explicit about whether he means the wisdom of philosophy, theology, or the Spirit's gift

128. Joseph Wawrykow suggests that reflection on q3 a8 can illuminate q1 of the Ia *pars* on *sacra doctrina*. In q3 a8 Thomas highlights that it was appropriate for the Son precisely as Wisdom to be the term of the assumption of human nature, with reference to 1 Cor 1:24: "Christ the power of God and the wisdom of God." Wisdom is the proper perfection of the human person as rational; participation in the Word of God who is Wisdom perfects the person in wisdom, and so it was fitting that the Word should be united to human nature for the consummate perfection of human beings. Question 3 a8 goes on to say that it is by sharing in the sonship of Christ that predestined humans are brought to the end of their heavenly inheritance, the end beyond their natural powers to which, *ST* Ia q1 a1 tells us, they are directed. Wawrykow suggests that in q1 a1 Thomas alludes to Christ as Wisdom with his use of Isa 64—"the eye has not seen, O God, besides you, what you have prepared for those who wait for you"—to illustrate the existence of revealed truths above the reach of reason in sacred doctrine, because this verse is closely linked with 1 Cor by Paul himself (1 Cor 2:9) as he reflects on the wisdom revealed in the Cross. So, Wawrykow suggests, if Thomas had Paul's usage in mind in Ia q1 a1, he would even here "be implying that the way to God as the beatifying end of human beings runs through the cross of Christ." Wawrykow, "Wisdom in the Christology of Thomas Aquinas," in *Christ among the Medieval Dominicans: Representations of Christ in the Texts and Images of the Order of Preachers*, ed. Kent Emery Jr. and Joseph Wawrykow (Notre Dame, IN: University of Notre Dame Press, 1998) 189–91.

129. See, e.g., *ST* Ia q39 a8, q45 a6 ad2, and chapter 1.

of wisdom,[130] his reference to the "consummate perfection of mankind" implies that he is thinking of the Spirit's wisdom, which flows from grace. The "eternal and immoveable perfection" to which the creature is reordered by participation in the likeness of the Word through wisdom seems clearly to be the perfection of beatitude.[131] Thomas's third reason why the Word should fittingly be the Person to assume human nature is, like his first, based on the intellectuality of human nature but focuses on this need for restoration after the Fall, for which the Incarnation was the remedy. Our first parents sinned through "an inordinate thirst for knowledge," and so, by the "Word of true knowledge," human beings should be led back to God, their proper end, by being restored by grace and perfected in wisdom.

Thomas's second reason in q3 a8 why the Word should be the Person assuming indicates a connection between participation in wisdom and adopted sonship. Because the Word is the Son of God, participation in the Word who is Wisdom fittingly brings about the end of the union, the fulfilling of the predestination of adopted sons. Thomas says that the fitness of the Word's assumption of human nature:

may be taken from its congruence with the end of the union, which is the fulfilling of predestination, namely of those who are preordained to the heavenly inheritance, which is owed only to sons, according to Romans 8:17: "If sons, heirs also." And so it was fitting that through him who is the natural Son, man should participate this likeness of sonship by adoption, as the Apostle says in the same place (Romans 8:29): "For those whom he foreknew, he also predestined to be conformed to the image of his Son."

A link, not fully explained here, can be inferred between wisdom and sonship because adopted sons participate in the Word who is the Son. Par-

---

130. Cf. *ST* Ia q1 a6, *corpus* and ad3; IIa IIae q45.

131. That Thomas is thinking of the dispensation of grace is also clear from the answer to the second objection, where he argues that it was fitting for the Word to become incarnate, because as God the Father made all things through the Word in the first creation, so he ought to have brought about the "second creation" through the Word, "in order that restoration should correspond to creation according to 2 Cor 5:19: 'For God indeed was in Christ reconciling the world to himself.'" Grace's perfection of the image is regularly described as a new creation in the *Summa*, and Thomas in his commentary on this passage from 2 Cor explains that as creation brings being out of nothingness, so grace gives new being to the one who has become nothing through sin, and so, "in a certain manner, the infusion of grace is creation" (*Sup II Corinthians, reportatio vulgata*, ch5 lect4).

ticipation in the Word of God by the wisdom that flows from the new creation of grace transforms human persons, bestowing a likeness of sonship, and so brings about the end of the union by reordering them to "eternal and unchangeable perfection," that is, to the inheritance of beatitude. As examined in chapter 6, Thomas makes the connection between wisdom and sonship more explicit in his treatment of the gift of wisdom elsewhere in the *Summa*.

Joseph Wawrykow points out that, with his reference to predestination, Thomas's "Wisdom Christology" is presupposed in this second argument in q3 a8.[132] The Word as Wisdom has a role in the perfection of each individual creature (especially of rational creatures by wisdom) and thus in the ordering of all creatures to God in the divine *ordinatio*. Wawrykow notes an emphasis on Christ as Wisdom from the outset of this article by his quotation in the *sed contra* of 1 Corinthians 1:24—"Christ, the power of God and the wisdom of God"—in conjunction with a text from John Damascene: "In the mystery of the Incarnation the wisdom and power of God are made known: the wisdom, for he found a most suitable discharge for a most heavy debt; the power, for he made the conquered conquer." Thomas has established in the Ia *pars* the sapiential context of predestination and has shown that God's work of bringing adopted sons to glory is the manifestation of God's wise plan to communicate the divine goodness. Thomas's claim in q3 a8 that the fulfilling of predestination fittingly takes place through the Son, who is the Word, is "but a restatement of the sapiential dimensions of this aspect of the communication of divine goodness."[133] Wawrykow's observation is supported by Thomas's treatment of adopted sonship in IIIa q23, where he devotes the first article to showing its fittingness in manifesting the divine goodness.

In q23 Thomas presents his most complete treatment of adopted sonship by grace in its relation to the natural sonship of Christ. This question falls, in the treatment of the Incarnation, at the end of Thomas's consideration of the consequences of the union, in a section on Christ's relationship to his Father.[134] It might at first seem strange that Thomas treats adopted sonship most fully here, rather than in the questions on grace, for instance.

132. Wawrykow, "Wisdom in the Christology of Thomas Aquinas," 184–85.
133. Ibid., 185.
134. This section (qq20–24) appears between Thomas's examinations of what belongs to Christ because of the union in himself (qq16–19) and in relation to us (qq25–26); see *ST* IIIa

But divine adoption cannot be understood except in relation to Christ. The question asks "whether adoption is befitting to Christ." Thomas's treatment of adopted sonship, though it focuses more on our adoption by grace, takes place in the context of establishing that Christ, as natural Son in the unity of his Person, has no need of adoption (q23 a4). In fact, it would not have been possible to address our divine adoption without the risk of Christological confusion, before establishing the duality of natures in the unity of Christ's person. In particular, it was necessary to show that Christ's possession of habitual grace flowed directly as an effect of the union in his Person to his human nature, and was not, as for us, added to a preexisting human nature. As an objector points out, it might be thought that Christ's grace is, like ours, the "grace of adoption":

Augustine says (*De Praedest. Sanct.* XV) that "by the same grace that man is Christ, as the grace, by the beginning of faith, any man is a Christian." But other men are Christians by the grace of adoption. Therefore, this man is Christ by adoption, and so he seems to be an adopted son.[135]

One who has read the earlier questions on the grace of union and habitual grace in Christ recognizes that the objector has failed to distinguish between them, or to recognize the difference between Christ's habitual grace and ours. In reply, Thomas distinguishes between the grace of union that makes Christ the natural Son and the habitual grace by which a human person becomes an adopted son, pointing out that

habitual grace in Christ does not make one who was not a son to be an adopted son, but is a certain effect of filiation in the soul of Christ, according to John 1:14: "We saw his glory ... as of the only-begotten of the Father, full of grace and truth."[136]

q16, prol. for this division. Christ, as one Person both fully human and divine, has a human will with its own proper operation, wholly and freely subjected to the divine will as its instrument (qq18–19). Because Christ's human will is both free and perfectly obedient, he is able, through the grace of headship, to merit both for himself and for others (q19 aa3–4). Christ's relation to the Father, then, is characterized by filial obedience, while his relation to us as a result is that of a mediator worthy of our adoration (qq25–26). Questions 20–24 discuss Christ's subjection to the Father (q20), his prayer (q21), and his priesthood (q22), before turning to two questions raised about things that may be said of Christ because of the Father's relation to him: whether it can fittingly be said that he is adopted (q23) and predestined (q24). As discussed in chapter 6, the question on adoption is the culmination of Thomas's treatment of Christ as exemplar of the obedient worship of God in charity and wisdom.

135. *ST* IIIa q23 a4 ob2.   136. *ST* IIIa q23 a4 ad2.

Even though Christ, like us, participates in the divine nature by habitual grace (which pertains to his human nature), he does not participate, like us, in divine sonship (which belongs naturally to his divine Person).

A defense against adoptionism is far from all that Thomas wishes to accomplish in IIIa q23, however. The first three articles of this question examine adopted sonship by grace and establish its relationship with the natural sonship of Christ. Like the rest of the section on the consequences of the union, the discussion in q23 about the relationship of adopted to natural sonship is governed by what has been established earlier in Thomas's treatment of the Incarnation, especially as to the grace of headship by which Christ is the model and principle of perfection for others. The purpose of the Incarnation was human salvation; because of it, humans also could become children of God. It might be said that adopted sonship by grace is a consequence of the union, for only on account of the Incarnation has it been made possible, and only in light of the Incarnation can we fully understand what it means. It makes sense to discuss our sonship in relation to Christ's, which is its exemplar cause—not only by way of distinction but also by way of explanation—in preparation for the treatment of Christ's predestination in relation to ours and his role as mediator uniting human beings to God.

Question 23 a1—"whether it is fitting that God should adopt sons"—places the entire question into the context of God's will to communicate the divine goodness to creatures; that is, the context of the divine plan of wisdom, or *ordinatio*, that manifests God's goodness. There is a parallel to the first articles of Ia-IIae q110 a1, on grace; IIa-IIae q23 a1, on charity; and IIIa q1 a1, on the Incarnation, in all of which Thomas emphasizes that God's motive in human sanctification is to communicate the divine goodness.[137] Like q110 a1, q23 a1 identifies divine adoption as the effect of God's predestination in his plan of goodness, with reference to Ephesians 1:5:

"He predestined us for the adoption of sons of God." But the predestination of God is not ineffective. Therefore God does adopt some to himself as sons. I answer that one adopts someone to himself as son inasmuch as out of goodness he admits him to a participation in his inheritance. Now God is infinite in goodness, from which it follows that he admits his creatures to a participation of good things, and especially

137. Cf. *ST* Ia q6 a4, q19 a2, q20 a2.

rational creatures, who, inasmuch as they are made to the image of God, are capable of divine beatitude. And this consists in the enjoyment of God, by which God himself is happy and rich through himself, inasmuch as he enjoys himself. Now anyone's inheritance is said to be what makes him rich. Thus, insofar as God in his goodness admits men to the inheritance of beatitude, he is said to adopt them.[138]

After this introduction, which evokes the discussions earlier in the *Summa* of grace as well as predestination and the perfection of the divine image in the beatific vision, Thomas expands on the traditional juridical notion that adoption bestows the right to an inheritance by explaining that one adopted by God is not only as a result deemed worthy but also actually made so by the transforming bestowal of grace:

Now divine adoption [makes one more rich than] human adoption, since God makes the one whom he adopts qualified (*idoneum*), by the gift of grace, to receive the heavenly inheritance; but a man does not make the one whom he adopts qualified; rather, he chooses the one who is already qualified for adoption.[139]

One is "made qualified" by grace in that it causes one to merit the inheritance, on account of God's predestining love, which causes goodness in those he elects, as Thomas established in the Ia *pars*.[140] God's purpose in doing so is simply to manifest the divine goodness:

Man works in order to supply his needs, but not God, to whom it is fitting to work in order to communicate the abundance of his perfection. So just as by the act of creation the divine goodness is communicated to all creatures in a certain likeness, by the act of adoption the likeness of natural sonship is communicated to men, according to Rom 8:29: "Those whom he foreknew to be conformed to the image of his Son."[141]

Again, as in Ia-IIae q110 a1, Thomas draws attention to the continuity and distinction between the gifts of creation and grace, the latter of which is a higher manifestation of the divine goodness, the effect of God's "special love" by which God "simply wishes the eternal good, which is himself, for the creature."[142] The deification of adopted sons by grace, by which they are made worthy of the heavenly inheritance, is the fulfillment of the divine will to "communicate by likeness its own good to others as much as possi-

---

138. *ST* IIIa q23 a1.
139. Ibid.
140. *ST* Ia q23 a4, a5; cf. Ia-IIae q110 a1.
141. *ST* Ia q23 a1 ad2.
142. *ST* Ia-IIae q110 a1.

ble" by ordaining those who participate in the divine goodness to God himself as their end.[143]

This likeness of the divine goodness, which is a participation of the divine nature, is adopted sonship; we participate in the divine nature specifically by being conformed to Christ as Son. It might be said that we participate in the divine nature in the manner of a son, sharing, insofar as it is possible for a creature, in the Son's relation to the Father. In doing so, we know from III q3 a8, we participate in the Son's personal property as Word by the perfection of wisdom. In III q23 a2 Thomas teaches that while the whole Trinity adopts the children of God, in the "spiritual regeneration of grace," different roles are appropriated to the divine Persons:

Adoptive sonship is a certain likeness of the eternal Sonship, as all things made in time are certain likenesses of what has been from eternity. Now man is likened to the splendor of the eternal Son by the light (*claritatem*) of grace, which is attributed to the Holy Spirit. Therefore adoption, though common to the whole Trinity, is appropriated to the Father as its author, to the Son, as its exemplar, to the Holy Spirit, as imprinting on us the likeness of this exemplar.[144]

The exemplarity of the Son on which Thomas is focusing in q23 a2 consists in the relation of being "begotten"; there is an analogy between Christ's unique natural generation from the Father and the regeneration of grace in the creature caused by the Trinity, such that it becomes "the son of the whole Trinity."[145] Those who are reborn as sons enter into a new relationship qualitatively like that of the Son.

In q23 a3 Thomas bases his argument that only rational creatures can be adopted, on the exemplarity of the Son as the Word, who by virtue of being begotten is one in nature and thus in communion with the Father. We learned in q3 a8 that adopted sons are conformed to the Word by being perfected in wisdom; now we see that this transformation of the creature, and its new relation of sonship, involves it in a new union with the Trinity like

143. *ST* Ia q19 a2.

144. *ST* IIIa q23 a2 ad3. In saying that "adoptive sonship is a certain likeness of the eternal Sonship: just as all that takes place in time is a certain likeness of what has been from eternity," Thomas seems to echo the teaching on the divine missions, which add to the eternal processions a temporal effect, as the exemplar of the perfection of the image by conformation to the Word and Love through wisdom and charity (*ST* I q43 a2 ad3, a5 ad2).

145. *ST* IIIa q23 a2 ad2.

that of the Word with the Father. The virtue of charity now moves to the foreground as the explanation of how sonship makes the rational creature capable and worthy of attaining the inheritance of beatitude:

The sonship of adoption is a certain likeness of natural sonship. Now the Son of God proceeds naturally from the Father as intellectual Word, existing as one with the Father himself. To this Word, therefore, something may be likened in three ways. First, with respect to the *ratio* of the form, but not its intellectuality ... In this way any creature whatsoever is likened to the eternal Word, as it was made through the Word. Secondly, the creature is likened to the Word, not only as to its form, but also as to its intellectuality ... and in this way the rational creature, even in its nature, is likened to the Word of God. Thirdly, a creature is likened to the eternal Word, as to the unity which he has with the Father; this comes about through grace and charity, hence our Lord prays (John 17:21–22): "That they may be one in us, as we also are one." And such a likeness perfects the *ratio* of adoption, for to those who are likened in this way the eternal inheritance is due. Whence it is clear that to be adopted belongs only to the rational creature; and still not to all, but only to those who have charity, which is "poured forth in our hearts by the Holy Spirit" (Romans 5:5); and so (Romans 8:15) the Holy Spirit is called "the Spirit of adoption of sons."

In this passage, in which Scripture texts from Romans as well as from John again come to the fore, Thomas highlights the notion of the unity of the Son with the Father as the mark of sonship. While all creatures are likened to the Word to varying degrees, only the rational creature is capable of adoption because it is like the intellectual Word of God "even in its nature" (i.e., by virtue of its natural faculties of intellect and will). As Thomas taught in Ia q93, however, such a natural likeness of intellectuality is not enough for the perfection of the image. The adopted son bears the greatest likeness to the Word, with respect not only to form and intelligibility in its nature but also to the Word's "oneness with the Father," the likeness of which in the creature is engendered by grace and charity.

There are striking parallels between q3 a8 and this passage from q23 a3, although the two emphasize different aspects of conformation to the Word in adopted sonship. As in q3 a8, this explanation revolves around the Word as exemplar both in creation and in the "second creation" of grace.[146] There is a progression of likeness of creatures to the Word, the most perfect being

---

146. *ST* IIIa q3 a8 ad2.

that possible for intellectual creatures. Question 3 a8, however, emphasizes the participation of rational creatures in the Word, who is "the concept of the eternal Wisdom," and Thomas argues that it is most fitting for the Word to perfect rational creatures (i.e., ontologically). The "consummate perfection of mankind" is to be conformed to the Word who is Wisdom, and in this transformation one becomes an adopted son, in whom the end of the Word's union with humanity can be accomplished.

In q23 a3 the topic is sonship itself, and there is a focus on the *unity* of the Word with the Father; the different degrees to which creatures are likened to the Word culminate not only with respect to a higher ontological transformation per se but also in the effects of such a transformation in a likening of relationship—a likeness, by means of grace and charity, to the unity of the Trinitarian communion in the creature's relationship with the Trinity. This highest level of relational likeness to the Word, however, rests on the ontological change of grace and the charity (and wisdom) that flows from it, which perfect the image so that it is capable of the supernatural activities of knowledge and love of God, effecting this new relation on the creature's part. Adopted sonship is thus identified in q23 a3 by the note of communion, a communion brought about by the activity of the Holy Spirit, which leads the sons of God (Rom 8:14)—by means of grace and charity—to the end of beatitude.

The Word's exemplary "unity … with the Father" thus has both ontological and relational aspects to which the adopted son is likened. In q23 a3 Thomas quotes John 17:21–22—"That they may be one in us, as we also are one." In his scriptural commentary on his passage he remarks that "there is a twofold unity of the Father and Son: a unity of essence and of love." The Son is united with the Father both in the one divine nature (i.e., ontologically), and in the "unity of love … because love, charity, makes one be with God" (i.e., relationally).[147] This bond of Love between Father and Son is, we know, the Holy Spirit. Thomas goes on to say,

The manner of this unity is added when he says, "I in them and you in me." They arrive at unity, because they see that I am in them, as in a temple: "Do you not know that you are God's temple and that God's Spirit dwells in you?" (1 Cor 3:16), by grace, which is a certain likeness of the Father's essence, by which you, Father, are in

147. *Sup. Ioh.* ch17 lect5 (2240).

me by a unity of nature: "I am in the Father and the Father in me" (Jn 14:10). And this is in order "that they may become perfectly one." Above he had said, "that they may be one," while here he says, "perfectly one." The reason for this is that the first time he was referring to the unity brought about by grace, but here to its consummation.[148]

By grace, adopted sons share in a likeness of the divine essence by a deifying participation in the divine nature, and grace's consummation is that all the disciples should become one with God and each other by the charity of the indwelling Holy Spirit, for "the purpose of God's gifts is to unite us in a unity which is like the unity of the Father and the Son."[149] The *Commentary on John* suggests that the effects of the exemplarity of the Word in *ST* IIIa q23 a3 extend, by the likeness of grace and charity that it causes in adopted sons, beyond the individual's attainment of the inheritance to the perfection in unity of the Church among all those whom it brings into communion.

Summary and Conclusion

Thomas's definition of grace as a participation in the divine nature, in relation to Christ, contributes to both his Christological and soteriological teaching, helping us to understand how and why Christ is able to bestow the gift of deification. Christologically, this definition helps to illustrate the full meaning of Christ's single personal *esse* in the union and also the distinction between his two natures. By the grace of union, divinity belongs to Christ not as a participated likeness of the divine nature but as a personal property. Yet because of the distinction of his two natures, Christ as human possesses habitual grace, which is a participation in the divine nature like ours.[150] Still, Christ's habitual grace, flowing from the union, is also unlike ours in that he participates in the divine nature in fullness, which gives this participation a soteriological significance, making him both our model and the causal exemplar of our deification.

---

148. Ibid. (2247).

149. Ibid. (2246).

150. Christ's human soul "is not divine through its own essence," but rather "through participation, by grace" because "together with the unity of person there remains distinction of natures" (*ST* IIIa q7 a1 ad1).

The Incarnate Word, in his fullness of habitual grace, is the "principle of perfection to human nature," so Christ in his humanity possesses the grace of headship, by which he participates the grace of the Holy Spirit to others. As Richard Schenk observes, for one to understand and believe the outward teaching of "the deeds and sayings of Jesus as *documenta et exempla*," one must also be led by the inner grace of the Holy Spirit given by Jesus to his disciples. There is thus a twofold cause of faith—revelation and grace.[151] Because of his fullness of grace, Christ both teaches us by his words and deeds and bestows the grace to believe in them. Christ himself is the highest pedagogical model of the activity of grace in a human soul, by his perfect docility to the actualization, by the divine *auxilium*, of the potential bestowed by his habitual grace—a docility for which he is disposed by the gifts of the Spirit. Christ the Son is the perfect example of filial obedience, and so, for those conformed to him by grace, deification—participation in the divine nature—is at the same time participation in his sonship.

The Son of God is one with the Father because he is the Father's "intellectual Word," eternally and immanently spoken in the divine mind, Wisdom begotten and beloved. The adopted son bears a likeness, in his relation to the Trinity, to this Word's unity of nature and love with the Father because he has been transformed in his nature by grace, in his will by the charity of the Holy Spirit, and in his intellect by the wisdom of the Word. This is the perfection of the image, of grace leading to glory, which bestows on adopted sons all of the theological virtues and gifts of the Holy Spirit to bring them to the eternal inheritance of beatitude. We see from III q3 a8 and q23 a3 that wisdom and charity have an especially prominent role in this journey of deification, and a special association with the Son and Holy Spirit in conforming adopted sons to the Son who is the Word. As in earlier parts of the *Summa*, Thomas indicates in the IIIa *pars* that by grace the rational creature is likened to the Word and Love by wisdom and charity. But he explicitly shows how, as grace likens the creature's faculties to the divine Persons, it brings about a likeness in the creature, as an individual, to the Son specifically as son. To be an adopted son is not only to be regenerated;

---

151. Schenk, "*Omnis Christi actio nostra*," 116–17. Cf. Thomas Aquinas, *Sup. Rom.* ch16 lect2: "Ad fidem duo requiruntur; quorum unum est cordis inclinatio ad credendum, et hoc non est ex auditu, sed ex dono gratiae; aliud autem est determinatio de credibili, et istud est ex auditu."

it is to engage in the grace-enlightened activities that are like those of the Son. It belongs to the one who is adopted by grace to be like the Son in that he is in relation to the Trinity as the Son is in relation to the Father, and on the part of the creature we can say that the activities of the intellect and will conformed to the Word and Love characterize this relation of sonship. The adopted son possesses and enjoys God himself in knowledge and love, and in doing this he is conformed to the Son, who, we know from the questions on the Trinity, is the "Word breathing forth love," the one who eternally loves the Father by the Holy Spirit.[152]

The exemplarity of the Son as Son, as Word and as giver of grace for the deification of human beings, can thus hardly be overemphasized. And precisely because the Son *is* Son, one in nature and love with the Father, deification also takes place through the exemplarity of the Holy Spirit. I noted in chapter 1 that the question on the divine missions in the beginning of the *Summa* emphasized the role of the Holy Spirit in sanctification. Now at the end, the complementary role of the Son comes more to the fore. The Son is the author of sanctification, the Spirit, who proceeds as Love, is the gift of sanctification itself.[153] As head of the body in the visible mission of the Incarnation, the Son bestows a graced participation in the divine nature through the instrumentality of his humanity. By this gift of the grace of the Holy Spirit, adopted sons receive the invisible missions of both Son and Holy Spirit.[154]

The following chapters turn to the specific effects of those missions in the rational creature chosen to be an adopted son—charity and wisdom flowing from grace. As the image is the principle of its own activities, its deification involves not only its transformation by grace to be a new kind

---

152. *ST* Ia q37 a2.

153. Thomas introduces this distinction in an article on the fittingness of the visible missions (*ST* Ia q43 a7 ad4): "It was necessary for the Son to be declared as the author of sanctification, as explained above. Thus the visible mission of the Son was necessarily made according to the rational nature to which it belongs to act, and which is capable of sanctifying." Because the rational nature is a principle of action, it fittingly signifies the Son as the author of sanctification, bestowing the Spirit's gift of sanctification on others temporally through his humanity in his visible mission, just as he is the principle of the Spirit in its eternal procession. The distinction that Thomas makes between the Spirit as the gift of sanctification, and the Son as its author, is unique to the *Summa*.

154. I.e., as discussed in chapter 1, in a certain manner, the invisible mission of the Word takes place through the "first gift" of the Father's love in the Holy Spirit.

of principle, likened to the one divine nature, but also the shaping of its activities by this infused virtue and gift, which assimilate its intellect and will to the Trinitarian Persons of Word and Love and so order it entirely to the knowledge and love of God. By virtue of its deification by grace, charity, and wisdom, the image becomes the free principle of the supernatural activities by which it moves to beatitude, led by the Holy Spirit, and so truly participates in the life of sonship that is perfected in deiformity.

CHAPTER 5

Charity in the *Summa theologiae*

The love of God has been poured out into our hearts by the Holy Spirit that has been given to us.

—Romans 5:5

Thomas's teaching on participation in Christ's sonship in the IIIa *pars* is the culmination of the picture of the journey of deification he has built throughout the *Summa*, beginning with his treatment of the divine missions and the perfection of the image in the Ia *pars*. We can expect, then, that what he has to say about charity and wisdom in the IIa *pars* will be relevant to connecting the Trinitarian and Christological dimensions of participation in the divine nature by grace. The deification that grace bestows transforms the intellect and will by the infusion of charity and wisdom in a special way among the other theological virtues and gifts, for these forms, properly intrinsic to the creature—and thus at the source of its free action—are the very same likening to the divine Persons of Word and Love, by a "representation of species," discussed in the treatment of the image. Charity and wisdom especially make the creature a "participator of the divine Word and Love proceeding, so as freely to truly know and rightly love God," in the divine indwelling.[1] So the deification by grace of the image, participating in the one divine nature, consists in a conformation, in the activities of intellect and will flowing from this nature, to the image of the Trinity, specifically because they are shaped by charity and wisdom. And

1. *ST* Ia q38 a1, q43 a3.

211

this ontological conformation to the image of the Trinity results in a conformation to the Son and a share in his relationship with the Father. Grace,
virtues, and gifts thus dispose the image to be freely moved in its actions by
the Holy Spirit, as obedient son, to the end of beatitude.

Charity's Communication of Beatitude by Fellowship with the Son

Charity is the greatest of the theological virtues, the infused *habitus* shaping the intellect and will that have God himself as their object "inasmuch as
they direct us rightly to God."[2] Faith, hope, and charity proportion the intellect and will of human beings who participate in the divine nature to obtain supernatural beatitude.[3] Thomas presents his treatment of charity and
"the corresponding gift of wisdom" in *ST* IIa-IIae qq23–46, following his
examinations of faith and hope, with their associated gifts. By comparison
to the latter two, Thomas devotes twice as many questions to charity, primarily to its acts and opposing vices (qq27–43) as well as to charity itself
(qq23–26), the precepts of charity (q44), and the gift of wisdom and its opposite, folly (qq45–46). Faith, hope, and charity all surpass natural human
virtues because of their higher end, but charity, as the "mother and root of
all virtues," is most perfect.[4] While faith and hope pass away in beatitude
and are replaced by vision and possession, charity and all the gifts remain
and are perfected in heaven.[5]

Thomas begins his examination of charity in IIa-IIae q23 a1 by drawing
upon the Gospel of John and Aristotle's *Ethics* to consider charity as a kind
of friendship, or mutual benevolent love, based on the communication of
goods. His analysis presupposes his earlier treatment of the passion of love,
where he discusses the love of friendship, its cause in apprehension of the
good and shared likeness, and its effects including union, mutual indwelling, ecstasy, and zeal for the good of one's friend.[6] He begins in the *sed contra* of q23 a1 by saying:

2. *ST* Ia-IIae q62 a1.
3. *ST* Ia-IIae q62 a1 c., ad1, ad3.
4. *ST* Ia-IIae q62 a4.
5. *ST* Ia-IIae 67, q68 a6.
6. *ST* Ia-IIae qq26–28. Recent studies on the natural love of friendship in Aquinas, and charity as friendship, include Daniel Schwartz, *Aquinas on Friendship* (New York: Oxford University
Press, 2007); James McEvoy, "The Other as Oneself: Friendship and Love in the Thought of St.
Thomas Aquinas," in *Thomas Aquinas: Approaches to Truth: The Aquinas Lectures at Maynooth,*

It is written (Jn 15:15): "I will not call you servants now, but my friends." But this was not said to them except by reason of charity. Therefore charity is friendship. I answer that according to the Philosopher in *Ethic.* 8.2, not every love has the *ratio* of friendship, but only the love which is with benevolence, when, that is, we love someone so as to wish good to them.[7]

After distinguishing this kind of love from that of concupiscence (which wishes the good of the loved object only for oneself), Thomas goes on to say that benevolence or well-wishing alone is nevertheless not enough for friendship, "for a certain mutual love is required, since friendship is between friend and friend, and this well-wishing is founded on some kind of communication." Between friends there is a communication of some good:

Since, therefore, there is a communication between man and God according to which he communicates his own beatitude to us, some friendship must be founded

---

1996–2001, ed. J. J. McEvoy and M. Dunne (Portland, OR: Four Courts Press, 2002), 16–37; Anthony Keaty, "Thomas's Authority for Identifying Charity as Friendship: Aristotle or John 15?" *Thomist* 62 (1998): 581–601; G. Mansini, "Similitudo, communicatio, and the friendship of charity in Aquinas," in *Thomistica*, ed. E. Manning (Leuven: Peeters, 1995); Walter Principe, "Loving Friendship According to Thomas Aquinas," in *The Nature and Pursuit of Love*, ed. D. Goicoechea (Buffalo: Prometheus, 1995); Paul Wadell, *Friends of God: Virtues and Gifts in Aquinas*, American University Studies Series VII: Theology and Religion 76 (New York: P. Lang, 1991); J. Bobik, "Aquinas on *communicatio*: The Foundation of Friendship and *caritas*," *Modern Schoolman* 64 (1986): 1–18; Jordan Aumann, "Thomistic Evaluation of Love and Charity," *Angelicum* 55, no. 4 (1978): 535–56; Robert Gleason, *The Meaning of Love: An Essay towards a Metaphysics of Intersubjectivity* (Glen Rock, NJ: Paulist Press, 1966); Jerome Wilms, *Divine Friendship According to Saint Thomas*, trans. M. Fulgence (Dubuque, IA: Priory Press, 1958). H. D. Simonin's early "Autour de la Solution Thomiste du Problème de L'Amour," *Archives d'Histoire Doctrinale et Littéraire du Moyen Âge* 6 (1932): 174–276, works toward an understanding of likeness as a cause of love that bears upon the love of friendship (i.e., addressing the "problem" of how love can at once be appetitive, and disinterested, or other-oriented). For recent discussion, see in particular D. M. Gallagher, "Desire for Beatitude and Love of Friendship in Thomas Aquinas," *Mediaeval Studies* 58 (1996): 1–47.

7. Anthony Keaty argues that Thomas's interpretation of charity as friendship is governed by his reading of John 15 rather than Aristotle in the sense that while Aristotle provides the categories by which to identify friendship's features, the specific content of Christian charity is that displayed in Christ's own benevolence and communication of good toward his disciples, which they are to imitate. The elevation of the disciples from servants to friends indicates the voluntary nature of charity, and it is "from the elevated status of being friends with Christ rather than servants that charity derives its excellence." The content of charity thus lies in friendship with Christ such that, having been told everything that Christ has heard from the Father (Jn 15:15), the disciples wish for others the highest good as known, loved, and manifested by Christ (Keaty, "Thomas's Authority for Identifying Charity," 600).

on this communication. About this communication, indeed, it is written in 1 Cor 1:9: "God is faithful, by whom you are called into the fellowship (*societatem*) of his Son." The love founded upon this communication is charity. From this it is clear that charity is a certain friendship of man for God.[8]

It would seem, however, as one objector proposes, that there cannot be friendship between human beings and God, since, as Aristotle teaches, "nothing is so appropriate to friendship as to dwell (*convivere*) with one's friend (*Ethic.* 8.5)," but "the conversation [i.e., familiar association, or *conversatio*] of God" and the angels, towards whom charity is directed, "is not with mankind," according to Daniel 2:11. Thomas's answer underscores the eschatological nature of charity and its progressive increase from grace to glory. Even for human beings on earth, in "the spiritual life of the mind," charity gives a fellowship (*conversatio*) with God and the angels, albeit imperfectly:

wherefore it is written (Phil 3:20), "our conversation is in heaven." But this conversation will be perfected in heaven, when "his servants shall serve him, and they shall see his face," as is said in Rev. (22:3–4). Therefore charity is imperfect here, but will be perfected in heaven.[9]

In fact, Thomas seems to be implying, Aristotle's quotation applies: by charity, we do dwell with God because God dwells in us, even now by grace but most fully in glory, where God will be "all in all" (1 Cor 15:28).

Charity is a theological virtue; that is, God is its proper object. Yet charity also extends to others for the sake of God. In further answers to objections, Thomas indicates the approach he will take in speaking of charity's object and order in qq25–26. Although Aristotle teaches in *Ethics* that friendship requires the return of love, and that the noblest kind of friendship is friendship for the virtuous, Thomas explains that friendship for someone extends to loving those whom the friend loves. So the friendship of charity can even extend to one's own enemies and to sinners, who are loved for God's sake, "to whom the friendship of charity is chiefly directed."[10]

We can draw at least three things from this introductory text on charity in q23 a1. First, the virtue of charity, by which human beings love God, and others for God's sake, is based on God's communication to us of a good; that is, it is based on God's love for us, by which he causally communicates

---

8. *ST* IIa-IIae q23 a1.   9. *ST* IIa-IIae q23 a1 ad1.
10. *ST* IIae-IIae q23 ad2–3.

every good. As detailed in previous chapters, Thomas often frames his treatments of the special gifts of God's love for humankind—grace, the Incarnation, adopted sonship—with a reference in the introductory article to the communication of the divine goodness by God's causal love, placing these discussions into the context of the divine *ordinatio*, established by God's will to manifest the divine goodness in the order and government of the universe, and especially of rational creatures called to beatitude. We cannot love God as God loves us, because God's love is the cause of goodness in us (by some participation of the divine likeness), while our love for God is a response to the divine goodness. "Mutual love" between a human being and God can only mean that God, in his love, causes in us a love that moves us toward the divine goodness by the participation of some likeness to God.[11]

Second, God's love for us directs us to beatitude by means of the love caused in us that moves us toward that end. The "communication of beatitude" on which our love for God is founded is God's willing of that supernatural end for us, a willing that transforms us by ordaining us to that end, by giving us the gifts that bring us there. Thomas returns with remarkable frequency throughout qq23–26, on charity itself, to the formula—found only in the *Summa theologiae*—that charity is a certain friendship of a human being for God founded upon the communication of eternal beatitude. It ap-

11. Louis Hughes points out that Thomas stresses more than Aristotle the latter's third condition for friendship—fellowship or "dwelling together"—making it not just a property of friendship but its basis in the friendship of charity. Hughes goes on to argue that one must understand what Thomas means by *communicatio* in q23 a1; he thinks that Thomas uses it to mean the sharing of something spiritual and noble in common "which is loved by all for the sake of all," i.e., God's beatitude. Louis Hughes, "Charity as Friendship in the Theology of Saint Thomas," *Angelicum* 52 (1975): 164–78, esp. 168. L.-B. Gillon, on whose analysis Hughes draws, touches on a relation between God's "active communication" of his gifts and the Aristotelian concord of wills necessary for friendship, but contrasts God's action as "efficient cause" of charity with charity's "foundation" in the common possession of the good of beatitude. "A propos de la théorie thomiste de l'amitié," *Angelicum* 25 (1948): 3–17, esp. 16–17. But I would argue that as used by Thomas here and elsewhere in the *Summa* in the case of a communication between God and human something is both shared and caused; communication of a good is a causing and therefore a sharing of that good in the creature by participation of what subsists in God. As a result, charity as friendship with God based on this communication must differ significantly from its analogate in natural friendship, and indeed from charity toward the neighbor, which is derivative from charity toward God. G. Mansini discusses differences between natural friendship and the friendship of charity, recognizing that charity toward God is the result of God's communication to us of a likeness of himself. "Similitudo, communicatio," esp. 12–13.

pears in each question, given as a premise for the argument of the *corpus* a total of eight times and twice in objections (where it is explained more fully in the answers to the objections).[12] In other words, Thomas thinks of it as an explanatory principle for every aspect of the treatment of charity—that charity is one virtue with the divine goodness as its end, that it is gratuitously infused, and proper to rational creatures with a capacity for eternal life (including angels), and that all things should be loved with respect to God as the first principle of beatitude—all have to do with charity's foundation on God's communication to us of a share in his own beatitude as final end.

Finally, God specifically communicates this beatitude to us by "calling us to the fellowship of his Son" (1 Cor 1:9). In what does Thomas think this fellowship with the Son consists? It would seem to be even more than friendship with Christ—who communicates to the disciples all that he has heard from his Father (Jn 15:15), manifesting God's love for them, and thus bringing them to love God and share with him his own happiness and virtue[13]—although certainly this is the way in which fellowship with the Son is revealed. In Thomas's commentary on 1 Corinthians, he specifies this fellowship in a way that makes clear that he is thinking of it in terms of the perfection of the image by grace:

He gives the reason for his promise, saying that "God will keep you firm," that you ought to hope, because "God is faithful ... by whom you were called to the fellowship of his Son Jesus Christ our Lord," that, namely, you may have fellowship with Christ, both in the present through the likeness of grace, according to 1 Jn 1:7: "if we walk in the light, as he is in the light, we have fellowship together with him," and also in the future through the participation of glory, Rom 8:17: "if we suffer with him, we will also be glorified with him." But God will not seem to be faithful, if he were to call us to fellowship with the Son and refuse it to us, inasmuch as it is through [God] himself that we are able to attain him. Whence it says in Joshua 1:5: "I will not leave you or forsake you."[14]

12. *ST* IIa-IIae q23 a1 c., a5 c.; q24 a2 c.; q25 a2 ob2, a3 c., a6 c., a10 c., a12 c., q26 a1 c., a2 c., a7 ob3. In the *Scriptum* Thomas comes closest to this idea when he says that "since charity is a certain friendship, which requires that friends live together, there can be no charity, unless there be a participation of the divine life, which is through grace" (*Scriptum* bk3 d27 q2 a4 qc4 c.). But he does not cast this explanation in terms of charity as founded on a share in future eternal beatitude.

13. See Anthony Keaty, "The Holy Spirit as Love: A Study in the Pneumatology of Thomas Aquinas" (PhD Diss., University of Notre Dame, 1997), esp. 175–80, and note 7 above.

14. *Sup. 1 Cor.* ch1 lect1.

The scriptural and doctrinal context into which Thomas places fellowship with the Son in this direct treatment of the verse indicates that for him it evokes the whole journey of the elect—of those God whom has called to that fellowship—to beatitude under the influence of grace.[15] Grace gives a "likeness" to Christ in that "we walk in the light, as he is in the light" (i.e., the light of grace) and that "we suffer with him" until we participate with him in the light of glory.[16] Our examination of Thomas's teaching on adopted sonship yields fuller insight into what this fellowship is: a participation in Christ's own sonship that is exercised specifically in activities shaped by charity and wisdom on the journey to beatitude. Fellowship with the Son is more than friendship with Christ; it is the friendship with God made possible by becoming like Christ as adopted sons, and so sharing the same end of beatitude with him through the free activities characteristic of sons. Charity is founded on God's communication of eternal beatitude to us by making us like his Son, who is one in nature and love with the Father.

Charity: Both Created Virtue and Participation in the Holy Spirit

In q23 a2, a3 Thomas establishes that while charity, as a virtue, is an intrinsic created *habitus* regulating the good human acts that unite us to God (and that thus have a voluntary and meritorious character), it is neverthe-

---

15. An earlier reference in the *Summa* to 1 Cor 1:9 in relation to charity's necessary connection to the other theological virtues confirms this interpretation: "Charity does not only signify love of God, but also a certain friendship with him, which adds to love a mutual return of love, with a certain mutual communication, as it says in *Ethics* 8. And that this pertains to charity is clear from 1 Jn 4: 'who remains in love, remains in God, and God in him.' And 1 Cor 1:9 says, 'God is faithful, by whom you were called into the fellowship of his Son.' This fellowship of human for God, which is a certain familiar *conversatio* with him, is indeed begun here in the present through grace, but perfected in the future through glory, both of which things are held by faith and hope." The familiar dwelling together of friend with friend required by Aristotle's definition of friendship is satisfied in charity, by which the disciple "remains in God and God in him" through an eschatological progress of growth in fellowship with the Son. To have charity is to dwell in God and have God dwelling within, now by grace and in the future by glory, and this is to be in a fellowship with God specifically as is the Son.

16. In Thomas's commentary on Philippians, he writes that this fellowship with the Son in 1 Cor 1:9 is a fellowship in his Passion, the fruit of justice, which by experiencing through the power of grace we will come to glory (*Sup. Phil.* ch3 lect2).

less a created *habitus* of an extraordinary kind (like grace, its principle). In a2 Thomas answers the question of "whether charity is something created in the soul." This article has much in common with I-II q110 a2, the parallel treatment of grace as a created *habitus*, though now Thomas is discussing a gift, not on the level of "the light of grace which is a participation of the divine nature," but on the level of "the infused virtues which are derived from and ordained to this light," shaping human activities flowing from the new nature toward a higher end.[17] In both places Thomas stresses that the habitual gift is given so that, by the possession of a form that is intrinsic, yet supernatural in origin, the person "may be moved sweetly and promptly by God to acquire eternal good."[18] God, "who moves all things to their due ends,"[19] adds such forms to the natural powers of his creatures to carry out the plan of his divine wisdom, by which "he orders all things sweetly" (Wis 8:1).[20] For both grace and charity, Thomas's explanation of how so excellent a gift can nevertheless be a created form revolves around the notion of an accidental participation in what is by nature divine.

Article 2 begins by addressing a disputed question pertaining to the gist of all these issues, and so to the very heart of Thomas's understanding of how God transforms and moves rational creatures, as free principles of their own activities, on the journey to beatitude. Thomas introduces the *corpus* with reference to Peter Lombard's discussion in the *Sentences* of whether charity is created:

The Master looks thoroughly into this question in d17 of Book 1 of the *Sentences*, and sets down that charity is not something created in the soul, but is the Holy Spirit itself dwelling in the mind. Nor does he mean to say that this movement of dilection by which we love God is the Holy Spirit itself, but that this movement of dilection is from the Holy Spirit without any mediating habit, whereas other virtuous acts are from the Holy Spirit as mediated by the habits of other virtues, for instance the habit of faith or hope or of some other virtue: and he said this on account of the excellence of charity.

17. *ST* Ia-IIae q110 a3.
18. *ST* Ia-IIae q110 a3; cf. IIa-IIae q23 a2: "For us to perform the act of charity, there should be in us some habitual form superadded to the natural power, inclining that power to the act of charity, and causing it to act with ease and pleasure."
19. *ST* IIa-IIae q23 a2.
20. This scriptural reference is found in both responses, underlining the role of grace and charity in the divine *ordinatio*.

Thomas responds that in fact, however, such a position takes away from the excellence of charity. His answer reveals the deep confidence he has in the order of divine wisdom, in which God, while always primary cause, works with creatures according to the nature he has given them. And this shows God's excellence. The excellence of a human being, as rational, is in voluntary action, in which the mind is a principle of its own movement, although moved by God, as Thomas established earlier in the *Summa*. For love to be a voluntary and meritorious act, it must proceed from an intrinsic principle: "given that the will is moved by the Holy Spirit to the act of love, it is necessary that the will also should be the efficient cause of that act." Charity thus requires a supernatural but intrinsic form added to the natural power of the will, by means of which the Holy Spirit moves it. Lombard's position, while attempting to preserve the primacy of divine causality in salvation, fails to attribute real freedom to the rational creature, and real primacy to God in his wise plan of providence.

The first objection and its response provide a key to the reason for Lombard's misunderstanding (as Thomas sees it). Lombard had supported his claim that "the Holy Spirit is the love with which we love God and neighbor" with extensive reference to Augustine, quoting from *DT* 8.7, where Augustine describes human charity as an analogy for the Trinity, and *DT* 15, where Augustine speaks of the Holy Spirit, who is Love, as God's love in us.[21] Lombard is aware that the question of causality is at issue here, as he goes on to quote Augustine in *DT* 15.17, where he says that "God is love" differs from such texts as "God is my hope" because God causes our hope but "is" love, just as God is spirit. Lombard refers to Romans 5:5, "the love of God is poured into our hearts by the Holy Spirit," to argue that in the

---

21. It must be said that here as elsewhere Lombard presses Augustine for more theological precision on this question than Augustine's rhetorical style or context was meant to convey. Augustine in *DT* 8, when he says, as Lombard reports it, to "love the love with which you love your neighbor, and you will love God, for God is love," is seeking for an analogy of the Trinity in human love; his argument is that charity loves itself in loving another so "you do see a trinity if you see charity." Again, although Augustine himself says in *DT* 15 that the Holy Spirit is the presence of love in us, he is being somewhat rhetorical in style and is primarily concerned with finding an analogy for the eternal procession of the Spirit (to which he says our love is more unlike than like). Augustine also says that the Holy Spirit stirs us, and moves us to love; in other words, there is ambiguity about whether Augustine means that the Holy Spirit is our love or is the cause of our love (as later commentators would claim).

mission of the Spirit the Spirit himself is sent from himself (a text from Augustine, *DT* 15 again the authority, that love both is God and is from God); Lombard's interpretation most basically points to his conviction that humans can only love God from God himself.[22]

In q23 a2 the first objection, although not naming Lombard, makes hidden reference to his text with its Augustinian authority:

It seems that charity is not something created in the soul. For Augustine says (*De Trin.* 8.7): "He who loves his neighbor, consequently, loves love itself. Now God is love. Therefore it follows that he loves God above all." Again he says (*De Trin.* 15.17): "It was said: God is charity, even as it was said: God is spirit." Therefore charity is not something created in the soul, but is God himself.[23]

In response, Thomas points out what he thinks is a misinterpretation of Augustine, and in doing so presents a teaching of its own significance to which he will return in subsequent questions:

The divine essence itself is charity, just as it is wisdom and goodness. Whence just as we are said to be good with the goodness which is God, and wise with the wisdom which is God, because the goodness by which we are formally good is a certain participation of divine goodness, and the wisdom by which we are formally wise, is a certain participation of divine wisdom, so too, the charity by which formally we love our neighbor is a certain participation of divine charity. For this manner of

---

22. Lombard notes questions and objections to his argument, which he acknowledges is not accepted "by most." First, how can charity increase in us if it is the Holy Spirit that is immutable? His answer is with reference to a text from Augustine, that "charity does not progress in us, but we progress in it." As Rosemann notes, this could be considered somewhat unsatisfactory, as it seems to require some kind of modulating principle in the person. "*Fraterna dilectio est Deus*: Peter Lombard's Thesis on Charity as the Holy Spirit," in *Amor amicitiae—On the Love That Is Friendship: Essays in Medieval Thought and Beyond in Honor of the Reverend Professor James McEvoy*, Recherches de théologie et philosophie médiévales Bibliotheca 6, ed. Thomas Kelly and Philipp Rosemann (Louvain: Peeters, 2004), 428. The objection is also raised that if our love and the love of God are both the Holy Spirit, it would be two different kinds of love, which is absurd. Lombard answers with an exegetical argument; these things are stated in Scripture and by authorities under different aspects. Finally, the objection is raised that Augustine, in *De doctrina christiana*, says that charity is a feeling or a motion of the mind. Lombard's answer points to a major area of focus for future perception of the difficulties of his teaching: he responds that charity here means only the act of charity, not a created virtue. The Holy Spirit unites directly with the mind to cause the act of charity without any mediating virtue. So the Holy Spirit itself is a kind of quasi-virtue. Lombard concludes by noting the excellence of charity above nature, which can thus be none other than God himself.

23. *ST* IIa-IIae q23 a2 ob1.

speaking is customary among the Platonists, with whose doctrines Augustine was imbued. And some not adverting to this have taken up from his words an occasion of error.[24]

Augustine, in Thomas's mind, was thinking of created charity in us as a participation of divine charity; he meant that when we love our neighbor and so love charity itself, we love God, in whom charity is essential and who is the cause of its participated likeness in us. In Thomas's view of participation this means that, in opposition to Lombard's erroneous interpretation, charity is "formal" in us: a proper, intrinsic, created *habitus*, which is truly the principle of charity's acts, while at the same time being a participation of God's own charity.

This teaching does not seem so remarkable in the context of Thomas's general view in the *Summa* of the participation of created perfections in their divine source, which would support the idea that Augustine is speaking analogically. But because divine charity—Love—is the proper name of the Holy Spirit, an implication follows that Thomas does not hesitate to draw. In q23 a3 he argues that charity is a virtue that unites us to God and so is the principle of good human acts. Yet if it is a virtue it is an accidental *habitus*, which would seem to mean it cannot be superior to the soul, its subject, again seemingly taking away from its excellence. Thomas answers just as he did to a similar objection in the questions on grace:[25]

Every accident is inferior to substance with respect to its being, since substance is a being through itself, while an accident has being in another. But with respect to the *ratio* of its species, an accident which is caused by the principles of its subject is lower in dignity than its subject, as an effect is inferior to its cause. But an accident which is caused by the participation of some superior nature is higher in dignity than its subject, inasmuch as it is a likeness of that higher nature, as light to something diaphanous. In this way charity is higher in dignity than the soul, inasmuch as it is a certain participation of the Holy Spirit.[26]

Just as Thomas taught earlier, that grace, as principle of the theological virtues, is a participation in the divine nature, he now presents charity, flowing from this principle, as a participation in the Holy Spirit.

How significant is Thomas's introduction of this formulation? It would

---

24. *ST* IIa-IIae q23 a2 ad1.
26. *ST* IIa-IIae q23 a3 ad3.

25. Cf. *ST* Ia-IIae q110 a2 ad2.

seem to help with the difficulty Lombard raises of understanding how the Holy Spirit "pours the love of God into our hearts" (Rom 5:5), intimately informing and moving the will while allowing it the freedom of voluntary action—for, as Thomas established throughout earlier parts of the *Summa*, a participated perfection belongs properly to the creature even as it likens it to the divine source. In Thomas's treatment of the natural passion of love, he had already quoted Dionysius as saying that "every love is a participated likeness of the divine love."[27] But charity is something more. That a created virtue is a participation not only in a divine perfection in general (as all created virtues are) but in a Trinitarian *Person* (i.e., in their personal property) seems a remarkable statement. And, as discussed in chapter 6, Thomas makes a similar statement about the gift of wisdom as a participation in the Son.

Thomas's earlier definition of grace as a participation in the divine nature in the *Summa* warrants the question of whether a connection exists between these definitions that offers insight into the Trinitarian structure of the deification of the image by grace. Although he never makes it entirely explicit, Thomas's teaching on grace, charity, and wisdom arguably implies that the image's participation in the divine nature, as principle of its own supernatural activities of intellect and will, unfolds as Trinitarian specifically through wisdom and charity, as participations by those powers in the likeness of the Son and Holy Spirit. Wisdom and charity, in a special way among the virtues and gifts, dynamically represent the species of these Persons, directing the image's supernatural activities of knowing and loving God, which flow from the principle of grace as the Persons proceed from the principle of the Father.

A brief overview of the use that Thomas makes of the definition of charity as a participation in the Holy Spirit can give us some initial insight into its significance. This formulation appears four times in the *Summa*'s treatment of charity (not including q23 a2, where charity is described as a participation in the divine love, although this now anticipates the perfection of this participation). After q23 a3, where the formula functions as an explanation for how a created virtue can be superior to the soul, it appears the other three times in q24, on the will as the subject of charity. First, it is placed in q24 a2, where Thomas argues that charity is infused. Quoting Romans 5:5,

27. *ST* Ia-IIae q28 a3.

he repeats that "charity is a friendship of man for God, founded on the communication of eternal beatitude." But this communication is according to the gifts of grace, which exceed nature. So charity cannot be in us naturally, nor can it be acquired through natural powers, but only "through the infusion of the Holy Spirit, who is the love of Father and Son, the participation of whom in us is created charity, as was said above." In q24 a5 Thomas considers charity's increase, not by addition as of one unit of charity to another (which would imply two distinct charities) but by the increased participation of a subject in charity, so that charity is intensified in the subject, as the latter is "more reduced to [charity's] act and more subjected to it." In answer to the objection that something new must be placed in the soul with charity's increase, as with its inception, Thomas answers that increase is not like infusion, as it involves only a change in quantity; when God increases charity, "he makes it exist more in the soul, such that the soul participates more perfectly the likeness of the Holy Spirit."[28] Finally, in q24 a7, Thomas argues that there is no limit to how much charity can increase in this life, "for charity itself according to the *ratio* of its proper species has no limit to its increase, since it is a certain participation of infinite charity, which is the Holy Spirit."[29]

How can we relate these references to what we already know about grace and charity, and how charity differs as a participation in the Holy Spirit from natural love, since that is also a participation in the divine love? Charity, flowing as an infused gift from grace, which deifies the subject on the level of nature, informs the will by a created virtue of supernatural origin for the God-like activities of that new nature (q23 a3). As we know from the Ia *pars*, the will already represents in the rational image the procession of the Holy Spirit as love proceeding,[30] for by this appetitive power, in its natural activity of loving creatures and loving God as the cause of creatures and so moving toward its object, it represents the Holy Spirit's dynamism as the divine Person with whom, as Love, love's property of movement toward

---

28. *ST* IIa-IIae q24 a5 ad3.

29. Ann Condit notes that of the three notions about charity presented by Thomas in IIa-IIae q23—that it is a kind of friendship, that it is a theological virtue, and that it is a participation in the Holy Spirit—he most stresses the latter. "The Increase of Charity," *Thomist* 17 (1954): 367–86, esp. 370.

30. I.e., by the exemplar causality appropriated to the Spirit; cf. *ST* Ia q45 a7 and chapter 1.

its object is associated.[31] By charity's more perfect participation of likeness, though, the will is more specifically likened to the Holy Spirit as the intra-personal Love of Father and Son (q24 a2). Charity is a participation in the love of Father and Son, who love each other principally, and all creatures, by the Holy Spirit.[32] So charity shares not only in Love's property of movement but also in its object, the divine Persons themselves, and creatures as ordered to God. An increase in charity, as a created virtue informing the will's action, means that the new potential placed in the will for this God-like action, is more fully actualized. The soul is made more subject to charity—that is, more likened to the Holy Spirit—and is more reduced to the act of charity, which is to love God as object (q24 a5). There is no limit to this increase of likeness and its subsequent activity in this life because the Holy Spirit as exemplar and the divine object of the activity are infinite; charity's perfection is in eternal life (q24 a7).

To put it in terms Thomas has used earlier in his discussion of movement of the will by grace, the charity-infused will becomes a more perfect moved mover toward the end of beatitude, in which the divine essence itself is the object of the soul's knowledge and love. The will is more perfectly like the Holy Spirit because it moves toward the same object; that is, it wills what God wills. When Thomas says that charity is a participation in the Holy Spirit, he is explaining *how* grace, by bestowing a participation in the divine nature, and thus in the divine Persons, reorients the creature to God, allowing it to be disposed for movement by the divine *auxilium* toward beatitude, in that it is inclined to will what God wills. This disposition is ultimately affected by the gifts of the Spirit, which are rooted in charity.

Charity, as a Participation of the Holy Spirit, Governs the Moral Life

If charity conforms the will to the Holy Spirit, directing it to beatitude, it is not hard to see why it must hold a significant place in relation to the other virtues and the gifts of the Holy Spirit in the journey of the moral life. It is precisely because charity is a participation in the Holy Spirit that it is the

31. Cf. *ST* Ia q36 a1, q45 a6.
32. *ST* Ia q37 a2.

highest of virtues, commanding all the others as their "mother and form," as well as being the root of the gifts of the Spirit that perfect the activity of the virtues by disposing them for movement by God. The intent of this argument is to illustrate Thomas's deeply pneumatological vision of the moral life, which, although not always explicitly elaborated as such, emerges in particular through his understanding of the very nature and centrality of the virtue of charity.

Charity's Excellence in Uniting Us to God

In IIa-IIae q23 aa4–6 Thomas begins to consider charity's principal role with respect to the other virtues. First, he examines what makes charity unique among them. Article 4 asks whether charity is a "special" virtue. Thomas is not just considering whether charity somehow stands out from other virtues, but whether charity can be said to have a specific object, as it seems that it extends to every moral act and is involved in every virtue (as one of the objections points out, Scripture commands that "everything be done in love").[33] Charity does have a special object—the divine goodness itself as the object of beatitude—and so is a specific kind of love. But, as the answers to the objections establish in anticipation of the following articles, charity, which has as its object this last end of life, commands the other virtues that have objects subordinate to this final end. That is, the objects are ordered, and therefore so are the virtues corresponding to them. So all virtues in a way depend upon charity, as the moral virtues depend upon prudence. "Love," according to 1 Timothy 1:5, "is the end of the commandments."[34]

The principle that, because charity's ultimate object is the divine goodness, charity orders all virtues with respect to itself, applies also to the various kinds of love that seem to create specific differences within charity. In a5 Thomas lays the groundwork for his detailed investigation in later questions of the primary and secondary objects of charity and the way in which these should be ordered. In discussing whether charity is one virtue, Thomas replies that although human friendships can be differentiated into species by their ends and objects, and by the kind of communion on which they are based, charity's "end is one, namely the goodness of God, and the commu-

---

33. 1 Cor 16:14; *ST* IIa-IIae q23 a4 ob2.
34. *ST* IIa-IIae q23 a4 ad1–3.

nication of eternal beatitude, on which this friendship is based, is also one."
So the love of neighbor, though it seems to have a different object, is not
a different charity than love for God, because the neighbor is loved out of
charity for God's sake.[35]

The theological virtues, with God as object, are all higher than the moral and intellectual virtues that have human reason as their rule, but among
the former, Thomas says in a6, charity is the greatest. Why does it matter
which is the greatest virtue? The hierarchical ordering of the virtues, with
charity at their head, was traditional scholastic practice, not least because
of the authority of 1 Corinthians 13:13, which is placed in the article's *sed
contra*. But there is a corresponding philosophical reason that will bear fruit
in subsequent discussions of charity's role among the virtues and gifts: the
virtue with the highest object orders all the others. Thomas may have in
mind a principle from the *De causis*, which he introduces elsewhere to explain the influence of the gift of wisdom: "the higher a virtue is, the greater
the number of things to which it extends" (*De causis* prop. 10.17).[36] Thomas
argues in a6 that, "among the theological virtues, the first place belongs to
that which attains God the most," that is, charity.

What, then, does it mean to attain God the most? Thomas's discussion
of the natural passion of love in Ia-IIae qq26–28 richly prepares the ground
for his treatment of the union of charity, as the highest kind of love, with
God as the beloved object. Love is a passion; all love transforms the lover.
The notion of a passion applies most properly to the concupiscible appetite
but also "in a wider and more extended sense" to the intellectual appetite,
or will, in which the love of charity, like all love, is a principle of movement.
The appetible object gives to the appetite "a certain adaptation to itself,
which consists in a pleasing affinity (*complacentia*) with that object, and
from this follows movement towards the appetible object."[37] Union results
from love because of this *complacentia* with the object; "the lover stands in
relation to that which he loves, as though it were himself or part of himself."[38] So while likeness is a cause of love,[39] it is also its effect in some re-

---

35. *ST* IIa-IIae q23 a5 ad1.
36. *ST* IIa-IIae q45 a3. Wisdom plays a similar role in relation to the intellectual virtues as
charity does to all of them.
37. *ST* Ia-IIae q26 a2.   38. *ST* Ia-IIae q26 a2 ad2.
39. *ST* Ia-IIae q27 a3.

spect, in that the will is proportioned to the beloved object apprehended by the intellect, and so inclined toward it.[40] In the love of friendship, willing good to the other as to oneself, one apprehends the friend as another self (*alter ipse*).[41]

Love thus results in a kind of mutual indwelling: "every love makes the beloved to be in the lover, and vice versa."[42] While speaking of "every love," Thomas gives charity as his prime example and 1 John 4:16 as his authority: "The one who abides in love abides in God, and God in him." The mutual indwelling of love takes place in both the apprehension and appetite. The beloved is in the lover's apprehension, and the lover is also in the beloved, desiring "an intimate knowledge of everything pertaining to the beloved, so as to penetrate into his very soul." Remarkably, Thomas's example of a lover is the Holy Spirit, "who is God's Love, [who] 'searches all things, even the deep things of God'" (1 Cor 2:10).[43] In the appetite, too, the beloved is in the lover because "the *complacentia* in the beloved is rooted in the lover's heart." In the love of friendship, strictly speaking, what is loved is the good willed to the beloved, rather than the beloved desired for oneself. Conversely, the lover is in the beloved, in the love of friendship, because "he counts what is good or evil to his friend as being so to himself, and his friend's will as his own."[44] In the love of friendship there is a likeness and union of wills.[45]

Thomas's examination of charity's excellence draws upon these teachings about love in general to explain that charity attains God the most because it unites us to God and so transforms us, in a sense, into the object of our love by conforming our will to God. In Ia-IIae, when Thomas con-

---

40. *ST* Ia-IIae q25 a2. As Paul Wadell puts it, "love perfects us not so much by movement towards the good, but by assimilation to the good," because, as Thomas explains in the beginning of the Ia IIae, "the form of any action comes from the end," from a transformation of the will that assimilates it to the object so as to be inclined toward it. *Friends of God*, 64; cf. *ST* Ia-IIae q1 a1, q9 a1.

41. *ST* Ia-IIae q28 a1.   42. *ST* Ia-IIae q28 a2, s.c.

43. In the context of Paul's teaching on the revelation given to those who have received the indwelling Spirit, this verse may refer to God's intra-Trinitarian love and to the activity of the Holy Spirit in the knowledge and love of humans for God. Thomas reflects on both aspects of this section of the text in his *Sup. 1 Cor.* ch2 lect2.

44. *ST* Ia-IIae q28 a2.

45. For a discussion of the relationship between love, mutual *extasis*, and union in the love of friendship in both the *Scriptum* and the *Summa*, see Peter Kwasniewski, "St. Thomas, Extasis, and Union with the Beloved," *Thomist* 61, no. 4 (1997): 587–603.

sidered the equality of the virtues in general, he already devoted an article (q66 a6) to whether charity is the greatest of the theological virtues. There he argues that although all of the latter are equal in having God as their object, faith (in what is not seen) and hope (in what is not yet possessed) remain at some distance from that end. But charity actually possesses the object, "since the beloved is, in a manner, in the lover, and the lover is drawn by desire to union with the beloved." There are two aspects to this possession, indwelling of the beloved, and union with it. In the question on the divine missions, Thomas used this same language of indwelling, regarding both intellect and will, when he said that in the gift of grace God is present to the creature "as the object known is in the knower, and the beloved in the lover," and so is possessed and enjoyed even in this life.[46] Both the knowledge of faith and the love of charity are involved in the divine indwelling by which God is present as object, for faith precedes charity, as knowledge precedes love.[47] But it is the union with God that charity brings about that allows the possession and enjoyment of God and makes charity the superior virtue. Similarly, in IIa-IIae q23 a6, Thomas says that even though the intellect is higher than the will, the intellect's own measure limits the excellence of the intellectual operation because the thing known is in the knower; but the excellence of the will's operation is in the measure of its object, as the operation is completed in union with its term. So "it is better to know than to love the things that are beneath us ... whereas the love of things that are above us, especially of God, ranks before knowledge."[48] Because it unites the will to the highest object, love of God can be more perfect in this life than knowledge of God.

In the love of friendship, the lover is in the beloved by a union of wills, so that the friend's will is one's own. As James McEvoy notes, within the logic of Thomas's use of the model of friendship for explaining charity, God and the self must become *alter ipse* to each other.[49] Yet while in natural friendship preexisting likeness to the other is a cause of love, in the case of charity toward God, as Mansini points out, likeness is love's effect, a conse-

---

46. *ST* Ia q43 a3.

47. *ST* Ia-IIae q62 a4. The divine mission in the intellect is not according to faith, however, but to wisdom, and it depends upon charity (see below).

48. *ST* IIa-IIae q23 a6 ad1; cf. Ia-IIae q26 a3 ad4.

49. McEvoy, "The Other as Oneself," 36.

quence of God's gift to us of a similarity with himself.[50] Union of the will with God is conformity of the will to God, and charity, which is friendship with God, truly conforms the will to God because it is a participation of the Holy Spirit.

Thomas seems to anticipate this teaching somewhat in his discussion of the theological virtues in Ia-IIae. In Ia-IIae q62 a3 he remarks that spiritual union marks out the operation of charity apart from faith and hope, which both raise the intellect and will to the supernatural end, because by charity

the will is, so to speak, transformed into that end. For the appetite of a thing is moved and tends towards its connatural end naturally; and this movement is due to a certain conformity of the thing with its end.[51]

In Ia-IIae q62 a1 Thomas had just established that grace as a participation in the divine nature gives rise to the theological virtues as new principles of human action proportionate to this new nature. It might be said that the creature receives a new "connatural end" toward which these virtues are directed. In fact, Thomas will say in his treatment of the gift of wisdom that charity gives a "connaturality with divine things," which is the basis of wisdom's judgment about ordering oneself toward that end.[52] In all love there is a proportioning of appetite to the object, giving it a connaturality for its end, thus making it a principle of movement toward that end;[53] in the case of charity flowing from grace, the image is newly proportioned to God as end.

Charity conforms the will to the Holy Spirit, in the creature who shares in the divine nature, so that the creature's movement tends toward its new end. This conformity is what brings about the union of the will with God. Charity's excellence, and its command of the other virtues because it unites the will to the highest object of the divine goodness, lies in the fact that it is a participation of the Holy Spirit. We already know that the efficient causality of God in moving the creature is appropriated to the Holy Spirit in the divine *auxilium*, reducing the graced potential of the creature to act. The Holy Spirit

50. Mansini, "Similitudo, communicatio," 12–13, and note 45.

51. *ST* Ia-IIae q62 a3.

52. *ST* IIa-IIae q45 a2.

53. See Gallagher's comments on this principle in which he explains Thomas's teaching that, in the case of a being endowed with cognition, the appetitive faculty becomes proportioned to its object by changing in response to it, which becomes a source of striving toward the object. "Desire for Beatitude and Love," 8–9.

is also at work as exemplar, bestowing this new potential through the created virtue of charity, and so at work in the direction of all the virtues to God.

Charity: Mother and Form of All the Virtues

In IIa-IIae q23 a7, a8 Thomas looks more closely at charity's role (and thus the role of participation in the Holy Spirit) in commanding the virtues. Article 7 asks whether any "true virtue" is possible without charity. This question is far reaching, as it touches on the issue of the sufficiency of the natural virtues without grace and the relationship of all the virtues, acquired and infused, to charity in the graced person. Thomas's account of the virtuous life, treated at length throughout the IIa *pars*, is summarized concisely in terms of the order of virtues with respect to the ultimate and universal good end (i.e., the last end of beatitude), and to the proximate and particular good ends that can be directed to that principal good.

At the beginning of the IIa *pars*, when Thomas first sketched his scheme of human action as ultimately specified by the only true last end of beatitude—the enjoyment of God, toward which all lesser ends are directed—his thought is shaped not only by Aristotle's philosophy of eudaimonism but also by Augustine's doctrine of *usus* and *fruitio*, which teaches for the Christian the right ordering of loves: one should love those things that are to be used (everything other than God) for the sake of that which is to be enjoyed (God alone).[54] As Anthony Keaty has observed, this teaching of Augustine in *De doctrina christiana* is also an important source in Thomas's treatment of the object and order of charity in IIa-IIae qq25–26, and shapes his view of charity as a "virtue friendship" oriented toward the final end.[55] These Augustinian teachings suffuse Thomas's treatment of charity in relation to the other virtues as well.

In q23 a7, building on his discussion of charity's excellence in attaining the highest object, Thomas says that charity orders the human person to the "ultimate and principal good of mankind, [which is] the enjoyment of God." A true virtue, simply speaking, is one directed to the principal good. This is so, by definition, for charity, whose object is the divine goodness itself. But what of the other virtues, those ordered to particular ends? Their ends may

54. See, e.g., references in Ia-IIae q1 a5, a6; q2 a7, a8; and q3 a1 to quotes from Augustine's *De civitate Dei* and *De doctrina christiana* that allude to this doctrine.

55. Keaty, *Holy Spirit as Love*, 170–75.

be truly good—so that they lead one by proximate steps toward the principal good—and then they can be called true virtues; or their ends may be only apparently good, leading one away. But without charity one is disoriented; one no longer has the principal good as ultimate end, and so no virtue can be directed to that good. Strictly speaking, "no true virtue is possible without charity." Thomas adverts to Augustine's teaching on the pagan virtues, which for Augustine must all be counterfeit, splendid as they may seem, as they fall short of the end of true happiness known only to those transformed and humbled by faith.[56]

Yet Thomas goes somewhat further than Augustine in admitting the possibility of true virtue, in an imperfect sense, even without charity. For Thomas, particular goods may be true goods even if they are not the final and perfect good—for example, the welfare of the state or the natural good that an individual not in the state of grace can work—though, as established in the questions on grace, this is limited in scope.[57] So long as an act without charity is not done "in accordance with lack of charity"—that is, for an end contrary to charity—but instead "in accordance with the possession of some other gift of God" such as faith, hope, or "even natural good which is not completely taken away by sin," such an act can be generically good. It can never be perfectly good, however, because "it lacks its due order to the last end."[58] The virtue producing such an act is always imperfect unless it is referred to the final and perfect good.

56. Cf. the reference to Augustine's *Contra Julianum* 4.3 in the *corpus* and ad1, where Augustine argues that even good actions performed by an unbeliever, as an unbeliever, are always sinful, because they are directed to an improper end. See Jennifer Herdt, *Putting on Virtue: The Legacy of the Splendid Vices* (Chicago: University of Chicago Press, 2008), for a helpful discussion of the treatment of the pagan virtues by both Augustine and Aquinas (among others), where she demonstrates the foundational importance of Augustine's thought on this question.

57. Cf. *ST* Ia-IIae q109 a2: "Because human nature is not altogether corrupted by sin, so as to be shorn of every natural good, even in the state of corrupted nature it can, by virtue of its natural endowments, work some particular good, such as to build dwellings, plant vineyards, and the like; yet it cannot do all the good natural to it, so as to fall short in nothing; just as a sick man can of himself make some movements, yet he cannot be perfectly moved with the movements of one in health, unless he is cured by the help of medicine." The extent to which Thomas opens a space for the operation of the natural virtues without grace is a matter of some debate (see the discussion and references in Herdt, *Putting on Virtue*, 73–76). In considering this question, recall that while Thomas does do so more than Augustine, at least formally, he still, like Augustine, always takes account of the damage done to human nature by sin, such that even much of the operation of natural virtue toward proximate ends is seriously compromised.

58. *ST* IIa-IIae q23 a7 ad1.

The presence of charity in the will, by elevating the will to the highest end, radically shapes the effective outcome of all other virtues.[59] In q23 a8 Thomas considers what it means that charity is called the form of the virtues. How exactly does charity "inform" them all? Thomas explains:

> In morals the form of an act is taken principally from the end, the reason being that the principle of moral acts is the will, whose object and, as it were, form, is the end. Now the form of an act always follows from a form of the agent. So it must be that in morals, that which gives an act its order to the end, gives the act also its form. Now it is clear, according to what was said above, that it is through charity that the acts of all other virtues are ordered to the last end. Therefore it also gives the form to the acts of all the other virtues: and it is just on this account that charity is called the form of the virtues, for these are called virtues as ordered to formed acts.

By charity, the human will is conformed to the divine will; that is, it is conformed to the last end and highest good, which is the object of the divine will. This conformation of the will by charity directs all one's moral acts to the last end; they will be acts of an agent who is always holistically acting toward that highest end. Every virtuous act of justice, temperance, and the like will be done with that end either actually or habitually in view. So these acts, and the corresponding virtues, will also be informed by the ultimate end as they are subordinated to it. They are like the manifold mental and physical actions of an athletic competitor who, having once oriented herself toward the goal, uses every skill to successfully win the prize. Charity informs the virtues by informing the will, by setting the context for virtuous operation in a will directed to God. And charity informs the will, directing it to God, because it is a participation in the Holy Spirit—for by this participation the will is conformed to the same object and activity as God's own. Because charity is a participation in the Holy Spirit, it directs other virtues to the last end by informing and so inclining the will in which they operate. By charity the will becomes deified in all of its operations, as the principle of God-like activities.

The answers to the objections in q23 a8 clarify some confusion that might arise from calling charity the form of the virtues. Charity is the form of the other virtues not as exemplar or essence (i.e., they are not specifical-

---

59. See Paul Wadell's discussion of charity as the form of the virtues in his argument for a charity-centered moral theology. *Friends of God*, chap. 3, esp. 96–109.

ly or substantially the same thing as charity), but rather "effectively (*effective*), insofar as it imposes the form on all, in the manner discussed above."[60] Charity is effectively the form of the virtues because, according to the explanation in the *corpus*, it orders the other virtues to the last end by informing the will, which is the principle of their acts. Charity is the "mother" of the virtues because it commands the virtues in this way. A mother conceives in herself by another, and charity "conceives the acts of the other virtues, by the appetite for the last end."[61] In the will that charity directs to the last end, the acts of the other virtues are born for the sake of this ultimate end, as the agent works in every way to attain it.[62]

---

60. *ST* IIa-IIae q23 a8 ad1.

61. *ST* IIa-IIae q23 a8 ad3.

62. My reading of q23 a8 differs somewhat from that of Michael Sherwin in *By Knowledge and by Love: Charity and Knowledge in the Moral Theology of St. Thomas Aquinas* (Washington, DC: Catholic University of America Press, 2005). Sherwin, as part of his valuable demonstration of the interdependence of charity and knowledge in Thomas's mature thought, argues that Thomas abandoned his earliest understanding in the *Scriptum* that love is the form of the beloved received in the will, which transforms the lover into itself, much as the intellect's object does in the cognitive faculty. In the *Summa theologiae*, Sherwin contends, there is "an absence of the language of form" in Thomas's analysis of love; where Thomas defines love as a transformation in the *Scriptum*, he instead describes it in the *Summa* as a *complacentia*, a pleasing affective affinity that is "the aptitude, inclination, or proportion existing in the appetite for the loved object" (70). In Sherwin's view, i.e., the notion of *complacentia* involves no assimilation to the beloved by love; love is a principle of action, not a resulting form. So Thomas moves to the insight that "formal causality belongs to the intellect, while efficient causality belongs to the will" (202). In his discussion of charity, Sherwin points out that in the *Scriptum* (bk3 d27 q2 a4 qc3 ad1) Thomas calls love the exemplar form of the virtues (because they participate in its likeness), while he denies that it is an exemplar cause in the *Summa* (q23 a8 ad1), saying rather that it is the form of the virtues "effectively, insofar as it imposes the form on all." Sherwin would agree that Thomas is saying by this that charity "directs the virtues to their ultimate end" because the form of an act is taken from the end. But he is concerned to show that the intellect actually orders to the end, while the will (and charity in the will) is itself ordered to the end by the intellect. So charity orders the other virtues insofar as the will moves the acts of the virtues toward the end recognized by the intellect. For this reason, Sherwin believes, Thomas denies that charity is an exemplar form of the virtues, affirming that it "is solely the efficient cause of the virtues" (199). In support of his point, Sherwin goes on to argue that in the *Summa* in general, unlike in the *Scriptum*, Thomas no longer describes divine goodness "as an exemplar form that is participated in by creatures," referring to Ia q44 a4, on creation, where Thomas discusses the divine goodness as a final cause. But Thomas establishes at the outset of the *Summa* that creatures are good by participation in the divine goodness, so that "everything is called good from the divine goodness, as the first exemplary, effective and final principle of all goodness" (Ia q6 a4). The divine goodness is exemplary, final, and efficient cause at once, as global primary

Charity and the Other Theological Virtues   With this in mind, we must briefly examine the way in which charity operates in relation to the other theological virtues, the acquired and infused moral virtues, and the gifts of the Holy Spirit in order to gain a clearer picture of how charity, as a participation in the Holy Spirit, governs all of the moral life. Enough has already been said about charity's relation to faith and hope to recognize that charity has a privileged place among the theological virtues. While all three have as their object "God himself, as the last end of all,"[63] faith and hope have a certain inherent imperfection in that they fall short of attaining the goal. Faith's object is God as First Truth, but not as yet seen directly by the intellect or senses.[64] Hope's object is eternal happiness, obtained from God, but only as apprehended by the wayfarer as a future good.[65] Unlike charity, which grows continuously from imperfection in this life to perfection in heaven,[66] faith and hope cannot be completely perfected because vision and possession replace them in eternal life. But, like charity, "faith and hope in things which are above the capacity of nature surpass all virtue that is in proportion to man."[67] The *habitus* of faith, hope, and charity are all infused together as principles of supernatural activity flowing from grace's participation in the divine nature. Generation of the acts of these *habitus*, howev-

---

cause. While affirming Sherwin's main point about the intellect's role in ordering the will to its end and his observations about Thomas's later abandonment of the idea of the virtues participating in charity (see note 60), I argue that Thomas does not abandon in the *Summa* the idea of the transformation of the will by charity into the beloved object—for in a real sense, charity transforms the will by a participation in the Holy Spirit into the divine object of its love. As noted above, in Ia-IIae q62 Thomas uses the same language as in the *Scriptum* about the will being transformed into its end by charity. Yet this does not mean that Thomas thinks of charity in the will as the terminus, rather than the principle, of the will's action. Participation in the Holy Spirit, in the perfection of the image, gives to the will a potential for higher action, perfecting it as a principle of the image's activities toward the supernatural end. Form is a principle of activity, and the new form of charity in the will is a new principle of action. Thomas's use of the language of *complacentia* to describe love in the *Summa* is not, in my opinion, an attempt to avoid the language of form; when Thomas says that it is a proportioning of the appetite to the beloved, which gives rise to an inclination, he seems to incorporate the idea of a transformation of the will in proportion to its end in much the same way as in the *Scriptum*. So I read Thomas as saying that charity informs the virtues by informing the will in which they operate by a participation in the Holy Spirit—so inclining the will for its operation toward the divine object known by faith.

63. *ST* Ia-IIae q62 a2.   64. *ST* IIa-IIae q1 a4.
65. *ST* IIa-IIae q17 a2.   66. *ST* Ia-IIae q67 a6.
67. *ST* Ia-IIae q62 a3 ad2.

er, takes place in a certain order on the basis of the faculties in which these principles exist. The intellect must apprehend something before it is hoped for or loved with the will; so in terms of their acts, faith precedes hope, and hope precedes charity.[68]

In terms of their perfection, however, faith and hope are incomplete until they are quickened by charity.[69] It is certainly possible for faith and hope to exist in one without charity (i.e., one who has lost the infused *habitus* of charity through sin), but only "inchoately," or imperfectly. According to Aristotle (*Ethics* 2.6), virtue requires not only doing the good but also doing it well. A virtue is not perfect if it produces acts that are good but done imperfectly.[70] Even though faith is an intellectual virtue, its act of belief, like hope's act, depends upon the perfection of the will; this is so because faith belongs to the intellect as commanded by the will.[71] Because faith's assent is to what is not seen, it involves the free choice of the will in believing, and so an act of faith is meritorious.[72] The act of belief proceeds from the intellect as moved by the will to assent and so requires a perfecting *habitus* in both powers.[73] Without charity, without the highest end as object, one's will is imperfect and so cannot perfectly command the assent of faith. Nor can one with such a will confidently look to God in hope of future bliss, based on the merits deriving from charity.[74]

The possession of charity thus makes the difference between living and lifeless faith. Faith works through charity, as the First Truth "is the end of all our desires and actions, as Augustine proves in *De Trin.* (1.8)."[75] Charity gives faith its form by directing the act of faith to the will's end, the divine Good—or, more precisely perhaps, First Truth apprehended as the highest good. Lifeless faith has perfection so far as the intellect is concerned (in that the intellect still infallibly perceives the truth), but not in the will; it does not assent to First Truth as one's highest good and last end of happiness.[76] Thomas goes so far as to say that, without charity, faith and hope "are not virtues properly so-called."[77] This is even stronger language than

---

68. *ST* Ia-IIae q62 a4
70. *ST* Ia-IIae q65 a4.
72. *ST* IIa-IIae q1 a4, q2 a1, a9.
74. *ST* Ia-IIae 65 a4; IIa-IIae q17 a2, a5, a6.
75. *ST* IIa-IIae q4 a2 ad3.
77. *ST* Ia-IIae q65 a4.

69. Ibid.; IIa-IIae q4 a7, q17 a8.
71. *ST* IIa-IIae q2 a1.
73. *ST* IIa-IIae q4 a2.

76. *ST* IIa-IIae q4 a4, a5.

he used with respect to the imperfection of natural virtues without charity, perhaps because the latter at least reach their proper ends, while the acts of lifeless faith and hope can never really be done well.

Thomas thus sees a kind of synergistic feedback system among the theological virtues, which, in the person on the way to beatitude, results in continuous progress: faith and hope lead to charity, while charity further enlivens the activity of faith and hope. In this life, charity depends upon faith and hope because the mutual fellowship of friendship with God,

which is a certain familiar *conversatio* with him, inchoate here in the present by grace, is perfected in the future by glory, both of which things are held by faith and hope. Just as someone cannot have a friendship with another if he disbelieves or despairs of having some fellowship or familiar *conversatio* with him, so also one cannot have friendship with God, which is charity, unless one has faith, by which he believes in this kind of fellowship and *conversatio* of man with God, and hopes that he can attain this fellowship. And so, charity can in no way exist [in this life] without faith and hope.[78]

Faith and hope are virtues necessary to the wayfarer's possession of charity, so that God may be believed in as the attainable object of eternal happiness and so loved as friend now and forever.

Once heaven is attained, though, the need for these virtues falls away: Christ, in full possession of the beatific vision here on earth, had neither faith nor hope but perfect charity.[79] Neither faith nor hope remains in heaven because the blessed see and possess God as the object of their knowledge and love.[80] Charity not only remains but is perfected. As the knowledge of faith gives rise to the love of charity on earth, so in heaven the knowledge of the vision causes perfect love, for "the more perfectly we know God, the more we love him."[81] And the converse is true; as charity enlivens faith and hope on earth, so in heaven, because charity disposes one by desire to receive the object of the beatific vision, "the one who possesses more charity will see God more perfectly, and be more beatified"—that is, vision and the enjoyment of its possession, the fulfillment of faith and hope—will be more perfect.[82] It makes sense that charity, which consists in the perfection of the

78. *ST* Ia-IIae q65 a5.   79. *ST* Ia-IIae q65 a5 ad3.
80. *ST* Ia-IIae q67 a5, a6.   81. *ST* Ia-IIae q67 a6 ad3.
82. *ST* Ia q12 a6. So there is a parallel between charity's movement of the will in the assent

divine image by grace so far as the will is concerned (i.e., by participation in the Holy Spirit), is the one theological virtue that perdures from the reception of grace to the state of glory, where it exists in fullness forever.

Charity and the Acquired and Infused Virtues   Charity's orientation of the whole person to beatitude elevates the acts of all of the virtues to the last end. Yet, in the whole acting person, each virtue still has its proper role in movement toward that end. Virtues are *habitus* perfecting the human powers of intellect and will in relation to the good; natural intellectual and moral virtues, arising from natural principles that direct the person to ends ruled by human reason, are acquired by habituation through the repetition of the virtues' acts.[83] Thomas follows a long theological tradition in holding that the graced person who has received the theological virtues directing him to the supernatural end also receives by infusion corresponding moral and intellectual virtues, which are proportionate to the theological virtues. These infused virtues do not themselves have God as object; they perfect the soul's activity toward things other than, yet in relation to, God.[84]

In the graced person the acquired and infused virtues coexist. While, materially, they observe the mean with respect to the same object (e.g., both acquired and infused temperance are concerned with the appropriate mean in the consumption of food), that mean is regulated differently in each case. According to the rule of human reason, one exercises natural temperance, moderating food for the sake of health; infused temperance operating according to the divine rule leads one to fast for the sake of prayer. Acquired and infused virtues are thus directed to different ends.[85] Yet, as Romanus Cessario points out, the two work together. The acquired and infused virtues produce different effects with respect to the passions disordered by sin.[86] In the *De virtutibus in communi*, Thomas explains that by the frequent habituating acts of the acquired virtues one gradually becomes accustomed

---

of faith by the intellect to First Truth and in the intellect's ready reception of First Truth itself as the object and medium of the beatific vision.

83. *ST* Ia-IIae q55 a3, q63 a2.

84. *ST* Ia-IIae q63 a3; see Romanus Cessario, *The Moral Virtues and Theological Ethics* (Notre Dame, IN: University of Notre Dame Press, 1991), 102ff.

85. *ST* Ia-IIae q63 a4.

86. Cessario, *Moral Virtues and Theological Ethics*, 121.

to resisting the attacks of concupiscence and actually feels these attacks less and less, while infused virtue ensures that one does not obey the concupiscence of sin, however strongly the attacks are felt.[87] The natural acquisition of a good *habitus* can prepare the ground for the operation of the infused virtues to some extent; one who has become accustomed to restricting their food intake for health reasons will find it easier to fast during Lent than if they had never developed their natural virtue of temperance. Cessario comments that, for instance, in individuals already disposed to live the Christian life, the virtues infused at baptism "discover the requisite psychological structure for their operation." Without grace, however, the acts of the natural virtues can never be meritorious.[88]

Acquired virtues can exist without charity, but they do so imperfectly. True and perfect moral virtues, which "produce good works in proportion to a supernatural last end" are those infused by God and exist only in one with charity. Thomas focuses on prudence to explain further why no moral virtue can exist perfectly without charity. All of the moral virtues depend for their proper operation on prudence, which has to do with making the right choices about the means to the end, and prudence in turn depends on the moral virtues to dispose the reason toward the right ends.[89] Because it is even more essential to be disposed toward the ultimate end than to other ends, prudence depends even more on charity to be perfect, and so do all the other virtues that require prudence's guidance.[90] All of the moral virtues are infused with charity as the means of carrying out the activities of the will toward the last end, so that charity "is the principle of all the good works that are referable to one's last end."[91]

One who has charity thus has all the infused moral virtues, so that the individual is equipped to carry out well all the various moral activities of life on the way to beatitude. Cessario notes, however, that some theologians in the late thirteenth century came to regard infused virtues as a superfluous construct. Duns Scotus, for instance, argues that because charity already

87. *De virt. in comm.* a10 ad14.

88. Cessario, *Moral Virtues and Theological Ethics*, 123.

89. *ST* Ia-IIae q65 a1. Josef Pieper explains it this way: "Only one who previously and simultaneously *loves* and *wants* the good can be prudent, but only one who is prudent can *do* good." *The Four Cardinal Virtues* (Notre Dame, IN: University of Notre Dame Press, 1966), 34.

90. *ST* Ia-IIae q65 a2.

91. *ST* Ia-IIae q65 a3.

supplies the supernatural end for the acquired virtues, and faith teaches how and to what extent they should be practiced, no others are necessary.[92] But for Thomas, to explain how one reaches beatitude, it is not sufficient (though it is essential) to say that human activity receives a new supernatural end. That activity and the capacities giving rise to it must also be elevated, as the whole acting person is transformed and made fit for everlasting life. As Cessario explains it, charity does not just add a new motive to an already existing acquired virtue; the *habitus* that make supernatural actions possible should themselves "include an intrinsic reference to grace ... The only alternative to affirming the existence of the infused virtue remains considering the action of grace as limited to altering the purposes, not the habits of the heart."[93] The supernatural activities of the graced believer are not only done with a new end but in an intrinsically different way so as to reach the new end. As elsewhere, Thomas gives full play to the causality of human action transformed by grace in the journey to beatitude. And none of this is possible without charity; as it is the form of the virtues, the new end toward which it directs the will causes the other virtues to be elevated as well.

In the exercise of the infused virtues, as in all things, Christ is exemplar. Cessario remarks insightfully that "the perfection of Christ's own virtues provides us with a key to interpret what formal difference the infused virtues make in one who is united to Christ." Christ possessed all of the virtues, even temperance, which it would seem was unnecessary in one whose passions were perfectly ordered. Thomas explains that "the more one remains free from base passions, the more perfectly temperate he is." Christ's temperance was infused, not acquired, and demonstrates the freedom of the Gospel that the Christian believer enjoys.[94]

These observations may have a connection to our earlier examination of charity and adopted sonship. Thomas's foundational understanding of charity as friendship with God is that it brings about "fellowship with the Son," by which God communicates to us his beatitude. So charity makes the believer an adopted son who shares one end of beatitude with Christ, attained in the freedom characteristic of sons. We now see more clearly how

---

92. Cessario, *Moral Virtues and Theological Ethics*, 102–3; he refers to Scotus, *Quaestiones in III librum Sententiarum* d36 no28.

93. Ibid., 107.

94. Ibid., 112–13. See *ST* III q7 a2 ad3.

this works itself out in the life of the believer. With charity, all of the moral virtues are infused, giving one the capacity to imitate Christ's own virtues. Through its command of the acquired and infused virtues, charity directs the moral life of adopted sons so that they live in a Christ-like way—conformed to Christ, with activities shaped by virtues like his. And what is crucial to the point is that one is conformed to Christ because, through charity, one is conformed to the Holy Spirit. Chapter 4 revealed that in his discussion of adopted sonship Thomas teaches that wisdom and charity have a special role in conformation to the Son, so that believers are, insofar as possible, one in nature and love with the Trinity; this is so because, by them, believers are conformed to the Word and Love. Now we can understand that charity, as a deifying participation in the Holy Spirit, conforms the will to the object and activity of God's own love, and in this way directs all of the virtues in a Christ-like way toward the end of beatitude so that one moves toward that goal in the freedom of an adopted son.

Charity and the Gifts of the Holy Spirit   "Those who are led by the Spirit of God are children of God" (Rom 8:14). Thomas's teaching on the gifts of the Holy Spirit expresses his conviction that the Holy Spirit is the primary mover in the journey of God's adopted children to beatitude. Habitual grace, as a participation in the divine nature, ultimately disposes the person to be moved by the *auxilium* of the Holy Spirit to that end; however, this effect of grace in the perfection of the image is mediated by the virtues and gifts of the Spirit flowing from it, which transform the person's powers and dispose those powers to be docile to the Spirit's action. We are now in a better position to understand how the gifts bring about this disposition because of their relation specifically to the virtue of charity. If the moral life consists in living by Christ-like virtues commanded by charity, it also involves living, like him, under the influence of the seven gifts of the Holy Spirit that can only exist with charity: filial fear, fortitude, piety, counsel, knowledge, understanding, and wisdom.

We saw that in Thomas's treatment of Christ's possession of the virtues and gifts he especially highlights Christ's gift of filial fear.[95] In adopted sons, this gift flows from the love of charity, by which "God becomes our Father,

---

95. *ST* IIIa q7 a6. See chapter 4.

according to Rom 8:15: 'You have received the spirit of adoption of sons, by which we cry out, *Abba*! Father!'"[96] The gift of filial fear causes one to revere God out of love, so as to fear offending and being separated from God. It is the first of the gifts of the Holy Spirit—and so the beginning of wisdom—that is the highest of them all, for by wisdom one orders one's life to the enjoyment of God as it is directed to this end "according to a certain participation of the divine nature by grace."[97] Because Christ possessed all of the gifts of the Holy Spirit in fullness, the gift of fear in his humanity made him perfectly docile to the promptings of the Holy Spirit. As perfectly obedient Son, entirely subject to the Father out of love, Christ is the perfect exemplar for adopted sons with respect to the gifts and infused virtues.

Not only the gift of fear but also all of the gifts of the Holy Spirit depend upon the presence of charity. In this respect they are similar to the infused virtues but are causally linked to charity in a different way. Thomas begins his treatment of the gifts in Ia-IIae q68 a1 by acknowledging a history of disagreement as to whether the gifts of the Holy Spirit are in fact distinct from the virtues, and if so, why. He accepts Gregory the Great's distinction of the virtues and gifts in the *Moralia on Job* but rejects various solutions that insufficiently explain this distinction—the gifts are not grouped together because they belong to a specific power, or because they help one to resist temptation, or because they alone conform us to Christ, for all these things apply to the virtues as well. In fact, Thomas seems to be saying, the gifts cannot be distinguished from the virtues because they perform a specialized function parallel to the virtues; this would simply make them another kind of virtue. Thomas instead grounds his explanation of the gifts in a scriptural locus: Isaiah 11:2–3 describes them in terms of "spirit" rather than "gift" ("the spirit of wisdom and understanding," etc.) The gifts are "in us by divine inspiration ... which denotes motion from without." What characterizes the gifts is that, rather than directly shaping human action toward the good measured by the rule of reason, even as elevated by the infused virtues, they open up that very action to a principle higher than human reason, the promptings of the divine *instinctus* appropriated to the Holy Spirit in the divine *auxilium*.[98]

96. *ST* IIa-IIae q19 a2 ad3.
97. *ST* IIa-IIae q19 a7. See chapter 3.
98. Cf. *ST* Ia-IIae q68 a2 ad1: "The gifts surpass the ordinary perfection of the virtues, not

The gifts are infused *habitus*, dispositions that make the graced creature "amenable to the promptings of God," disposing the powers of the soul, shaped by the theological virtues, to be docile to the movement of the Holy Spirit.[99] The gifts thus dispose the person to be easily moved by God to the operation of all of the virtues, by the constant activity and presence of the Holy Spirit. If charity directs all of the virtues to the supernatural end by causing the will to participate in the Holy Spirit, and so be united to its divine beloved object, we can begin to see why it is so closely related to the gifts: through charity, the Holy Spirit is made present and active in the soul, dwelling in the one who loves as the beloved in the lover. Thomas makes this explicit in subsequent articles of q68 but first establishes the necessity of the gifts, and the manner of their operation, which extends to every aspect of the moral life. In the *Summa* Thomas treats each gift in association with an infused virtue, whose operation it perfects by making it more amenable to the Holy Spirit's prompting. As Servais Pinckaers notes, this plan manifests Thomas's conviction that the gifts, and thus the promptings of the Holy Spirit, are active in every Christian throughout the whole of the moral life.[100]

---

as regards the kinds of works (as the counsels surpass the commandments), but as regards the manner of working, in respect of man being moved by a higher principle." See chapter 3 for a discussion of the divine *instinctus* and its relation to the movement of auxiliary grace. As noted there, Thomas placed increasing emphasis on the primacy of divine action in his later works, in association with more frequent references to a text from Aristotle's *Eudemian Ethics* (7.14), where the latter argues for the necessity of an exterior mover of the will. Thomas refers to a related text in this work in Ia-IIae q68 a1 with reference to the divine *instinctus*. Servais Pinckaers notes that the highest number of incidences to the word *instinctus* occurs in Ia-IIae q68, on the gifts. *The Pinckaers Reader: Renewing Thomistic Moral Theology*, ed. John Berkman and Craig Titus, trans. Sr. Mary Thomas Noble et al. (Washington, DC: Catholic University of America, 2005), 388. Ulrich Horst's thorough study of the development of Thomas's thought on the gifts shows the importance of Thomas's use of this text as well as Augustine's *Commentary on the Sermon on the Mount* as he moved from an early conception of the gifts as simply operating in a suprahuman mode by overriding human faculties to his later understanding that the gifts dispose one to be moved in every aspect of the formed Christian life by the divine *instinctus*. *Die Gaben des Heiligen Geistes nach Thomas von Aquin* (Berlin: Akademie Verlag, 2001), 57, 78–79, 167–68.

99. *ST* Ia-IIae q68 a2, a5.

100. Servais Pinckaers, "Morality and the Movement of the Holy Spirit: Aquinas' Doctrine of *instinctus*," in *The Pinckaers Reader*, chap. 20, esp. 391. For an in-depth discussion, see Marie-Joseph Nicolas, "Les dons du Saint-Esprit," *Revue Thomiste* 92 (1992): 141–52, and the article by Père Labourdette on which Nicolas comments: M.-M. Labourdette, *Dictionnaire de*

Thomas's explanation of why the gifts are needed to perfect the opera-tion of the theological virtues reveals his understanding of the ubiquity and primacy of God's action moving the creature to the supernatural end. Hu-man reason elevated by grace is human reason nonetheless. The theological virtues, although they bestow a perfection higher than that of nature, are yet possessed in a way that is imperfect compared to natural virtues. Com-pared to the capacity of the virtues of natural reason to reach the connatural end, the theological virtues can attain their end only imperfectly, as God can never be fully known and loved by human beings:

As ordered to the ultimate supernatural end, to which reason moves, according as it is in a manner, and imperfectly, formed by the theological virtues, the motion of reason does not suffice, unless it receive in addition the *instinctus* and motion of the Holy Spirit, according to Rom 8:14, 17: "Those who are led by the Spirit of God are sons of God; and if sons, heirs also," and Ps 142:10: "Your good spirit will lead me into the right land," because none can attain to the inheritance of that land of the blessed except by being moved and led there by the Holy Spirit. And so to achieve that end, it is necessary for man to have the gift of the Holy Spirit.[101]

As Thomas argues in his treatment of grace, if God moves and perfects rational creatures even in their natural operations, the divine help is even more necessary for adopted sons to reach the supernatural end. This help is not only given by the extrinsic promptings of the Holy Spirit but also by the intrinsic *habitus* of the gifts, which specifically enable them to respond to those promptings in all the different areas of the moral life. The gifts are not for Thomas the special province of extraordinary people but are for all those destined for beatitude—that is, they are necessary for salvation.[102]

Spiritualité, vol. 3, s.v. "Dons du Saint-Esprit: Part IV of Saint Thomas et la théologie thomiste," 1610–35

101. *ST* Ia-IIae q68 a2.

102. Ibid. John of St. Thomas makes this point in his classic treatment of the gifts of the Holy Spirit in Thomas's doctrine. Cf. *The Gifts of the Holy Ghost*, trans. Dominic Hughes (New York: Sheed & Ward, 1951), chap. 2.16. A number of recent authors have also pointed out this fact, including Nicolas, "Les dons du Saint-Esprit"; Labourdette, "Dons du Saint-Esprit"; Pinck-aers, *Pinckaers Reader*, 384–95; Wadell, *Friends of God*, 123; and most recently Horst, *Die Gaben des Heiligen Geistes*. Nicolas remarks that the theology of the gifts, founded on the gift of char-ity in the Holy Spirit, is the theology of holiness, and so "the foundation of the universal call to holiness, because it shows how this call is inscribed in the very soul of the baptized" (151–52, my translation). There is, however, debate as to the mode of action of the gifts. James Stroud, in "Thomas Aquinas' Exposition of the Gifts of the Holy Spirit: Developments in His Thought

Thomas argues that the gifts perfect the whole person as the moral virtues perfect the appetite; the moral virtues make the will respond readily to the command of reason, while the gifts make the person docile to the movement of the Holy Spirit. The gifts "abide" in one (i.e., they are permanent dispositions, or *habitus*) because the Holy Spirit himself is within, according to John 14:17: "He shall abide with you and shall be in you." Thomas defends the idea that the gifts are intrinsic *habitus*, as he does in the case of grace and charity, because as *habitus* shaping the powers of the soul they allow the human person to act in true freedom even as God acts on them. The human subject, as a rational instrument, "is so acted upon by the Holy Spirit that he also acts himself, insofar as he has a free-will. Therefore he needs a habit."[103] In fact, it might be said, the gifts dispose the person for the

---

and Rival Interpretations" (PhD diss., Catholic University of America, 2012), outlines the history of reception of Thomas's teaching on the gifts, identifying the long predominant "standard two modes account" stemming from John of St. Thomas and represented by many influential Thomists, such as Garrigou-Lagrange in, e.g., "Le mode suprahumain des dons du Saint-Esprit," *Vie spirituelle* 7 (1923): 124–36. This model argues that "there are two modes of action in man towards his supernatural end: one human and one above/beyond the human. In the human mode, the human person with the infused virtues acts without the gifts of the Holy Spirit toward his supernatural end. In the above/beyond the human mode (*supra humanum modum*), the human person with gifts of the Holy Spirit acts toward his supernatural end" (1–2; see 69–111). I.e., the infused virtues may operate without the gifts; however, in the second mode, the gifts help them to operate with greater facility or perfection in specific instances. But Stroud shows that proponents of the standard model, relying more on the *Scriptum*, do not take into account the development of Thomas's thought in the *Summa theologiae*. The alternative account that scholars such as Servais Pinckaers and Angela McKay advance is more faithful to Thomas's fully developed thought, which distinguishes instead between one mode of human action by the acquired virtues toward the connatural end, and another by the infused virtues and gifts toward the supernatural end. In this model, which is in accord with my own findings, the gifts are understood to be always at work in the graced person moving toward beatitude. Joseph de Guibert, SJ, initiated the early twentieth-century debate with Garrigou-Lagrange as to Thomas's evolution in terminology, which Garrigou-Lagrange denied; see De Guibert, "Dons de Saint-Esprit et le mode d'agir ultrahumain d'apres Saint Thomas," *Revue d'Ascétique et de Mystique* 3 (1922): 394–411. Cf. Servais Pinckaers, "Morality and the Movement of the Holy Spirit," in *The Pinckaers Reader*, chap. 20, 385–95, esp. 391; Angela M. McKay, "The Infused and Acquired Virtues in Aquinas' Moral Philosophy" (PhD diss., University of Notre Dame, 2004). See also Cruz Gonzalez Ayesta's related discussion and critique of the school of John of St. Thomas on the gifts in *El Don de Sabiduría según Santo Tomás* (Pamplona: Ediciones Universidad de Navarra, 1998), esp. 68–88. Ayesta, also observing development in Thomas's thought, contends that the tradition of interpretation following John of St. Thomas leads to a mistakenly psychological view of them, which proposes a division between the ordinary ascetic and extraordinary mystical life (e.g., 20).

103. *ST* Ia-IIae q68 a3 ad2.

action of cooperating grace, by which the mind "both moves and is moved" by God.[104]

The perfection of "all human forces" for this action—so that they can "be moved by the *instinctus* of God, as by a superior power"—means that both intellect and will are the subjects of the gifts. The gifts operate in every aspect of human thought and willing, and therefore in the whole moral life. To each theological and cardinal virtue is assigned a corresponding gift. As Thomas remarks, they "extend to everything to which the virtues, both intellectual and moral, extend."[105] The gifts also operate to perfect the theological virtues, but, Thomas explains further, the gifts are related to these in a different way. His reason sheds further light on the role of charity with respect to the gifts:

104. *ST* Ia-IIae q111 a2. Nicolas argues that the grace of the gifts is operating grace because an act of the gifts in which one is moved by the divine *instinctus* is the result of an "immediate divine motion," not "the fruit of deliberation or reasoning, the final moment of a whole process, but an immediate participation of the spirit in that which God sees and wills for the one whom he inspires." "Les Dons du Saint-Esprit," 144. Nicolas is particularly thinking of the act of infused prudence, which can manifest the foolishness of the cross in contradiction to the reasoned action of ordinary prudence. Thomas's own explanation of the reason for the necessity of a *habitus* for the gifts seems to indicate that the answer is more complex, however; the gifts dispose the free will to be a more perfect moved mover in the activity of all the virtues. Thus they dispose for the ready choice of means and execution of the virtuous act, the province of the free will and so of cooperating grace. This is clear in light of the discussion of operating and cooperating *auxilium* in chapter 3. While operating grace causes the interior act of the will in each act of charity (directing it to the supernatural end), its exterior act must take place under the influence of cooperating grace; likewise, the exterior acts of the moral and intellectual virtues that have to do with the means to the end, while directed interiorly by charity toward the last end, are caused by cooperating grace (and can therefore be meritorious). Therefore, as the gifts bestow a disposition in the free will for all the virtues to be easily moved to their acts, once operating grace has moved the will to the highest end, they dispose the person for the action of cooperating grace. A comment by Pinckaers is relevant: "This is the peculiar effect of inspiration or of the gifts: to achieve the unity of action between the superior principle, which is God's Spirit, and the interior principles which are the virtues, at the level of our free and reasonable will, at the source of our actions." *Pinckaers Reader*, 389. The notion that the gifts dispose one for operating grace is perhaps at work in the thought of those who would argue that Thomas envisions the infused virtues and gifts as governing a "mystical life" distinct from ordinary Christian life, in which one is increasingly passive under the divine influence; e.g., R. Bernard's comment that "there can be no better cooperation for [the soul] than that of complete abandonment" ("La vertu infuse et le don du Saint-Esprit," *La Vie Spirituelle* 42 [1935], suppl. 67) and Wadell's discussion in support of this view that under the gifts we are "moved by divine agency instead of our own" (*Friends of God*, 131).

105. *ST* Ia-IIae q68 a4.

The mind of man is not moved by the Holy Spirit, unless it is united to him in some way, as the instrument is not moved by the craftsman except by contact, or some other union. But the primary union of man [with God] is by faith, hope and charity. So these virtues are presupposed to the gifts, as the roots of the gifts. So all the gifts correspond to these virtues, as being derived from them.[106]

The Holy Spirit's gifts are only at work in the human mind that is united to God, a union to which all the theological virtues contribute but that is ultimately the effect of charity. This union must be present for the gifts to do their work of rendering the person docile to the Spirit's promptings even with respect to the theological virtues themselves.[107]

Therefore charity must be present:

The Holy Spirit dwells in us through charity, according to Rom 5:5: "The charity of God is poured forth in our hearts by the Holy Spirit, who has been given to us," just as our reason is perfected by prudence. Just as all the moral virtues are connected together in prudence, so the gifts of the Holy Spirit are connected together in charity, so that whoever has charity has all the gifts of the Holy Spirit, none of which can be had without charity.[108]

As prudence governs the appetitive power disposed by the moral virtues, the Holy Spirit with its gifts governs the soul. For the gifts of the Spirit to be present and at work, the Holy Spirit itself must be present in the special mode belonging to those in whom God "dwells as in his own temple"— that is, in the Spirit's divine mission "according to the mode of charity" that brings about the divine indwelling, in which the soul is likened to the Holy Spirit.[109] Thomas is not saying that God's causal power is somehow limited by God's "location" with respect to the soul, but rather that by charity the soul is disposed with respect to God's action. The Holy Spirit dwells in one by charity because by charity the will participates in the Holy Spirit. The will that participates in the Holy Spirit is united to it not only by likeness

---

106. *ST* Ia-IIae q68 a4 ad3. While Thomas holds that all of the gifts correspond to the theological virtues, he particularly associates certain ones with each virtue in his treatments of them: understanding and knowledge with faith, fear with hope, and wisdom with charity. Treatments of the other gifts are found in the treatment of the cardinal virtues: counsel (prudence), piety (justice), fortitude (fortitude). Thomas assigns the gift of fear to temperance also (IIa-IIae q141 a1 ad3).

107. See also *ST* Ia-IIae q68 a8.   108. *ST* Ia-IIae q68 a5.

109. *ST* Ia q43 a3, a5 ad2.

but also because by virtue of that likeness it loves God as beloved object in a bond of union. It is this union by assimilation, making of the mind a united instrument, that prepares all of the faculties to be docile to the Spirit's action via the gifts. As charity's participation in the Holy Spirit is the reason why it commands the other virtues, so it also explains why charity is the root of the Spirit's gifts.[110]

And because charity endures in heaven—that is, because the Spirit's mission continues to the blessed[111]—so also do the gifts. In heaven, where charity is perfected, the gifts will exist perfectly, as they did in Christ, whose charity was perfect in his earthly life. In heaven the minds of the blessed are perfectly docile to the movement of the Holy Spirit because they are perfected in good by the gifts.[112] Charity, then, from the beginning of the Spirit's mission in the soul, commands the virtues, and roots the gifts, orienting the person throughout their life toward beatitude. By charity's participation in the Holy Spirit, flowing from grace's participation in the divine nature, "the love of God is poured into our hearts by the Holy Spirit" given to God's adopted children. Through charity, the indwelling Spirit, whose grace is the New Law of freedom written on our hearts,[113] bestows on God's children a freedom that grows ever greater with charity's increase—the true

110. John of St. Thomas emphasizes the connaturality that charity bestows for the operation of the gifts, especially the intellectual gifts (e.g., *Gifts of the Holy Ghost*, 3.39). I examine this further in connection with the gift of wisdom.

111. *ST* Ia q43 a6 ad3.

112. *ST* Ia-IIae q68 a6, c., ad1. Thomas considers objections that the gifts seem to be given in order to aid the *viator*, in the state of ignorance and temptation, and some, such as fortitude, seem peculiar to the active life that will cease in heaven. He responds with an interpretation of Gregory's *Moralia* on the gifts, attempting to show that Gregory describes each gift in terms of something that passes away and something that remains in heaven; e.g., in the case of wisdom Gregory "says that 'wisdom strengthens the mind with the hope and certainty of eternal things,' of which, two, hope passes, and certainty remains" (ad2). Thomas proposes that although the gifts will not work with respect to the same matters as in the active life, "all the gifts will have their respective acts about things pertaining to the contemplative life, which is the blessed life" (ad3). Although his explanations are somewhat unsatisfactory, he provides more specific answers in his questions on the individual gifts as to their acts in the state of glory; so in the case of fortitude, its act in heaven "is to enjoy full security from toil and evil" because "the gifts do not have the same acts in heaven as on the way, for they exercise their acts there in connection with the enjoyment of the end" (*ST* IIa-IIae q139 a1 ad2). In heaven, then, the gift of fortitude seems to dispose one for unwavering firmness of mind in enjoyment of the beatific vision.

113. *ST* Ia-IIae q106 a1, q108 a1.

freedom that Pinckaers describes as "freedom for excellence," freedom for
the movement toward eternal life.[114] The central unifying role that Thomas
gives to charity with respect to all the virtues and gifts demonstrates again
his thoroughly pneumatological understanding of the journey to beatitude.
It also contributes to his holistic vision of this journey; although distinctions must be made in the examination of the virtues and gifts, ultimately
it is the whole acting person, with all of his faculties properly ordered by
charity, who mounts up freely to perfection. In this journey, charity, as a
participation in the Holy Spirit, is the director of the whole person to beatitude, not only by its intrinsic orientation of the will to the last end, and thus
its command of the virtues, but also as the root of the gifts that dispose the
person for the Spirit's extrinsic leading.

Charity and the Holy Spirit's Role in the Journey to Beatitude

There are clear parallels between IIa-IIae q24, on the will as the subject of
charity, and Ia-IIae q109, on the necessity of grace. These parallels demonstrate that in his treatment of charity, Thomas is expanding on the same
topic of divine action in the journey to beatitude he had already introduced, and making more explicit its pneumatological character. Throughout the articles of q109, as discussed in chapter 3, Thomas sketches a model
of the need for grace, both habitual and auxiliary, at every stage of the journey. Articles 1–4 discuss the limited capacity of intellect and will to know
the truth and do the good, and to love God and fulfill the commandments
without grace. Grace is needed for fallen humanity to will and act for supernatural good, and even to perfectly reach natural good ends. Thomas notes
that sin has corrupted the will more than the intellect,[115] following his earlier teachings (drawn from Augustine) on the will as the first mover in sinful
acts, and original sin's basic nature as concupiscence.[116] Grace is necessary to
merit eternal life (a5), to prepare oneself for grace (a6), to rise from sin (a7),
to avoid sin (a8), to continue in the good (a9), and to persevere in good to
the end of life (a10).

In IIa-IIae q24 Thomas examines the infusion and growth of charity in

114. See *Pinckaers Reader*, 390–95; Servais Pinckaers, *The Sources of Christian Ethics,* trans.
Sr. Thomas Mary Noble (Washington, DC: Catholic University of America Press, 1995), chap. 15.
115. *ST* Ia-IIae q109 a2 ad3.
116. Cf. *ST* Ia-IIae q74 a2, q82 a3, and references to Augustine therein.

the will throughout this journey, and the possibility of its loss in those who do not have the gift of perseverance. In q24 a1 he establishes that the will is the subject of charity because the will's object is the good as apprehended by the intellect, and the divine good, as the object of charity, is known by the intellect alone.[117] Charity, flowing from the gift of grace, elevates the healed will's operation to this supernatural end (cf. Ia-IIae q109 a2).[118] As Thomas had already said in Ia-IIae q109 a3, while

> nature loves God above all things inasmuch as he is the beginning and end of natural good ... charity loves him as he is the object of beatitude, and inasmuch as man has a spiritual fellowship with God.[119]

In q24 a2, where Thomas discusses charity's infusion as a participation of the Holy Spirit, he argues that charity, "poured forth in our hearts by the Holy Spirit" (Rom 5:5), must be an infused gift because it is "a friendship of man for God, founded upon the communication of eternal beatitude." Such a communication is "not according to natural goods but to gifts of grace, because, as it says in Rom 6:23, 'the grace of God is everlasting life.'" Charity thus surpasses the natural faculties (which could not attain this end). In Ia-IIae q109 a5, on whether humans can merit everlasting life without grace, Thomas introduces his answer with this same text from Romans 6:23, and twice refers to the Gloss on this text, as he argues there too that, as everlasting life is an end exceeding natural human faculties, the gift of grace, preparing the will, is needed to produce the works that attain to this end. Question 24 a2 explains that charity, likening the will to the Holy Spirit, prepares it for such supernatural works by directing it to the divine good and commanding the other virtues to that end, as well as being the root of the gifts that dispose one to be moved by the Holy Spirit. So Thomas argues in Ia-IIae q114 that merit is attributed chiefly to charity through the power of the Holy Spirit moving us to everlasting life.[120]

In Ia-IIae q109 the activity of the Holy Spirit in this journey, by virtue of its association with the gift of grace, was clear but mostly implicit. The Spirit's role in the journey becomes more explicit in the questions on charity, however. Both Ia-IIae q109 a6 and IIa-IIae q24 a3 consider the possible role

---

117. See Sherwin, *By Knowledge and by Love.*
118. On the insufficiency of the will without grace, especially to do or will supernatural good.
119. *ST* Ia-IIae q109 a3 ad1.
120. Cf. Ia-IIae q114 aa3–4.

of prior disposition on the part of the human recipient for the gift of grace or charity. Question 109 a6 asks, "Can one prepare oneself for grace, without the help of grace?" and q24 a3, "Is charity infused according to natural capacity?" The answer to both is no. Thomas emphasizes in both questions his mature teaching on the prevenience of the divine motion in the preparation of the human will, focusing in q109 a6 on the need for God's help, in the gifts both of habitual grace, and of the divine *auxilium* moving the soul to its act.

In q24 a3, however, the role of the Holy Spirit comes much more openly to the fore with reference to both of these gifts. Thomas begins in the *sed contra*:

It is written in Jn 3:8, "The Spirit breathes where he wills," and in 1 Cor 12:11, "One and the same Spirit works all these things, dividing to each one as he will." Therefore charity is not given according to natural capacity, but according to the will of the Spirit distributing his gifts.

Throughout the rest of the *corpus*, Thomas attributes the quantity of charity infused in each "solely to the grace of the Holy Spirit who pours out charity" and "who divides his gifts according to his will." This attribution to the Spirit of the quantity of infusion of the habitual form of charity is followed in the answer to the first objection by a reference also to the Spirit's activity in the operating *auxilium* of conversion, as Thomas explains that though there may be a preparation for the reception of grace, "the Holy Spirit prevenes even this disposition or effort, by moving man's mind either more or less, as he wills. So the Apostle says (Col 1:12): 'He has made us worthy to share the lot of the saints in light.'" The special role of the Holy Spirit in the journey to glory, often enough implicit in the questions on grace, can now be understood more explicitly because in the gift of charity flowing from grace the Holy Spirit has "poured out the love of God into our hearts (Rom 5:5)" by bestowing a participation in himself.

Charity's role in the journey emerges even more clearly in q24 aa4–9, where Thomas discusses charity's increase and perfection. There are no complete parallels to these articles in the remaining ones (aa7–10) of Ia-IIae q109, for there the focus was on the need for grace on the journey in spite of the ongoing human tendency toward sin, whereas in discussing the growth of charity Thomas is for the moment attending to the potential of those who have been given grace to overcome it.[121] Yet the obstacle of sin is not far from his thoughts, as he returns in q24 aa10–12 to consider the loss of charity through sin, and one can make connections to the picture of the more difficult aspects of the journey traced in q109 aa7–10, on grace. Even where Thomas focuses only on the increase of charity in the good will, however, he adverts to the causal picture he established earlier of the primacy of the divine agency, especially in supernatural action, which yet allows the free and proper activity of the will as a moved mover.

Thomas's discussion of charity's increase, as a supernatural *habitus*, both builds on and surpasses discussions earlier in the *Summa* about *habitus* and their increase in general. In fact, the closest structural parallels to q24 aa4–6—whether charity can increase, whether it does so by addition, and whether every act of charity increases charity—appear in Ia-IIae q52, on the increase of *habitus*, which contains three articles with the same subjects regarding *habitus* in general. Natural, or acquired, virtues in the will can be both caused and increased by the repetition of acts, that is, by habituation.[122] Infused virtues, which dispose one for an end above nature, can be caused by divine infusion alone—and so Augustine defines them as virtues that "God works in us without us"[123]—but the acts of these virtues can "strengthen the already existing *habitus*," disposing for its increase.[124] These acts are inspired by grace, and in them both divine and human agency are at work.[125] As any *habitus* increases, its subject participates more perfectly in the form.[126]

Thomas establishes in q24 a4 that charity can increase:

---

121. Although in a related article on merit (Ia-IIae q114 a8) in the questions on grace, Thomas argues that one can merit an increase in grace and charity by condign merit—i.e., the merit that derives from the activity of the Holy Spirit moving one to eternal life—such that one called to the goal reaches it step by step.

122. *ST* Ia-IIae q51 aa3–4.

123. Cf. Ia-IIae q63 a2: Human virtue ordained to the good which is delimited according to the rule of human reason can be caused by human acts, inasmuch as acts of this kind proceed from the reason, under whose power and rule such good is established. On the other hand, virtue ordaining man to good as delimited by the divine law, and not by human reason, cannot be caused by human acts, the principle of which is reason, but is caused in us only by divine operation. And so, defining virtue of this kind, Augustine places in the definition of virtue: 'which God works in us without us.'"

124. *ST* Ia-IIae q51 a4 ad3.

125. For a helpful discussion of the question of divine and human agency in the infused virtues, in Aquinas as well as in a wider historical context, see Herdt, *Putting on Virtue*, 86–91.

126. *ST* Ia-IIae q52 a1, q66 a1.

Augustine says (*On John*) that "charity merits to be increased, that having grown it may merit to be perfected."[127] I answer that the charity of the way can increase. For, we are called wayfarers because we tend towards God, who is the ultimate end of our beatitude. On this way we progress further the nearer we draw to God, who is not approached by movements of the body, but by affections of the mind. And charity brings about this nearness, because through it the mind is united to God. And therefore it is of the *ratio* of the charity of the way that it can be increased, for if it were not increased, progression along the way would cease. And therefore the Apostle calls charity the way, saying in 1 Cor 12:31, "I will show you a more excellent way."

The movements of charity, by which it constantly grows greater, are the steps by which we approach God, until the perfect charity of heaven is attained.[128] The central role of charity in the journey to beatitude thus cannot be overestimated; this journey is nothing other than the soul's progress in charity until it reaches union with God.

In q24 a5 Thomas says that growth in charity takes place not by addition but by an increasing likeness to the Holy Spirit, in which the soul participates more and more perfectly, as charity exists more within it.[129] Charity increases "as its subject participates charity more and more; that is, as it is more reduced to [charity's] act, and made more subject to it"; charity increases "solely by intensification."[130] Thomas echoes his description in Ia IIae q52 a2 of the increase of *habitus* in general, not by addition but by intensity, through an increasingly more perfect participation in a form, as the subject's potential is more fully actualized by an agent. But Thomas is describing an intensification in the possession of the habitual form of charity, by a reduction to act that can only be attributed to the Holy Spirit (cf. q24 a3), and the focus is on divine agency. As in Ia-IIae q109, he is thinking of the dual divine action of God in bestowing a supernatural *habitus* and actualizing its potential through the divine *auxilium*.

But this is only one side of the story; the moved will is also a mover, and the exterior human act must involve the cooperation of the free will,

---

127. *Tractate 74*.

128. In q24 aa4–9 the influence of Augustine, whose original teaching this was, is particularly clear. This idea is found in Augustine's *Tractate 32 on John*, in which he preaches on Jn 7:37–39, about Christ's giving of the Holy Spirit, "whose greatest benefits are in us because through him the charity of God has been poured out in our hearts."

129. *ST* IIa-IIae q24 a5 ad3.

130. *ST* IIa-IIae q24 a5 c., ad1.

to allow the possibility of merit. Question 24 a6 considers to what extent charity's increase is due to the human actor moved by God. The article asks whether charity increases with every act of charity. In Ia-IIae q52 a3 Thomas made the point that not all acts of a *habitus* increase it; rather, acts done carelessly or in some way with an intensity underproportioned to the *habitus* will eventually result in its decrease. Each individual act of a *habitus* may not have a direct effect but may cumulatively dispose toward a subsequent increase or decrease, as many morsels of food increase an animal's size, or many drops of water hollow out a stone. The acts of infused virtues work something like this: unlike those of acquired virtues, acts of infused virtues do not directly cause growth in the virtue, because God alone does that, but they dispose their possessor well or ill for the reception of an increase of the virtue from God.[131]

In q24 a6 Thomas first warns that if an act of charity is done with tepidity or slackness, "it does not conduce to a more excellent charity, but rather disposes one to a lower degree." Then, using the simile of an animal's bodily increase through many morsels of food that cumulatively dispose for—but do not each actually cause—a growth spurt, he goes on to argue:

Charity does not actually increase through every act of charity, but each act of charity disposes to an increase of charity, insofar as one act of charity makes man ready to act again more promptly according to charity, and this readiness increasing, he breaks out into an act of more fervent love, and strives to advance in charity, and then charity increases in act.

Each act of charity stimulates the desire for God, sharpening one's hunger for union with him and so disposing one well for the acts leading to that union. In response to the first objection, Thomas clarifies that every act of charity merits two things: everlasting life, bestowed later, and an increase in charity, bestowed "when we strive for that increase." God alone moves one to the exercise and grants the increase, but we too have a cooperative and meritorious role in disposing our will by fervently carrying out the acts of charity, and so moving closer to God. The quality of one's acts of charity can contribute to a growing likeness to the Holy Spirit—and so a nearer approach to beatitude, but, as Thomas says in later articles, sinful acts can also dispose for, or entirely cause, its loss.

131. On this, see Wawrykow, *God's Grace and Human Action*, 225.

Thomas considers in aa7–9 the trajectory of perfection in charity followed by the soul on its way to beatitude, and in aa10–12 the loss of charity through sinful acts. His teaching on both is shaped by the notion of charity as a participated form higher than nature, which raises the person to an end beyond nature. In a7 Thomas argues that no limit can be fixed to the increase of charity for the one who is still a wayfarer because "it is a participation of the infinite charity which is the Holy Spirit." God, who is the cause of charity, has infinite power, and the subject's capacity for charity increases whenever charity increases. Charity stretches the rational creature's capacity, "enlarging our hearts," according to 2 Corinthians 6:11.[132] Charity can increase indefinitely for the wayfarer because its end is not in the present but in a future life.[133] And yet there is a clear distinction between even the perfect charity of the wayfarer and that of the blessed, which Thomas compares to the difference between a line and a surface.[134] Because of the fullness of knowledge in the beatific vision, charity in heaven has a kind of three-dimensional richness.

In a8 Thomas describes charity's incremental perfection. No creature can love God perfectly as he loves himself, but "on the part of the lover, charity is perfect when he loves as much as he can." The charity of the saints is perfect as the charity of *viatores* cannot yet be, because in heaven

the whole heart of man is always actually borne towards God … and this is not possible in this life, in which, because of the weakness of human life, it is impossible to think always actually of God and to be moved by love towards him.[135]

The perfection of charity possible to a wayfarer (and attained by some) is to try earnestly to give oneself to God and to divine things, except when one must attend to the needs of this life. Finally, one who has charity attains its perfection in the most basic kind of way "when he habitually [even if not actually] gives his whole heart to God, by not thinking or desiring anything contrary to the love of God." As noted below, the language of "habitual or actual" love of God, which Thomas uses here, connects this article to his treatment of the perfection of the image.

In a9 Thomas describes the progress of perfection in charity for the wayfarer in more practical terms, according to the three traditional degrees

132. *ST* IIa-IIae q24 a7 ad2.   133. *ST* IIa-IIae q24 a7 c., ad1.
134. *ST* IIa-IIae q24 a7 ad3.   135. *ST* IIa-IIae q24 a8.

of the spiritual life: beginners, whose struggle is against sin (and who according to a8 would have at least habitual charity); proficients, who strive to progress in good; and those who are perfect, whose chief aim is union with and enjoyment of God (both of whom would have charity in varying degrees, actually). For the completion of this trajectory one would have to return to Ia q12, on the beatific vision (see chap. 1), where Thomas said that those who have more charity will have a fuller (more actual) participation in the light of glory—be made more deiform—and so see God more perfectly because their greater desire has disposed them to receive the object of their desire.[136] The more charity enlarges the human heart in this life—the more the soul participates in the likeness of the Holy Spirit and strives toward God, moved by the Spirit to actually love God—the more one will be like God and enjoy God in heaven.

The degrees of perfection in habitually or actually loving God that Thomas traces in IIa-IIae q24 aa7–9 clearly reflect those in Ia q93 on the perfection of the image, where he said that the graced image "actually or habitually knows and loves God, though imperfectly," while the image possessing the likeness of glory knows and loves God fully and actually, and so perfectly represents the divine Persons of Word and Love.[137] Now we can understand how the soul, participating the Holy Spirit by charity in act, more perfectly "represents the species" of Love as it grows in charity and so is deified, with respect to the will, as the Trinitarian image of God.

In aa10–11 Thomas considers the possibility of charity's decrease or loss. The charity of heaven cannot be lost, for the blessed see the object of their desire, the divine essence, "the very essence of goodness," and love it wholly and actually.[138] The charity of the wayfarer is not fully actualized, though—and so long as the movement of the mind is not always actually directed toward God, the possibility remains that it can be lost. As in the growth of charity, Thomas takes into account both divine and human causality in charity's loss. But while charity can progressively increase in this life with our meritorious cooperation, it cannot incrementally diminish but can only be lost by our failure to cooperate with God. Charity is caused by God alone, not by human acts, so, as Joseph Wawrykow points out, Thom-

---

136. *ST* Ia q12 a6.   137. *ST* Ia q93 a7.
138. *ST* IIae-IIae q24 a11.

as "disallows talk of 'decrease'" with respect to charity; unlike an acquired virtue, no stable *habitus* is formed in the person on account of repeated acts of an infused virtue, which a single defective act might undermine but not destroy. Rather, as one mortal sin destroys the communion between the human being and God, it removes charity entirely.[139]

Charity cannot be lost by simply not performing the acts of charity, unless a sin is involved, as the *habitus* of charity would otherwise remain.[140] As Thomas says in Ia-IIae q109 a8, however, one cannot avoid venial sins, or remain free of mortal sin for long, without the help of grace. Venial sins, and even the cessation of acts of charity, do contribute to charity's loss by disposing one for that loss, and mortal sins destroy charity entirely, because they are directly contrary to charity and merit the punitive withdrawal of God's love.[141] Although charity in act cannot lead to sin, when "charity is not acting actually," consent may be given to a motive for sin.[142] Charity can be lost in this life because of the changeability of the free will. In practice, God's constant help is needed to keep and grow in the *habitus* of charity.[143]

The primacy of divine action in salvation is seen in q24 of Thomas's treatment of charity, as it was in the questions on grace, by his teaching that growth to the full measure of charity belongs only to those who have the gift of perseverance, and so can avoid sin to the end. As in Ia-IIae q109 a10, Thomas draws in q24 a11 on Augustine's mature anti-Pelagian writings to underline the need for this special operating *auxilium* to remain in the good until the end.[144] Although charity may be lost by the weakness of the

---

139. Joseph Wawrykow, "Theological Virtues," in *The Oxford Handbook of Aquinas*, ed. Eleonore Stump and Brian Davies (Oxford: Oxford University Press, 2012).

140. God, as cause, does not take back his gift except in punishment for sin; so charity could only be lost by sin, either directly or by way of punishment.

141. *ST* IIa-IIae q24 a10. Venial sins involve disordered affections for things directed to the end of union with God, mortal sins turn away from that end itself.

142. *ST* IIa-IIae q24 a11, c., ad4.

143. Cf. *ST* IIa-IIae q24 a12: "Charity, being an infused habit, depends on the action of God who infuses it, who stands in relation to the infusion and safekeeping of charity, as sun does to the infusion of light in the air." Mortal sin places an obstacle that immediately cuts off the influx of charity by God into the soul because by disobedience one prefers sin to God's friendship.

144. On operating grace and the gift of perseverance, see Wawrykow, *God's Grace and Human Action*, 266–76. As discussed in chapter 3, Wawrykow draws from the earlier work of Henri Bouillard (*Conversion et grâce chez S. Thomas d'Aquin* [Paris: Aubier, 1944]), on Thomas's use of these works of the later Augustine in his theology of grace, and J. Patout Burns (*The Devel-*

unaided will in consenting to sin, it cannot fail through sin on the part of charity's cause, the Holy Spirit who dwells in those who have charity and who "infallibly works whatever he wills":

> It is impossible that these two things should be true: that the Holy Spirit should move someone to the act of charity, and that the same person should lose charity by sinning, for the gift of perseverance is counted among the "benefits of God, by which those who are freed are most certainly freed," as Augustine says in the book *De praedestinatione sanctorum*.[145]

Those who receive the gift of perseverance from the Holy Spirit—and so become more perfectly like and effectively moved by the Holy Spirit—will reach the end of beatitude. This final parallel in IIa-IIae q24 with Ia-IIae q109 serves to underscore the role of charity, and thus of the Holy Spirit as exemplar and efficient cause, in the working-out of the entire graced journey to beatitude. The Holy Spirit is the pattern and motor, through charity in the will, of grace's movement of the human person to eternal life.

Romans 5:5 in the *Summa*

In this regard it is worth noting the significant presence throughout the *Summa*—in key loci having to do with various aspects of the image's journey to beatitude—of Romans 5:5: "Hope does not disappoint, because the charity of God has been poured out into our hearts by the Holy Spirit who has been given to us." This is a central scriptural text for Thomas with respect to the notion of charity as a participation in the Holy Spirit, and the

---

opment of Augustine's Doctrine of Operative Grace* [Paris: Études augustiniennes, 1980]), who discusses the development of Augustine's own teaching on the operating grace of perseverance necessary for the predestined. Cf. Augustine, *De correptione et gratia*, Corpus scriptorum ecclesiasticorum latinorum 92, ed. Georges Folliet (Vienna: Verlag der Österreichischen Akademie der Wissenschaften, 2000); "*De dono perseverantiae* and *De praedestinatione sanctorum*," in *Aux moines d'Adrumète et de Provence. Saint Augustine: Texte de l'édition bénédictine*, Oeuvres de Saint Augustin: Bibliothèque Augustinienne 24 (Paris: Desclée, 1962). An English translation of the latter two is available: *Saint Augustine: Four Anti-Pelagian Writings*, trans. John Mourant and William J. Collinge, intr. William J. Collinge (Washington, DC: Catholic University of America Press, 1992).

145. Thomas actually refers to either the introduction or chapter 14 of *De dono perseverantiae*, where this phrase appears; *De dono pers.* was transmitted as the second volume of *De praed. sanctorum*.

Spirit's causality in bringing the creature to eternal beatitude—the goal of the "hope which does not disappoint." In the questions on charity itself, it appears as the authority in the *sed contra* of IIa-IIae q24 a2, on the infusion of charity, where Thomas makes his principal argument that participation in the Holy Spirit causes charity. It is also present in the background of q23 a2, on charity as something created in the soul. Romans 5:5 played a significant role in the history of debate about the identification of the Holy Spirit with charity, to which this article refers. Lombard uses it as his own authority where he identifies the two in I d17 of the *Sentences*, interpreting it in light of a text from Augustine, where, in the *DV* 15, the latter refers to Romans 5:5 in his argument that the source of human love for God is God's own love. In q23 a2 Thomas adverts to and refutes Lombard's opinion, arguing that Augustine (formed as he was by "Platonist" teachings) meant that human charity is a participation in divine love. Thomas teaches that charity is not, as Lombard thought, the Holy Spirit itself at work in us *without* us, but rather that the will, participating in and so conformed to the Spirit, with the same activity and end, works freely as a deified principle of action under the Spirit's influence. Romans 5:5 therefore carries a certain weight for Thomas as a text that conveys the notion of charity as a participation in the Holy Spirit—and thus also the notion of the Spirit's presence and activity in the journey to beatitude.

Thomas refers directly to Romans 5:5 twenty times in the *Summa*, first in the question on the divine missions, where he explains that the Holy Spirit is the giver of grace, which disposes the soul to receive the divine indwelling of the Persons.[146] It appears twice elsewhere in the Ia *pars* with reference to the charity of the angels.[147] The bulk of the references occur in the IIa *pars* in a series of contexts that effectively sketch major aspects of the "advance of the rational creature to God" through grace, and the virtues and gifts directed by charity to eternal life: questions on the infused virtues, gifts, fruits, New Law (fulfilled by charity and making one fit for beatitude), grace, charity, wisdom, joy, freedom of obedience, spiritual judgment, patience, and spiritual freedom from sin.[148] In the IIIa *pars*, Romans

---

146. *ST* Ia q43 a3 ad2.

147. To make the point that it is caused by God; *ST* Ia q60 a5 ob4, q108 a4 ob2.

148. *ST* Ia-IIae q65 a2 ob2, q68 a5, q70 a3, q91 a5, q98 a1, q107 a1 ad2, q109 a3 ob1; IIa-IIae q19 a6 ob2, q24 a2, q28 a1, q44 a1 ob2, q45 a6 ob1, q60 a1 ob2, q136 a3, q183 a4 ad1.

5:5 is the key scriptural referent in q23 a3 for Thomas's argument that adopted sonship, as a participation in the sonship of Christ by the "Spirit of adoption" (Rom 8:15), belongs only to those who have charity; it also appears in a question on sacramental character, in relation to charity as that which marks out the saints as ordained to eternal life.[149] In other words, by simply examining the loci where references to Romans 5:5 appear in the *Summa*, one could form a somewhat comprehensive map of Thomas's theology of deification in its Trinitarian cause, moral unfolding, and Christological exemplar. If, as I argue here, this text carries for Thomas the notion of the Holy Spirit's activity in deification as participated exemplar and mover, then the presence and activity of the Holy Spirit can truly be said to permeate his entire presentation of the journey of the image to beatitude in the *Summa*.

A comparison with the use of Romans 5:5 in Thomas's other works, based on the *Index Thomisticus*, reveals an interesting contrast: it appears with relative infrequency in works that treat charity from Thomas's early to midcareer—such as the *Scriptum, De veritate*, and *Summa contra Gentiles*[150]—but significantly more often (besides the *Summa*) in three scriptural works from Thomas's middle to late years—the *Catena aurea* and the *Commentary on Romans* and *Commentary on John*, written just before or over the same period of time as the *Summa*.[151] The *Catena* contains seven citations of the

---

149. *ST* IIIa q23 a3, q63 a3 ob3.

150. *Scriptum* bk1 d14 q2 a1 qc1 sc1 (the Holy Spirit is given temporally); bk3 d13 q2 a2 qc2 ad1 (the Holy Spirit diffuses charity throughout the mystical body); d27 q2 a2 c. (charity is a theological virtue that fits us for friendship with God); and a4 qc4 sc1 (charity cannot be unformed). *DV* q27 a2 sc2 (the grace of the Holy Spirit precedes, and is other than, charity). *SCG* III.151.7; IV.18.3 (the Holy Spirit causes the perfection of the human mind); IV.21.1 (in loving God we are made like the Holy Spirit, who is the love of Father and Son). Although in the *Summa contra Gentiles* Thomas does not yet systematically speak of charity as a participation in the Holy Spirit (but see IV.17.22), his teaching in *SCG* IV on the role of the Spirit in creation and salvation, and the way in which "the love by which we love God is properly representative of the Holy Spirit" (IV.21.1–2), is similar to that in the *Summa theologiae*. In some respects, owing to the organization of the material on the Holy Spirit into a single locus, his teaching here is more accessible. Jean Pierre Torrell dates all of these works as completed by 1265, the last being *SCG* IV, probably completed in 1264–65. *Saint Thomas Aquinas*, vol. 1, *The Person and His Work*, trans. Robert Royal (Washington, DC: Catholic University of America Press, 2003), 332–34.

151. Torrell accepts dates for the *Catena* between 1265 and 1268; the existing *Commentary on Romans* (possibly a second version) from 1271 to 1272; and the *Commentary on John* prob-

verse (all from separate loci in Augustine's *Commentary on John*), while in Thomas's own John commentary he makes reference to it eleven times, four of these associated—as in *ST* IIIa q23 a3—with Romans 8:14–15, in the context of teaching on the charity belonging to adopted sons, led by the Spirit of God.

Although space does not permit a full examination of these developments, Thomas's exegesis of Romans 5:5 in the *Commentary on Romans* sets forth his most explicit teaching on charity as a participation in the Holy Spirit, which directs the whole of the moral life toward God:

> The charity of God can be taken in two ways: in one way, for the charity by which God loves us: "He loved you with an everlasting love" (Jer 31:3); in another way for the charity [of God] by which we love God: "I am sure that neither death nor life will separate us from the love of God" (Rom 8:39). In both ways "the charity of God is poured into our hearts by the Holy Spirit who has been given to us." For the Holy Spirit, who is the love of the Father and Son, to be given to us, is for us to be brought to participation in the Love who is the Holy Spirit, by which participation we are made lovers of God. The fact that we love him is the sign that he loves us: "I love those who love me" (Pr 8:17); "Not that we loved God but that he first loved us" (1 Jn 4:10). The charity by which he loves us is said to be poured into our hearts, because it is clearly shown in our hearts by the gift of the Holy Spirit impressed in us: "By this we know that he remains in us," etc. (1 Jn 3:24). But the love by which we love God is said to be poured into our hearts, that is, because it extends itself to the perfecting of all the moral habits and acts of the soul; for, as it says in 1 Cor 13:4, "Charity is patient, it is kind," etc.[152]

Thomas presents here a number of the same ideas that can be found in different places in the *Summa theologiae*, brought together into one narra-

---

ably to 1270–72. The first would be concurrent with the Ia *pars*, and the latter two with the IIa and IIIa *pars*, of the *Summa theologiae*. *Saint Thomas Aquinas*, vol. 1, 337–41, esp. 431. As Thomas Prügl points out, drawing from the work of Torrell and others, Thomas's commentary on Rom 1–8 can be considered an *expositio*; i.e., a commentary that Thomas prepared for publication rather than one drawn from the notes of his students (the latter being *reportationes*), as were most of his others (which are thus entitled *lectura* rather than *expositiones*). The commentary on Rom 1–8, which contains Thomas's "perfectly developed teachings on grace," thus shows clear evidence of his mature thought. "Thomas Aquinas as Interpreter of Scripture," in *The Theology of Thomas Aquinas*, ed. Rik Van Nieuwenhove and Joseph Wawrykow (Notre Dame, IN: University of Notre Dame Press, 2005), 386–415, esp. 387–88, 390. Cf. Torrell, *Saint Thomas Aquinas*, vol. 1, 250–57.

152. *Sup. Rom.* ch5 lect1.

tive: God's love is the source of our love for God because our love is a participation in the Holy Spirit, the Love of Father and Son, so that we share in God's own love for himself. We not only receive from God's love the created gift of grace and charity, but also possess and enjoy the indwelling of the divine Persons through this gift. And, finally, the gift of charity perfects all of our moral activities. So, Thomas says, "hope does not disappoint" because "God does not deny himself to those whom he loves," and for those who love him, "it is clear that he has prepared eternal goods."[153]

Thomas's commentary on the scriptural text here, as elsewhere, provides insight into the coherence of his teaching in the *Summa*. Possibly, given the development in his use of this text and others from Romans, one can propose that reflection on Paul's teaching in Romans led Thomas to a deeper understanding of charity as a participation in the Holy Spirit in adopted sons led by the Spirit, which influenced his mature works.[154] As a corollary development, even a cursory examination of the evolution of Thomas's arguments against Lombard's identification of charity and the Holy Spirit in *Sentences* I d17 provides hints that Thomas comes, in his thought on this matter, to a deeper appreciation of the importance both of the primacy of the Holy Spirit's causality, and the freedom (and therefore meritoriousness) of human action, in the journey of the image to beatitude. Further research would be required to confirm this hypothesis, but findings are suggestive.[155]

---

153. Ibid.

154. E.g., a search for text from Rom 8:14–15 reveals a similar distribution to that of Rom 5:5 in Thomas's works. Not surprisingly, most of the references in the *Summa* for 8:14 ("those who are led by the Spirit of God are the children of God") are concentrated in the IIa *pars*, and for 8:15 ("You did not receive a spirit of slavery to fall back into fear, but you received a spirit of adoption, through which we cry, '*Abba*, Father!'") are in the IIIa *pars*. Thomas often associates these texts with the notion that charity, belonging to adopted sons by grace, casts out or replaces fear (e.g., *Sup. Ioh.* ch2 lect1; *Sup. Rom.* ch8 lect3). Bouillard has noted the influence of Paul's writings, especially Romans, in the development of Thomas's thought on the movement of the soul by grace (*Conversion et grâce*, 138).

155. Thomas stresses both of these things more in the *Summa*'s treatment of charity than in the *Scriptum*, in part simply because he has developed a clearer general understanding of the relationship between divine and human action in his later work, possibly because of organizational differences: in the *Scriptum*, charity's infusion by the Holy Spirit, and its created status, is treated in a completely separate place (in bk1, in the context of the questions on the Trinity) from its essence and operations as a virtue of the will (in the questions on charity in bk3 dd27–31). The first consequence is some disconnection of the two. In the *Summa* Thomas addresses all of these matters together in IIa-IIae qq23–24, and it is integral to his understanding in the *Summa* of

At any rate, Thomas's reflection on the Pauline teachings on charity and the Holy Spirit deeply shapes his mature thought on the deification of God's adopted children.

Summary and Conclusion

The connections discussed in this chapter between the questions on charity and Thomas's mature teaching on the perfection of the image by grace indi-

---

the deification of the image by grace that charity, precisely as a participation in the Holy Spirit, through the Spirit's mission in the gift of grace, shapes the operations of the will in the likeness of the Spirit toward the supernatural end, allowing for human agency to be subordinated to the divine action. At least two other texts also deserve examination in relation to this question: the disputed question *De caritate* (*S. Thomae Aquinatis Quaestiones Disputatae*, vol. 2, *De Virtutibus: De caritate*, ed. P. Bazzi et al. [Turin: Marietti, 1965]), dated by Torrell to the same period (1271–72) as the writing of the IIa-IIae (*Saint Thomas Aquinas*, vol. 1, 336), and Thomas's second treatment (the recently rediscovered *Lectura Romana*) of the *Sentences,* which includes bk1 d17. A Latin text of the latter is available in *Lectura romana in primum Sententiarum Petri Lombardi,* ed. Leonard Boyle and John Boyle (Toronto: PIMS, 2006), 190–201; a comparative annotated English translation of this and other texts on love in Thomas's works was recently published by Peter Kwasniewski and Joseph Bohn, *On Love and Charity: Readings from the "Commentary on the Sentences of Peter Lombard" by Thomas Aquinas,* trans. Peter Kwasniewski and Joseph Bohn, intr. Peter Kwasniewski (Washington, DC: Catholic University of America Press, 2008). An earlier English translation of the *De caritate* also exists: *Saint Thomas Aquinas on Charity,* trans. Lottie H. Kendzierski (Milwaukee: Marquette University Press, 1960). The *De caritate*'s argument against Lombard's position (*DC* a1) stresses the necessity that "actions of the will proceed from an intrinsic principle," so that they be voluntary and meritorious, albeit moved by the Holy Spirit. The *Lectura Romana* of bk1 d17 is remarkably different from the earlier *Scriptum* both in organization and content. One significant shift is that in the earlier version Thomas holds in this distinction, with regard to charity's infusion and increase, that one can dispose oneself to receive it (e.g., q2 a1 ad4, a2 ad4). This accords with his position in the earlier *Scriptum* that "to the one who does what he can, God does not deny grace," a position he would later reject when he became aware of the danger of semi-Pelagianism through his reading of the later Augustine, as shown by Bouillard's *Conversion et grâce* and Wawrykow's *God's Grace and Human Action* (see note 131 above and note 70 in chapter 3). This position no longer appears in a parallel passage in the later version (q2 a1 ad4). It makes sense that, as complete primacy in causality is accorded to the Holy Spirit, the participated secondary causality of the human agent can also emerge with its proper freedom and force. A fine essay on this topic by Dominic Doyle has recently come to my attention, in which Doyle makes some points similar to those made here; e.g., that Aquinas comes to emphasize both the divine transcendence and the dignity of the instrumental role of human agency in salvation, in the context of his teaching on charity as intimate friendship between human being and God: "The Development of Aquinas' Understanding of Charity, with Special Reference to His Refutation of Lombard's Identification of Charity with the Holy Spirit," in *Thomas Aquinas: Questions on Love and Charity*, Rethinking the Western Tradition Series, ed. Robert Miner (New Haven, CT: Yale University Press, forthcoming).

cate that, at the time of the *Summa*, he thought of charity in the context of its role in grace's deifying activity in the divine *ordinatio* for the predestined. In the *Summa*, the reason for this is clear; charity as a participation in the Holy Spirit describes the perfection of the image by grace with respect to the will, by a participation in the divine procession of Love; that is, by the orientation of the will and all of its operations to the object of God's own love, God himself. It is by charity's inclination of the will to God and its command of the moral life led by the Holy Spirit that the journey to beatitude is completed. The identification of charity as a participation in the Holy Spirit thus appears multiple times in Thomas's treatment of charity in contexts that have to do with the way in which charity is infused and increases in the will on this journey. In the *Summa*, then, not only does Thomas several times identify charity as a participation in the Holy Spirit, but he also clearly places this notion into a context that explains what this participation means in terms of the perfection of the divine image and its activity on the journey to beatitude, in God's plan of predestination for the elect.

We also saw at the beginning of this chapter that in the *Summa* Thomas introduces the questions on charity by considering it as a kind of friendship, founded on God's communication of his own beatitude to us, by calling us into the fellowship of the Son. Through this description, uniquely expressed and frequently used in his treatment in the *Summa*, Thomas frames charity as the primary virtue of adopted sons, who share one end of beatitude with the Son through the loving activity characteristic of God's children. We can now see how this characterization of charity relates to Thomas's subsequent analysis of it as an infused created virtue that is a participation of the Holy Spirit. To be an adopted son, on the way to beatitude, is to participate in the Holy Spirit in one's will by charity, so as, by the activities of the deified will shaped by the virtues and gifts under the influence of charity, and moved by grace, to receive beatitude as one's final end.[156]

Joy and peace, two of the effects of charity's act of love, give a foretaste to the wayfarer of heaven, where "the joy of the blessed is full to perfection"

---

156. Thomas expresses a similar idea in his *Commentary on Ephesians*: "The Son is by nature like to the Father, and so principally and in himself beloved, and so naturally and in the most excellent way beloved by the Father. We are sons by adoption, inasmuch as we are conformed to his Son, and so have a certain participation in the divine love. Jn 13:35. 'The Father loves the Son, and has handed everything over to him; whoever believes in the Son, has eternal life.'" *Sup. Eph.* ch1 lect2.

and every desire is unified and set at rest by being ordered to God as to one goal.[157] As Thomas established in Ia q12, on the beatific vision, the one with more charity will participate more fully in the light of glory in his intellect, and so will see God more clearly. The connection between the perfection of the will by charity and the perfection of the intellect by wisdom, culminating in the image's deiformity in the beatific vision, is the subject of chapter 6. Charity's perfection of the will by participation in the Holy Spirit is completed by wisdom's perfection of the intellect by the Son who is the Word. This Trinitarian perfection of the image, brought about by the divine missions, finds its completion in the perfect contemplative worship of the beatific vision, the fulfillment of the journey of adopted sonship.

157. See *ST* IIa-IIae q28 a3, q29 a3.

CHAPTER 6

Wisdom, Charity, and Christ

The Spirit of the Lord shall rest upon him, a spirit of wisdom and of understanding.

—Isaiah 11:2

Thomas concludes his treatment of charity in the IIa-IIae *pars* with q45, on the gift of wisdom. Having established that charity, as a created participation in the Holy Spirit, perfects the will of the children of God, orienting all of their activities toward God on the journey to beatitude, and having considered in subsequent questions the implications of this orientation in the ordering of charity and its effects, Thomas examines how the Spirit's gift of wisdom perfects charity's operation toward the possession and enjoyment of God. Thomas was original in the *Summa theologiae* in associating each gift of the Spirit with a corresponding virtue, which it perfects by disposing the person to be amenable to the promptings of the Holy Spirit in the activity of that virtue.[1] How, then, does wisdom perfect charity? And why does it do so? As an intellectual gift, it would seem that wisdom might not correspond to charity, which perfects the will. How are the two related?

Some have suggested that wisdom's role in perfecting charity in the IIa-IIae is unclear, or that their association is simply due to charity's posi-

---

1. On this innovation and others in the development of Thomas's thought on the gifts, see Edward D. O'Connor, ed., "Appendix 4: The Evolution of St. Thomas's Thought on the Gifts," in *St Thomas Aquinas: Summa Theologiae*, vol. 24, *The Gifts of the Spirit (1a 2ae. 68–70)* (New York: McGraw-Hill, 1963), 110–30.

tion as the greatest of the theological virtues, and wisdom's as the greatest gift.[2] Were this all that could be said, the true reasons for both the elevated status and the correspondence of charity and wisdom would remain for the most part unexplained. But there are good reasons why the gift of wisdom is deeply interdependent with charity: on the level of the acting person, as a charity-informed knowledge that in turn perfects charity by ordering its activities, and on a deeper level as the intellect's participation in the Son in his divine mission, corresponding to charity's participation by the will in the Holy Spirit. Together charity and wisdom are the deifying virtue and gift *par excellence* of God's adopted children. And, because Christ in his fullness of grace, charity, and wisdom is the principle and model of adopted sonship, in the second half of this chapter I consider how the children of God are "conformed to the image of the Son" (Rom 8:29) by wisdom-perfected charity through the instrumentality of Christ and his sacraments.

Wisdom in the *Summa*

It belongs to the one who has the gift of wisdom, Thomas says in q45 a1, to "judge and set in order all things according to divine rules." Thomas builds upon the foundation laid earlier in this article, and from the outset of the *Summa*, in his teaching about wisdom in general. The notion of wisdom is central to Thomas's understanding of the pursuit of theology, or *sacra doctrina*, the subject of the *Summa*. And, as Wawrykow suggests, this informs the *Summa* from its beginning with the idea of formation in theology as conformation to Christ.[3]

In *ST* Ia q1 a6, on *sacra doctrina* as wisdom, Thomas identifies three kinds of wisdom: the wisdom of the philosophers (i.e., first philosophy or metaphysics), the wisdom of *sacra doctrina*, and the gift of wisdom. The wise person considers the highest principles and judges and orders other matters in their light. Wisdom is able to judge and order because, according to Aristo-

---

2. See ibid., 125–26, and his discussion of M.-M. Labourdette's *La charité (Cours de théologie morale, 2a2ae. 23–46* (Toulouse: Studium dominicain, 1959–60), 267.

3. I.e., the likeness to God brought about through theological activity has for Thomas a specifically Christological dimension because it is a conformation to Wisdom. Joseph Wawrykow, "Wisdom in the Christology of Thomas Aquinas," in *Christ among the Medieval Dominicans: Representations of Christ in the Texts and Images of the Order of Preachers*, ed. Kent Emery Jr. and Joseph Wawrykow (Notre Dame, IN: University of Notre Dame Press, 1998), 189–91,

tle in *Metaphysics* 1.2, to which Thomas alludes, knowledge of the first principles and causes is knowledge of the final cause, the good or end for which things are to be done. Because one knows the end, one understands what is needed to achieve it. As Thomas explains:

In the genus of building, the craftsman who plans the form of the house is called wise, and architect, with respect to the inferior craftsmen who trim the wood and prepare the stones; so it is said (1 Cor 3:10): "As a wise architect I have laid the foundation."

The master architect understands the science of building and so can order the work done to attain the final structure. "The one who considers simply the highest cause of the whole universe, which is God, is most of all called wise. Hence wisdom is also said to be the knowledge (*cognitio*) of divine things, as is clear from Augustine [*DT* 14.1]."[4] As an intellectual virtue, wisdom—whether metaphysics or *sacra doctrina*—is an acquired habit of the speculative intellect, the greatest of the intellectual virtues because its object is "the supreme cause, which is God, as stated at the beginning of the *Metaphysics*."[5] All wisdom, then, in some way directs one to order everything to God as end.[6]

In the *Summa* and other works after his midcareer, Thomas makes use of Aristotle's discussion in the *Nicomachean Ethics* X, of wisdom's contemplative activity as the highest—and so most delightful—operation of the intellect, and therefore of human life.[7] In his commentary on the *Ethics*,

4. *ST* Ia q1 a6.

5. *ST* Ia-IIae q66 a5. Wisdom is a kind of science that is higher than and includes every other in that, considering the highest causes, it judges not only their conclusions but also their first principles; *ST* Ia-IIae q57 a2 ad1–2. It is because *sacra doctrina* is the highest wisdom that it is nobler than the other sciences (*ST* Ia q1 a5; although Thomas does not explicitly say this in the body, it is clearly what he has in mind. Cf. the *sed contra:* "Other sciences are called the handmaids of this one: 'Wisdom sent her maids to invite to the tower' [*Prov.* 9:3]").

6. Cf. *ST* Ia q1 a1. See M.-J. Le Guillou, *Le Christ et l'Église: Théologie du Mystère* (Paris: Éditions du Centurion, 1963), and its English translation by Charles Schaldenbrand, *Christ and Church: A Theology of the Mystery* (New York: Desclee, 1966), for an in-depth examination of the notions of mystery and wisdom in biblical and patristic perspective, which Le Guillou argues are at the heart of the structure and ecclesiology of the *Summa*. The *sacra doctrina* of the *Summa*, illuminated by reflection on Thomas's treatment of wisdom and mystery in his biblical commentaries, is the communication of God's own wisdom revealed in Christ, which is the foundation of God's communication to human beings of divine beatitude.

7. E.g., *ST* Ia-IIae q3 a5; IIa-IIae q152 a2, q167 a1 ad1, q180 a4; *DV* q18 a1; *De Anima* q16.

Thomas explains that the highest of human activities is the contemplation
of truth that belongs to wisdom, both because the intellect is the highest
faculty and because "among the objects that can be known, the highest are
the intelligible, and especially the divine."[8] Metaphysical wisdom considers
matters related to being, which constitute the indemonstrable first principles of philosophy "since universal being is the proper effect of the supreme
cause, which is God."[9] *Sacra doctrina* is "wisdom above all human wisdom,
not just in any one genus, but simply speaking," because it is the consideration of God as the highest cause, not only as the philosophers knew him
through creatures but "also so far as he is known to himself alone and communicated to others through revelation."[10] All wisdom contemplates the
truth of God as the cause of the universe that is ordered to him—that is, as
the cause of the divine *ordinatio*. *Sacra doctrina* does so not only from the
viewpoint of God as first cause of the hierarchy of divine effects, however,
but also as God sees himself and all creatures proceeding from him, in the
light of the divine plan of creation and salvation known only by revelation.
Whereas the principles of metaphysics are abstracted from a consideration
of existing beings, the principles of *sacra doctrina* come from God's own
knowledge (*scientia*), "through which, as through the highest wisdom, all
our knowledge is set in order."[11] Thomas has argued in q1 a2 that *sacra doctrina* is indeed a science, or a kind of knowledge, because it proceeds from
established principles. Yet these are known not by the light of the natural
intellect, but by the light of a higher science—that of God and of the blessed—principles revealed in Scripture. God's own wisdom is thus the source
of ours.[12] The knowledge of God as cause, through God's effects, which is

8. *Sententia Libri Ethicorum* X lect10 ch7 no8.

9. *ST* Ia-IIae q66 a5 ad4.

10. *ST* Ia q1 a6. Cf. Ia-IIae q62 a2; *SCG* II.4.

11. *ST* Ia q1 a6 ad1. God is, of course, the "master architect" of the universe through the divine wisdom. Cf. *ST* Ia q14 a8, q22 a2.

12. In his *Commentary on the Metaphysics* Thomas draws from but goes beyond Aristotle in
saying that knowledge of God actually imparts a share in God's wisdom—that there is a causal connection between the knowledge that God has and ours. Aristotle, in his argument that
metaphysics, as wisdom, is the highest science, remarks that this science is the most honorable
because it is the most divine; i.e., it deals with God as a first principle and with knowledge that
"God alone can have, or God above all others" (*Metaphysics* 983A.9). In Thomas's *Commentary*
he remarks that "God alone has it [this knowledge] in a perfectly comprehensive way. And he
has it maximally, inasmuch as it is also had by men in their own way, although it is not had by

possible to natural reason, is surpassed by the knowledge of God in his essence for the intellect strengthened by grace and taught by revelation; imperfect now by faith, this knowledge is made perfect by direct vision of the divine essence in heaven.[13]

Because those who are intent on the contemplation of truth are moved by love of truth, and delight in obtaining it, both intellect and will are involved in wisdom's act of contemplation, which brings happiness.[14] As Aristotle teaches in the *Ethics*, the highest human happiness "consists principally ... in the contemplation of divine things,"[15] although the speculative virtues of which the Philosopher spoke can bring only the imperfect happiness to be had in this life.[16] Thomas also opens his treatise on Boethius's *De hebdomadibus* with a dense scriptural reflection on the delight of the contemplation of wisdom, both human and divine, which he compares to play.[17] So, Kieran Conley argues, even metaphysical wisdom has an affective dimension in its orientation to God as final cause; its act of contemplation, seeing reality as ordered to its highest cause—the "highest intelligible" that is "the very object of happiness"—results in a certain happiness, albeit one only perfected in the future life.[18]

In q1 a6 ad3, however, Thomas distinguishes a third kind of wisdom in

---

them as their own possession but as something borrowed (*mutuatum*) from him" (*In duodecim libros Metaphysicorum Aristotelis expositio* bk1 lect3 no13). Although Thomas refers in this text to the acquired wisdom of metaphysics, not *sacra doctrina* or the infused gift of wisdom, he employs a principle familiar from the *Summa* with regard to human knowing, especially of divine things: it is a participation in divine knowledge.

13. *ST* Ia q12 aa12–13.   14. *ST* IIa-IIae q180 a1.

15. *ST* Ia-IIae q3 a5.   16. *ST* Ia-IIae q3 a6 ad1.

17. *Exposito Libri Boethii De ebdomadibus*, prol. Thomas reflects on Sir 32:15–16. In the Vulgate, "praecurre prior in domum tuam, et illuc advocare et illic lude, et age conceptiones tuas." Thomas explains that to pursue the contemplation of wisdom one must collect all of one's thoughts within the mind and play there, for wisdom is like play both in that it holds the greatest delight and is pursued for its own sake, as one considers different conceptions through which the knowledge of truth is acquired. Thomas refers to Prov 8:30—"cum eo eram cuncta conponens et delectabar per singulos dies ludens coram eo omni tempore"—to link the play of human wisdom to that of God in creation. The same verse is connected to the *otium contemplatio sapientiae* in *Scriptum* bk1 d2 q1 a5 expos., and in *SCG* it is a scriptural authority for the teaching that joy and delight are found in divine Wisdom, which is God (I.91.13).

18. *ST* Ia-IIae q66 a5 ad2. For a thorough discussion of this point and a systematic comparison of the three types of wisdom identified by Thomas, see Kieran Conley, *A Theology of Wisdom: A Study in St. Thomas* (Dubuque, IA: Priory Press, 1963).

addition to philosophical wisdom and the wisdom of *sacra doctrina*: the Holy Spirit's gift of wisdom, by which the spiritual person judges the things of God by inclination rather than by cognition or acquired knowledge:

Since judgment pertains to wisdom, there is a twofold wisdom according to a two-fold mode of judging. For one may judge, in one way, by inclination (*per modum inclinationis*), as he who has the *habitus* of a virtue rightly judges about those things having to do with acting virtuously, insofar as he is inclined to them; hence in the *Ethics* X it is said that the virtuous person is the measure and rule of human acts. In another way, by cognition (*per modum cognitionis*), as someone instructed in the science of morals is able to judge about virtuous acts, even if he does not have the virtue. The first mode of judging about divine things pertains to that wisdom which is placed among the gifts of the Holy Spirit: "The spiritual man judges all things" (1 Cor 2:15). And Dionysius says (*Div. Nom.* 2): "Hierotheus was taught not by learn-ing alone, but also by undergoing divine things (*patiens divina*)." The second mode of judging pertains to that doctrine which is acquired by study, though its princi-ples are held from revelation.

The gift of wisdom, which judges by inclination, has an even closer re-lationship with the will than the wisdom of *sacra doctrina*, for it flows from connaturality with the divine things bestowed by charity.

The reference to 1 Corinthians 2:15 in the passage above is significant in relation to this connection with charity. In his commentary on 1 Corinthi-ans, Thomas explains further his understanding of the "spiritual man [who] judges all things." One is called spiritual, Thomas says, because "his intellect is illuminated and his affection and will are kindled by the Spirit of God." In his commentary, too, Thomas gives the quote from the *Ethics* X to explain why such a one can judge all things, explaining that the spiritual person is virtuous and so has sound judgment because "his intellect is illuminated and his affections are ordered by the Holy Spirit."[19] Although Thomas does not distinguish between judging by cognition and by inclination, and al-though in some parts of this section of his commentary it is unclear wheth-er he is talking about the wisdom of theology given by revelation or the gift of wisdom, here at least he is clearly referring to a virtuosity of judg-ment that is the effect of the Spirit's gift rather than of acquired knowledge. And he describes an illumination of the intellect and enkindling of the af-fections in the will in language reminiscent of the words he uses in *ST* Ia

---

19. *Sup. 1 Cor.* ch2 lect2 117–18.

q43 to describe the effects of grace in the missions, especially in relation to the mission of the Word, which bestows wisdom.[20] In the context of the Scripture passage, Thomas goes on in his commentary to say that the Spirit gives Christians "the mind of Christ": "that is, we receive in ourselves the wisdom of Christ to make us able to judge."[21] The wisdom of theology is a human pursuit, an acquired intellectual virtue that judges the things of God by means of the knowledge gained through study, although its principles are obtained by revelation; the gift of wisdom allows one to judge "not by learning alone, but also by undergoing (*patiens*) divine things."

The Gift of Wisdom

Thomas's initial description of the gift of wisdom in IIa-IIae q45 a1 is similar in many respects to his treatment of *sacra doctrina* as wisdom in Ia q1 a6.[22] Thomas again follows the Aristotelian maxim that *sapientis est ordinare* and refers to 1 Corinthians 2:15:

According to the Philosopher [in *Metaphysics* 1.2], it belongs to the wise person to consider the highest cause, through which a most certain judgment can be made about other things, and according to which all things should be set in order. The "highest cause" can be taken in two ways, either simply speaking, or as in some genus. So the one who knows the highest cause in some genus, and through it is able to judge and order all the things which belong to that genus, is said to be a wise person in that genus, as in medicine or architecture, according to 1 Cor 3.10: "As a wise architect I have laid a foundation." However, the one who knows the highest cause simply speaking, which is God, is said to be a wise person simply speaking, inasmuch as he is able to judge and set in order all things according to divine rules (*regulas divinas*). Now man acquires this mode of judging through the Holy Spirit, according to 1 Cor 2:15: "The spiritual person judges all things"; because, as it says in the same, "the Spirit searches all things, even the depths of God." Whence it is manifest that wisdom is a gift of the Holy Spirit.[23]

20. Cf. *ST* Ia q43 a5 ad2–3.

21. *Sup. 1 Cor.* ch2 lect2 121.

22. For an in-depth reading of *ST* IIa-IIae q45, see Cruz Gonzalez Ayesta, *El Don de Sabiduría según Santo Tomás* (Pamplona: Ediciones Universidad de Navarra, 1998), whose conclusions in some respects overlap my own but who also provides, as subsequent notes will indicate, an analysis of Thomas's texts in light of his reception in the tradition.

23. *ST* IIa-IIae q45 a1.

Although Thomas said in Ia q1 a6 that *sacra doctrina* is the highest human wisdom simply speaking, it seems from this passage that theology alone is not enough to make one a wise person *simpliciter* after all. The gift of wisdom differs from theological wisdom, as Thomas has already indicated in Ia q1 a6, in that it is acquired not through study but as an infused gift of the Holy Spirit. As we know from Thomas's general theology of the gifts, this means that the person receives an enduring *habitus* through which the Holy Spirit easily moves him to wisdom's acts.

In the *sed contra* of q45 a1 Thomas prefaces the *corpus* above with the same quotation from Isaiah 11:2 that anchors his explanation in Ia-IIae q68 a1 of the distinction between gifts and virtues—"The Spirit of the Lord shall rest upon him, a spirit of wisdom and of understanding."[24] The gift, as a *habitus* of the speculative intellect, has a more perfect manner of working than the virtue because it makes one amenable to the extrinsic motion of the Spirit's prompting. While one might be able to pursue *sacra doctrina* as a purely theoretical field of study with an intellect unenlightened by grace, it seems that it is only in the graced intellect, possessing the infused virtues and gifts (and thus believing and loving what one learns), that the wisdom of *sacra doctrina* can fully bear fruit, through the operation of the gift under the influence of the Holy Spirit.[25]

In his answers to objections in q45 a1 Thomas again distinguishes the intellectual virtue of wisdom, "which is acquired by human study," from the gift, which "descends from above" (Jas 3:15). He further distinguishes the gift of wisdom from faith, and from fear and piety, all of which are closely related to the operation of the gift in the adopted sons of God. Faith—the virtue operative in assenting to the revealed principles of *sacra doctrina*[26]— is presupposed to the gift of wisdom, for "faith assents to the divine truth itself, whereas it belongs to the gift of wisdom to judge according to the divine truth."[27] Piety, "which pertains to the worship of God," manifests both

---

24. The next verse appears in the *sed contra* of IIIa q7 a6, on Christ's possession of the gift of fear.

25. Note that Thomas again inserts the verse from 1 Cor 2:15 on the "spiritual man," adding a quote from 1 Cor 2:10 about the Holy Spirit who knows and reveals the hidden things of God; in his commentary he explains that this is why God "reveals his wisdom through the Holy Spirit" (*Sup. 1 Cor.* ch2 lect2 102).

26. See, e.g., *ST* Ia q1 a1 ad1; IIa-IIae q1 a1.

27. *ST* IIa-IIae q45 a1 ad2.

faith and wisdom. Both piety and fear can be called wisdom because "if one fears and worships God, this shows a right judgment about divine things."[28] Filial fear, which derives from reverent love, is itself linked to piety in those who are children of God. Piety's highest form, as a virtue, pays filial homage to God as "first principle of being and government";[29] the gift of piety pays worship and duty to God as Father.[30] The one who has the gift of wisdom, then, can be expected to believe, fear, and worship God as an adopted son or daughter, judging and ordering all things in light of this reverent worship "according to the divine rules."

"To Judge and Order According to Divine Rules"

Is there any significance to this specification of Thomas in q45 a1 that the one with the gift of wisdom is able "to judge and set in order all things according to divine rules (*regulas divinas*)"? While judging and ordering pertains to wisdom in general, a survey of the articles of q45 indicates that Thomas seems to associate doing so "according to divine rules" with the gift in particular. This phrase appears in four out of the six articles of q45 and is referred to in other terms in the remaining two articles. The notion finds a context elsewhere in the *Summa*, in the multiple places where Thomas employs the idea of the human reason participating in and being governed by the divine reason. Even on the natural level, as discussed in chapter 1, the human intellect is a participation in the light of the divine intellect.[31] So the eternal reason is ultimately the measure or rule of human reason.

Thomas often expresses this in terms of the notion of the eternal law. The eternal law is "the very idea of the government of things in God the ruler of the universe," the rule by which God regulates everything according to the wise plan of divine providence.[32] Everything in the universe, as it is subject to divine providence, is ruled and measured by the eternal law, but especially the rational creature, which is

subject to divine providence in a more excellent way, inasmuch as it is made a participator in providence, by providing for itself and others. Whence it also participates in the eternal reason, by which it has a natural inclination to its due act and

28. *ST* IIa-IIae q45 a1 ad3.
30. *ST* IIa-IIae q121 a1.
32. *ST* Ia-IIae q91 a1.

29. *ST* IIa-IIae q101 a1.
31. *ST* Ia q12 a2, a5.

end. And this participation of the eternal law in the rational creature is called the natural law.[33]

It is particularly as participating in divine providence and its unfolding in the divine government that the rational creature participates in the eternal law; it is the mark of the *imago Dei* to share in the working out of the divine *ordinatio* for itself, as principle of its own activity moved by God, and especially in the case of its own salvation (see chaps. 2 and 3). Even on the natural level, the image in some sense "judges and orders things according to divine rules" when it exercises philosophical wisdom, ordering matters governed by reason under the natural law with respect to God as the highest cause.[34]

The divine rules manifested by the natural law, however, are limited in scope compared to those made known by the New Law of grace—externally by the aid of revelation and its study in *sacra doctrina*, and internally by the intellect enlightened by grace and prompted by the Holy Spirit (i.e., both in the virtue of theological wisdom and the gift).[35] Because the divine plan of providence is the work of God's wisdom and love, the perfection of participation in this plan in the creature takes the form of wisdom and love.[36]

33. *ST* Ia-IIae q91 a2.

34. John Rziha's valuable study on Thomas's doctrine of human participation in the eternal law by nature and grace as the foundation of his moral theology came to my attention when this work was substantially completed. Rziha provides a helpful overview of the twentieth-century retrieval of the notion of participation by Thomists and examines how Thomas's unique doctrine of participation shapes his understanding of the way that humans, participating in the eternal law, are "moved and governed" by God to attain their end (as all creatures are), and also participate cognitively in this process through the activity of their reason. Humans attain the supernatural end insofar as they participate in the divine nature and are moved by the Holy Spirit, their reason formed by the acquired intellectual virtues, faith, and the gifts of the Holy Spirit. Although Rziha's approach and concerns differ somewhat from this project, and he does not explore the supernatural perfection of the human person in terms of conformation to the divine image or to Christ's sonship, many of his insights and conclusions about Thomas's understanding of divine and participated human causality in the moral journey of sanctification overlap and confirm what I have argued while providing greater depth in some areas. *Perfecting Human Actions: St. Thomas Aquinas on Human Participation in Eternal Law* (Washington, DC: Catholic University of America Press, 2009).

35. Cf. *ST* Ia q12 a13; Ia-IIae q106 a1 ad2.

36. In *ST* IIa-IIae q45 ad3 Thomas distinguishes the gift of knowledge from the gift of wisdom by saying that, on account of the former, the intellect is aided in its act of judgment according to human ideas, but by the gift of wisdom according to the divine ideas. As noted in

The law of grace, which is a more perfect participation in the eternal law than the natural law, is necessary for human beings ordained to a supernatural end of beatitude out of all proportion to their natural faculties.[37] The wisdom of *sacra doctrina* considers and judges things in the light of the revealed knowledge possible in this life, of God in his essence, and the divine plan of creation and salvation. So it enables the creature to participate more perfectly in the divine plan of providence and government, by an acquired capacity to order everything, like God, to God as the object of knowledge and love. But even an unlettered believer, ignorant perhaps of many of the more exalted mysteries of their faith (thus lacking in the intellectual virtue of wisdom) but trusting in what has been revealed, will by the gift of wisdom successfully "judge and order all things by the divine rules," so as to attain salvation because of a simple grasp of the goal by loving faith.[38] The capacity to do so in a salvific manner most basically pertains to the gift, although it is assisted and deepened by study of *sacra doctrina*.

The Gift of Wisdom's Source in Charity: Undergoing Divine Things

In q45 a2, on whether wisdom is in the intellect, Thomas examines wisdom's close relationship to charity. He indicates that charity informs the gift of wisdom in a way that differentiates the gift from the acquired virtue of theological wisdom. "Wisdom," he says,

---

chapter 1, the divine ideas are those *rationes* existing in the mind of God, by which God causally knows the universe in its ordered hierarchy; they are at the basis of creation and providence (cf. Ia q15 a2). Furthermore, the ideas are especially associated with the Son, who proceeds as the Word of the divine intellect—because he is represented by the proper species of every creature, of which the divine ideas are the exemplars—and to whom is appropriated wisdom (cf. Ia q15 aa2–3, q45 aa6–7). So by the gift of wisdom we join with God in judging according to a God's-eye view of the universe, including our own place within it, with an intellect especially conformed to the Word.

37. *ST* Ia-IIae q91 a4 c., ad1.

38. *ST* IIa-IIae q45 a5. On this, see Bruce Marshall, "*Quod Scit Una Vetula*: Aquinas on the Nature of Theology," in *The Theology of Thomas Aquinas*, ed. Rik van Nieuwenhove and Joseph Wawrykow (Notre Dame, IN: University of Notre Dame Press, 2005), 1–35. Marshall makes reference to Thomas's comment in the *Collationes Credo in Deum* that none of the philosophers before Christ's coming could know as much about God, and what is necessary for life, as one old woman knows by faith after Christ's coming (1). For Thomas the faith and wisdom of the *vetula* presupposes an ecclesial context in which *sacra doctrina* informs the teaching handed on to all the faithful.

denotes a certain rectitude of judgment according to divine reasons. Rectitude of judgment can be twofold, however. In one way, through the perfect use of reason; in another, according to a certain connaturality about the things judged. So for instance, in those things pertaining to chastity, one who has studied moral science judges rightly through the investigation of reason, but the one who has the habit of chastity judges rightly about them through a certain connaturality. Thus to have right judgment about divine things by the investigation of reason pertains to wisdom which is the intellectual virtue, but to have right judgment about these things according to a certain connaturality for them pertains to wisdom as a gift of the Holy Spirit, as Dionysius says, in *De Div. Nom.*, ch. 2, that Hierotheus was perfected in divine things "not only by learning, but also by undergoing (*patiens*), divine things." Now this kind of undergoing-with (*compassio*) or connaturality for divine realities is brought about through charity, which unites us to God, according to 1 Cor 6 (17): "whoever is joined to God is one spirit [with him]." So therefore wisdom which is the gift has its cause in the will, namely charity, but its essence in the intellect, whose act is to judge rightly, as said above.[39]

As discussed in chapter 5, Thomas thinks that all of the gifts depend upon the presence of charity in the will because charity especially joins the human person to God by the will's participation in the Holy Spirit.[40] By conforming the human will to the divine will, which has God as its object, charity in a sense gives the will a new connatural end.[41] The human mind that has this connaturality, and so has become a united instrument with the Holy Spirit, is able to be effectively and continuously moved by the Spirit via the gifts.[42] It might appear that wisdom is no different from the other gifts in this respect.

But Thomas seems to think that the work of the gift of wisdom especially depends upon the connaturality with God arising from charity—in fact, that charity shapes the very character of wisdom's activity. Distinguishing the gift of wisdom from the gift of knowledge, for instance, he writes,

To know what must be believed pertains to the gift of knowledge, but to know in themselves (*secundum seipsas*) those things that are believed, by a kind of union with them, pertains to the gift of wisdom. Therefore the gift of wisdom corresponds more to charity which unites the human mind to God.[43]

---

39. *ST* IIa-IIae q45 a2 c.
40. Cf. *ST* Ia-IIae q68 a4 ad3, a5.
41. Cf. *ST* Ia-IIae q62 a3. I.e., one proper to its new participation in the divine nature by grace.
42. Cf. *ST* Ia-IIae q68 a4 ad3, a5.
43. *ST* IIa-IIae q9 a2 ad1.

The gift of wisdom makes possible a more intimate knowledge—one might say the kind of knowledge one friend has of another. Charity brings about the friendship, or "connaturality with divine things," which alone makes one able to judge and order all things according to the divine rules most perfectly.[44] Thomas Gilby points out that Thomas speaks in many places in the *Summa* of a kind of knowledge of God motivated and deepened by love, which unites the knower to the known as loved and so allows for an intimate knowledge of the beloved, by affinity.[45] As Kieran Conley puts it, "the intellect experiences the object, connaturalized and made present in the will by love, and illumined by affectivity ... the intellect judges the object, now seen in the light of love."[46] By the gift of wisdom the creature not only knows about God's goodness but is also united to it, contemplating God's loveliness and judging things in that light.[47] So Thomas alludes in q45 a2 to a traditional etymology of the Latin *sapientia* as sweet or savored (*sapida*) knowledge to argue that it is closely related to charity.[48] Notably, he does the same in his description of the Son's mission as wisdom in the intellect, making it clear that he refers there to the gift (rather than the virtue) of wisdom as well.[49]

In both IIa-IIae q45, on the gift of wisdom in the intellect, and in Ia q1 a6, where he distinguishes the intellectual virtue from the gift, Thomas places the quotation from Dionysius's *Divine Names* on being taught not only by learning but also by undergoing or "suffering" (*patiens*) divine things. This phrase, difficult to translate precisely in English, was subject to varied interpretation even in Thomas's day. His use of it sheds some light

44. Cf. *ST* IIa-IIae q45 a4.

45. Thomas Gilby, "Appendix 10: The Dialectic of Love in the *Summa*," in *St Thomas Aquinas: Summa Theologiae*, vol. 1. (1a 1), *Christian Theology*, ed. Thomas Gilby (New York: McGraw-Hill, 1964), 124–32.

46. Conley, *Theology of Wisdom*, 117.

47. T. R. Heath, ed., "Appendix 4: The Gift of Wisdom," in *St Thomas Aquinas: Summa Theologiae*, vol. 35, *Consequences of Charity (2a 2ae. 34–46)* (New York: McGraw-Hill, 1964), 200–202, esp. 201.

48. *ST* IIa-IIae q45 a2 ad1. But Thomas recognizes that the traditional interpretation may not apply to a verse from Sir 6:23—"the wisdom of doctrine is according to her name" in the Vulgate—which has been translated from the Greek.

49. He speaks too of a certain perception or "experiential knowledge" (*ST* Ia q43 a5 ad2): "Et ideo signanter dicit Augustinus quod filius mittitur, cum a quoquam cognoscitur atque percipitur, perceptio enim experimentalem quandam notitiam significat. Et haec proprie dicitur sapientia, quasi sapida scientia, secundum illud Eccli. VI, 'sapientia doctrinae secundum nomen eius est.'"

on how he understands the gift of wisdom to relate to charity. In his own commentary on the *Divine Names* he writes that *patiens divina* means "not only receiving the knowledge of divine things in the intellect, but also loving them, united to them through the affection." Applying again the principle from the *Ethics* X, he argues that just as a virtuous person can judge rightly about things pertaining to that virtue, so can one united to divine things by affection judge rightly about them.[50] Ysabel de Andia, in her study on the meaning and later reception of the phrase *pati divina* in Dionysius and Thomas, observes that Thomas cites it in the context of his treatments of the passions of the soul as well as of the gift of wisdom. She considers these references in light of the affective and sapiential "double context" of the formula *pati divina* as received by the western Middle Ages in the Latin translations of Dionysius and his scholiasts.[51]

De Andia points outs that in his questions on the passions of the soul Thomas explains the *pati divina* in terms of the passion of love, by which the soul is affectively drawn and united to God.[52] And in his treatments of the gift of wisdom Thomas employs the Dionysian reference to distinguish between the mode of judging of the intellectual virtue of wisdom (by cognition) and that of the gift (by inclination), as in IIa-IIae q45 a2. De Andia

---

50. *In de divinis nominibus* ch2 lect4: "Doctus est ista quae dixit *ex quadam inspiratione diviniore*, quam communiter fit multis, *non solum discens, sed et patiens divina*, idest non solum divinorum scientiam in intellectu accipiens, sed etiam diligendo, eis unitus est per affectum. Passio enim magis ad appetitum quam ad cognitionem pertinere videtur, quia cognita sunt in cognoscente secundum modum cognoscentis et non secundum modum rerum cognitarum, sed appetitus movet ad res, secundum modum quo in seipsis sunt, et sic ad ipsas res, quodammodo afficitur. Sicut autem aliquis virtuosus, ex habitu virtutis quam habet in affectu, perficitur ad recte iudicandum de his quae ad virtutem illam pertinent, ita qui afficitur ad divina, accipit divinitus rectum iudicium de rebus divinis."

51. Ysabel De Andia, "'Pati divina' chez Denys l'Aréopagite, Thomas d'Aquin et Jacques Maritain," in *Saint Thomas d'Aquin*, Les Cahiers d'Histoire de la Philosophie, ed. Thierry-Dominique Humbrecht (Paris: Cerf, 2011), 549–89, esp. 558.

52. De Andia, "*Pati Divina*' chez Denys l'Aréopagite," 561–63; see *ST* Ia-IIae q22 a3 ad1, with reference to the quote from Dionysius: "Dicendum quod passio divinorum ibi dicitur affectio ad divina, et coniunctio ad ipsa per amorem." See also q22 a1, where Thomas argues that the soul, apart from its role with respect to the body, can be said to be passive, or undergo passions (*pati*) only in "the larger sense, according to which, to receive anything is to be passive ... as the air is said to be passive, when it is illuminated. This, however, is more to be perfected than to be passive." Of this meaning of passion as reception, Thomas quotes Aristotle (*De Anima* 1.5): "to sense and to understand are in a certain manner to be passive." Also see q26 a2, on love as a passion.

argues that Thomas uses the notion of the *pati divina* to signify a distinction between a purely speculative and affective knowledge of divine things, the latter of which he associates with the gift of wisdom.[53] For instance, in *ST* Ia q64 a1, in explaining that the fallen angels are deprived of the knowledge of truth that can only come from charity and wisdom, Thomas says,

The cognition of truth is twofold, one which is had through grace, and another which is had through nature. And that which is had through grace is [also] twofold, one which is only speculative, as when some hidden divine things are revealed to someone. The other is affective, producing love of God; and this properly pertains to the gift of wisdom.[54]

The gift (as opposed to the virtue) of wisdom flows in a special way from charity such that it "has its cause, which is charity, in the will, but its essence in the intellect, whose act is to judge rightly."[55] So the spiritual person, "by reason of the *habitus* of charity, has an inclination to judge rightly of all things in conformity with the divine rules" through the gift of wisdom, in the light of love.[56] And the operation of the gift of wisdom also produces the love of God. In a special way among the gifts, charity is not only "the virtue making the operation of the gift possible, but becoming an integral part of its operation."[57]

---

53. De Andia, "'*Pati Divina*' chez Denys l'Aréopagite," 566–70. De Andia associates the gift of wisdom with an "affective or experiential knowledge" that tastes the sweetness of the Lord (567–68); see, e.g., *ST* IIa-IIae q97 a2 ad2: "There is a twofold knowledge of the divine goodness or will. One is speculative; and in this, it is not lawful to doubt or prove whether God's will is good, or whether God is sweet. The other is an affective or experiential (*affectiva seu experimentalis*) knowledge of the divine goodness or will, by which one experiences in oneself the taste of divine sweetness and the *complacentia* of the divine will, as Dionysius says of Hierotheus, *De Div. Nom.*, II, that he learned about divine things by compassion for them (*ex compassione ad ipsa*). And in this way we are admonished to prove God's will and taste his sweetness." Cruz Ayesta, *El Don de Sabiduría*, 133–34, makes the point that in his mature works Thomas does not equate the connatural knowledge to be had by charity in the gift of wisdom with tasted or experiential knowledge in the sense of a mystical or apophatic knowledge of God, as was held in the interpretative tradition following John of St. Thomas. Ayesta argues that the *cognitio affectiva* that Thomas attributes to the gift of wisdom is best interpreted as related to or even synonymous with practical knowledge; that is, it helps one to discern the end and order oneself to it (135–36).

54. *ST* Ia q64 a1.   55. *ST* IIa-IIae q45 a2.

56. *ST* IIa-IIae q60 a1 ad2.

57. T. R. Heath, "Gift of Wisdom," 201. De Andia observes that charity "does not only imply a 'connaturality' with the thing loved, but is also the cause of the mutual inhabitation of the

Wisdom's Perfection of Charity: Ordering the Things to Be Loved

In q45 a3 Thomas provides a corollary teaching that, for the one who has read the questions on charity, sheds light on the way in which charity directs all of a person's acts first to the love of God, then to other things with respect to that first love. The article asks "whether wisdom is merely speculative, or practical also." Thomas replies that the gift of wisdom

both considers and consults [divine things], considering them according as divine things are contemplated in themselves, and consulting them according as it judges human things through divine things, directing human actions by divine rules. Thus that wisdom which is a gift is not only speculative but also practical.[58]

To an objection that the virtue of wisdom is only speculative, Thomas explains that wisdom as a gift is even more excellent than the intellectual virtue because "it attains more closely to God, through a certain union of the soul with him," and so it has a greater scope, extending to both contemplation and action. Wisdom's primary activity is the contemplation of divine things, which, Thomas says, "is the vision of the principle," but it also "directs human acts according to divine rules."[59]

In IIa-IIae q180, where Thomas examines the contemplative life itself, he describes intellectual contemplation of the divine truth, understood as an "appetible good"; charity is at work, for love in the will motivates this contemplation: "we are urged to the vision of the first principle, namely God, by the love of God ... inasmuch as through loving God we are aflame to gaze on his beauty."[60] Because obtaining what we love is delighting in it, contemplation of this highest object terminates in a delight, even in this life, which "surpasses all human delight," to be exceeded only by the con-

---

beloved in the lover ... it is charity which allows an 'enjoyment' of the Divine Persons, which is the perfect form of the *pati divina*." "'*Pati Divina* chez Denys l'Aréopagite," 573.

58. *ST* IIa-IIae q45 a3.

59. *ST* IIa-IIae q45 a3 ad3: "Ad tertium dicendum quod prius est considerare aliquid in seipso quam secundum quod ad alterum comparatur. Unde ad sapientiam per prius pertinet contemplatio divinorum, quae est visio principii; et posterius dirigere actus humanos secundum rationes divinas. Nec tamen in actibus humanis ex directione sapientiae provenit amaritudo aut labor, sed potius amaritudo propter sapientiam vertitur in dulcedinem, et labor in requiem."

60. *ST* IIa-IIae q180 a1 c., ad1-2.

templation of heaven.[61] Although Thomas treats the contemplative life in q180 as an occupational state belonging to those "who are chiefly intent on the contemplation of truth," he indicates in the preceding question that contemplative and active aspects can be distinguished in all human life, for the human intellect itself is both speculative and practical. Human pursuits that are "directed to the necessities of the present life" belong to the active life; those that are "directed to the consideration of truth" belong to the contemplative.[62]

In q45 a4, a5 Thomas makes it clear that the gift of wisdom belongs to all who have grace and charity and so are without mortal sin, for "God loves those who love him (Prov 8:17). Now it is written, (Wis 8:28) that God 'loves none but those who dwell with wisdom.'" Not all attain the same degree of the gift of wisdom; those with the greatest wisdom can contemplate divine things and also communicate them to others, and they can order both themselves and others according to divine rules. But all are able to contemplate divine things and direct their affairs according to divine rules in the measure that suffices for their salvation.[63] The gifts are active in everyone who has habitual grace and necessary for salvation. The gift of wisdom gives to all of God's adopted children the capacity to exercise contemplation of the truth to the degree possible in their state of life, and to order the moral life to this end.

Wisdom is practical as well as speculative, for divine things provide the rule for the contingent things with which human action is concerned; so wisdom guides human action in all other matters on the basis of the truths contemplated.[64] Wisdom in turn perfects charity—because the will is moved by the objects presented to it by the intellect, we can deduce that wisdom in the reason properly judges and orders the objects to be loved by charity in the will, so that, united first to God in love, it loves others for God's sake, doing all things in accord with love for God.[65] Wisdom is practical because it works through charity. Thomas notes that, although the moral virtues are directed to external actions, and the contemplative life to the consideration of truth, "the moral virtues belong to the contemplative life dispositively" by curbing the passions and causing peace in the soul—

61. *ST* IIa-IIae q180 a7 c., ad3.
62. *ST* IIa-IIae q179 a2 c., ad3.
63. *ST* IIa-IIae q45 a5.
64. *ST* IIa-IIae q45 a3 ad2–3.
65. Cf. *ST* IIa-IIae q25 a1.

the peace of order, which is especially the effect of wisdom.[66] In the soul participating by charity in the Holy Spirit, charity properly directs the moral virtues to the end of beatitude. The operation of wisdom in the reason thus orders charity's own direction of the whole moral life toward beatitude, which in turn disposes one for beatitude's contemplation.[67]

Wisdom, then, both derives from charity and results in its perfection. It is a kind of knowledge stimulated by charity, which in turn helps charity to be properly ordered by judging and ordering the objects that the intellect presents to the will, according to the divine rules, so that it loves God above all and everything else in relation to God. To judge and order things in this way is to have a good will, because the goodness of the human will depends on conformity to the eternal law, and sin is a defection from it. If human reason ruling the will even on the natural level depends on the divine reason, even more so, "where human reason is deficient [i.e., in supernatural matters], it is necessary to have recourse to the eternal reason."[68] A good will is one conformed to the divine will, in having God's goodness as its end;[69] the rectitude of the will thus depends on conformity to the eternal law.[70] Charity, in a profound sense, conforms the will to God by participation in the Holy Spirit, so that it has God itself as the object of its love, toward which it directs its love of all other things.[71] In such a will the gift of wisdom orders charity. In the first article of the questions on charity, although Thomas has not yet treated the gift of wisdom, he notes that

charity is regulated, not by the reason, as human virtues are, but by God's wisdom, and transcends the rule of human reason, according to Eph 3:19: "The charity of Christ, which surpasses all knowledge."[72]

---

66. *ST* IIa-IIae q180 a2.

67. It is perhaps worth noting Thomas's remark in *ST* IIa-IIae q45 a3 ad3: "from the direction of wisdom there results no bitterness or toil in human acts; but rather, by wisdom, bitterness is changed to sweetness, and labor to rest" ("Nec tamen in actibus humanis ex directione sapientiae provenit amaritudo aut labor, sed potius amaritudo propter sapientiam vertitur in dulcedinem, et labor in requiem"). It seems possible to speculate that here is an echo of the Pentecost sequence *Veni Sancte Spiritus*, in use in the medieval liturgy by Thomas's time, in which the effects of the Holy Spirit's gifts are enumerated: "In labore requies, in aestu temperies, in fletu solatium."

68. *ST* Ia-IIae q19 a4.   69. *ST* Ia-IIae q19 a9.

70. *ST* Ia-IIae q21 a1.   71. Cf. *ST* Ia-IIae q19 a10.

72. *ST* IIa-IIae q23 a1 ad2. In Thomas's *Sup. Eph.* (ch3 lect5), he treats the passage from which this text comes at length, providing a beautiful exegesis that weaves together reflections

To have charity like Christ's is to have the gift of wisdom, which, by a participation in divine wisdom, conforms human to divine reason so that the will acts in all things according to the divine rules, participating successfully in the divine *ordinatio* for the creature's salvation.[73]

Two questions in Thomas's treatment of charity that deal with charity's order seem to corroborate the view that wisdom perfects charity by ordering its objects. The question on wisdom immediately follows q44, on the precepts of charity, which examines the scriptural commands of the Old Law to love God and neighbor. Question 44 in effect asks about the cause of charity's right ordering (under the Old Law), a question fully answered only in q45 (which gives its cause in the New Law). In the final article (q44 a8) Thomas explains that the order of charity must come under the commandment of charity because "the order of charity pertains to the *ratio* of the virtue, since it is based on the proportion of love to the beloved." In the *sed contra* Thomas argues that "whatever God works in us by grace, he first teaches us by his Law." He refers to the Vulgate translation of Songs 2:4—*ordinavit in me caritatem* ("he set in order charity in me")—to argue that as God causes the order of charity in us by grace, it must have first come under the precept of the law.[74] By following this article on the right ordering of charity (as commanded by the Law) with q45 on the gift of wisdom, Thomas is demonstrating how God causes by the New Law of grace the order of charity that the commands of the Old Law foreshadow.

Thomas also makes Songs 2:4 his authority in the *sed contra* of IIa-IIae q26 a1, at the outset of an earlier question devoted to the order of charity.[75]

---

on the charity of Christ as the manifestation of the surpassing love of God and the perfection of our own charity, exemplified in Christ's love shown in the Passion.

73. It is specifically because the right will is properly ordered toward God as last end that it merits before God (*ST* Ia-IIae q21 a4)—and so, one can infer, why charity and wisdom in that will are essential to the one who merits. Thomas places merit in the context of the common good, such that it is one's duty to refer all things not only to God as last end per se but also, as God is governor and ruler of the universe, to act rightly toward other individuals in the community. So to act in all things "according to the divine rules" is praiseworthy as being good for all. Cf. Ia-IIae q21 a3.

74. *ST* IIa-IIae q44 a8.

75. Thomas would likely have been familiar with St. Bernard of Clairvaux's *Commentary on the Song of Songs*. On Sg 2:4, Bernard writes of the way in which wisdom determines the order followed by affective charity by assessing everything at its true value so that one loves God before all else and everything else for his sake. Bernard says of such a person: "Give me such a

There he is more explicit about the way in which order (and by implication the role of the gift of wisdom) is integral to the *ratio* of charity:

The love of charity tends to God as to the principle of beatitude, upon the communication of which the friendship of charity is founded. And so it is necessary that there be some order applied in the things loved out of charity, based on relation to the first principle of this love, which is God.[76]

Charity, because it is the virtue that specifically tends toward the last end *qua* last end, which is the first principle, above all "implies relationship to the first principle. And thus in charity above all, order is considered with respect to relation to the first principle."[77] In q45 and q180 Thomas identifies wisdom's act of contemplation as "vision of the first principle." Although Thomas does not yet explicitly mention wisdom in q26 a1, we can understand that the gift of wisdom in the reason first "sees" God, the first principle, and all things in relation to God by contemplation, and so orders the will in its activities, made capable by charity of being united to that first principle; it is thus on account of wisdom's activity in the reason that order is said to be in charity in the will.[78] The gift of wisdom in particular is nec-

---

one, I say, and I shall boldly pronounce him wise, who undoubtedly savors things as they are in reality, who in truth and confidence can boast and say: *'he set love in order in me'* ... O Wisdom, who reaches from end to end mightily in establishing and sustaining things, and disposing all things sweetly in blessing and ordering the affections! Direct our actions, as our temporal necessity demands, as your eternal truth requires, so that each of us may securely boast in you and say: *'he set love in order in me.'* For you are the power of God and the Wisdom of God, Christ the spouse of the Church, our Lord and God of all, who is blessed forever. Amen" (*Serm.* 50.8; PL 183, 1024C-D). Bernard's (and Thomas's) thought is evidently shaped not only by Augustinian themes but also by meditation on the *O antiphons* sung in the liturgy in the days preceding Christmas and popular in the Middle Ages. These antiphons, drawing from multiple Scripture texts, reflect on the mystery of the Incarnation; the first is addressed to the Messiah as the Wisdom of God: "O Wisdom, you came forth from the mouth of the Most High and, reaching from beginning to end, you ordered all things mightily and sweetly. Come, and teach us the way of prudence."

76. *ST* IIa-IIae q26 a1.

77. *ST* IIa-IIae q26 a1 ad1: "Ad primum ergo dicendum quod caritas tendit in ultimum finem sub ratione finis ultimi, quod non convenit alicui alii virtuti, ut supra dictum est. Finis autem habet rationem principii in appetibilibus et in agendis, ut ex supradictis patet. Et ideo caritas maxime importat comparationem ad primum principium. Et ideo in ea maxime consideratur ordo secundum relationem ad primum principium."

78. *ST* IIa-IIae q26 a1 ad3: "Order belongs to reason as the faculty that orders, and to the appetitive power as to the faculty that is ordered. It is in this way that order is said to be in charity."

essary to perfect charity because it is essential to charity to be properly ordered to God.

Wisdom makes one able to assess the true order of things to be loved—an order based on their relation to the first principle. This order of relationship to God in turn derives from the divine *ordinatio*, in which, as described in chapter 1, things are more or less like God to the extent that they participate in the divine goodness (and are therefore truly lovable). God is the first principle of happiness on which the fellowship of charity is based; self and others are loved on account of shared likeness to God.[79] David Gallagher, in his study of the apparently problematic relationship between Thomas's teachings on the "self-oriented" desire for beatitude and on the "other-oriented" love of friendship for God, notes insightfully that the doctrine of participation helps to explain Thomas's position: one should love God even more than oneself because God's goodness, the unparticipated source of one's own, is also therefore one's own highest goodness.[80]

In the subsequent articles of q26 Thomas explores the shape of the hierarchy of love for God, self, and neighbor. It becomes apparent that wisdom's task is not quite so simple, with respect to one's neighbors, as ordering charity's activities according to a God's-eye view of the relative goodness of beings in the universe—at least in this life. Although the neighbor who is better deserves to be the object of greater love because he is nearer to God, the lover naturally loves those who are closer to him more intensely in the good he wishes them for their salvation.[81] Thomas resolves this seeming opposition between likeness to God's goodness and nearness of relationship as priorities in love in the final article of q26, on whether the order of charity endures in heaven. There, "one will simply love those who are better, in the love of charity":

For the whole blessed life consists in the ordering of the mind to God. Thus the whole order of love in the blessed will be observed in relation to God, so that each one will love more and hold nearer to himself the one who is nearer to God.

In heaven, it will no longer be necessary for each person to help those closely connected with them to salvation, and so they will simply love the

79. *ST* IIa-IIae q26 a2 c., ad1.
80. D. M. Gallagher, "Desire for Beatitude and Love of Friendship in Thomas Aquinas," *Mediaeval Studies* 58 (1996): 1–47, 36–38.
81. *ST* IIa-IIae q26 aa6–7.

better more.[82] The reason for loving those nearest to us more intensely than those who are better is to help them to salvation, and this too wisdom judges in accord with the divine will. The gift of wisdom, then, ordering charity, as it conforms the human to the divine reason, judges and orders according to a participation in the divine *ordinatio*, which is specific for each of the elect, within the network of their relationships, on the journey to beatitude.

Wisdom Belongs to the Children of God: Participation in the Likeness of the Son

Because wisdom flows from charity, it belongs to all those who have grace and are without mortal sin. All such "children of the kingdom" have a connaturality or union with divine things by which they judge and order everything in relation to God, in their own life and sometimes even in the affairs of others.[83] In q45 a6 Thomas argues for the correspondence of the seventh beatitude ("blessed are the peacemakers") with the gift of wisdom.[84] For each of the gifts, Thomas examines its connection with one of the beatitudes on the basis of Augustine's treatment in his *De sermone Domini in monte*. This article could at first seem like only an appendix to the earlier articles of q45, simply completing this systematic scheme. But Thomas's treatment in a6 reveals a deep insight into the connection of the gift of wisdom to the Gospel teaching that those who make peace "shall be called the children of God," one that places his entire teaching on wisdom into a new perspective.

Thomas refers in the *sed contra* to Augustine's teaching that "wisdom is fitting to peacemakers, in whom there is no movement of rebellion, but [only] obedience to reason."[85] He relates Aristotle's connection between

---

82. *ST* IIa-IIae q26 a13. G. Mansini also makes this point, noting that Thomas follows the same principle in the *De caritate*. "Similitudo, communicatio, and the friendship of charity in Aquinas," in *Thomistica*, ed. E. Manning (Leuven: Peeters, 1995), 23.

83. *ST* IIa-IIae q45 a4 c., ad3; a5 c., ad2.

84. Thomas understands the beatitudes as acts of the graced person on the journey to beatitude, which unfold as perfect fruits of the Spirit rooted in charity (Ia-IIae q69 a1, q70 a1, a2, a3), in a characteristically eschatological framework; see J. P. Torrell, *Saint Thomas Aquinas*, vol. 2, *Spiritual Master*, trans. Robert Royal (Washington, DC: Catholic University of America Press, 2003), 215–20; Olivier Bonnewijn, *La béatitude et les béatitudes: Une approche thomiste de l'éthique* (Rome: Pontificia Università lateranense, 2001); D. Mongillo, "Les béatitudes et la béatitude. Le dynamique de la Somme de théologie de Thomas d'Aquin: Une lecture de la Ia-IIae q. 69," *Revue des sciences philosophiques et théologiques* 78 (1994): 373–88.

85. Thomas may be quoting from memory. In fact, Augustine's actual text refers to a link

wisdom and order, already central to the discussion, to another text of Augustine:

The seventh beatitude is suitably fitted to the gift of wisdom, both as to the merit and as to the reward. To the merit pertains what is said, "blessed are the peacemakers." Now they are called peacemakers who make peace, whether in themselves or also in others. In both cases this is attained because those things in which peace is established are put in due order, for "peace is the tranquility of order," as Augustine says, *De civ. Dei* xix [13]. Now it belongs to wisdom to order, as is clear from the Philosopher, in the beginning of the *Metaphysics* [1.2]. And thus to be a peacemaker is fittingly attributed to wisdom.[86]

As he does in an earlier question on the beatitudes in general, Thomas frames his reply in terms of merit and reward, an indication that he is thinking within the context of his teaching on the journey of the elect to beatitude.[87] In that earlier question he says that those things set down as merits are "a kind of preparation for, or disposition to happiness, either perfect or inchoate," while the rewards are that happiness, either perfect as in heaven or as yet partially realized and to be hoped for by the wayfarer.[88] Peacemakers are blessed—that is, they are prepared for beatitude and merit it—because of their wisdom, for peace is established by the order that wisdom brings about.

---

between wisdom and order: "Wisdom is fitting to peacemakers, in whom all things are already ordered, and no adverse motion rebels against reason, but the whole obeys the human spirit, which itself obeys God; about whom this is said: 'Blessed are the peacemakers'" (*De Serm. Dom. in Monte* bk1 ch4).

86. *ST* IIa-IIae q45 a6 c.

87. Olivier Bonnewijn, in his careful study of the beatitudes, examines the way in which beatitude as the goal of the moral life is the key concept in the *Summa*'s moral theology. He traces the link between moral action and the beatific vision, arguing that beatitude describes the perfection of human action under the influence of the gifts. That is, beatitude is the highest instance of excellent human action, in which the human person acts most fully under the influence of grace; it is thus also the highest instance of the subordination of human to divine action, manifesting the "communion between the two *operantes*" (447). The beatitudes are the excellent acts that link human activity on earth and in heaven, activity that, because it conforms one to the image of Christ, is Christiform. For a helpful summary of the argument, see *La béatitude et les béatitudes*, 437ff. Bonnewijn's argument accords well with mine; if beatitude is a central theme of the *Summa*, deification is too. He focuses on the goal, I on the transformation necessary to arrive there; he on excellent action, I on how such action conforms us to God by participation, adapting us for God's own beatitude by likeness to the divine nature/Persons.

88. *ST* Ia-IIae q69 a2.

The source of this "tranquility of order," and its relationship to charity, is made clear in an earlier question devoted to peace itself. Peace is one of the interior effects of charity, along with joy and mercy. Peace arises from union within oneself or with others. One's heart is at peace when the sensitive and rational appetites are united, working together to move toward one end. This interior union is peace in the truest sense. Concord arises between persons when there is a union of appetites among them, although this may not necessarily entail the interior peace of each one.[89] Because charity brings about union with God and others, and because by charity "God is loved with the whole heart, so that we refer all things to him," union with God results in a unifying of the soul's appetites within, although one that can be perfect only in eternal life. As a result of charity, too, concord comes about, because we love our neighbor as ourselves and wish to do his will as if it were our own.[90] Peace, then, is the fruit of well-ordered charity—and so is the work of the gift of wisdom. Union with God by charity and wisdom thus results not just in an external concord of wills with God and others, but in true peace, flowering in the peace of beatitude, where all desire will be at rest in the perfect "contemplation of wisdom" in the beatific vision.[91]

Furthermore, because God is not only the object but also the participated exemplar of the intellect and will in the one who knows and loves God by grace, the meritorious rectitude of the will required for beatitude is rooted most deeply in a total transformation into God's likeness in the intellect and will by deification, which is adopted sonship. In his general treatment of the beatitudes, Thomas remarks that "to be conformed to God by a certain adoptive filiation belongs to the gift of wisdom," and that "to establish peace in oneself or with others shows one to be an imitator of God, who is the God of unity and peace, and so the reward given is the glory of divine filiation, which is to be perfectly conjoined to God in consummate wisdom."[92] The gift of wisdom is the highest reward in the kingdom of heaven, for "the highest dignity in the king's house belongs to the king's son."

---

89. *ST* IIa-IIae q29 a1.

90. *ST* IIa-IIae q29 a2 ad4, a3.

91. See *ST* Ia-IIae q3 a8, q5 a4; because all desire will be immovably satisfied in heaven, the beatific vision cannot be lost once possessed. From this repose of the will in God following upon the vision in the intellect comes the delight of beatitude (Ia-IIae q4 aa1–2).

92. *ST* Ia-IIae q69 a3 ad1, a4 c., ad3.

Thomas specifies the nature of this likeness of sonship bestowed by wisdom even further in q45 a6, when he explains that the reward of peacemakers, which is their beatitude, is that "they shall be called the children of God":

Now those are called children of God inasmuch as they participate in the likeness of the only-begotten and natural Son of God, according to Rom 8 (29): "whom he foreknew to be conformed to the image of his Son," who is Wisdom begotten. And thus, by gaining the gift of wisdom, man attains to the sonship of God.[93]

Peacemakers shall be called the children of God because they participate by wisdom in the likeness of the Son. For Thomas, all who have grace and charity, and thus are adopted sons, participate by grace in the divine nature (on the level of their nature) and by charity in the Holy Spirit (in their will). The gift of wisdom in a special way completes the deification of the image's faculties on the journey to beatitude by bestowing in the intellect a participation in the Son, the Word, "who is Wisdom begotten."

What Thomas says here confirms and elucidates his teaching in Ia q43 that in the gift of grace the intellect is likened by wisdom to the Son, "the Word breathing forth Love."[94] Thomas already has in mind in his treatment of the Trinity, the roles of wisdom and charity in concretely manifesting the invisible missions of Word and Love in the rational creature, by which God comes to dwell in it as the "known in the knower and the beloved in the lover."[95] The deepest reason for the unique relationship between charity and wisdom lies in their joint representation, in the graced *imago Dei*, of the Trinitarian Persons, such that the image knows and loves God in a filial way, "conformed by the Spirit of adoption to the image of the Son."

Wisdom, Faith, and Faith's Gifts

It might be asked, however, why Thomas thinks that the intellect is especially likened to the Son in his invisible mission by wisdom, rather than by faith or one of its associated gifts (understanding and knowledge). Wisdom is, of course, ineluctably associated with participation in the sonship of the Word who is Wisdom begotten. But how does this scripturally rooted claim make

93. *ST* IIa-IIae q45 a6.
94. *ST* Ia q43 a5 ad2.
95. *ST* Ia q43 a3; cf. also Ia q8 a3 and the discussion in chapter 2.

sense in light of the perfection of the image? After all, faith is the theological virtue perfecting the intellect, which makes us capable of supernatural knowledge of God in this life. By the light of faith the intellect gives assent to matters of faith, so that the person acquires "little by little" the knowledge necessary for salvation on the way to the full vision of God in eternal life.[96] In the *Summa's* examination of grace, Thomas even explicitly draws a parallel between faith as a participation in the divine knowledge, charity as a participation in the divine love, and grace as a participation in the divine nature to argue that just as faith and charity transform the powers of intellect and will, disposing them toward the supernatural end, so grace, which is their "principle and root," transforms the essence of the soul as the principle of the powers.[97] If the procession of the Word is the exemplar of the intellect in creation, and the divine missions add to the processions a further temporal effect, by which the rational creature "is made a participator of the divine Word and Love proceeding so as to know God truly and to love God rightly,"[98] why is the infused virtue of faith, elevating the intellect for supernatural knowledge, not identified with that effect?[99] If charity is a par-

---

96. *ST* IIa-IIae q2 a3. In the *De veritate* Thomas calls the light of faith an "initial participation" of the full supernatural knowledge of God in the vision. *DV* q14 a2: "For this reason also, for man to be ordained to the good which is eternal life, there must be some initial participation of it in him to whom it is promised. However, eternal life consists in the full knowledge of God, as is clear from John [17:3]: 'Now this is eternal life,' etc. Consequently, we must have within us some initial participation of this supernatural knowledge. We have it through faith, which by reason of an infused light holds those things which are beyond our natural knowledge."

97. *ST* Ia-IIae q110 a4; cf. a3 ad3: "Unde relinquitur quod gratia, sicut est prius virtute, ita habeat subiectum prius potentiis animae, ita scilicet quod sit in essentia animae. Sicut enim per potentiam intellectivam homo participat cognitionem divinam per virtutem fidei; et secundum potentiam voluntatis [participat] amorem divinum, per virtutem caritatis; ita etiam per naturam animae participat, secundum quandam similitudinem, naturam divinam, per quandam regenerationem sive recreationem."

98. *ST* Ia q38 a1.

99. The reader may recall that the eternal processions of the Word and Love flow from the Father, their principle and so, we know from the questions on creation, are the exemplars of the powers of intellect and will flowing from the principle of the rational nature. The image of nature thus can be said to participate in some respect the likeness of the divine nature and its processions, for it is a principle of its own activity and represents the species of the Word and Love in the rational activity of its intellect and will. But by the divine missions (which add to the processions a further temporal effect), the image being perfected by grace truly participates in the divine nature in every respect, for, as principle of the supernatural activities of intellect and will, it shares not only in the divine nature's intellectual nature and activity but also, most

ticipation in the likeness of the Holy Spirit, why is wisdom, and not faith, especially identified as a participation in the likeness of the Son?

The question is instructive. The first thing to be said is that faith, as Thomas remarks in his discussion of the gift of wisdom, is always presupposed to wisdom in this life.[100] Without faith there can be no charity, and without charity there can be none of the gifts. Faith is thus always operative—before vision replaces it—as a principle of the gift of wisdom, elevating the intellect to God as First Truth.[101] The "participation in the divine knowledge" of what is given by revelation, which living faith bestows by its assent, is the necessary substrate of wisdom's operation in this life. Wisdom in a sense perfects both faith and charity because all of the gifts of the Spirit in the cognitive power, including wisdom, are "ordained to supernatural knowledge, which, in us, takes its foundation from faith."[102] With respect to what is proposed for belief, one needs the gift of understanding (which assists the intellect to "penetrate into the heart" of what is said), wisdom (enabling one to judge rightly about divine things), and knowledge (to judge human things in relation to God), as well as counsel to apply knowledge in particular circumstances.[103] The gift of wisdom thus cooperates with the gifts of the Spirit perfecting faith. As discussed above, however, Thomas thinks that wisdom corresponds more integrally to charity than to faith because it orders charity and charity is its direct cause, uniting the mind to God and so allowing for wisdom's certitude of judgment based on connatural knowledge "of the very things we believe in themselves, by a kind of union with them."[104]

Living faith and its gifts are thus all active in the intellect of one with the gift of wisdom; as discussed in chapter 5, however, faith can exist without charity and the gifts in a lifeless state, and so faith alone is insufficient even for such perfection of participation in the divine knowledge as is possible in this life. There can be an assent of the will to the matters of faith—as in the case of the demons—on the basis of a conviction that what is said is true because God is speaking, but without an assent to what is said as good.

---

importantly, in its own divine object and end. On this last point, see the discussion of parallels between Ia q93 on the image and Ia q14 on God's knowledge in chapter 2.

100. *ST* IIa-IIae q45 a1 ad2.

101. *ST* IIa-IIae q1 a1; cf. q4 a7, q45 a1 ad2.

102. *ST* IIa-IIae q8 a6.

103. *ST* IIa-IIae q8 a6; cf. Ia-IIae q68 a4.

104. *ST* IIa-IIae q9 a2 ad1.

If one does not willingly embrace the propositions of faith, their truth is not self-evident; the demons recognize, reluctantly, that the teaching of the Church is from God but "do not see the things themselves that the Church teaches, for example, that there are three Persons in one God."[105] In other words, in one with only lifeless faith, there is no union with God as the known in the knower and the beloved in lover, for there is not the instruction of the intellect that "bursts forth in love" and so is a likening to the Word breathing forth Love as the created term of the divine missions. For this charity is required, with wisdom that perfects it, according to Ia q43 a5 ad2, in which Thomas associates charity and wisdom with the kindling of the affection and perfection of the intellect in the invisible missions of the Spirit and Son.

Furthermore, even living faith in itself could not bestow a participation in the likeness of the Son that endures and is perfected in the journey from this life to the next. That is because faith—although the necessary beginning of deification in this life—has in itself no potential for the deiformity of heaven. Faith and hope are virtues of the wayfarer, no longer needed or operative in beatitude, where they will pass away. Faith does not remain in the blessed, but wisdom—with the other gifts of the Spirit flowing from charity—does.[106] I say more in chapter 7 about the operations of the beatified intellect; here it is enough to point out not only that wisdom's perfection of the intellect endures from this life to the next, but also that wisdom and charity govern the activity of the blessed, for wisdom's loving contemplation of the divine essence is the substance of eternal life. In beatitude, wisdom completely transforms the person into a child of God, in the likeness of the Son, and wisdom's perfection of charity is complete.

Can the effect of the Son's invisible mission, which Thomas identifies as "wisdom" in Ia q43 a5, be exclusively identified with the gift of wisdom?[107] In Thomas's discussion of the divine indwelling in the *Summa*, the association of this wisdom with the gift of charity in the Spirit's mission seems to indicate that at least Thomas is thinking of the gift of wisdom as a principal effect of the Son's mission; as already noted, Thomas's etymological explanation of *sapientia* as "savored knowledge" in both Ia q43, on the divine

---

105. *ST* IIa-IIae q5 a2.
106. *ST* Ia-IIae q68 a6 c., ad2–3.
107. I am grateful to Bernhard Blankenhorn, OP, for raising this question.

missions, and II II q45 a2, on the gift of wisdom, provides a textual link as well. In a general sense, however, all knowledge of the truth—and so *a fortiori*, all graced knowledge of God—is a participation in the likeness of the Son, the Word, who is Truth itself.[108]

In his *Commentary on John* Thomas considers how the faithful become sharers in this truth as they are "taught all things" by the Holy Spirit (Jn 14:26). In the divine missions, he says, the children of God are conformed by the Holy Spirit to the Son, who, "since he is begotten Wisdom, is Truth itself"; and so the effect of the missions of Son and Spirit is that the children of God become "sharers in the divine wisdom and knowers of the truth."[109] As Thomas will say later in his commentary on John 17:17, when believers are "sanctified in the truth," they are made to share in the perfection and holiness of the Word, who is the Truth.[110] The effects of the Son's mission in the intellect are brought about with the help of the Holy Spirit: "The Son, since he is the Word, gives teaching to us; but the Holy Spirit enables us to grasp it."[111] The conformation of the intellect to the Word is a participation in Truth made possible by the mission of the Holy Spirit, who with charity "gives an understanding from within," "makes us know all things by inspiring us," and "makes us participate in the wisdom of the Son" as he leads the children of God from within through his gifts.[112] And so, as Emery puts it, "the indwelling of the divine Persons appears … as the blossoming of the welcome given to the Truth, or rather as the *Trinitarian dimension of the event that takes place in the adherence to the Truth*."[113]

The likening of the intellect to the Word that takes place in the divine missions is, it seems, not only a likening by means of the gift of wisdom. And yet, because in the missions there is an adherence to the Truth in love,[114] it is especially by the gift of wisdom that this likening takes place.

---

108. On this, see Gilles Emery, *Trinity, Church, and the Human Person* (Naples, FL: Sapientia Press, 2007), 92–93.

109. *Sup. Ioh.* ch14 lect6 (#1958).   110. *Sup. Ioh.* ch17 lect4 (#2229).

111. *Sup. Ioh.* ch14 lect6 (#1958).   112. *Sup. Ioh.* ch14 lect6 (#1958–60).

113. Emery, *Trinity, Church, and the Human Person*, 97. Italics in original.

114. *ST* I q43 a5 ad2: "The Son is sent not in accordance with every and any kind of intellectual perfection, but according to the intellectual illumination which breaks forth into the affection of love, as is said in John 6 (45): 'Everyone that has heard from the Father and has learned, comes to me.'" In his Gospel commentary on this passage Thomas says: "He learns the word who grasps it according to the meaning (*rationem*) of the speaker; now, the Word of the

The gift of wisdom is integrally associated with the Spirit's mission in charity, which makes one adhere to the Truth, and so it has a special role in conforming disciples to the Word in the divine missions. In his commentary on
John 17:26 Thomas sheds further light on the connection of the effects of
the Son's mission with that of the Spirit in the divine indwelling. He gives
two explanations for what Jesus meant when he said, "I have made known
to them your name ... that the love with which you have loved me may be
in them, and I in them." First, "The Father loves all those in whom the Son
is present; and the Son is in them insofar as they have knowledge of the
truth"; that is, the Father will love all those who participate in the Word.
Second, "As you have loved me, so they, by participating in the Holy Spirit,
may love. And by that fact I will be in them as God in a temple, and they
in me, as members of the head: 'He who abides in love abides in God, and
God abides in him' (1 Jn 4:16)."[115] The love of the Father and Son—that is,
the love of the Father for those in whom the Son is present because of their
participation in the Word—is participated in by the faithful in the mission
of the Holy Spirit, which causes them to love and welcome the Word, so
that God dwells in them and they in God. Love causes one to welcome the
truth, as Emery notes, and in the relationship between charity and truth the
order of the mission of the Son and Holy Spirit is expressed: "truth flowers
in charity" as the Word bursts forth in Love, and "charity moves the mind
to grasp the truth and give it its assent."[116]

The assistance of the gift of wisdom especially perfects this adherence to
God by charity. Among the intellectual gifts of the Spirit that enable participation in the Truth, even the gift of understanding, without wisdom,
would not be sufficient, for it is not enough to apprehend, however deeply,
what is true without orienting oneself to it with wisdom's judgment that
one should adhere to this truth.[117] This is perhaps one reason wisdom, of all
the gifts, is the highest, and the one that "directs both the human intellect
and affections."[118] While the effect of the Son's divine mission includes ev-

---

Father is breathing forth love: he, therefore, who grasps it with the fervor of love, learns; Wisdom 7:27: 'She transfers herself into holy souls, and makes them prophets and friends of God'"
(*Sup. Ioh.* ch6 lect5 (#946).

115. *Sup. Ioh.* ch17 lect6 (#2270).

116. Emery, *Trinity, Church, and the Human Person*, 107, 109.

117. *ST* IIa-IIae q8 a6.

118. *ST* Ia-IIae q68 a4 ad5; because it is the "directing principle" of both the gifts of under-

ery kind of perfection of the intellect that participates in the Word, the gift of wisdom represents and perfects, in a special way, all of the others. And so it is to the gift of wisdom that the "glory of divine filiation consisting in perfect union with God" belongs.[119]

Wisdom, Charity, and Christ

We are now in a position to consider how Christ—through his perfection of grace, charity, and wisdom—reveals the way to the beatitude communicated by fellowship with him through the "Spirit of adoption." In chapter 4 we saw that Christ in his humanity, possessing the fullness of participation in the divine nature by grace because of the hypostatic union, possessed in this life also the perfection of all the virtues and gifts proper to his state as both *comprehensor* and *viator*. So he was led most perfectly by the Holy Spirit in filial obedience and love. Christ's charity and wisdom, among all the virtues and gifts that were supereminently his, must be the greatest of any human. His fullness of habitual grace (i.e., his perfect participation as human in the divine nature) makes his humanity the instrument of his divinity, so that as Head he is both principle and model of grace for our salvation. This fullness of grace plays out in the fullness of his charity and wisdom, flowing from the root of grace. He participates humanly by charity and wisdom in the likeness of the Holy Spirit and Son to the maximum possible extent.

As John Boyle points out, when Thomas argues for Christ's fullness of grace, he does so in part with an eye to the role of Christ's perfect knowledge and love of God, operating in his obedient self-offering for our salvation.[120] As principle, by his divine nature working through the instrumentality of his humanity, Christ can bring others to a like deiformity by grace, charity, and wisdom, and therefore to the full obedience to God on earth and enjoyment of God in beatitude, which he alone already possessed *in via*.[121] And, as

---

standing and of fear, according to Isa 11:2. On wisdom's precedence among the gifts, see Ia-IIae q68 a7.

119. *ST* Ia-IIae q69 a4.

120. John F. Boyle, "The Structural Setting of Thomas Aquinas' Theology of the Grace of Christ as He Is Head of the Church in the *Summa Theologiae*" (PhD diss., University of Toronto, 1989), 215.

121. Cf. *Comp. theol.* 213; *ST* IIIa q10 a4.

model, he most clearly manifests to us what perfect human participation in the divine love and wisdom looks like. The latter, one can infer, is the underlying reason why "every action of Christ is our instruction," as Thomas stresses in his exposition of Christ's life on earth. What Christ did and suffered for our salvation reveals God's wisdom and love for us because he is the living Word made flesh, the living Word of God's *sacra doctrina*. For our salvation this loving wisdom is made visible in Christ through his exemplary participation in the Word and Love, teaching us by his own manifest wisdom and charity how to be adopted sons.

The Charity of Christ Crucified, and Ours

What is the pattern that Christ, in his own charity and wisdom, provides for the life of sonship? I noted in chapter 4 that from the beginning articles of the IIIa *pars* Thomas emphasizes that the Incarnation makes known the wisdom and goodness of God, through Christ who is the "power of God and the wisdom of God" (1 Cor 1:24). In the Apostle's text, Christ manifests God's power and wisdom especially through the weakness and foolishness of the cross, an insight on which Thomas does not fail to build.[122] In the IIIa *pars* Thomas examines the mysteries of Christ's life from conception to exaltation at the right hand of the Father, all of which have salvific efficacy insofar as they are the cause and model of our own sanctification.[123] Much could be said of each of them, for in all Christ's meritorious charity is displayed, in the conformity of his will to God. Yet nowhere does Thomas stress so clearly and so often the causal and pedagogical role of Christ's charity in bringing about our salvation, as in his treatment of the Passion. Christ crucified is a kind of icon of charity perfectly ordered by wisdom, and so he reveals both God's love for us and the way to participation in that love.[124]

Like the Incarnation itself, the Passion of Christ was not, absolutely speaking, necessary for the deliverance of humanity from sin, but was most fitting and in keeping with God's mercy and justice.[125] There was no more fitting way for God to deliver the human race than through the Passion of Christ, Thomas says in IIIa q46 a3, first of all because:

122. See Wawrykow, "Wisdom in the Christology of Thomas Aquinas," 182–91.
123. Cf., e.g., *ST* III q34 a3. See Torrell, *Saint Thomas Aquinas*, vol. 2, 131ff.
124. Cf. *Sup. Eph.* ch3 lect5.
125. *ST* IIIa q46 a1, ad3.

through this we know how much God loves us, and so are moved to love God, in which the perfection of human salvation consists. Whence the Apostle says (Rom 5:8): "God commends his charity towards us, because while we were enemies, Christ died for us."

Although God could have willed to deliver humanity from sin in some other way,[126] Christ's suffering out of love for us on the Cross reveals God's love, through Christ's love for us, and elicits our own love in return. The second reason for the fittingness of the Passion follows from the first. Christ's Passion was fitting because it gives us an example of every virtue "required for human salvation"; it teaches us how to reach "the perfection of human salvation" belonging to the love of God, for all of the virtues are directed by charity, perfected by wisdom.[127] In several works Thomas gives a list of the virtues Christ displays on the Cross, which he compares with Augustine to "the chair of the Master teaching."[128] Christ "suffered for us, leaving an example" (1 Pet 2:21) by his obedience, humility, constancy, justice, fortitude, patience, and charity.[129]

---

126. *ST* IIIa q46 a2.

127. As Thomas points out in his *Commentary on John* (ch15), the only commandment Christ gives his disciples to keep is the practice of charity; but this one includes all the others because "charity is the root and end of all the virtues" (lect. 2) and makes of those who share in the divine wisdom revealed to them by Christ the "friends of God [Wis 7:27]" (lect. 3).

128. *ST* IIIa q46 a4.

129. See *ST* IIIa q46 a3, a4; *SCG* IV.55; *Comp. theol.* 227; *Collationes Credo in Deum* 4. A remarkable passage in Thomas's *Commentary on Philippians* is also worth examination. He treats Phil 2:5, Paul's exhortation to the Philippians to be humble, in order to experience (in the Vulgate, *sentire*, to sense or feel) in themselves what is also in Christ Jesus, who humbled himself, even to death on a cross. Thomas provides a concise prescription for conformation to Christ through the five spiritual senses: "Primo videre eius charitatem, ut ei conformemur illuminati. Is. 33:17: regem in decore suo videbunt, et cetera. 2 Cor. 3:18: nos autem omnes revelata facie gloriam Dei speculantes, et cetera. Secundo audire eius sapientiam, ut beatificemur. 3 Kg 10:8: beati viri tui, et beati servi tui, hi qui stant coram te, et audiunt sapientiam tuam. Ps. 17:45: in auditu auris obedivit mihi. Tertio odorare gratias suae mansuetudinis, ut ad eum curramus. Sg. 1:3: trahe me post te, curremus in odorem unguentorum tuorum. Quarto gustare dulcedinem eius pietatis, ut in Deo semper dilecti simus. Ps. 33:9: gustate et videte quoniam suavis est dominus. Quinto tangere eius virtutem, ut salvemur. Mt 9:21: si tetigero tantum fimbriam vestimenti eius, salva ero. Et sic sentite quasi tangendo per operis imitationem." It is Christ's charity, wisdom, grace, piety, and power that we experience through imitation. This passage bears both resemblances and differences to significant treatments of the spiritual senses by other thirteenth-century theologians—in particular William of Auxerre's *Summa Aurea*—and so seems to deserve further study. On William's teaching, see Boyd Taylor Coolman, *Knowing God by Experience: The*

In the context of Christ's voluntary suffering, obedience comes to the fore as the manifestation of his charity. Thomas emphasizes in the *Summa* the voluntary nature of Christ's suffering as he treats the causes of Christ's Passion. Christ died out of obedience, and so out of charity: "Christ suffered out of charity and out of obedience for the same reason; because he fulfilled the precepts of charity out of obedience, and was obedient, out of love, to the Father's command."[130] Thomas explains in his commentary on John 15 that Christ's obedience is the model for those who "abide in God's love," and so "keep his commandments":

Christ shows that he abided in the Father's love because in all things he kept the Father's commandments. For he submitted to death: "He humbled himself, becoming obedient unto death, even death on a cross" (Phil 2:8), and refrained from all sin ... And so he says, "I abide in his love," because there is nothing in me, as man, opposed to his love.[131]

Christ's human obedience was thus the manifestation of his charity: because charity inspired his human will, it was voluntarily united with the Father's will that he should be delivered up for our salvation.[132] It was also the manifestation of his perfect wisdom, for in a good will charity is ordered in conformity to the divine will by the gift of wisdom. And so he "laid down his beloved life for the good of charity," suffering in the loss of this life a pain greater than any other, "both because it flowed from a greater wisdom and charity ... and because he grieved at once for all sins."[133]

In IIIa q48 Thomas presents a series of articles examining the various

---

Spiritual Senses and the Knowledge of God in the Theology of William of Auxerre (Washington, DC: Catholic University of America Press, 2004).

130. *ST* IIIa q47 a2 ad3; cf. a1.

131. *Sup. Ioh.* ch15 lect2.

132. *ST* IIIa q47 a3 c., ad2. That there was no contrariety of wills in Christ, even in the face of death, is a consequence of the hypostatic union in that Christ's human will is perfectly subordinated as instrument of his divine will; the obedience of his human will is further specified as the consequence of his perfect charity flowing from his fullness of grace. It is thus his charity—i.e., his perfect participation in the Holy Spirit—that makes his human will the perfect instrument of his divinity. Because of this charity, he is able to merit condignly for himself and others. See Ia-IIae q114 a4, a6; IIIa q18 a6, q19 a4. If Christ's charity makes his human will the instrument of his divinity, it is his wisdom, perfecting charity, that does the same in his intellect.

133. *ST* IIIa q46 a6 ad4. Thomas comments in q46 a9 ad4 that Christ willed to suffer while he was still young, first "to commend more his love, by giving up his life for us while he was still in his most perfect state of life."

"modes" in which Christ's suffering effected our salvation. Because Christ's humanity is the instrument of his divinity, "all of Christ's actions and sufferings operate instrumentally by the power of his divinity for human salvation." Christ's Passion is thus the efficient cause of human salvation.[134] In the first four articles of q48 Thomas considers multiple ways in which the Passion brought about its effect. Underlying all of these to some extent is the teaching found in the first two reasons for the fittingness of the Passion—that it manifests Christ's love, revealing God's love, and teaching us how to love in God in return.[135]

First, the Passion caused our salvation by way of merit (q48 a1). As a consequence of the hypostatic union, Christ as Head possesses the fullness of grace, which he bestows on his members, and so by the Passion merited salvation for both himself and us. But in fact Christ merited for us as Head from the first moment of his conception—specifically by the perfection of his charity as the cause of merit.[136] Thomas does not think that Christ's charity was any greater in the Passion than in the other mysteries of his life, and yet the Passion has a "special effect ... because of the nature of this work, which was suitable for such an effect, as is clear from the arguments above on the fittingness of Christ's Passion."[137] He explains that "it was necessary for Christ to suffer" in order to remove "certain obstacles" on our part, by which "we were impeded from obtaining the effects of his preceding merits."[138]

What are these obstacles? When Thomas argued earlier that the Passion was fitting because it reveals God's love for us, his authority was Ro-

---

134. *ST* IIIa q48 a6, ad2. John Boyle remarks that all of the modes of the Passion's divine efficiency are instances of instrumental causality in that all are aspects of his human operation. "Structural Setting of Thomas Aquinas' Theology," 283–84.

135. The other three reasons Thomas gives for the fittingness of the Passion are also related to the various ways in which the Passion caused our salvation: third, the Passion was fitting because it merited justifying grace and glory (cf. q48 a1); fourth, by it we are "introduced to (*inducta*)," or brought to the realization of, the greater need to refrain from sin because we have been "bought with a great price" (cf. q48 a4); and fifth, as humanity was overcome by the devil, so one who is human should overthrow the devil, and by dying conquer death (cf. q48 a4 ad2). The third and fourth at least may be related to Christ's charity (as the cause of merit) and ours in response.

136. *ST* IIIa q19 a4, a34 a3; cf. q8; Ia-IIae q114 a6. On charity as the cause of merit, see Ia IIae q114 a4.

137. *ST* IIIa q48 a1 ad3.   138. *ST* IIIa q48 a1 ad2–3.

mans 5:8: "God commends his charity towards us, because while we were enemies, Christ died for us." In his scriptural commentary on this passage, Thomas remarks that Christ's death was meritorious and satisfied for our sins not in that it was a death per se (nor certainly on account of the malice of the killers), but because Christ died out of obedience to the Father, and love for us, so that all, even his killers, could be "reconciled to God" (Rom 5:10) and turned from enemies into friends.[139] Thomas quotes this verse again when he discusses the effects of the Passion, beginning with the forgiveness of sins (q49 a1); there the first reason he gives for the Passion being the cause of forgiveness of sins is that it "arouses our charity," for "it is by charity that we obtain pardon for our sins." The foremost "special effect" of the merit of the Passion, applied to us, is to remove the first obstacle to our salvation, our own refusal, through sin, to love God.[140]

Because Christ suffered so greatly out of love and obedience, his Passion "satisfied perfectly for our sins," and so caused our salvation by way of satisfaction (q48 a2):

He properly satisfies for an offense who presents to the offended one something which he loves as much or more than he hated the offense. But Christ, by suffering out of love and obedience, presented to God a recompense greater than was required for the offense of the whole human race. First, indeed, on account of the magnitude of the charity from which he suffered. Second, on account of the dignity of his life which he laid down for satisfaction, that of God and man. Third, on account of the extent of the Passion and the magnitude of the pain assumed, as said above. And so the Passion of Christ not only sufficed, but also superabundantly satisfied for the sins of the human race, according to 1 Jn 2:2: "He is the propitiation for our sins; and not for ours only, but also for those of the whole world."[141]

The Father loves Christ's love and obedience, which were so great in the Passion that they outweighed every offense of the human race. Christ, who was sinless, satisfied not for himself but for those joined to him by faith

---

139. *Sup. Rom.* ch5, lect2.

140. And so in the gift of justification there is not only the remission of sins but also the conversion of the free will from sin toward God by faith quickened by charity; cf. *ST* Ia-IIae q113 a4 ad1. Cf. note 126; III q49 a1. Le Guillou notes observantly that Christ merits for us "because he enables us to merit in Him and through Him as His members, by permitting us, through our human activity which has been gathered into Himself, to construct in ourselves the image of God." Schaldenbrand, *Christ and Church*, 262.

141. *ST* III q48 a2.

and charity in the mystical body—because "the head and members are like one mystic person ... the satisfaction of Christ belongs to all the faithful as to his members."[142] Christ's charity, revealed in the Passion, was so great that its value even superabundantly satisfied for the malice of his killers, for whom he prayed on the Cross, "in order to show the abundance of his charity, on account of which he suffered."[143]

It is in Thomas's discussion of the Passion as a sacrifice (q48 a3) that we see most clearly why, out of all Christ's works, his charity is especially manifested in the Passion. "He delivered himself up for us, an oblation and a sacrifice to God for an odor of sweetness" (Eph 5:2). Thomas's placement of this verse in the *sed contra* of a3 is illuminated by his scriptural commentary on this passage, where he says that Paul is speaking of "the sign of immense charity," which we are called to imitate by "walking in love" as "beloved children" of God (Eph 5:1).[144] Thomas draws much from Augustine in q48 a3, explaining that

A sacrifice is properly said to be something done for the honor properly owed to God, to appease him. And so Augustine says in *De civ. Dei* 10, "A true sacrifice is every work which is done so that we may adhere to God in charity, referred to that blessed end by which we can truly be blessed." Now Christ, as Augustine adds, "offered himself in the Passion for us"; and this work in which he voluntarily bore the Passion was most acceptable to God, since it came forth from charity. Whence it is manifest that the Passion of Christ was a true sacrifice.

God is given the honor owed to him, and so appeased, by the proper ordering of human hearts to him in charity, so that their works are referred to the end of beatitude; that is, restoration of the proper order of things from the disorder of sin appeases God. Christ restores that order on our behalf by his self-offering in charity for us so that we could again be directed to God.

As Thomas points out in his treatment of sacrifice in the IIa *pars* (as an external act of the virtue of religion), its principal part is the inward sacrifice of devout self-offering to God.[145] This self-offering of devotion has charity as its proximate cause, for "love makes one ready to serve one's friend," and it also nourishes charity, for "all friendship is safeguarded and increased by the practice and consideration of friendly deeds."[146] Every act done out of

---

142. *ST* III q48 a2 ad1.
144. *Sup. Eph.* ch 5, lect 1.
146. *ST* IIa-IIae q82 a2 ad2.

143. *ST* III q48 a2 ad2, q47 a4 ad1.
145. *ST* IIa-IIae q85 a2, a4.

reverence for God, in order to cling to him in charity, has the nature of a sacrifice.[147] Charity is thus the inner cause of sacrifice, and true devout sacrifice makes one cling to God. Christ's sacrifice was perfect, exceeding those of the Old Law, in that it was an offering of human, mortal, and sinless flesh, and that "being the offerer's own flesh, it was acceptable to God on account of his charity in offering up his own flesh."[148] Christ's charity was manifested especially in his obedience. This obedience, "better than sacrifices," led him to the sacrifice of the Passion, and because he was "obedient out of love to the Father's command," his sacrifice was acceptable and suitable for reconciling humanity to God.[149] Christ's loving obedience in the Passion supersedes the disobedience of human sin and so is pleasing to God on our behalf.[150] Sacrifice effects reconciliation because its inner reality is the obedient self-offering in love that unites one to God. So the Passion "acts by way of a sacrifice, insofar as through it we are reconciled to God."[151]

In offering this sacrifice of himself, Christ was our redeemer (q48 a4, a5). His Passion freed humanity from the bondage of sin and the debt of punishment, for it was "a kind of price by which we were liberated from both obligations." Something offered in satisfaction is a price given to redeem oneself or another from sin and debt:

Now Christ made satisfaction, not by giving money or something of that kind, but giving that which was of the greatest value—namely, himself—for us. And so Christ's Passion is called our redemption.[152]

Christ, in love, paid the "price of our redemption, his own precious blood" to God so that humans could belong fully to God, for by removing sin it allowed us once again to be "united to God by the union of charity."[153] Christ's redemption is thus no merely extrinsic act by which some high price might be paid without regard to the engagement of those who are ransomed. When Thomas turns to the effects of the Passion, he points out that

---

147. *ST* IIa-IIae q85 a3, ad1.   148. *ST* IIIa q48 a3 ad1.

149. *ST* IIIa q47 a2 c., ad3.

150. And so, by his obedience, Christ fulfills and surpasses all the precepts of the Old Law: the moral precepts, based on the commands of love for God and neighbor; the ceremonial precepts, ordained for sacrifices and oblations; and the judicial precepts, ordained to compensation for wrongdoing (*ST* IIIa q47 a2 ad1).

151. *ST* IIIa q48 a6 ad3, q49 a4.   152. *ST* IIIa q48 a4.

153. *ST* IIIa q48 a3 ad1, ad3.

Christ as Head redeems his members from sin by suffering out of love and obedience on their behalf, "as if a person by some meritorious action of his hands, were to redeem himself from a sin which his feet had committed."[154] Christ's love and obedience belong to his whole mystical body. And the Passion has the effect of removing sins on our part because it arouses our charity in response. The charity of Christ in the Passion is both the cause and the model for our sanctification.

Conjoined to Christ's Passion

When Thomas examines the effects of the Passion (q49), he is concerned not only with enumerating its benefits (liberation from sin, the devil's power, and the debt of punishment; reconciliation with God and the opening of Heaven's gate; and the exaltation of the body for Christ), but also establishing the way in which these effects are communicated. Because Christ's humanity was the instrument of his divinity, his suffering in the flesh had a kind of universal and transtemporal efficacy for the forgiveness of sins and the bestowal of the other benefits of the Passion, "just as if a doctor were to make a medicine by which all diseases could be cured, even in the future."[155] But Christ's Passion "needs to be applied to each individual" in order for each to obtain its effects.[156] Throughout the articles of q49 Thomas teaches that this personal appropriation of the effects of the Passion takes place through faith, charity, and the sacraments, "which derive their power from Christ's Passion."[157] For those "who are conjoined to Christ's Passion" in this way, personal sin is cleansed and God is appeased by the sacrifice of Christ for their offenses.[158] The gate of heaven—that is, the possibility of eternal beatitude—opens wide to those who "communicate in his Passion through faith and charity and the sacraments of faith."[159]

What does it mean to be "conjoined to Christ's Passion"? By the sacraments, beginning with baptism, "we are likened to him sacramentally, according to Rom 6:4: 'For we are buried together with him by baptism into death.'"[160] And by "faith living through charity," Christ's Passion is applied

---

154. *ST* IIIa q49 a1.   155. *ST* IIIa q49 a1 ad3.
156. *ST* IIIa q49 a1 ad4.
157. *ST* IIIa q49 a1 ad4, ad5; a3 ad1–3; a4; a5.
158. *ST* IIIa q49 a4.   159. *ST* IIIa q49 a5.
160. *ST* IIIa q49 a3 ad2.

"not only to our minds but also to our hearts."[161] The reason these things make us communicate in the Passion is that they conform us to Christ in the Passion. We share in the effects of the Passion because we become like Christ crucified. The inner reality of the sacramental likening to Christ, which takes place through the sacraments, is nothing other than the conformation of mind and heart to Christ through the grace of the sacraments, which transforms the person into an adopted son of God.[162] The sacraments are instrumental causes of Christ's grace, extensions of the uniquely conjoined instrumentality of Christ's own humanity, which confer a participated likeness in the divine nature by grace, from which flow the perfections of the virtues and gifts.[163] So they confer the deifying participation of intellect and will in the likeness of Word and Love by wisdom-perfected charity, built on faith, which belongs to adopted sons.

The transformation wrought by faith, charity, and the sacraments must then take the form in us, as in Christ the Son, of sacrificial obedience. By their likening to God through charity and wisdom, the life of the sons of God wears the aspect in this life of the Passion, and in the next of glory. Those who have received "the spirit of adoption of sons," who are "incorporated with him as members," and therefore conformed to their Head, are conformed to his suffering and death in their mortal bodies so as to be brought with him to immortal glory (cf. Rom 8:17).[164] The final effect of

---

161. *ST* IIIa q49 a1 ad5.

162. E.g., the *res tantum* or reality of baptism is inward justification, which is the result of (living) faith, and to which belong regeneration (i.e., adopted sonship) and enlightenment (*ST* IIIa q66 a1 ad1). Thomas does not explicitly name the *res* of Confirmation as such, but says that it is "the sacrament of the fullness of grace," so that those who receive it "are conformed to Christ, inasmuch as from the first instant of his conception he was 'full of grace and truth,' as it says in Jn 1:14" (IIIa q72 a1 ad4). The *res tantum* of the Eucharist, which is "the consummation of the spiritual life and the end of all the sacraments," is the unity of the mystical body of the Church (the effect of charity; IIIa q73 a3). Thomas distinguishes between the way in which baptism and the Eucharist conform one to the Passion: "Baptism is the sacrament of the death and Passion of Christ inasmuch as one is reborn in Christ by the power of his Passion. But the Eucharist is the sacrament of the Passion of Christ inasmuch as one is perfected in union with the suffering Christ. Whence, just as Baptism is called the 'sacrament of faith,' which is the foundation of the spiritual life, so the Eucharist is called 'the sacrament of charity,' which is the 'bond of perfection' (Col 3:14)" (IIIa q73 a3 ad3).

163. *ST* IIIa q62 a2, a3, a5.

164. *ST* IIIa q49 a3 ad3. For a discussion of some ideas in this and following sections in relation to the notion of liturgical asceticism, see also Daria Spezzano, "Conjoined to Christ's

the Passion for Christ's members is the full enjoyment of God in beatitude, which he already experienced in his soul even on the Cross.[165] Christ's human soul was deiform and beatified even in this life because he participated fully in the likeness of Word and Love by his perfection of wisdom and charity flowing from his fullness of grace in the hypostatic union. These made of his human free will the perfectly obedient instrument of his divinity (see chap. 4). Just as there is a link between the deification of Christ's humanity and its obedient instrumentality, there is a connection between our deification and the obedience of our own free will to God, which makes of us instruments in our own salvation insofar as we are "led by the Holy Spirit as sons of God." We are likened to Christ not just in any way but precisely in the cruciform shape of his Passion—that is, we are conformed to him by wisdom-perfected charity that not only turns us away from sin and shapes a sacrificial life of filial obedience, but also brings us to the perfection of that obedience in the deiformity of beatitude.

Christ's Priesthood and Ours

The deified life of adopted sons, conformed to Christ's Passion in sacrificial obedience and perfected in the contemplation of the beatific vision, is at its heart a life of worship. Christ in the Passion was our high priest and sacrifice of the New Law, the principle and model of true worship of God. The conformation to Christ—which takes place through faith, charity, and the sacraments—gives to adopted sons a participation in Christ's priesthood, both in the external deputation to engage in the rites of divine worship and, in a deeper sense, in the interior worship of God that finds its fulfillment in the worship of the blessed.

Christ as Priest and Sacrifice of the New Law   Christ is the model of true worship in the sacrifice of the Passion, for he was both priest and sacrifice for us. Thomas anticipates q48 a3, on the Passion as sacrifice, in q22 a2, on Christ as priest and victim. His use of the same key authorities in both articles provides a clear textual link. In the *sed contra* of both articles, Ephesians 5:2 appears—"He delivered himself up for us, an oblation and a sacri-

---

Passion: The Deifying Asceticism of the Sacraments According to Thomas Aquinas," *Antiphon* 17, no. 1 (2013): 73–86.

165. *ST* IIIa q46 a8, q49 a5 ad1.

fice to God for an odor of sweetness"—and in the beginning of the *corpus* there is a quote from Augustine's *De civ. Dei* 10: "Every visible sacrifice is a sacrament, that is, a sacred sign, of the invisible sacrifice." The invisible sacrifice is "that by which one offers his spirit to God"; as in q48 a3, Thomas refers in q22 a2 to Augustine's teaching that "whatever is offered to God to raise one's spirit to God, can be called a sacrifice." As Thomas emphasizes the charity of Christ as the inner reality of this sacrifice in q48 a3, he also underlines the primacy of its interior aspect of self-offering.

Thomas goes on to argue that Christ's priestly self-offering fulfilled the ceremonial precepts of the Old Law, which required sin offerings, peace offerings, and holocausts, or "wholly burnt offerings." It did this by obtaining for us the gifts of remission of sins, grace (to adhere to God, "in which peace and salvation consist"), and glory (in which we are wholly united to God). So Christ in his humanity "was not only priest, but also perfect victim, being at once victim for sin, victim for peace-offering, and holocaust."[166] Christ was a victim not on account of the will of those who killed him—for they were not offering a sacrifice to God—but on account of "the will of the sufferer, who freely offered himself to suffering."[167] And in this free self-offering to God, as human, he "raised humanity's spirit" to God, obtaining for us justification, grace, and glory—the gifts necessary for perfection of the divine image in the journey to beatitude.[168]

Thomas's concern with how Christ as priest and victim fulfills the Old Law precepts is significant in relation to his emphasis on the importance of the interior self-offering of Christ's sacrifice and its interior effects in us. In the background is his teaching on the Old Law, with its judicial, moral, and ceremonial precepts, and the New Law of grace, which fulfills and surpasses the first. The purpose of the whole Law is love of God and neighbor; external works of divine worship commanded by the ceremonial precepts (to which sacrifice belongs) express outwardly the subjection to God of the interior acts of faith, hope, and love.[169] The outward worship of the body manifests and helps to bring about the interior worship of the soul, which "consists in the soul being united to God by the intellect and affections."[170]

---

166. *ST* IIIa q22 a2. And so (a3) the priesthood of Christ expiated sins, because it satisfies for sins, and by its power we receive grace to turn from sin.

167. *ST* IIIa q22 a2 ad2.   168. *ST* IIIa q22 a2.

169. *ST* Ia-IIae q99 a1 ad2, a3.   170. *ST* Ia-IIae q101 a2.

All worship in this life prefigures the true worship of heaven, where "the external worship will not consist in anything figurative, but solely in the praise of God, proceeding from the inward knowledge and affection, according to Isa 51:3: 'Joy and gladness shall be found there, thanksgiving and the sound of praise.'" The "burdensome" external worship of the Old Law, which prefigured both the future interior worship of glory and the sacrifice of Christ, gave way to the greater perfection of the New Law. This, foreshadowing more clearly the worship of heaven, prescribes fewer external acts, as it consists chiefly in the inner working of the grace of the Holy Spirit.[171] Because "the kingdom of God consists chiefly in internal acts," the New Law commands only those that lead to or result from grace (e.g., the sacraments, and good works in keeping with "faith working through love").[172] There is therefore a kind of trajectory of perfection from the Old Law to the New to the worship of heaven toward an increasing interiority, or "truth," dependent on the inner working of the Holy Spirit through grace. Thomas's teaching that Christ's sacrifice as priest and victim especially fulfills the Old Law sacrifices by his interior self-offering thus presents Christ as the source and model of New Law worship, of inward grace given to humans to move them to acts of faith working through love.

Christ's sacrifice thus has the effect of uniting humanity with God, and in this, as priest, he is our mediator. At the end of q48 a3, on the sacrifice of the Passion, Thomas quotes Augustine in the *De trinitate*, on Christ as the

one true mediator reconciling us with God through the sacrifice of peace, that he might remain one with him to whom he offered, become one with those for whom he offered, and himself be the one who offered, and who was offered.[173]

Augustine is speaking in this passage of Christ's mediatorship as high priest, who offers his own body as the flesh of sacrifice. The final question in Thomas's treatment of the mystery of the Incarnation in itself (IIIa q26) treats Christ as mediator of God and humanity.[174] There he teaches that a mediator "conjoins" and unites those between whom he mediates, in that

---

171. *ST* Ia-Iae q101 a2, q107 a4, q108 a1.   172. *ST* Ia-IIae q108 a1.
173. *DT* 4.14.

174. This question comes at the end of a section on the consequences of the union, in relation to Christ himself, in relation to his Father, and in relation to us. It is a fitting end to the treatment of the Incarnation in itself, but it also caps in particular the dual consideration of Christ's relationship to his Father and to us.

he "transfers" (*defert*) to one what belongs to the other. Christ, as the one in whose very Person God and humanity are conjoined, unites and so reconciles humanity to God as the perfect mediator. In his humanity he conjoins humans to God by "presenting the commands and gifts of God to mankind, and by making satisfaction and interceding for mankind to God."[175]

In q22 a1 Thomas makes it clear, following Augustine, that it is as priest that Christ is mediator, transferring the unifying gifts of satisfaction and deification between God and humans:

The proper office of a priest is to be a mediator between God and the people, inasmuch as he hands over to the people divine things; whence *sacerdos* means "giver of divine things" according to Malachi 2:7: "They shall seek the law at his mouth," namely, the priest's; and again, inasmuch as he offers the people's prayers to God, and, in a manner, makes satisfaction to God for their sins; whence the Apostle says (Hebrews 5:1): "Every high-priest taken from among men is ordained for men in the things that pertain to God, that he may offer gifts and sacrifices for sins." Now this is most fitting to Christ. For through him divine gifts are bestowed on men, according to 2 Peter 1:4: "By whom," namely Christ, "he has given us most great and precious promises, that by these you may be made partakers of the divine nature." He also reconciled the human race to God, according to Colossians 1:19–20: "In him," namely Christ, "all the fulness was pleased to dwell, and through him to reconcile all things." Therefore it is most fitting to Christ to be a priest.

Christ unites God and humans, as priest, in the sacrifice of his Passion, by offering to God the satisfaction owed to him by humanity and by bestowing on humans the deifying gift of grace—a participation in the divine nature that belongs properly to God.

Participation in Christ's Priesthood   It is through the grace of the sacraments, applying to us the effects of the Passion, that we are conformed to Christ's sacrificial priesthood and so to his perfect worship of the Father.

---

175. *ST* IIIa q26 a1, a2. Christ is mediator as human, not as God. A mediator is distant from both the extremes that he unites, and joins them by giving to one what belongs to the other. Christ as human is distant from God by nature, and from humans by dignity of grace and glory, and "transfers" (*defert*) to humans what is God's, while giving to God what is required from humanity (a2). It might be said that as the hypostatic union permits the communication of idioms, it also makes possible a "communication of properties" in the sense that they are communicated by participation from God to humanity through the mediatorship of Christ's humanity.

The sacraments are the instrumental means of our deification, involving us too in that instrumentality. Thomas teaches that sacramental grace both removes the defects of sin and "perfects the soul in those things pertaining to the worship of God (*cultum Dei*) according to the religion of the Christian life" because, through the Passion, Christ both delivered us from sin and "inaugurated the rites of the Christian religion by offering 'himself, an oblation and a sacrifice to God' (Eph 5:2)."[176] Christ's sacrifice, which Thomas calls the "immense sign of charity" in his commentary on this text from Ephesians, was the beginning of the sacramental system by which Christians receive the effects of that sacrifice. The principal effect of the sacraments is grace, but baptism, confirmation, and orders also bestow a sacramental character, a spiritual mark or seal in the soul, which Thomas compares to the mark received by ancient soldiers to indicate their deputation to service:[177] "Since by the sacraments men are deputed to something spiritual pertaining to the worship of God, it follows that through them the faithful are signed (*insigniantur*) with some spiritual character." The character signifies the spiritual power to either receive or bestow divine things "according to the rite of the Christian religion."[178]

This power is instrumental, like the power of the sacraments themselves, so the minister (and also, we can infer, the recipients) of the sacraments plays an instrumental role in the communication of the divine gifts in the sacramental rites.[179] That is, the spiritual power signified by the character allows all the baptized to participate instrumentally in the deifying reception of grace conferred through the sacraments, and ordains those in Holy Orders to further participate in its bestowal.[180] Baptized Christians who par-

176. *ST* IIIa q62 a5.

177. *ST* IIIa q63 a1.

178. *ST* IIIa q63 a2. Thomas quotes from Dionysius's *EH* 2: "God in 'a certain sign gives a participation in himself to those approaching baptism'; and he adds, 'perfecting them to be divine and the communicators of divine things.'" Here, as in several other questions on the sacraments, Dionysius is the authority on the instrumentally mediated transmission of grace through the sacraments, one that, as in this quote, is the transmission of a deifying participation in divinity. Cf., e.g., IIIa q60 a4, q64 a1.

179. *ST* IIIa q63 a2. Thomas addresses the instrumentality of the recipients in his treatment of the fruitful reception of the sacraments (see below).

180. Space does not permit a special consideration of the instrumental role of the ordained priesthood, to which Thomas devotes considerable attention, as an instrument of Christ's action in bestowing divine gifts on the faithful. Relevant discussions appear in Theophil Tschipke,

ticipate in the rites of divine worship are thus extended instruments of the Godhead, to whom belongs the principal power of deifying through the sacraments. In the transmission of grace, their instrumentality, like that of the sacraments they administer or receive, derives from the instrumentality of Christ's humanity in the Passion to which they are "conjoined" by faith, charity, and the sacraments (cf. q49).[181]

That Thomas uses the word "conjoined" to describe both the union of Christ's humanity and divinity, and the union of the faithful to his Passion by conformation to him, underscores the close instrumental relationship between the faithful and Christ in general and in the transmission of the sacraments in particular. The instrumentality of the faithful participates in that of Christ, for the sacramental character is a participation in Christ's priesthood, from which the character "flows like an instrumental power:"[182]

Each of the faithful is deputed to the reception or handing on to others of those things which pertain to the worship of God. And to this is properly deputed the sacramental character. Now the whole rite of the Christian religion is derived from the priesthood of Christ. And so it is clear that the sacramental character is specially the character of Christ, to whose priesthood the faithful are configured according to the sacramental characters, which are nothing other than participations of the priesthood of Christ, derived from Christ himself.[183]

The participation in Christ's priesthood that the sacramental characters bestow gives to the faithful the instrumental power, deriving from Christ, who has the "full power of the spiritual priesthood" to carry out the rites of the Christian religion.[184] And because Christ's perfect priesthood, which is eternal, is the principal agent, the participations in his priesthood that are

---

L'humanité du Christ comme instrument de salut, Studia Friburgensia: Neue Folge 94, trans. P. Secretan, intr. B. D. de La Soujeole (Fribourg: Academic Press, 2003); Le Guillou, *Le Christ et l'Église*; Matthew Levering, "Holy Orders and Ecclesial Hierarchy in Aquinas," in *Rediscovering Aquinas and the Sacraments: Studies in Sacramental Theology*, ed. Matthew Levering and Michael Dauphinais (Mundelein: Hillenbrand, 2009), 85–101.

181. Cf. *ST* IIIa q64 a1, a3.   182. *ST* IIIa q63 a5 ad1.
183. *ST* IIIa q63 a3.
184. *ST* IIIa q63 a5. As far as I have been able to discover, Thomas describes sacramental character as a participation in Christ's priesthood only in the *Summa theologiae*; as in other areas of his thought, he seems to have come to a full understanding of the way the rational creature participates instrumentally in its own sanctification, always subordinated to yet operating freely under the influence of the primary divine causality.

the characters are also indelible in the soul, "not from any perfection of its own, but from the perfection of Christ's priesthood."[185] Sacramental character, as an instrumental power in the soul, remains as long as the soul remains—even when the soul is without grace.[186]

Thomas's discussion of participation in Christ's priesthood, in association with the teaching on character, seems to refer strictly to the deputation as minister or recipient by the characters of baptism, confirmation, and orders to the external worship of God carried out in the Christian rites.[187] That is, simply by being marked out as deputed to these rites, which were inaugurated by Christ's sacrifice of himself on the Cross, one participates in his priesthood, even if one is not united to God by grace and charity. Formally speaking, engagement in the Christian rites is an external act of worship, as the offering of an outward sacrifice, and it is this to which character refers. Yet we have seen that Christ's priestly sacrifice on the Cross satisfied for our sins because it was the visible sign of the "immense charity" of his interior self-offering in love—and the principal part of sacrifice is the "inward spiritual sacrifice, whereby the soul offers itself to God."[188] The notion of participation in Christ's priesthood by the deputation of sacramental character seems to open to a larger conception of participation in his true worship of the Father, the true worship of the New Law of grace, for those who are conformed to his Passion by "faith, charity and sacraments." Every act done in order to adhere more closely to God in loving obedience can be called a sacrifice and true worship. A graced life of sacrificial filial obedience, shaped by charity and wisdom to be like that of Christ crucified, makes one participate more fully in the interior reality of Christ's priesthood, so that one's whole life can be said to be directed toward the worship of God.

In fact, throughout the question on sacramental character, Thomas seems to have in mind the necessary relationship between inward and ex-

---

185. *ST* IIIa q63 a5, ad1.

186. E.g., in apostates (*ST* IIIa q63 a5 ad2), or in wicked ministers, who are still able to confer the sacraments instrumentally (though not suitably or morally; *ST* IIIa q66 a5 c., ad3, a6).

187. At the end of the question on character, however, Thomas notes in answer to an objection that although not every sacrament imprints the character that deputes one to actions pertaining to the "worship of the priesthood of Christ," "every sacrament makes one a participator in Christ's priesthood, from the fact that he obtains from it some effect" (*ST* IIIa q63 a6 ad1).

188. *ST* IIa-IIae q86 aa2–3.

ternal worship of God on earth in attaining the end of worship in the vision of heaven. In several places he presents a comparison or parallel between character and the other—principal—effect of the sacraments: grace. Each of these can be said to mark the faithful for a particular end, and each bestows in them a seal (*signaculum*):

> Now the faithful are deputed to two things. First, indeed, and principally, to the enjoyment of glory. And to this they are signed with the sign of grace, according to Ezek. 9:4: "Sign the *thau* on the foreheads of those who weep and mourn"; and Rev 7:3: "Do not harm the earth or sea, nor the trees, until we sign the servants of our God on their foreheads." Secondly, the faithful are deputed to receiving or handing on to others those things pertaining to the worship of God. And this properly speaking is the sacramental character.[189]

Grace "seals" the person for the interior act, character for the exterior act, of worship. The sign of grace is the seal of the Holy Spirit, the gift of God's love, which deputes the faithful to future glory.[190] The Holy Spirit "signs" the believer by the gift of participated charity as the pledge of future inheritance.[191] This gift configures the Christian to Christ, who stamps the "character" of the Holy Spirit in human hearts to conform them to his sonship.[192] Thomas also calls grace the seal of predestination, a "character" by which the faithful of Christ are marked out for eternal life as "the result of charity and

---

189. *ST* IIIa q63 a3. Thomas's scriptural references link the seal of grace to the sign of the Cross. In the only other two places where Thomas refers to the *thau* in Ez 9:4 (once in conjunction with the same quote from Revelation), he identifies it directly as the sign of the Cross (*Sup. II Cor.* ch1 lect5 [45–46]; *Sup. Rom.* ch1 lect6). In the passage from the *Commentary on 2 Corinthians* he links the sign of the Cross, the sign of faith and of eternal life configuring the faithful to Christ, with the pledge of the Holy Spirit, in whom that life is received.

190. *ST* IIIa q63 ob1, ad 1 (cf. Eph 4:30). Cf. *Sup. Eph.* ch4 lectio; *Sup. II Cor.* ch1 lect5.

191. In his commentary on Eph 1:13–14—"you were signed with the Holy Spirit of promise, who is the pledge of our inheritance"—Thomas remarks that the distinctive sign of the Holy Spirit is charity "poured out into our hearts"; the Spirit gives the promise of eternal inheritance to those he makes children of God, and as the pledge or even the "earnest," or partial prepayment, "of our inheritance," he communicates charity to us as "a particular and imperfect participation in the divine charity ... which is to be perfected." *Sup. Eph.* ch1 lect5.41–43.

192. *De pot.* q10 a4: "Habetur autem ex sacra Scriptura quod per spiritum sanctum configuramur filio, secundum illud Rom. VIII, 15: 'accepistis spiritum adoptionis filiorum'; et Galat. IV, 6: 'quoniam estis filii, misit Deus spiritum filii sui in corda vestra.' Nihil autem configuratur alicui nisi per eius proprium characterem ... Spiritus autem sanctus est a filio tamquam proprius character eius; unde dicitur de Christo, II Cor. I, 21–22: 'quod signavit nos, et unxit nos et dedit pignus spiritus in cordibus nostris.'"

grace" in distinction to the servants of the devil.[193] The sacramental character is itself a kind of sacrament of the internal seal of grace bestowed, "a sign of the invisible grace conferred in the sacrament."[194] Grace is given interiorly to those who receive the sacramental character so they can worthily carry out their service.[195] The relationship between the two seals of grace and character is based on that between their two ends; external worship (the end of sacramental character) is ordained to glory (the end of grace);[196] this is so because the purpose of external worship in this life is the true interior worship of the believer, which is fulfilled in the eternal worship of God in heaven.[197]

Deification through the Sacraments: Fruitful Reception

To be fully conformed to Christ through the sacraments, and so obtain the saving effects of his Passion, one must be fully engaged in receiving them by faith working through charity. As instrumental causes of grace employed by God in the divine *ordinatio*, and causally dependent on Christ's own sanctifying activity, the sacraments deify, conferring a participated likeness of God's own divine nature.[198] As instruments, too, the sacraments work in their own proper manner as signs; a sacrament is "a sign of a holy thing insofar as it makes men holy."[199] That is, they "effect what they signify," or cause

193. *ST* IIIa q63 a1 ad1, a3 ad3.

194. I.e., the character is the *res et sacramentum*, the grace the *res tantum* (in the case of baptism, the interior justification of the sinner). *ST* IIIa q63 a3.

195. *ST* IIIa q63 a4 ad1.

196. Thomas answers an objection that sacramental character must not endure in heaven because there is no external worship there; it will remain, he says, because, "although external worship does not endure after this life, its end remains." *ST* IIIa q63 a5 ob3, ad3.

197. It is perhaps worth mentioning a text from Thomas's scriptural commentary on Ps 4:7—"The light of your face, O Lord, is signed upon us"—the verse he associates in the *Summa* with the threefold perfection of the image by nature, grace, and glory. Thomas says that this light places in the soul a likeness to God's truth and so the ability to know the good (in his treatment of the image he associates its perfection with glory). He relates the "signing of the light of God's face on us," again to Ephesians' teaching that "we are signed with the sign of the Spirit" (cf. Eph 1:13, 4:30) and to "the sign of the cross given in Baptism, which we should daily impress on ourselves. *Songs* 8: 'Place me as a sign upon your heart.'"

198. *ST* IIIa q62 a1. John Boyle's research shows that Thomas was unique in structuring the *Summa* so that his treatment of the sacraments flowed from that of Christology, reflecting his view of the instrumental causality of the sacraments, which are part of Christ's own salvific activity. "Structural Setting of Thomas Aquinas' Theology," 43.

199. *ST* IIIa q60 a2.

grace by signifying.[200] This is so because, as Thomas stresses repeatedly, human beings, as embodied, require sensible things to convey spiritual realities "for soul and body together constitute a unity."[201] And, conversely, to access the spiritual reality of the sacraments, one must engage their meaning with intellect and will. The sacraments "cause by signifying" because humans are symbol makers and readers, embodied rational creatures who attain invisible through visible realities, to whom "it is proper to discover the unknown by means of the known."[202] In other words, the divine wisdom providentially institutes the sacramental economy in precisely the way that is appropriate for the salvation of the individuals of human nature God has created—in the same way as the Incarnation was, and in dependence upon it.[203]

Sacraments as instrumental causes engage the person precisely as signs and so require an offering, or obedience, of the intellect and will in faith and charity. This is, in a sense, the very conformation to Christ in sacrificial obedience that opens the person to receive the effects of his Passion. To put it another way, though Thomas holds the common medieval view that the instrumental power bestowed on the priesthood of the baptized through character is only "passive"—the power of reception—he actually envisions this reception in a dynamic mode. Each individual who participates in the sacraments, led by the grace of the Holy Spirit, must be fully engaged in mind and heart to receive the sacramental effects because the sacraments cause grace by signifying to persons to bring them into a share in the Trinitarian divine life.[204]

200. *ST* IIIa q62 a1 ad1. Thomas does not use the common scholastic term *significando causant* in the *Summa*, although he does in *DV* q27 a4 ad13, q28 a2 ad12.

201. *ST* IIIa q62 a1 ad2. And so the sign of the sacrament includes not only its material reality but also the actions and words that make it complete. The words of the rite express the intention of the minister necessary to the sacrament. Cf. IIIa q60 a6, q62 a4 ad4, q64 a8. The ritual aspects of the celebration of the sacraments, to which Thomas assigns at least an article for each, serve to increase its solemnity and arouse devotion and fruitful reception on the part of those participating in it. Cf., e.g., IIIa q66 a3 ad5, a7 ad2, a10, q83.

202. *ST* IIIa q60 a2. Thus there is a link between Thomas's sacramental theology and his doctrine of analogy. In both, his anthropology is informed by Dionysius's teachings on God as the supereminent and invisible source of all perfections as well as the consequent mediating role of sensible things in lifting the mind to God's invisible reality; e.g., Ia q4 aa2–3, q13 a3 ad2; IIIa q60 a4, q64 a4 ad1.

203. *ST* IIIa q61 a1.

204. This important topic, which touches on some modern critiques of Thomas's so-called "productionist" view of sacramental causality—e.g., by Louis-Marie Chauvet in *Symbol and*

Baptism: Sacrament of Faith

Living faith—informed by charity—already preveniently inspired by the Holy Spirit, leads to the desire for baptism and is necessary for the reception of baptismal grace. Without living faith, one may be baptized and receive the baptismal character, "but not unto salvation."[205] With living faith, one may even be saved without the sacrament of baptism, although the desire for baptism it inspires should normally result in the reception of the sacrament.[206] Faith in Christ's Passion, from which the sacraments derive their power, is the principal reason for the remission of sins through the sacraments.[207] Sacramental baptism, for those well disposed, fully applies the effects of the Passion by the complete remission of sin and its penalty, and bestows a greater share of grace and the virtues, than the baptism of desire alone.[208] Still, the essential condition of salvation is "mental" incorporation

---

Sacrament (Collegeville: Liturgical Press, 1995)—cannot be fully addressed here. Liam Walsh and especially Bernard Blankenhorn have both provided valuable responses to Chauvet. See Liam Walsh, "The Divine and the Human in St. Thomas's Theology of Sacraments," in *Ordo sapientiae et amoris: Hommage au professeur Jean-Pierre Torrell, OP*, ed. Carlos-Josaphat Pinto, OP (Fribourg: Éditions Universitaires, 1993), 321–52; "Sacraments," in *The Theology of Thomas Aquinas*, ed. Rik Van Nieuwenhove and Joseph Wawrykow (Notre Dame, IN: University of Notre Dame Press, 2005), 326–64; and Bernard Blankenhorn, "The Instrumental Causality of the Sacraments: Thomas Aquinas and Louis-Marie Chauvet," *Nova et Vetera* 4, no. 2 (2006): 255–94. Blankenhorn presents an especially thorough examination of the development of Thomas's understanding of sacramental causality as instrumentally bestowing a real participation in Christ's saving mysteries. He notes the same kind of shift from disposing to participatory instrumental causality as has been discussed here with regard to the instrumentality of Christ's humanity, the working of grace, and the sacraments. See also Colman O'Neill, "The Role of the Recipient and Sacramental Signification," *Thomist* 21 (1958): 257–301, 508–40. Although I was unaware at the time of O'Neill's contribution, my unpublished manuscript "The Disputed Question of Instrumental Causality in the Sacramental Theology of St. Thomas" (2004) attempts to answer Chauvet by examining how, in the larger scheme of God's plan of loving wisdom to share the divine life with rational creatures, he allows them to share instrumentally in the causality of the sacraments by means of their engagement in the signs appropriate to their nature. I draw from this manuscript here.

205. *ST* IIIa q68 a8 c., ad4; cf. a4 ad3.

206. *ST* IIIa q68 a2. The baptism of desire, though salvific in the case of those who die without being able to receive the sacrament they sought, is not envisioned as an alternative to the normal ecclesial reception of the sacrament, which would be sinful to defer beyond the proper time (a3).

207. *ST* IIIa q62 a5 ad2.

208. *ST* IIIa q68 a2 ad2, q69 a4 ad2.

into Christ by living faith; even before Christ's coming, those saved by faith in this way became members of his body.[209]

In those who are sacramentally baptized, disposition plays an essential role in determining the extent to which they will receive baptism's effects. Those who approach baptism with greater devotion "receive a greater share of the grace of newness, just as he who draws closer to a fire receives more heat, although the fire, in itself, gives forth its heat equally to all."[210] On the other hand, those who approach insincerely will hinder its effect. To the objection that "all who have been baptized in Christ Jesus, have put on Christ" (Gal 3:27)—that is, even those who are insincere—Thomas explains:

To be "baptized in Christ" can mean two things. In one way, "in Christ" means to be in conformity with Christ. And thus, whoever is baptized in Christ, being conformed to him through faith and charity, "puts on Christ" by grace. In another way some are said to be baptized in Christ, inasmuch as they receive the sacrament of Christ. And so, all put on Christ through the configuration of character, but not all through the conformity of grace.[211]

There could be no clearer statement of the necessity of faith and charity—and especially of charity, because without it faith is dead—for true conformation to Christ and thus the reception of the sacramental effects. One must be both "corporally" or visibly (by the character), and "mentally" or inwardly, incorporated into Christ to receive the full effects of membership in his body and participation in his grace: regeneration; "spiritual sense, consisting in the knowledge of truth"; and fruitfulness of good works through the "spiritual movement which results from the *instinctus* of grace"[212]—that is, the leading of the Holy Spirit. By the true conformation to Christ of inward devotion in the reception of the sacraments, and thus conformation to the true worship of his priestly sacrifice, the faithful become well-disposed instruments of the Holy Spirit.[213]

---

209. *ST* IIIa q68 a1 ad1, a2.

210. *ST* IIIa q69 a8.

211. *ST* IIIa q69 a9 ad1. When the insincerity is overcome, the recipient will obtain baptism's primary effect, sanctifying grace (a10).

212. *ST* IIIa q69 a5 c., ad1.

213. But the Holy Spirit has already been at work to inspire faith and conversion in those who receive the sacraments fruitfully.

The Eucharist: Sacrament of Charity

As Christ's perfectly ordered charity—principle and model of ours—came to the fore in Thomas's treatment of the Passion, so charity is also the key note in his treatment of the Eucharist, the memorial of Christ's Passion:

Baptism is the sacrament of the death and Passion of Christ inasmuch as one is regenerated in Christ by the power of his Passion. But the Eucharist is the sacrament of the Passion of Christ inasmuch as one is perfected in union with the suffering Christ (*in unione ad Christum passum*). So, just as Baptism is called the "sacrament of faith," which is the foundation of the spiritual life, the Eucharist is called "the sacrament of charity," which is the "bond of perfection," as it says in Col 3:14.[214]

The Eucharist is called the sacrament of charity because it perfects its recipients "in union with the suffering Christ"—that is, in union with the immense charity of his Passion. The Eucharist is the greatest of all sacraments, and perfects them as their end, because it contains Christ himself and unites one to him, which is the goal of all the sacraments.[215] Union is the effect of charity—the union of each believer with Christ and with each other in Christ's body—and so, Thomas will say, the *res* of the Eucharist is the unity of the Church.[216]

We can understand that the Eucharist especially makes one share in and so be conformed to Christ's charity because it is the sacrament of his sacrifice, re-presented in memorial. Christ crucified as victim is made truly present in the "sacrifice which is offered every day in the Church," for it "is not distinct from that which Christ himself offered, but is a commemoration of it."[217] The true presence of Christ's self-offering in the Eucharist is both the perfection of the New Law and the gift of his love to his disciples. As the memorial of Christ's Passion, containing his own body, the Eucharist fulfills the sacrificial figures of the Old Law, chief among them the paschal lamb.[218] And so it was fitting that the Lord instituted this new sacrament at the Last Supper, in the hour of his Passion, as successor to the old. Out of love for his disciples, too, Christ gave them the memorial of his Passion. He wanted to "leave himself with them under the sacramental species," and so that the

214. *ST* IIIa q73 a3 ad3.

216. *ST* IIIa q73 a3.

218. *ST* IIIa q73 a6.

215. *ST* IIIa q65 a3.

217. *ST* IIIa q22 a3 ad2, q73 a3 ad3, q83 a1.

sacrament would be held in greater veneration he "instituted this sacrament at his last parting" with them

because the last words spoken, especially those from departing friends, are committed more to the memory; since then affection for friends is more inflamed, and the things which affect us most are imprinted most profoundly in the soul.[219]

The true presence of Christ crucified in the sacrament is thus fitting for three reasons: because it is the sacrifice of the New Law, more perfect than the old; because it belongs to the perfection of our faith to believe in his unseen presence; and because it belongs to Christ's love, "out of which for our salvation he assumed a true body of our nature." Christ "promises us his bodily presence as a reward" at the end of our journey to him "because it is the special feature of friendship to live together with friends, as the Philosopher says (*Ethic.* IX)." Even in our earthly pilgrimage, however, he gives us his bodily presence in the sacrament to unite us with himself: "Hence this sacrament is the sign of supreme charity, and the uplifter of our hope, from such familiar union of Christ with us."[220]

Charity brings union with God; this is the end of the Christian life, and that in which its perfection radically consists.[221] It is because of charity that the New Law is the law of perfection.[222] That Thomas calls the Eucharist the "sacrament of charity, which is the 'bond of perfection'" (cf. Col 3:14), is significant, for he describes charity this way in several other places where he speaks of it as the perfection of the whole spiritual life. Martyrdom, for instance, is the most perfect of virtuous acts because it is "the greatest proof of the perfection of charity," suffered in imitation of Christ's own obedience unto death.[223] Charity "binds" all the other virtues together for the end of union with God. In Thomas's scriptural commentary on Colossians 3:14–17, he remarks that the Apostle is urging the Colossians to both charity and wisdom because they are first among the virtues and gifts, and perfect all the others—"charity informs all the virtues, wisdom directs them." Charity unites all the virtues to the ultimate end, while wisdom instructs us, leads us to devotion and true worship, and directs all our actions to be done in the name of Christ.[224] It is charity ordered and perfected by wisdom that is

---

219. *ST* IIIa q73 a5.
221. *ST* IIa-IIae q184 a1.
223. *ST* IIa-IIae q124 a3 c., ad2.

220. *ST* IIIa q75 a1.
222. *ST* Ia-IIae q107 a1.
224. *Sup. Col.* ch3 lect3.

the bond of perfection. The Eucharist, as "the sacrament of charity, which is the 'bond of perfection,'" is the sacrament that is the "consummation of the spiritual life," especially given for its perfection by charity well ordered by wisdom in anticipation of the ultimate end of union with God.[225]

The notion of the Eucharist as the sacrament of charity illuminates Thomas's explanation of the suitability of the names given for the Eucharist in the Christian tradition, for each of them has to do in some way with Christ's charity in the Passion, and charity's perfecting effects in us on the way to heaven. The Eucharist signifies the past, present, and future. It is called a *sacrifice* (and therefore also *host* or victim) because it commemorates the Passion, "which was a true sacrifice" (i.e., springing from charity). Because it brings ecclesiastical unity in the present (the effect of charity), it is called *communion*. Thomas quotes John Damascene: "it is called communion since we communicate through it with Christ, both because we participate in his flesh and deity, and because we communicate and are united to each other through it." It "foreshadows the enjoyment of God which will be in heaven" (the fruit of charity), and so it is called *viaticum*, because it provides the way of arriving there. It is also called *Eucharist*, or "'good grace,' because 'the grace of God is everlasting life' (Rom 6:23); or because it really contains Christ, who is full of grace." And in Greek, Thomas points out, it is called *metalepsis*, which means "assumption," because, "as Damascene says, 'by this we assume the deity of the Son.'"[226]

Thomas is actually building on a threefold scheme for the way in which all of the sacraments "signify our sanctification" as past, present, and future, which he has already laid out in an earlier question on the sacraments in general. The sacraments are signs of "the cause itself of our sanctification, which is the Passion of Christ, and the form of our sanctification, which

---

225. Cf. *ST* IIIa q73 a2. Michael Dauphinais points out that in his *Commentary on John* Thomas interprets the Bread of Life discourse in Jn 6 in terms of wisdom; "wisdom must be Eucharistic" because Christ is "the true wisdom, who alone can completely satisfy the human creature" (315). One is transformed into Christ the incarnate Word by an eating, which is both sacramental and spiritual—i.e., when the Eucharist is "received in its full sapiential reality" (317). "*And They Shall All Be Taught by God*: Wisdom and the Eucharist in John 6," in *Reading John with St. Thomas Aquinas: Theological Exegesis and Speculative Theology*, ed. Michael Dauphinais and Matthew W. Levering (Washington, DC: Catholic University of America Press, 2005), 312–17.

226. *ST* IIIa q73 a4.

consists in grace and the virtues, and the ultimate end of our sanctification, which is eternal life"[227]—that is, they are signs of God's power at work throughout the journey to beatitude. In his brief explanation for the names of the Eucharist, Thomas thus sketches out the way in which it is the consummate sign of the cause, present form, and end of our sanctification. In all of these ways, the Eucharist is therefore the sign of charity—for growth in charity, perfected by wisdom, is the way in which we progress in the perfection of the divine image, being sanctified by coming continually closer to God and the deiformity of eternal life.[228] And this is why the Eucharist ultimately signifies our participation in "the deity of the Son."

Effects of the Eucharist   The Eucharist's principal effect is the bestowal of grace because in it we receive Christ, the source of "grace and truth" (Jn 1:17), and because it represents his Passion, for "this sacrament works in us the effect which Christ's Passion worked in the world." So the Eucharist, as spiritual food and drink, gives the spiritual sustenance, growth, restoration, and delight that can only come from grace. And the Eucharist, by the unity it symbolizes, is the sign of charity that flows from grace.[229] All of the sacraments bestow grace, but by the Eucharist, in a special way, "grace receives increase, and the spiritual life is perfected, so that one may come to be perfect in himself by being conjoined with God."[230] The Eucharist brings about these effects of charity because through it not only is the *habitus* of grace and charity bestowed, but charity "is furthermore aroused to act, according to 2 Cor 5:14: 'the charity of Christ urges us.'" So the soul is spiritually restored through the sacrament

in that it is spiritually delighted, and in a certain manner inebriated with the sweetness of the divine goodness, according to Songs 5:1: "Eat, friends, and drink; and be inebriated, my most beloved."[231]

---

227. *ST* IIIa q60 a3.   228. *ST* IIa-IIae q24 a4.

229. *ST* IIIa q79 a1.   230. *ST* IIIa q79 a1 ad1.

231. *ST* IIIa q79 a1 ad2. Paul Murray points out Thomas's use elsewhere of this verse, and discusses the recurring figure in his writings of inebriation associated with wisdom, grace and divine love. "Drunk on Wisdom: St. Thomas and St. Catherine of Siena," *Angelicum* 82 (2005): 637–49. In Thomas's commentary on Ps 35, Thomas compares the fountain of life and sweetness pouring forth in the Holy Spirit, and making one drunk in the spirit, to an intoxicating fountain of wine (638). Murray notes the link that Thomas makes in his commentary on Jn 2 (the wedding at Cana) and elsewhere between "wine and the spirit of the Gospel," as opposed

Thomas also compares the "inebriation" of charity actively experienced in the Eucharist to a living and deifying fire, again quoting John Damascene, who in the *De fide orthodoxa* compares the Eucharist to the burning coal taken from the altar and placed on the lips of the prophet Isaiah (*De fide orth.* 4.13; cf. Isa 6:6): "'For a burning coal is not simply wood, but it is united to fire; thus too the bread of communion is not simply bread, but is united to divinity." He follows this quote with one from Gregory, in a homily for Pentecost: "The love of God is not idle, for it works great things, wherever it is."[232]

As noted in chapter 3, Thomas uses the metaphor of the burning coal to express the notion of participation in the divine nature. God's love, the Holy Spirit, sets the sacrament "on fire" with divinity, and we participate in that love through charity. So the Eucharist deifies us especially through charity: in a later article, to argue that venial sins impede the effect of the Eucharist because they hinder "the fervor of charity," Thomas once again quotes the same text of Damascene:

The fire of that desire which is in us, being taken up from this coal—that is, from the fiery enkindling of this sacrament—will burn up our sins, and illuminate our hearts, that by participation of the divine fire we may be kindled into fire and deified.[233]

The Eucharist participates to us, as instrumental cause, a share in the "fire" of the divine nature by which we are deified, arousing in us the fervent charity in act by which we are likened to the Holy Spirit.

And so, as grace leads us on the journey to heaven, the second principal effect of the Eucharist that Thomas names is the attainment of glory. Again, it is because the Eucharist contains Christ and represents his Passion that it brings us to glory, "because it was by his Passion that Christ opened

---

to the water of human wisdom (638, 643). Thomas, like St. Catherine of Siena after him, did not hesitate to assign due importance to the "passionate fervor—the 'inebriation' to use his own word—which forms part of living faith" (644). Peter Kwasniewski has shown that, from his earliest writings, Thomas associates the notion of love's *extasis* with the fervor of charity that inflames the lover, uniting and transforming them into the divine beloved. "The Ecstasy of Love in Aquinas's *Commentary on the Sentences*," *Angelicum* 83 (2006): 51–93. Thomas applies this to the Eucharist as the sacrament of charity in the *Scriptum* bk4 d12 q2 a1 qc1 ad3 (76). As Kwasniewski notes, Thomas retains this "erotic" element in his doctrine of love throughout his career, both with respect to God's love and ours (86–93).

232. *ST* IIIa q79 a1 ad2. Cf. Gregory, *In Evang.* bk2 hom30.
233. *ST* IIIa q79 a8; cf. *De fide orth.* 4.13.

to us the entrance to eternal life."[234] As the effects of the sacraments are the effects of the Passion, in the background is Thomas's teaching that the Passion opens the gates of heaven by delivering us from sin.[235] The remission of sins in baptism first opens the gates of heaven,[236] but in discussing the Eucharist Thomas seems to stress not just the possibility of eternal life but also the assistance given to attain it. The food of the Eucharist foreshadows the perfect spiritual refreshment and unity to be experienced in glory, which is known in anticipation by grace. Yet, just as we must first suffer with Christ so as afterward to be glorified with him (Rom 8:17), "so this sacrament does not immediately bring us into glory, but gives us the power of obtaining glory, and therefore it is called *viaticum*."[237] That is, the Eucharist is food for those who are being conformed to Christ as adopted sons on the way to beatitude: "if sons, heirs also; heirs indeed of God, and joint heirs with Christ; yet so if we suffer with him, we may also be glorified with him."[238]

Recall once again Thomas's teaching on the beatific vision, that the one who has more charity will have a greater participation in the light of glory, and so a greater deiformity, on account of their desire to see God.[239] On earth we "undergo divine things" through charity and wisdom, in the mode of the Passion—because of the need for purification from sin—so that a connaturality is brought about in us for those divine realities.[240] The activity of the blessed, freed from sin, is the unmediated experience and fruition of divine things in the contemplation of the beatific vision by wisdom-perfected charity. The Eucharist, through its effects of grace and glory, feeds the fire of our charity on the journey to heaven so as to bring us to the greatest possible likeness to—and enjoyment of—God.

As the Eucharist is food for growth in charity, Thomas considers its role in various phases of the journey to beatitude, just as he did for grace and charity.[241] And as the activity of the Holy Spirit in leading adopted sons

---

234. *ST* IIIa q79 a2.

235. *ST* IIIa q49 a5. Cf. the line from the Office hymn *Verbum supernum* written by Thomas for the feast of Corpus Christi: "O salutaris hostia, quae caeli pandis ostium." *Officium de festo Corporis Christi ad mandatum Urbani Papae IV dictum festum instituentis: Opera omnia*, vol. 29, ed. E. Fretté and P. Maré (Paris: Apud Ludovicum Vivès, 1876), 335–43.

236. *ST* IIIa q69 a7.   237. *ST* IIIa q79 a2 ad1.

238. Rom 8:17; cf. *ST* IIIa q48 a3 ad3.   239. *ST* Ia q12 a6.

240. *ST* IIa-IIae q45 a2.

241. Cf. *ST* Ia-IIae q109; IIa-IIae q24; and comparisons in chapters 3 and 5.

emerged as central in those discussions, so here too it plays a hidden but important role. By the Eucharist especially, one might say, we participate in the likeness of the Holy Spirit by being conformed to the charity of Christ's Passion. Having established the role of the Eucharist in bringing the elect to beatitude by grace and glory, Thomas examines its effects with respect to sin, the obstacle to this end. Mortal sins exclude one from reception of the Eucharist, for those who are in mortal sin are spiritually dead and cannot receive the food of the living; they "cannot be united with Christ, which is the effect of this sacrament."[242] We saw in the questions on charity that even one mortal sin destroys charity completely because charity is a *habitus* infused by God, not acquired by us. Mortal sin "places an obstacle to the outpouring of charity by God into the soul," as sin is chosen over God's friendship.[243]

Venial sin does not merit this complete withdrawal of God's gift, and so does not diminish the *habitus* of charity, although it can lessen the fervor of charity's act.[244] For this reason, venial sins can partially hinder the effect of the Eucharist. But by the same token, the Eucharist can so excite charity's act as to take away venial sins because "the power of charity, to which this sacrament belongs, is greater than that of venial sins."[245] The measure in which the punishment due to sin is removed through the Eucharist is "according to the measure of the devotion and fervor" of the one receiving it in union with Christ by charity.[246] The Eucharist has the effect of arousing charity, with beneficial consequences for progress toward beatitude, but its effects also depend upon the prior condition of the recipient, who must nurture by the devotion of charity the proper and meritorious disposition for receiving the gift of charity's increase.[247]

For this reason Thomas stresses repeatedly the essential role of devotion in the reception of the Eucharist, even more so than in that of baptism, where the effect of character can be received even without it. The very substance of the Eucharist's work is charity, and so merely "sacramental eating" without spiritual union with Christ has no effect. To receive the full effect of the sacrament, one must eat it both sacramentally and spiritually, and it

---

242. *ST* IIIa q79 a3.
244. *ST* IIa-IIae q24 a10; IIIa q79 a4.
246. *ST* IIIa q79 a5.

243. *ST* IIa-IIae q24 a12.
245. *ST* IIIa q79 a4 ad1, ad3.
247. Cf. *ST* IIa-IIae q24 aa4–7.

is possible to receive its effects even by the "spiritual eating" of desire.[248] It is this spiritual eating that the angels enjoy in heaven, where they "eat Christ spiritually inasmuch as they are united with him in the enjoyment of perfect charity, and in clear vision (which is the bread we hope for in heaven), and not by faith, as we are united to him here." So on earth the faithful spiritually eat the "bread of angels" as they receive Christ in the sacrament, "which is ordained to the enjoyment of heaven."[249] Spiritual eating belongs only to the just; mortal sinners eat sacramentally, but to their condemnation.[250] Thomas insightfully characterizes the sacrilege they commit as rooted in falsehood: by their action they profess to be united with Christ and his body, but in truth they act against the charity of Christ in a false sign of friendship.[251]

Those who eat spiritually do so to the extent of their devotion; it is for this reason, Thomas explains, that the Church prescribes a fast before reception:

the greatest devotion is called for at the moment of receiving this sacrament, because it is then that the effect of the sacrament is bestowed, and such devotion is hindered more by what goes before than after it.[252]

Likewise, the solemnity of celebration; the beauty or fittingness of the liturgical actions, surroundings, and music; and the words of the rite are all meant to inspire the devotion that allows one to receive fruitfully.[253] A reverential fear of God, inspired by love, should dictate to each one's conscience whether he has sufficient devotion to receive the Eucharist daily.[254] The sacrament of the Eucharist itself is "completed in the consecration of the matter"—that is, in the transformation of the species into Christ's body

---

248. *ST* IIIa q80 a1.   249. *ST* IIIa q80 a2 c., ad1.

250. *ST* IIIa q80 a4.

251. *ST* IIIa q80 a4; cf. a5 ad2. Following Jerome, Thomas compares the reception of the Eucharist by fornicators to the kiss of Judas, though not as to the gravity of their offense compared to his.

252. *ST* IIIa q80 a8 ad6.

253. *ST* IIIa q83, esp. a3, a4, a5. Thomas provides similar arguments for the fittingness of the rite of baptism (e.g., q66 a10). Sr. Thomas Augustine Becker provides an examination of the role of solemnity in the liturgy in inspiring the devotion needed for fruitful reception. "The Role of *Solemnitas* in the Liturgy According to Saint Thomas Aquinas," in *Rediscovering Aquinas and the Sacraments: Studies in Sacramental Theology*, ed. Matthew Levering and Michael Dauphinais (Mundelein: Hillenbrand, 2009), 114–35.

254. *ST* IIIa q80 a10 ad3.

and blood[255]—but its purpose is not fulfilled until the recipients enjoy union with Christ as living members of his body. The purpose of the real presence of Christ in the Eucharist, whose sacrifice of love is represented in memorial, is to bring about the communion of all the faithful for whom he has merited salvation.

The Eucharist and the Church   It is for this reason that the true presence of Christ is not the *res* but the *res et sacramentum* of the Eucharist; his presence is itself a sacrament of the Eucharist's deepest reality and final corporate effect, the unity of the Church on earth and in heaven. Christ's perfect sacrifice in the Passion was a sacrament or visible sign of his well-ordered charity, the charity perfected by wisdom in which his members participate by sharing his fullness of grace, and which unites them with each other and with God in the friendship founded on the communication of beatitude by fellowship with the Son.[256] The members of Christ's mystical body are incorporated into him most perfectly by charity in this life and by glory in the next.[257] And, as Thomas points out in his *Commentary on John*, incorporation and perseverance in the mystical body come about through spiritual eating of the Eucharist, by which one attains to its *res*. The one who "eats the flesh and drinks the blood" of Christ will "have eternal life" when, being transformed into Christ as his member by spiritual eating, one is not only made divine and "inebriated with divinity" but also brought into the unity of the Church by the Holy Spirit, who unites us as members of the Church to Christ by faith and love and also merits in us the Resurrection.[258]

The communion of the Church comes about as Christ's members, eternally incorporated in him by baptism and deified by charity and wisdom, are "conformed to the image of the Son" (Rom 8:29), and so united and led by the Spirit to beatitude. The *res* of the Eucharist is thus ultimately the deiformity of the Church, because the participation of all of the members in the Trinitarian communion brings about its unity. Christ, through the

---

255. *ST* IIIa q80 a1 ad1.

256. Of this friendship Le Guillou remarks that it is "founded on the communication of wisdom: it is communion with wisdom," because "from the communication of Wisdom flows the *communion* of charity." Schaldenbrand, *Christ and Church*, 246.

257. *ST* IIIa q8 a3.

258. *Sup. Ioh.* ch6 lect6.

Holy Spirit, is the principle of unity in the Church because as head he is the author of grace to the members of his body, bestowing on them through the instrumentality of his Passion a deifying share in his own perfect charity and wisdom, which takes the form of this communion.[259] He effects this unity instrumentally through the sacraments by giving the faithful an instrumental participation in his priesthood, which, lived fully, bears fruit in lives of true worship. In God's providential plan for human salvation, Christ's members receive the deifying grace that brings them to eternal life through the sacramental economy of the New Law within the communion of the Church.

Summary and Conclusion

Thomas's teaching on the gift of wisdom, which flows from and perfects charity, completes the picture of deification by conformation to the Trinitarian image. By wisdom-perfected charity, adopted sons participate in the likeness of the Son and Holy Spirit so that their intellects and wills are conformed to the Word and Love, ordering them rightly on the way to beatitude. Through the gift of wisdom, the Holy Spirit leads the children of God through the suffering and sacrifice of this life to the perfection of charity in the next. Thomas wrote on "life everlasting" at the end of the *Collationes Credo in Deum* as his own life was drawing to a close. "The first thing that should be known about eternal life," he says, "is that man is intimately conjoined to God. For God himself is the reward and end of all our labors." This "conjoining" fulfills the highest potential of both intellect and will, for it consists in "perfect vision" and in "the most perfect love, for the more one knows, the more one loves." It also consists in "the highest praise, as Augustine says (*de Civ. Dei* 22), 'We will see, and we will love, and we will praise.' And Isaiah (51:3): 'Joy and gladness will be found in her; the act of thanksgiving, and the voice of praise.'" Entering into the joy of heaven, the blessed

---

259. Le Guillou makes the related argument that the notion underlying all images of the Church—body, people, temple, communion, etc.—is "that of communion in the divine Wisdom through the communication of beatitude; the Church is made up of that part of humanity which has been refashioned in the image of the Image, but it can arrive at its genuine existential condition only through the condition of Christ the Head," who is the Word. Schaldenbrand, *Christ and Church*, 303–4.

find the "perfect satiation of all desire," which God alone, as the "supreme Good," can fulfill and infinitely exceed.[260] And so there is perfect peace, the tranquility of order uniting all desires in enjoyment of the highest good, which is the work of wisdom;[261] as Augustine says, "no one rests except in God; 'You have made us, O Lord, for yourself, and our hearts are not at rest until they rest in you.'"[262]

The enjoyment of contemplating God on earth is imperfect compared to that of heaven, "of which it is written (Prov. 35:9): 'You will give them drink from the torrent of your delight.'"[263] The fullness of joy and peace, the fruits of charity well ordered by wisdom, overflows in the blessed, conjoined to God in loving contemplation of the vision, as on earth they have been conjoined to Christ in the loving obedience of his Passion.[264] Christ in his fullness of grace, charity, and wisdom is the principle and model for his members of how to lead the deified life so as to attain beatitude. It is a life of worship in the communion of his body the Church, participating in his sonship and his priesthood, "undergoing divine things" with him, by sacrifice on earth and by deiform joy in heaven. Wisdom and charity conform God's adopted children to the Word and Love and so "to the image of the Son," making them instrumental causes, through their own Spirit-led activities, in their journey to eternal life.

260. *Collationes Credo in Deum* 15. I am following the text, based on the Leonine edition, given by Nicholas Ayo in *The Sermon-Conferences of St. Thomas Aquinas on the Apostle's Creed* (Notre Dame, IN: University of Notre Dame Press, 1988). On the dating, see pp. 2–3.

261. *ST* IIa-IIae q29 a2 ad4.   262. *Collationes Credo in Deum* 15.
263. *ST* IIa-IIae q180 a7 ad3.   264. *ST* IIa-IIae qq28–29.

CHAPTER 7

Deification in the *Summa theologiae*

> *He predestined us for adoption to himself through Jesus Christ, in accord with the purpose of his will, in praise of the glory of his grace, by which he has graced us, in his beloved Son.*
>
> —Ephesians 1:4–6

This examination of Thomas Aquinas's teaching in the *Summa theologiae* on grace, charity, and wisdom justifies the claim that he thinks of human salvation as deification. The "advance of the rational creature towards God," through "Christ, who as man, is our way to God,"[1] takes place as the creature is deified by increasing likeness to the Trinitarian image, and conformed to the image of the Son, coming with the Son to his eternal inheritance. In Thomas's mature thought, the deification of human persons by participation in God's own love and wisdom is the greatest example of God's gracious will to communicate the divine goodness. While always remaining the transcendent primary cause of human sanctification, God allows humans to share in the proper activities of the divine life, in the greatest measure possible to them, so that they participate as free agents in their own journey toward union with him. God's wisdom and love in the divine *ordinatio* are thus especially manifested in the deification of adopted sons, who are involved by grace in working out their own salvation.

1. *ST* Ia q2, prol.

Thomas's theology of deification in the *Summa* is not always explicit, however—following the structure of the work, it becomes apparent only step by step, framed in terms of a rich complex of interrelated concepts. This final chapter shows synthetically how the reading of the questions on grace, charity, and wisdom undertaken in this volume allows us to perceive throughout the *Summa* a theology of deification that, though sometimes hidden, is always at work. Drawing on the results of the preceding analysis, I first consider how the theme of deification develops as the *Summa* proceeds, arguing that this development must be placed in the context of Thomas's larger pedagogical plan for the work. Then a more systematic synthesis shows how his teaching on the deifying role of grace, charity, and wisdom integrates the elements of Thomas's doctrine of deification found throughout the work.

The End of the Journey

Because deification describes the very process of human salvation and sanctification in the *Summa*, its full meaning in Thomas's theology develops from the beginning to the end of the work, in accord with Thomas's plan to "teach the knowledge of God, not only as he is in himself, but also as he is the source of things and their end, and especially of rational creatures."[2] One way of seeing this is to consider how, as the *Summa* unfolds, Thomas fills out with increasing clarity his description of the supernatural end of human life, and explains more fully the nature of the transformation required to attain it. Chapter 1 explained that from the outset of the *Summa* Thomas teaches that human beings are directed to God, and that human capacities and action must be transformed to reach this supernatural end if they are to find their highest fulfillment. Reading the first question of the *Summa*, on *sacra doctrina*, we know only that although human salvation requires knowledge of the end, it "surpasses the grasp of human reason."[3] By the end of the Ia *pars*, however, we understand that this end is nothing less than the direct vision of God, and that it is reached as the creature, already created to the image of God, is made deiform by the light of glory, fully likened to the Trinitarian Persons in intellect and will by the knowledge and

2. Ibid.
3. *ST* Ia q1 a1.

love of God. We know, too, that this goal is attainable only by grace, leading to glory for the predestined in God's wise plan of providence. The IIa *pars* fleshes out this picture much more, with its examination of human action elevated by grace on the journey to beatitude. We learn that God—working with and through human capacities deified by grace, charity, and wisdom—leads them by the Holy Spirit to the end of communion with himself in fellowship with the Son. By the time we reach Thomas's discussions in the IIIa *pars* of the grace of Christ and adopted sonship, and the way in which sacraments conform Christians to Christ, we understand much more about the end and how it is reached: humans who come to share in God's own beatitude, likened to the divine nature and Persons, and freely led by the Spirit, are conformed "to the image of the Son," sharing in his own life of loving obedience and worship of the Father.

The difference between Thomas's descriptions of the end of human life and the concomitant transformation of the human creature in the first and last parts of the *Summa* has to do not only with the fact that he is focusing on different theological topics, but also with the progress of his pedagogy as he builds an increasingly nuanced picture of human salvation. He is concerned in the Ia *pars* with the divine nature and the way in which God providentially participates the divine perfections to creatures—and especially to humans made to the image of God by virtue of their rationality. The Ia *pars* thus primarily presents the transformation of the image for the end of glory in terms of the perfection of its intellectual operation by assimilation to the Trinitarian exemplar. Thomas adverts to the special role of grace, charity, and wisdom in effecting this transformation but does not yet explain just how grace, virtues, and gifts make God himself the object of the image's knowledge and love. He also sets God's transforming gift into the context of predestination early on, but he is most concerned at this point to show that this predestination brings into play a causal chain in which grace is prevenient and human freedom is also preserved; God in his love predestines the elect to receive grace, which moves the free will to merit glory, and so predestination has God's goodness as both its source and end in the divine *ordinatio*.

In the IIIa *pars*, on the other hand, Thomas is concerned with the Incarnation and how it effects human salvation. The focus is on Christ, who is the source of grace and the principle and model of human sanctification for those who participate in his sonship. The Word became incarnate not only to save human beings from the effects of sin but also to raise them to "the full participation of divinity, which is mankind's true beatitude and the end of human life."[4] In the IIIa *pars* Thomas presents this end of beatitude more often in terms of the inheritance of sons, who as a result of their predestination have been conformed, by lives of love and wisdom flowing from their participation in Christ's grace, "to the image of the Son." The conformation of humans by grace to the image of the Trinity, treated in the Ia *pars*, is thus also a conformation to Christ and a share in his relationship to the Father. The nature of predestination's effects is now more clearly understood—they consist in this transformation and this end, in which God's wisdom and love for humans in Christ is most clearly revealed.[5]

What links Thomas's differing accounts of the end in the Ia and IIIa *pars*, and his descriptions of the transformation required, is his teaching in the IIa *pars* on grace, charity, and wisdom, deifying the image so that the "Spirit of adoption" can lead it on the journey to beatitude. The questions in the IIa *pars* on grace, charity, and wisdom integrate the Ia *pars* (the Trinity and the divine missions) and IIIa *pars* (Christology and adopted sonship) with respect to Thomas's theology of deification. They help to explain the relationship between them; that is, by the time Thomas presents his teaching on adopted sonship in the IIIa *pars*, we understand just how grace's participation in the divine nature, giving rise to participation by the intellect and will in Word and Love through charity and wisdom, concretely takes the form in the acting person, of a participation in Christ's sonship, and a life conformed to his own.

A Theology of Deification in the *Summa*

Thomas's teaching on the deifying role of grace, charity, and wisdom can thus be extended backward and forward from the IIa *pars* to shed light on

4. *ST* IIIa q1 a2.

5. In an interesting essay, Gilles Mongeau notes that Thomas often uses the rhetorical technique of textual crossovers and repetition to develop his teaching on key ideas as the *Summa* unfolds, "such that the full meaning of the key term or idea only emerges at the very end, once the student has 'navigated' the process by which the meaning emerges." "The Spiritual Pedagogy of the *Summa theologiae*," *Nova et Vetera* 2, no. 1 (2004): 91–114, esp. 98.

the presence of a coherent, though not always obvious, theology of deification throughout the *Summa*. Only in this work does Thomas give parallel descriptions of grace as a participation in the divine nature and charity and wisdom as participations in the likeness of Spirit and Son. Taken together, they help to reveal a deep connection between his treatments of the divine nature and missions, the Trinitarian image on its journey to beatitude through the moral life, adopted sonship through Christ and his sacraments, and the beatific vision. With Thomas's mature conception of the deifying role of grace, charity, and wisdom in mind, the reader of the *Summa* is better able to understand why conformation to the image of the Trinity is also conformation to the image of the Son—and at the same time a process taking place through the graced creature's own moral activities on the journey to eternal life.

The Invisible Missions in the Moral Life of the *Imago Dei*

This project has examined several loci in the *Summa* that give accounts, from different perspectives, of the perfection of the rational creature. In Ia q43 Thomas says that in the gift of grace the invisible missions conform the soul to God, assimilating its will to the Holy Spirit by charity, and its intellect to the Word by wisdom, so that God becomes the indwelling object of its knowledge and love. Ia q93, on the image, presents a corresponding teaching. Grace and glory perfect the image so that it actively "represents the species" of Word and Love in its intellect and will by knowledge and love of God as its proper object. Thomas's treatment in the IIa *pars* of the moral life characterizes the movement of the graced image toward God as a process, in which its nature and powers of intellect and will are so elevated by grace, charity, and wisdom (ordering all the virtues and gifts) that it can participate actively and meritoriously as a secondary cause in its own journey to beatitude. These three perspectives on the advance of the rational creature to God are clearly related to each other by the idea of the transformation of the creature by grace such that its intellect and will are directed toward God. But is it possible, with the tools Thomas provides, to do more than simply note the common theme of these narratives?

The *Summa*'s identification of grace as a participation in the divine nature, from which charity and wisdom flow as participations in the likeness of Spirit and Son, helps us to see more clearly the central construct into which each of these accounts provides a different pedagogical window. A partial synthesis between Thomas's teaching on the divine missions and image appeared at the end of chapter 2, where I argued that Ia q43 and q93 are connected as treatments of cause and effect with respect to the two central aspects of the creature's sanctification by grace: God's presence to the soul as object and the resulting assimilation of the creature to the Word and Love, as its intellect and will are actively elevated to this new intentionality. In light of Thomas's teaching on the IIa *pars*, we see that grace perfects the representation of the species of Word and Love in the image, especially through the virtue of charity and the gift of wisdom, as participations in the Spirit and Son. It is through these infused *habitus* that the creature knows and loves God above all things, sharing in God's own knowledge and love of himself. The intellect participating in the Son by wisdom, with God as its object, produces an inner word that is a likeness of the Word, Wisdom begotten, and from this word proceeds a love of God in the will that is a participated likeness of the Holy Spirit who is Love.[6] The temporal effects that the invisible missions add to the eternal processions of Word and Love can now be identified more precisely as wisdom and charity, the active representation of the species of Son and Spirit by participation in the divine Persons. So, as charity and wisdom deify the will and intellect by a participation in the dynamic life of the Trinity, the creature truly participates in the divine nature. It is especially through charity and wisdom, then, that grace "deifies" the creature in the transformation of its nature as the principle of its active orientation to God.

In representing the species of the divine Persons by charity and wisdom, so that all of the creature's activities are shaped and ordered to God as end, the image conformed to the Trinity by grace becomes at the same time the principle of its own supernatural activities. In this regard, it is significant that Thomas refers to grace both as the "root of the invisible missions" (in the question on the divine missions) and as the "root and principle of the infused virtues and gifts" (in a question on grace).[7] This dual characterization of grace gives insight into an implicit link in Thomas's thought between his Trinitarian and moral theology. The image's ontological transfor-

---

6. See chapter 2; cf. *ST* Ia q93 a8.
7. *ST* Ia q43 a5 ad3; Ia-IIae q110 a3 ad3.

mation into the Trinitarian likeness that takes place through grace in the divine missions is specifically a transformation of the creature's powers of intellect and will through charity and wisdom that enables it to participate as a moved mover in its own journey to beatitude. As discussed in chapter 3, participation in the divine nature by grace, as the principle of the virtues and gifts, gives one the necessary disposition to be led by the Holy Spirit's *auxilium* because the intellect and will are well ordered by the filial obedience of the children of God, in whom charity is perfected by wisdom.

The deification of the image and its faculties by grace, charity, and wisdom can thus be located at the heart of Thomas's understanding of the moral life. To say that grace is the root of both the invisible divine missions and the infused virtues and gifts is to say that the missions deify through the infused virtues and gifts, all of which are governed by charity and ordered by wisdom for the creature's sanctification. I have noted throughout this book that Thomas comes in his later works to a profound appreciation of both the primacy of divine causality, and the proper role of secondary created causality in God's wise plan of providence for the universe, especially in the case of the free activity of rational beings. Thomas's theology of deification provides a link between his treatments of the Trinity and moral life in the *Summa*, which also demonstrates in a striking way the fruits of his mature understanding of the participation relationship between God and the rational creature made to and perfected in the divine image.

Wisdom, Charity, and Adopted Sonship

The perfection of the *imago Dei*, because it is a progressive participation in the likeness of the Trinitarian Persons by charity and wisdom, is also a conformation "to the image of the Son," *qua* Son, and a participation in his sonship. As detailed in chapter 4, Thomas emphasizes in the Ia and IIIa *pars* that the Son who is the Word is exemplary in the deification of human beings on multiple levels, through the visible and invisible missions, in a complementary relationship with the Holy Spirit.[8] In the visible mission

---

8. Thomas reflects on the complementarity of the divine missions in his *Commentary on John* on the text "The Paraclete, the Holy Spirit whom the Father will send in my name, will teach you all things" (Jn 14:26). The Holy Spirit comes in the name of the Son because he is the Spirit of the Son and "conforms us to the Son because he adopts us as children of God: 'You have received the spirit of adoption by which we cry out, Abba! Father!' (Rom 8:15)." The Spirit

of the Incarnation, Christ as head is the author of sanctification, bestowing through the instrumentality of his own graced humanity, as exemplary cause and model, the gift of the grace of the Holy Spirit. With respect to participation in the divine nature by grace, Christ is exemplar cause through his fullness of grace in his visible mission; with respect to participation of the human in the divine intellect by wisdom, he is exemplar as Word in the invisible mission; with respect to participation of the individual in sonship, he is exemplar as the natural Son of God. As the *Summa* unfolds, Thomas links the various ways in which the Son, who is the Word and Wisdom begotten, is the exemplar of the adoption of grace in rational creatures.[9]

Chapter 4 compared references in the Ia *pars* (q33 a3) and in the IIIa *pars* (q3 a8 and q23) to adopted sonship as a participation in the Son's natural filiation. In each of these places Thomas sketches a progression of likeness to the second Person of the Trinity as exemplar, in which creatures participate according to their degree of similarity to God—by trace (irrational creatures), rational nature (image), grace, or glory. In Ia q33 a3 Thomas presents the adopted sonship of grace and glory simply in terms of an ordination to the inheritance of glory—that is, rational creatures share in the Son's filiation insofar as they are heirs with him to eternal life. There is no reference as yet to the means by which grace accomplishes this "conformation to the image of the Son" and brings about a share in his inheritance. In the IIIa *pars*, on the other hand, with references to the progression of likeness of creatures to the Word who is Wisdom (q3 a8), and who as the Son is one in nature and love with the Father (q23 a3), Thomas more clearly indicates

---

teaches the faithful all things because "just as the effect of mission of the Son was to lead us to the Father, the effect of the mission of the Holy Spirit is to lead the faithful to the Son. Now the Son, since he is begotten Wisdom itself, is Truth itself: 'I am the Way, and the Truth, and the Life' (Jn 14:6). And so the effect of this kind of mission is that men be made participators in divine wisdom and knowers of the truth. The Son, therefore, gives teaching to us, since he is the Word; but the Holy Spirit makes us capable of his teaching (*doctrinae eius capaces facit*)" (ch14 lect6). Thomas seems to be saying that the Spirit adopts us as sons precisely in that the gift of wisdom (by which we connaturally "taste" and so understand divine things) conforms us to the Son, and it is through this conformation that we come to the Father.

9. In speaking of the exemplarity of the Son, Thomas is using the language of appropriation. The whole Trinity effects adoption by grace, but different roles are fittingly appropriated to the divine Persons: "Adoption, though common to the whole Trinity, is appropriated to the Father as its author; to the Son as its exemplar, to the Holy Spirit, as imprinting on us the likeness of this exemplar" (*ST* IIIa q23 a2 ad3).

how adopted sons attain the inheritance of glory—through the activities proper to sons, of the graced intellect and will informed by wisdom and charity, which bring the creature to communion with God.

Only the reader who has been attentive to Thomas's presentation of the questions on grace, charity, and wisdom in the IIa *pars* will recognize fully why this is so. To be an adopted son is to be in relation to the Trinity as the Son is to the Father, precisely because one's intellect and will participate in the likeness of the Son and Holy Spirit, such that with the Son and Holy Spirit, God is the object of one's knowledge and love. The adopted son, participating in the divine nature by grace, loves God by a will conformed to the Holy Spirit with an intellect conformed to the Word—and just in this way attains and enjoys the inheritance of beatitude proper to the Son. And so,

to be adopted belongs to the rational creature alone; not indeed to all, but only to those who have charity, which "is poured forth in our hearts by the Holy Spirit" (Rom 5:5); for which reason the Holy Spirit is called "the Spirit of adoption of sons" (Rom 8:15).[10]

Grace makes of the rational creature an adopted son because it causes that creature to know and love God in the likeness of the Son, who loves the Father by the Holy Spirit.

Thomas's pairing of Romans 5:5 and 8:14 in III q23 a3 above is revealing. Chapter 5 proposed that Thomas's identification of charity as a participation in the Holy Spirit, drawn from his interpretation of Romans 5:5, not only expresses his understanding of charity's role in directing the moral life of the image on the journey to beatitude by perfecting its will, but also illuminates his teaching that charity's friendship with God is "founded on the communication of beatitude by fellowship with the Son." This is so because charity, as a participation in the Holy Spirit, allows one to share in the Son's own eternal communion with the Father through the Holy Spirit. Charity is the primary virtue of adopted sons, who share one end of beatitude with the Son because they act in all things out of love for the Father, as he does. Love for God, as a deifying participation in the divine love, is the effect of God's love, his gracious will to communicate his own beatitude to the elect, by causing them to act so as to merit it by grace. As Thomas points out in one of his scriptural commentaries, to be an adopted son is first to be loved

10. *ST* IIIa q23 a3.

by the Father as is the Son; because our adoption as sons conforms us to the image of the Son, we enjoy "a certain participation in the divine love," which belongs first to the Son, who is beloved of the Father "naturally, and in a most excellent way."[11] This share in the divine love is the cause of our predestination to beatitude and actually takes effect in us through our participation in it by means of the charity "poured forth in our hearts by the Holy Spirit." So charity, perfected by wisdom, conforms us to Christ and gives us a destiny like his.

Thomas especially associates the gift of wisdom with charity in the *Summa*, as it is rooted in charity and also perfects it. It flows from charity in a special way among the gifts, because it particularly depends upon the connaturality with God that charity gives; wisdom is a kind of loving knowledge that arises from the savored experience of divine things. Wisdom's highest act is contemplation; it allows one to consider the highest things, and so to "judge and order all things according to divine rules" in the light of love. In chapter 6 I argue that wisdom's work in the intellect perfects charity in the will by judging and ordering charity's objects, so that charity directs and unites the whole person more perfectly to God as the principle of beatitude, conforming the human to the divine will. I propose too that Thomas especially links wisdom with charity because he thinks not only that it perfects charity in this way, but also that wisdom as a participation in the likeness of the Son by the intellect corresponds with charity's participation in the Holy Spirit by the will. By inference, wisdom orders charity well because participation in the Son by the intellect perfects participation in the Holy Spirit by the will.

Because the intellect is conformed to the Word, it judges and orders in accord with the divine reason and so perfects the will's activity of loving God above all, and everything else for God's sake, which conforms it to God's own Love in the Holy Spirit. Charity and wisdom together are thus the primary deifying virtue and gift that direct all the others, ordering God's adopted children in the journey of their moral lives toward God. In this way, rational creatures participate in the loving wisdom by which God providentially orders all things, including their own salvation, in the divine *ordinatio*. So wisdom is associated with the beatitude of peacemakers, for

11. *Sup. Eph.* ch1 lect2.

peace is the "tranquility of order," the fruit of union with God for those who "shall be called the children of God."

Faith, filial fear, and filial piety all work together with wisdom in an eminent way in adopted sons, so that they live a well-ordered life of loving obedience and worship of God. Christ provides a pattern for this deified life of sonship. I argued in chapter 6 that the exemplary role of Christ's wisdom-perfected charity, flowing from his fullness of grace as Head, is particularly clear in Thomas's treatment of Christ's priesthood and sacraments. Christ crucified is an icon of God's love for us, and his voluntary suffering the greatest example of perfect charity and wisdom, manifested in his obedience to the Father. The saving and deifying power of Christ's priestly Passion, communicated through the sacraments, consists especially in his sacrificial love. This charity of Christ is both the cause and model of the sanctification of his members. By the sacraments Christians are conjoined to Christ's Passion because they are conformed, by the grace of the sacraments, to his sacrificial love and obedience in the Passion and receive the final effect of the Passion in beatitude.

The deification bestowed by the sacraments, as it is a conformation to Christ's charity and wisdom, takes the shape of filial obedience and therefore of true devotion. Adopted sons, participating in Christ's priesthood, exercise the true exterior and interior worship as he did, by the outward sacramental character and the inward seal of grace. By fruitful reception, fully engaged as instruments in their own sanctification through the virtues and gifts, they are deified and move toward the end of glory by the *instinctus* of the Holy Spirit within the communion of the Church. So through grace, charity, and wisdom (directing all the virtues and gifts), the whole mystical body participates in the likeness of the divine Persons, and with and through the Son is led by the Holy Spirit to share in the divine communion of knowledge and love enjoyed by the Persons in beatitude.[12] The final reality of the Eucharist, the sacrament of charity, is thus not only the Church's unity but also its deiformity.

---

12. It is not surprising that Thomas follows his treatment of adopted sonship in the IIIa *pars* with a question on Christ's predestination, which Thomas argues is the exemplar of ours, both because, according to Paul in Rom 8:29, we are predestined specifically to the adoption of sons, "which is a participated likeness of natural sonship," and because we, like Christ in his humanity, obtain the end of predestination through grace, which is most manifest in him, from "whose fullness of grace we have all received" (Jn 1:16; *ST* IIIa q24 a3).

The Deified Life of Adopted Sonship as the Manifestation of God's Glory

If Christ is the principal and primary model of the deified life, those who participate in his sonship by grace, charity, and wisdom will reveal the divine glory and beauty just as he did. Thomas continually returns to the theme of God's salvation and deification of the elect through grace, virtues, and gifts as a supreme manifestation of the divine goodness in God's sapiential plan for the universe. God's goodness and wisdom are manifest in those whom he perfects in the divine image, whose lives ordered by charity and wisdom not only liken them to the divine Persons but also make them instruments in their own journey to beatitude, in the freedom of adopted sons, led by the Holy Spirit. In Thomas's *Commentary on Romans* he argues that those who are "conformed to the image of the Son" (Rom 8:29) attain the inheritance of beatitude with Christ by their adoption and also share his splendor:

The adoption as sons is nothing more than this conformity, because a person adopted into the sonship of God is conformed to his true Son. First, in the right to the inheritance as was stated above (v. 17): "If sons, then heirs, heirs of God and fellow heirs with Christ." Secondly, in sharing his splendor. For he is begotten of the Father as the "splendor of his glory" (Heb 1:3). Hence by enlightening the saints with the light of wisdom and grace, he makes them be conformed to himself.

Those who have the light of wisdom and grace manifest God's glory, for the Son's splendor is his wisdom—in Thomas's commentary on Hebrews 1:3 (the Son "is the splendor of [God's] glory"), which he quotes in the passage above, he clearly identifies the two. Explaining that glory means "knowledge and praise of the divine goodness," which can belong perfectly to God alone, he says that the Word is the splendor of Wisdom, shining forth as the Father's knowledge of himself.[13] In the *Summa*'s treatment of the Tri-

---

13. *Sup. Heb.* ch1 lect2: "Since splendor is that which is emitted first from something shining, wisdom is truly something shining. Eccles. 8:1: 'the wisdom of a person shines in his face.' Hence it is that the first conception of wisdom is as of a certain splendor. The Word of the Father, therefore, who is a certain conception of his intellect, is the splendor of Wisdom, by which he knows himself. And thus the Apostle calls the Son 'the splendor of his glory,' that is, of the divine knowledge of his renown. In which it is shown that he is not only wisdom, but Begotten Wisdom. Isa 62:1: 'Until her just one comes forth as splendor,' etc."

nity, Thomas also associates splendor especially with the co-eternity of the Son as "the Word, which is the light and splendor of the intellect, as Damascene says (*De fide orth.* 3.3)."[14] And in the question on adopted sonship he says that in adoption of sons by the Trinity "one is likened to the splendor of the eternal Son [as exemplar] by the light of grace."[15] Thomas's scriptural commentaries help us to understand that in the multiple places in the *Summa* where he speaks of adopted sonship "conforming us to the image of the Son" (Rom 8:29) he is thinking not only of our share in the inheritance of beatitude but also of how we share in wisdom's splendor, in which the knowledge and praise of the divine goodness (i.e., God's glory) shines forth.

These two aspects of conformation to the Son are related—because the gift of wisdom causes adopted sons to participate successfully in the divine *ordinatio* for their salvation, it manifests the divine goodness. Thomas says in his commentary on Ephesians 1:5–6 that the final cause of the predestination of adopted sons is "the praise of the glory of God's grace" so that "we should praise and know the goodness of God," for "the only motive for God's predestinating will is to communicate the divine goodness to others."[16] As the creature is conformed to the Word by wisdom in the intellect, so it is also conformed to the Word insofar as it is through the Word that God carries out the divine plan of wisdom for the universe and for each individual creature, manifesting his glory. The predestination of the elect to beatitude, toward which they move by participation in the Word and Love through wisdom-perfected charity, fully reveals the splendor of God's glory—the knowledge and praise of the divine goodness—in the divine plan of providence.

14. *ST* Ia q39 a8, q34 a2 ad3.

15. *ST* IIIa q23 a2 ad3.

16. Predestination causes both glory and grace, by which the elect can merit eternal life through the activity of their free will, to carry out God's plan of providence (*ST* Ia q23 a5). In *Sup. Eph.* ch1 lect1 Thomas makes the same argument that "there are two effects of predestination, grace and glory. Within the realm of what is willed, grace can be identified as a reason for the effects which are oriented towards glory." But he notes too that grace and glory constitute a progressively more perfect twofold likeness to the Son of God for adopted children. What the Apostle says about those who are "predestined to the adoption of children through Jesus Christ" (Eph 1:5) can refer to the imperfect likeness to the Son by grace in this life, but "more probably refers to the perfect assimilation to the Son of God which will exist in the Fatherland." And the final cause of predestination is specified in the words "for the praise of the glory of his grace," that is, that we should praise and know the goodness of God. So the end of predestination, which conforms us to the Son, is the knowledge of God's goodness.

To manifest God's glory by conformation to the Son in wisdom is also to participate in his divine beauty, for the splendor of the Son's wisdom is an aspect of his beauty.[17] Wisdom's act is contemplation, flowing from charity, in which the interior devotion of true worship is rooted. And so, a deified life of true worship is a beautiful life, conformed to that of the Son. The contemplative life of heaven—and even that on earth—is beautiful in itself, for

beauty ... consists in a certain clarity and due proportion. Now each of these is found radically in the reason, to which belongs both the light manifesting [beauty] and due proportion in ordering other things. And so, as the contemplative life consists in the act of reason, beauty is found in it, in itself and essentially. Whence, Wis 8:2 says about the contemplation of wisdom, "I became a lover of her beauty."[18]

The act of contemplation is beautiful because it contemplates God's own beauty, loving the goodness of the divine truth.[19] The contemplation of wisdom delights in God's truth with surpassing love so that "through loving God, we are aflame to gaze on his beauty."[20] By this contemplation one is conformed to that truth, participating in the wisdom and beauty of the Word who is Truth. To live by the gift of wisdom and the virtue of charity,

17. Splendor (brightness, or clarity) is an aspect of species, or beauty, which Hilary appropriates to the Son; Thomas in turn attributes this part of the Son's beauty to the light of the divine intellect proceeding. The other parts of beauty, integrity, and proportion he associates with the Son's perfect sharing of the Father's nature and representation of the Father's image (*ST* Ia q39 a8). One might infer that by "the light of wisdom and grace" adopted sons share in all aspects of the Son's beauty; it is by participating in his divine nature and being perfected in the divine image that they share in his splendor—and so with him reveal the Father's glory.

18. *ST* IIa-IIae q180 a2 ad3.

19. The source of all beauty is God, who is "the cause of the harmony and clarity of the universe," according to Dionysius (*On Divine Names* 4; see *ST* IIa-IIae q145 a2). Beauty has a relation to both goodness and truth, for it "adds to goodness a relation to the cognitive power" (*ST* I-IIae q27 a1 ad3; cf. Ia q5 a4 ad1; IIa-IIae q145 a2 ad1; *De divinibus nominibus* ch4 lect3.); that is, the apprehension of the beautiful understands the true to be good and so gives delight in the true. Cf. Jan Aertsen, *Medieval Philosophy and the Transcendentals: The Case of Thomas Aquinas*, Studien und Texte zur Geistesgeschichte des Mittelalters 52 (New York: E. J. Brill, 1996), 359. Aertsen provides a discussion of Thomas's understanding of beauty in relation to the transcendentals of being, unity, truth, and goodness. See also Daniel Gallagher, "The Analogy of Beauty and the Limits of Theological Aesthetics," *Theandros: An Online Journal of Christian Theology and Philosophy* 3, no. 3 (Spring/Summer 2006) for a summary and evaluative discussion of current Thomist theological aesthetics.

20. *ST* IIa-IIae q180 a1, a7.

contemplating the beauty of God manifested especially through the Son, is also to manifest with him God's beauty.

Because wisdom and charity belong to all who are in the state of grace, one may infer that Thomas does not refer the beauty of the contemplative life only to the cloister (although there it may be lived to its highest degree) but to the vocation of each of the faithful to true worship, fulfilled in the beatific vision. This contemplative dimension of life must be the source of activity for all God's adopted children, for wisdom is both contemplative and practical, moving from knowledge of the highest cause to the right-ordering of all loves toward that divine source and end.[21] In his discussion of "honesty"—moral goodness that is worthy of honor—Thomas observes that "spiritual beauty consists in one's conduct being well-proportioned with respect to the spiritual clarity of reason."[22] The spiritual beauty of wisdom shines in all that is honest or virtuous, for, according to Plato, the sight of what is honest arouses "a wonderful love of wisdom."[23]

All of God's adopted sons, conformed to the image of the Son, share in his true worship of the Father, and so with him reveal the divine beauty. Their worship is on earth a configuration to Christ's Passion, but in heaven it is a life of perfect vision, love, and praise, configured to his glory. The indwelling of God known and loved by wisdom and charity, likening adopted sons to the Son and Holy Spirit, thus shines forth in the splendor of a moral life oriented to beatitude, which makes the goodness of the divine truth manifest. So, for Thomas, the deified life is a beautiful life—a life governed by charity and wisdom, rooted in contemplation, lived in union with God and others for God's sake—which foreshadows heaven and manifests God's beauty and glory. It is a life configured to the beautiful life of the Incarnate Word.

Wisdom, Charity, and Deiformity

Beatitude is the highest perfection of wisdom and charity in adopted sons. God alone perfectly knows and so loves himself. Yet in the beatific vision the created intellect, participating in the light of glory, is made "deiform," sharing to the highest degree in the divine likeness by actual knowledge and

---

21. See *ST* IIa-IIae q45 a3, q182 a4.

22. *ST* IIa-IIae q145 a2. Temperance especially serves to free the intellect from base desires, allowing it to rise to higher things; *ST* IIa-IIae q141 a2 ad3; q143.

23. *ST* IIa-IIae q145 a2 ad1. Thomas is quoting Tully, *De Officiis* 1.5.

love of God (see chap. 1). In Ia q12 Thomas argues that the glorified intellect is strengthened by a more perfect likeness to the divine intellect so as to be disposed to receive the vision of the divine essence itself as its form—to see God, insofar as it is possible for a creature, as God does. He adds that those who have more charity will have a fuller participation in the light of glory and so will be more deiform

because where there is the greater charity, there is more desire; and desire in a certain manner makes the one desiring apt and prepared to receive the object desired. So the one who has more charity, will see God more perfectly, and be more beatified.[24]

But exactly what Thomas thinks the deiformity of the intellect is, on the part of the creature, and how charity in the will increases deiformity are not yet fully explained in Ia q12. As the *Summa* unfolds, we understand better how the intellect is likened to God, and how charity not only disposes one by desire for its even greater increase but does so precisely by conforming the will to the likeness of the Holy Spirit. In the invisible missions to the blessed the supernatural "kindling of the affections" by charity and the "illumination of the intellect" by wisdom are perfected, and the soul's participation in Word and Love reaches its highest similitude.[25]

The image of glory receives the fullness of the divine indwelling and likeness in the vision, as the divine essence informs the souls of the blessed:

they see him, and in seeing him, possess him as present, having the power to see him always; and possessing him, they enjoy him as the ultimate fulfillment of desire.[26]

Beatitude requires vision in the intellect and comprehension and enjoyment in the will. These three elements of beatitude correspond to faith, hope, and love, of which they are the final outcome—for perfect happiness consists in attaining the last end, to which the human person is ordered by both intellect and will. In beatitude, perfect knowledge of the end in the intellectual vision replaces the imperfect knowledge of faith, and the comprehension or "laying hold of" this end now present, attains what has been hoped for by the will, which can at last repose in loving enjoyment, possessing its beloved.[27] Charity alone remains in heaven, where it is perfected,

---

24. *ST* Ia q12 a6.   25. *ST* Ia q43 a6 ad3; cf. Ia q43 a5 ad3.
26. *ST* Ia q12 a7 ad1; cf. a1 ad4
27. *ST* Ia-IIae q4 a3. Thomas points out that the comprehension of God by a created intellect in beatitude does not refer to a complete "inclusion of the comprehended in the comprehendor"

"for vision is a cause of love, as is said in *Ethic.* 9 [5]. And the more perfectly God is known, the more perfectly he is loved."[28] In the will of the blessed, charity reaches its greatest operation so that the "whole heart of man is always actually borne towards God."[29]

The deiformity of the beatific vision is thus not a static state of conformity to the divine likeness, although the image's journey toward the divine likeness has reached completion. Rather, the deiformity of the soul in glory consists in its most active participation in the divine life of knowledge and love eternally enjoyed by the Trinitarian Persons. Loving contemplation of the divine essence is the highest activity of adopted sons. In glory, their intellect, participating to the greatest possible extent in the likeness of the Word, exercises perfect wisdom's highest act: contemplation of the divine truth. Their will, participating fully in the likeness of the Holy Spirit, exercises perfect charity's highest act in union with and enjoyment of God. And as wisdom flows from and perfects charity in this life, so in glory the contemplative activity of the vision is the result of their dynamic synergy.[30] The life of deiformity, because it is a participation in the likeness and activity of the divine Persons, is a life of sonship fully exercised.

In this life, while all the infused virtues and gifts are operative in the graced soul, charity and wisdom have a special governing role in bringing about the divine indwelling and likeness because of their integrated activity in directing the mind in all things toward God. In the deiformity of glory, as in the deification of grace, charity and wisdom have a governing role among the virtues and gifts that endure in heaven. The moral and intellectual virtues remain and are perfected, at least formally, inasmuch as the minds of the blessed are perfectly ordered (i.e., by charity), although the material element of these virtues, which concerns the active life, passes away.[31] The gifts, too, remain and are perfected, because in glory the human mind is perfectly subject to the Holy Spirit's movement; all of their operations are now direct-

---

(as if God were finite and so able to be fully known by a finite being), but rather to a laying-hold of (*tentionem*) what is present and possessed. Note too that while delight is an effect flowing from charity, it is not itself what charity seeks (Ia-IIae q4 a2 ad3).

28. *ST* Ia-IIae q67 a6 ad3.

29. *ST* IIa-IIae q24 a8.

30. The contemplative life of heaven, although in a different mode from that on earth, is yet continuous with it, "by reason of charity, in which it has both its beginning and end." *ST* IIa IIae q180 a8 ad1.

31. *ST* Ia-IIae q67 aa2–3.

ed to the knowledge and love of God in the contemplative life of heaven.[32]

Thomas especially associates the gift of understanding, insofar as it makes the intellect capable of apprehending the divine essence, with the light of glory. Understanding is a "supernatural light" that enlightens the mind for a penetrating knowledge of supernatural truth, to which belongs the vision of God promised to the clean of heart, a vision inchoate on earth and perfect in heaven.[33] But wisdom's judgment must direct and complete understanding's apprehension of truth by adherence to the truth. In a passage on Christ's beatific knowledge, where Thomas argues that the soul of Christ, because it is united to the Word, "more fully receives the light in which God is seen by the Word himself than any other creature," he begins by observing:

The vision of the divine essence belongs to all the blessed according to a participation in the light flowing into them from the fountain of the Word of God, according to Ecclus., 1:5: "The fountain of wisdom is the Word of God on high."[34]

The "light in which God is seen by the Word himself," that Christ and all the saints share, is the light of the divine wisdom participated through the Word. The souls of the blessed in heaven are most like Christ, in whom charity, wisdom, and all the gifts find their fullest operation.

The deiformity of the light of glory is the conformity of the intellect to the divine essence, which comes about, in response to the direct vision of God, as the Holy Spirit moves the soul to loving knowledge of God through all the gifts flowing from charity's assimilation to the Spirit, especially understanding and wisdom. In turn, charity in the will is totally ordered by the wisdom of the Word to union with God. So we now better understand Thomas's claim in Ia q12 a6 that the illumination of the intellect by the light of glory belongs more perfectly to the one who has more charity. The perfection of the creature's love of God in glory depends on the knowledge of the vision, but that knowledge in turn depends on the perfection of its love and the gifts flowing from it. And in this knowledge and love the soul is conformed perfectly to the Word and Love. In glory, the splendor of the gift of wisdom shines most radiantly, "bursting forth into the affection of love" in the perfect likeness of "the Word breathing forth Love,"[35] and so manifesting God's goodness by fully conforming the saints to the image of the Son.

32. *ST* Ia-IIae q68 a6 c., ad2–3.
33. *ST* IIa-IIae q8 a1, a4, a7. Cf. *Scriptum* bk3 d32 q1 a3 ad 6.
34. *ST* III q10 a4.   35. *ST* Ia q43 a5 ad3.

Conclusion

Taken together, Thomas's mature teachings on grace, charity, and wisdom allow us to perceive an underlying theology of deification at work throughout the *Summa theologiae*—profoundly scriptural, Christological, and pneumatological in character—with extensive connections to his doctrines on the Trinity, image, moral life, Christ, and sacraments. Thomas's definitions in the *Summa* of grace as a participation in the divine nature, and charity and wisdom as participations in the likeness of Holy Spirit and Son, help us to trace sometimes-hidden connections between these different areas of *sacra doctrina* and to see that, for Thomas, deification is God's gracious means of salvation for predestined human creatures in the divine *ordinatio*. This providential plan proclaims God's goodness. To understand that a participation in the divine nature and Persons transforms the graced image into the principle of its own supernatural activities is to acknowledge the all-encompassing primacy of divine causality, and therefore also the graciousness of God's gift of human freedom. Thomas came in his later work to a full recognition of both of these, and so shaped his theology of deification.

Deification for Thomas in the *Summa* is at once fully "Triniform"—on the level of the active faculties, the invisible missions conform the image to the Trinity—and "Christiform"—on the level of the individual, the human person participates in Christ's grace and sonship and so is conformed "to the image of the Son," in his visible mission, by the "Spirit of adoption" (Rom 8:15, 29). The teaching that God's adopted children are deified by personal conformation to God through grace, charity, and wisdom in the *Summa* is the flowering of Thomas's lifelong teaching that God's wisdom creates and restores all things, manifesting his goodness. God predestines his adopted children "out of pure love" to "praise the glory of his grace" (Eph 1:6) because "the divine predestinating will has no other reason than to communicate the divine goodness to his children."[36] The Father shares himself generously with those who are "called the children of God" in a self-offering of wisdom and love poured out in them through the gift of grace, which grows to its full flood in glory when they have become "like him," for they "see him as he is" (1 Jn 3:1–2).

36. *Sup. Eph.* ch1 lect1.11, 13.

A Brief Survey of Deification in the Christian Tradition before Aquinas

To describe "the advance of rational creatures towards God,"[1] Thomas draws from Scripture and the theological patrimony of East and West for a traditional Christian vocabulary associated with what Norman Russell has called the "metaphor of deification."[2] Like the Church Fathers, Thomas employs in the *Summa* a range of scripturally based terms: assimilation, participation, the communication of divine goodness, perfection of the divine image, conformity to Christ, adoption by grace (through Christ and the Holy Spirit), and unifying likeness of the soul to God by knowledge and love in the beatific vision. The early Church drew widely on Scripture for the vocabulary to express a cluster of related notions that would come to be understood as deification. These scriptural notions describe a new destiny made possible for the believer who, redeemed and restored by the grace of the Incarnation, is lifted to the ultimate vocation of assimilation to God in the vision of eternal life (1 Cor 13:12; 1 Jn 3:2) and a participation in divine incorruption and immortality (1 Cor 15:52). This vocabulary centered around the themes of the creation of the human person in the image and likeness of God (Gen 1:26–27); filial adoption (e.g., Rom 8:14; Gal 4:5; Eph 1:5), and the imitation of God or of Christ (Mt 5:44–48; Eph 5:1).[3] Besides the Genesis account of creation in the divine image, a few other Old Testament passages were loci of patristic attention regarding deification—such as Psalms 82:6, referred to by Jesus in John 10:34–35 ("I have said you are gods, and all of you, sons of the Most High")[4]—but it was from the New

---

1. *ST* Ia q2, prol.

2. Norman Russell, *The Doctrine of Deification in the Greek Patristic Tradition* (Oxford: Oxford University Press, 2004), 1.

3. I.-H. Dalmais, *Dictionnaire de Spiritualité*, vol. 3, s.v. "Divinisation—patristique grecque," 1370–89.

4. Justin Martyr (in the *Dialogues with Trypho* 124) was the first Christian writer to link

Testament that patristic authors drew most of the early Christian terminology and teaching associated with Christian deification, in particular from the Pauline and Johannine writings.

The Pauline Epistles present a model of participatory union with Christ (through the Holy Spirit) in which the abovementioned themes of creation and likeness, filial adoption, and the imitation of God or Christ all play a role.[5] Paul describes life in Christ, the second Adam, as "a new creation" (2 Cor 5:17). Baptism into Christ brings believers into a new relationship to God, as adopted sons and heirs, able to address God as Father (Rom 8:15; Gal 4:5–7). In Romans 8, Paul expands upon the role of the Spirit of Christ, the "Spirit of adoption," who "leads the sons of God" in freedom (8:2, 8:14–17; cf. 2 Cor 3:17), according to God's plan of goodness to bring them to glory (8:29–30). Paul's understanding of the fullness of the Christian destiny of sonship is thus eschatological; immortality and incorruption will belong to those who have put on Christ, who "shall bear the image of the heavenly man" (1 Cor 15: 49), having received the "pledge of the Spirit" (2 Cor 5:5). Jules Gross notes that, for Paul, incorporation with Christ, which "divinizes" the Christian, also joins them to the Father and Holy Spirit; "while being christocentric, Pauline mysticism ... has the divine Spirit as its active principle."[6]

The author of the Letter to the Ephesians continues the theme of adoption and inheritance for the predestined, "sealed with the promised Holy Spirit" through Christ, in whom, as head of the body (Eph 1:22–23), God carries out his plan of goodness to "sum up all things in Christ in heaven and earth" (1:10) "for the praise of the glory of his grace" (1:6). Russell points out that although Paul urges his hearers to follow his example of conformation to Christ—and the author of Ephesians exhorts, "be imitators of God" (5:1)—the emphasis in the Pauline writings is on participatory union rather than imitation, a real union with "Christ in you, the hope of glory" (Col 1:27) expressed in a variety of images.[7] In the Letter to the Hebrews, similar themes of participation in Christ and in the Holy Spirit (3:14, 6:4), adoption, and its eschatological fulfillment (2:10–13, 12:5–8) appear, although

---

this verse to the notion of deification, and Irenaeus soon associated it with the Pauline teaching on the adoption of the sons of God in baptism. Russell, *Doctrine of Deification*, 99, 106.

5. The following discussion of scriptural sources of vocabulary associated with deification is indebted to Russell, *Doctrine of Deification*, 79–89. Stephen Thomas, although not writing for an academic audience, also effectively demonstrates the biblical foundations of the doctrine of deification. *Deification in the Eastern Orthodox Tradition: A Biblical Perspective* (Piscataway, NJ: Gorgias Press, 2008).

6. Jules Gross, *La divinisation du chrétien d'après les pères grecs: Contribution historique à la doctrine de la grâce* (Paris: J. Gabalda, 1938), 103; Paul A. Onica, trans., *The Divinization of the Christian According to the Greek Fathers* (Anaheim, CA: A&C Press, 2002), 85.

7. Russell, *Doctrine of Deification*, 85.

the emphasis is on the mediation of Christ in giving believers access to the Father (9:24, 10:20).[8] As discussed in earlier chapters, 2 Peter 1:2–4 provides the most direct reference to Christian deification in the Scriptures.

The Johannine writings also provide several key scriptural loci to which the patristic tradition referred its teaching on deification. In the prologue to the Gospel of John, Christ is introduced as the divine Word who is light and life by nature, and through whom light and life are given to human beings; receiving the Word, they receive the "power to become children of God" (Jn 1:4–12). Believers are reborn from above through baptism (3:3–8) and receive the life of the Holy Spirit imparted by Christ to his disciples (Jn 20:22). In the Eucharist they share in life through the one who is "the Bread of Life" (Jn 6:35–51). Christ's self-description as the vine, in whom the branches must remain if they are to bear fruit, underlines the relationship of participation in which he is the divine source of spiritual life and love, upon which the life and love of believers depends (Jn 15:5). The children of God, participating in Christ, the "light of the world" (Jn 8:12), are also "children of light" (Jn 12:36), who see the way to the Father illuminated by the Word. Knowledge and vision are thus associated in the Johannine writings with the sonship that participation in Christ bestows; this vision and assimilation are ultimately eschatological, for those who are "God's children now" will, when vision is granted, "be like him, for [they] shall see him as he is" (1 Jn 3:2).[9]

Russell argues that the early Greek Fathers metaphorically spoke of deification in two related ways: "the ethical approach takes deification to be the attainment of likeness to God through ascetic and philosophical endeavor," while "the realistic approach assumes that human beings are in some sense actually transformed by deification."[10] The ethical approach employs a more philosophical model and language of imitation and likeness, relating to the ascetic and contemplative life and focused on the practice of virtue. The realistic approach adopts a language of participation, often related to the sacraments of baptism and the Eucharist, and draws much from the Pauline writings.[11] The realistic approach has two aspects—ontological and dynamic—the former referring to "human nature's transformation in principle in the Incarnation," and the latter concerned with "the individual's appropriation of this deified humanity, through the sacraments."[12] Among the early Greek Fathers, the ethical approach is typical of Clement of Alexandria and the Cappadocians, while the realistic approach is characteristic of Justin, Irenaeus, Origen, and Athanasius. The two approaches "begin to converge" in Cyril of Alexandria's teaching on the restoration of divine life in the Holy Spirit to humanity through the deified flesh

8. Ibid., 86.
10. Ibid., 2.
12. Ibid., 2–3.

9. Ibid., 87.
11. Ibid., 2, 9.

of Christ, appropriated to each believer through the sacraments and moral life;[13] with him, in the East, "the theology of divinisation reaches its full development."[14] Notably, Cyril frequently employs 2 Peter 1:4 in his teaching and was a possible influence for Thomas in his use of the vocabulary of grace as a "participation in the divine nature."[15] A doctrine of deification is later passed through Dionysius and Maximus the Confessor to the Byzantine tradition and transmitted through translations of their writings to medieval Latin theologians, including Thomas. Dionysius was particularly influential in the transmission of Greek patristic teaching on deification to the medieval West, so a brief exposition of his teaching is relevant.[16]

Deification is a central theme in the Dionysian *corpus*. To use Russell's categories, Dionysius's approach contains both realistic and ethical/philosophical dimensions; Dionysius defines deification as "the attaining of likeness to God and union with him so far as possible."[17] This likeness and union have an intellectual dimension; the goal of all those being deified "consists of an inspired participation in the one-like perfection, and in the one itself, as far as possible. It consists of a feast upon that sacred vision which nourishes the intellect and divinises everything rising up to it."[18] Yet Dionysian apophaticism forbids positive intellectual knowl-

---

13. Ibid., 13–14; cf. 191–92, 204.

14. Dalmais, *Dictionnaire de Spiritualité*, 1390. For a thorough discussion of Cyril's theology of deification, see Daniel Keating, *The Appropriation of Divine Life in Cyril of Alexandria* (Oxford: Oxford University Press, 2004).

15. Russell, *Doctrine of Deification*, 12, 200–202. See also chapter 4.

16. For a discussion of Dionysius's widespread influence on medieval thought, see Paul Rorem, *Pseudo-Dionysius: A Commentary on the Texts and an Introduction to Their Influence* (New York: Oxford University Press, 1993), esp. 215ff. For an interesting introduction to this topic, see Jean LeClercq, "Influence and Non-Influence of Dionysius in the Western Middle Ages," in *Pseudo-Dionysius: The Complete Works*, ed. and trans. Colm Luibheid (New York: Paulist Press, 1987), 25–32. For recent significant treatments of Maximus on deification, see Paul Blowers, *Exegesis and Spiritual Pedagogy in Maximus the Confessor* (Notre Dame, IN: University of Notre Dame Press, 1991); Lars Thunberg, *Microcosm and Mediator* (Chicago: Open Court, 1995); Jean-Claude Larchet, *La Divinisation de l'homme selon saint Maxime le Confesseur* (Paris: Cerf, 1996); Andrew Louth, *Maximus the Confessor* (New York: Routledge, 1996). Russell provides a valuable condensed analysis. *Doctrine of Deification*, 262–95. Maximus, extremely important in the Eastern tradition, was less often cited as an authority than Dionysius by Western medievals but was still influential; John Scot Eriugena translated his *Ambigua* commenting on Dionysius's texts along with Dionysius's works. Henri Dondaine observes that Eriugena does not cite Maximus but "exploits him magnificently." "L'objet et le 'medium' de la vision béatifique chez les théologiens du XIIIe siècle," *Recherches de théologie ancienne et médiévale* 19 (1952): 60–130, 65n20.

17. Dionysius, *EH* 1.3; Russell, *Doctrine of Deification*, 248, cf. 255.

18. Dionysius, *EH* 1.3 (376A). (Luibheid, *Pseudo-Dionysius*, 198.) All of the following quotes of Dionysius's works come from this volume unless otherwise noted.

edge of God: "The union of divinized minds with the Light beyond all deity occurs in the cessation of all intelligent activity."[19] While the Godhead in itself remains transcendent and unknowable, imitation of God illuminates and so deifies the human intellect in a mediated fashion by participation in the divine light according to each one's place in the universal hierarchy of heaven and earth.[20] As hidden cause of this hierarchy, God is known through the divine theophanies, the manifestations of God in his divine attributes and powers, by which "the formless God is represented in forms."[21]

Dionysius employs, in the service of Christianity, a Neoplatonic scheme of the hierarchical procession and return of all things to God inherited from Proclus and others.[22] For the pagan Neoplatonists, this was a philosophical explanation for the emanation and return of the Many from the One; Dionysius transforms it into a Christian vision of God's providential creation and hierarchical ordering of each creature to himself. The knowledge of God mediated through this hierarchy deifies the intellectual creature. Dionysius defines a hierarchy in the third chapter of the *Celestial Hierarchy* as "a sacred order, a state of understanding and an activity approximating as close as possible to the divine." These three characteristics, as Rene Roques points out, denote the structure and dynamism of the Dionysian universe.[23] As sacred order, the hierarchy (both celestial and ecclesiastical) of the triadic ranks of angels and humans

19. Dionysius, *Divine Names* 1.5 (593C). (Luibheid, *Pseudo-Dionysius*, 54.) As Vladimir Lossky has argued, in Dionysius's negative theology, deification is ultimately a mystical experience, not a purely intellectual union. *The Mystical Theology of the Eastern Church* (New York: St. Vladimir's Seminary Press, 2002), 25–43.

20. On earth, through the ecclesiastical hierarchy, "The divine Light, out of generosity, never ceases to offer itself to the eyes of the mind ... and it is on this that the divine hierarch models himself when he generously pours out on everyone the shining beams of his inspired teaching ... In godlike and hierarchical fashion he gives to all who approach his guiding light and does so in harmonious and orderly fashion and in proportion to the disposition of each one towards the sacred." Dionysius, *EH* 2.3 (400B). (Luibheid, *Pseudo-Dionysius*, 205.)

21. Dionysius, *CH* 1.3 (180C). (Luibheid, *Pseudo-Dionysius*, 157.) In *The Divine Names* Dionysius contrasts the hidden unchanging unity of God with the distinctions or processions by which God shares his perfections (*DN* 2 [636]), enlightening those who are being drawn to him through the rays of divine illumination (*DN* 1.2 [589A]).

22. E.g., "'Every good endowment and every perfect gift is from above, coming down from the Father of lights.' But there is something more. Inspired by the Father, each procession of the Light spreads itself generously towards us, and, in its power to unify, it stirs us by lifting us up. It returns us back to the oneness and deifying simplicity of the Father who gathers us in. For, as the sacred Word says, 'from him and to him are all things.'" Dionysius, *CH* 1.1 (120B). (Luibheid, *Pseudo-Dionysius*, 145.) See Rorem, *Pseudo-Dionysius*, 51–52. Stephen Gersh discusses the history of Christian Neoplatonism's adaptation of this scheme. *From Iamblichus to Eriugena* (Leiden: E. J. Brill, 1978).

23. René Roques, *L'univers dionysien* (Paris: Aubier, 1954), 30.

exhibits a perfect harmony, which reflects the will of God,[24] who is himself the "transcendent source of all order and of all hierarchy."[25] The state of understanding of each member of the hierarchy is the knowledge of God proper to their rank, a knowledge that is inseparable from their divinisation.[26] This knowledge is transmitted from one level to the next; only the first rank of heavenly beings receives illumination directly from God himself, for they are the most like him.[27] The activity of the hierarchy consists of this transmission and brings about purification, illumination, and perfection for its members;[28] perfection consists ultimately in a unification of the intellect, a deiform vision in which God is the center of perspective.[29] Every member of the hierarchy shares the goal of the hierarchy "to enable beings to be as like as possible to God and to be one with him ... For every member of the hierarchy, perfection consists in this, that it is uplifted to imitate God as far as possible," and even that it participates in God's work by passing on that illumination to others.[30]

In spite of the philosophical elements in his doctrine of deification, Dionysius shows his indebtedness to the realistic tradition in his teaching that deification takes place for human members of the hierarchy by means of the sacraments and symbols of the earthly liturgy. The capacity of each intellect to receive the divine light differs radically between the earthly and heavenly hierarchy, for the mode of reception of that light differs for corporeal and noncorporeal beings.[31] The way in which human beings participate in the "one," being uplifted to gaze on the divinizing splendor of God, is through perceptible symbols. A symbolic process of enlightenment is necessary to our nature, which is both corporeal and intellectual, for we require material means to guide us upward by functioning as images of higher immaterial realities: "This divine ray can enlighten us only by being upliftingly concealed in a variety of sacred veils which the Providence of the Father adapts to our nature as human beings."[32] Those sacred veils are the symbols given through the

24. Ibid., 38.

25. Dionysius, *CH* 8.2 (241C). (Luibheid, *Pseudo-Dionysius*, 169.)

26. Roques, *L'univers dionysien*, 120.

27. Dionysius, *CH* 7.2 (205B–208D). (Luibhied, *Pseudo-Dionysius*, 161–64.)

28. Ibid., 7.3 (209C). (Luibheid, *Pseudo-Dionysius*, 165.)

29. Roques, *L'univers dionysien*, 95.

30. Dionysius, *CH* 3.2 (165AB). (Luibheid, *Pseudo-Dionysius*, 154.)

31. "We see our human hierarchy ... as our nature allows, pluralized in a great variety of perceptible symbols lifting us upward hierarchically until we are brought as far as we can be into the unity of divinization. The heavenly beings, because of their intelligence, have their own permitted conceptions of God. For us, on the other hand, it is by way of perceptible images that we are uplifted as far as we can be to the contemplation of what is divine. Actually, it is the same one whom all one-like beings desire, but they do not participate in the same way in this one and the same being." Dionysius, *EH* 1.2 (373A-B). (Luibheid, *Pseudo-Dionysius*, 197.)

32. Dionysius, *CH* 1.2 (121C). (Luibheid, *Pseudo-Dionysius*, 146.) Aquinas refers to this passage in his discussion of sacramental signs in *ST* III q60 a4.

hierarchy in Scripture and the liturgy, which we must penetrate by spiritual exegesis. It is specifically Jesus Christ, "source and perfection of every hierarchy,"[33] who mediates the illumination given to penetrate the hidden meaning of the liturgical symbols, allowing us to move from the effect (the perceptible symbol) to its divine cause and goal.[34] Russell points out that "although Dionysius is a writer generally recognized to be the most strongly Neoplatonic of the later Greek ecclesiastical authors, his use of the concept of deification occurs more frequently in his discussions of the sacraments than in any other context," showing that "he stands in the tradition of Origen, Athanasius, and Cyril, even if he uses a different vocabulary."[35]

In the West, Augustine is the chief and most influential patristic witness to a doctrine of deification, though Tertullian is the first to introduce its Latin terminology.[36] Augustine presents deification in terms of a salvific reform of the divine image through faith, a process of cleansing illumination directed toward the vision of God,[37] through the mediation of the Word made flesh, who "by becoming a sharer (*particeps*) of our mortality, has made us sharers of his divinity."[38] Like many of the Greek Fathers, Augustine employed the Neoplatonic concept of participation to frame his teaching on deification,[39] the content and significance of which

33. Dionysius, *EH* 1.2 (373B). (Luibheid, *Pseudo-Dionysius*, 197.)

34. "We … when we think of the sacred synaxis must move in from effects to causes and in the light which Jesus will give us, we will be able to glimpse the contemplation of the conceptual things clearly reflecting a blessed original beauty. And you, O most divine and sacred sacrament: Lift up the symbolic garments of enigmas which surround you. Show yourself clearly to our gaze. Fill the eyes of our mind with a unifying and unveiled light." Dionysius, *EH* 3.III.2 (428C). (Luibheid, *Pseudo-Dionysius*, 212.)

35. Russell, *Doctrine of Deification*, 253.

36. Gustave Bardy, *Dictionnaire de Spiritualité*, vol. 3, s.v. "Divinisation—chez les Pères Latins," 1390. For more recent treatments of Augustine's doctrine of deification, see José Oroz Reta, "De l'illumination à la déification de l'âme selon saint Augustin," *Studia Patristica* 27 (1993): 364–82; Robert Puchniak, "Augustine's Conception of Deification, Revisited," in *Theōsis: Deification in Christian Theology*, ed. Stephen Finlan and Vladimir Kharlamov (Eugene, OR: Pickwick, 2006), 122–33; Gerald Bonner, "Augustine's Conception of Deification," *Journal of Theological Studies*, n.s., 37 (1986): 360–86; Victorino Capànaga, "La deificaciòn en la soteriología augustiniana," in *Augustinus Magister 2* (Paris: Etudes augustiniennes, 1955), 745–54; Russell, *Doctrine of Deification*, 329–32; and Keating, *Appropriation of Divine Life*, 227–51.

37. See, e.g., *Conf.* 13.3.4; *De doctrina christiana* 1.10.

38. *DT* 4.2.4: "Adiungens ergo nobis similitudinem humanitatis suae abstulit dissimilitudinem iniquitatis nostrae, et factus particeps mortalitatis nostrae fecit nos participes divinitatis suae." CCSL 1.164. Augustine uses this Athanasian formula in a number of places, e.g., *Serm.* 192.1: "Deos facturus qui homines erant, homo factus est qui Deus erat," PL 38.1012; *Enarr. in ps.* 52.6: "Filius enim Die particeps mortalitatis effectus est, ut mortalis homo fiat particeps divinitatis." PL 36.616.

39. See Bonner, "Augustine's Conception of Deification," 373; Oroz Reta, "De l'illumination à la déification," 374ff.

were derived from Scripture and Christian tradition.[40] The ascent to God, taking place through grace, is a journey away from "the land of dissimilitude"[41] toward union with God as adopted children.[42] This is a journey of knowledge and love that takes place in an ecclesial context and is completed eschatologically for the *totus homo deificatus* in the possession and enjoyment of God himself.[43] Augustine may be compared to Cyril in his teaching that "the deification of human beings is the purpose for which the Word became incarnate and is appropriated by them in baptism"; however, unlike Cyril, Augustine does not appeal directly to 2 Peter 1:4, perhaps because of the use made of it by the Pelagians.[44] While Augustine's use of terms derived directly from *deificare* is limited compared to the frequency with which Dionysius and some other Eastern Fathers used the terminology of *theosis*, Augustine clearly does teach that in becoming God's adopted children humans are "deified by his grace," becoming by grace what God is by nature.[45] The recent discovery of new sermons by Augustine, one of which has deification as the central theme, adds significantly to the evidence that Augustine preached that God is a "deifier" who wishes "not only to vivify us but also to deify us."[46] Even where Augustine does

40. Although Augustine's emphasis on the healing and liberating activity of grace necessitated by human sin leads him at times to express his theology of deification somewhat differently than the Greek Fathers, Oroz Reta argues that Augustine also teaches, like them, the elevating and deifying activity of grace in terms of illumination and glorification. "De l'illumination à la déification," 372–73.

41. *Conf.* 7.10.16.

42. E.g., *Ep. (ad Honoratus)* 140.4.10: "Nos quoque per eius gratiam facti sumus, quod non eramus, id est filii Dei; sed tamen aliquid eramus, et hoc ipsum aliquid multo inferius, hoc est filii hominum. Descendit ergo ille, ut nos ascenderemus, et manens in sua natura factus est particeps naturae nostrae, ut nos manentes in natura nostra efficeremur participes naturae ipsius, non tamen sic; nam illum naturae nostrae participatio non fecit deteriorem, nos autem facit naturae illius participatio meliores." CSEL 44.162.

43. *Sermo* 166.4 (PL 38.909).

44. Russell, *Doctrine of Deification*, 331–32.

45. *Enar. in Ps.* 49.2: "Manifestum est ergo, quia homines dixit deos, ex gratia sua deificatos, non de substantia sua natos." CCSL 38.575. Bonner notes fifteen instances where Augustine uses such terms, and does not consider all of them significant. "Augustine's Conception of Deification," 369, 378.

46. "*Sermon 23B-Dolbeau 6–Mainz 13*," in *The Works of St. Augustine III/11: Newly Discovered Sermons*, ed. and trans. Edmund Hill (Hyde Park, NY: New City, 1997), 37–47. François Dolbeau originally discovered the sermons in Mainz and published them in *Vingt-six sermons au peuple d'Afrique, retrouvé à Mayence*, Collection des études augustiniennes: Série Antiquité 147 (Paris: Institut d'Études Augustiniennes, 1996). Puchniak provides an interesting analysis of the sermon identified as Dolbeau 6, in which he proposes that Augustine, preaching in a pagan context on North Africa in 404, was circumspect in his use of deification language lest it be misunderstood in pagan terms; yet he also takes the occasion of this sermon to introduce a

not employ the language of *deificare*, other soteriological metaphors closely associated with deification—for example, divine adoption, new creation, and especially incorporation with Christ—deeply shape his understanding of Christian salvation.[47]

Apart from one often-quoted passage referring to 2 Peter 1:4 in Leo the Great's *Sermon 21* for Christmas Day,[48] Augustine and Dionysius were the most frequently used patristic sources for teachings on deification in the medieval West. Eriugena, whose works include a commentary on Dionysius's *Celestial Hierarchy*, made the earliest complete Latin translation of Dionysius in the ninth century.[49] In his *Periphyseon*, Eriugena attempts to reconcile Dionysian apophaticism with the Augustinian confidence that the ultimate human vocation is to see God.[50] Drawing also from Maximus, he proposes that the vision of God mediated through the divine theophanies—images, or reflections of the divine essence—deifies the saints.[51] Other translations of the Dionysian *corpus* also circulated in the twelfth and thirteenth centuries. Henri Dondaine notes that Albert the Great and Thomas Aquinas used Eriugena's translation and that of John Sarracenus (1167). But a text with notable influence in the Franciscan tradition was Thomas Gallus's early thirteenth-century *Extractio*, a modified paraphrase of the whole Dionysian *corpus*, which posited a union of dilection with God superior to intellectual cognition to explain Dionysius's doctrine of apophaticism. Dondaine remarks insightfully that the version used by different schools influenced their history of interpretation.[52] John Damascene's *De fide orthodoxa*, translated in the twelfth century by Burgundio of Pisa and known to Thomas Aquinas, was also a source of Greek patristic teaching, including that of the Cappadocians, Cyril, Dionysius, and Maximus.[53]

---

polemical contrast between true deification and the falsehood of idols. "Augustine's Conception of Deification, Revisited," 126–33.

47. David Meconi, SJ, *The One Christ: St. Augustine's Theology of Deification* (Washington, DC: Catholic University of America Press, 2013).

48. "Agamus ergo, dilectissimi, gratias Deo Patri, per Filium ejus, in Spiritu sancto, qui propter multam misericordiam suam, qua dilexit nos, misertus est nostri; 'et cum essemus mortui peccatis, convivificavit nos Christo,' ut essemus in ipso nova creatura, novumque figmentum. Deponamus ergo veterem hominem cum actibus suis; et adepti participationem generationis Christi, carnis renuntiemus operibus. Agnosce, o Christiane, dignitatem tuam, et 'divinae consors factus naturae,' noli in veterem vilitatem degeneri conversatione redire." PL 54.192.

49. Paul Rorem, *Eriugena's Commentary on the Dionysian Celestial Hierarchy* (Toronto: Pontifical Institute of Mediaeval Studies, 2005).

50. See Dondaine, "L'objet et le 'medium,'" 63–65.

51. *Periphyseon* I.9 (CCCM 161). See also Eriugena's treatment of the theophanies in discussing Jn 1:18 ("no one has ever seen God"); *Comm. Jn.* I, 25. Édouard Jeauneau, ed., *Jean Scot: Commentaire sur l'Evangile de Jean*, Sources Chrétiennes 180 (Paris: Cerf, 1972), 114–27.

52. Dondaine, "L'objet et le 'medium,'" 68–71.

53. E.g., John's description in *De fide* 3 and 4 of the orthodox teaching on Christ's deified

Twelfth-century monastic authors, such as Bernard of Clairvaux, primarily presented deification in terms of an ascent to God through the transformation of love.[54] Scripture was the foundational source for reflection on deification for monastics and scholastics alike. The Scripture text "he who is united to the Lord becomes one spirit with him" *qui adhaeret Domino unus spiritus est* (1 Cor 6:17), a foundation of Cistercian mysticism, was central to Bernard's mystical theology,[55] according to which the soul formed in the divine image is conformed to the likeness of its spouse the Word, and so deified, by a union of wills brought about through love.[56] This verse was also a favorite of Albertus Magnus (who sometimes quotes Bernard in connection with it) in discussions of charity and union with God,[57] and was significant for Aquinas in his treatments of the role of charity and wisdom in union with God through participation in Christ's sonship.[58] Not surprisingly, it also played a role in twelfth- and thirteenth-century debates over Peter Lombard's identification of charity and the Holy Spirit.[59]

---

humanity, and the deifying power of the Eucharist, drawing from sources such as Cyril of Alexandria and Maximus. Thomas refers to this text, e.g., in *ST* III q79 a1, a8. A translation of John's text is available in *De Fide Orthodoxa: Versions of Burgundio and Cerbanus*, ed. E. M. Buytaert (St. Bonaventure, NY: Franciscan Institute, 1955).

54. M.-A. Fracheboud, *Dictionnaire de Spiritualité*, vol. 3, s.v. "Divinisation—Moyen Age—auteurs monastiques du 12e siècle," 1405ff.

55. Étienne Gilson, *The Mystical Theology of St. Bernard*, trans. A. H. C. Downes (Kalamazoo, MI: Cistercian, 1990), 119–29, 238–39n177.

56. See, e.g., Bernard of Clairvaux, *De diligendo Deo* 10.28: "O amor sanctus et castus! o dulcis et suavis affectio! o pura et defecata intentio voluntatis! eo certe defecatior et purior, quo in ea de proprio nil jam admistum relinquitur: eo suavior et dulcior, quo totum divinum est quod sentitur. Sic affici, deificari est." PL 182, 991A; *In Cantica canticorum* 61, 62, 71, 80–83.

57. E.g., *Sup. Ioh.* 2.11, in *Opera Omnia*, vol. 24, ed. A. Borgnet (Paris: Vivès, 1899), 100b—"Secundae nuptiae sunt Dei et hominis in uno spiritu in gratia charitatis conjuncti. I ad Corinth. vi, 17: 'Qui adhaeret Domino, unus spiritus est'"—*Summa theologiae* II tr4 q14 m4 a2, in *Opera Omnia*, vol. 32, ed. A. Borgnet (Paris: Vivès, 1895), 201ab—Dilectio autem charitatis elevat creaturam supra se, ita quod totam se reponat in dilecto increato quod est Deus, etiamsi nihil debet sibi fieri. Et ut dicit Bernardus, confitetur quam bonus, non quoniam sibi bonus, et adhaeret Deo in uno spiritu. I ad Corinth. VI, 17: 'Qui adhaeret Domino, unus spiritus est'"—*ST* II tr10 q37 m1, in *Opera Omnia*, vol. 32, 407a—"Adhuc, Dionysius in eodem capite: 'Interpretatio hierarchiae est quantum est possibile similitudo ad Deum et unitas.' Quaeratur ergo, Quomodo sit similitudo, et quomodo unitas? Et si forte dicatur, quod est unitas in consensione voluntatum, sicut dicit Apostolus, I ad Corinth. VI, 17: 'Qui adhaeret Domino, unus spiritus est.' Hoc videtur parum esse: quia etiam hic in via multi per charitatem sic Deo uniuntur."

58. See chapter 4.

59. Lombard, *Sent.* I d17. *Magistri Petri Lombardi Sententiae in IV Libris Distinctae* (Rome: Collegium S. Bonaventurae, 1971), 141–52, esp. 142. E.g., Alexander Hales, in his "Glossa on the *Sentences* I.17.25," quoting Bernard's Sermon 71 on the Song of Songs, argues that God and human can become one not in essence but only by an agreement of wills. *Magistri Alexandri de*

Thirteenth-century treatments of deification often take place in the context of questions related to the beatific vision and—because of the introduction of Aristotelian texts—to the need for a created medium of grace (and glory) in the soul.[60] By the thirteenth century, the great majority of scholastic authors, rejecting the opinion of Peter Lombard, held there to be a created form of grace (or charity) divinely infused into the soul, assimilating it to God and making it pleasing to him. The Halesian *Summa theologica*, widely read especially in the Franciscan schools, defines this assimilation brought about by grace in terms of deiformity,[61] which is a likeness of the whole Trinity insofar as it gives a similitude of the divine attributes appropriated to each Person: power to the Father, truth to the Son, and goodness to the Holy Spirit.[62] Bonaventure, often drawing much from both Augustine and Dionysius, speaks of deification in terms of the condescension of grace and return of the soul to God through love. Grace places a deiform *habitus* in the soul (specifically, in the will), which makes a new creation of fallen nature, assimilating it to the Trinity, making it pleasing, and uniting it to God.[63] Beatitude consists in an "inflowing of God in the soul, which is at once deiformity and satiety;"[64] the deiformity of the light of glory "makes the eye of the soul able to see God."[65] Albert

---

Hales Glossa in quotuor libros sententiarum Petri Lombardi (Florence: Quaracchi, Collegium S. Bonaventura, 1951), 177–78. Aquinas makes a similar argument in *De virtutibus* q2 a1 ad3, where he addresses Lombard's claim: "Cum dicitur, 'qui adhaeret Deo, unus spiritus est'; non designatur unitas substantiae; sed unitas affectus, quae est inter amantem et amatum." See chapter 5 for further discussion of Aquinas's response to Lombard.

60. See chapter 1 for further discussion of debates concerning the beatific vision. The following summary review of early thirteenth-century views on deification is indebted to Humbert-Thomas Conus, *Dictionnaire de Spiritualité*, vol. 3, s.v. "Divinisation—Moyen Age—théologiens du 13e siècle," 1413ff.

61. Alexander Hales, "*Summa theol.*, III inq. 1 tr. 1 q2 c1 a1 sol," in *Doctor irrefragibilis Alexandri de Hales Ordinis Minorum Summa Theologica iussu et auctoritate Rmi P. Pacifici Perantoni*, vol. 4 (Florence: Quaracchi, Collegium S. Bonaventura, 1948).

62. Ibid., tr. 1 q6 c3 and 6.

63. See, e.g., *Breviloquium* 5.1. *Opera Omnia*, vol. 5 (Florence: Quaracchi, Collegium S. Bonaventura, 1882), 252a–253b. Christopher Cullen observes that "the East has tended to understand salvation in terms of theosis or divinization, the West in terms of justification. Bonaventure's doctrine of deiformity seems to be the middle ground between the two views. Our being reconciled to God, while consisting in the grace of justification, also involves being made Godlike." *Bonaventure* (New York: Oxford University Press, 2006), 156. Cullen notes the influence of both Dionysius and Augustine on Bonaventure's theology of grace: Bonaventure describes grace as "hierarchizing" the soul (*Itinerarium* 4.4; *Opera Omnia* 5, 307a), while he also draws from Augustine in his treatment of grace and free will (e.g., *Brevil.* 5.3; *Opera Omnia* 5, 255b). *Bonaventure*, 157–59.

64. *In Sententiae* IV d49 part1 a1 q1. *Opera Omnia* 4, 569b.

65. *In Sententiae* III, d14, a1 q3 ad6. *Opera Omnia* 4, 306b.

the Great stresses even more strongly the necessity of a created medium in the re-
creation of the soul by grace and its elevation to the beatific vision in glory, a medium that, far from placing an obstacle between the soul and God, is itself a new disposition of the soul given by God to permit union with him.[66] Albert, who wrote
extensive commentaries on the Dionysian *corpus* and for whom Dionysius was a
frequent authority, underscores the idea that grace is a perfection of the soul that
makes it deiform, assimilated to God and participating in him.[67] As Maria Burger
has shown, when Albert was writing his Dionysian commentaries, Thomas worked
extensively as his student assistant, commenting in his own hand on comparisons
of Eriugena's and Sarracen's translations of Dionysius.[68] In Albert's commentaries
on the Gospels, he also speaks of deification in terms of filiation, by assimilation to
the Son through the Holy Spirit.[69] Thomas draws from the traditional vocabulary
of deification in a structured way throughout the course of the *Summa* to suit his
pedagogical purposes, continually adding theological depth to his depiction of the
rational creature's deifying progress toward likeness and union with God.

66. *De divinis nominibus* 13.27; *Sent.* I d17, II d26 a1; in *Opera Omnia*, vols. 14, 25, 27, ed. A.
Borgnet (Paris: Vivès, 1892–93),.

67. *De coel. hier.* 1.1, 3.1; *Sent.* II d26 a10 ad2; in *Opera Omnia*, vols. 14, 27.

68. Maria Burger, "Thomas Aquinas' Glosses on the Dionysius Commentaries of Albert
the Great in Codex 30 of the Cologne Cathedral Library," in *Via Alberti: Texte—Quellen—Interpretationen*, Subsidia Albertina 2, ed. Ludger Honnefelder, Hannes Mohle, and Susana Bullido del Barrio, trans. M. Tracey (Münster: Aschendorff, 2009), 561–82. Including his own commentary *De divinibus nominibus*, Thomas's own works are replete with references to Dionysius;
M.-D. Chenu notes that Dionysius is quoted 1,702 times, the second-most frequent authority
after Augustine. *Toward Understanding Saint Thomas: Translated with Authorized Corrections
and Bibliographical Additions*, Library of Living Catholic Thought, trans. A. M. Landry and D.
Hughes (Chicago: H. Regnery, 1964), 127. For discussions, see, e.g., T. C. O'Brien, "Appendix
3: The Dionysian Corpus," in Blackfriar's *Summa*, vol. 14, ed. Thomas Gilby, OP (New York:
McGraw-Hill, 1975), 182–93; Fran O'Rourke, *Pseudo-Dionysius and the Metaphysics of Aquinas*
(Notre Dame, IN: University of Notre Dame Press, 2005); Andrew Hofer, OP, "Dionysian Elements in Thomas Aquinas' Christology: A Case of the Authority and Ambiguity of Pseudo-
Dionysius," *Thomist* 72 (2008): 409–42; and works by Ysabel de Andia such as "'Pati divina'
chez Denys l'Aréopagite, Thomas d'Aquin et Jacques Maritain," in *Saint Thomas d'Aquin*, Les
Cahiers d'Histoire de la Philosophie, ed. Thierry-Dominique Humbrecht (Paris: Cerf, 2011),
549–89, and *L'Union à Dieu chez Denys l'Aréopagite* (Leiden: E. J. Brill, 1992).

69. *In Matt.* 6.9; *In Luc.* 11.2; *In Ioh.* 6.44; in *Opera Omnia*, vols. 20, 23, 24.

The Disputed Question of "Created Grace" in the *Summa theologiae*

Anna Williams has pointed out that in the *Summa theologiae* Thomas scarcely mentions the category of "created grace" (*gratia creata*) as such. In the context of her study of Aquinas and Gregory Palamas, as traditional representatives of Eastern and Western views of sanctification, Williams seeks to map the common ground between the two traditions regarding the doctrine of deification.[1] The question of created grace is "one of the thorniest points of contention between East and West." But Williams raises the interesting and significant question of whether Thomas really held this doctrine as firmly as has been supposed, or even if he perhaps avoided it, given the dearth of references to the term in the *Summa*.[2] The answer to this question is germane to principal points made in this book; if Thomas hesitated to use the notion of created grace, it would undermine the argument for the importance of grace precisely as an interior principle, infused but proper to the creature, in his view of the human journey to beatitude.

I would note first that the idea of the grace given to the human person as something created is not absent from the *Summa*, and, *pace* Williams, the terminology does appear in the questions on grace.[3] Nevertheless, while Thomas certainly re-

---

1. A. N. Williams, *The Ground of Union: Deification in Aquinas and Palamas* (New York: Oxford University Press, 1999). See the introduction to this volume for further discussion of Williams's work, which played an important role in stimulating contemporary discussion of Aquinas's doctrine of deification.

2. Williams, *Ground of Union*, 87.

3. Ibid. Williams states that no use of the term *gratia creata* appears in the treatise on grace; however, in *ST* Ia-IIae q110 a2 ad3, Thomas says that according to the way in which accidents are said to have being, by inhering in a subject that has being, "grace is said to be created, in that humans are created according to it; that is, they are constituted in new being, from nothing, that is, not from merits; according to Eph 2 (10): 'Created in Christ Jesus in good work.'" "Pro-

tains the notion in the *Summa theologiae* of the "new creation" (cf. Gal 6:15) in association with grace and the graced image, it is true that explicit references to created grace are much reduced in comparison to his more frequent use of the term in
parallel places in earlier works. One might add to Williams's evidence, for instance,
parallel articles in earlier works to *ST* q110 a1, which asks "whether grace implies
anything in the soul." In the *Scriptum* the title is "whether grace is something created in the soul" and in the *De veritate* "whether grace is something created positively
in the soul."[4] Williams challenges the validity of speaking of created grace in relation to the *Summa* at all, given Thomas's "extreme hesitation in using it,"[5] and spec-
ulates that he "avoids" it because "he saw precisely the kind of problem with it that
the Orthodox see"; that is, it seems to place God and his grace on opposite sides of
the absolute distinction between Uncreated and created.[6]

Williams acknowledges that Thomas "insists on the working of divine grace
through forms established in the human recipient of grace," but argues that he adverts to grace as created only as a way of signaling the finite creaturely status of
the human subject in which its effects are received.[7] Williams draws this conclusion from a primary reference for Thomas's use of "created grace" in *ST* IIIa q7 a11,
which asks whether the grace of Christ is infinite. There Thomas refers in the *sed
contra* to grace as "something created in the soul" in preparation for his argument
that Christ's habitual grace is finite with respect to its existence in Christ's finite human soul, though not with respect to its nature as a universal principle of grace for
humanity. Williams points out that Thomas uses the term in this instance to make
a statement not about grace in general but about the created nature of Christ's human soul, to which the grace of Christ, in itself infinite, is conformed. Thomas
writes in the *corpus* that Christ's habitual grace as a being "must be a finite being,
since it is in the soul of Christ, as in a subject, and Christ's soul is a creature having
a finite capacity; hence the being of grace cannot be infinite, since it cannot exceed
its subject."[8] Williams interprets this to mean that "the assumption of his notion of

---

prie loquendo, nullum accidens neque fit neque corrumpitur, sed dicitur fieri vel corrumpi, secundum quod subiectum incipit vel desinit esse in actu secundum illud accidens. Et secundum
hoc etiam gratia dicitur creari, ex eo quod homines secundum ipsam creantur, idest in novo
esse constituuntur, ex nihilo, idest non ex meritis; secundum illud ad Ephes. II, 'creati in Christo Iesu in operibus bonis.'" Cf. also *ST* Ia q43 a3, discussed in chapter 1 and mentioned below,
where Thomas clearly refers to grace as a created gift.

4. Cf. *Scriptum* bk2 d26 a1; *DV* q27 a1.   5. Williams, *Ground of Union*, 87.
6. Ibid., 88.   7. Ibid., 88–89.

8. A similar argument can be found in Alexander Hales's *Summa theologica* about grace in
general, in response to an objection that grace cannot be created because it is a good worthy of
infinite good. "Nullum bonum creatum potest esse dignum bono infinito; sed gratia est bonum
dignum bono infinito, quia facit animam dignam bono infinito; ergo non est creata": "Gratia

created grace is that grace is anhypostatic," assuming the "limitations of its subject when enhypostasized."[9] So "the effects of grace in human persons are analogous to [the] essential grace," which "most truly and fundamentally, is *gratia increata*, the Holy Spirit, God *ipse*."[10] That is, to call grace created is only to name the effect of uncreated grace in the created person, a transformation "changing the subject's status from creature to Creator," for "grace considered as gift is not created, nor is the effect of grace created."[11]

In this regard, Williams finds it significant that in *ST* I-IIae q110 a1, "in responding to an objection using the term *created grace*, Aquinas omits to use the term himself."[12] The second objector argues that God quickens the soul immediately, as the soul quickens the body: "Therefore nothing can come as a medium between God and the soul. Hence grace implies nothing created in the soul." Thomas replies by distinguishing between God's efficient causality of the soul's life and the soul's formal causality of the life of the body, taking advantage of the analogy to introduce the notion of grace as a form caused by God in the soul, informing it without medium just as the soul informs matter. As Thomas goes on to say in a2, this form is habitual grace. God "gives life" to the soul by causing in it the new form of grace.

In response to Williams's argument, in the parallel articles to q110 a1 in the *Scriptum* and *De veritate*—although Thomas uses the language of "created grace" frequently enough, in accord with common scholastic categories for this *quaestio*[13]—he

---

creata uno modo est finita, alio modo infinita. Simpliciter enim finita est quantum ad subiectum in quo est; in comparatione vero infinita est quantum ad illud a quo est, quia est a gratia increata, quae est infinita Bonitas." The *Summa* goes on to say that grace can be said to be finite with respect to its essence, but infinite according to its power, in that it can make the soul worthy of infinite good, "for the infinite good, which is uncreated grace is *per illam* [i.e., created grace] possessed and received by the rational creature." *Summa theol.* III inq I tract. I qII ad6.

9. Williams's statement that, nevertheless, "grace considered as gift is not created," based on ad1 (*Ground of Union*, 89), is unwarranted, however; there Thomas explains the scriptural text "God does not give the Spirit by measure [to his Son]" and explains that this can refer to habitual grace insofar as Christ is the giver of grace; thus insofar as he is the principle for the habitual grace given to others. It is somewhat problematic to make Thomas's discussion of Christ's habitual grace the basis of conclusions about whether he understands the gift of grace in human persons ordinarily to be finite—i.e., created—because unlike other humans Christ had the fullness and complete perfection of habitual grace that in a sense could be said to be infinite (cf. *DV* q29 a4).

10. Williams, *Ground of Union*, 89.   11. Ibid.

12. Ibid., 88.

13. The distinction between uncreated and created grace in connection with the gift of habitual grace by the Holy Spirit seems to have developed in the course of reflection on Lombard's d26 in book II of the *Sentences*, on operating and cooperating grace, and therefore in the context of the question of Pelagianism and the cooperation of grace and the free will with

presents essentially the same objection and reply as in the *Summa* in both places, referring to created grace in the objection and to God's efficient causality of the soul's life versus the soul's formal causality in the reply (with no mention there of created grace either).[14] It seems, then, that the difference between objection and reply in q110 a1 that Williams observes is not enough to warrant the claim that Thomas is particularly "avoiding" the use of the term here; he is simply bringing forward earlier material. Nevertheless, in the whole of a1, the term does not appear at all, unlike the earlier treatments; Thomas uses only language associated with the notion of grace as a *habitus*, God's bestowal of a form in the soul, language also present in the earlier treatments (where it is clearly identified with grace as "something created in the soul") but that Thomas apparently considers sufficient in the *Summa*. A similar shift can be observed in a comparison of *DV* q29 a1, "whether there is created grace in Christ," and *ST* IIIa q7 a1, "whether in the soul of Christ there was any habitual grace."[15]

Is Thomas avoiding reference to created grace while retaining the language of habitual grace in his later work in order to keep God and his grace on the same side of the distinction between uncreated and created, as Williams proposes? Williams is attempting to delineate the difficult question of how Thomas "keeps two poles together in creative tension": he both maintains the Christian distinction between Creator and creature and affirms "the reality of the interaction between these two ontologically distinct realms."[16] As Williams recognizes, Thomas employs the doctrine of participation throughout the *Summa* to negotiate this relationship.[17] Certainly, "created grace" names the effect of uncreated grace in the transformation of the human person, as all created effects are participated likenesses of the divine perfections that are realized in the subject. Yet Williams seems to overstate the case for Thomas's intention to keep grace on the divine side of the divide between Uncreated and created. This is most clearly seen in her related discussion of Thomas on created charity:

---

which Lombard is dealing via Augustinian texts. The distinction seems to be found first in 1245 in the Halesian *Summa theol.* (III inq I tract. I qII), in which it is specifically asked, *utrum gratia sit res creata vel increata?* This question, which became standard, is preceded, however, by Alexander's own reference to "gratia, communiter dicta ad creatam et increatam" in the *Glossa Sententiarum* II dist. 26.6, indicating that this language was already current in the schools. Cf. Albertus Magnus, *In II Sent.* d26 a1; Bonaventure, *II Sent.* d26 q2; Thomas Aquinas, *Scriptum* bk2 d26 a1.

14. There are some interesting differences in the use of authorities, however, and in the *Scriptum* Thomas does not name God's causality of the soul's life as efficient, merely remarking that God is not the formal cause of the soul (unless as exemplar) and so vivifies the soul through a mediating form. Cf. *Scriptum* bk2 d26 a1 obs, ad5; *DV* q27 a1 ob1, ad1.

15. Cf. *Scriptum* bk3 d13 a1.   16. Williams, *Ground of Union*, 81.

17. E.g., ibid., 95.

When Aquinas refers to charity as an accident (II-II.24,4 ad 3), he presumably does not mean it is so in any absolute sense; such an interpretation is ruled out by his previous identification of charity with divine essence. However, his terming charity an accident corresponds with his notion of the human person's charity as created; when charity dwells within a human subject, it remains God's possession and therefore, in some sense, remains an alien element within the human being.[18]

Such a view seems to diminish the full sense in which the participated perfection of charity (and grace) is properly *of* the creature, precisely by virtue of its origin in the divine exemplar.

Thomas's doctrine of participation permits creatures to truly and properly possess the substantial divine perfections in a participated manner without ontological confusion. A principle of this doctrine is that the participating subject receives a participated perfection belonging in totality to the source in a particular manner that limits or restricts it according to the mode of the subject. Every participated perfection in creatures, beginning with existence itself, is an effect of its uncreated divine cause, a certain determinate negation, or limited reception of its infinite participated source; in Thomas's later works he speaks of this in terms of the limitation of act by potency.[19] But this does not make existence anhypostatic, for instance. Even perfections belonging to nature, such as existence and goodness, are ways in which creatures participate in what is uncreated and substantial only in God. As similitudes of the divine perfections, they no less properly belong to the creature through its substantial form, which is constituted by the way in which God knows the creature as a likeness of himself.[20]

All participated perfections can in an extended sense even be said to be accidental in that the perfections themselves are not the substantial form of the creature. Thomas sometimes calls participated *esse* an accident in that *esse* is substantial only in God; however, he carefully distinguishes this from the Avicennian position that *esse* is something differing from and superadded to the essence from outside. Rather, *esse* is the actuality of the substance, that by which the essence is what it is.[21] In the case of grace, Thomas terms it an accidental, not substantial, form of the

18. Ibid., 81. Chapter 5 touches on Thomas's response to Peter Lombard's doctrine that charity is the Holy Spirit *ipse*, on which Williams is commenting here.

19. William Norris Clarke, *Explorations in Metaphysics* (Notre Dame, IN: University of Notre Dame Press, 1994), 93–96.

20. *ST* Ia q6 aa3–4.

21. See, e.g., *Quodlibet* II q2 a1 ad2: "Esse est accidens, non quasi per accidens se habens, sed quasi actualitas cuiuslibet substantiae," and Rudi te Velde's discussion of this text in *Participation and Substantiality in Thomas Aquinas* (Leiden: E. J. Brill, 1995), 73–76. Joseph Owens points out that because being gives actuality to the created essence, the act of being is accidental to the essence just in the sense that it is a prior constituent necessary to make the essence a re-

soul because it is higher than the soul as a participation in the divine goodness that is above human nature; it participates in what is substantial only in God: "What is substantially in God, becomes accidental in the soul participating the divine goodness."[22] In addition, charity is a virtue, which by definition is an accidental habit.[23] Charity and grace differ from other accidental forms, however, in that as they make the creature participate in a higher nature they are more excellent than the soul in which they have being, even though the accidental mode of being per se is less perfect than that of substance.[24] Thomas's characterization of created grace and charity as accidental forms does not imply that he considers them to be "alien elements" within the human being; rather, by teaching that they involve a participation in a higher nature, he is building on a trajectory that is in continuity with his teaching on creation while still accounting for the radically superadded character of the order of grace as the new creation.

Thomas has been at pains before in his treatment of grace in the *Summa* to insist on the properly intrinsic quality of a *habitus* in his general consideration of human action—and to identify grace as an entitative *habitus* is to say that it properly and actually belongs to the creature as an intrinsic created quality. Thomas's general displacement of the language of created grace—though it is still present to some degree—by that of habitual grace in the *Summa* fits well into the overall scheme that he has established in this work. He certainly considers habitual grace to be a created gift in continuity with all of the ways in which the divine perfections can be increasingly participated in the hierarchy of creatures—a scheme he has fully established in discussing the divine *ordinatio*. This is not to confuse the gifts of grace with those of nature; grace is clearly a second gift, a new infused disposition that elevates nature, but for all that, the same principles that apply to all ways of participating the divine perfections are in place. We have seen in earlier parts of the *Summa* that the new disposition of the light of grace proportions the created intellect to God, making of the soul itself a kind of medium by which God is known more perfectly, as the image is increasingly likened to God by an assimilation to the Word and Love. The form of grace is a new disposition of the soul that likens it to God, so that God may be possessed and enjoyed. It is a change, a new quality or perfection in the creature, which allows it to enjoy the uncreated gift of the divine

---

ality, not as an accidental subsequent to the essence. The primary efficient cause gives the act of being by participation, and in doing so constitutes the essence. "The Accidental and Essential Character of Being in the Doctrine of St. Thomas Aquinas," in *St. Thomas Aquinas on the Existence of God: Collected Papers of Joseph Owen* (New York: State University of New York Press, 1980), 92–93.

22. *ST* Ia-IIae q110 a2 ad2.

23. *ST* IIa-IIae q23 a3 ob1.

24. *ST* Ia-IIae q110 a2 ad2; IIa-IIae q23 a3 ad3; IIa-IIae q24 a4 ad3.

Persons dwelling within it. Thomas distinguishes early in the *Summa* between the gift of the divine Persons themselves and the "created gift" of grace that allows the creature to enjoy the divine indwelling.[25]

In contrast to Williams, I argue that Thomas's move in the *Summa* away from the language of "created grace," while maintaining the notion of habitual grace, does not indicate "extreme hesitation" on his part to use the former because it might suggest a false distinction between God and his grace.[26] Rather, I propose that he certainly considers grace, as a participation in the divine nature by the creature, to be created—that is, newly and properly belonging to *this* creature as an intrinsic quality—and still refers to it as such occasionally. But in the *Summa* Thomas has already established that the absolute distinction between God and his creatures does not prevent, and indeed is the necessary context for, any divine perfection to be shared with creatures. To be created means to participate in the divine likeness from the first moment of existence, and God works in his rational creatures by bestowing upon them forms as principles of their own activities that will bring them to their proper ends. Thomas places the gift of habitual grace within the larger framework of the divine *ordinatio*, and preferentially using the language of *habitus* emphasizes not so much that it is, like all perfections, a created gift, but that it is an intrinsic quality that brings about the free operation of its rational subject.

25. *ST* Ia q43 a3 ad1.
26. Williams, *Ground of Union*, 88.

Bibliography

Primary Texts

Works of Thomas Aquinas

"*Collationes Credo in Deum.*" Latin text (Leonine edition) and English translation in *The Sermon-Conferences of St. Thomas Aquinas on the Apostle's Creed*, edited by Nicholas Ayo. Notre Dame, IN: University of Notre Dame Press, 1988.

Compendium theologiae seu Brevis compilatio theologiae ad fratrem Raynaldum: Opera omnia iussu Leonis XIII P. M. edita, vol. 42, 5–191. Rome: Editori di San Tommaso, 1979. Translated by Cyril Vollert as *Light of Faith: The Compendium of Theology*. St. Louis: B. Herder, 1947. Reprint, Manchester, NH: Sophia Institute Press, 1993.

"*Contra errores Graecorum ad Urbanum papam.*" In *Opera omnia iussu Leonis XIII P. M. edita*, vol. 40A. Rome: Santa Sabina, 1969.

De ente et essentia: Opera Omnia, vol. 43, 315–81. Rome: Editori di San Tommaso, 1976. Translated by Armand Maurer as *On Being and Essence*, 2nd ed. Toronto: PIMS, 1968.

"*De perfectione.*" In *Opera omnia iussu Leonis XIII P. M. edita*, vol. 41B, *De perfectione spiritualis vitae*. Rome: Santa Sabina, 1970.

"*Expositio Libri Boetii de Hebdomadibus.*" In *Opuscula Theologica*, vol. 2, edited by M. Calcaterra. Turin: Marietti, 1954.

In duodecim libros Metaphysicorum Aristotelis expositio, 2nd ed. Edited by M. R. Cathala and R. M. Spiazzi. Turin: Marietti, 1971.

Lectura romana in primum Sententiarum Petri Lombardi. Edited by Leonard Boyle and John Boyle. Toronto: Pontifical Institute of Mediaeval Studies, 2006. Translated by Peter Kwasniewski and Joseph Bohn in *On Love and Charity: Readings from the "Commentary on the Sentences of Peter Lombard" by Thomas Aquinas*. Washington, DC: Catholic University of America Press, 2008.

"*Officium de festo Corporis Christi ad mandatum Urbani Papae IV dictum festum instituentis.*" In *Opera omnia*, vol. 29, edited by E. Fretté and P. Maré, 335–43. Paris: Apud Ludovicum Vivès, 1876.

Opera Omnia. Iussu impensaque Leonis XIII P. M. edita. Rome: Ex Typographia Polyglotta S. C. de Propaganda Fide, 1882–.

Scriptum super libros sententiarum, 4 vols. Edited by P. Mandonnet and M. F. Moos. Paris: P. Lethielleux, 1933–47. Translated by Peter Kwasniewski and Joseph Bohn in *On Love* and Charity: Readings from the "Commentary on the Sentences of Peter Lombard" by *Thomas Aquinas.* Washington, DC: Catholic University of America Press, 2008.

S. *Thomae Aquinatis Catena aurea in quatuor Evangelia,* 4 vols., 2nd ed. Edited by A. Guarenti. Turin: Marietti, 1953. Translated by M. Pattison, J. D. Dalgairns, and T. D. Ryder as *Catena aurea: Commentary on the Four Gospels Collected Out of the Works of the Early Church Fathers,* 4 vols., 1st ed. Introduction by J. H. Newman. Parker, Oxford, 1841. Reprint, Southampton: Saint Austin Press, 1997.

S. *Thomae Aquinatis Liber de Veritate Catholicae Fidei contra errores Infidelium.* Edited by Ceslai Pera. Turin: Marietti, 1961. Translated by Charles J. O'Neil as *Saint Thomas Aquinas: Summa contra Gentiles.* Notre Dame, IN: University of Notre Dame Press, 1975.

S. *Thomae Aquinatis Quaestiones disputatae,* vol. 1, *De Veritate,* 9th ed. Edited by Raymond Spiazzi. Turin: Marietti, 1953. Translated by Robert W. Mulligan, James V. McGlynn, and Robert W. Schmidt as *Truth,* 3 vols. Chicago: Henry Regnery, 1952–54.

S. *Thomae Aquinatis Quaestiones disputatae,* vol. 2, *De Virtutibus: De caritate.* Edited by P. Bazzi et al. Turin: Marietti, 1965. Translated by Lottie H. Kendzierski as *Saint Thomas Aquinas On Charity.* Milwaukee: Marquette University Press, 1960.

S. *Thomae Aquinatis Quaestiones disputatae,* vol. 2, *Quaestiones disputatae de potentia,* 10th ed. Edited by P. M. Pession. Turin: Marietti, 1965.

S. *Thomae Aquinatis Quaestiones disputatae de anima: Opera Omnia,* vol. 24/1. Edited by B. C. Bazan. Rome-Paris: Commissio Leonina-Éditions du Cerf, 1996.

S. *Thomae Aquinatis Quaestiones disputatae de malo: Opera omnia,* vol. 23. Rome-Paris: Commissio Leonina-J. Vrin, 1982.

Summa theologiae. Instituti Studiorum Medievalium Ottaviensis, 5 vols. Ottawa: Commissio Piana, 1953. Translated as *Fathers of the English Dominican Province.* New York: Benzinger Brothers, 1948. Reprint, Allen, TX: Christian Classics, 1981.

"Super Epistolam ad Colossenses Lectura." In *Super Epistolas S. Pauli Lectura,* vol. 2, edited by R. Cai, 125–61. Rome: Marietti, 1953.

"Super Epistolam ad Ephesios Lectura." In *Super Epistolas S. Pauli Lectura,* vol. 2, edited by R. Cai, 1–87. Rome: Marietti, 1953. Translated by F. R. Larcher and M. L. Lamb in *Commentary on the Letters of Saint Paul to the Galatians and Ephesians.* Edited by J. Mortenson and E. Alarcón. Lander, WY: Aquinas Institute for the Study of Sacred Doctrine, 2012.

"Super Epistolam ad Galatas Lectura." In *Super Epistolas S. Pauli Lectura,* vol. 1, edited by R. Cai, 563–649. Rome: Marietti, 1953.

"Super Epistolam ad Hebraeos Lectura." In *Super Epistolas S. Pauli Lectura,* vol. 2, edited by R. Cai, 335–506. Rome: Marietti, 1953. Translated by C. Baer in *Commentary on the Epistle to the Hebrews.* Edited by R. M. McInerny. South Bend, IN: St. Augustine's Press, 2005.

"Super Epistolam ad Philipenses Lectura." In *Super Epistolas S. Pauli Lectura,* vol. 2, edited by R. Cai, 89–123. Rome: Marietti, 1953.

Super Epistolam ad Romanos Lectura, in *Super Epistolas S. Pauli Lectura,* vol. 1. Edited by R. Cai, 1–230. Rome: Marietti, 1953.

"*Super Epistolam ad Titum Lectura.*" In *Super Epistolas S. Pauli Lectura*, vol. 2, edited by R. Cai, 301–26. Rome: Marietti, 1953.

Super Evangelium S. Ioannis Lectura, 5th ed. Edited by Raphael Cai. Turin: Marietti, 1952. Translated by James A. Weisheipl and Fabian R. Larcher as *St. Thomas Aquinas, Commentary on the Gospel of St. John*. Albany, NY: Magi Books, 1980.

Super librum De Causis expositio. Edited by H. D. Saffrey. Fribourg-Louvain: Société Philosophique-Nauwelaerts, 1954.

"*Super primam Epistolam ad Corinthios Lectura.*" In *Super Epistolas S. Pauli Lectura*, vol. 1, edited by R. Cai. Rome: Marietti, 1953.

"*Super Psalmos.*" In *Opera omnia*, vol. 14, *In psalmos Davidis expositio*, 148–312. Parma: Typis Petri Fiaccadori, 1863.

"*Super secundam Epistolam ad Corinthios Lectura.*" In *Super Epistolas S. Pauli Lectura*, vol. 1, edited by R. Cai, 437–561. Rome: Marietti, 1953.

Other Primary Texts

Abelard, Peter. *Theologia summa boni.* Edited by Constant J. Mews. Turnhout: Brepols, 1987.

Albertus Magnus. *Opera Omnia.* Edited by A. Borgnet. Paris, 1890–99.

Alexander of Hales. *Doctor irrefragibilis Alexandri de Hales Ordinis Minorum Summa Theologica iussu et auctoritate Rmi P. Pacifici Perantoni*, vol. 4. Florence: Quaracchi, Collegium S. Bonaventura, 1948.

———. *Magistri Alexandri de Hales Glossa in quattuor libros sententiarum Petri Lombardi.* Bibliotheca franciscana scholastica medii aevi 12. Florence: Quaracchi, Collegium S. Bonaventura, 1951.

Aristotle. *The Basic Works of Aristotle.* Edited by Richard McKeon. New York: Random House, 1941.

Augustine. "*Epistula 140 (ad Honoratus).*" In *S. Aureli Augustini Hipponensis Episcopi Epistulae 124–184.* Corpus scriptorum ecclesiasticorum latinorum 44, edited by Al Goldbacher. Vienna: Verlag der Österreichischen Akademie der Wissenschaften, 1904.

———. "*Sermone 166.*" In *Sermones selecti duodeviginti: Stromata patristica et mediaevalia*, vol. 1, edited by C. Lambot, 61–63. Utrecht: Spectrum, 1950.

———. *Confessiones.* Corpus christianorum series latina 27. Turnhout: Brepols, 1954.

———. *De Doctrina Christiana.* Corpus christianorum series latina 32. Turnhout: Brepols, 1962.

———. "*De dono perseverantiae.*" In *Aux moines d'Adrumète et de Provence. Saint Augustine: texte de l'édition bénédictine.* Oeuvres de Saint Augustin: Bibliothèque Augustinienne 24. Paris: Desclée, 1962. Translated by John Mourant and William J. Collinge as *Saint Augustine: Four Anti-Pelagian Writings.* Washington, DC: Catholic University of America Press, 1992.

———. "*De praedestinatione sanctorum.*" In *Aux moines d'Adrumète et de Provence. Saint Augustine: Texte de l'édition bénédictine.* Oeuvres de Saint Augustin: Bibliothèque Augustinienne 24. Paris: Desclée, 1962. Translated by John Mourant and William J. Collinge in *Saint Augustine: Four Anti-Pelagian Writings*. Washington, DC: Catholic University of America Press, 1992.

⸻. *Tractatus in Evangelium Iohannem*. Corpus christianorum series latina 36. Turnhout: Brepols, 1962. Translated by John Rettig as *Tractates on the Gospel of John*. Washington, DC: Catholic University of America Press, 1995.

⸻. *De sermone Domini in monte*. Corpus christianorum series latina 35. Turnhout: Brepols, 1967.

⸻. *De diversis quaestionibus octoginta tribus, q51, Corpus christianorum series latina 44, 78–82. A*. Turnhout: Brepols, 1968. Translated by David Mosher in *Saint Augustine: Eighty-Three Different Questions*, 85–88. Washington, DC: Catholic University of America Press, 1982.

⸻. *De Trinitate*. Corpus christianorum series latina 50–50A. Turnhout: Brepols, 1968. Translated by Edmund Hill as *The Trinity*. Hyde Park, NY: New City Press, 1991.

⸻. *Sermon 23B-Dolbeau 6–Mainz 13: Vingt-six sermons au peuple d'Afrique, retrouvé à Mayence*. Collection des études augustiniennes: Série Antiquité 147. Edited by François Dolbeau. Paris: Institut d'Études Augustiniennes, 1996. Translated by Edmund Hill as *The Works of St. Augustine III/11: Newly Discovered Sermons*, 37–47. Hyde Park, NY: New City, 1997.

⸻. *De correptione et gratia*. Corpus scriptorum ecclesiasticorum latinorum 92. Edited by Georges Folliet. Vienna: Verlag der Österreichischen Akademie der Wissenschaften, 2000.

⸻. *Ennarationes in psalmos 51–60*. Corpus scriptorum ecclesiasticorum latinorum 94. Edited by H. Müller. Vienna: Verlag der Österreichischen Akademie der Wissenschaften, 2004.

Bede. *In epistulas septem catholicas*. Corpus christianorum series latina 121. Turnhout: Brepols, 1983.

Bernard of Clairvaux. "*Sermones super cantica canticorum*." In *Sancti Bernardi Opera*, vols. 1, 2. Rome: Editiones Cistercienses, 1957–58. Translated by a Religious of C.S.M.V. as *Commentary on the Song of Songs*. London: Mowbray, 1952.

⸻. "*Liber de diligendo Deo*." In *Sancti Bernardi Opera*, vol. 3. Rome: Editiones Cistercienses, 1963. Translated by Terence Connolly as *On the Love of God*. Techny, IL: Mission Press, 1943.

Biblia Latina cum Glossa Ordinaria: Facsimile reprint of the editio Princeps Adolph Rusch of Strassburg, 1480/81. Edited by Karlfrid Froehlich and Margaret T. Gibson. Brepols: Turnhout, 1992.

Bonaventure. *Opera Omnia*, vols. 4–5. Edited by P. P. Aloysii. Florence: Quaracchi, Collegium S. Bonaventura, 1882.

Cyril of Alexandria. *A Commentary on the Gospel According to St. Luke by S. Cyril, Patriarch of Alexandria*. Oxford: Oxford University, 1859.

⸻. *Thesaurus de sancta et consubstantiali Trinitate*. Patrologia Graeca 75, 9–656. Paris: J. P. Migne, 1859.

Dionysius. *On Divine Names, Celestial Hierarchy, and Ecclesiastical Hierarchy*. Translated by Colm Luibheid as *Pseudo-Dionysius: The Complete Works*. New York: Paulist Press, 1987.

John Damascene. *De Fide Orthodoxa: Versions of Burgundio and Cerbanus*. Edited by E. M. Buytaert. St. Bonaventure, NY: Franciscan Institute, 1955.

———. *De Fide Orthodoxa*. Translated by Frederick Chase as "An Exact Exposition of the Orthodox Faith." In *Saint John of Damascus: Writings*. Fathers of the Church 37. New York: Fathers of the Church, 1958.

John Scot Eriugena. *Commentary on John. Jean Scot: Commentaire sur l'Evangile de Jean*. Sources Chrétiennes 180. Edited by Édouard Jeauneau, 114–27. Paris: Cerf, 1972.

———. *Periphyseon I*. Corpus christianorum continuatio mediaevalis 161. Edited by Édouard Jeauneau. Turnhout: Brepols, 1996.

Lombard, Peter. *Sententiae in IV libris distinctae, editio tertia*, 2 vols. Edited by Ignatius Brady. Grottaferrata: Editiones Collegii S. Bonaventurae ad Claras Aquas, 1971.

Secondary Literature

Aertsen, Jan A. *Medieval Philosophy and the Transcendentals: The Case of Thomas Aquinas*. Studien und Texte zur Geistesgeschichte des Mittelalters 52. New York: E. J. Brill, 1996.

Aumann, Jordan. "Thomistic Evaluation of Love and Charity." *Angelicum* 55, no. 4 (1978): 535–56.

Ayesta, Cruz Gonzalez. *El Don de Sabiduría según Santo Tomás*. Pamplona: Ediciones Universidad de Navarra, 1998.

Bardy, Gustave. *Dictionnaire de Spiritualité*, vol. 3, s.v. "Divinisation—chez les Pères Latins," 1389–98.

Barnes, Corey. *Christ's Two Wills in Scholastic Thought: The Christology of Aquinas and Its Historical Contexts*. Toronto: Pontifical Institute of Mediaeval Studies, 2012.

Becker, Sr. Thomas Augustine, OP. "The Role of *Solemnitas* in the Liturgy According to Saint Thomas Aquinas." In *Rediscovering Aquinas and the Sacraments: Studies in Sacramental Theology*, edited by Matthew Levering and Michael Dauphinais, 114–35. Mundelein: Hillenbrand, 2009.

Bernard, R. "La vertu infuse et le don du Saint-Esprit." Supplement, *La Vie Spirituelle* 42 (1935), 67.

Blankenhorn, Bernard. "The Instrumental Causality of the Sacraments: Thomas Aquinas and Louis-Marie Chauvet." *Nova et Vetera* 4, no. 2 (2006): 255–94.

Blowers, Paul. *Exegesis and Spiritual Pedagogy in Maximus the Confessor*. Notre Dame, IN: University of Notre Dame Press, 1991.

Bobik, J. "Aquinas on *communicatio*: The Foundation of Friendship and *caritas*." *Modern Schoolman* 64 (1986): 1–18.

Bonner, Gerald. "Augustine's Conception of Deification." *Journal of Theological Studies*, n.s., 37 (1986): 360–86.

Bonnewijn, Olivier. *La béatitude et les béatitudes: Une approche thomiste de l'éthique*. Rome: Pontificia Università Lateranense, 2001.

Bougerol, J. G. "The Church Fathers and the Sentences of Peter Lombard," and "The Church Fathers and *auctoritates* in Scholastic Theology to Bonaventure." In *Reception of the Church Fathers in the West*, vol. 1, 113–64, 289–35. New York: E. J. Brill, 1997.

Bouillard, Henri. *Conversion et grâce chez S. Thomas d'Aquin*. Paris: Aubier, 1944.

Bourassa, François. "Adoptive Sonship: Our Union with the Divine Persons." *Theological Studies* 13 (1952): 309–35.

Boyle, John F. "The Structural Setting of Thomas Aquinas' Theology of the Grace of Christ as He Is Head of the Church in the *Summa Theologiae*." PhD diss., University of Toronto, 1989.

Boyle, Leonard. *The Setting of the* Summa theologiae *of Saint Thomas*. Toronto: Pontifical Institute of Mediaeval Studies, 1982.

Burger, Maria. "Thomas Aquinas' Glosses on the Dionysius Commentaries of Albert the Great in Codex 30 of the Cologne Cathedral Library." In *Via Alberti. Texte—Quellen—Interpretationen*. Subsidia Albertina 2, translated by M. Tracey, edited by Ludger Honnefelder, Hannes Mohle, and Susana Bullido del Barrio, 561–82. Münster: Aschendorff, 2009.

Burns, J. Patout. *The Development of Augustine's Doctrine of Operative Grace*. Paris: Études augustiniennes, 1980.

Busa, R., ed. *Index thomisticus: Sancti Thomae Aquinatis operum omnium indices et concordantiae*, 50 vols. Stuttgart: Frommann-Holzboog, 1974–80. Available online at www.corpusthomisticum.org, edited by Enrique Alarcón, SJ, for the Fundación Tomás de Aquino.

Capànaga, Victorino. "La deificaciòn en la soteriología augustiniana." In *Augustinus Magister 2*. Paris: Études augustiniennes, 1965.

Cavadini, John. "The Structure and Intention of Augustine's *De trinitate*." *Augustinian Studies* 23 (1992): 103–23.

Cessario, Romanus. *The Moral Virtues and Theological Ethics*. Notre Dame, IN: University of Notre Dame Press, 1991.

———. "Aquinas on Christian Salvation." In *Aquinas on Doctrine: A Critical Introduction*, edited by Thomas G. Weinandy, Daniel A. Keating, and J. P. Yocum, 117–38. T&T Clark: New York, 2004.

Chenu, Marie-Dominique. "Le plan de la Somme théologique de saint Thomas." *Revue thomiste* 47 (1939): 93–107.

———. *Introduction à l'étude de s. Thomas d'Aquin*. Montreal: Études médiévales, 1964. Translated by A. M. Landry and D. Hughes as *Toward Understanding Saint Thomas: Translated with Authorized Corrections and Bibliographical Additions*. Library of Living Catholic Thought. Chicago: H. Regnery, 1964.

Clarke, William Norris. *Explorations in Metaphysics*. Notre Dame, IN: University of Notre Dame Press, 1994.

Condit, Ann. "The Increase of Charity." *Thomist* 17 (1954): 367–86.

Conley, Kieran. *A Theology of Wisdom: A Study in St. Thomas*. Dubuque, IA: Priory Press, 1963.

Conus, Humbert-Thomas. *Dictionnaire de Spiritualité*, vol. 3, s.v. "Divinisation—Moyen Age—théologiens du 13e siècle," 1413–32.

Coolman, Boyd Taylor. *Knowing God by Experience: The Spiritual Senses and the Knowledge of God in the Theology of William of Auxerre*. Washington, DC: Catholic University of America Press, 2004.

Crowley, Paul. "*Instrumentum divinitatis* in Thomas Aquinas: Recovering the Divinity of Christ." *Theological Studies* 52 (1991): 451–75.

Cullen, Christopher. *Bonaventure*. New York: Oxford University Press, 2006.

Cunningham, Francis. *The Indwelling of the Trinity: A Historico-Doctrinal Study of the Theory of St. Thomas Aquinas*. Dubuque, IA: Priory Press, 1955.

Dalmais, I.-H. *Dictionnaire de Spiritualité*, vol. 3, s.v. "Divinisation—patristique grecque," 1370–89.

Dauphinais, Michael A. "Loving the Lord Your God: The *imago Dei* in Saint Thomas Aquinas." *Thomist* 63, no. 2 (1999): 241–67.

———. "*And They Shall All Be Taught by God*: Wisdom and the Eucharist in John 6." In *Reading John with St. Thomas Aquinas: Theological Exegesis and Speculative Theology*, edited by Michael A. Dauphinais and Matthew W. Levering, 312–17. Washington, DC: Catholic University of America Press, 2005.

De Andia, Ysabel. *L'Union à Dieu chez Denys l'Aréopagite*. Leiden: E. J. Brill, 1992.

———. "'Pati divina' chez Denys l'Aréopagite, Thomas d'Aquin et Jacques Maritain." In *Saint Thomas d'Aquin*. Les Cahiers d'Histoire de la Philosophie, edited by Thierry-Dominique Humbrecht, 549–89. Paris: Cerf, 2011.

De Guibert, Joseph. "Dons de Saint-Esprit et le mode d'agir ultrahumain d'apres Saint Thomas." *Revue d'Ascétique et de Mystique* 3 (1922): 394–411.

Dodds, Michael. "The Doctrine of Causality in Aquinas and *The Book of Causes:* One Key to Understanding the Nature of Divine Action." In *Aquinas' Sources: The Notre Dame Symposium, Proceedings from the Summer Thomistic Institute 2000*, edited by Timothy Smith. South Bend, IN: St. Augustine's Press, 2008.

Dondaine, Henri-F. "A propos d'Avicenne et de S. Thomas: De la causalité dispositive a la causalité instrumentale." *Revue thomiste* 51 (1951): 441–53.

———. "L'objet et le 'medium' de la vision béatifique chez les théologiens du XIIIe siècle." *Recherches de théologie ancienne et médiévale* 19 (1952): 60–130.

———. "Cognoscere de Deo 'quid est.'" *Recherches de théologie ancienne et médiévale* 22 (1955): 72–78.

Doolan, Gregory T. *Aquinas on the Divine Ideas as Exemplar Causes*. Washington, DC: Catholic University of America Press, 2008.

Doyle, Dominic. "The Development of Aquinas' Understanding of Charity, with Special Reference to His Refutation of Lombard's Identification of Charity with the Holy Spirit." In *Thomas Aquinas: Questions on Love and Charity*. Rethinking the Western Tradition, edited by Robert Miner. New Haven, CT: Yale University Press, forthcoming.

Emery, Gilles. *La Trinité créatrice: Trinité et création dans les commentaires aux Sentences de Thomas d'Aquin et de ses précurseurs Albert le Grand et Bonaventure*. Bibliothèque Thomiste 47. Paris: J. Vrin, 1995.

————. *Trinity in Aquinas.* Introduction by Jean Pierre Torrell. Ypsilanti, MI: Sapientia Press, 2003.

————. "The Personal Mode of Trinitarian Action in Saint Thomas Aquinas." *Thomist* 69, no. 1 (2005): 31–77.

————. "Trinity and Creation." In *The Theology of Thomas Aquinas*, edited by Rik Van Nieuwenhove and Joseph Wawrykow, 58–76. Notre Dame, IN: University of Notre Dame Press, 2005.

————. *The Trinitarian Theology of St. Thomas Aquinas.* Translated by Francesca Aran Murphy. New York: Oxford University Press, 2007.

————, Ed. *Trinity, Church and the Human Person: Thomistic Essays.* Naples, FL: Sapientia Press, 2007.

Erb, Heather McAdam. "Pati Divina." In *Faith, Scholarship and Culture in the 21st Century*, edited by Alicia Ramos and Marie I. George, 73–96. Washington, DC: Catholic University of America Press, 2002.

Ernst, Cornelius, Ed. *St. Thomas Aquinas: Summa Theologiae*, vol. 30, *The Gospel of Grace: 1a2ae 106–114.* New York: McGraw-Hill, 1964.

Fabro, Cornelio. "The Intensive Hermeneutics of Thomistic Philosophy: The Notion of Participation." *Review of Metaphysics* 27, no. 3 (1974): 449–91.

————. "Le *Liber de bona fortuna* de *L'Ethique à Eudème* d'Aristote et la dialectique de la Providence divine chez saint Thomas." *Revue Thomiste* 88 (1988): 556–72.

Fakhry, M. *Islamic Occasionalism, and Its Critique by Averroës and Aquinas.* London: Allen & Unwin, 1958.

Farthing, J. L. "The Problem of Divine Exemplarity in St. Thomas." *Thomist* 49 (1985): 183–222.

Fracheboud, M.-André. *Dictionnaire de Spiritualité*, vol. 3, s.v. "Divinisation—Moyen Age—auteurs monastiques du 12e siècle," 1399–413.

Fraigneau-Julien, B. "L'inhabitation de la sainte Trinité dans l'âme selon saint Cyrille d'Alexandrie." *Revue de Sciences Religieuses* 30 (1956): 135–56.

Gallagher, Daniel. "The Analogy of Beauty and the Limits of Theological Aesthetics." *Theandros: An Online Journal of Christian Theology and Philosophy* 3, no. 3 (Spring/ Summer 2006).

Gallagher, David M. "Desire for Beatitude and Love of Friendship in Thomas Aquinas." *Mediaeval Studies* 58 (1996): 1–47.

Garrigou-Lagrange, Reginald. "Le mode suprahumain des dons du Saint-Esprit." *Vie spirituelle* 7 (1923): 124–36.

Gavrilyuk, Paul. "The Retrieval of Deification: How a Once-Despised Archaism Became an Ecumenical Desideratum." *Modern Theology* 25 (2009): 647–59.

Geiger, Louis-Bertrand. *La participation dans la philosophie de s. Thomas d'Aquin.* Paris: J. Vrin, 1952.

————. "L'homme, image de Dieu. A propos de *Summa Theologiae*, I, 93, 4." *Rivista di Filosofia Neo-scolastica* 66 (1974): 511–32.

Geiselmann, J. R. "Christus und die Kirche nach Thomas von Aquin." *Theologische Quartalschrift* 107 (1926): 198–222, and 108 (1927): 233–55.

Gersh, Stephen. *From Iamblichus to Eriugena.* Leiden: E. J. Brill, 1978.

Gilby, Thomas. "Appendix 10: The Dialectic of Love in the *Summa.*" In *St Thomas Aquinas: Summa Theologiae,* vol. 1, *Christian Theology (1a 1),* edited by Thomas Gilby, 124–32. New York: McGraw-Hill, 1964.

———. "Introduction." In *St Thomas Aquinas: Summa Theologiae,* vol. 3, *Knowing and Naming God (Ia 12–13),* edited by Herbert McCabe, xix–xl. Manchester: Blackfriars, 1964.

Gilleman, G. *The Primacy of Charity in Moral Theology.* Translated by W. F. Ryan and A. Vachon. Westminster, MD: Newman Press, 1959.

Gillon, L.-B. "A propos de la théorie thomiste de l'amitié." *Angelicum* 25 (1948): 3–17.

Gilson, Étienne. *La théologie mystique de saint Bernard.* Paris: J. Vrin, 1934.

Gleason, Robert. *The Meaning of Love: An Essay towards a Metaphysics of Intersubjectivity.* Glen Rock, NJ: Paulist Press, 1966.

Gross, Jules. *La divinisation du chrétien d'après les pères grecs: Contribution historique à la doctrine de la grâce.* Paris: J. Gabalda, 1938. Translated by Paul A. Onica as *The Divinization of the Christian According to the Greek Fathers.* Anaheim: A&C Press, 2002.

Habets, Myk. "Reforming Theōsis." In *Theōsis: Deification in Christian Theology,* edited by Stephen Finlan and Vladimir Kharlamov, 146–67. Eugene, OR: Pickwick, 2006.

Hallonsten, Gösta. "*Theosis* in Recent Research: A Renewal of Interest and a Need for Clarity." In *Partakers of the Divine Nature: The History and Development of Deification in the Christian Tradition,* edited by Michael J. Christensen and Jeffrey A. Wittung, 281–93. Madison, NJ: Fairleigh Dickinson University Press, 2007.

Heath, T. R. "Appendix 4: The Gift of Wisdom." In *St Thomas Aquinas: Summa Theologiae,* vol. 35, *Consequences of Charity (2a 2ae. 34–46),* edited by T. R. Heath, 200–202. New York: McGraw-Hill, 1964.

Herdt, Jennifer. *Putting on Virtue: The Legacy of the Splendid Vices.* Chicago: University of Chicago Press, 2008.

Hofer, Andrew. "Dionysian Elements in Thomas Aquinas' Christology: A Case of the Authority and Ambiguity of Pseudo-Dionysius." *Thomist* 72 (2008): 409–42.

Horst, Ulrich. *Die Gaben des Heiligen Geistes nach Thomas von Aquin.* Berlin: Akademie Verlag, 2001.

Hughes, Louis. "Charity as Friendship in the Theology of Saint Thomas." *Angelicum* 52 (1975): 164–78.

John of St. Thomas. *The Gifts of the Holy Ghost.* Translated by Dominic Hughes. New York: Sheed & Ward, 1951.

Jordan, Mark. *Rewritten Theology: Aquinas after His Readers.* Oxford: Blackwell, 2006.

Kärkkäinen, Veli-Matti. *One with God: Salvation as Deification and Justification.* Collegeville, MN: Liturgical Press, 2004.

Keating, Daniel A. *The Appropriation of Divine Life in Cyril of Alexandria.* Oxford: Oxford University Press, 2004.

———. "Justification, Sanctification and Divinization in Thomas Aquinas." In *Aquinas on Doctrine: A Critical Introduction,* edited by Thomas G. Weinandy, Daniel A. Keating, and J. P. Yocum, 139–58. New York: T&T Clark, 2004.

————. *Deification and Grace*. Naples, FL: Sapientia Press, 2007.

Keaty, Anthony. "The Holy Spirit as Love: A Study in the Pneumatology of Thomas Aquinas." PhD diss., University of Notre Dame, 1997.

————. "Thomas's Authority for Identifying Charity as Friendship: Aristotle or John 15?" *Thomist* 62 (1998): 581–601.

Kwasniewski, Peter A. "St. Thomas, Extasis, and Union with the Beloved." *Thomist* 61, no. 4 (1997): 587–603.

————. "The Ecstasy of Love in Aquinas's *Commentary on the Sentences*." *Angelicum* 83 (2006): 51–93.

Labourdette, M.-M. *Dictionnaire de Spiritualité*, vol. 3, s.v. "Dons du Saint-Esprit: Part IV of Saint Thomas et la théologie thomiste," 1610–35.

Larchet, Jean-Claude. *La divinisation de l'homme selon saint Maxime le Confesseur*. Paris: Cerf, 1996.

LeClercq, Jean. "Influence and Non-Influence of Dionysius in the Western Middle Ages." In *Pseudo-Dionysius: The Complete Works*, edited by Colm Luibheid, 25–32. New York: Paulist Press, 1987.

Le Guillou, M.-J. *Le Christ et l'Église: Théologie du Mystère*. Paris: Éditions du Centurion, 1963. Translated by Charles Schaldenbrand as *Christ and Church: A Theology of the Mystery*. New York: Desclee, 1966.

Leroy, Marie-Vincent. Review of *Thomas d'Aquin: Les clés d'une théologie*, by Albert Patfoort. *Revue thomiste* (1984): 298–303.

Levering, Matthew W. "Holy Orders and Ecclesial Hierarchy in Aquinas." In *Rediscovering Aquinas and the Sacraments: Studies in Sacramental Theology*, edited by Matthew W. Levering and Michael Dauphinais, 85–101. Chicago: Hillenbrand, 2009.

Lonergan, Bernard. *Grace and Freedom: Operative Grace in the Thought of St. Thomas Aquinas. Collected Works of Bernard Lonergan*, vol. 1. Edited by Frederick E. Crowe and Robert Doran. Toronto: University of Toronto Press, 2000.

Lossky, Vladimir. *The Mystical Theology of the Eastern Church*. New York: St. Vladimir's Seminary Press, 2002.

Louth, Andrew. *Maximus the Confessor*. New York: Routledge, 1996.

Lucas, Daria. "Participation and Communion: Divinization through the Liturgy in the Thought of Thomas Aquinas." M. Lit. Stud. thesis, University of St. Mary of the Lake/Liturgical Institute, 2003.

Lyons, H. "The Grace of Sonship." *Ephemerides Theologicae Lovanienses* 27 (1951): 438–66.

Mansini, G. "Similitudo, communicatio, and the friendship of charity in Aquinas." In *Thomistica*, edited by E. Manning, 1–26. Leuven: Peeters, 1995.

Marshall, Bruce D. "*Ex occidente lux*? Aquinas and Eastern Orthodox Theology." *Modern Theology* 20, no. 1 (2004): 23–50.

————. "*Quod Scit Una Vetula*: Aquinas on the Nature of Theology." In *The Theology of Thomas Aquinas*, edited by Rik Van Nieuwenhove and Joseph Wawrykow, 1–35, 192–221. Notre Dame, IN: University of Notre Dame Press, 2005.

McEvoy, J. J. "The Other as Oneself: Friendship and Love in the Thought of St. Thomas

Aquinas." In *Thomas Aquinas: Approaches to Truth. The Aquinas Lectures at Maynooth, 1996–2001*, edited by J. J. McEvoy and M. Dunne, 16–37. Portland, OR: Four Courts Press, 2002.

McGrath, Alister. "The Influence of Aristotelian Physics upon St. Thomas Aquinas' Discussion of the 'Processus Iustificationis.'" *Recherches de théologie ancienne et médiévale* 51 (1984): 223–29.

McKay, Angela M. "The Infused and Acquired Virtues in Aquinas' Moral Philosophy." PhD diss., University of Notre Dame, 2004.

Meconi, David, SJ. *The One Christ: St. Augustine's Theology of Deification*. Washington, DC: Catholic University of America Press, 2013.

Merriell, D. Juvenal. *To the Image of the Trinity: A Study in the Development of Aquinas' Teaching*. Toronto: Pontifical Institute of Mediaeval Studies, 1990.

———. "Trinitarian Anthropology." In *The Theology of Thomas Aquinas*, edited by Rik Van Nieuwenhove and Joseph Wawrykow, 123–42. Notre Dame, IN: University of Notre Dame Press, 2005.

Mongeau, Gilles. "The Spiritual Pedagogy of the *Summa theologiae*." *Nova et Vetera* 2, no. 1 (2004): 91–114.

Mongillo, D. "Les béatitudes et la béatitude. Le dynamique de la Somme de théologie de Thomas d'Aquin: Une lecture de la Ia-IIae q. 69." *Revue des sciences philosophiques et théologiques* 78 (1994): 373–88.

Murray, Paul. "Drunk on Wisdom: St. Thomas and St. Catherine of Siena." *Angelicum* 82 (2005): 637–49.

Nicolas, M.-J. "Les dons du Saint-Esprit." *Revue Thomiste* 92 (1992): 141–52.

O'Brien, T. C. "Appendix 3: The Dionysian Corpus." In Blackfriar's *Summa*, vol. 14, edited by Thomas Gilby, 182–93. New York: McGraw-Hill, 1975.

O'Connor, Edward D. "Appendix 4: The Evolution of St. Thomas's Thought on the Gifts." In *St Thomas Aquinas: Summa Theologiae*, vol. 24, *The Gifts of the Spirit (1a 2ae. 68–70)*, edited by Edward D. O'Connor, 110–30. New York: McGraw-Hill, 1963.

O'Neill, Colman. "The Role of the Recipient and Sacramental Signification." *Thomist* 21 (1958): 257–301, 508–40.

O'Rourke, Fran. *Pseudo-Dionysius and the Metaphysics of Aquinas*. Notre Dame, IN: University of Notre Dame Press, 2005.

Oroz Reta, José. "De l'illumination à la déification de l'âme selon saint Augustin." *Studia Patristica* 27 (1993): 364–82.

Owens, Joseph. "The Accidental and Essential Character of Being in the Doctrine of St. Thomas Aquinas." In *St. Thomas Aquinas on the Existence of God: Collected Papers of Joseph Owen*. New York: State University of New York Press, 1980.

Patfoort, Albert. "L'unité de la *Ia Pars* et la mouvement interne de la Somme théologique de S. Thomas d'Aquin." *Revue des sciences philosophiques et théologiques* 47 (1963): 513–44.

———. *Thomas d'Aquin: Les cléfs d'une théologie*. Paris: FAC éditions, 1983.

Pieper, Josef. *The Four Cardinal Virtues*. Notre Dame, IN: University of Notre Dame Press, 1966.

Pinckaers, Servais. *The Sources of Christian Ethics*. Translated by Sr. Thomas Mary Noble. Washington, DC: Catholic University of America Press, 1995.

———. *The Pinckaers Reader: Renewing Thomistic Moral Theology*. Edited by John Berkman and Craig Titus. Translated by Sr. Mary Thomas Noble, Craig Titus, Michael Sherwin, and Hugh Connelly. Washington, DC: Catholic University of America, 2005.

Principe, W. H. "Loving Friendship According to Thomas Aquinas." In *The Nature and Pursuit of Love*, edited by D. Goicoechea. Buffalo: Prometheus, 1995.

Prügl, Thomas. "Thomas Aquinas as Interpreter of Scripture." In *The Theology of Thomas Aquinas*, edited by Rik Van Nieuwenhove and Joseph P. Wawrykow, 386–415. Notre Dame, IN: University of Notre Dame Press, 2005.

Puchniak, Robert. "Augustine's Conception of Deification, Revisited." In *Theōsis: Deification in Christian Theology*, edited by Stephen Finlan and Vladimir Kharlamov, 122–33. Eugene, OR: Pickwick, 2006.

Reichberg, G. M. "The Communication of the Divine Nature: Thomas's Response to Neoplatonism." *Proceedings of the American Catholic Philosophical Association* 66 (1992): 215–28.

Rikhof, Herwi M. "Trinity." In *The Theology of Thomas Aquinas*, edited by Rik Van Nieuwenhove and Joseph P. Wawrykow, 36–57. Notre Dame, IN: University of Notre Dame Press, 2005.

Rocca, Gregory. *Speaking the Incomprehensible God*. Washington, DC: Catholic University of America Press, 2004.

Rogers, Eugene. "The Eclipse of the Spirit in Thomas Aquinas." In *Grammar and Grace: Reformulations of Aquinas and Wittgenstein*, edited by Jeffrey Stout and Robert MacSwain, 136–53. London: SCM Press, 2004.

Rondet, Henri. "La divinisation du chrétien." *Nouvelle revue théologique* 71 (1949): 449–76, 561–88.

Roques, René. *L'univers dionysien*. Paris: Aubier, 1954.

Rorem, Paul. *Pseudo-Dionysius: A Commentary on the Texts and an Introduction to Their Influence*. New York: Oxford University Press, 1993.

———. *Eriugena's Commentary on the Dionysian Celestial Hierarchy*. Toronto: Pontifical Institute of Mediaeval Studies, 2005.

Rosemann, Philipp W. "*Fraterna dilectio est Deus*: Peter Lombard's Thesis on Charity as the Holy Spirit." In *Amor amicitiae—On the Love That Is Friendship: Essays in Medieval Thought and beyond in Honor of the Reverend Professor James McEvoy*. Recherches de théologie et philosophie médiévales, Bibliotheca 6, edited by Thomas Kelly and Philipp Rosemann, chap. 21. Louvain: Peeters, 2004.

Russell, Norman. *The Doctrine of Deification in the Greek Patristic Tradition*. Oxford: Oxford University Press, 2004.

Rziha, John. *Perfecting Human Actions: St. Thomas Aquinas on Human Participation in Eternal Law*. Washington, DC: Catholic University of America Press, 2009.

Sánchez Sorondo, Marcelo. *La gracia como participación de la naturaleza divina según San-*

to Tomás de Aquino. Bibliotheca Salmanticensis 28. Introduction by Cornelius Fabro. Salamanca: Universidad Pontificia de Salamanca, 1979.

Schenk, Richard. "*Omnis Christi actio nostra est instructio*: The Deeds and Sayings of Jesus as Revelation in the View of Thomas Aquinas." In *La doctrine de la révélation divine de saint Thomas d'Aquin.* Studi Tomistici 37, edited by Leo J. Elders, 104–31. Vatican City: Libreria Editrice Vaticana, 1990.

Schockenhoff, E. "The Theological Virtue of Charity (IIª IIae qq. 23–46)." In *The Ethics of Aquinas.* Moral Traditions Series, edited by S. J. Pope, 244–58. Washington, DC: Georgetown University Press, 2002.

Schwartz, Daniel. *Aquinas on Friendship.* New York: Oxford University Press, 2007.

Shanley, Brian J. "Divine Causation and Human Freedom in Aquinas." *American Catholic Philosophical Quarterly* 72, no. 1 (1998): 98–122.

———. *The Treatise on the Divine Nature, Summa Theologiae I 1–13.* Indianapolis: Hackett, 2006.

Sherwin, Michael S. *By Knowledge and by Love: Charity and Knowledge in the Moral Theology of St. Thomas Aquinas.* Washington, DC: Catholic University of America Press, 2005.

Sickenberger, J., Ed. *Die Lukaskatene des Niketas von Herakleia.* Texte und Untersuchungen zur Geschichte der altchristlichen Literatur 22/4. Leipzig: Akademie Verlag, 1902.

Simonin, H. D. "Autour de la Solution Thomiste du Problème de L'Amour." *Archives d'Histoire Doctrinale et Littéraire du Moyen Âge* 6 (1932): 174–276.

Sokolowski, Robert. *The God of Faith and Reason: Foundations of Christian Theology.* Notre Dame, IN: University of Notre Dame Press, 1982.

Somme, Luc-Thomas. *Fils adoptifs de Dieu par Jésus Christ: La filiation divine par adoption dans la théologie de saint Thomas d'Aquin.* Paris: J. Vrin, 1997.

Spezzano, Daria. "Conjoined to Christ's Passion: The Deifying Asceticism of the Sacraments according to Thomas Aquinas." *Antiphon* 17, no. 1 (2013): 73–86.

Stroud, James. "Thomas Aquinas' Exposition of the Gifts of the Holy Spirit: Developments in His Thought and Rival Interpretations." PhD diss., Catholic University of America, 2012.

Sullivan, J. E. *The Image of God: The Doctrine of St. Augustine and Its Influence.* Dubuque, IA: Priory Press, 1963.

te Velde, Rudi A. *Participation and Substantiality in Thomas Aquinas.* Leiden: E. J. Brill, 1995.

Thomas, Stephen. *Deification in the Eastern Orthodox Tradition: A Biblical Perspective.* Piscataway, NJ: Gorgias Press, 2008.

Thunberg, Lars. *Microcosm and Mediator.* Chicago: Open Court, 1995.

Torrell, Jean Pierre. "Imiter Dieu comme des enfants bien-aimés." In *Novitas et Veritas Vitae: Aux Sources du Renouveau de la Morale Chrétienne,* edited by Carlos-Josaphat Pinto de Oliveira, 53–65. Fribourg: Éditions Universitaires, 1991.

———. "Le Christ dans la 'spiritualité' de saint Thomas." In *Christ among the Medieval Dominicans: Representations of Christ in the Texts and Images of the Order of Preachers,* edited by Kent Emery Jr. and Joseph Wawrykow, 197–219. Notre Dame, IN: University of Notre Dame Press, 1998.

———. *Saint Thomas Aquinas*, vols. 1 and 2. Translated by Robert Royal. Washington, DC: Catholic University of America Press, 2003.

Trottmann, Christian. *La vision béatifique: Des disputes scolastiques à sa définition par Benoît XII.* Rome: École Française de Rome, 1995.

Tschipke, Theophil. *L'humanité du Christ comme instrument de salut de la divinité.* Studia Friburgensia: Neue Folge 94. Introduction by B. D. de La Soujeole. Translated by P. Secretan. Fribourg: Academic Press, 2003.

Wadell, Paul J. *Friends of God: Virtues and Gifts in Aquinas.* American University Studies Series 7: Theology and Religion 76. New York: P. Lang, 1991.

Walsh, Liam. "The Divine and the Human in St. Thomas's Theology of Sacraments." In *Ordo sapientiae et amoris: Hommage au professeur Jean-Pierre Torrell, OP*, edited by Carlos-Josaphat Pinto, OP, 321–52. Fribourg: Éditions Universitaires, 1993.

———. "Sacraments." In *The Theology of Thomas Aquinas*, edited by Rik Van Nieuwenhove and Joseph Wawrykow, 326–64. Notre Dame, IN: University of Notre Dame Press, 2005.

Wawrykow, Joseph P. *God's Grace and Human Action: "Merit" in the Theology of Thomas Aquinas.* Notre Dame, IN: University of Notre Dame Press, 1995.

———. "Wisdom in the Christology of Thomas Aquinas." In *Christ among the Medieval Dominicans: Representations of Christ in the Texts and Images of the Order of Preachers*, edited by Kent Emery Jr. and Joseph Wawrykow. Notre Dame, IN: University of Notre Dame Press, 1998.

———. "Grace." In *The Theology of Thomas Aquinas*, edited by Rik Van Nieuwenhove and Joseph Wawrykow, 192–221. Notre Dame, IN: University of Notre Dame Press, 2005.

———. "Hypostatic Union." In *The Theology of Thomas Aquinas*, edited by Rik Van Nieuwenhove and Joseph Wawrykow, 222–51. Notre Dame, IN: University of Notre Dame Press, 2005.

———. *The Westminster Handbook to Thomas Aquinas.* Louisville, KY: Westminster John Knox Press, 2005.

———. "Christ and the Gifts of the Holy Spirit According to Thomas Aquinas." In *Kirchenbild und Spiritualität. Dominikanische Beiträge zur Ekklesiologie und zum kirchlichen Leben im Mittelalter. Festschrift für Ulrich Horst zum 75. Geburtstag*, edited by Thomas Prügl and M. Schlosser, 43–62. Paderborn: Schöning, 2007.

———. "Theological Virtues." In *The Oxford Handbook of Aquinas*, edited by Eleonore Stump and Brian Davies, 287–310. Oxford University Press, 2012.

Whidden, David L. *Christ the Light: The Theology of Light and Illumination in Thomas Aquinas.* Minneapolis: Fortress Press, 2014.

Wilkins, Jeremy. "Trinitarian Missions and the Order of Grace According to Thomas Aquinas." In *Philosophy and Theology in the Long Middle Ages: Essays in Honor of Professor Stephen Brown*, edited by K. Emery, R. Friedman, and A. Speer. Leiden: E. J. Brill, 2011.

Williams, A. N. *The Ground of Union: Deification in Aquinas and Palamas.* New York: Oxford University Press, 1999.

Wilms, Jerome. *Divine Friendship According to Saint Thomas*. Translated by M. Fulgence. Dubuque, IA: Priory Press, 1958.

Wippel, John. "Thomas Aquinas and Participation." In *Studies in Medieval Philosophy*, vol. 17. Washington, DC: Catholic University of America Press, 1987.

———. "Metaphysics." In *The Cambridge Companion to Aquinas*, edited by Norman Kretzmann and Eleonore Stump, 93–95. Cambridge: Cambridge University Press, 1993.

———. *The Metaphysical Thought of Thomas Aquinas: From Finite Being to Uncreated Being*. Washington, DC: Catholic University of America Press, 2000.

Index

Abelard, Peter, 55n128

Adam, 164–65, 172–74

adoption: adoptive sonship, 142–50, 192–207, 334–42; and charity, 205, 336–37; vs. Christ's natural sonship, 58–59, 195, 200–207; as deification, 146, 192–207, 334–36; degrees of, 58–59, 196–97; divine goodness as motive for, 202–4; and filial fear, 149–50; God's glory manifested in, 339–42; by grace, 142–43; juridical vs. meritorious perspectives on, 194–96, 203; as participation in Christ's sonship, 192–207; predestined, 194, 202–4; rational nature required for, 204–5; and sacraments, 304–5; and wisdom, 199–200, 286–89, 339–42; and worship, 273, 326–27, 338, 341–42. *See also* deification; filiation

Aertsen, Jan, 341n19

Albert the Great, 31–32, 185n90, 357–58

analogy, 21n11, 86–88, 314n202

Aristotle, 28–29, 113, 121, 141, 179–80n76, 185, 212–14, 235, 266–70, 271

Augustine, 6–7, 65n156, 65n157, 74n3, 84, 90, 92–94, 99n81, 118, 122–23, 149n134, 161–62, 201, 219–21, 230–31, 251–52, 256–57, 258, 286–87, 307, 353–55

Ayesta, Cruz Gonzalez, 271n22, 279n53

baptism, 309, 311, 313n1194, 315–16. *See also* sacraments

Barnes, Corey, 181n82

beatific vision. *See visio Dei*

beatitude: charity in progress to, 248–57; communication as charity's cause, 215–17; divine vs. human causality in, 126–29; Eu-

charist as food for journey to, 322; as goal of will, 107; grace needed to attain supernatural, 18–19, 111–12; and Holy Spirit, 148, 249–50; New Law ordered to, 117; theological virtues order to, 137–38; wisdom perfected in, 292, 326–27, 343–44. *See also* deification; glory; *visio Dei*

beauty, 341–42

Becker, Sr. Thomas Augustine, 324n253

Bede, 134n98

being. *See* existence

Bernard of Clairvaux, 283–84n75

Blankenhorn, Bernard, 315n204

Boethius, 24

Bonaventure, 31, 55n128, 56n129, 357

Bonnewijn, Olivier, 287n87

Bouillard, Henri, 121–23, 256n144

Boyle, John, 295, 299n134, 313n198

Burger, Maria, 358

Burns, J. Patout, 256–57n144

Catena aurea, 132, 259–60; on John, 96n76; on Luke, 132–33; on Mark, 134; on Matthew, 161n18

causality, 20–30, 47–49, 120–29, 181–84; Christ's instrumental in his humanity, 179–90; divine vs. creaturely, 27; divine vs. human, 125–29; divine vs. secondary, 47–49, 106; exemplar, 50–61; God as origin of all, 125–26; primacy of divine, 120–29; sacramental, 303–4; of Trinitarian Persons, 41–43, 50–61. *See also* ideas, divine; grace; *ordinatio*; participation; predestination; will

Cavadini, John, 92n65

Cessario, Romanus, 237–39

charity, 212–64, 280–86, 317–24; and acquired and infused virtues, 237–40; and adoption, 205, 336–37; baptism's full effect requires, 316; as bond of perfection, 318–19; of Christ, 177, 295–302; communication of beatitude foundation of, 215–17; *complacentia*, 226–27; connaturality given by, 230; created vs. divine, 220–21; as created *habitus*, 217–21; in deification, 332–33, 336–38; divine goodness as object of, 225–29; and Eucharist, 317–19, 321; as fellowship with Christ, 216–17; as form of virtues, 230–33; as friendship, 212–17; as gift of divine goodness, 214–15; and gift of wisdom, 275–86; gifts of Holy Spirit require, 177, 240–48; God attained by, 226–29; as highest virtue, 225–30; increase vs. loss of, 251–57; to neighbor, 285–86; as participation in Holy Spirit, 221–24, 229, 246–47, 282; in Passion, 296–303; perfected in *visio Dei*, 234–37, 343–45; in progress to beatitude, 247–57; and sacrifice, 301–3; sin destroys, 256–57; and theological virtues, 235–37; union with divine will, 227–30; *visio Dei* requires, 39–40; wisdom orders objects of, 280–86

Chauvet, Louis-Marie, 314–15n204

Chenu, Marie-Dominique, 20

Christ: vs. Adam, 164–65, 172–74; beauty of, 341; charity as fellowship with, 216–17; charity of 177, 295–302; condign merit of, 174–75; divine mission of Word, 63–64, 67–70, 334–35; exemplar as human, 172–78, 295–303; exemplar as Son or Word, 58–59, 197–98, 208–9, 338; filial fear of, 176–78; gifts of Holy Spirit to, 176; grace of, 160–71; habitual vs. auxiliary grace in, 166–71, 173–78, 201–2; habitual grace vs. union in, 166–71, 184–90, 201–2; grace of headship, 184–90; humanity as instrument of divinity, 179–90; infused virtues in, 239–40; love for disciples, 157; as mediator, 307–8; mystical body of, 301, 303, 325–26, 338; not adopted, 195, 201–2; obedience of,

177–78, 298; Old Law fulfilled by, 306–7; participates grace to others, 179–90; perfects human nature, 165; in predestination, 199–200; presence in Eucharist, 317–18; priesthood of, 305–11; sacrifice of, 301–2; sonship of, 192–207; unity with Father, 206–7; as Wisdom, 55, 197–200, 339. *See also* God; Incarnation; Passion; Son; Trinity; Word

Christian distinction, 25

Church, 324–26

Clarke, William Norris, 28–29n37

Collationes Credo in Deum, 275n38, 297n129, 329–27

Colossians, Letter to the, 3:10, 85; 3:14–17, 318

Commentary on Colossians (Sup. Col.), 85n41, 180n79, 318n224

Commentary on 1 Corinthians (Sup. I Cor.), 154–55, 164, 216n14, 227, 270n19, 271n21, 272n25

Commentary on 2 Corinthians (Sup. II Cor.), 113n30, 118n55, 199n31, 312n189

Commentary on Ephesians (Sup. Eph.), 132n92, 154n5, 155n7, 156–57, 194n115, 263n156, 282n72, 296n124, 301n144, 312n190–91, 337n11, 340n16, 346n36

Commentary on Galatians (Sup. Gal.), 143

Commentary on Hebrews (Sup. Heb.), 132n92, 155n7, 156, 194n115, 339

Commentary on John (Sup. Ioh.), 132n92, 135n101, 157, 180n76, 193, 194n115, 206–7, 260, 293–94, 297, 325

Commentary on the Metaphysics, 268–69n12

Commentary on Philippians (Sup. Phil.), 155n8, 217n16, 297n129

Commentary on the Psalms (Sup. Psalmos), 116–17, 117n49, 135

Commentary on Romans (Sup. Rom.), 118, 144n121, 147–48, 195, 260–61, 300, 312n189, 339

Commentary on Titus (Sup. Tit.), 132n92, 158

Compendium theologiae, 186

Condit, Ann, 223n29

Conley, Kieran, 269, 277
contemplation, 267–69, 280–81, 341–42
convenientia creaturae ad Deum, 86–88
Corinthians, First Letter to the, 1:9, 216–17;
    1:24, 55n128, 200; 2:9, 18–19; 2:10, 227,
    272n25; 2:15, 270–71, 272n25; 6:17, 157, 276,
    356; 15:46–47, 164–65
Corinthians, Second Letter to the, 3:17,
    118n55; 5:19, 199n31
creation, Trinitarian causality of, 41–43,
    50–61. *See also* ideas, divine; participation
Crowley, Paul, 191n109
Cullen, Christopher, 357n63
Cyril of Alexandria, 133, 162n20, 163n22,
    349–50

Dalmais, L.-H., 350
Dauphinais, Michael, 96n75, 319n225
de Andia, Ysabel, 278–79
De ente et essentia, 27n35, 179–80n76
De Guibert, Joseph, 244n102
deification, 192–207, 328–46, 347–58; adop-
    tion as, 146, 192–207, 334–36; charity in,
    332–33, 336–38; defined, 1, 6; vs. deiformity,
    7–8, 342–45; divine goodness as motive
    for, 202–4; and divine missions, 332–34;
    Eastern vs. Western views of, 11–14; end of,
    329–31; ethical vs. realistic treatments of,
    349; fire metaphor for, 179–80, 321; God's
    glory manifested in, 339–42; via grace, 332–
    34; history of doctrine, 347–58; and moral
    life, 333–34; sacraments as instruments of,
    190–92, 309–13, 338; structure of, 333; two
    poles of, 9–10, 362; wisdom in, 332–33,
    336–38. *See also* adoption; beatitude; partic-
    ipation; Peter, Second Letter of; *visio Dei*
Dionysius, 6–7, 25, 26n31, 31, 33, 183, 276,
    277–78, 309n178, 341n19, 350–53
divinization. *See* deification
Dondaine, Henri-F., 182n86, 350n16, 355
Doyle, Dominic, 262n155
Duns Scotus, John, 238–39

election, 47
Emery, Gilles, 52, 54, 68n165, 293, 294

Ephesians, Letter to the, 1:5–6, 202, 340;
    1:13–14, 312n191; 5:1–2, 301, 305, 309,
    348
Eriugena, John Scotus, 355
Ernst, Cornelius, 64n152
Eucharist, 317–26, 349. *See also* sacraments
existence: caused by God, 25–29; as God's
    essence, 22, 26–28; as participated perfec-
    tion, 22
Expositio Libri Boethii de Hebdomadibus,
    24, 269

faith: baptism as sacrament of, 315–16; and
    charity, 234–36; replaced by vision, 236–37,
    292; and wisdom, 289–92
Fakhry, Majid, 113n30
Farthing, J. L., 43n82
fear: as beginning of wisdom, 149–50; filial,
    149–50, 176–78
filiation: adopted vs. natural, 200–207;
    degrees of, 58–59, 196–97; as deification,
    334–36; wisdom as cause of, 288–89. *See
    also* adoption; Christ
Fra Angelico, 5
free will, 47–48, 107–10, 113–15, 121–28. *See
    also* will
friendship: charity as, 212–17; as union of
    wills, 227, 228–29. *See also* charity

Gallagher, Daniel, 341n19
Gallagher, David M., 229n53, 285
Gallus, Thomas, 355
Gavrilyuk, Paul, 11–13
Geiselmann, J. R., 181–82, 183n88
gifts. *See* Holy Spirit
Gilby, Thomas, 37–38n64, 277
Gillon, L.-B., 215n11
glory, 36–40, 77, 155, 339–42; and charity,
    39–40; Eucharist as food on journey to,
    321–22; God's, 339–42; light of as medium
    of *visio Dei*, 36–39; as perfection of image,
    77; and predestination, 340. *See also* beati-
    tude; grace; *visio Dei*
Glossa Ordinaria, 81–82, 117, 134, 154n3,
    155n6, 162n19, 164, 249

God: accessibility to rational creatures,
86–90; attained by charity, 226–29; beauty
of, 341–42; essence as existence, 22, 26–28;
as final cause, 44–45; as first cause of creation, 25–29, 47–49, 125–26; as first cause
of free will, 109–10, 112–13; freedom of,
45; government of, 109; incommunicable
nature and name, 135–36; as intellectual,
74–76; knowledge of, 42–45, 92–95; as
object of rational nature, 88, 91–95; predestination of, 45–49; primacy in grace,
120–29; providence of, 45–49; *ordinatio*
of, 43–50; as Trinity, 51; wisdom of, 44,
46. *See also* Christ; goodness, divine; Holy
Spirit; ideas, divine; Trinity
goodness, divine, 41–45; charity as gift of,
214–15; as charity's object, 225–29; deification manifests, 339; divine *ordinatio* manifests, 200; grace as participation in, 138–42,
203; as motive for adoption, 202–4; predestination caused by, 48, 200; as principle
of creaturely goodness, 29; sanctification
manifests, 45–46
grace: in Adam vs. Christ, 172–74; as *auxilium*, 115, 118–29, 240–41, 252; of Christ,
160–71, 173–78, 184–90, 201–2, 208;
Christ's habitual vs. auxiliary, 173–78;
Christ's habitual vs. of union, 166–71,
184–90, 201–2; created, 118, 141, 362–65;
defined, 3; deification caused by, 332–34;
development of Aquinas's teaching on,
121–24, 126–29; in divine missions, 63–69;
as effect of Eucharist, 320–21; as *gratia gratum faciens*, 63; God's primacy in, 120–29;
and *habitus*, 115–18, 121–25, 129–60, 363;
of headship, 184–90; Holy Spirit as gift of,
65–66; Holy Spirit as giver of, 64–67; as
New Law, 116–19; operating vs. cooperating, 126–29, 245n104, 256; as participation
in divine goodness, 138–42; via predestination, 340n16; in perfection of image,
77; as principle of merit, 143; as principle
of supernatural activities, 129–30, 137–38,
141–43; progressive increase, 68–69; in
Scriptum, 184–88; as seed planted by Holy

Spirit, 143–45; theological virtues from,
137–38, 142–43; will requires to attain beatitude, 111–12. *See also* adoption; *habitus*;
missions; *ordinatio*; predestination
Gregory the Great, 247n112, 321

habitus: charity as created, 217–21; defined,
114; gifts of Holy Spirit as, 242–45; grace
as, 115, 117–19, 121–30, 139–42; increase and
decrease of, 251–57; theological virtues as,
137–38. *See also* grace; virtue
Hales, Alexander, 356n59, 357n61, 360–61n8
Hallonsten, Gösta, 11–12
happiness. *See* beatitude
Heath, T. R., 279
Hebrews, Letter to the, 1:3, 339
Herdt, Jennifer, 231n56, 251n25
Hilary of Poitiers, 86–86, 96n76
Holy Spirit: charity as participation in,
221–24, 229, 246–47, 282; condign merit
from, 147; divine mission of, 63–70; as
Gift, 60–61, 65–66; gifts of, 240–48; gifts
to Christ, 176–78; as goodness, 55; grace
given by, 64–67; *instinctus* of, 119, 147–48,
242–45, 316; leads the journey to beatitude,
147–48, 248–51, 257; as Love, 51–61; as
New Law of grace, 117–19; perseverance
from, 256–57; as pledge of beatitude, 148;
seed of grace planted by, 143–45; wisdom
as gift of, 269–89. *See also* charity; God;
missions; Romans; Trinity
Horst, Ulrich, 242n98
Hughes, Louis, 215n11
human nature: baptism as regeneration
of, 158; Christ's in participating grace to
others, 180–81; habitual grace in Christ's,
168–71; as intellectual, 75–76; perfected
by Christ, 165; proportion to God, 86–90;
sacraments fitted for, 69–70, 313–14; as
sensible, 69–70; stages of perfection of,
76–83; and theological virtues, 137–38. *See
also* will; image; intellect, created

ideas, divine, 42–43, 87–88, 274–75n36
image, 28, 57–61, 72–104; Christ as of Father

58–60; and divine missions, 98–103; end of created, 329–31; as formal likeness, 57–61; glory as perfection of, 77; God as object of, 88, 91–95; intellectual nature as, 74–76; vs. likeness, 95–97; as medium for knowledge of God, 92–95; progressive perfection of, 76–83; proportion to God, 86–90; representation of species of Word and Love in, 85–95, 289; vs. trace, 57; Trinitarian character of, 83–95. *See also* human nature; intellect, created

Incarnation: fittingness of, 160–62; fittingness of Word for, 197–200; hypostatic union in, 166–67; timing of, 163–65. *See also* Christ; missions, divine; Passion

indwelling, divine, 63, 68n165, 98, 100–103, 148, 228, 292–95, 332–34, 343

intellect, created: God as object of, 88, 91–95; as image of God, 74–76; medium of perceiving God, 31, 32, 36–39; natural limitations of, 40; perfected by knowledge of source, 35; proportion to God, 31–35, 86–90; required for adoption, 204–5; Trinity mirrored in, 57–61. *See also* human nature; image

John Chrysostom, 31, 33
John Damascene, 95–96, 170, 180n80, 200, 319, 321, 355
John, First Letter of, 3:2, 19, 35, 37, 39, 145
John, Gospel of, 349; 1:14–16, 165, 170–71, 186, 187, 193, 201, 338n12; 1:17, 154, 320; 10:36, 135n101; 14:26, 293, 334n8; 15:10, 298; 15:15, 213, 216; 17:17, 293; 17:21–22, 206; 17:26, 294
John of St. Thomas, 243n102
Jordan, Mark, 155n6
justification, 56, 122, 128, 300n140, 304n162, 306, 357n63

Keating, Daniel, 2n7, 13–15, 162n20, 163n22, 350n14
Keaty, Anthony, 213n7, 230
knowledge, gift of, 240, 246n106, 274n36, 276, 289, 291
Kwasniewski, Peter, 321n231

Law, New, 116–19; beatitude as end of, 117; Eucharist as sacrifice of, 317–18; grace as, 116–19; vs. natural law, 274–75; worship in, 307
Le Guillou, M.-J., 267n6, 325n256, 326n259
Leo, Pope, 162
LeRoy, Marie-Vincent, 20
light of glory. *See* glory
likeness. *See* image
liturgy, 282n67, 284n75, 314n201, 322n235, 324, 352–53. *See also* sacraments
Lombard, Peter, 61n143, 65n156, 65n157, 95–97, 141, 162n19, 218–22, 258, 256–57n59
Lonergan, Bernard, 49, 123, 126, 127–28
Lossky, Vladimir, 351n19
love. *See* charity

Mansini, Guy, 215n11, 228–29, 286n82
Marshall, Bruce, 275n38
Maximus the Confessor, 350n16
McEvoy, James, 228
McKay, Angela, 244n102
merit: in adoption, 194–96, 203; Christ's condign, 174–75; grace as principle of, 143; Holy Spirit's condign, 147; of Passion, 299
Merriell, D. Juvenal, 73–74, 78–82, 84, 90, 94n72, 97n77, 98
missions, divine, 61–70, 98–103, 156, 332–35; complementary, 334–35n8; and deification, 332–34; double relation of, 62–63; grace as root of, 63–64; of Holy Spirit, 63–70; and image, 98–103; need for visible, 69–70; visible vs. invisible, 63; wisdom as effect of Son's, 292–95; of Word or Son, 67–70, 334–35. *See also* grace; Incarnation; indwelling
Mongeau, Gilles, 331n5
Murray, Paul, 320–21n231
mystical body. *See* Christ

neighbor, love of, 285–86
Neoplatonism, 25, 28–29, 35, 44–45, 75, 182–83
Nestorianism, 166, 351
Nicolas, M.-J., 243n102, 245n104

obedience, 304–5

Officium de festo Corporis Christi, 322n235

ordinatio, divine, 43–50; God as omnicausal in, 125–26; manifests divine goodness, 42–45, 200, 340; and New Law, 116; participation by wisdom in, 274, 283. *See also* causality, predestination, providence

Origen, 133–34n97

Owens, Joseph, 363–64n21

participation, 23–30, 129–50, 179–207; of Christ's grace to others, 179–90; in Christ's priesthood via sacraments, 309–13; in Christ's sonship as deification, 192–207; created grace as, 363–65; defined, 24; in divine goodness, 138–42; in divine nature, 129–50; in divine providence, 116–17, 124, 136, 273–75, 340; in existence, 22–23, 26–29; fire metaphor for, 22, 173, 179–80; in Holy Spirit as charity, 221–24, 229, 246–47, 282; in Passion via sacraments, 303–4; principle, 168, 171, 179, 183–84; in Son or Word, 199, 200, 286–89, 292–95. *See also* causality; ideas, divine

Passion, 296–307; baptism applies salvation of, 315–16; Christ's members conjoined to, 303–5; fittingness of, 296–97, 299n135; as meriting salvation, 299–301; obedience in, 298; Old Law fulfilled by, 306–7; as redemption, 302–3; sacraments as participation in, 303–4; as sacrifice, 301–2, 305–7; as satisfaction for sin, 300–301

Patfoort, Albert, 20, 117

pati divina, 275–79

peace, 286–89

Pelagianism, 122

perseverance from Holy Spirit, 256–57

Peter, Second Letter of, 1:4, 14, 129–42, 153–59, 160, 162, 168, 349–50, 354–55. *See also* deification; participation

Pieper, Josef, 238n89

Pinckaers, Servais, 108n13, 242, 244n102, 245n104

predestination, 45–49; and adoption, 194, 202–4; divine goodness as cause of, 48; and

human freedom, 47–49; glory via, 340n16; God's glory manifested in, 340; and grace, 139–40; wisdom of Christ in, 199–200. *See also* causality; grace; *ordinatio*; providence

procession and return, 20–21, 25, 29, 35, 75

providence, divine, 44, 46–48; and government, 107, 109, and law, 116–17; participation in, 116–17, 124, 136, 273–75, 340. *See also* causality; *ordinatio*; predestination

Prügl, Thomas, 260n151

Psalms, 4:7, 81–82, 116–17, 313n197; 35:10, 38; 81:6, 135; 84:12, 168n34

Puchniak, Robert, 354–55n46

Q. D. De anima, 132n92, 155–56n9, 267n7

Q. D. De caritate, 261–62n155, 286n82

Q. D. De malo, 108n13, 113n30

Q. D. De potentia, 182–83, 312n192

Q. D. De veritate, 31–38, 81–82, 90, 131, 182–83, 267n7, 290n96, 362

Q. D. De virtutibus in communi, 237–38

religion, virtue of, 301, 305. *See also* worship

Reta, Oroz, 354n40

Rikhof, Herwi, 62n147, 64

Romans, Letter to the, 5:5, 219–20, 222–23, 257–62, 348; 6:23, 249; 8:2, 118; 8:14–17, 147–48, 194, 206, 260, 261n154, 336; 8:29, 59, 158, 192–94, 196, 338n12, 339

Roques, René, 351

Rosemann, Philipp W., 220n22

Russell, Norman, 347, 348, 349, 350, 353

Rziha, John, 274n34

sacra doctrina, 17–18, 40–41n74, 198n128, 266–69, 275

sacraments, 146, 192–92, 308–26; baptism as regeneration, 158, 315–16; character as participation in Christ's priesthood, 309–13; devotion's role in, 316, 323–24; and divine missions, 69–70; fruitful reception of, 313–14; human nature fitted for, 69–70, 313–14; as instruments of deification, 190–92, 309–13, 338; as participation in

Passion, 303–4; *res tantum* of, 304n162. *See also* baptism; Eucharist; liturgy

sacrifice, 301–3

Schenk, Richard, 162n19, 208

Scriptum super libros Sententiarum, 68n165, 81–82, 97, 121–23, 131, 181–82, 184–88, 197, 261–62n155

Sherwin, Michael, 253–54n62

Simonin, H. D., 213n6

sin: Eucharist's effects hindered by venial, 323–24; free will limited by, 108; grace needed because of, 120–21, mortal destroys charity, 256–57; Passion as satisfaction for, 300–301; venial disposes for charity's loss, 257; venial removed by charity in act, 323

Sokolowski, Robert, 25

Somme, Luc-Thomas, 140n109, 194–97

Son: as exemplar, 58–59; 196–97, 201–2, 208–9; as Image of Father, 59, 75; invisible mission of, 67–68. *See also* adoption; Christ; Trinity; Word

Songs, Song of, 2:4, 283; 8:6, 117n49, 313n197

sonship. *See* adoption; Christ; filiation

Sorondo, Marcelo Sánchez, 131n90

Spezzano, Daria, 304–5n164, 315n204

Stroud, James, 243–44n102

Sullivan, J. E., 74n3

Summa contra Gentiles, 29n37, 54, 56, 113, 122, 132, 181–82, 259n150

Summa theologiae: Ia q1, 266–70; Ia q12, 30–40; Ia q14, 87–91; Ia q19–23, 44–50; Ia q43, 61–70, 98–103; Ia q93, 71–97; Ia-IIae q62, 137–38, 120–21, 124; Ia-IIae q68, 241–48; Ia-IIae q109, 248–51; Ia-IIae q110, 125, 138–42; Ia-IIae q111, 126–29; Ia-IIae q112, 146; Ia-IIae q113, 300n140; Ia-IIae q114, 147–49, 174–75; IIa-IIae q23, 212–33; IIa-IIae q24, 248–57; IIa-IIae q45, 271–89; IIIa q1, 160–65; IIIa q7–8, 168–79, 187–90; IIIa q23, 200–207; IIIa q48, 298–302; structure of, 17, 20–21, 62, 159, 329–31

Super librum De Causis expositio, 106, 168

te Velde, Rudi A., 24n20, 28n31, 43n83, 182–83

theosis. See deification

Torrell, Jean-Pierre, 20, 98, 119, 192n111, 259–60n151

Trinity, 50–70, 83–95; activity *ad extra* of, 52–61; appropriations, 55–56, 58, 119, 198, 204, 335n9; causality in creation, 53–54; causal roles of Persons, 55–56, 204; image vs. trace of, 57; names of Persons, 51–53, 58–60; processions, 51–54; rational creature's likeness to, 57–61, 83–95; unity of Son or Word with Father, 206–7. *See also* Christ; God; Holy Spirit; image; missions, divine; Word

Tschipke, Theophil, 181n82, 183n88

understanding, gift of, 246n106, 289, 291, 294, 345

virtue: acquired vs. infused, 237–40; charity as highest, 225–30; charity directs, 230–33; and gifts of Holy Spirit, 241–46; as good *habitus*, 114; hope, 234–36; intellectual, 267; prudence, 238; theological, 137–38, 142–43, 234–37; and *visio Dei*, 176–77. *See also* charity; faith; *habitus*; wisdom

visio Dei, 30–40, 326–27, 342–45; charity perfected in, 234–37, 343–45; charity required for, 39–40; as deiformity, 342–45; as direct knowledge of God, 93; in *De veritate* vs. *Summa theologiae*, 33–37; Eucharist perfects charity required for, 322; via light of glory, 36–39; medium of, 31, 32, 36–39, 93–95; as perfection of image, 93–95; and proportion between created intellect and God, 31–35; and theological virtues, 176–77; wisdom in, 343–45. *See also* beatitude; deification; glory

Waddell, Paul J., 245n104

Wawrykow, Joseph, 46n94, 123–24, 127, 162n19, 163n23, 175–77, 198n128, 200, 255–56, 266

Whidden, David L., 180n76

Wilkins, Jeremy, 63n152

will, 48–49, 107–14; and grace, operating

will (*cont.*)
  and cooperating, 126–28; freedom of, 47–
  48, 106–12, 115, 121; God as first cause of,
  109–10, 112–13; interior vs. exterior acts of,
  127; of means to beatitude, 107; rectitude
  of, 282–88; sin limits, 108; and voluntary
  action, 112. *See also* causality; charity; free
  will; *ordinatio*; predestination
William of Auvergne, 30
Williams, Anna, 7n20, 8–15, 359–65; on
  created grace, 359–65; on two poles of deification, 9–10, 362
Wippel, John, 23n17
wisdom, 265–96; and adoption, 199–200,
  286–89, 339–42; Christ or Word as Begotten, 55; of Christ, 295–302; and contemplation, 280–81, 341–42; in deification,
  332–33, 336–38; as effect of divine mission,
  292–95; vs. faith, 272, 289–92; fear as beginning of, 149–50; gift of caused by charity, 275–79; as gift of Holy Spirit, 269–89;
  of God, 44, 46; God's glory manifested
  in, 339–42; and Incarnation of Word, 197–
  200; judges and orders according to divine
  rules, 273–75, 281, 283, 337; orders objects
  of charity, 280–86; as participation in divine providence or *ordinatio*, 274, 283, 340;
  as participation in likeness of Son or Word,
  67, 199–200, 274–75n36, 286–89, 292–95,
  340; peace caused by, 286–89; perfected in
  beatitude, 292; of philosophers, 266–68;
  as play, 269; speculative and practical,
  280–82, 342; of *sacra doctrina*, 268–69; and
  splendor, 339; in *visio Dei*, 343–45
Wisdom, Book of, 8:1, 44, 125, 218, 284n75
Word, 51–54; as exemplar, 197–98; 204–7;
  fittingness for Incarnation, 197–200; participation in, 60; unity with Father, 206–7;
  wisdom as participation in likeness of, 67,
  199–200, 289, 295, 340. *See also* Christ;
  Son; Trinity
worship: and adoption, 273, 326–27, 338,
  341–42; Christ as model of, 305–13; in
  heaven, 313, 326–27, 341–42; inward and
  outward, 70n171, 305, 311–13; and sacramental character, 308–13, 338; and wisdom,
  273, 318, 326–27, 341–42. *See also* liturgy;
  religion; sacraments